The Materialist Conception of History

The author and the editor: Karl Kautsky with his grandson John Kautsky in Vienna, about 1926, when he was writing *The Materialist Conception of History*.

KARL KAUTSKY

❦ The Materialist Conception of History

Abridged, annotated, and introduced by
John H. Kautsky
Translated by
Raymond Meyer
with John H. Kautsky

Yale University Press
New Haven and London

Set in Bembo type by Rainsford Type, Danbury, Conn.
Printed in the United States of America by Bookcrafters,
Inc., Chelsea, Mich.

Library of Congress Cataloging-in-Publication Data
Kautsky, Karl, 1854–1938.
[Materialistische Geschichtsauffassung. English]
The materialist conception of history / Karl Kautsky ;
abridged, annotated, and introduced by John H. Kautsky ;
translated by Raymond Meyer with John H. Kautsky.
    p.   cm.
Translation of: Die materialistische Geschichtsauffassung.
Bibliography: p.
Includes index.
ISBN 0-300-04168-3
1. Historical materialism. I. Kautsky, John H., 1922–
II. Title.
D16.9.K37513 1988   87-34028
335.4'199—dc19   CIP

The paper in this book meets the guidelines for
permanence and durability of the Committee on
Production Guidelines for Book Longevity of the
Council on Library Resources.

10 9 8 7 6 5 4 3 2 1

I dedicate this book to my dear Luise, the mother of my sons, my staunch comrade, my untiring and understanding helpmate in my work, the enthusiastic, brave champion of our common ideals.

—K.K.

Contents

Preface by John H. Kautsky   xv

Introduction by John H. Kautsky   xxi

Author's Preface (v)★   lxv

Volume One. Nature and Society

PART ONE. MIND AND WORLD

Section 1. The Object of Investigation (3)   3

1. The Nature of the Materialist Conception of History (3)   3
2. The Materialist Conception of History among the
   Marxists (12)   4

Section 2. Materialism and Idealism (19)   7

1. Materialism (19)   7
2. The Revolt against Materialism (29)   8
3. Belief in God (31)   9
4. The Meaning of Life (34)   11
5. Ethics (39)   13
6. Atom and Mind (44)   14

Section 3. Kant (50)   16

1. Materialism before Kant (50)   17

★The numbers in parentheses are the page numbers in the unabridged German edition.

2. The Materialist Component of the Kantian Theory (52)   17
3. The Limits of Cognition (54)   17
4. Crossing the Boundary (59)   19
5. The Ideality of Space (67)   19
6. The Ideality of Time (75)   20
7. Necessity (78)   21
8. Freedom (89)   24
9. The Moral Law (96)   24
10. The Leap from Necessity into Freedom (105)   26

Section 4. Theory and Practice (110)   28

1. Action and Cognition (110)   28
2. The Certainty of Knowledge (112)   30
3. Action and Necessity (115)   31
4. Causality or Functional Dependence (119)   33

Section 5: The Dialectic (128)   34

1. Ego and Environment (128)   34
2. The Dialectic of Self-Initiated Development (130)   35
3. The Dialectic of Perfection (136)   37
4. The Conservative Nature of the Mind (141)   38
5. The Adaptation of Thoughts to One Another (144)   40

PART TWO. HUMAN NATURE

Section 1. Heredity (169)   45

1. Acquired Characteristics (169)   45
2. Crossbreeding (176)   46
3. Individual and Species (178)   47
4. Environment and Species (186)   49
5. Marx and Darwin (196)   52
6. The Transformation of the Animal into Man (200)   53
7. The Human Psyche (206)   54

Section 2. Man—An Egotistical Being (220)   58

1. The Drive for Self-Preservation and Pleasure (220)   58
2. The Drive for Self-Preservation and Egoism (224)   59
3. Malthus and Darwin (231)   61

Section 3. Man—A Social Being (241)   64
1. Egoism and Sympathy (241)   64
2. Darwin's Discovery of Animal Morality (252)   65
3. Drives and Morality (258)   68
4. Society as an Organization (264)   70

5. The Closed Society (273)   72
6. War (279)   74
7. Internal Differentiation of Society (289)   78
8. Collective Thinking (291)   79

Section 4. Man—A Sexual Being (307)   85

1. Preservation of the Species (307)   85
2. The Care of Offspring and the Forms of Marriage (309)   86
3. The Original Forms of Marriage (320)   88
4. The Prohibition of Incest (330)   91
5. The Freudian Hypothesis (334)   91
6. The Harmful Effects of Inbreeding (341)   93
7. The Valuation of Sexual Drives (349)   95
8. The Origin of Sexual Modesty (354)   96

Section 5. Other Characteristics of the Human Psyche (361)   97

1. The Animal and Beauty (361)   97
2. Art in the Animal and in the Human World (371)   98
3. Art and Economy (381)   100
4. Man's Urge to Inquire (386)   102
5. Man with his Contradictions (391)   104

Section 6. Adaptation in Nature (401)   108

1. Progress and Adaptation (401)   108
2. Passive Adaptation (406)   110
3. Active Adaptation (412)   111

Part Three. Human Society

Section 1. Race (479)   116

1. Man's Original Home (479)   116
2. The Migrations (483)   117
3. The Separation of the Races (489)   120
4. The Mixing of the Races (493)   121
5. The Struggle of the Races as the Driving Force of
       History (500)   123
6. Racial Antagonisms (510)   125
7. Superior and Inferior Races (517)   127
8. Class and the Faculty of Thought (524)   130
9. Sex and the Faculty of Thought (533)   135
10. Special Endowments of the Races (536)   137
11. "National Character" in Historiography (542)   139
12. "National Character"—A Mystery (555)   141
13. Racial Ties of Blood (562)   143
14. Race and Language (563)   144

Section 2. Technology (570) 146

1. Anthropogeography (570) 146
2. The Impetus to Historical Development (576) 148
3. The Intelligence of the Inhabitants of the Forest and of
    the Grassland (582) 151
4. Plaiting (587) 152
5. Digging (598) 154
6. Defense and Attack (608) 156
7. The Production of Tools (622) 159
8. Fire (627) 161
9. Of Invention (634) 163
10. The Development of the Steam Engine (639) 165
11. The Steamship and the Locomotive (645) 166
12. Novelty in Technical Progress (654) 168
13. Novelty in Social Ideas (662) 170
14. Advantages Due to Fertility and Mineral Wealth (675) 176
15. Advantages Due to Geographical Location (682) 179
16. Changing Advantages Due to Natural Factors (691) 180

Section 3. The Economy (701) 183

1. Natural and Artificial Organs (701) 183
2. Working Together (707) 185
3. Working for One Another (713) 188
4. Technology, Economy, and Obtaining Food (723) 192
5. Agriculture and Industry (731) 193
6. The Mode of Production (737) 196
7. Property (741) 199
8. Landed Property (751) 202
9. The Development of Property (757) 205
10. The Conservative Character of Property (771) 209
11. Organ and Environment (779) 213
12. The Dialectic and Evolution (789) 217
13. Mode of Production and Mental Character (794) 219
14. Individual and Society (799) 221

Section 4. Marx's Preface (805) 224

1. Will and Mode of Production (805) 224
2. Base and Superstructure (811) 227
3. Christianity and Revolution (819) 231
4. The Base in the Last Analysis (830) 232
5. Production of Life as Production of Human Beings (837) 234
6. Production of Life as Preservation of Life (850) 237

7. Economy and Natural Science (863) — 239
   a. Knowledge of Nature and Technology (863) — 239
   b. Views of Nature and of Society in Ideology (875) — 243

Volume Two. The State and the Development of Mankind

PART FOUR. CLASS AND STATE

Section 1. Definitions (3) — 249

1. How Long Have There Been Classes? (3) — 249
2. The Concept of Class (8) — 250
3. Occupations (19) — 254
   a. The Division of Labor (19) — 254
   b. Intellectuals (21) — 254
4. Occupational Antagonisms (28) — 257
5. Abolition of Classes and Abolition of Occupations (31) — 259
6. Class, Occupation, and Estate (38) — 262
7. The Concept of the State (42) — 264
8. The Marxist Conception of the State (52) — 265

Section 2. The Origin of the State and of Classes (61) — 267

1. Engels' Hypothesis (61) — 267
2. Critique of Engels' Hypothesis (67) — 269
3. Slavery (74) — 272
4. The Conquest State (81) — 274

Section 3. The First States (94) — 277

1. Sedentary Agriculturalists (94) — 277
2. Nomadic Herdsmen (99) — 279
3. The Nomads' Capacity for Creating States (107) — 281
4. The Founding of the State (110) — 282
5. The Expansion of the State and of the Tribe (121) — 286
6. Association of Tribes (127) — 287
7. The Tendency of the State to Expand (131) — 288
8. Imperialism (143) — 291

Section 4. Effects of the State (147) — 293

1. Economic and Political Means (147) — 293
2. Communism and Private Property (151) — 294
3. Trade (156) — 294
4. Usury (163) — 296
5. Trading Peoples (168) — 298
6. Writing (170) — 299
7. Science (178) — 300
8. Money (185) — 303
9. Accumulation of Treasures (194) — 305

10.   Irrigation Works (204)   307
11.   Irrigation Systems and State Government (213)   309
12.   The City—Industry and Art (226)   310
13.   Rise and Decline (238)   314
14.   Civilization and Its Decay (250)   318

Section 5. The First Forms of the State (262)   320

 1.   Aging of the State and Aging of Civilization (262)   320
 2.   The Democracy of the Vanquished (264)   320
 3.   The Democracy of the Victors (271)   323
 4.   Aristocrats and Art (275)   325
 5.   The Aristocracy and Science (280)   325
 6.   Monarchy (285)   328
 7.   The First Class Struggles (299)   332
       a. The Exploited Are Weak and Divided (299)   332
       b. Vying for the Ruler's Favor (306)   335
       c. The Immobility of the Orient Despite All
           Disturbances (310)   337
 8.   The Downfall of the State (314)   338

Section 6. The City-State (324)   341

 1.   The Origin of the City-State (324)   341
 2.   Class Struggles in the City-State (331)   343
 3.   Democracy and Exploitation in the City-State (340)   346
 4.   Mixed Forms of the State (350)   349
 5.   The Fall of the City-State (357)   351
 6.   The Socialism of Antiquity (364)   353

Section 7. The Capitalist Industrial State (371)   355

 1.   Industrial Capitalism (371)   355
 2.   The Progressive Force of Industrial Capitalism (377)   357
 3.   The Spirit of Capitalism (382)   358
 4.   State and Town in the Middle Ages (388)   360
 5.   Free Labor (395)   363
 6.   Asceticism (402)   365
 7.   The Emergence of Industrial Capital (410)   369
 8.   Progress and Social Revolution (416)   370
 9.   Modern Democracy (422)   372
10.   Capital in the Democratic State (429)   375
11.   The National State (437)   379
12.   The Growth of the State Apparatus (446)   382
       a. Army, Commerce, Customs (446)   382
       b. Education, Justice, Health Services (451)   384
       c. Taxes (456)   385
       d. Change in the Character of the State (458)   386
13.   Politics as a Vocation (459)   387

14. Force and Democracy (469) 390
15. Charisma (479) 395
16. The Intellectuals (487) 397

Section 8. Abolition of Classes and of the State (499) 400

1. The Decline of the Proletariat (499) 400
2. The Rise of the Proletariat and the Struggle for
   Democracy (505) 402
3. The Rise of the Proletariat and the Reduction of
   Working Time (514) 406
4. The Victory of the Proletariat (523) 410
5. Roads to Socialism (530) 412
6. The Undermining of Capitalism (539) 418
7. Crises (542) 419
8. The Limits of Capital Accumulation (546) 421
9. Accumulation in Agriculture (552) 422
10. The Presuppositions of the Necessity of Socialism (560) 425
11. The Intensification of Class Antagonisms (564) 427
12. Economy and Politics (578) 434
13. The Conditions for the Socialization of Production (586) 437
14. The Transformation of the State (597) 443
15. The Abolition of the State (602) 446

*Section 9. Marx's Explanation of the Motive Forces of Social
Development* (614) 450

1. Marx's Preface Once Again (614) 450
   a. Class Struggle in History (614) 450
   b. The Impact of Economic Transformations on
      Ideology (620) 454
   c. The Development of the Productive Forces in Society
      (621) 455
   d. Every New Mode of Production Is Tied to Material
      Conditions (625) 457
   e. Mankind Sets Itself Only Tasks That It Can Solve
      (627) 458
2. The Further Development of the Materialist Conception
   of History (629) 460

PART FIVE. THE MEANING OF HISTORY

Section 1. Uniqueness in History (639) 465

1. The Practical Significance of the Materialist Conception
   of History (639) 465
2. The Materialist Conception of History and
   Historiography (643) 467

3. Practical Tasks of Historiography (649)   468
4. History as Teacher (655)   470
5. The Singular in History (660)   471
6. The General and the Particular in History (666)   473
7. General and Particular Laws (675)   476
8. Historical Laws (678)   477
9. The Separation of the Particular from the General (685)   480
10. The Individual in History (690)   482
11. Individual and Class Struggle (698)   485
12. The Creative Individual (707)   488

Section 2. Will and Science in History (711)   489

1. The Origin of Volition (711)   489
2. Teleology and Causality (714)   490
3. Pure and Applied Science (720)   493
4. The Power of the Will (730)   494
5. Marx and Jehovah (736)   496

Section 3. The Goal of the Historical Process (741)   497

1. Prognoses Derived from Experience (741)   497
2. Prognoses in Society (746)   499
3. Transcendent Prognoses (757)   504
4. Astronomical Conceptions of History (761)   505
5. Ascent to Freedom (769)   506
6. Ascent to Morality (776)   508
7. Ascent to Humanity (783)   511
8. Ascent to Health and Strength (794)   513
9. Ascent to Happiness and Contentment (806)   515
10. Ascent to Perfection (819)   517
11. The Law of Progress (825)   519
12. The Limits of Progress (835)   522

Bibliography   529
Index   543

JOHN H. KAUTSKY

Preface

This preface could well begin with the same words as Karl Kautsky's own preface: "With the completion of the present work, a wish I have had for decades has been fulfilled." Nearly forty years ago, when I was working on my doctoral dissertation on the political thought of Karl Kautsky at Harvard, my uncle Benedikt Kautsky, who had himself a quarter of a century earlier assisted his father in his work on *The Materialist Conception of History*, and I developed the idea of producing an abridged edition of its two volumes. Nothing came of that idea then, as both of us became involved in other kinds of work. My uncle has long since died, and my own interests have tended to move away from Karl Kautsky's writings.

Still, I have remained very much aware of the great influence my grandfather had on my intellectual development, most obviously through his writings and more subtly through my father, and of the tremendous debt I owe him. It is therefore a source of great satisfaction to me that I could now, near the end of my academic career, repay a little of that debt by making what Kautsky regarded as his most important work more widely available than it has been for quite some time.

Of course, I have not produced the present edition merely to fill a personal need. In the past forty years, there has been a significant growth of interest in Karl Kautsky, making the republication of his principal work more important. In my introduction, I mention a number of reasons that may explain the strange fact that in spite of this growing interest this work has been largely ignored, but two obvious ones are no doubt its inordinate length and the absence of an English translation. A half-century after Kautsky's death, the time seemed reasonably propitious for the appearance of an abridged version of *Die materialistische Geschichtsauffassung* in English.

(The same version is being published in the original German, also in 1988, by the Verlag J. H. W. Dietz in Bonn, the publisher of most of Kautsky's writings through more than a century.)

From the outset, I was determined to reduce the length of Kautsky's original two-volume text quite drastically. At the same time, no section of it was to be eliminated in its entirety, for different readers are likely to be interested in different aspects of the work and all of them should be aware of its total scope. I also sought not to delete any material merely because it has been proved wrong by later developments or by later research or, of course, merely because I disagreed with it or even because it seemed unimportant from my point of view. In making my editorial decisions, I sought to retain what seemed important to Kautsky and what seemed to be important to his argument regardless of whether I considered that argument strong or weak, valid or invalid, attractive or unattractive. I did not regard it as my function to improve Kautsky's work, let alone to censor it, but sought to retain as much of it and to change as little of its character as possible in a far-reaching abridgment.

Following these principles, I managed to reduce Kautsky's text to exactly one-third of its original length. At the same time, of the 222 chapters in the entire two volumes, only one was completely omitted (as were the two appendices to Parts I and II). On the other hand, of the 1,733 pages of text in the original version, only eight escaped any deletions whatsoever.

Thus, two-thirds of the original *Die materialistische Geschichtsauffassung* could be omitted from this abridged edition, mostly by the deletion of individual words, sentences, and paragraphs. The process of cutting proved to be relatively easy for me and, I hope, not very damaging to Kautsky's work, given its peculiar character of that of an old man intent on reviewing a long lifetime of productive thought. Writing of his book shortly after its publication, he said that in his earlier writings he had always preferred brevity and the omission of details on the assumption that there would be later opportunities to deal with his subjects more fully. "But this time I felt that I was addressing my readers for the last time in a wide context: that what I did not say now would never be said by me" ("Eine Selbstanzeige," p. 166).

Thus, Kautsky's original work contains innumerable nonessential passages—often a paragraph or two, sometimes even a few pages—that could be omitted or summarized here, usually by retaining a few of Kautsky's own words (and sometimes in my words). This is particularly true of the huge amount of illustrative material Kautsky cites in support of his generalizations, which often involves not only references to but discussions of specific instances of animal behavior or historical events. Numerous quotations could be abbreviated, summarized, or mostly just identified, especially when Kautsky's comments on them make their content clear. To be sure, some reference to the issues raised in quotations and Kautsky's responses to them had to be retained, for his subjects and especially his emphases can in part be understood only as responses to ideas prevalent in German academic and Marxist circles of his time.

In hope that my abridgment has made Kautsky's work more readable and perhaps, in some respects, even a better book, for it is now more tightly organized, the unity of its argument may be more apparent, the forest may be more visible now that many trees have been cut down. But if these are advantages, a price certainly had to be paid for them. Obviously, Kautsky's generalizations may now not appear as well supported by evidence as they were in the original. More generally, the present version is inevitably less rich than that original. Not only are Kautsky's arguments, illustrations, and allusions often interesting both for their substance and as indicators of the state of scholarship in his time, but they contain the more charming and sometimes humorous elements of his work. Yet they often had to be summarized or omitted here as is also true of most of his ironic and witty comments, many reserved for the chauvinism, militarism, and racism of German professors of his day. It is unfortunate that my abridgment may thus reinforce Kautsky's reputation as a dry, pedantic, and humorless writer, though such adjectives certainly do not accurately describe his personality.

All deletions of more than a word or two are indicated by ellipses (. . .), except where I have inserted my own summary passages in brackets to take the place of or describe longer passages by Kautsky or quotations by other writers. Wherever possible, I let Kautsky's own summary passages indicate the content of longer passages I had eliminated, but where my deletions would have interrupted the flow of his argument or where sources he cites or quotes needed to be identified, I inserted my own brief summaries or citations. The summaries are no more than that, designed to reflect Kautsky's views; they do not serve as my editorial comments. Still, they were not written by Kautsky, and I therefore set them apart from his text by placing them in brackets and printing them in italics. On the other hand, all words in italics that are not enclosed in brackets appear in italics in Kautsky's original version.

I have followed Kautsky's own convenient practice of indicating in the text itself the sources to which he refers or which he quotes. His original work contains very few footnotes, all of which I could omit. Thus, all footnotes in the present edition were added by me. I have sought to keep their number to a minimum. They serve one of two functions. Many provide cross-references to relevant passages and should also help to call attention to the unity of the argument of the book. As the chapters in this abridged edition are mostly quite short, cross-references could generally be made not to pages but to chapters identified, for example, as IV:8:13, that is, Part IV, Section 8, chapter 13 (parts, sections, and chapters are indicated in the running heads). Almost all footnotes other than cross-references refer to other works by Kautsky. Many themes taken up in this book had been treated by him in earlier works, and in his preface he himself calls *The Materialist Conception of History* the "quintessence of my life's work." It seemed reasonable, therefore, to let the present edition serve in part as a guide to Kautsky's other writings on related subjects. As a result, all of Kautsky's book-length works are mentioned in my footnotes, but only some of his articles, since he wrote well over a thousand of them. All works by Karl Kautsky are cited in the text and in footnotes without the author's name.

Dr. Raymond Meyer of Palo Alto, California, has produced an extraordinarily careful and accurate translation of the abridged text of *Die materialistische Geschichtsauffassung*. I compared it word for word with the German original and made such changes as I thought desirable, mostly quite minor ones. Hence, I assume ultimate responsibility for the translation as it appears here, even though Dr. Meyer did the great bulk of the work on it.

Aside from the well-known and insuperable difficulty of translating with a single word the German *Geist* (and *geistig*) and *Aufhebung* (and *aufheben*), only the following need be mentioned about our translation. We render *Gemeinwesen*, a term Kautsky constantly applies to human communities from the horde and tribe to the modern state, for lack of a better word as "polity." The more literal translation as "commonwealth" seems even clumsier and is often quite inappropriate, and the word "community" generally had to be reserved to translate *Gemeinschaft*, which Kautsky uses for various human associations, like families, gentes, churches, occupations, and classes, as well as tribes and states, while "mark community" is used to render *Markgenossenschaft*.

To avoid using the clumsy nouns "the human" or "human being" as frequently as Kautsky uses the very ordinary German word *Mensch*, we felt compelled to translate this term simply as "man." It would also be awkward constantly to refer to it by "he or she," and to alternate the masculine and feminine pronouns would seem affected. The reader who dislikes sexism, as we do, will, we hope, blame the English language rather than Dr. Meyer or me for our consistent use of "man" and "he" to refer to Kautsky's *Mensch*. Above all, it would be ironic and unfortunate, given his position on the equality of the sexes, if our usage made Kautsky appear as sexist.

In order to make this edition more useful to the English-speaking reader, I have wherever possible substituted English translations (or, as in the case of Darwin and Spencer, English originals) for works in German and, in a few cases, French cited or quoted by Kautsky, and I also replaced earlier editions with more recent ones. The search for these English-language and/or more recent editions and for the appropriate page references in them took me beyond the Washington University Library and its interlibrary loan system to the Library of Congress and the libraries of Harvard, Columbia, and the University of Chicago and, in Vienna, to the Austrian Nationalbibliothek and the University Library as well as the libraries of the Chamber of Labor and of the Association for the History of the Labor Movement.

In the case of the works of Marx and Engels, I have wherever possible substituted for Kautsky's citations references to the two most accessible English-language collections, the eight-volume Marx Library published by Vintage Books in New York, 1973–81 (which is identical with the Pelican Marx Library published by Penguin Books in England) and Karl Marx and Frederick Engels, *Selected Works in Three Volumes* (Moscow: Progress Publishers, 1969). If a publication is reprinted in both collections—as, for example, the Communist Manifesto is—my first page reference is to the appropriate volume in the Marx Library followed by a reference to *MESW* and the volume and page numbers in the *Selected Works*.

Among the English translations I cite are, of course, also those of a number of Kautsky's works. Some of them are quite poor and even inaccurate, and I have therefore not hesitated to introduce changes when I quote them in order to render the German original more correctly. In a few instances, I have also changed a word here and there in the translation of writings by Marx and Engels, where the version I cite seems to be inaccurate.

I owe a profound debt of gratitude to Dr. Raymond Meyer for his excellent translation and for his effective and pleasant cooperation with me. I am also grateful to the libraries I mentioned above and to Professor Rudolf Pritz and the Kunstverein Wien for helping to make my stay in Vienna in the summer of 1985 possible. Washington University provided me with a grant to cover the cost of translation, with a sabbatical leave in the fall of 1984, and with some research grants. I deeply appreciate this support and I thank Marilyn Schad for efficiently and patiently transcribing the entire manuscript on the word processor. Above all, however, I am grateful to my wife, Lilli, for cheerfully putting up with and giving moral support to a husband who spent all too much time editing, checking translations and references, indexing, and proofreading.

When I wrote my introduction, some sections of a long, incomplete, and unpublished essay on Karl Kautsky as a social scientist proved helpful. I had written it in 1958–59 while a research fellow at the Harvard Russian Research Center and now resurrected it from a dusty file. Though a bit belatedly, I gladly acknowledge my debt to Harvard and to the Rockefeller Foundation for making my stay there possible and to my late friend and colleague Morris Watnick, who helped me revise the essay at the time. The manuscript of the introduction was read by Raymond Meyer and by my present colleagues Barbara Salert, Robert Salisbury, and Peter Schwartz, all of whom I thank for their valuable comments and helpful suggestions.

JOHN H. KAUTSKY

Introduction

Why a New, Abridged Edition
of The Materialist Conception
of History?

Karl Kautsky's long and extraordinarily productive career as a writer, which
had made him the most authoritative theoretician, interpreter, and popu-
larizer of Marxism in the generation after that of Marx and Engels, came
to an end with his death on October 17, 1938. He died shortly after the
Munich crisis resulting in the dismemberment of the land where he had
been born eighty-four years and one day earlier. In the subsequent few
years, the world, including the scholarly world, was preoccupied with
matters other than those Kautsky had been concerned with, and in the post–
World War II period of the cold war and of revolution in underdeveloped
countries, Marxism came to be widely identified with Communism, and
there was little interest in Kautsky's democratic and determinist variety of
Marxism. Thus a man who in his lifetime had been the object of a huge
polemical literature, expressing agreement or disagreement with him,[1] received little scholarly attention.

It was only in the 1950s and 1960s that some scholarly articles and chapters
on Kautsky appeared.[2] Then, beginning in the 1970s, with growing interest

1. Werner Blumenberg's Kautsky bibliography, *Karl Kautsky's literarisches Werk*, itself indispensable to any study of Kautsky's work, mentions (on p. 17) 350 reviews and 450 articles,
big and small, about Kautsky and lists (on pp. 135–40) 67 of the more important articles and
20 books and pamphlets wholly devoted to Kautsky.

2. Brill, "Karl Kautsky," who could begin by saying "Karl Kautsky is today an almost
unknown name"; Cole, *A History of Socialist Thought*, especially III, ch. 5; Rubel, "Le magnum

in the history of Marxism and of the German Social-Democratic Party and in one or two cases perhaps also due to the development of Eurocommunism,[3] a number of books were devoted to Kautsky.[4] However, with three exceptions,[5] all of these works either totally ignore or barely mention *Die materialistische Geschichtsauffassung*, and a recent Kautsky reader[6] contains no excerpts from it.

How is one to explain this general lack of attention to a work that Kautsky (in his preface) called "the quintessence," "the foundation," and "the result" of his life's work? That the two volumes were never reprinted since they were published in 1927 and, in an unchanged second edition, in 1929 and that, as far as I know, they were never translated into any foreign languages (except Polish)[7] is one important reason, but itself requires some explana-

opus de Karl Kautsky"; Matthias, "Kautsky und der Kautskyanismus"; Osterroth, "Karl Kautsky"; Lichtheim, *Marxism*, part V, ch. 5; John Kautsky, "J. A. Schumpeter and Karl Kautsky"; Irrlitz, "Bemerkungen über die Einheit"; Steinberg, *Sozialismus und deutsche Sozialdemokratie*, especially ch. III; Laschitza, "Karl Kautsky und der Zentrismus." See also my dissertation, "The Political Thought of Karl Kautsky," and my article, "Kautsky, Karl" in the *International Encyclopedia of the Social Sciences*. This list of articles on Kautsky is not complete and, in particular, omits the more polemical and the more specialized ones. Among some later relevant writings are the following: Panaccione, "L'analisi del capitalismo in Kautsky"; Salvadori, "La concezione del processo rivoluzionario in Kautsky"; Geary, "Difesa e deformazione del marxismo in Kautsky"; Papcke, "Karl Kautsky und der historische Fatalismus"; Kolakowski, *Main Currents of Marxism*, II, ch. 2; Lübbe, "Einleitung"; Bronner, "Karl Kautsky and the Twilight of Orthodoxy"; Geary, "Karl Kautsky and German Marxism." For a more complete listing of works on Kautsky published before 1980, see the bibliography in Hünlich, *Karl Kautsky*, especially pp. 331–36.

3. On the intriguing relation of Kautsky's thought to Eurocommunism and on some relevant literature, see my article, " Karl Kautsky and Eurocommunism."

4. Waldenberg, *Myśl Polityczna Karola Kautsky'ego w okresie sporu z Rewizjonismem* (Karl Kautsky's Political Ideas during the Period of his Controversy with Revisionism); Waldenberg, *Wzlot i upadek Karola Kautsky'ego* (Karl Kautsky's Rise and Fall), 2 vols., Italian translation: *Il Papa Rosso, Karl Kautsky*; Holzheuer, *Karl Kautskys Werk als Weltanschauung*; Projekt Klassenanalyse, *Kautsky: Marxistische Vergangenheit der SPD?*; Waldenberg, *Kautsky*; Salvadori, *Kautsky el la Rivoluzione Socialista*, English translation: *Karl Kautsky and the Socialist Revolution*; Steenson, *Karl Kautsky*; Hünlich, *Karl Kautsky und der Marxismus der II. Internationale*; Mende, *Karl Kautsky—vom Marxisten zum Opportunisten*; Gilcher-Holtey, *Des Mandat des Intellektuellen. Karl Kautsky und die Sozialdemokratie;* Geary, *Karl Kautsky;* Panaccione, *Kautsky e l'ideologia socialista*.

5. Maximilien Rubel's article is mostly a summary of *Die materialistische Geschichtsauffassung*, Waldenberg's *Kautsky* contains about twenty pages each of selections from it and commentary on it, and Mende, *Karl Kautsky*, pp. 143–78, passim, discusses some points made in it. Steenson, in his excellent biography of Kautsky, devotes three and a half pages to it.

6. Goode, ed., *Karl Kautsky: Selected Political Writings*.

7. *Materialistyczne pojmowanie dziejow.* To my knowledge, only four brief sections of *Die materialistische Geschichtsauffassung* have heretofore been published in English: II, 614–28 as "The Driving Force of Social Evolution" in the *New Leader;* of this, II, 622–28 was reprinted in Laidler and Thomas, eds., *The Socialism of our Time*, pp. 325–34; I, 818–20, 830–32, 837 in Hook, *Marx and the Marxists*, pp. 163–65; II, 38–42 in Bottomore and Goode, eds., *Readings*

tions.[8] For at least two decades after its publication, in the period of Fascism and World War II, the times were not propitious for a work of this kind. Also, it was written when Kautsky was no longer as active and as influential politically as he had been for three or four decades before the 1920s. Hence those interested in Kautsky's political role or in specific earlier phases of history may have regarded *The Materialist Conception of History* as irrelevant to their concerns. Finally, large portions of the work are devoted to matters not usually dealt with by Marxists and hence perhaps of little interest to those concerned with Marxist literature. It may, in part, be for this reason that some, particularly those not in sympathy with Kautsky's natural-science approach, have sometimes treated it with some disdain, irony, and even ridicule.[9] Another factor responsible for Kautsky's work not being widely read or, one suspects, not being read carefully or in its entirety even by some of those who commented on it was no doubt its inordinate and forbidding length of about 1,800 pages.

Why, then, should Kautsky's *Materialist Conception of History* still—or again—be of interest today? The work touches on so many subjects and fields of knowledge that no one person with his or her particular tastes and interests can answer that question for others. One can, however, at least say that anyone concerned with Kautsky's thought must pay attention to what he himself regarded as his principal work. Even those who wish to focus only on Kautsky's role or ideas before the 1920s cannot reasonably

---

in *Marxist Sociology*, pp. 103–07; and II, 473–78 in Beetham, ed., *Marxists in face of Fascism*, pp. 245–50.

8. Many other works by Kautsky appeared in numerous editions and translations. Blumenberg provides a (quite incomplete) listing of over nine hundred foreign language editions in twenty-six languages. Since the 1970s, the Verlag J. H. W. Dietz Nachf. in Bonn, the original publisher of most of Kaustky's works, has republished eight of his books, and others have been republished in German, English, French, Spanish, Italian, and other languages.

9. Thus, Perry Anderson, *Arguments within English Marxism*, p. 62, refers to "Kautsky's *Die Materialistische Geschichtsauffasung* [as] a superficial, universal compendium of evolution, from the picanthrope to Palmerston." Had he read the work, Anderson would have discovered that, as Kautsky himself describes it, it actually ranges (without ever mentioning Palmerston) from "the protozoa . . . [to] the threshold of the state of the future" (p. 465). See also Lichtheim, *Marxism*, p. 265, n. 1. The most extensive critique of Kautsky's work, published in 1929, is Karl Korsch, "Die materialistische Geschichtsauffassung. Eine Auseinandersetzung mit Karl Kautsky," a mixture of brilliant insights, misunderstandings, distortions, and biting irony written on the pervasive assumption that to prove a statement wrong it is sufficient to show that it differs from Marx's view and/or was agreed to by a "bourgeois" thinker. More positive, but thoughtful and not uncritical articles by contemporary Marxist writers reviewing *Die materialistische Geschichtsauffassung* include Braunthal, "Kautskys materialistische Geschichtstheorie"; Wiener, "Kautskys Darlegung des historischen Materialismus"; Schifrin, "K. Kautsky und die marxistische Soziologie"; and Rónai, "Kautskys Klassen-und Staatslehre." Wholly negative reviews written from a Communist perspective include Rappoport, "Der Autorevisionismus Karl Kautskys"; Paschukanis, "Die neuesten Offenbarungen Karl Kautskys"; Messin, "Eine neue Revision der materialistischen Geschichtsauffassung"; and one review in a scholarly journal by Meusel.

ignore his statement of what he feels was the conception guiding his work throughout much of his life. By the same token, anyone interested in the intellectual history of Marxism, of German Social Democracy, or of the Second International cannot afford to ignore *The Materialist Conception of History*.

However, this book can be of interest also to some who are not particularly concerned with its author or even with relevant aspects of the history or the ideas of Marxism or of Social Democracy. Stretching across the natural and social sciences, *The Materialist Conception of History* is unique in its scope among Marxist works. It may be of interest as one of the last attempts to integrate such a wide range of knowledge. Historians of science, particularly those concerned with the history of Darwinian and also Lamarckian ideas and of their impact on social theory and social science, may want to pay attention to Kautsky's work.

There are other aspects of *The Materialist Conception of History* that various specialists in intellectual history may find significant, such as Kautsky's reactions to Kant, to Max Weber, and to Freud. Kautsky's conception of ethics, of race, and of heredity—to mention three subjects discussed by him at great length—may well intrigue those who trace the development of ideas on them. Finally and perhaps most obviously, Kautsky's ambitious attempt to formulate a consistent conception of history should be of interest to historians, historical sociologists, and philosophers of history. Also, his interpretation of world history—to be sure, the world of a Central European intellectual in the early twentieth century was smaller than ours—from the beginnings of states and even of mankind down to the present and even the future might well fascinate many a lay reader.

The present work, then, can interest different readers for different reasons. What follows in this introduction will inevitably reflect my own interests. I will not even summarize all the contributions *The Materialist Conception of History* may be thought to be making nor will I generally yield to the temptation to argue with Kautsky and to point out where it seems to me that he was right or wrong. I will also, reluctantly, refrain from comparing or relating his thought to that of Marx and other Marxists, for that would inevitably draw me into the morass of Marx interpretation and force me far to exceed the proper scope of an introduction. All I hope to do here is to point to some aspects of and some problems with Kautsky's work as a contribution to social science. Before doing so, however, I may offer a few brief remarks to remind us that Kautsky represented what was universally regarded as orthodox Marxism before World War I; to indicate how he deals with Marx and Engels in the present work; and to argue that it is in some ways a late-nineteenth-century or pre–World War I work, though it was written a decade after the war.

Kautsky and Marxism

Since Kautsky's time, an immense variety of Marxisms has developed. On the one hand, there are ideas of revolutionary intellectuals in underdeveloped countries, from Lenin and Trotsky in turn-of-the-century Russia to numerous political leaders following or adapting their thought in Asia, Africa, and Latin America in the past half-century, and then there are ideas of ideologists of established revolutionary regimes. On the other hand, in industrialized countries, Marx has been reinterpreted along different lines, Hegelian and Freudian, critical-theoretical and existentialist, humanist and individualist, phenomenological and structuralist, ecological and feminist. Anyone who has derived his conception of what constitutes Marxism from one or more of these interpretations will hardly recognize Kautsky as a Marxist at all.

Yet, Kautsky knew Marx personally (in 1881) and from 1885 to 1888 he worked closely with Engels, who from 1881 to his death in 1895 carried on a correspondence with him that fills some four hundred printed pages.[10] In 1883, *Die Neue Zeit* was founded by Kautsky, which may be said to mark the beginning of Marxism as a school of thought. He edited it for thirty-five years and made it the leading international Marxist journal of its time. The initial wide dissemination and popularization of Marxism was largely due to two early works by Kautsky, *The Economic Doctrines of Karl Marx* of 1887, published in twenty-five German editions and in at least fifty editions in twenty other languages, and his commentary of 1892 on the Erfurt Program (translated into English as *The Class Struggle*), published in nineteen German editions and at least forty-four complete and another twenty-three partial editions in eighteen other languages. In 1891, he had himself drafted the "section on principles" (that is, on Marxist theory) of the Erfurt Program, the first Marxist program of the German Social-Democratic party. Marx's heirs and Engels entrusted Kautsky with the task of preparing for publication Marx's manuscript for a fourth volume of *Capital*,[11] and Kautsky prepared the "Volksausgabe" of *Das Kapital*, the most reliable German edition of its time of Marx's three-volume work. In the two decades between Engels' death and the First World War, Kautsky was clearly regarded as the most authoritative interpreter of Marxism by all the major Marxist theorists.

All these Marxist credentials do not make Kautsky's ideas somehow more valid or more significant than ideas that have been called Marxist in the

---

10. Benedikt Kautsky, ed., *Friedrich Engels' Briefwechsel mit Karl Kautsky.*
11. Marx, *Theorien über den Mehrwert*, 3 vols. The English translation, based on a different edition, is *Theories of Surplus Value*, 3 vols.

period since World War I, nor does the fact that they are so different from the latter prove that these latter have not, in one way or another, been inspired by some aspects of Marx's Marxism. The historical record does, however, make it difficult to believe that Kautsky—and with him an entire generation of Marxists beginning with Engels who had worked with Marx in a uniquely close collaboration for four decades—had totally misunderstood Marx. An alternative interpretation—that Kautsky spent much or all of his adult life deliberately distorting and misinterpreting Marx—is so silly as not to merit any comment.

It seems not unreasonable to assume that Kautsky was, in fact, closer to Marx than many more recent writers, because the latter have, since World War I, responded to environments different from those that shaped Marx and Kautsky, environments industrially either much more backward or much more advanced than Western Europe in the late nineteenth century. Still, my point is not at all that Kautsky offers the only possible or the only valid interpretation of Marx.[12] Nor do I expect that, after many decades in which Marxism has been linked to everything from psychoanalysis to existentialism and from five-year plans to guerrilla warfare, the republication of the principal work of the principal Marx interpreter of the immediate post-Marxian period would reshape or clarify to any substantial extent the popular or scholarly image of Marxism.

However, Kautsky's Marxist credentials do indicate that his magnum opus represents what was quite generally regarded as orthodox or classical Marxism in the third of a century between Marx's death and World War I. In view of the tremendously far-reaching and varied permutations and reinterpretations Marxism has undergone since that time, it seems useful to be reminded of what was thought of as Marxism in the period when Marx's ideas first spread beyond a narrow circle.

The Materialist Conception of History, Marx and Engels

The question might be raised here whether Kautsky's "orthodox" Marxism was not more akin to the thought of Engels than that of Marx. In recent years, many commentators have, after all, come to distinguish between and even to contrast the views of the two founders of Marxism, and Kautsky is then usually associated with Engels rather than Marx. This is obviously

---

12. Two important works by Marx—his early *Economic and Philosophical Manuscripts* and the *Grundrisse*—had not yet been published when Kautsky wrote his *Materialist Conception of History*.

not the place to go into the matter of his relation to the two, much less their relation to each other, but we may briefly note what Kautsky's own attitude on it may have been, as it is reflected in his *Materialist Conception of History*.

Kautsky saw no conflict between the thoughts of Marx and Engels and commonly he refers to them jointly either by name or as "our masters" or "teachers" (*Meister*). In a passage at the very beginning of the present work (not reproduced in this edition), he says of them: "The two collaborated so closely that the work of one is also that of the other" (1929 ed., I, 3).

As to his *Materialist Conception of History*, Kautsky is careful to emphasize (I:1:2) that he presents his own conception of history here, not a commentary on Marx and Engels, and that there can therefore be no argument as to whether he understands some particular Marxian statement correctly. He immediately adds, however, that he owes his conception of history "to my great teachers" and that he does not "depart from the foundation of their thought." Kautsky was clearly convinced that his conception of history, though arrived at via a very different route from Marx's and Engels', was "in complete agreement" with theirs with respect to both methods and results (III:4:1).

While the present work is certainly not a commentary on Marx and Engels, it does contain such commentary, notably, two chapters on Engels' interpretation and use of the dialectic (I:5:2–3), one chapter on his notion of the "production of human beings" as a determinant of social change (III:4:5), and four chapters on his hypothesis on the origins of classes and the state (IV:2:1–4); there are as well six chapters on Marx's summary statement of his conception of history in his preface to his *Contribution to the Critique of Political Economy* (III:1:1, 2, 4, 6; IV:9:1). There we find Kautsky in some explicit disagreements with his teachers. The chapters on Engels serve to distinguish his own views from Engels' and contain some quite sharp criticism of the latter, but the chapters on Marx interpret Marx's statements to coincide, as far as possible, with Kautsky's own conception of history. Where they differ, Marx's sentences are not so much criticized as they are said to be in need of revision in the light of knowledge not yet available in Marx's time (notably IV:9:1a,b,c, 2).

Thus, though Kautsky was closer to Engels, with respect both to their personal contacts and their common anthropological and natural-science interests, than he was to Marx, he emphasized his differences with the former more than those with the latter. Generally, he differs more—and is more aware of his differences—with both Marx and Engels in the present work than in his previous writings, but this in no way keeps him from seeing himself, as he did for six decades until his death, as a faithful disciple of both his teachers.

A Late-Nineteenth-Century Work Written in the 1920s?

Kautsky was seventy-three years old when *The Materialist Conception of History* was published, and it is clearly the work of an old man who wanted to sum up his life's work and particularly to return to some of his early ideas to integrate them with later ones and to take account of recent literature. While the work as a whole is quite different from anything he had written before and much of it is wholly original, much, on the other hand, elaborates, supports, and modifies ideas he had developed more briefly decades earlier, especially in his *Ethics and the Materialist Conception of History* (1906), *Vermehrung und Entwicklung in Natur und Gesellschaft* (1910), and *Are the Jews a Race?* (1914).

Particularly in the first volume of *The Materialist Conception of History*, Kautsky returns to the subjects that had occupied him in the 1880s and even earlier, when he was in his twenties and thirties. He is fond of quoting some of his own early writings, reprints three of them, written in 1876, 1883, and 1884, as appendices in *Die materialistische Geschichtsauffassung* (they are omitted in the present edition) and says in the preface (in a passage also omitted here) that he wishes he could have reprinted more of them. It is also striking how many of the sources Kautsky refers to are works of the nineteenth century.[13] This suggests how heavily Kautsky relied on work he had done in his earlier years, particularly in areas touching on fields like biology, anthropology, ethnology, and demography. Some of his views having been shaped when he was young, he continued in his old age to rely on the sources that had shaped them.

It is probably fair to say, then, that with respect to the state of scientific knowledge on which it rests, *The Materialist Conception of History* is more nearly a work of the late nineteenth or pre–World War I twentieth century rather than of the 1920s. In any case, this is certainly true with respect to the attitude of unquestioning optimism pervading it. Kautsky is completely convinced that the growth of industry, science, and technology inevitably is associated with progress toward democracy and socialism. To him, World War I did not mark the end of an era, as it has come to be seen in our time, but was merely a serious interruption of an age of progress with things already returning to "normal" by the time he was writing in the mid-1920s (Preface; V:1:1).

The Materialist Conception of History, then, should be read and, I believe,

---

13. Of 147 works—not including writings by himself, by Marx and Engels, and by classical writers from Greek and Roman ones to Hegel and Goethe—quoted or cited by Kautsky in this abridged edition, half (73) were first published before 1900 and of these nearly half (32) first appeared before 1875, i.e., before Kautsky was twenty-one.

is of interest as a document illustrating the state of a particular type of social science a century ago and of Marxism in the generation after Marx's death.

An Attempt at Value-free Social Science

Since Kautsky's day, the paths of Marxism in most of its proliferating varieties on the one hand of Western academic social science on the other have diverged to the point where they appear to be incompatible to many on both sides. The republication of Kautsky's *Materialist Conception of History* may serve to remind us that there was once a time when Marxism and social science were thought by Marxists to be identical as attempts to explain social phenomena in terms of scientifically based theories; then, it was they who attacked academics for not being good social scientists.[14]

To Kautsky, Marxist "materialism" is a method (I:2:1), and this "materialist method . . . is the method of natural science. The materialist conception of history means nothing but the application of this method to society . . . " (I:3:4). Kautsky's approach to the study of society is positivistic and, in principle, value-free. He saw that the social scientist is involved in the conflicts he analyzes, and he recognized that such involvement introduces value judgments into the social sciences from which natural science remains free. "But in social science, too, these value judgments are not of the essence of science but constitute a foreign body, . . . a source of mistakes. The more it is possible to exclude them, the less prejudiced the investigator, the less will the product of his research be subject to scientific objections."[15] But how can Marxism be both a value-free science of society and the ideology of the proletariat, one of the participants in social conflict? Kautsky's way out of the dilemma is to separate the two. He thinks of Marx's socialism as value-oriented applied science based on the value-free pure

---

14. While *The Materialist Conception of History* is clearly a scholarly work that seeks to base its statements on evidence and cites plenty of scholarly—and by no means only Marxist—sources, it was not written primarily for an academic audience. In fact, Kautsky here and there treats German professors with some irony or contempt, for, in the period of his political activity, they tended to be conservatives and, above all, chauvinist nationalists. In an ideologically deeply divided society, Kautsky was clearly writing for a Marxist audience, though obviously a scholarly one. On the other hand, to judge by the absence of reviews in non-Marxist scholarly journals, his work was largely ignored in academic circles.

15. "Drei kleine Schriften über Marx," p. 321. See also V: 1:5 and V: 3:12, below, on value judgments as "a source of error." Kautsky had already written in 1906 that, while the proletariat required a moral ideal in its class struggle, that ideal "has no place in scientific socialism, the scientific search for the laws of the development and movement of the social organism," it "becomes a source of error in science when it presumes to set the goals for the latter." *Ethics*, p. 202.

science of economics and industry (V: 2:3), and he says of the materialist conception of history that "as a purely scientific theory, it is, certainly, by no means tied to the proletariat"; it is merely attractive to the proletariat, which in itself proves nothing as to the validity of the conception (p. 478).

Kautsky always thought of himself as much more of a social scientist in search of objective truth than as a politician in quest of power. Even many of his most polemical works contain long segments of historical, anthropological, and other social and even natural-science analyses, and *The Materialist Conception of History* is obviously meant to be a wholly scientific work.[16] Still, Kautsky does not live up to his ideal of excluding value judgments as sources of error even here. He often expresses his sympathies and antipathies quite openly, and he also introduces the pseudo-objective concept of the interests of society—which generally turn out to coincide with his value preferences. This is, of course, a device widely used by social scientists and universally employed by politicians, but it is difficult to square with a view of society as divided by conflict, such as Kautsky obviously held. Apparent as Kautsky's value positions are, however, what is noteworthy about *The Materialist Conception of History* is how little advocacy or condemnation it contains, that it is wholly devoted to building an explanatory theory of history and, in this sense, is clearly a work of social science.

Natural and Social Science

In the context of turn-of-the-century Marxism, it is not so much what Kautsky thought of as his natural-science approach to the study of history and society that is the most striking aspect of *The Materialist Conception of History* as his concern with subjects in the natural sciences, like biology, zoology, and even physics, and on the borderlines between the natural and social sciences, like physical anthropology, psychology, genetics, and demography. Kautsky himself considered this the most innovative contribution of his work. In an article summarizing and defending that work, he wrote of it as "that side of my book on the materialist conception of history that is especially close to my heart, because I believe that I have here expanded Marxism, not only in details, but in principle, and have filled a large gap in its world view."[17]

From our point of view here, the question in this connection is not how

---

16. It is probably because Kautsky wanted to keep current political controversy out of it that *The Materialist Conception of History* contains barely more than a few hints on the subjects of Bolshevism and the Soviet Union, though he was intensely involved in their analysis and in polemics about their nature and prospects at the very time he wrote the present work.

17. "Natur und Gesellschaft," p. 481. See also p. 461, below.

well Kautsky's statements in natural science fields stand up in the light of present-day knowledge nor, for that matter, even whether they were valid by the standards of his own time. It seems unlikely to me that he could have kept up with current developments and been familiar with and understood the most advanced work being done in all the fields he touched on. Though he was obviously acquainted with much scientific literature, many of his views may well have been one-sided and outdated. Indeed, Kautsky was himself keenly aware of being a layman in the natural sciences (see, for example, *Vermehrung und Entwicklung*, p. vii; and I: 4:4, II:1:1, below), and of the "embarrassing position" in which he was placed as such by his need to deal with natural science subjects.[18]

Kautsky's excursions into natural science fields are of interest to us, not as contributions to these fields, but because they are characteristic of his view of the materialist conception of history as wholly compatible with natural science and, indeed, as linked to it. Pursuing an interest that can be traced back to his earliest writings, Kautsky attempted to encompass the study of development in nature and society in a single, consistent system of thought, to reconcile them in what in a favorite and recurrent—and difficult to translate—phrase he calls a *widerspruchsloser Gesamtzusammenhang*, a totality or complex of interrelations (or a total context) free of contradictions. He thought that he had achieved this in his *Materialist Conception of History*—and regarded it as the greatest accomplishment of his work.

Kautsky's conception, then, rests, as he states in his preface, on "the recognition of the uniformity of the processes of nature and of society." He seeks a "law to which human as well as animal and plant development is subject," and he finds it in that "every change both of societies and of species is to be explained by a change in the environment. . . . New forms of organisms and of social organizations arise through adaptation to a changed environment" (p. 461; see also III:2:12). However, within this general law more specific laws govern different realms within nature and society. Plants adapt only "passively," animals adapt also "actively" (II:6 :2–3 and IV:9:2),[19] and men, in addition and very importantly, adapt by creating artificial organs, as we will discuss below. Here we merely need to stress that, contrary to a view often ascribed to him, Kautsky did not offer a simple natural-science explanation of social development and history, he did not assert that human societies are governed merely by the same laws of development as is organic nature. Indeed, he repeatedly emphasized the opposite, especially in the present work, but also in earlier ones (Preface,

18. *Are the Jews a Race?*, pp. 18–19. See also *Vermehrung und Entwicklung*, pp. 16–17.

19. Relying on a number of experiments and scientific authorities and unable otherwise to explain adaptation, Kautsky insisted that acquired characteristics can be inherited. II: 1:1 and II: 6:3, and *Are the Jews a Race?*, pp. 37–43.

I:2:2, II:1:5, III:2:12, III:3:11, IV:9:2, V:1:7–8; *Vermehrung und Entwicklung*, p. viii; *The Social Revolution*, pp. 14–15).

Darwinism and Neo-Lamarckism

Kautsky's interest in the natural sciences and particularly in evolution in nature is often seen as linked to his Darwinian background. Kautsky himself stresses his debt to Darwin and the fact that he enthusiastically studied Darwin as a young man,[20] and this has, in turn, been emphasized by much of the literature on Kautsky.[21] Here I therefore merely need to note that Kautsky's relationship to Darwinism is not quite so simple as is suggested by his being described as a Darwinist.

In the fragment of his autobiography, written a decade after the present work, Kautsky recalls that when he was twenty Darwin's proof in *The Descent of Man* that "man is, beginning with his animal state, a social being with social instincts appropriate to such a being, [that] morality is nothing but the totality of these instincts," affected him "like a revelation."[22] Under Darwin's influence, at the age of twenty-two he developed his early materialist conception of history with emphasis on the "social drives" of men. He says that he merely had "to modify and deepen"[23] that conception when, two years later, he adopted the Marxian materialist conception of history after becoming familiar with Engels' *Anti-Dühring*. He now accepted without question Engels' view of dialectical development in nature (which he criticizes in the present work; I:5:2–3) until neo-Lamarckism developed around the turn of the century and induced him to turn again to natural science, as he did in his *Vermehrung und Entwicklung* (1910), and to adopt "a far-reaching revision of my old Darwinism."[24]

Writing specifically of his *Materialist Conception of History* two years after its completion, Kautsky says:

20. *Vermehrung und Entwicklung*, pp. v–vii; "Karl Kautsky," p. 120; and I: 1:2, II: 3:2, below. Blumenberg's bibliography lists seven articles by Kautsky on Darwinism written between 1875 and 1882.

21. See especially Steinberg, *Sozialismus und deutsche Sozialdemokratie*, pp. 48–53; Steenson, *Karl Kautsky*, pp. 18–19, 24–30, 63–66; and Kupisch, "Einleitung," pp. xi–xx. See also Matthias, "Kautsky und der Kautskyanismus," pp. 152–54; Holzheuer, *Karl Kautskys Werk als Weltanschauung*, pp. 19–21; and Steinberg, "Karl Kautsky und Eduard Bernstein," p. 56.

22. *Erinnerungen und Erörterungen*, pp. 379, 214. See also ibid., pp. 378–81; *Ethics*, pp. 71, 99; and II: 3:2, below.

23. *Erinnerungen und Erörterungen*, p. 216.

24. Ibid., p. 221. See also ibid., p. 394.

For Marx, the mass is the carrier of development, for Darwin it is the individual, though not as exclusively as for many of his disciples. He by no means rejected the doctrine of Lamarck who regarded the progressive adaptation of organisms to the environment as the most important factor in their development. But the main thing for Darwin was not the same effect of the environment on all individuals of the same species, that is, a mass phenomenon, but the occasional and accidental peculiarities of particular individuals by which each of them is either favored or disadvantaged in the struggle for existence. . . . In the past three decades, [Lamarckian] thoughts, modernized and adjusted to newer knowledge, have gained . . . new strength. . . . These neo-Lamarckian ideas got a powerful hold on me. The more I occupied myself with them, the clearer it became to me that they could be reconciled with the materialist conception of history in quite another way than original Darwinism. A materialist neo-Lamarckism, freed not only of all the naiveté of its origins but also of all mysticism, which some of its followers seek to inject into it, seemed to me to assert in biology the same principle that Marx had revealed for society in the materialist conception of history.[25]

In his autobiography, Kautsky says that it was this "higher unity" of the neo-Lamarckian view of development in nature and of the Marxian view of development in society that he pursued systemically and presented at length in his *Materialist Conception of History*.[26]

That Kautsky, from his neo-Lamarckian perspective, disagrees with Darwin becomes quite evident in the following pages (especially II:1:3–4, II:2: 3. See also *Are the Jews a Race?*, pp. 25–37). It is all the more surprising that, in contrast to his later emphasis on the influence on his *Materialist Conception of History* of neo-Lamarckism, that term does not even appear in the two volumes themselves, and only in one sentence close to the end of the second volume does Kautsky say that development in nature can be explained by a "modernized Lamarckism" (p. 520). Lamarck's name is barely mentioned, as when Kautsky notes that Marx and Engels never commented on Lamarckism. "In their time, there was as yet no antagonism between Lamarckism and Darwinism" (1929 ed., I, 199). On the other hand, Darwin is frequently quoted and referred to in *The Materialist Conception of History*. In fact, in the index to the unabridged German original, there are almost four dozen references to him in the first volume, more than to any other author in that volume except Marx. No wonder that many readers may be struck by Darwin's influence on Kautsky and may overlook Lamarck's.

On the one hand, then, Kautsky saw the struggle for existence, not, as Darwin had, as a conflict between individuals of the same species, but as a struggle of species with each other and especially with the environment, thus shifting his emphasis from the individual to the mass. On the other hand, he

25. "Natur und Gesellschaft," pp. 485–86.
26. *Erinnerungen und Erörterungen*, p. 222.

remained faithful to what Darwin's *Descent of Man* had "revealed" to him in his youth—that man was a social animal and especially that his moral behavior was due to social drives inherited from his social animal ancestors. These social drives are to Kautsky a major component of human nature.

Human Nature

But why was Kautsky so interested in human nature? He saw it as a constant element that merely adapts to changes in the environment and hence cannot account for change, that is, for history (I:1:1, II:1:7, II:5:5), but he stressed that man's adaption to his environment could not be understood without reference to his inherited nature, and so he devotes about a sixth of his magnum opus to an analysis of human nature. This analysis is typical of what Kautsky called his materialism, which refused to exempt the human mind, like human society, from the single realm of nature. His effort is directed at establishing the basic nature of man, that is, the mental characteristics with which he entered history. To find these, Kautsky again and again returns to the animal world, and, far from drawing a clear dividing line between the animal and man, he is intent on demonstrating that at least the beginnings of all basic human characteristics may be found among animals. The essentially human in man is the animal, for everything non-animal is a product of history.

Relying heavily on the reports of explorers and travelers rather than the kind of systematic scientific literature one could draw on today, Kautsky devotes much space to descriptions of the behavior of animals, especially the social apes, and of still surviving primitive people. He thought that drawing a line connecting the two was the only way to ascertain the direction of the development in the transition from animal to man that rested on facts rather than speculation and would at least produce hypotheses (p. 57).

By this method, Kautsky arrived at the conclusion that man entered history with a set of inborn drives, including the drive of individual self-preservation, the sex drive that serves to preserve the species, and a social drive, developed by social animals for the preservation of society. Drives leading man to desire knowledge and beauty, too, are seen as inherited from animals. For some aspects of this subject matter, Kautsky could refer to his earliest writings. In particular, he develops his "materialist" explanation of ethics in terms of the social drives (II:3:2–3, III:3:3), an explanation deriving moral phenomena from natural rather than supernatural sources and linking man to the animal rather than setting him apart from it, as he had proposed it two decades earlier in his book *Ethics and the Materialist Conception of History*. Thus Kautsky here integrates into his conception of history, as its starting point, ideas he had derived from his zoological and anthropological interests and had advanced at various times through half a century.

Rationality and Freud

It is clear from Kautsky's conception of human nature as made up of a variety of drives passed on to man by his animal ancestors and especially from his emphasis on social drives that his conception of history has nothing in common with that crude interpretation of the Marxist view according to which it assumes that man is "basically" moved only by materialistic or selfish interests. That interpretation must have been as common in Kautsky's day as it is in ours, for he considered it necessary to dispose of it at the beginning of his work, devoting the first four pages of the original version to this task (see also II:5:5).

More interesting than Kautsky's rejection of this interpretation is the distinction between conscious and unconscious motives implied in his explanation of human nature in terms of inborn drives.[27] Kautsky draws this distinction quite explicitly in the present work (II:5:5), where he opposes the Marxian conception of history to the overestimation of the influence of reason on human behavior, a view he had already expressed in 1883 in his first article in *Die Neue Zeit*.[28] Yet, one senses a certain ambiguity in Kautsky's thinking on the rationality of man. On the one hand, he stressed that "the unconscious plays a big role in society and history" (p. 106). On the other hand, he assumed that individuals and classes become aware of their class interests and act accordingly and that, at least in the case of the proletariat, "scientific understanding" and no "mere appeal to the feelings" (V:2:4) plays a crucial role in this process. While this is not necessarily inconsistent with Kautsky's emphasis on the unconscious, one can hardly read this book without being struck by the pervasive optimism inspiring it, the firm conviction that the advance of science, democracy, and socialism cannot be stopped, which seems to rest on the faith that knowledge must triumph over ignorance, reason over irrationality. Emotionally, if not intellectually, Kautsky may have been more a child of the eighteenth-century Enlightenment, which he accused of overestimating the role of reason in human behavior (p. 106), than he knew or cared to admit.

Kautsky's somewhat ambivalent position on the question of human irrationality is reflected in his attitude toward Freud. Kautsky nowhere systematically discussed the theories of his great Viennese contemporary but does refer to some of them in a number of passages in the present work. On the one hand, he acknowledged "gladly . . . that psychoanalysis, also in its Freudian version, is important for Marxism insofar as it opposes the

27. On his view of the relationship of reason to the drives, see I: 4:1, II: 1:7, p. 80, II: 5:5.

28. "Die sozialen Triebe in der Tierwelt," p. 73; reprinted in *Die materialistische Geschichtsauffassung* (1929), I, 441.

hitherto common underestimation of drives in man" (p. 107). On the other hand, he attacked psychoanalysis exactly because it assumed that man was not conscious of his real motives. Thus, he rejected the Oedipus complex, because no one is aware of sexually desiring his mother, and he seeks to disprove the child's desire to see his parents' genitals by suggesting that he could recall no such desire on his part.[29]

Kautsky wrote that he had not yet found any result of psychoanalysis that would throw light on the historical process, but there was no objection to others employing it in the study of history, provided they had some understanding not only of psychoanalysis but also of history and economics (II:1:7). Kautsky was also careful to withhold judgment on the value of psychoanalysis for medicine (II:1:7, II:4:5), but he stressed that research into the unconscious required "self-criticism, sobriety, and precision," while Freud unfortunately tended to be guilty of "arbitrary constructions, exaggerations and premature hypotheses," and many of his disciples had taken over from "their master not his genius but his excesses" (II:1:7).

In an essay written a few years after the present work ("Die Fabel von der Naturnotwendigkeit des Krieges"), Kautsky attacked three then recent books, including Freud's *Civilization and its Discontents*, for holding war to be a result of man's aggressive nature and hence inevitable, rather than a result of certain historical developments in human society. Here his view of man as naturally peaceable and social, because he is descended from herbivorous social animals, clashes with Freud's picture of man as asocial and aggressive. The clearest distinction between Freud and Kautsky, then, is not on the question of whether man is moved by reason or by what Kautsky calls drives, but on the question of the nature and the role of these drives.

Environmental Change— The Motor of Evolution and History

The drives that constitute human nature do not drive history. The dynamic element in history, as in nature, is a changing environment; human history,

---

29. *Die materialistische Geschichtsauffassung* (1929), I, 335 and 218–19, passages omitted in the present edition. For Kautsky's explanation of the feelings characteristic of the Oedipus complex with reference to social relations specific to particular historical conditions rather than to natural-sexual relations, see V: 3:7. Kautsky's lack of sympathy with Freud becomes strikingly obvious in the irony and ridicule with which he treats Freud's excursions into social science and especially anthropology. In particular, he takes issue with the notion that it is possible to learn about the psyche of early primitive man by studying neurotics produced by modern industrial civilization, an assumption on which Freud's *Totem and Taboo: Some Points of Agreement Between the Mental Lives of Savages and Neurotics* is based (II: 1:7).

like evolution in nature, is a process of adaptation. Just as plant and animal organisms do not change once they have adapted to their environment, neither does man. That the human mind is conservative and does not initiate change and is hence "ultimately" not responsible for anything new (that is, for history) is a point Kautsky repeatedly stresses (for example, I:5:4, III 2:12, III: 3:11).

As mentioned above, Kautsky's central goal in writing his *Materialist Conception of History* was to place human society and history in the "total context" of nature. To do this, he felt that he had to demonstrate that something new could develop, that there could be change and hence history, even though the human mind could not, on its own initiative, create anything new. The mind was no exception to the general law of nature that nothing could be created out of nothing. Man did not stand above nature, and hence no supernatural factors need be adduced to account for history (see especially, III:2:12, III:3:11).

In thus dismissing any explanation of social change as resulting from the brilliance or divine inspiration of great inventors and thinkers as no real explanation at all, Kautsky sought not only to advance his "materialist" conception of history as against what he called "idealist" ones; he also opposed "great men" theories of history, as they were prevalent in Germany in his time, and made the "masses" a crucial factor in history. It is only their response to environmental change, which is merely made explicit by great individuals, that has lasting effects in history (V:1:10–12), just as it is the impact of environmental change on entire species rather than on particular individuals that is responsible for evolution in nature, as Kautsky held in contrast to Darwin.

If environmental change is the motor of all change, both in nature and in human society, what is it that starts the motor and keeps it going? In nature, Kautsky assumes, changes in the environment, for example, in climate and vegetation, are due to the cooling and shrinking of the earth's surface and even to changes in the position of the earth in the universe. Man, however, more and more creates his own environment, a concept by which Kautsky means not only man's physical surroundings but his social ones, his institutions and ideologies (III:3:11). In the course of his evolution, man was subject to changes that made him develop greater intellectual and manual powers than all other animals. These enabled him to respond to new demands of the environment by creating artificial organs—tools, weapons, methods, social institutions, and rules. A totally new element was thereby introduced into the process of evolution. Man's artificial organs not only served him to solve the problems they had been consciously fashioned to meet, but not being part of his body, they and their products in turn became part of his environment. As such, they posed new and unforeseen problems for man, which required further adaptation through the creation of further artificial organs. This never-ending interaction between man and his artificial environment was, according to Kautsky, the driving force of the development of human societies (III:3:11, IV:9:2).

> Every social innovation, which in the last analysis is to be traced back to a new kind of social labor that, for its part, originates in the last analysis from a new technology, becomes a new environment once it has been carried through. This new environment poses new problems for men and impels them to solve these problems with new means. This, in turn, leads to the creation of new organs and organizations that, for their part, again become parts of the social environment and give it a new form. In this manner, the process of social development continues ever onward, once transformations of man's natural environment have got it going, even when nature remains completely constant. It is a mechanism that generates its own motive force, after it has once been set in motion by an impulse coming from nature. [p. 216]

The totally new elements in historical change are those results of the activity of the human mind, of inventions that were not foreseen by the mind. Since they appear in the environment before they appear in the mind, Kautsky can call them parts of the environment rather than the mind. "The problems arising out of the new inventions and constituting the impulse to further development were not foreseen and intended, but form a power that operates independently of men's volition and knowledge and, rather, determines their direction. It is on the recognition of this that our materialist conception of history rests" (p. 522). Kautsky must, of course, admit that even the unforeseen consequences of inventions are consequences of mental activity, as when he says: "The new in history . . . is certainly a result of the human mind, but not one that was in the mind earlier than in reality" (p. 215). What he really describes, then, is a process of interaction between environment and mind, as he himself stresses. But this makes the designation of the environment as the "ultimate" motor and the mind as "conservative," that is, requiring an impulse from without in order to move, seem rather arbitrary. Yet this is a conception that Kautsky must insist on.

Natural Science and Property—Base or Superstructure?

Kautsky was convinced that his scheme of historical development agreed with the scheme Marx had outlined in his "Preface to *A Contribution to the Critique of Political Economy*": A legal, political, and ideological superstructure is changed by preceding changes in a base consisting of "relations of production" that themselves correspond to "material productive forces." When challenged by a reviewer of his work that "not technology—the *forces of production*—but the *relations of production* are according to Marx the real foundation of society,"[30] Kautsky replied that, while Marx distinguished sharply between the economy and technology, between the social and the material elements in the process of production, he viewed the two as closely connected, "but the technical element as the primary one."[31]

Kautsky is particularly concerned with the relationship between natural science and technology. He notes that Marx had not mentioned natural science in his "Preface," but it was surely part of the "intellectual life process" he had assigned to the superstructure. Yet for Kautsky, "there can be no doubt...that knowledge of nature is among the 'productive forces'" (p. 239), that is, in the base. Indeed, Kautsky goes so far as to identify natural science as "the changeable factor" among the productive forces. "The development of the 'material productive forces' is therefore basically just another name for the development of knowledge of nature. Accordingly, an intellectual process, that of gaining knowledge of nature, appears as the bottom base of the 'real foundation,' the 'material substructure' of human ideology." Not surprisingly, however, Kautsky finds "knowledge of nature" also in the superstructure: religion, philosophy, and art all rest on it. He can only conclude that "from the perspective of the materialist conception of history, the role played in history by knowledge of nature is a very complicated matter" (p. 240; see also p. 227).

Also, having stated that science is the only changeable factor among the productive forces, Kautsky argues that it is technology—and specifically the unforeseen and unintended consequences of technical innovations—that advances science by making more facts of nature known to man. Technology and mind—base and superstructure—are interacting, then, and it is difficult to see one as primary and the other as secondary. As Kautsky himself concludes, "Technology, economy, and understanding of nature are intimately interrelated" (III:4:7a).

A similarly "intimate" interrelationship exists between the roles Kautsky assigns to technology and to property. He emphasizes that it is not technology alone that determines the mode of production in a given society (III:3:4 and 6). Among the other factors that determine it, the most important is the property system (III:3:6 and 10), which, as a legal relationship, is a part of the superstructure and thus itself derived from the mode of production. Property, then, is both one of the principal determinants of the mode of production and itself "ultimately" determined by it. Kautsky may escape the chicken-and-egg character of the interaction between technology and property by seeing it, like everything in a conception of history, as taking place in time. The property system is the product of an earlier mode

30. Schifrin, "K. Kautsky und die marxistische Soziologie," p. 162.

31. "Natur und Gesellschaft," p. 497. In support, Kautsky quotes Marx, *Capital*, I, 493–94, n. 4.

of production and, being extremely conservative (III:3:10), persists to modify subsequent modes of production until it is modified by them. "In the long run . . . the forms of property cannot be in contradiction to the material conditions of production. In the last analysis, it is always the latter that determine the relations of production" (p. 227). But at the same time he also asserts that "the way in which each technical innovation is employed, how it affects the processes of men working with and for one another, what social relations men enter in the course and as a result of these processes, all these things depend on the particular system of property" (p. 211).

Are Base and Superstructure Distinguishable?

With respect to the relationship of technology both to property and—what is even more important for his attempt at the formulation of a materialist conception of history—to science and mental activity generally, Kautsky is unable to escape from the cycle of interaction between base and superstructure. But does he wish to escape from it? Here he appears ambivalent. Kautsky not only recognizes, as any reasonable thinker must, that various factors in history and society—technological, economic, institutional, ideological—are all interrelated and interacting, but he stresses this and at times positively glories in the complexity of his conception of history and makes a virtue of it (for example, III:4:4). He emphasizes that it "cannot be said that base and superstructure always stand in a relation of cause and effect to one another. They influence each other in constant interaction. Certain legal, political, and religious views are conditioned by certain economic circumstances, but the reverse is equally true" (p. 229).

The distinction between base and superstructure is nevertheless not useless according to Kautsky, because the materialist conception of history is designed to explain movement rather than static conditions. Its function is to explain the rise of new phenomena in society. New ideas always rise on a new economic base, but they do not do so immediately. The human mind being a conservative element, old ideas and social institutions based on them are not discarded until they become quite incompatible with the new base (III:4:2). Therefore, "the attempt to explain completely the entire spiritual and intellectual content of an era by its economy will never succeed" (p. 232); see also III:4:2). Only new ideas are based on the economic conditions of that era. Old ideas have to be explained with reference to economic conditions of the period when they were new. Thus, Christian ideas of the present day may have to be explained in terms of an economic base existing in the times of the Reformation, of Jesus, or of the Old Testament prophets.

Such "intellectual forms transmitted [from earlier periods] do not belong to the results, to the superstructure, but to the conditions, to the base of the new economy as well as to the base of the new forms of consciousness corresponding to the new economy" (p. 233). In saying this, Kautsky would seem to draw the logical consequence of the recognition of the reciprocal relationship between base and superstructure and thereby to go beyond it by arguing that the superstructure of one historical epoch becomes the base of another one. As he states bluntly, the image of the superstructure can be used only to describe the constant relationship between economy and ideology, "the statics of society; in its dynamics it ceases to have any substance" (p. 460). He is even more outspoken on the matter when he says that "an individual phenomenon in history . . . whether it is of an economic, ideological or other kind, . . . will function in some respects as base, in others as superstructure. Only for the phenomena in history that are *new* at a particular time does Marx's statement about base and superstructure hold good unconditionally" (p. 234).

Here base and superstructure are not merely interrelated and interacting, they can no longer be distinguished by their character: an ideological element can be base, an economic one superstructure (except when the element is new, that is, "in the last analysis"—a matter we will turn to in a moment). The same point is explicitly made by Kautsky when he stresses at some length that it would be "crudely materialistic" to think of the base as consisting entirely of material things, the superstructure as made up merely of ideas. Intellectual work is part of the productive forces, indeed "all the productive forces" at the disposal of society are to "be ascribed to the development of man's knowledge." Even more clearly, the relations of production are "determined very strongly by mental factors, by men's needs and by their knowledge." "On the other hand, the ideological superstructure is not at all of a purely mental nature." Social consciousness requires material means of communication, science needs laboratories and observatories, art requires instruments and materials, religion relies on buildings and material symbols (III:4:2).

Determination Only in the Last Analysis

If one side of Kautsky's ambivalence is his emphasis on the interrelatedness and even the indistinguishability of base and superstructure, which surely casts doubt on the analytical utility of the scheme, the other side is his insistence on the retention of that scheme of base and superstructure. Yet, he had no choice about taking either position. On the one hand, as a sensible student of society and history, he was keenly aware of the complexity of the social world, he tried to do it justice in his work, and he detested analyses he liked to call *schablonenhaft*, that is, based on preconceived, simplistic patterns. On the other hand, Kautsky was committed to the scheme of base and superstructure. It was probably politically, possibly emotionally, and certainly intellectually unthinkable for him to give up what he regarded as Marx's and Engels' greatest contribution and the basis of their entire work (I:1:1). Furthermore, it was also the basis of a half-century's attempts on his own part to analyze contemporary and past societies, attempts he could well consider by and large successful.

To be sure, in *The Materialist Conception of History*, written toward the end of his life, Kautsky was not incapable of looking back critically on some aspects not only of his own earlier work but also of that of Marx and Engels, and he clearly now had doubts about the concepts of base and superstructure, which he says must not be interpreted too literally (III:4: 2). But the distinction between environment (including man-made environment) and organism (including the human mind) as, respectively, the dynamic and the conservative elements, the mover and the moved, in nature and in history is of the very essence of the present work. On it rests Kautsky's attempt "to comprehend the history of humanity in harmony with the laws of nature" (p. 215) and to reject idealistic and religious views placing the human mind beyond the operation of deterministic laws.

How, then, could Kautsky reconcile his use of a scheme distinguishing a base and superstructure or, at any rate, a dynamic and a conservative element in history with his recognition that these elements were in fact interacting reciprocally rather than as cause and effect? As is already clear from a number of quotations above, Kautsky attempts to do this by the simple device of introducing the concept of "the last analysis." There is, of course, interaction, he says, but in the last analysis or ultimately the base always determines the superstructure. Kautsky does not merely assume in passing that determination takes place only in the last analysis; he stresses it repeatedly (for example, I:1:1, III:3:13, III:4:2 and 4, IV:8:2).

Now, obviously, there is nothing objective about what is in the last analysis or ultimate or basic or fundamental. These are concepts in the mind of the observer, and different observers can differ, as they might on what is important or significant. To Kautsky, however, describing a factor in these terms does not mean that it is important. Indeed, a basic factor, like technology, might be much less important in accounting for a particular phenomenon than a nonbasic one, like ideology. Kautsky's "last analysis" must be interpreted more literally as referring to the beginnings, the origin of a thing.

As I noted, Kautsky stressed that among the ideas and institutions of an age some always have been inherited from preceding ages and are hence explicable only with reference to the economic conditions of these earlier ages. "Thus, in order to understand the total ideology of our time, we must go back into the remote past. Only then will we succeed in laying bare all its economic origins. But we will always find, if we dig deep enough, that all ideas are rooted in economic conditions. That is the meaning of the image of base and superstructure. The relations between the two factors are not so simple as they appear at first glance" (p. 231).

Not only does Kautsky have to admit, in what is surely an understatement, that for practical purposes of historical research the problem of going back into the remote past involves a "quite laborious task, which cannot always be carried out completely" (p. 233). But there is, again, no objective way for the historian of knowing when he has dug "deep enough." One suspects that the materialist historian does not find an economic determinant when he has dug deep enough, but, rather, he feels that he has dug deep enough when he finds an economic determinant. But what if he digs deeper? Will he not find that the economic change that was responsible for a new idea was itself brought about by some ideological change, for example, a scientific discovery? Thus Kautsky cannot break out of the cycle of interaction—there is no last analysis—until he has gone back to the very last analysis, that is, the very first origin of technological change, the first use of tools by very early man.

Why Men Have a History

Given the difficulties with Kautsky's scheme of technological determinism—difficulties he himself was quite aware of but could not escape from—what contribution does his treatment of the subject make toward the formulation of an acceptable conception of history and thus to social science?

First, one must give Kautsky credit for grappling seriously with problems that Marx had tantalizingly raised and left unresolved to be variously interpreted by innumerable analysts of his thought. Clearly, Kautsky's *Materialist Conception of History* is important both as a searching, sympathetic but not uncritical interpretation of Marx's conception of history in the light of Kautsky's analysis and as an attempt at an interpretation of history in the light of a modified and elaborated Marxist conception of history.

Second, just as Marx's emphasis on the economic factor in history can be seen as a major contribution to historiography, whether one accepts his economic determinism or not, so can Kautsky's emphasis on technology, whether we recognize it as the "ultimate" motor of history or not. It is certainly a useful counterweight to conceptions of history still predominant in Kautsky's day and by no means dead today that explain history with reference to such factors as the spirit of the times, which merely need to be explained themselves, or to such relatively unchanging factors as geography and climate, racial or national character, or culture.

If these are major contributions of Kautsky's works, he would nevertheless have regarded them as incidental to his principal objective of formulating a conception of history along natural science lines. Here we might first of all express sympathy with the attempt, carried out with remarkable consistency through a sweeping survey of much of human history, to exclude any metaphysical or supernatural factors as explanations of change, never to treat the human mind as uncaused cause of what is new in history.

But this attempt, admirable as it may be, rests on reliance on the questionable concept of the last analysis and ultimate causation. Must Kautsky's work be written off as a failure, then, after all? If he had attempted to explain specific historical events or even entire periods as mere reactions to recent technological change, it would indeed be a failure. But, in principle, that was clearly not his intention. On the contrary, he decried efforts to do so as bound to fail and stressed that no event or period can be fully explained by the economic conditions of its own time. A quarter-century before the present work, he had written, "One cannot explain the history of a period from its own economic history alone but must take into account the entire preceding economic development and, in addition, its products, beginning with prehistory [*von der Urzeit an*]. . . . The materialist historian must begin each of his investigations *ab ovo*."[32]

In going back to the "Urzeit" and the *ovum*, that is, to his last analysis, Kautsky explains, not some events or phases of history, but history itself. He raises the intriguing question of why man, unlike all other animals, has a history or, at any rate, a history different in kind from that of all other animals. And he finds the answer in seeing early man adapting to a change in his environment by using tools that, as they become part of the environment, require further adaptation. Once this beginning is explained, all further history can be seen as a further process of adaptation to an environment that is ever changing as a result of these adaptations. Now, the question of why human beings have a history is of little interest to most historians and social scientists, Marxist and non-Marxist, but it was central to Kautsky's concern in the present work and it should, indeed, be a question central to any conception of history.

Kautsky makes an important contribution to such a conception by seriously tackling the question, by trying to ascertain why and how primitive man came to use tools and thus to modify his environment (III:2:1–9). He stresses consistently that the beginnings of the relevant developments are to be found among animals, that there is no sharp dividing line between man and the animal, that, in short, man is part of nature and that there are explanations consistent with laws of nature even for the fact that man has a history, which proceeds differently from evolution in the rest of nature.

---

32. "Bernstein und die materialistische Geschichtsauffassung," p. 10. See also V: 1:9, below. Kautsky had made the same point as early as 1883 in "Ein materialistischer Historiker," p. 540.

Technological Change as the
Independent Variable

But what about history as most historians understand it, apart from the question of its beginnings? Kautsky obviously means to make a contribution to its understanding, too, by his technological determinism, his materialist conception. Here, by admitting and, indeed, insisting that the economic and "ultimately" the technological base is determinative only in the last analysis, he reintroduces all kinds of noneconomic and nontechnological factors as equally determinative of whatever is to be explained. As we saw, he cannot escape from the cycles of interaction among the various factors (and sometimes cannot even clearly distinguish between them)—simply because there is, in fact, no escape. Here technological determinism is no help.

However, even if one recognizes that one cannot break out of the cycles of interaction, one can only explain something with reference to something else; one must, in order to explain one's dependent variable, choose an independent variable. Thus, even if one knows that the base does not in fact determine the superstructure in some last analysis, because there is no last analysis, one can very conveniently and usefully for analytical purposes choose that base as one's independent variable to explain "superstructural" elements, like politics and ideologies. One can recognize that one can always dig deeper and can—indeed, one must for practical purposes—refuse to dig beyond a certain point.

In analyzing specific events or phases of history, Kautsky does not—because he cannot—go back to the beginning of human history for an explanation, though he suggests that this ought to be done (V: 1 : 9). Rather, in his practice, he explains new political and ideological phenomena with reference to contemporary or recent economic and technological changes. This method often proves quite successful in that it permits him to gain many fascinating insights that can advance one's understanding of history whether one cares about questions of ultimate causation or not.[33] Kautsky, to be sure, mistook a useful analytical device for a description of relationships existing in historical reality. He thought that his independent variable was given as such in reality rather than chosen by him. That, however, does not make the device he chose less useful and fruitful and the insights provided by it less valuable.

---

33. Thus, the question whether it was "ultimately" new religious ideas that were responsible for the development of modern capitalism or whether these ideas were themselves rooted in economic change may well be pointless, but surely Max Weber's work inspired by this question and the debate it, in turn, inspired—to which Kautsky contributed on IV: 7 : 3 and IV: 7: 6–7—have been extremely valuable.

In short, then, one can think of Kautsky's conception of history as involving two attempts at a "materialist" explanation of history, that is, an explanation that denies to the human mind an ultimately creative or dynamic role. One of these seeks to explain the beginnings of human history, and thus the fact that men have a history at all, in the context of his general view of change as a process of adaptation. Once history, that is, the process of adaptation to an ever-changing man-made environment, has got started, Kautsky admits, in principle, all possible nontechnological factors, including, above all, the human mind, as determinants of specific historical phenomena and periods—though they are said to be less than ultimately determinative. But, in practice, since he assumes that ultimately technological change is responsible for all other change and since he will not dig deeper to go from his last analysis to some imaginable more final one, Kautsky emphasizes technological change as his explanatory variable not only, first, as he seeks to account for the fact of human history, but, second, also as he analyzes specific aspects of human history.

The State and Classes

It is neither possible nor necessary to summarize Kautsky's analysis of human history here, but a few remarks on some of its aspects may be appropriate. First, history is to Kautsky the history of man from his beginnings and of man all over the earth. Class-divided societies, from this perspective, constitute an "exception, a mere episode in the history of human society" (p. 250). But while Kautsky devotes about a fourth of the present work, in his sections on race, technology, and the economy, to early or what is often called prehistoric man, he can develop his story at all historically, that is, as one of chronological development, only from the beginnings of classes and states, notably the great empires of antiquity, and that story takes up most of the second half of his work. Also, in fact, history is still to him, as it was to the majority of Western intellectuals of his time, the history of the West (though he briefly develops some interesting thoughts on Chinese and Indian history, IV:4:13, IV:8:5).

Kautsky rejects at some length Engels' theory of classes developing within primitive communities and of the state then emerging as a tool of the dominant class (IV:2:1–3). To it, he counterposes his own theory, which he had first advanced as a young man, of both classes and states arising simultaneously as a result of the conquest of agrarian villages by nomadic pastoralists—a conquest that, to be sure, can take place only if certain economic conditions are present. The pastoralists now living off the peasants superimpose themselves on the latter as a ruling class and, uniting a number of villages under their sway, erect the state as an instrument of suppression and exploitation (IV:2:4 and IV:3:1–7).[34]

It may well seem that Kautsky ascribes an immensely important role to the state in his conception of history. Trade, banking, and money, writing and science, irrigation and flood control works, urbanism, art and architecture are all discussed in a section entitled "Effects of the State." All of them, however, are seen merely as arising out of conditions associated with the existence of the state, which is itself defined as an institution representing the ruling class or classes. Unlike Hegel's thought and some more recent neo-Marxian theorizing, Kautsky sees the state not as an actor, or as independent of classes (pp. 270–71),[35] it is not reified—though his choice of words may sometimes seem to suggest it. It is "only an abstraction. . . . The state has no will, no purposes, and no goals. Only men have them, men who rule in the state and through the state" (p. 388). The only actors in history are human beings—individuals, groups, classes.

When Marx generalized about history, he tended to project backward into the past the trends he saw in capitalism. He saw history being driven forward by growing tensions between developing forces of production and conservative relations of production, tensions that are expressed in the form of class struggles and are ultimately resolved by social revolutions. Kautsky was more interested in and better informed about premodern history than Marx could be. He stressed not only that there were no classes during most of human history, but even when there are classes and class rule, as in early states and under oriental despotism, there are hardly any class struggles (IV:5:7a and b); and when there are class struggles and even revolutions, as in the ancient city-states, especially in Greece (IV:6:2–3), they do not bring about new relations of production. If the forces of production develop at all, they serve only the luxury of the exploiters; the exploited continue to live in the old way and hence cannot visualize or seek new relations of production. Precapitalist societies are doomed to stagnation or cycles of rising civilization and decay, cycles that can be renewed not from within but only through conquest by less civilized but more vital outsiders (IV:4:13, 14, IV:5:7c, 8, IV:6:5, IV:9:1a).

"What Marx in 1859 regarded as a general law of social development

---

34. When I wrote my study *The Politics of Aristocratic Empires* a few years ago, I found that much of what Kautsky had to say on the formation and early forms of states and the functions and character of aristocracies (IV: 3:1–5, 8) stands up quite well in the light of more recent research.

35. Kautsky does mention Greek tyranny, Roman Caesarism, and French Bonapartism emerging in a situation where hostile classes hold each other in balance, but he does so in connection not with the role of the state, let alone its autonomy, but with the rise of dictatorships (IV: 8:14).

reveals itself today, strictly speaking, to be only the law of this development since the rise of industrial capitalism" (p. 454; see also IV:9:2). Thus, to have emphasized that in the precapitalist world there were no social revolutions in the Marxian sense was a major contribution by Kautsky to Marxist interpretations of history, for this view makes it possible to account for the social stability of polities governed by aristocracies from their beginnings millennia ago down to our own century.

Kautsky traces the crucial difference between capitalism and the earlier economy back to the difference between medieval Western towns and the cities of antiquity and the Orient (IV:7a, IV:6:1–3, IV:7:4) and to the growth of free labor in the former (IV:7:1, 5–6).[36] Industrial capitalism differs fundamentally from earlier modes of production and exploitation in that it continues to create productive forces and wealth, thus permitting the regeneration of society from within (IV:7:2), and, by developing the forces of production for mass production rather than mere luxury, it changes the living conditions of the mass of the exploited. Class struggles and political revolutions can now lead to social revolutions, because for the first time the conditions for new forms of production are present. In the English and French revolutions, the new forces of production and the elements of industrial capitalism representing them (that is, the independent urban petty bourgeoisie that contains the beginnings of industrial capital as well as of the proletariat) come to collide with the traditional property system and the political system of feudalism. It is only now that the class struggle becomes the motor of history, moving society forward to higher forms (IV:7:8, IV:9:1a).

The State and Class Struggles Under Capitalism

Out of the struggle of the new industrial classes against feudal and clerical royalist regimes arises a new form of democracy (IV:7:9). It "brings about complete equality of rights for . . . all adult members of the polity" (p. 374), making the modern democratic state fundamentally different from all earlier states, though exploiting and exploited classes continue to exist within it. The position of the bourgeoisie rests not, like that of earlier exploiters, on political-military power but on its economic indispensability, and class conflicts are no longer fought out by force of arms once democracy is assured

---

36. Much of Kautsky's extended discussion of these subjects is carried on with reference to Max Weber's work, which Kautsky both greatly admired and frequently disagreed with (e.g., IV: 5:7a, IV: 6:2, IV: 7:1, 3, C-7; see also IV: 4:8–9 and IV: 7:15).

(IV:7:10). With the growth of modern democracy goes the striving for the national, that is, language-based, state (IV:7:11). "Like the progress of industry, that of the self-determination of peoples is irresistible" (p. 380). National states do not seek conquests if their neighbors, too, are national states. Thus, "in this modern democratic state, neither the exploitation of the working class within it nor its relationship with its neighbors rests upon the military might of its ruling class" (p. 381).

Kautsky notes that as the old suppressive functions of the state recede, new functions grow. Democracy brings universal military service, and armies and armaments expand tremendously—though Kautsky, writing in the 1920s, expected an early trend in the opposite direction! Systems of transportation, communication, education, and medical care all grow as do the taxes to pay for them (IV:7:12). In recognizing that the new functions of the state are important to the exploited, too, Kautsky adds a significant corrective to the traditional Marxian view of history and of the state. In precapitalist times, government served the interests of the ruling class; the Marxian conception of government as an organ of the ruling class is not inappropriate with reference to the aristocracy. In modern societies, however, governments perform more and more functions that serve also the interests of the lower classes. In Kautsky's view, then, the working class can and does advance toward the realization of its political and economic goals already under capitalism, and the class struggle assumes less and less violent forms with the development of capitalism.

Because of its new functions, the exploited no longer aim to destroy the state, but wish to take control of the government. And they become more and more capable of doing so, struggling first for democracy and then for its use to influence the state in their interest. The government continues to serve the maintenance of exploitation, and, indeed, the workers become dependent on the state in a new way, "but democracy also makes it possible to wrest this whole immense state apparatus with its irresistible power out of the hands of the great exploiters that still hold it today and thus to turn the apparatus of domination into an apparatus of emancipation" (IV:7: 12d).

With the growth of governmental functions, bureaucracy grows, but it more and more has to share power with numerous organizations—corporations, trade unions, cooperatives, political parties—many of which develop their own professional bureaucracies. Parliaments, representing a majority of the people, install, control, and dismiss governments and make laws and thus control the bureaucracy. But once the voters have learned to make use of their rights and have organized in mass parties (which represent class interests and specific methods of pursuing them) and once they are informed by a free press, they in turn control parliaments (IV:7:12d, 13). Press, party, and parliament "if they have sufficient power, are the organs through which the people, that is, its strongest class and political method at a given time, rules the state, controls the state apparatus, that is, the bureaucracy, and gives it direction" (p. 389).

As to class struggle, Kautsky does not share what he calls "a crudely simplistic conception of Marxism" (p. 372) that sees modern society as simply divided into the proletariat and the bourgeoisie, but repeatedly emphasizes its complexity and the multiplicity of classes and the variety of conflicts and cooperation within and between them. Indeed, he stresses the complexity of the class structure even in ancient and oriental societies (IV: 5:7a) as well as conflicts between producers and consumers (IV:1:2) and between different professions and occupations (IV:1:4). He notes in particular the varied important roles in politics of the intellectuals who constitute no class at all (IV:7:16), and had repeatedly stressed the rapid growth of the intelligentsia and of white-collar workers for about thirty-five years before he wrote the present work (see IV:7:16, *n.* 30). Matters are further complicated by the fact that political parties in modern democracies do not coincide with classes. Not only do parties represent different "methods" as well as different class interests (IV:7:13), but bourgeois parties, though representing primarily the interests of the bourgeoisie, are composed of "very different strata, classes, and parts of classes," mostly peasants and petty-bourgeois but also intellectuals and workers (IV:8:3).

While referring to insights regarding modern societies, which Kautsky developed by amending notions commonly propounded by Marxists, we should also note his view of the development of proletarian class consciousness and class parties pursuing socialist goals. Much more than the proletariat's economic antagonism to capital, it is the political antagonism over the question of democracy that he holds responsible for this development. Initially driven into the struggle for democracy and the suffrage by the bourgeoisie itself, the proletariat becomes independent as it expands that struggle to one for universal suffrage (IV:8:2). "Universal suffrage and fully developed democracy in general are a result and an achievement of the proletarian class struggle" (p. 405)—but, Kautsky adds, only in countries that pass through a stage of princely absolutism and a centralized government with a powerful bureaucracy and a standing army. "What significance the struggle for democracy . . . had for the proletariat . . . becomes evident if we compare the countries of Europe, where such struggles were necessary, with . . . the United States, where the workers encountered an already considerably developed democracy" (p. 405). Kautsky here puts his finger on a crucial difference between Western European and American politics, resting on the absence of an aristocracy in American history, and he ascribes to it the failure to form a large labor party in the United States. Not being particularly interested in—or well informed about—American politics, however, he does not pursue the matter.

Democracy

Kautsky, then, conceived of the modern state under capitalism as a democracy and in particular saw a close link between the development of democracy and the rise of the proletariat. Democracy is not bourgeois nor is it merely formal (IV:7:9; pp. 374, 387, 393, 405); it entails real rights for all citizens, but it is not, of course, equivalent to socialism. Exploitation and hence class antagonism and class struggle continue to grow with the development of capitalism (IV:8:11), and class conflicts are reflected in the politics of parties, parliament, and the press. Kautsky notes that financial campaign contributions by capitalists are still important and that capitalists can pay to have their interests advanced in the press. "In this area, the superior strength of big capital vis-à-vis the propertyless makes itself oppressively felt" (p. 390). Also, Kautsky is deeply concerned with the growing cost of armies and armaments (IV:7:12a and p. 430). But whatever happens under democracy that Kautsky may not like, he does not regard as its fault, but, on the contrary, as a remnant of predemocratic days that can and will be corrected by the further progress of democracy. Democracy "as such" is clearly a wholly good thing to Kautsky.[37]

To a generation that has come to identify Marxism as virtually the antithesis of democracy, Kautsky's unquestioning devotion to democracy may seem to be the most remarkable aspect of his work. In fact he was, in this respect as in others, a good representative of the orthodox Marxism of the Second International and of German Social Democracy in the Wilheminian empire. His faith in democracy is a persistent and consistent theme of his works, from his authoritative commentary on the Erfurt Program of 1892 and, notably, his *Parlamentarismus and Demokratie* (first published under a different title in 1893), through his anti-Revisionist writings, beginning in 1899, including *The Road to Power* of 1909, often described as his most radical book, to the anti-Communist writings of his last two decades.

In the present work, too, Kautsky sees democracy only as a solution to problems; he does not treat it as posing problems. Thus, while in other contexts he stresses the growing complexity of the technological and social world, he does not seem worried about the ability of voters to understand it and to make decisions or to control their representatives who must do so. He recognizes the inevitability of bureaucracy, but does not tell us at all realistically how it is to be subjected to popular control. From a present-

---

37. Indeed, in one passage he speaks of "the idea of democracy" in contrast to the kind of democracy practiced by the bourgeoisie (p. 405), thus doing for democracy precisely what he rightly accused Hegel and Lassalle of doing for the state, i.e., divorcing the "idea" from the reality (IV: 1:7).

day perspective, Kautsky's conception of democracy often seems quite un-realistic and innocent of a host of problems, for example, with respect to questions of representation and voting behavior, public opinion and mass communications.

Why would an analyst as aware of the complexity of modern politics as Kautsky was hold such a simple view of democracy? Of course, most of the huge body of scholarly work on democratic politics that exists today was not available in Kautsky's time, and some decades ago even scholars in democratic countries tended to speak of democracy in what seems to us idealized and naive terms. But one must also refer to Kautsky's own back-ground to explain his attitude toward democracy. He did not really have much firsthand experience with democratic politics. As a young man, he spent a few years in Switzerland (1880–82 and 1884) and in England (mostly 1885–88), but he was never either a participant in or a student of the politics of these countries. His political experience was acquired in the imperial Vienna of the late 1870s and some of the 1880s and, above all, beginning in 1890 in Wilheminian Germany. In both countries, he was almost con-stantly involved in conflicts within the Social-Democratic Party and learned not only about other parties, the weak parliaments, and especially the press—all of which he stresses in the present work as the principal organs of democracy—but also about governments dominated by monarchs, bu-reaucrats, and military men rather than republican executives controlled by parliaments elected by universal suffrage.

Throughout Kautsky's active political career as a party writer and editor and adviser to party leaders (except for its last few years in the early Weimar Republic), democracy was to him not the existing political system but a hoped-for alternative to the unsatisfactory present. Like most opposition politicians, Kautsky was more concerned with the defects of the status quo than with the details of the future order he desired. As a goal and hence an ideal, democracy—in this respect not unlike socialism—seemed to him ob-viously both highly desirable and quite inevitable, but its functioning was never clearly visualized.

Further, for a Marxist whose political views were shaped in the last quarter of the nineteenth century, it was not farfetched to see the rise of democracy and of political labor movements as going hand in hand. To Kautsky, the growing socialist parties would demand and advance democ-ratization and, in turn, benefiting from it, they would, once democracy was achieved, sooner or later inevitably come to power and would then intro-duce socialist changes through democracy. The prediction rests on the as-sumptions that with advancing industrialization the number and political power of workers must increase and that at least most of them must become socialists. Although in the late twentieth century, these assumptions have become unrealistic, in Marx's day they involved brilliant insights, and they were still quite sensible and supported by a great deal of evidence in Kautsky's times, especially given the fact that *The Materialist Conception of History* reflects in part views and experience shaped long before it was written.

The Corporation, the Welfare State, Fascism

If one looks back at Kautsky's work with the benefit of hindsight, it is striking how he ignored or underestimated the importance of the development in his own time of the corporation, of social or welfare policy, and of Fascism. The relevance to his argument at least of the first two of these could have been fairly obvious even in the 1920s so that Kautsky's lack of attention to them supports the impression that his *Materialist Conception of History* is in good part the product of his interests and experience as they were shaped in earlier decades. The significance of Fascism was much harder to appreciate in the early 1920s, but here, too, Kautsky's preconceptions tended to obstruct his understanding.

Kautsky's image of capitalism still seems, in good part, to rest on a conception of individual capitalists operating their enterprises. He mentions the growth of cartels and trusts, and he is certainly aware of the development of corporations (IV:8:11), saying in passing even that they need a bureaucracy of their own (IV:7:13). But he sees corporations as run by the magnates of finance capital (IV:8:11). Kautsky refers to the person of the capitalist becoming superfluous and his individual initiative being replaced by "stable regulation and organization" (p. 437), but he comes no closer than that to any discussion of the growth of the corporate managerial bureaucracy, of the separation of ownership from control, and of the possible differences between the motivations and behavior of managers and capitalists. Generally, he speaks of capitalists (see, for example, IV:7:13) or, more vaguely, of capital, rather than of managers or corporations, as actors in the economy and in politics.

Kautsky put tremendous emphasis in many of his writings, including the present one, on the political benefits workers derive from democracy—the opportunity to become politically active and educated, to organize unions and parties, to have their own press, to participate in local governments, and eventually to gain power locally and nationally. It is all the more striking, then, that he is virtually silent on the social and economic changes brought about, at least in part, in response to pressure by organized labor and socialist parties. In one sentence, he notes that "like the struggle for democracy, so-called social [welfare] policy or social reform also tends to raise the proletariat" (p. 408; see also IV:8:2 and 10). When Kautsky shows how the modern state—unlike all previous ones—has functions that serve the interests of the exploited as well as of the exploiters, he mentions only education and, quite briefly, medical care (IV:7:12b), and in another context, he stresses the importance of the reduction of the working day for the intellectual and political rise of the proletariat (pp. 407–08). Otherwise, he does not deal at all with government regulation of industry and business in the interest of consumers and, particularly, of labor, nor with the great variety of social insurance and welfare benefits being provided in all industrialized countries. Though greatly expanded since Kautsky's time, these programs were by no means unknown or even entirely new then.[38]

In retrospect, it seems clear that the most far-reaching change brought about in modern societies by socialist parties—though not only by them— is the establishment of welfare states. To Kautsky, however, the crucial change socialist parties were bound to introduce was still the socialization of the means of production. He wrote the present work in Vienna in the 1920s, at the very time a Social-Democratic city administration introduced pioneering social welfare measures, perhaps most visibly in the field of public housing. Yet, Kautsky mentions socialist control of Vienna only in a brief passage (partly deleted in the present edition) as offering an opportunity to the proletariat to "introduce the beginnings of socialist production on a larger scale" (p. 438).

In this work, published midway between the two world wars and between Mussolini's and Hitler's seizure of power and just a few years before the onset of the Great Depression, Kautsky could say, "With every year by which we distance ourselves from the World War and the mercenary mentality it created, with which the process of production returns more onto its normal track and the number of the unemployed and the desperate diminishes, there also dwindles more and more the prospect that the violence-prone among the capitalists will be able to halt the advance of the working class under democracy by unleashing a civil war, to remove democracy itself."

Italian Fascism was to him a unique phenomenon, due to special circumstances like the disruption of World War I and especially the splitting of the Italian proletariat by the Communists, who frightened the capitalists and weakened the proletariat. These conditions "are limited to a particular country and a particular point in time and will not be very easily repeated" (p. 394). Kautsky compares the Italian Fascists to earlier American Pinkertons and calls them paid thugs, hired by shortsighted and frightened capitalists who did not understand that such armed bandits would eventually threaten their property and persons, too. Only in Italy, with its exceptionally large population of declassed elements, could such thugs be found in suf-

38. Kautsky had in letters to Bernstein of 21 August 1897 and 1 August 1898 stated bluntly that "social policy" had never interested him. The relevant two sentences are quoted in Steinberg, *Sozialismus und deutsche Sozialdemokratie*, p. 84, n. 251.

ficient numbers to be effective. In industrialized countries and particularly in Germany, Kautsky asserts with confidence, they simply do not exist in such numbers (IV:7:14).

What Kautsky says to explain Italian Fascism is by no means all irrelevant, but obviously it is not adequate. Later, he found it even more difficult to explain the rise of Fascism in industrialized Germany with its powerful labor movement, and perhaps for that reason he wrote relatively little on the subject even after the Nazis came to power in 1933.[39] An antidemocratic and antisocialist mass movement of the dimensions of Nazism simply did not fit into Kautsky's conception of modern politics.[40] Of course, Kautsky was not alone in this respect. Good explanations of Fascism—a novel phenomenon—were rare in its early years and especially by 1927, when Nazism was only a small storm cloud on the German horizon. Indeed, the question of the social bases of Fascism and especially of its relationship to capitalism—which Kautsky ought to have answered—remains highly controversial to this day. One can at least note that Kautsky stated clearly that Fascism would not everywhere be the response of capitalism to the rise of labor in democracy (p. 394). He thought that dictatorships were a phenomenon of early industrial capitalism with an immature proletariat, not of advanced capitalism (IV:8:14), as other Marxists came to see it.

The Future of Underdeveloped Countries

If Kautsky did not and could not understand Western democracy as we do today and if he did not appreciate some major political tendencies of his own time, he certainly could not know about the political developments in the underdeveloped world, which have become clearer and aroused the interest of numerous Western scholars—or, indeed, have taken place—only since World War II. I deal here with Kautsky's thoughts on the subject only

39. In "Einige Ursachen und Wirkungen des deutschen Nationalsozialismus," Kautsky devoted a few pages (pp. 237–42) to an attempt to explain Nazism, "a complex phenomenon." He did so with reference to the consequences of the depression and of the Versailles treaty. See also my n. 29 at the end of IV: 7:14. The demoralizing effects of the depression on German workers are also stressed in *Grenzen der Gewalt*, pp. 23–25. Other writings of 1931–34 dealing wholly or in part with Nazism are summarized in Salvadori, *Karl Kautsky*, p. 349–63.

40. Kautsky and part of his immediate family became themselves victims of Nazism. He fled from Vienna to Czechoslovakia on March 12, 1938, when Hitler's troops marched into Austria, and died in exile in Amsterdam seven months later. His eighty-year-old-wife, Luise, caught in German-occupied Holland, died in December 1944 in Auschwitz, where their youngest son, Benedikt, who spent seven years in German concentration camps, was a prisoner at that time.

to point up, with the benefit of hindsight, both some of the limitations imposed on him by his perspective and some valid insights he could derive from it.

Given his long-standing interest in Russian revolutionary developments,[41] Kautsky could draw some highly suggestive parallels between Russia in the past and present and China and India in the present and future and contrast them to Western European history. He stressed the absence of a petty bourgeoisie in the history of these non-Western countries (IV:7: 10, IV:8:5) and of the democratic tradition it had initiated (IV:7:4–10). Most important, he was aware of the key role of intellectuals in the revolutions of underdeveloped countries, men who seek to apply the revolutionary experience and the socialist theories of the West in an environment where they are not—or not yet—applicable. However, Kautsky shows no sensitivity here to the revolutionary potential of the peasantry, as he had in his earlier writings on Russia,[42] and he does not mention peasant revolts even when he deals with the Chinese and Mexican revolutions (IV:8:5).

If Kautsky is aware of some of the differences between the political consequences of what I have called modernization from within, as it occurred in Western Europe, and modernization from without, as represented by Russia and the underdeveloped countries,[43] he nevertheless could conclude only that the different historical tracks (IV:7:10) all lead to the same goal where industrial capital has become dominant, because the latter and its laws of motion are the same everywhere (IV:8:5). Here the limitations under which Kautsky was laboring become apparent, limitations imposed on him in general by a Eurocentric perspective common among European intellectuals of his time and in particular by his Marxism, a special variety of Eurocentrism. He could conceive of revolutions only as bourgeois or proletarian or as containing elements of the two, for example, being bourgeois in content but carried out by the proletariat. He could not see that they could be wholly different—as revolutions of modernizing intellectuals in underdeveloped countries, including the Russian one, have in fact turned out to be. Writing in 1925, he could refer to the Russian revolution "as the *last* of the bourgeois revolutions of Europe—and as the *first* of the bourgeois

41. For references to a few of Kautsky's writings on Russia, see my footnotes 12 in IV: 7:9, 25 in IV: 7:14, und 9 in IV: 9:1d. Kautsky's more significant writings on the subject are well summarized in Salvadori, *Karl Kautsky*, pp. 100–108, 218–25, 251–318, and a number of post-1917 ones are reprinted in Lübbe, ed., *Kautsky gegen Lenin.*

42. See "Die Bauern und die Revolution in Russland," and "Triebkräfte und Aussichten der russischen Revolution." On the prospects of the March 1917 Revolution, see "Die Aussichten der russischen Revolution," written in April 1917, which concludes by stating that the peasantry is the decisive factor in the Russian Revolution and one that has no parallel in West European history.

43. See my *Political Consequences of Modernization,* esp. pp. 44–49.

revolutions of Asia. And yet it came also as the first of the revolutions of our age in which the proletariat wielded decisive power."[44]

In his chapter significantly entitled "Roads to Socialism" (IV:8:5), there emerges a picture of non-European politics—or at least the politics of countries Kautsky sees as dominated by industrial capital, like those of Latin America, China, and India—in which the proletariat and the achievement of democracy play a central role. Even in Russia, "the strength and independence of its proletariat and of democracy" (p. 414) must necessarily grow as industry grows. It is a picture far removed from the reality even of Kautsky's day and one, it is safe to say by now, that has proved to be a dismal failure as a prediction.

Half a century later, we cannot help asking how Kautsky could have been so wrong. Both ignorance and wishful thinking obviously played their part, the latter all the more strongly as it was uninhibited by sound knowledge. Yet Kautsky was not alone or even exceptional in these respects. At least through the 1950s, a widespread belief in the West was that decolonization meant self-determination and would therefore result in the establishment of democratic regimes. Kautsky, who correctly foresaw the end of colonialism—he takes British withdrawal from India for granted two decades before it occurred—at least seemed to think that a period of native dictatorship would normally intervene between political revolutions, like the fall of the Romanovs, the Manchus, and the British in India (IV:8:5), and the establishment of democracy. As to Russia, wrong as he was in his expectations of a collapse of the Soviet regime, at least he did not share the illusions about its actual or potential proletarian or "socialist" character as he understood that term—illusions still held by some major democratic Marxist leaders and thinkers, especially in the first, pre-Stalinist decade of Soviet rule when Kautsky was writing. This position is clearer in some of Kautsky's writings on the character and prospects of the Soviet regime than in the present work, where only a few paragraphs deal with or hint at this subject.

The Marxian dictum about the industrially more developed country showing to the less developed one the image of its own future, which Kautsky quotes as unshaken truth in his chapter "Roads to Socialism," was in many ways an insightful forecast when it was written sixty years earlier. But it began, as we can now see, to be misleading about the time Kautsky repeated it. The process of industrialization initiated in England turned out to be a model for only part of the world, yet Marx's and Kautsky's assumptions—which posit an identity between industrialization and the rise of capitalism and an inextricable linkage between these and the rise of the proletariat, of democracy and, eventually, of socialism—rest on the analysis

44. "Was uns Axelrod gab," p. 120.

of this process. Modernizing revolutions in underdeveloped countries and then an industrializing regime and society like the Soviet one that were neither bourgeois nor proletarian, neither capitalist nor socialist nor democratic (as he used these adjectives) were unimaginable to Kautsky because there was no historical precedent for them. He was still in the same position as Marx of having only the Western European development of industry and politics available as a model. Therefore, he used only the Marxian concepts and categories that had served him well in his analysis of Western European politics, irrelevant as they proved to be to the novel process of history unfolding in his time.

The Realistic Approach to Socialism

Kautsky's generation was the last that could still manage largely to ignore the underdeveloped countries. In his work of some seventeen hundred pages, only a single chapter of fewer than ten pages and a few scattered paragraphs are devoted to the subject of their future. But what about Kautsky's thoughts on the future of industrialized countries? It can be summarized in the single word "socialism," for there was no doubt in Kautsky's mind that, with the growth of capitalism, the rise of democracy and, through it, the political victory of the proletariat and hence of socialism were inevitable. Yet there is no systematic discussion in *The Materialist Conception of History* that shows how Kautsky visualized socialism. There are only various passages indicating Kautsky's approach to certain problems of the future society under socialism and of the transition to it. These passages reflect two somewhat distinct attitudes, one quite realistic and practical, the other expressing far-reaching hopes for a much better society. This hopeful attitude rests in part, of course, on Kautsky's indomitable optimism and his socialist ideology, as distinguished from his social science. But he could also maintain it because of his quite sensible reluctance and refusal to make specific predictions as to the socialist future, which I shall note below.

Kautsky says that "socialism is for us only a means to an end, to the final goal of the complete emancipation of the proletariat" (p. 427). If that could be achieved within capitalism more easily and with fewer sacrifices, the socialist goal would have to be given up. Kautsky, of course, does not expect this, but he reasons that the socialist mode of production must satisfy the proletariat more than the capitalist one, it must provide it with more material goods, knowledge, and freedom. It would be foolish to expect workers to retain socialism if it did not do so (IV:8:10).

But that socialism will be superior to capitalism, at least from the proletarian point of view—which Kautsky often identified with that of "society" (IV:8:1)—does not mean that under socialism society will somehow be perfect. Kautsky disagreed with Engels' suggestion that organization of production under socialism is tantamount to men controlling their history, and he says that solving present-day social problems through socialism will not solve all future problems (IV:9:2). Socialism involves—and is virtually defined by Kautsky as—the end of exploitation and classes and hence of class conflict, but he clearly expects other conflicts to persist or to arise. There will certainly be "complete" democracy, which would presumably be pointless if there were no more conflicts in society. Kautsky refers to the force of majorities, once determined by free elections, being irresistible against individuals and minorities (p. 448). In another context he says that the conflicts between those who resist innovations and those who welcome them will "of course" always exist, even in classless societies (p. 454).[45]

Kautsky also seems quite realistic in his discussion of the conditions most favorable to the transition to socialism—he finds them in capitalist prosperity (IV:8:13)—and of the reasons why the payment of compensation for expropriated capitalist enterprises may be desirable (III:3:10; IV:7:10). Socialization of industry can involve cooperative and communal as well as state ownership, but even in the latter case must not mean administration by the traditional bureaucracy (IV:8:4). Kautsky stresses that special organizational forms would have to be created, adapted to the interests of producers and consumers in each branch of industry and transportation, and he thinks of socialization as a gradual process of development involving a great deal of learning and experimentation (p. 411). He also faces up to the problem of workers' productivity under socialism, which, in turn, involves the difficult problem of creating a new "proletarian class morality," and he thinks that morality will be the more attainable the more extensive is democracy within the enterprise so that workers regard it as their own (IV:8:13). Finally, Kautsky expresses grave doubts that the social sciences and especially economics are sufficiently advanced to be able immediately to adapt the entire immensely complex process of production to the needs of the working masses so as to satisfy them fully and to attain a maximum of production (V:3:10).

As to the "withering away of the state" under socialism, to which Kautsky devotes an entire chapter (IV:8:15), he agrees that some aspects of government, like the political police and eventually the military, would disappear, but others would grow, for example, in the fields of education and health care and, above all, of the regulation of the huge process of production. All of this is to be handled "in as democratic, as flexible and

---

45. "New contradictions, new problems, new struggles will arise in socialist society." "Gustav Mayers Engels-Biographie," p. 346.

unbureaucratic a manner as possible, yet without eliminating all bureauc-racy. For no large organization can manage any longer today without bu-reaucracy, once it has responsibility for tasks requiring specialized knowledge and complete devotion on the part of those entrusted with carrying them out" (p. 448; see also IV:7:13). The state, then, does not wither away, but its functions change once there are no more classes and the government represents the majority rather than exercising power over it (IV:8:15).

The Idealized Image of Socialism

If Kautsky deals with some aspects of the transition to socialism and even of the future socialist society as quite practical problems, there are also numerous vaguer passages on that society in the present work. Many of them contrast socialism to capitalism and simply suggest that whatever or at least much that is bad under the latter will be taken care of under the former. Mostly, Kautsky just assumes this will happen as a consequence of the absence of exploitation and classes, but does not discuss in any detail the process by which it will come about.

Socialism will bring equality of property of all parts of the population (p. 448), and "the abolition of classes, of the antagonisms between poverty and wealth with all the many social differences they give rise to" (p. 523). With socialism, we are approaching "a condition of general far-reaching humanity", that is, respect for the human personality. Cleanliness and nu-trition will improve, and hence men and women will be healthier and stronger (V:3:8). There will be equality of education (p. 448), and "so-cialism will make the rapidly growing diversity of scientific production and of intellectual and artistic production in general accessible to the entire laboring mass of all occupations" (V:3:12).

"Along with exploitation, the antagonisms among nations arising out of exploitative tendencies will disappear" (V:3:6). Already before the ad-vent of socialism, that of "universal democracy" in all industrialized coun-tries and the consequent self-determination of nations should lead to "the abolition of armies and of war by means of a league of these states" (IV:7:11). Once the major countries of the world have "socialist-democratic governments" and there is no more war and hence no interest in strategic boundaries, states can be shaped entirely and everywhere on the basis of the self-determination of nationalities and can yield "a number of important functions to the League of Nations," which becomes indispensable "for the construction of the new society that will take the place of the capitalist one" (IV:8:15).

Perhaps one can grant Kautsky that some of these remarks—all of them brief assertions rather than careful analyses—are in line with historical trends he could detect in his time. But he ignores countertrends and all kinds of huge problems involved in the immense changes he projects. No doubt he was unaware of many of these problems, but he also did not wish to deal with them, in part probably simply because they were unpleasant to face but in part also because of his reluctance to make predictions about the still distant future.

The concept—or the fiction—of the collectivity or the society as a political actor, acting, of course, in what Kautsky thinks of as the interest of society, is not only, as I noted earlier, hard to reconcile with a conception of history emphasizing that societies are divided by conflict, but it also permits him to fail to analyze or even recognize the problem of the relation of the individual to society under democracy and hence also under socialism. On the one hand, he knows that individual freedom must be limited in any society simply by the fact of social living, and he even sees individual dependence on society growing with social development and the division of labor. Individuals can subjectively *feel* free if they voluntarily accept social restrictions as necessary and useful. Individuals who are "refractory or un-mindful of their duty" may have to be subject to compulsion, but the greater the majority that makes the rules, the smaller the number of resisters, and the greater the community of interest between majority and minority, the less will compulsion be felt as a limitation of freedom (V:3:5). Where Kautsky once deals with the question of how the "collectivity" functions as a political actor, he stresses that it can act "only if it has organized itself and . . . entrusted individual men with the task of carrying out the will of its majority" (IV:7:13). And, as I just noted, he says that the force or weight of the majority determined in free elections becomes irresistible against individuals or minorities. There is no mention here of any limitations on majority decisions in the form of individual or civil liberties.

On the other hand, there is Kautsky's pervasive emphasis on democracy. Certainly that means to him, above all, majority rule through universal suffrage and parliamentary government, but it does also involve civil liberties. Thus, he refers to the freedoms of association, of assembly, and of the press as aspects of democracy (IV:7:9) and particularly stresses the first of these (IV:7:13). While he thinks of these freedoms often principally as indispensable to the rise of the proletariat rather than as individual liberties and similarly demands freedom of expression for minorities without mentioning it as an individual right (V:2:4; but see pp. 244–45), he denounces socialists who might demand such freedoms for their movement but would, once they are in power, deny them to their opponents (IV:8:14).

Furthermore, Kautsky expects that under socialism "the differentiation of human personalities, which up to now has affected only some strata of society, will become a universal phenomenon," and he refers to it as "individualism" (p. 511). With the universal availability of education and the expansion of leisure time, socialism will provide "a hitherto unheard of possibility of the free development of the individual personality" (p. 524). It will "facilitate the full development by everyone of all his potentialities"— but Kautsky limits this to "potentialities the promotion of which is in the interest of society." "The individual [can] make copious use of these fully developed potentialities, entirely as he pleases, . . . at least in his leisure hours"—but only, Kautsky adds, "insofar as they are not socially harmful" (pp. 523–24).

By thinking of society as making decisions, Kautsky can avoid the key political questions of who within the society will decide what is in the interest of society and what is socially harmful and how and by whom those who make these decisions are to be selected and controlled and influenced, in short, how power is to be distributed and wielded within society. Such questions can hardly be answered by the mere employment of the concepts of majority and minority, with the majority under socialism evidently thought of by Kautsky as very large and quite homogeneous and hence quite like—and certainly representing—society. All too generally, Kautsky substitutes for analytical answers to political questions the mere word "democracy." Often he seems to imply that everything will be taken care of, if it is handled democratically; and under socialism, which adds freedom from exploitation and from economic inequality to democracy's freedom from political inequality and repression, things will be taken care of even better.

Socialism and Social Science

Why, then, does Kautsky devote so little space and thought in his massive work on *The Materialist Conception of History* to the socialist future of the industrialized countries that he expected with complete confidence? As far as the transition to socialism is concerned—a transition Kautsky considered sufficiently imminent after World War I to analyze in some detail—a major reason is probably simply that he had, in 1922, just a few years before he wrote the present work, published *The Labour Revolution*. It is a substantial book on the political and economic problems that would confront a new socialist government and deals at some length with matters like the bureaucracy, planning, socialization, and others hardly touched on in *The Materialist Conception of History*. Presumably, Kautsky did not want to repeat himself here.[46]

46. In a passage omitted from this edition, Kautsky stated that the subject of the transition to socialism was beyond the scope of the present work. "This is not the place to develop and

But what about the future under socialism once the transition is completed? Why does Kautsky not think and write in far more detail about what he is advocating? His answer, I believe, would be that he is merely projecting present-day tendencies into the future and thus predicting the coming of socialism and, indeed, demonstrating its inevitability (V:3:2), but he is not advocating it. As he says at the end of the present work, the task of scientists is not to console or to please but to discover and proclaim the truth, whether it is pleasing to them and others or not. To be sure, if it is pleasing, like the prediction of socialism, so much the better politically. It may then help inspire enthusiasm and presumably political action, but inspiration is not the principal task of science and of the materialist conception of history (V:3:12).

Socialism is a goal that the working class must pursue, "whether [it] knows it or not. [It is] not an ideal that a theorist has conceived or that a poet has dreamed up and yearned for, but an ideal that is given with its class position" (p. 443; see also IV:8:4 and V:3:2). Kautsky's task, as he perceived it, then, was not to dream or propose what a socialist society ought to look like, but to predict what would inevitably come about. Yet Kautsky also stressed repeatedly that our ability to predict is quite limited. "Regardless of how greatly our methods of social research might be improved, it will never be able to determine in advance the totality of coming social transformations and it will always be able to foresee only those transformations closest in time" (p. 218–19). As the Marxian prediction of coming socialism rests on experience, "it does not reach farther than our experience up to the present allows us to see. Its limits are thereby set. It [permits us] . . . only to recognize those coming solutions that are to be expected for problems already existing today, as far as the means and the forces for their solution are already developing and observable today" (p. 503).

When Kautsky wrote *The Materialist Conception of History*, he thought that at least Britain and Germany were on the verge of the beginning of the transition to socialism (IV:7:14, IV:8:12). But the socialist society resulting from this transition seemed to him still in the more distant future, and hence he stated repeatedly that "the forms of socialism that ultimately, after various trials and errors, prove to be the most suitable may look quite different from those we envision today" (p. 442; see also III:3:12). He stressed that the forms of production under socialism would vary in different countries and in different time periods and for different branches of the economy and concludes that socialism is not "a rigid, immutable formation of a perfect society; rather it refers to the direction that the further development of society will take under proletarian leadership" (p. 418).

---

justify the program of Social Democracy" (*Die materialistische Geschichtsauffassung* (1929), II, 524).

Like Marx, Kautsky was anxious to distinguish his scientific socialism from utopian socialism. He thought it would be foolish and futile to plan or foretell the socialist future, for societies are not planned and built like houses; they evolve out of existing conditions (III:4:2). Given that point of view, then, Kautsky may seen inconsistent in predicting as much about the socialism of the distant future as he does rather than being blameworthy for predicting too little. The predictions he does make and his rosy image of the future socialist society that emerges from them are, of course, a result of his emotional and ideological commitment to socialism rather than a result of careful social science analysis.

As a socialist, however, he sought to advance the cause of socialism only quite incidentally by depicting the benefits of the future society in glowing colors. He saw his contribution to socialism and the labor movement, as he saw Marx's and Engels' (p. 174), to be not a statement of values but the social-scientific analysis of the past and the present—which, he was convinced, would prove the inevitability of socialism in the future. Just as in the three volumes of Marx's *Capital*, so in the two volumes of Kautsky's *Die materialistische Geschichtsauffassung*, there is little explicit concern with socialism. Kautsky's magnum opus, like most of his work, was not meant to be, and overwhelmingly is not, devoted to advocacy or propaganda. It is a work of social science analysis and, for better or worse, it should be judged as such today.

Author's Preface

With the completion of the present work, a wish I have had for decades has been fulfilled, but also one that many others had expressed to me. How often have we Marxists been charged with basing all our thought and action on the materialist conception of history, but having neglected to give a systematic and comprehensive account and justification of this conception. This deficiency came to contradict ever more glaringly the practical and theoretical significance of Marxism, which dominates from year to year more strongly the labor movement and thereby the entire present-day development of society and of the state.

But this very significance of Marxism increasingly claims the strength and energy of all its adherents for the pressing tasks of the present, so that they have hardly any time and tranquility left for purely theoretical comprehensive work. . . . A peculiar coincidence of personal and general political circumstances has, however, for almost a decade now, given me the opportunity to devote myself entirely to theoretical labor and thus to provide a thorough foundation for the materialist conception of history, such as we have heretofore lacked and so urgently need.

The split of the German Social-Democratic Party that occurred during the World War took from me, in October 1917, the editorship of *Die Neue Zeit*, which until then had claimed my time and attention without interruption for thirty-five years. To be sure, this did not render me unemployed. The problems of the revolution, first of the Russian, then of the German, occupied me fully, and this activity was followed by the work of collecting and editing the German documents on the outbreak of the World War,[1] which kept me busy until the end of 1919. Then, however, I had the free time and the calm to undertake the work that had for long been close to my heart. Unfortunately, its completion required far more time than I had expected. At first, the work proceeded smoothly and rapidly, despite a half-year interruption caused by a journey to *[Transcaucasian]* Georgia (August 1920–January 1921). . . . Soon after *[October 1921]*, however, I interrupted my work in order to complete my book on the proletarian revolution [The Labour Revolution], in which I summed up the lessons for the proletarian class struggle that can be drawn from the experiences of the last revolution. I finished this book in June 1922.

When I returned to *The Materialist Conception of History*, I was no longer satisfied with the way I had treated the subject. I had fallen into the old error of our previous studies of the topic, I had summarized too much and had restricted myself too much to allusions, as I had done previously in my small book *Ethics and the Materialist Conception of History*, which, along with my work *Vermehrung und Entwicklung in Natur und Gesellschaft* [Propagation and Development in Nature and Society], is the preparatory study for the present work. . . . Therefore, I discarded what I had already written and began anew, in a different manner. In the meantime, however, my state of health had become much worse. . . . In view of my diminished capacity to work . . . , I began to doubt whether I would be able to complete the book in accordance with my new plan. I sketched out the train of thought and singled out certain chapters that I considered especially important in order to elaborate them. In this way, I thought that, should my strength fail prematurely, I would still be able to leave behind a torso of the book out of which my sons could make something. But I had never worked in this fashion, and the isolated chapters would not turn out right.

So I started over once again from the beginning, this time systematically developing one chapter out of the other in keeping with my new plan and completely finishing each one in its proper place. The further I advanced in this work, the more frequently I felt compelled, for the sake of completeness, to discuss questions that had not been a matter of concern for me up to then and that I had not yet thoroughly investigated. This made new studies necessary. Other questions I had studied, to be sure, but a half century earlier. Here it was necessary to familiarize myself with the current state of knowledge. And so I made only slow progress. Nevertheless, I succeeded in carrying on to the conclusion of the task.

I may call my work, in its present form, comprehensive, for it treats all fields that are, to my knowledge, relevant to an understanding of the ma-

---

1. *Outbreak of the World War.* See also *The Guilt of William Hohenzollern* and *Delbrück und Wilhelm II.*

terialist conception of history. That is not, of course, to say that my work is definitive. That is something no scientific work can ever be. Nor is it exhaustive. The materialist conception of history is founded, on the one hand, on the recognition of the uniformity of the processes of nature and of society; on the other hand, it shows, within what is general in the evolution of the world, what is particular in the development of society. To explain both the one and the other, so many and so diverse fields must be investigated and illuminated that, given the present-day state of scientific knowledge, perhaps several dozen experts would have to devote the best part of their lives to the task, if an exhaustive grounding and presentation of the materialist conception of history is to be provided. . . .

As with all my writings, in this work, too, I have attached the greatest importance to its being clear, easy to read, and generally understandable. To be sure, this goal cannot always be achieved. . . . There are only a few chapters in my book in which the subject matter precluded a treatment of it that can be easily understood, but these are, unfortunately, located at the beginning of this work, in Part I. I would regret it if my readers let themselves be deterred from reading further by these difficulties. . . . I have attempted to write the different parts, indeed often also individual chapters so that each of them can be understood in itself. If the reader finds the first part too difficult, he . . . can ignore it for the time being. . . . Indeed, for readers who are not interested in either philosophy or natural science and ethnology, it might even be practical to begin directly with the fourth part, which treats of the state and classes, areas in which alone Marxism is usually sought. A complete understanding of the materialist conception of history does require knowledge of all five parts. Furthermore, each individual part will be fully grasped only if the preceding ones from which it proceeds are known. . . .

Since my account of it had to show all sides of the materialist conception of history, I could not always present new ideas. Often enough, I had to repeat ideas that were already well known, especially those originating with Marx and Engels, but also not a few that I myself had already developed earlier. As I was not writing a textbook, however, I did not feel obliged to discuss all ideas with a thoroughness corresponding to their importance. Where I had nothing new to say and there was no danger of a misunderstanding, I treated even important ideas only briefly. On the other hand, where I had something new to present or had to deal with controversial matters, I sometimes wrote at great length, even on secondary questions. . . .

Of course, I have not mentioned all the books that have gone into the making of the present work. To this end, I would have to list all the books I have read in more than half a century, including a great many that I no longer have at hand and of which I have even lost the excerpts I made from them. On the other hand, I must admit that it was impossible for me to study thoroughly all the works relevant to each of the questions I have treated. Such a requirement can be made only for a monograph of limited scope. . . . Unfortunately, it was not possible for me to obtain all the books I would like to have used. The largest part of the present work was composed in Vienna, where the conditions for obtaining rare scholarly and scientific works from abroad were very unfavorable in the postwar period. Still, the fulfillment of all my desires in this regard would only have delayed the completion of my work, would only have expanded it, without changing its fundamental ideas, which have been established for a long time. I would merely have added another detail here and there. . . .

I was helped not a little in my labors by the fact that a number of socialist parties that were interested in my work freed me for several years from the burden of gainful employment. An especially strong interest in my exposition *[of the materialist conception of history]* was shown by the party executive of the German Social-Democratic Party, which made it possible to print this voluminous book very quickly. I would like to express here my gratitude to all of them, as well as to my three sons, Felix, Karl, and Benedikt, who, each with his particular expertise, aided me by word and by deed. The index was compiled by Benedikt.[2] Lastly, I must also mention my dear wife, who has taken the most lively interest in all my writings since the beginning of our marriage, with whom I have discussed each one of them and have scrutinized and polished all my manuscripts, and who has always given me valuable suggestions, especially to make my presentations clearer and more easily understandable. This is true to an especially high degree of the present work.

It constitutes the quintessence of my life's work. It presents the method that has been the basis of my work for half a century. This method had already been formulated a generation before I became acquainted with it; numerous successes of its authors had already confirmed its fruitfulness. Since then, further studies by the masters and their disciples have reaffirmed it ever more strongly, while at the same time refining the method itself and developing it further. Hence I now present this method not just as the basis, but also as the result of my life's work.

As such, I dedicate this work to the one who has been most closely associated with my life's work during the greater half of my existence, to my Luise. In the first half of my life, there was another woman who influenced me in the most decisive manner, my mother. At an early age, she instilled in me a lively enthusiasm for high ideals. Should it still be possible for me to write my memoirs, as I plan to do, then I shall dedicate

---

2. Felix was a mechanical engineer, Karl a physician, and Benedikt an economist. The index of the present edition was, of course, compiled by the editor, but the original one proved helpful in its preparation.

that work to her. I note this now, as I must count on the probability that it will not be granted to me to complete that work.[3]

In my childhood, the atmosphere of 1848 still prevailed in my parents' house. In that atmosphere, I became filled, as soon as I began to think politically, with hatred of Austria, with the wish that it be smashed in order to bring about the liberation of its different nations who were shackled to one another. The aftereffects of the Paris Commune of 1871 did not then push the goal of national liberation aside, but broadened it into the goal of social liberation. It took on clearer forms when I came into contact with the Social-Democratic movement in 1874. In it and through it, I became acquainted with the materialist conception of history, which fascinated me. I adhered to it with the more conviction, the more I recognized, in applying it, how many new truths it opened up to me in the study of the past and how greatly it contributed in practice to making the advance of social democracy almost uninterruptedly victorious and irresistible. . . .

The materialist conception of history does not deny the power of the human will. But it shows that that will is enduringly victorious and invincible only when it is active in the direction given by economic conditions and when it stays within the limitations of what is possible at a particular time, which are set by these conditions. A will that disregards those limits cannot achieve anything lasting, but must ultimately fail, even if it achieves momentary successes and strives to defend them with extreme ruthlessness and bloody terrorism. Because of its limitation of the effectiveness of volition, the theory of historical materialism was, in times of revolution, easily perceived by the untrained masses and by individuals who used them as a troublesome leaden weight that paralyzed the revolutionary will. Some remained adherents of the materialist conception of history, but reinterpreted it in important points to change it into its opposite. Others rejected it entirely and proclaimed the omnipotence even of a volition without basis and without limits, if only it were energetic enough.

The excitement caused by the World War is beginning to subside. The economic abnormalities resulting from it are beginning to give way once again to normal economic conditions in which the force of economic laws is again manifesting itself. At the same time, the division of the laboring masses is more and more coming to an end. Despite the reaction that is still dominant at present, the strength of the Social-Democratic movement

3. Kautsky began work on his memoirs, *Erinnerungen und Erörterungen*, only in September 1936, having in the meantime written two major books on war, *Krieg und Demokratie* and *Sozialisten und Krieg*. By the time of his death on October 17, 1938, he had completed the story of his life only to the beginnings of his editorship of *Die Neue Zeit* in 1883, but even this fragment comprised more than five hundred pages when it was published in 1960.

is beginning to grow again, and it is resuming its temporarily interrupted victorious advance. This does not mean, however, a mere continuation of the movement as it proceeded prior to 1914. The Revolution . . . has created a new political foundation, on which the proletarian class struggle can be conducted more successfully than before, and it has proletarianized immense masses of petty-bourgeois individuals and filled immense masses of the indifferent and the fainthearted with interest for political and social matters and with an awareness of their strength. As soon as these new masses have been sufficiently organized and educated, their entry into the ranks of the Social-Democratic movement must make this movement irresistible and confer on it complete political power. It will achieve this power under economic conditions that will enable it immediately to undertake steps toward the emancipation of labor.

With growing trust in the old Social-Democratic movement, there must also awaken again and grow interest in the old theory, on which Marx and Engels founded their practice, the theory of the materialist conception of history. And more than ever, it now becomes necessary to acquaint the masses with that theory, if the practice of social democracy is to be able to achieve the maximum of that which its rapidly growing power will soon permit it to accomplish. The understanding of the materialist conception of history is now less than ever a purely academic matter. The dissemination of this understanding is becoming more than ever an important practical condition of socialist successes.

I do not mean that recognition of the materialist conception of history should be a prerequisite for adherence to the Social-Democratic Party. This party must be open to everyone who wants to join in the struggle of the proletariat for its emancipation, the struggle against all oppression and exploitation, no matter how an individual might support that desire theoretically, by materialist, Kantian, or Christian principles, or in some other way. But the most fruitful, most successful method of carrying on this struggle and bringing it to a victorious conclusion is provided, we are convinced, by the materialist conception of history—though only when it is not merely recognized, but also understood and intelligently applied. The greatest truth can have disastrous effects, if it is reduced to a few catchphrases that are mechanically parroted and applied, without thought and investigation of reality.

Nothing would make me happier than to succeed with my book in arousing livelier interest in the materialist conception of history as well as pointing out the wealth of problems that this conception encompasses, spreading a clear understanding of it, and counteracting all mechanical thinking in its application. I have set for the present work the task of promoting in this way the emancipation of laboring humanity. May it be equal to this great task!

Vienna, September 1927   Karl Kautsky

VOLUME ONE
 Nature and Society

PART ONE

Mind and World

Section One
The Object of Investigation

CHAPTER ONE

The Nature of the Materialist Conception of History

... Of the many great achievements of the two intellectual giants Engels and Marx, the most significant by far is their materialist conception of history. It became the firm foundation of their immense common lifework. Their entire socialism, indeed, the entire nature of the modern labor movement cannot be comprehended without this conception of history, which is their basis. ...

If the materialist conception of history really maintained that men act only from economic motives or material interest, then it would not be worthwhile for us to concern ourselves with it at length. ... Certainly *[Marx and Engels]* saw in the economy the fundamental motive force of history. However, in holding this position they were engaged not in psychology but in history. They did not want to explain the *universally human*, but the *historically particular*. They were not investigating the question of why men think and act, why they have ideas and ideals and let themselves be guided by them, but rather the question of why these ideas and ideals are very different in different times. ... And they found that the ultimate cause of changes of ideas is to be sought in changes of the economic conditions in which men live. That is something completely different from the assumption that men are always determined only by material *interests*. ...

It is not claimed that the link between a particular idea or institution and the economic factors in which it is grounded is always direct and clearly evident. ... Marx always held only the view that the economic factors were determinative in the *last* analysis. Intermediate links and interactions can in some circumstances heavily obscure the linkage. . . . [1]

[*Kautsky argues that Marx's work in economics, particularly* Capital, *rests on the materialist conception of history.*][2]

The Materialist Conception of History among the Marxists

What was for Marx and Engels the basis of all their work, what made it so magnificent and fruitful, did not always obtain justice at the hands of their successors. . . . These are frequently Marxists who, to be sure, recognize the materialist conception of history in theory but disregard it completely in practice. The temptation to do this is especially great for socialists in economically backward countries. According to Marx's conception of history, socialism is a product of certain economic conditions, that is, of a highly developed industrial capitalism. And no mass movement can be created arbitrarily through the volition of a few individuals, be they ever so devoted and ever so energetic. This insight often imposes limits on the practical goals that the socialists of a country set themselves at any given time and on their methods of actions, limits that are felt to be oppressive and are repeatedly transgressed by people of passionate nature. Sooner or later, the cause of Marxism must always pay for this with a defeat.

[*In two pages, Kautsky refers to Marxists who analyzed the materialist conception of history more fully and systematically than Marx and Engels themselves ever did: those who, like himself,[3] also sought to test it in its application to historical research—Paul Lafargue, George Plekhanov, Antonio Labriola, Franz Mehring, Otto Bauer, and Heinrich Cunow—and those who sought to reconcile it with the philosophy of Kant—Eduard Bernstein, Ludwig Woltmann, Karl Vorländer, Max Adler, and Alfred Braunthal—and he also mentions Nikolai Bukharin*][4] whose materialism leaves nothing to be desired with respect to its crudity. . . .*

It was not to be expected that the original unity of the school would long endure. The greater the success of a comprehensive view and the more

1. This point is elaborated in III:4:4, below.

2. For other comments by Kautsky on Marx's and Engels' materialist conception of history, see *Ethics*, pp. 105–19, and *Die historische Leistung von Karl Marx*, esp. pp. 7–15.

3. Kautsky cites his series of articles in *Die Neue Zeit* of 1896–97 directed against Belfort Bax, "Was will and kann die materialistische Geschichtsauffassung leisten?" It was introduced by "Die materialistische Geschichtsauffassung und der psychologische Antrieb," and concluded by "Utopistischer und materialistischer Marxismus." To this might be added "Bernstein und die materialistische Geschichtsauffassung."

4. The relevant works of these authors cited by Kautsky are listed in the bibliography.

numerous those become who share it, the more varied the shadings among them. . . . Today Marxism has even become a fashion with which many flirt who have never read anything written by Marx or Engels or one of their followers. Many call themselves Marxists, of whom Marx, if he were still alive today, would repeat the witticism he made in the 1870s about a juvenile, rash remark made by one of his most ardent but also most imaginative disciples: "If that is Marxism, then I am no Marxist." . . .

The differences of standpoint among the Marxists—differences which have their origin in individual, social, and national differences—have become so great that it is not to be expected that any one conception of Marxism would be generally recognized as the one in agreement with Marx's views. . . . It is not my intention to increase the number of commentaries on Engels' and Marx's statements by yet one more. The task that I set myself here is a different one. What I present in the pages that follows is a grounding and justification of my *own conception of history*, which represents the guiding thread as well as, in the present form, the result of my life's work in the service of Marxism. It is certainly true that I owe the conception of history I develop here to my great teachers. I have, however, made this method my own through fifty years' work and through its application in theory and in practice. Since I give here an exposition of my own conception, any controversy about whether I correctly understand this or that statement of Marx is obviated from the outset. No one will want to claim that I misunderstand myself.

Should the reader object that he is interested in Marx's and not in my conception of history, then I may reply that each of the other expositors of historical materialism in fact also presents only his own conception. We have all learned from Marx and rely on his research and his thoughts as our basis. But each of us sees them and sees reality with his own eyes. If I present my own conception of history here for the most part without referring to Marx's and Engels' statements, I do not thereby depart from the foundation of their thought on which I stand. But, in doing so, I hope to cause the discussion to cease revolving around the interpretation of isolated statements and to be devoted completely to substance alone. I, too, will not be able to do entirely without referring to particular writings of Marx and Engels. But by presenting as my own the conception of history that I owe to them, I gain the freedom to develop it in another context than my teachers did and thus to open up insights that they did not communicate to us, that they perhaps did not even have.

After all, I did not receive my conception of history as a finished product. I already possessed a conception of history before I became acquainted with that of Marx. Only gradually, after much searching and groping, did I transfer into my own original conception ever more Marxist features and came to prove their fruitfulness in my efforts in theory and practice. Finally, it came . . . completely to agree with Marx's conception. But, still, my point of departure had been a different one and it provided me with an interest in phenomena to which Marx and Engels gave less attention. Even though I learned an immense amount from them, some things I learned from others, too. That goes without saying, after all.

The beginnings of my historical thinking were naturally formed only a generation after Marx and Engels had arrived at their conception of history: in the 1870s. Darwinism was at that time the theory that occupied the whole world. There was no such thing yet at the time Marx and Engels created the materialist conception of history. They had started out from *Hegel*; I started out from *Darwin*. The latter occupied my thoughts earlier than Marx, the development of organisms earlier than that of the economy, the struggle for existence of species and races earlier than the class struggle.

As long as I think independently, I think historically. Early in my life I began to strive for a conception of history. Initially, however, it was linked for me with natural-scientific, not with economic thinking. To be sure, socialist literature soon made me aware of the importance of the economic factor. As my economic knowledge progressed, my recognition of the importance of this factor for historical development also grew, but my interest in the natural factor in history persisted; and I continued my endeavor to relate the historical development to the development of organisms.

As early as 1876, I conceived the plan of writing a universal history on the basis of the conception of history that I had then devised. I was not yet twenty-two years old—only when one is very young does one make such bold plans. It was to be a "developmental history of mankind." The historical materialism of a Marx and Engels had not yet been brought to my attention. . . . And my knowledge of economics was still very deficient. The development of humanity seemed to me then to be the result of a struggle between communism and individualism, by which I understood . . . different kinds of drives bred in men through the different forms of the struggle for existence.[5]

The labor of years was still necessary, a labor supported by intimate contact with Engels from 1881 on, with Marx unfortunately only briefly, and the perfecting of my knowledge of economic history as well as the assiduous, systematic application of the materialist method to the investigation of various historical periods, in order for me to master this method to such a degree that it was no longer alien to me but became my own. As such I explain it in what follows.

5. Kautsky reproduced in unchanged form, "with all its errors," his 1876 "Draft of a Developmental History of Mankind" in *Die materialistische Geschichtsauffassung*, (1929), I, 155–65. It is omitted from the present edition. See also II: 3:2, below.

CHAPTER ONE

Materialism

. . . Even those who today still wish to regard historical materialism as nothing more than a working hypothesis will have to admit that it has given science a rich yield. However, a hypothesis cannot remain in this stage permanently. Either its application results in growing contradictions that it is unable to eliminate and that require that it be modified, restricted, or abandoned altogether. Or the hypothesis is successfully integrated without contradiction into the totality of known complexes of interrelations, into the "universal plexus." Then it may claim general scientific validity as a theory at least as long as the totality of the known interrelations is not increased by significantly new knowledge which gives a new character to that totality and requires that the theories constructed on its basis be more or less reshaped. Historical materialism, too, has not remained an empirical hypothesis, that is, an isolated hypothesis arrived at through the mere observation of facts, but instead has been organically incorporated into a great worldview, with which it stands and falls. . . .

What has proved untenable is a materialism that promises . . . to explain all phenomena, including those of the human mind, through the mechanics of matter. . . . But the materialism of Marx and Engels is contained in their *method. [Kautsky quotes Engels,* Ludwig Feuerbach, *p. 361, and* Anti-Dühring, *p. 42.]* The reference by materialism to matter means nothing else than the acknowledgment that the world outside of us really exists, is not mere appearance, not a product of the thinking brain. . . . In the case of the materialist method used by Marx and Engels, *[there is the additional]* demand not to regard each of the things outside of us separately as immobile and unchanging, but rather to investigate these things in their movements and changes, in their becoming and their perishing, in the totality of their interrelations. . . .

The more comprehensive the chain of interrelations to which we link an object, an idea, a process, an interrelation, the more closely does the object of our investigation become known. The scientific ideal consists in the discovery of the universal complex of interrelationships of all phenomena. That would be the attainment of absolute truth. The attainment of this goal is inconceivable. . . . When we succeed in solving a problem, then as a rule the solution does nothing more than raise new problems that we did not see before. It is, however, necessary at least to strive to bring all complexes of relations that we have recognized into a totality of interrelations that is free of contradiction. This task, though, becomes increasingly more difficult with the progress of the sciences and of the division of labor among them. The disparity between the totality of knowledge in society and the totality of the individual's knowledge is becoming ever more immense. . . . Be that as it may, every researcher must strive to achieve as wide a horizon as possible. In any case, he must integrate all the knowledge that he has at his disposal into a universal complex of interrelations, and the latter should be such that it is compatible with the totality of the complexes of interrelations in the other sciences.

This is the method that underlay what Marx and Engels designated as dialectical materialism, and with the help of which they founded the materialist conception of history. . . . Not the possession of the truth but the path to truth was most important to them. In this respect, one may well say that the materialist conception of history is not bound to a materialist philosophy. It is compatible with every worldview that makes use of the method of dialectical materialism or at least does not stand in irreconcilable contradiction to it. . . . However, that is not to say by any means that our conception of history is compatible with every kind of philosophy. . . . And we have every reason to hold fast to the name of *materialist* conception of history . . . in order to attest clearly that it conflicts with every kind of *idealist philosophy*.

CHAPTER TWO

The Revolt against Materialism

No matter how various the forms might be in which materialism appears, in one respect they are all in agreement. They conceive all of the phenomena of this world as in a single totality of interrelations, from which nothing is excluded that we are conscious of, the phenomena of a mental and social kind as well as all others.

For our cognitive capacity there is nothing outside the complex constituted by the totality of phenomena and thus outside "nature." That is by no means to say that the totality of interrelations is not divided into different large fields, each of which has its own peculiar character and exhibits particular kinds of interrelations that are lacking in other fields. We find that nature is divided into organic and inorganic. The latter in turn shows various aggregate states, gaseous, fluid, and solid, each of which obeys particular laws. In the world of organisms, of individuals, who strive to safeguard the existence of their individuality and to reproduce it, we find the great division into living beings without demonstrable consciousness, and those with marked consciousness. Within the latter we in turn find the division into animals that remain limited to their natural organs and those that are capable of creating for themselves additional, artificial ones: human beings. Finally we find social organizations of human beings that in turn exhibit their own interrelations. . . . The fact that each of these fields has its own special problems need not at all contradict their being interrelated in a totality. It merely means that knowledge of one of these fields is not sufficient to give one knowledge of the others, that, for example, a knowledge of mechanics and chemistry does not suffice to solve all the riddles of life.

Nevertheless, we find again and again attempts in philosophy to set off a particular domain of phenomena from the totality of interrelations and to oppose it to the latter as a world unto itself: the world of the human mind and its social expressions. Mind in opposed to "matter," society to "nature"; the sciences are divided into the natural sciences and the humanities and social sciences [Geisteswissenschaften].[1] . . . From time immemorial idealism has vigorously arisen alongside *[materialism]*. There were too many spiritual and emotional needs, in part those received from tradition, in part newly emerged ones that materialism did not satisfy.

CHAPTER THREE
Belief in God

The need for causality, the urge to discover relations between causes and effects in its environment is innate even in the animal. . . . In the case of man, as his intelligence and technology grow, the domain of the relations that he seeks to discover also becomes larger.[2] His need for knowledge of the causes of things grows more rapidly than the conditions for the satisfaction of this need. . . . His fantasy and his ability to form abstractions develop relatively rapidly. . . . His critical capacity grows considerably more slowly, as does the logical capacity that does not tolerate any contradiction in our thinking. Thus from the progress of thought there first arises a wealth of hypotheses as unclear as they are premature. . . . Among these premature hypotheses is also the assumption that there are gods.

Primitive man . . . does not yet distinguish between animate and inanimate nature. In inorganic nature, too, he encounters things that . . . appear to him to be endowed with sensation, with volition and agency that are often conceived of by his undisciplined fantasy as boundless. *[Kautsky here*

1. See also V:2:2, below.
2. See II:5:4, below.

quotes Lucien Lévy-Bruhl, How Natives Think, *p. 85.]* Long ago, before the beginning of his written history, man had already reached the point of attributing all events, the causes of which were not clearly evident, to the action of personal beings, which were imagined very vaguely, but which . . . readily took on human form. However, they were much stronger than him and provided with various powers that were superhuman but were desired by human beings, such as the ability to remain invisible, to fly, not to die, etc. . . .

Like many later hypotheses, this primitive assumption, too, was intended not only to aid in understanding the environment, but also in influencing it. Men reflected on the causal relations in their environment, because they needed to grasp them in order to give a more purposeful form to their own activity. If the success of each of our actions is dependent on the intervention of one of these great unknown beings, the gods, then it is best to win his favor. . . . In doing this, one makes use of the same means that one employs to influence great earthly lords: petitions, flattery, and what is especially effective, bribery with an abundance of sacrificial offerings. *[This endeavor]* is among humanity's first attempts to influence its environment.

If one did all that in a thoroughgoing way, then one acquired a considerable degree of certainty with regard to the unknown powers of the world. This feeling of security was disagreeably prejudiced when, in antiquity, in connection with the beginning of natural science, there arose a more or less materialist philosophy of nature, which regarded all things as being in a single complex of interrelations, in which there was no room for the intervention of divinities. . . . These were not immediately slain by materialism, but they were certainly pensioned off. . . . Materialism was all the more repulsive as it was erected, in antiquity and also still in the seventeenth and eighteenth centuries, upon a backward knowledge of nature, which, as a practical matter, hardly allowed the scientific mastery of the forces of nature to take the place of the invocation of the gods. And materialism left many spiritual and emotional needs unsatisfied, especially in times of social decline, when the footing disappeared that the individual had at other times found in the community and when everyone fearfully searched for a superhuman savior and redeemer, since he despaired of finding him among men. . . .

Now if more ancient materialism still came to terms with primitive, personal gods, more recent materialism is completely atheistic and rejects even the newer, refined ideas of God. Regardless of how little the God of the more recent deists might intervene in the course of the world, he is not, as were the gods of the ancient materialists, a figure who is wholly dispensable for the explanation of the world; rather he is its creator and originator. Without him, the world appears to be inconceivable. He stands outside the totality of interrelations and above it. With this assumption the materialist method is irreconcilable.

The Meaning of Life

... With the development of transport, of technology, of science, the naive notion recedes [that] man or the place where he lives is the center, not merely of *his* own world, but of the world in general. As it recedes, another advances ever more into the foreground, one that arises from the fact that man is the most ingenious being on earth, the one who by means of his intelligence subjugates more and more creatures and even natural forces, compels them to serve him or renders them harmless. No longer does his body appear to be the center of the world, but rather his mind. Not the mind of an individual, but the totality of mental activities of men socially bound together. . . . Materialism, which places man into the totality of the interrelations of nature, in which he seems ever tinier the more natural science progresses, is difficult to reconcile with man's presumptuousness vis-à-vis his environment. . . .

The anthropocentric conception of the world brought forth a way of thinking that has continued to exert a strong influence: the assumption of a world purpose. From its beginnings, men's knowledge—and the animals' as well—has been intimately linked with their action. . . . Every action, however, presupposes a purpose, which the actor has set himself and which he seeks to attain through his actions. The fundamental purpose of life is, for man as for the animal, given with life itself. It consists in the preservation of life. No species of creatures endowed with consciousness that is not endowed with strong impulses of self-preservation and reproduction would be able to preserve itself. These impulses dominate the mental faculties, which are nothing but organs in the struggle for existence, for self-preservation. . . . But the achievement of this paramount purpose requires, in the most diverse situations and under the most diverse conditions, the setting of subpurposes. . . .

The mental life both of men and of the higher animals involves not only the correct recognition of causal relations, but also the discovery of and the striving for correct specific ends and means, that is to say, those which correspond to the principal end of the preservation of the species. Not only causal, but also teleological thinking is a necessity of life for them. When man asks about everything that happens, why it happens, then this "why" easily takes on two meanings. It asks not merely *for the cause*, but also *for the purpose* of the event. However, such a purpose is not always evident. One then ends up searching for, in addition to the purposes that men and animals consciously set for themselves, all kinds of other hidden purposes in one's environment, in nature, and in that special domain of nature that we call society. But there is no such thing as a purpose per se. Every purpose that we know is set by an individual and serves this individual. Without its relationship to this individual it ceases to be a purpose. . . .

Man's anthropocentric point of view, although it has been consciously abandoned, has continued to be unconsciously effective to the present time. It is this point of view that allows man to proclaim his own ends as world ends, as a tendency toward continuous perfection inherent in the very nature of the world. Perfection being understood, of course, from the human standpoint as the most perfect adaptation of the world to human needs and wants,[3] whether in this vale of tears or in a better world still located in the clouds. . . . But what being would be capable of setting purposes for the world? The old primitive gods could not have done it. Like men, each one of them pursued private momentary ends within the world. . . . They had originated in primitive times, in which the social and natural environment hardly changed for the individual. . . . The urge to know the world's purpose arose in times when the traditional social conditions were rapidly changing. In such circumstances it was but a small step to pose the question of the why of this process of transformation, not only as regarded its causes but also with respect to its purpose. And this easily became the question of the purpose of the world in general, which naive man simply equated with his immediate environment.

. . . A new divinity was sought, a single god or one who rules over the other gods with despotic omnipotence . . . who not only creates the cosmic system and sets in it motion, but also confers on it its purpose, just as human reason sets purposes for itself. Thus we gain the possibility of seeing in all the troubles and afflictions of our time only transitional stages, which lead to the fulfillment of the world's purpose that has been established by the ordering hand of an all-powerful and all-knowing world reason. That this world reason, when examined more closely, did not rise above the level of human reason and was guided exclusively by human considerations was not noticed by those in need of consolation. . . .

The materialist conception, which adheres to experience, was incompatible with this comforting doctrine of a rational world purpose. Experience shows us only animals and men who set for themselves particular purposes for the general purpose of their preservation and reproduction; it also shows us organisms that are purposeful, that is, adapted to the purposes of their preservation and reproduction, but beyond that it shows us no purposes in the world, let alone a world purpose.[4] That seemed to a great many a bleak conception. And it is, indeed, cheerless in its effect in times of social decay as well as for groups of people who are threatened with decline or even with destruction. To be sure, the correctness of a conception is not measured by whether it is comforting or cheerless. . . . No normal person will maintain that a concrete object he imagines exists merely because

3. For Kautsky's critique of Engels' belief in perfection, see I: 5 : 3, below.
4. See also V : 3 : 3, below.

he needs it. But the more we rise from palpable things to the highest abstractions, the more easily does this consideration insinuate itself into philosophical thinking. . . .

CHAPTER FIVE
Ethics

In addition to numerous psychological motives, there was also significant objective reason for resisting pre-Marxist materialism. It could not account for ethical phenomena. The manner in which it sought to derive them all from feelings of pleasure or aversion, from the individual's calculations of his advantage and disadvantage, could not be convincing. It required that one accept the claim that the good is that which is enduringly agreeable and advantageous, that it is in the interest of the individual to love his fellow man and to stand by him in his troubles, that only shortsightedness can fail to see this . . . [It further maintained that] striving after pleasure did not have to coincide with mere sensual pleasure, which is of transitory nature and easily harms the individual or at least leaves him unsatisfied. . . . But how were the sense of duty, the voice of conscience, the complete devotion of one's personality to impersonal goals, the suffering of torture and death for the sake of great social ends to be explained by the striving after pleasure or gain? . . .

Striving after pleasure, egoism, is only one side of the human spirit. Another of its sides expresses itself in a sense of obligation vis-à- vis our fellow men and the community we live in or the social group one belongs to. This feeling does not arise from mere deliberation and a higher degree of insight; it is often stronger in the ignorant than in the educated and often operates without any reflection as an irresistible impulse. Where does this contradiction in man come from that resolves itself into the contradiction of good and evil in us? How can we come to know the good and separate it from evil?

This problem had appeared already in antiquity under those social conditions that had also awakened the need to assume a world purpose set by a world reason. The attempt to solve the ethical problem was made in the context of this assumption. There thus arose not only a new worldview but also a new method of thinking. [Early Greek philosophy, stimulated by commercial contacts, sought to explain nature. But with the sudden growth of Athenian wealth and power, some came to question the traditional customs and obligations toward the state. Many thinkers were now preoccupied with man's social nature, which they tried to explain from the individual's inner life.]

While materialism, moving along the pathways of the old natural philosophy, sought to understand the human mind as a piece of nature, its adversary placed the mind outside of nature. From this standpoint, the contradiction in man between the good and the evil in him appeared . . . as the opposition of mind and nature (or matter). Man has arisen from nature. From it he got those impulses to pleasure and to gain that the materialists note in him. But man also received in his reason a spark of that divine world reason that gives to the cosmic mechanism its purpose. Thus man is "half animal, half angel." What is evil in him is the animal, the natural, the sensual. The good is the spiritual, the supernatural, the heavenly. Not from observation of the external world, but rather only from observation of his own better self can he attain knowledge of the good. And this observation yields much more certain knowledge than that of the external world. For our senses are deceptive; truth reposes in the mind alone, and I know nothing with greater certainty than that I think. . . .

Both the idealist and the materialist methods have achieved the most varied results. But to the present day, the antagonism of these two methods of thought has not been overcome. . . . [5]

CHAPTER SIX

Atom and Mind

I believe that I have indicated the most important roots of the opposition of idealist thinking to the materialist method, *[but a major objection by idealists to materialism, namely, that it cannot explain phenomena of the mind, has not been discussed.]* It is correct that the problem of those phenomena that are called mental is by no means solved yet. We have not yet traced them back to their ultimate origins. But is that not true for a good many natural phenomena? . . . This ignorance is no reason to exclude any phenomenon from the totality of interrelations, to regard it as outside the latter. To be sure, given the present state of our knowledge, the appearance of mind means that there is a leap in nature, just as does the appearance of life. . . . Certainly nothing is more difficult to explain than how such leaps in nature occur. Despite all leaps, however, the unity of all phenomena in nature continues to be firmly accepted. Only the leap to the mind is supposed to be a reason for not treating the latter as a natural phenomenon.

. . . Many mental phenomena have already been scientifically investigated. . . . And every program of knowledge in this area shows us mental life ever more intimately linked with physical states, especially with those of the nervous system and its center, the brain. It cannot at all be foreseen how far natural science will yet advance in its investigation of the psyche. . . . Since every solution to one of these riddles that has been achieved so far is due to the materialist method, we have no reason to renounce it in

5. See also Kautsky's chapter on "Ancient and Christian Ethics" in *Ethics*, pp. 11–25.

this area. By diverting us from this method, the idealist conception directly hinders the investigation and solution of the problems of the mind.

Let us assume—without conceding it—that the nature of the mind makes it impossible ever to fathom with natural-science methods the manner in which it came to pass at a certain point in time that, in a previously inorganic world, under certain conditions of this world, organic beings with life and sensation arose out of certain highly complicated chemical combinations. Here is the real difficulty of the problem. The further development of life and mind does not pose any insurmountable difficulties. But does idealist philosophy place the animal world outside the context of nature? Indeed, strictly speaking, it ought to exclude the plant world from it, too, for the origination of life does not at the present time appear less mysterious than that of sensation. Up to now, though, probably no idealist philosopher has dared to assign to the realm of the mind even only the animal world, let alone the entire world of organisms. When the realm of the mind is discussed, it is always understood to refer only to the human mind. . . . No one has yet spoken of the immortality of the souls of toads and beetles, and yet their psychic life could be explained just as little as that of humans if the materialist method must fail for all eternity even with regard to the simplest sensation. . . .

The objection made against materialism that it is unable to explain the mind proves to be at bottom only a result of that arrogance of man vis-à-vis his environment, of which we have already spoken. . . . The new natural science, primarily by means of the theory of the origin of species, has once again removed the line separating man from the animal that the mind had allegedly formed. We even owe to experimentation with animals very important revelations about how mental phenomena come about. . . . One can argue about the degree and the nature of the difference between the human and the animal mind. But no one will be able to deny that the simplest mental processes—sensation and volition, but also judgment—occur just as much in animals as in men. And it is the simplest, not the most complex mental processes that are difficult to subject to a materialist explanation, or rather to explain at all, for the idealist considers them inexplicable and as not requiring explanation. . . .

Although today's "mind" or "soul" must be accorded to animals, another way has been found to restore the gap separating man from the animal. The difference between understanding and reason was invented. Kant, in particular, sharply opposes them to one another. Understanding is concerned with the processing of facts of sense experience; in contrast, reason is concerned with speculation about the loftiest truths. Man shares understanding with the animals; reason, however, is to be found only in man. Reason is what is divine in man. . . . That gives rise to a new difficulty, though. For a partition is thereby erected not between man and the animal, but between primitive man and civilized man. . . . A cultural development of many millennia was necessary before the preconditions were present for the creation of high-level abstractions, which rose far above sense experience. . . . If only reason is divine, immortal, outside the context of nature, then not all, but only relatively few men in all humanity until now have partaken of the divine. . . . If one regards all men as possessing the "divine" spark, . . . then one must admit that the same spark has not been denied to animals either.

No matter what partitions one might erect within the world of organisms endowed with mental capacities, none provides a reason, or even makes it merely permissible, to remove the human mind or one of its stages from the totality of interrelations in nature and to consider it as a thing itself that functions and is to be understood outside this totality.

Section Three
Kant

[*Kautsky devoted a sixty-page section of his work to a discussion of and argument with Kant's philosophy in response to attempts in his time to reconcile Kant with Marx. He cites particularly the philosophers Karl Vorländer and Max Adler as being engaged in this enterprise. Such philosophers insist "... on the idea of free will and of a moral law beyond and above all history, all time, and all space. This view is to be reconciled with the materialist conception of history, which rests on the strictest causality of human will and loses its very basis without it"* (Die materialistische Geschichtsauffassung (1929), I, 65). *This Kant-Marx synthesis went far to meet the needs of German university students sympathetic to socialism, "so we cannot simply ignore the questions of the moral law and of freedom of will, as Kant poses them" (ibid.). However, Kautsky fears that some of his readers might find some of the following chapters difficult or of little interest and suggests that they may "without impairing their understanding of my later analysis" (ibid., p. 66) skip the chapters on the identity of space and time and "at worst" even all the subsequent chapters in the section of Kant.*][1]

1. The section on Kant is drastically abbreviated here, both because Kautsky himself regarded his debate with Kant as a less than essential part of his work and because he had, two decades earlier in his controversy with the Revisionists, made his principal points much more briefly in a chapter on "Kant's Ethics" in his *Ethics and the Materialist Conception of History*, which has been translated into English (and also twelve other languages). All the lengthy quotations from Kant, mostly from his *Prolegomena to Any Future Metaphysics*, *The Critique of Pure Reason*, and *The Critique of Practical Reason*, and also from the neo-Kantian Friedrich Albert Lange, *The History of Materialism*, and Kautsky's statements of agreement and, mostly, disagreement with them have been omitted. Only passages stating Kautsky's own views have been retained as well as almost the entire last chapter on the leap from necessity to freedom.

CHAPTER ONE
Materialism before Kant

[Very briefly sketching the history of materialism and linking it to economic development and growth of natural science, Kautsky says with reference to Hellenistic Alexandria:] With progress of knowledge the methods of the exact natural sciences developed and in consequence the materialist method developed also. *[Further on, he continues with reference to modern times:]* With this rapid growth of the natural sciences there arose the more recent natural-scientific materialism, most prominently located in the seventeenth century and the beginnings of the eighteenth century in England, later in the eighteenth century in France and in the nineteenth century in Germany. This materialism was already built on extensive detailed factual knowledge in the natural sciences and on precise methods of research, in which rigorous testing and critique of the results achieved in particular instances were not lacking.

But now, as in antiquity, its weak side was still ethics, that is, the nature of man in society. A new science of society was, it is true, already coming into being, but it was only in its beginnings and had not yet found the method that would have made it possible to incorporate it into the totality of interrelations of things or phenomena. As in antiquity, the materialists continued to deduce the social nature of man not from the nature of society, but from the nature of the isolated individual to be analyzed in the manner of the natural sciences. Consequently, the materialists had to fail in this area again and again and to arrive at conceptions that were artificial and internally contradictory. . . .

CHAPTER 2
The Materialist Component of the Kantian Theory

Kant recognizes that the world outside of us is real, not a product of our brain. Only through our senses do we learn of the external world. . . . But this cognition is conditioned not only by the nature of external things, but also by the nature of our cognitive capacity. We therefore see things not as they are, but as they appear to us. . . . *Critical* materialism can quite well come to terms with the Kantian distinction between things in themselves and phenomena.

CHAPTER THREE
The Limits of Cognition

. . . It is possible to attain very precise mental images of the external world, the world of things in themselves. To be sure, we cannot know an isolated, unchanging thing as it is. Our mental image of it is always conditioned by the nature of our mental apparatus. But this is not the case when we receive mental images of several things simultaneously or mental images of successive changes of one or several things, while our physical state has not changed. . . . Then we find in each of these mental images something common to all of them: our cognitive capacity, which remains the same. If we compare our different mental images with one another, we can disregard this subjective factor, which is the same for all of them . . . In other words: The *differences* between the things external to me, which are shown to me by my senses, really exist, they are real differences. They are not produced by my cognitive capacity. The same is true of the *changes* that one and the same thing undergoes vis-à-vis a mental apparatus that remains constant. . . .

And there is still more. To the relations among the things external to me that I can know there also belong the relations of other human beings to the same thing that I observe, that are having an effect on me. Inasmuch as I assume that other human beings are organized in the same way as I am, I may conclude that their perceptions communicated to me confirm the perceptions I have attained if they are in agreement with them. In this way, I succeed in excluding to a high degree the subjective moment from my cognition of the external world. . . .

If we cannot know the things in themselves in isolation, we can nevertheless know their differences and interrelations and their motions and changes. Is that alone not a great deal? To be sure, the differences we can become aware of remain differences of mental *images* and not of *things* in themselves. Thus the manner in which we become conscious of differences is just as determined by the nature of our cognitive capacity as is the individual mental image. But that in no way changes the fact that with these differences we are made conscious of real differences between the things in themselves. . . .

Sensory deceptions can occur when the senses and their central organ are not normal but affected by disease. . . . No sensory perception can be considered as real and certain that is accessible to one individual alone and that another cannot also attain. . . . Certain knowledge is thus not possible for the isolated human being, but only for man in society. It is a social function. . . .

Our senses are limited, however. They show us, to be sure, *real* differences among things, but by no means *all* differences among things. . . . There are certainly . . . differences we can neither observe directly nor discover indirectly through their effects on other objects; differences the existence of which we do not have even the faintest idea. They can be innumerable. . . . An apparent identity, that is, a failure to observe differences between two phenomena, need not indicate a real identity of the things in themselves underlying the phenomena. . . . This latter boundary, though, is not a rigid barrier; it is constantly being pushed forward. Man's capacity to become aware of differences increases in the course of his historical development. He is able to invent technical aids and methods that ... significantly increase the cognitive capacity of his nervous system. ...

However, we do not pay attention even to all the differences between things of which our senses inform us. ... Even in the case of actual sense impressions much is overlooked or intentionally put aside as unimportant. That is even more true of our recollections. Only what seems important to us is retained. ... What is perceived differs widely in the various stages of social development. That is true even of mere sense impressions. ... It is all the more true, of course, of complicated mental processes.

Our knowledge is, then, even more relative than Kant assumed. It is not dependent on a cognitive capacity that always remains the same, but rather on one that changes with the technology and the peculiar mental character of society in history. Besides, our knowledge is constantly progressing. ... Of no problem may it be said ... that we will never solve it, but only, as long as it is not solved, ... that we do not know the solution. However, we must never expect a solution that brings us closer to an absolute truth. For the upshot of every solution is that it confronts us with new, larger problems. ... There is no absolute knowledge, but only a process of cognition the end of which cannot be foreseen. This is the epistemology of the materialist conception of history.

CHAPTER FOUR

Crossing the Boundary

... If we have the strength to forgo the absolute, if we remain within the boundaries of experience, then we are already committed to the materialist method, that is, the method of natural science. The materialist conception of history means nothing but the application of this method to society— taking its peculiar character into consideration, of course. Just like the natural sciences, it too concerns itself only with the world of phenomena, for society, human beings other than myself, are also only phenomena for me. And Kant himself admitted that in the world of phenomena causality and necessity obtain. ...

CHAPTER FIVE

The Ideality of Space

... Of course, certain *capabilities* must be innate to our thinking apparatus, ... but this apparatus can produce *knowledge* only after the external world has affected it and imparted experiences to it. ... By the way, these capabilities are innate only for present-day man, that means, they are inherited. His ancestors had to acquire them in remote, prehistorical times. . . .

. . . The *capacity* to receive certain impressions from certain stimuli of the external world . . . must surely be innate if the organism is to arrive at certain perceptions. However, that is not at all to say that the form of these perceptions is innate in us. As if there could be a form in itself that, detached from any content, existed prior to its content! . . . Form is conditioned by content, and without content it is a mere word. . . .

. . . Man (and likewise, the animal) orders all his visual and tactile impressions according to their situation relative to himself. . . . *[He]* combines *[them]* as the idea of space. The ability to make *[spatial]* distinctions must certainly be present a priori in my brain. And the order of the distinctions is certainly quite subjective; it is not inherent in the things external to the subject. In nature, that is, in the external world, there is no right and no left, no above and no below, no front and no behind. . . . But this order of things external to me according to subjective viewpoints does not at all mean that nothing external to me corresponds to it and that it does not originate from experience. . . . Regardless of how our idea of space might come into being, the spatial differences and changes (motions) of the things we observe are caused by differences and changes in the external world; they are not given in our brain a priori. If one were to assume this, then one would have to consider as a product of our mind the entire world that is visible to us and can be touched by us . . . What remains of our perception of the external world, if all forms, distances, and movements of bodies exist only in my head, and nothing that calls forth these perceptions is to be found outside us? . . .

CHAPTER SIX
The Ideality of Time

. . . Time becomes a word without content and without meaning if one disregards the succession of phenomena. . . . Like the perception of spatial and all other differences, the perception of temporal differences is dependent on certain mental capabilities which, a priori innate, have to be present in me. In the case of space, these capabilities are those of sight and touch; in the case of time, they are one's *memory*, the *capacity of recollection*. . . . For the animal it is a matter only of its personal recollections; in the case of man, thanks to language and writing, these are joined by the recollections transmitted from earlier generations. Finally human intelligence reaches a level permitting man to obtain, from present-day mute witnesses of a past that goes back beyond the existence of humanity, information about that early time. . . .

My idea of time is . . . divided into two halves with the most contradictory characteristics, on one side the past, on the other the future. In the former, there is determinacy and immutability; in the latter, we see only indeterminacy and freedom. My consciousness of the past arises from the impressions that successively enter my memory; in contrast, the future is present in our unconscious psychic life earlier than in our consciousness. It lives in us as the drive to self-preservation, to the prolongation of life. This prolongation, however, cannot be conceived other than as a prolongation of my life as it has occurred hitherto and as I remember it. The drive to self-preservation, therefore, leads necessarily to the prolongation beyond the present of the line of the past, projected out of the memories of my preceding life. Thus the two quite opposite ideas of past and future join in the idea of a unitary time. . . .

With time, just as with space, we come to the conclusion that, if it is an a priori idea, all changes and movements of the world that we believe we perceive are only products of our mind, that thus either the entire world exists only in our head or our cognitive capacity is a clever means for transforming the external world into the crudest deception for us. . . .

CHAPTER SEVEN

Necessity

. . . We have come to the conclusion that the organization of our cognitive capacity indeed does not show us isolated things external to us as they are, but does certainly show us a relationship between ourselves and these things, and that we are quite capable of becoming aware of the differences among these, of their motions and their changes. . . . If the phenomena we regard as movements and changes of the things external to us really happen, then they also happen in spaces and times that are real. Then the regularly oc-curring sequences are also real; they are by no means categories that exist in our mind prior to all experience. To be sure, the formation of experience is dependent on certain capabilities of the mind that inhere in it a priori, prior to experience, as dispositions, but they become effective factors only through application and practice. . . .

As we see that the impulse to search for causes is active even in animals,[2] so too do we see in them also the instinctual recognition of the necessary sequence of certain phenomena. . . . The assumption of necessity is present much earlier as an animal instinct than as a human idea. The instincts are given to the individual a priori. But they become an inexplicable mystery if we assume that the species, too, has always possessed them a priori. Like all its attributes, it must have acquired them through the effects of its

---

2. See II: 5:4, below.

environment. To the instinctual beginning points of the feelings of causality and necessity are joined, in the case of the higher animals and most of all in the case of man, conscious observations, from which he draws conclusions as to many causal and necessary interrelations. Thus we reach a root of these concepts that is not present a prior but originates from experience, not only for the species, but also for the individual.

The events that men observe are divided into two groups: those that occur only once . . . and those that repeat themselves from time to time, one particular phenomenon being followed again and again in the same fashion by another. For the first no rule can be formulated. We call them accidental. The manner of the repetition of the others forms their rule, their law. . . . This observed regularity or conformity to laws easily appears to us as necessity, by which we understand nothing but the opposite of accident. But the regularity of the recurrence of a sequence of phenomena is of interest to us, as we shall see, above all in regard to our practice, our future. We conclude that because, according to our observations, a process has heretofore always taken place in the same way, it must also be so in all future times. However, the mere observation of a frequent recurrence of a series of events of the same kind gives us no absolute guarantee for this conclusion, but only a high degree of probability. In this regard Hume and Kant are completely right.

Man is, however, not content to consider each of the individual regularities in isolation. When his observations frequently recur, he also finds regular relations among individual regularities, and again regular relations among these relations, of an ever-higher order until finally all regularities are joined in a total complex of relations, in which every individual regularity supports the other or is at least integrated into the complex of the others in a manner free of contradiction. Through these interrelations among all of the observed regularities, every single one of them becomes a scientific certainty.

. . . The scientifically demonstrated necessity or conformity to a law is not absolute. It is valid only under certain conditions. As these change, the law can also change. It is always only relative. . . .

. . . The idea of necessity became *fatalism*. The conception that certain regularities, laws, become evident in all events that repeat themselves became transformed into the conception that a necessity could also be discovered for the singular event that does not repeat itself, a necessity the individual could not escape from, no matter what he did. We must mention this conception here because the materialist conception of history has often been called fatalistic. However, it is clear that a rule cannot possibly be found for what is singular, what does not recur. . . . Here no conformity to law or necessity can be identified and hence any fatalism is excluded. But it is certainly true that, as our knowledge progressed, the more the range of the interrelations observed by us grows, the more precise the aids to and the methods of our research become, the more does the range of singular events shrink, at least relatively, in comparison with the abundance of the observed regularities. And even in each of these singular events we are able to discover ever more elements for which laws have already been ascertained.

Thus the conviction takes root in us that ultimately all events in the world are based on relations that conform to laws, that every phenomenon has its cause not only in the sense of an occasion, which can also be accidental, but in the sense of a cause which is an inevitable link in an endless chain of causes and effects. According to this conviction, there is no accident in the world; the opposition between accident and necessity does not exist outside of us, but rather within us. Everything seems to us to be an accident, the cause of which is unknown to us or the singular appearance of which we have not yet been able to resolve completely into elements that are recurrent and that therefore display a regularity. In this sense we can say that there is no accident, that there is nothing singular, nothing unique.[3]

Since our knowledge is limited, however, since we will never succeed in exhausting the infinity of the world, we will hardly ever succeed in reducing to laws all that is singular and accidental. Especially in the case of the most complicated of the phenomena known to us, the psyche of a human individual in its interactions with the psyches of other men, we will perhaps always encounter occurrences that mock all the rules known to us. But nevertheless, even in man's mental life we discover more and more laws. And these, not the singularities, determine the historical activity of the human race.[4]

The more comprehensive the total complex of regularities is, into which we are able to integrate, without contradiction, every one of the regularities we have ascertained, the more securely is our scientific knowledge of the laws of nature founded. But their certainty is valid only within this complex. New facts, new methods are continually expanding the total complex of our knowledge. If they fit into it as we have hitherto conceived of it, then they confirm it. But ... from time to time there appear newly identified regularities that contradict the previous order of the total complex or of one of its parts. Then much becomes uncertain that until then seemed to be beyond doubt. Some observed regularities have to be reexamined; some are recognized to be erroneous; some are brought into another relation with other regularities. The whole edifice of relations must be modified until

3. A quarter century earlier, Kautsky had defined science as "the knowledge of the *necessary*, regular relationships of phenomena" and said of Marx and Engels that they "brought the field of history into the realm of necessity with greater success than their predecessors and thus raised history to a science." "Bernstein und die materialistische Geschichtsauffassung," p. 7.

4. See V:1:6–12, below.

everything again fits together harmoniously and without contradiction, until a new total complex of a higher order is produced.

The same expansion of the total complex that makes our scientific knowledge of the laws of nature ever more certain makes us again and again aware of the fact that all knowledge is only relative. Thus we continually realize anew that, like everything in this world, its necessities, too, are only relative and are valid only under certain conditions . . . But is a relative necessity still a necessity at all? It is possible that linguistic usage always takes the word necessity absolutely. But, of course, that does not prove that our conception is wrong; at most it could be a reason for no longer using the word necessity, and for replacing it with regularity or law. As we shall see, however, the concept of necessity continues to exist for us as a practical matter. And we must also cling to it theoretically, if we refuse to recognize anything intermediate between necessity and accident, if we stand for the view that everything in the world takes place either necessarily or without regularity.

We must categorically reject the apriority of causality and necessity, just as we rejected the apriority of space and time. And we must be glad that we can do this for good reasons, for like the apriority of time and of space, the apriority of causality and necessity would only be a means of lying to ourselves about relations in the world that do not exist outside of ourselves and to make the world itself completely unknowable for us.

CHAPTER EIGHT
Freedom[5]

CHAPTER NINE
The Moral Law

A moral law can be valid only for beings that live socially. That, however, suffices to make it a fact of experience that can be understood only within the total complex of phenomena, not outside of it. . . .

That mysterious power of duty and conscience that governs our action to such a great extent works quite impulsively, mostly without lengthy reflection. It does not express itself in a general, bloodless moral law that required strenuous philosophical mental labor to be dis-

---

5. This chapter, all of it devoted to an argument with Kant, is omitted in the present edition.

tilled out of the most abstract concepts. The real moral law is effective with compelling power in every human being, even in the most ignorant savage who is entirely incapable of any kind of higher abstraction. It is not effective, however, as a striving for a general legislation beyond time and space, but rather in the form of very definite, concrete commands. These do not require long reflection and are immediately accepted as inviolable, as, for example, the commands: You shall not wed your sister; you shall defend your community; you shall not steal from your comrade; you shall not eat forbidden foods; you shall fight for your god; . . . etc. The sense of duty becomes most intense in time of struggle for the existence of the community, and consequently this "noble," "sacred" feeling has been linked with a great deal of murder and destruction in the history of humanity up to now. . . .

Up to this time the natural sciences have formed the mainstay of materialism. In matters pertaining to society, even the most impassioned materialists showed themselves to be either helpless or, reluctantly and unwittingly, devoted to the idealist method. Kant combined idealism in social matters with materialism in natural matters. The natural scientists may well come to terms with Kant. On the other hand, his attempts to apotheosize into an eternal, rigid, absolute moral law the moral laws that determine social life and change with time and place must today be rejected by those who have gained from the development of the social sciences since Kant the conviction that the study of society in accordance with the materialist method offers the only way of getting to the root of the moral law.

The Kantian view does not constitute the complement but rather the diametrical opposite of this view, that of the materialist conception of history. And far from improving Marx's theory, it denies precisely that which is the great historical achievement of the materialist conception of history. For if the latter is correct, then it has succeeded in closing the gap in our experiential knowledge that was previously wide open in materialism and again and again gave idealism new access to our thinking in spite of the materialist advance of the natural sciences. Kant, however, sought to keep this gap open forever.[6] It can be pointed out that, according to Kant's viewpoint, too, man's freedom of will does not bring forth any other actions than those brought about by causal necessity; that this freedom only permits us to regard them from another perspective. This view is not only quite sterile for science, which strives for knowledge and not for moral judgments; it also creates an ambiguity that is not conducive to natural science clarity. No matter how much one, even as a Kantian, regards history as a mere empirical science, Kant's concept of freedom of the will nevertheless again

---

6. Kautsky had sought to close this gap in his *Ethics*. On ethics, see also II : 3 : 1–3, below.

and again opens a little back door to smuggle in elements that are apt to break through causal necessity in human volition and behavior and thus also in human history[7]. . . .

Nonetheless, there are Kantian Marxists, Kantian adherents of the materialist conception of history. And the achievements of some of them have been outstanding. But not, it seems to me, *because* of their Kantianism but in *spite* of it. Their accomplishments would have been more significant still if they were based on the materialist method consistently applied.

What we, after Kant, want to accept into this method as an enduring attainment is not his categorical imperative, but another imperative, which Feuerbach already drew from his critique of cognition, the demand: *be content in your research with the world as it is given*, . . . the world of appearances and its conception by the senses. . . .

CHAPTER TEN

The Leap from Necessity into Freedom

Before we leave the question of freedom, we still have to consider a sentence that has been given the most varied interpretations. In his *Anti-Dühring*, Friedrich Engels states that the introduction of socialist production "... is humanity's leap from the realm of necessity into the realm of freedom" (Engels, *Anti-Dühring*, p. 310). Now one thing is clear from the outset: The freedom of which Engels speaks here cannot be freedom in Kant's sense, the causelessness of man's rational will, its ability to begin a movement of its own accord without any cause. If Engels had used the word in this sense, then that would mean that socialism executes humanity's leap out of the world of phenomena, the only world we can be aware of, into the unknowable intelligible world, that socialism strips away from men everything they have in common with the animal world and transforms them into pure angels. Of course, Engels did not say such nonsense. The freedom he is referring to is not the Kantian one, but rather that Hegelian one that arises from our understanding of necessity, so that we voluntarily do what we have recognized as necessary. On this point Engels remarks: "Freedom does

---

7. On freedom of will, see also the next chapter and, III:2:2, III:4:1, and V:2:1–2, below, and, among Kautsky's earlier writings, especially the chapter on freedom and necessity in *Ethics*, pp. 59–65, and the chapter on "Economic Development and Will" in *The Road to Power*, pp. 35–42.

not consist in the dream of independence of natural laws, but in the knowledge of these laws, and in the possibility this gives of systematically making them work towards definite ends" (p. 125).

Today anarchy of the private producers independent of one another prevails in production. The laws governing the economy assert themselves in very painful crises, which the individual confronts helplessly and which even society is incapable of mastering. Men are the slaves of their own economic circumstances. If, however, society acquires possession of the means of production, then it can organize production according to a plan in order to shape it corresponding to its understanding of the laws of the economy. In this way, men cease to be slaves of the economy; they become its masters and thereby free. "It is only from this point that men, with full consciousness, will fashion their own history; . . . that the social causes set in motion by men will have, predominantly and in constantly increasing measure, the effects willed by men" (pp. 309–10). The passage concludes with the statement about the leap from the realm of necessity into that of freedom.

From these remarks some people have concluded that Engels means that the materialist conception of history is valid only for the age of capitalism, that it is no longer applicable to socialism. . . . That would be correct only if Engels had said that with socialism man ceases to be within the chain of the causal necessities that appear in human history. . . . Freedom *in the sense of Hegel and Engels* . . . does not by any means annul historical necessity and hence the materialist conception of history, even though it can considerably change the way in which history runs its course.

Of course, Engels' formulation is only a metaphorical one, which, like any simile, should not be taken without a grain of salt. The coming socialist society will not be the first in human history that disposes of the critically important means of production and is thereby able to organize production according to a plan. We find that such organizations predominate into the period of developed commodity production, that is, during the largest part of human history. To that extent there was already "freedom" in the distant past and it was only capitalism that brought us the realm of "necessity." On the other hand, the distant past was certainly ruled by another necessity to a very high degree, by the necessity of natural events. Understanding of the laws of nature was slight, man was dependent to a high degree on natural events, which seemed to be a series of unpredictable caprices. In this respect, it was precisely capitalism, with its immense rapid development of the natural sciences and of technology, that brought us a great measure of freedom. That freedom, to be sure, was paid for with a growing dependence of men on social forces confronting them as overpowering and uncontrollable, indeed, often as quite unpredictable.

Our task now is to join to the great measure of freedom through domination of natural forces, which we have gained through industrial capitalism, the economic freedom of which that capitalism has robbed us. That will certainly result in a high degree of freedom. But one must not take the leap to this freedom too literally. The sphere of the economy, to whose laws we are subject, has been enormously expanded by capitalism. . . . The expansion of the modern economy to a world economy contributes perhaps even more to the difficulty of comprehending and controlling it than does private property in the means of production. . . . Socialism cannot come—this our experiences up to now have shown us—for all sectors of the world economy at once. It will start from individual, industrially highly developed countries, and in these from individual branches of industry especially well suited for a socialist organization of production. As long as all occupational branches of a country and all countries of the world economy are not organized in a socialist manner, the economic freedom that socialism brings will not be universal.

Even after the general realization of socialism, human freedom will of course remain limited, just like our knowledge of the world on which this freedom is founded. We shall never completely fathom all problems posed by nature, and we will hardly be able ever to foresee all consequences even of our social activity. Therefore, instead of speaking of a leap from the realm of necessity into the realm of freedom, one would probably do better to speak only of an extension of the province of freedom within the realm of causal necessity, the boundaries of which are unassailable[8]. . . .

Section Four
Theory and Practice

CHAPTER ONE:

Action and Cognition

Up to now we have considered the process of cognition only from the standpoint of the contemplating and thinking human being. The philosophers content themselves with this standpoint. But man, like the animal, is not merely a contemplating and thinking, but also an acting being. And from his action there issues no less a wealth of knowledge than from his contemplation. When we consider the mental faculties and their functioning—the "mind"—. . . as phenomena that do not be-

---

8. For further comments by Kautsky on Engels' famous passage, see IV:9:2, below.

long to a world other than the one given to us through our senses, then we find that the organs of free movement and those of intelligence develop together in the animal organism, the ones conditioning the others. Both kinds are equally necessary for the preservation of the organism in the struggle for existence.[1]

When we speak of free movement or movement by one's own will, we do not, of course, mean by that a kind of movement initiated by itself without having a cause. It is, however, a movement that is not, like a reflex movement found even in plants, directly triggered by an external stimulus. In the case of organisms with voluntary movement, a nerve center is interposed between the stimulus and the movement, a brain that receives the stimulus but does not necessarily have to pass it on immediately to the organs of movement. At first the stimulus produces only an activity of the brain, in which it meets with a number of memories of earlier impressions. The effect of the stimulus depends on the inherited capacities and tendencies of the brain and its acquired experiences and habits. It depends on them whether the brain merely stores the stimulus, in order to enrich its experiences, or whether and in what way the brain is induced by it to bring about a purposive movement of the organism.

The final purpose served by the brain is not determined by it. This purpose is given with the organism itself and consists in the survival and reproduction of the latter. Thus we are by no means free in our choice of our primary purpose. However, our mental capacity is able to a certain degree to choose among different means it considers appropriate for attaining this purpose. . . . This *ability to choose* gives the appearance of *freedom of will*. But in reality its mental power will always press the organism to choose, among the given possibilities of action, that one which promises to achieve the greatest effect with an affordable expenditure of strength. When this command is transgressed, either deficient knowledge is responsible or a repressing of knowledge by blinding passions or emotions, such as hate, love, fear, anger, or by instincts and habits. In no case is the apparently arbitrary movement performed by the organism in a given case under the influence of all these factors a causeless and in that sense a free movement.

What has been said does, however, make it evident that an organism has to possess a cognitive capacity that is all the more highly developed, the more numerous and complicated the organs directed by its brain become and the more complicated the circumstances are in which the organism must maintain itself. Thus the organs of movement and the organs of

---

1. Kautsky had dealt with this point in his chapter on "Self-Movement and Intelligence," *Ethics*, pp. 76–84.

cognition develop in constant interaction with each other. This process of development explains the nature of our cognitive capacity. It serves the organism's conscious, purposive action and has therefore evolved only those abilities that are required for this task. In order to act appropriately, the organism must above all be able to distinguish among the things of its environment, so that it knows which ones it has to seek out and which ones it has to avoid. It must also be able to perceive changes of things in space and in time and, finally, to observe regularly recurring sequences and on the basis of such observations to foresee future useful or harmful events and to prepare itself for them. . . . On the other hand, it is a matter of indifference for the behavior of the organism that it know what every single thing in its environment is in itself. . . .

The limits of cognition are, then, given with its practical origin, and it is understandable why our organism inherited only specific capacities of cognition from its animal ancestors. It can strengthen these capacities and make them more effective through increased use. Through technical aids, including mathematics, it can make accessible to them perceptions that would have to remain denied to the simple natural organs; but through no kind of mental effort can it add a new capacity to its inherited mental capacities. . . .

The intimate connection between action and cognition . . . also tells us that within its limitations cognition must be real. For only on this presupposition is conscious, appropriate action possible. If the cognition of conscious beings were only appearance, then they would have had to perish long ago through senseless action. Our practical successes show us in how high a degree we are capable of knowing the reality around us.[2]

CHAPTER TWO
The Certainty of Knowledge

. . . . My entire mental being is set in motion only by external impulses. It expresses itself through the way in which it reacts to these impulses, of necessity going beyond mere sensation and thinking. My behavior provides the best test of my ego. . . .

It was not until a class was formed freed from the toil of everyday life that the possibility was created of research and thinking that was practically disinterested in the success of its activity and that saw and sought to solve problems going beyond what was of practical interest Only thereby was

---

2. On action and knowledge, see also V:2:1–2, below.

the possibility given of scientific, methodical work going beyond "sound common sense." But also the possibility of unbounded speculations, which were curbed only when science began not merely to observe and to speculate, but also to be practically active—practical not in the sense of everyday practice, which serves man's self-preservation, but in the sense of a new scientific practice in the service of disinterested research. Thanks to this practical work, especially that of experiments, modern natural science has taken on a materialist character—removed equally far from both skepticism and idealism—that is completely different from the materialism of antiquity, which was based on mere speculation. The fact that idealism, even if only in the form of Kant's "critical" idealism, still finds room in the social sciences can be attributed not least of all to the circumstance that practical experiments are not feasible in this area.

    . . . The many inappropriate actions of men, that is, actions that yield a quite different result from what we intended, show that our cognitive capacity is still quite deficient. This should not surprise us, for animal and human organs are, after all, . . . the product of an evolution. . . . Each of them, however, is perfect enough to assure the existence of its possessor at least reasonably well, not as a consequence of a mystic teleology of nature, but simply because organisms with less perfect organs cannot maintain themselves in their struggle with the environment, a process that is going on and went on uninterruptedly, as the numerous remains of extinct animal species attest. . . .

CHAPTER THREE:

Action and Necessity

. . . The fact that we (and even the higher animals) are capable in a significant measure of conscious, purposive action proves that we possess to an important degree the capacity to recognize real causal relations outside ourselves. On the other hand, the intimate connection of action with the struggle for existence makes it understandable that the need to investigate causal relations and the tendency to regard them as necessary are innate in us as properties that the higher animals that preceded us already had acquired and passed on to us. Action is, to be sure, just as closely linked with our need for freedom as with our recognition of necessity. . . . However, by this freedom one should not understand freedom of the will. . . . Rather, what is of interest already to [primitive man], indeed, already to the animal, is *freedom of action*.

    . . . The realm of recognized necessity is the past, which can no longer be changed in any way. . . . The future lies unknown and free before us; its shape depends to a great extent on our action. Precisely because we know that, we act. But this knowledge . . . cannot determine *how* we act at every particular moment. This can only be effected by the fact that, on the one hand, we expect, in the external world, certain situations as the necessary consequences of those presently given and, on the other hand, we assume of every movement we perform that its necessary consequence will be an effect that is required in order for us to shape the movement of the external world to our advantage in the given case. . . .

Unfortunately, however, the world we live in is of an extremely complicated nature. There is hardly an occurrence in which quite a large number of causes do not work together; no situation that does not bear in its womb the most varied effects. So it is enormously difficult to foresee necessary relations for the future with some certainty and to organize our behavior accordingly. Necessary, that is, regular or lawlike relations, can be known with certainty only for the simplest events. In order to recognize in the events of the external world that which is in accordance with laws, it is above all necessary to strip them of an abundance of nonessential details and to hold fast only to their essential features, which are considerably easier to grasp. This is done either by means of systematic experimentation or through abstraction. . . . It is not always possible to discover causal relations with certainty by means of experiment, of systematically simplified and systematically varied practice. Then only abstraction works, the comparison of numerous cases of the same kind that have been observed, either through practical action or through mere contemplation. Each case will display its peculiarities that do not occur in others. These must be disregarded, abstracted from. Only some features will be common to all cases. They are the essential ones. Their regular recurrence appears as the aspect of the phenomena that conforms to laws and is necessary.

Through experiment and abstraction we can, with great certainty, attain knowledge of numerous necessary or lawlike relations. The certainty of our knowledge grows . . . when, through the advances of our abstractive activity, the many individual laws are combined without contradiction into a small number of general laws. Thus, we arrive at ever-higher principles governing the total complex of interrelations. But even this certainty of knowledge can be considered complete only when it proves itself in practice. . . . Through the intimate connection of theory and practice, the certainty of both increases. But just as theory will never succeed in penetrating to the ultimate causes of being, so too will it never succeed in resolving all the complex phenomena of practice into simple forms and thereby confer on human action complete certainty. . . . Unwanted, unforeseen consequences of our activity play an immense role in the history of mankind.

Causality or Functional Dependence

Up to now we have always spoken only of cause and effect and of necessity. But may we still do that, in view of the results that modern physics has arrived at?... As a mere layman... I am, unfortunately, endowed only with common sense in the field of physics, and I am clearly aware that that does not suffice in science. *[In eight pages, Kautsky quotes and discusses several lengthy passages from Mach,* The Analysis of Sensations, *pp. 89–90, 96, and* Knowledge and Error, *pp. 205–206, and also from Friedrich Adler,* Ernst Machs Überwindung des mechanischen Materialismus, *p. 170, proposing the replacement of the concept of cause and effect with that of functional dependence. He then concludes the following.]*

By a cause one understands, after all, a cause of movement.... A new movement stems from the collision of two bodies moving in different directions.... or, to express the matter in a less crudely materialistic manner, every new movement has its origin in a collision of opposites. Thus the concept of the struggle of opposites, "the father of all things," is very closely related to that of cause. In contrast, the modern conceptions, which want to replace the concept of causality with another, have a more quietistic character, one preferring calm. They need not exclude the struggle of opposites, but are not closely connected with it. *[Kautsky refers here to the work not only of Mach but also of Max Verworn.]* Causality, on the other hand, incessantly directs attention to it. That makes it congenial to the conception of history of dialectical materialism. That, of course, would be no reason to accept causality if it were not also scientifically tenable. Should the concept of causality be generally abandoned in science and replaced by Mach's or Verworn's conception of lawlike relations, then the materialist conception of history would have to take that into account. Neither the one nor the other of the two conceptions is incompatible with it....

I owe so much to Mach that, in spite of great theoretical reservations, I accepted with sympathy the suggestion of my friend Fritz Adler that I replace the "vulgar" view of cause and effect with that of Mach, and I attempted to apply it practically in my work. However, unfortunately, I achieved no success with the concept of function. I would blame that on my own inadequacy if others had obtained better results. But I do not know of anyone who has known how to put functional dependence to good use in historical research or achieved any particular successes with it. And for that reason I consider myself justified in adhering to the... concept of causality, and indeed to... the struggle of opposites as the cause of all motion and development.

Section Five
The Dialectic

CHAPTER ONE

Ego and Environment

. . . The question is by no means whether the mind is an active or passive element, but whether it can, as the only phenomenon in nature, function as its own cause, without having first experienced a determining impulse. Not the activity of the mind but only the nature and the origin of this activity are subject to question. In order to understand this clearly, we start out from the assumption that the mind is one of the tools of the animal organism in the struggle for existence.[1] . . . From the beginnings of its functioning in the simplest animals in which it first appears, the mind encounters two factors: on the one hand, the body of the organism, which produces the mental functions, a body with certain innate needs and capacities. Let us call it the "ego." On the other hand, there is its environment. . . . It is this environment that poses the problems the mind has to solve.[2] The more it understands its own needs and capacities as well as the differences and relationships among the objects in the environment, the better it solves them.

. . . The resolution of the antagonism betwen ego and environment consists in adaptation. . . . Either the ego adapts itself to the environment through certain changes or actions or it is able to shape certain parts of the environment in such a manner that they are adapted to its own purposes or, finally, some mutual adaptation takes place. . . . This is not to say that every change or movement of the organism called forth by external stimuli is or must be appropriate. Many can be quite indifferent and some even inappropriate. But only those organisms will develop and maintain themselves whose appropriate reactions to external stimuli preponderate over the inappropriate ones. The appearance of consciousness, of the awareness of the environment and of the organism's own needs and capacities serves to make it easier for the reaction to external stimuli to occur in an appropriate manner.

The process of movement and development in the organic world outlined here is a dialectical process, that is, it is a process that begins with an affirmation, is continued by a negation, and is concluded by a negation of the negation, that is, an affirmation. It was in this sense that Hegel used the word, and Marx and Engels took it over from him. The starting point

1. See I:4:1–2, above.
2. See also I:5:4, III:2:9–13, and V:1:12, below.

of each process of adaptation is an organism, the ego, the affirmation, the "thesis." It is opposed by its environment, the "nonego," the negation of the organism, the "antithesis." The final result is the overcoming of the opposition, the negation of the negation, the renewed affirmation of the organism through adaptation, the "synthesis." Thereby the process returns to its starting point, the individual that maintains itself. It may have changed in the course of the process in such a way that the starting point is raised to a higher level. In that case, what occurs is not a circular movement but development.

It seems very doubtful to me that the movement of the entire world, the inorganic as well as the organic, fits into this scheme. To be sure, in the inorganic world, too, every new movement arises out of the antagonism or collision of opposed elements. However, the result . . . is not always a synthesis and certainly not a return to the starting point.

CHAPTER TWO

The Dialectic of Self-Initiated Development

The dialectic described here agrees with the Hegelian one in form but is of an entirely different kind. For Hegel, thesis and antithesis are not, as are organism and environment, two quite different things affecting each other, but the thesis already contains its own contradiction, its negation. This negation grows and finally overcomes and transcends the thesis, the starting point of the process. But the negation, too, contains the seed of its own negation, which finally leads to the synthesis and the renewed affirmation of the thesis but on a higher level. Marx and Engels took over this conception of the dialectic from Hegel, but, as Engels put it in his essay on Feuerbach [p. 362], they "turned [it] off its head . . . and placed [it] upon its feet again." To Hegel, the dialectic was a movement of the mind [or spirit] produced by the mind itself that sets the world in motion and effects historical development. Marx and Engels "materialized" it, they turned it into a law of motion of the material world as well as of thought.

[Kautsky here quotes Engels' Anti-Dühring, p. 149, and comments:] In this description, the conception of the negation is particularly striking. The germinating of the seed and the growth of the animal out of the egg are conceived of as negations of the seed and the egg. . . . [But] every organism passes through a number of stages in the course of its existence and its forms change incessantly. If giving up its past form and assuming a new one constitutes a negation of the earlier form, then the individual is engaged in a continuous process of negation. . . . Even more questionable than the conception of the negation is that of the negation of the negation. Here a real negation of the individual is being referred to. The plant dies after it has borne seeds, the butterfly dies after it has laid its eggs. The newly produced seed or the newly laid egg constitutes the return to the starting point of the process, the seed or the egg, from which the individual had originated. But the production of seeds and eggs and the death of the organism that produced them by no means coincide temporally. The former always occurs earlier than the latter. The negation of the negation and the synthesis, the return to the thesis, are then, by no means identical, although they may follow one another in quick succession in the case of some organisms. . . .

. . . Here we investigate the question whether the processes of movement and development in the world really *always* assume the form of the Hegelian dialectic-thesis, antithesis, synthesis with return to the starting point. I consider this assumption to be correct for the organic world, but not at all in the way Engels illustrates it here. He regards movement and development not as the reciprocal effect of two factors, the individual and the environment, on one another but merely as the self-initiated movement of one factor, the individual, and he seeks the antithesis as well as the thesis in the same individual.[3] Evidently, this is still a strong aftereffect of the Hegelian model, which also explained movement in terms of only one factor, the mind, positing, out of itself, its own negation.

As a scheme to characterize some processes, but not as a general law, the dialectical negation of the negation in the Hegelian sense can, under certain circumstances, be quite appropriate. I have myself repeatedly applied it in this way but have become very cautious in doing so, because it is easily subject to a certain arbitrariness. . . .

With respect to the Hegelian scheme of the dialectic as the necessary form of the movement and development of all phenomena in the world, there arise grave doubts particularly after it has been subject to materialist "inversion."[4] But it is by no means settled that Marx and Engels regarded this scheme as a general, necessary law of motion of the world. *[There follow two more quotations from Engels' Anti-Dühring, pp. 154 and 147, from which Kautsky concludes:]* That is to say, we need not at all to accept the dialectic everywhere a priori as the necessary scheme of development; rather, we must discover it where it does occur. . . . It became very fruitful for the Marxian conception of history, which by no means submitted to it slavishly. . . .

3. On this disagreement between Engels and Kautsky with respect to the evolution of man, see II:1:6, below.

4. This word ("Umstülpung") is taken from Marx's postface to the second edition of *Capital*: "With [Hegel, the dialectic] is standing on its head. It must be inverted, in order to discover the rational kernel within the mystical shell." *Capital*, I, 103.

[Marx and Engels] were at pains to approach nature and history "free from preconceived idealist crotchets" *[Engels, Ludwig Feuerbach, p. 361].* The Hegelian dialectic therefore never seduced them to indulge in forced constructions and never misled them to substitute for research the invention, with the aid of the Hegelian "idealist crotchet," of imaginary interrelationships. The [dialectic] served them merely to direct their attention to the contradictions and conflicts of society, which work toward new "syntheses," and to facilitate their investigation. The Hegelian dialectic was for them merely a "heuristic principle," not absolute truth. . . . They regarded it not as a routine to be followed mechanically that made all further research unnecessary, but as one of the lights that illuminate the path of research.[5]

The Dialectic of Perfection

In Engels' illustrations of the dialectic, we find, aside from self-movement, an element of an idealist rather than materialist nature, that of the steady perfection of the world through the dialectical process. . . . In the above-mentioned illustrations of the dialectic Engels points out, still without qualification, that it always means a further development of the organism due to its inherent nature, a development he even designated as perfection.[6] *[Kautsky then objects to Engels' identification of a quantitative increase as perfection, as in his example of a plant that grew out of a single seed producing many seeds, and especially to Engels' citing improvements in plants artificially produced by gardeners to meet human tastes or needs as an illustration of perfection in nature.]*

Hegel could discover in the world steady progress toward growing perfection, because he saw a world-reason at work in it setting purposes. But where can materialist thinking find a world-purpose? And if there is none, what is the origin of the striving for steady perfection through the dialectical process? Man can set purposes for himself in nature and can adapt particular phenomena of his environment to his purposes, and he can see this as perfection from *his* point of view. But it would be anthropocentric thinking to regard this as perfection of the *world*[7]. . . . In nature there is, certainly, constant development, but this is not synonymous with perfection or even always with upward development. . . .

5. Kautsky had made the same point in "Bernstein und die Dialektik," p. 40.
6. The translation of *Anti-Dühring* used here renders Engels' word "Vervollkommnung" as "improvement." "Perfection" is a better translation in this context.
7. See I:2:4, above.

Perfection is basically nothing other than appropriateness to a purpose. . . . Every organism has its own purposes, which in the last analysis can be traced back to the purpose of its preservation and reproduction. In this sense, an organism will be all the more perfect, the better it is adapted to this purpose of self-preservation of the individual and of the species. Now, it is impossible to say that this adaptation and perfection grow in the course of the evolution of organisms, that the more highly developed ones . . . are better adapted and more capable of living and of maintaining themselves than those more simply constructed. . . . One cannot possibly say that the human species is better adapted for its preservation than the species of earthworms.[8] It is, therefore, not correct that the process of development always means an advancement to ever-greater perfection.

And likewise one cannot say that the negation of the negation in the Hegelian sense always leads back to the starting point—on a higher level, to be sure—of the dialectical process. In society, it is true, every change of a social institution amounts to its negation. . . . But . . . there are institutions to which men never return after they have once gone beyond them. . . . And the same is true of the development that the individual plant or animal organism goes through from the moment of its conception to its demise. Even if one chooses to call each of the stages of this development a negation of the preceding ones, nowhere in it can a return to an earlier stage be discovered. . . .

It is evident that the Hegelian dialectical scheme is not generally, but often only in a very forced manner and frequently not at all, applicable to nature and society if one simply "inverts" it. For its materialist application, it is not enough merely to turn it off its head and place it upon its feet, but one must also completely change the path which the feet follow. We achieve agreement of the thought with the facts only if we seek what is dialectical in the scheme, not in the *direction* of the development, but in the *motive force* of the development of organisms and regard as such the dialectical reaction of the individual organism to its environment. . . . [9]

CHAPTER FOUR

The Conservative Nature of the Mind

. . . .Although in a different sense than Hegel, we regard the dialectical process primarily as a mental one, as the struggle of an aware and consciously acting being with its environment. At least only this kind of dia-

8. See II:6:1, below.
9. Kautsky returned to his discussion of Engels' view of the dialectic in *Erinnerungen und Erörterungen*, pp. 216–22.

lectical process need concern us here, where we are dealing with the materialist conception of history.

The mind is a very highly active, restless element, but no change of direction, no new goal or ideal, no new thought or new knowledge, arises in it without a cause... without an impulse from without. Because the environment is constantly undergoing change and unceasingly presents us with problems we must solve if we want to maintain ourselves, for that reason the mind is in continuous, restless movement.... The active nature of the mind does not, however, go so far that it spontaneously engenders problems that the external world does not offer it.... If it has found a solution of a problem, then it remains faithful to it,... as long as no new facts turn up that cause it to appear as mistaken or at least as inadequate. Most of the problems that everyday life poses for us recur anew in the same way again and again.... Under constant conditions, the same solution is found again and again for such problems. This solution becomes a habit that one accepts from one's ancestors and considers, without further reflection, as self-evident. Man passionately resists any modification of it as a violation of his essential being. Very compelling new facts must turn up that are incompatible with the old ideas before these are abandoned.... The human mind, or rather the mind of animals generally, does not hanker after innovations but is *conservative.*...

Every change in the relationship of man to the external world creates new problems. Such changes are effected not only through a change in the external world, but also through a change in the animal or human organism itself.... However, these changes in the organism are of two kinds. Either they occur necessarily in certain phases in the course of every normal individual of the same species. Then the problems that arise from *[these changes]* are new for the individual but not for the species.... Or it is a matter of phenomena that are peculiar not to the species, but only to particular individuals. Such phenomena, like sicknesses, can represent new phenomena and call forth new problems that require new solutions. Such changes... will, however, as a rule, be traceable in the last analysis to particular influences of the external world on the individual or its ancestors.

Problems always arise for the individual from the relationship between its innate character and the external world, and new problems arise only from a modification of this relationship, never from a change of the mind coming out of itself. There are no innovations without the mind. Without new ideas there is no new conscious practice. But the impetus to the new ideas, if they are new not merely for the individual but for the species, is given by the external world.[10] ... The mind be-

10. See also I:5:1, above, and III:2:9–13, V:1:12, below.

comes revolutionary only where its environment has already been revolutionized.

The Adaptation of Thoughts to One Another

The conflicts between the ego and its environment are not the only ones the mind must overcome. . . . The more diverse the sense organs are, the more diverse are also the impressions that the organism, the "ego," receives from the same point of the external world. But it is not only the senses that become ever more diverse in the course of evolution, but also the organs of movement. . . . Only such higher kinds of organisms are capable of life in which, along with the organs' division of labor, there also develops a central organ. It combines the impressions the various senses receive from the same object into a unitary image in *[the organism's]* consciousness. On the other hand, it subjects the different organs of movement to a unitary volitional impulse that brings about their unified cooperation for a common end. . . . The adaptation, without contradiction, of impressions and movements to one another is, from its beginnings, one of the tasks of the mind, that is, of the central organ of the sensory and motor nerves, of the brain. This task emerges, just as those discussed in the preceding sections, from the nature of the mind as a tool of the organism in the fight for its self-preservation. To the extent that this task remains confined to the functioning of the sensory and motor organs, it is carried out completely instinctively, without the organism becoming conscious of it. . . .

Memory is among the most important faculties of the mind. The more experiences are collected in my memory, the less is my thinking and willing determined by the momentary impulses from the external world and the more are these impulses controlled by the totality of my experiences. . . . But, this totality of my experiences, even more than the sense impressions of the moment, would form a wild chaos, if the mind did not order it and integrate all experiences, to the extent that they have been kept alive in consciousness, into a total complex free of contradiction. This operation cannot be unconscious. Here consciousness must work and here it has to perform the most difficult labor. To create order, it must join what is similar, separate what is different, abstract what is common from similar phenomena, and order these abstractions, too, to subsume finally all of them under one or a very few principles. For man, this activity takes on enormous dimensions. . . . To order, without contradiction, all the huge research material *[made available by language, writing, and technology]* is a gigantic task. And yet the human mind works at it indefatigably, for every contradiction in its own thoughts is intolerable to it, in accordance with the natural disposition of the mind that is present even in the animal.

To be sure, Engels declares, drawing here, too, on Hegel, that contradictions are present not only in our thinking but also in reality. *[Kautsky quotes Engels, saying in his* Anti-Dühring, *p. 132, that "motion itself is a contradiction," and proceeds to deny it.]* The word "contradiction" can be understood in two ways. On the one hand, as the expression of a conflict, on the other, as the expression of the incompatibility of two phenomena or thoughts. That there are conflicts in the world, no one denies. . . . The only question is whether a contradiction, as something incompatible, is also possible. The determination that two phenomena are or are not compatible with one another is, however, a judgment, and judgments exist only in my consciousness, which can make mistakes, not in the external world. The contradiction to which Engels referred was contained in his *definition* of motion. . . . This contradiction in the definition gives us a reason for seeking another definition, but not for claiming that in reality something can not merely appear to be but actually be simultaneously compatible and incompatible with something else. . . .

[The] process of logical thinking is as much a dialectical one as that of the overcoming of the conflicts between the ego and its environment. It, too, ends with a synthesis. . . . Both processes, however, are fundamentally different, because in one the environment confronts the ego, whereas the other takes place merely in our consciousness. . . . To be sure, the impressions, sensations, and thought that the mind orders are called forth by the external world. But they are shaped by the mind, and the more comprehensive the domain of experiences and the further advanced the process of their ordering is, the more distant one becomes from the external world. *[One is removed from it]* through the growing pyramid of abstractions that is built up on the basis of the totality of experiences, so that the point reaching toward the heavens often no longer knows anything of the ground on which it rests. In this second kind of dialectic, the ideas seem to be alone among themselves. Here we seem to be in the realm of pure reason, which brings forth its new knowledge from itself. . . . From there it is no longer far to the assumption that the mind, in contrast to all other phenomena of this world, has the ability to move itself of its own accord and to transpose this, its own movement, onto the world, to impart impulses to the latter without itself receiving any from it, to be merely cause and not also effect. . . .

That is not to deny that the ideas and the mental creations of men in general, hence also their social institutions, do have the tendency to make themselves independent of the external world. However, when the idea attains such an independent life, its development ceases, it petrifies. Engels points to the state and religion as examples of such independence.[11] They have a great historical role even when they are independent of society, but then they function not as a *driving force* but as a *hindrance* of development. They constitute a driving force of development only when they are very closely connected with newly emerging social conditions and receive their impulses from the external world. This is due to the conservative nature of the mind mentioned above, which manifests itself in the adaptation of thoughts to one another as well as in the adaptation of thoughts to facts. . . .

Since not all men have the same mental endowments and the same opportunities for observation, the new facts that are incompatible with the old edifice of ideas will always be noted at first only by isolated preeminent minds. But the mere recognition that the old conceptions do not suffice would not be enough to bring about their end. In order to effect that, the thinkers who have recognized the untenability of the old structure of ideas must also be able, without contradiction, to relate the new facts to the old ones to the extent that the old facts are recognized as valid by the innovators; that is, these thinkers must be able to erect a more or less comprehensive new system of thought. . . . *[The innovator needs great knowledge, rich imagination disciplined by critical ability, and a strong character to face the resistance of ideas that had become independent of the environment.]* Unfortunately, admiration of the bearers of the new thought easily makes one overlook its original source. A new idea will arise and succeed in obtaining recognition only when the external world through a change gives an impulse for it, and one that is sufficiently strong.[12] With this statement we have arrived at the fundamental idea of historical materialism, but in so doing we have anticipated some things, since we have not yet dealt with the relationship between man and society, but only with that between a conscious organism and its environment. . . .

Not only *cognition* but also *volition* is among the mental phenomena. Its basis is given before all experience, thus a priori, with the organism and its innate drives. But how this volition expresses itself in every given case vis-à-vis the external world depends as much on the latter as on the organism. The individual acts of the will are therefore determined as much by our knowledge of the external world as by our physical constitution.[13] The more varied the external world and the more numerous the problems it confronts us with, the more numerous and diverse the purposes that the

11. Kautsky here evidently refers to Engels, *Ludwig Feuerbach*, pp. 369–75.
12. On innovations, see also III:2:12–13, below, and on creative individuals, see V:1:12, below.
13. Kautsky returns to this point in V:2:1–2, below.

individual's will sets itself. The more necessary is it then to order them without contradiction, in a coherent system of purposes, if the organism's powers are not to exhaust themselves in actions that contradict, cancel, paralyze one another.

The whole labor of knowing the external world, of adapting thoughts to facts and thoughts to each other, would be useless if it did not lead to a system of purposes. In the case of the social animals, this process is made more complicated by the fact that they have not only purposes of the individual, but also purposes of the society to which they belong. These, too, are basically purposes of individuals, for only a thinking organism can set purposes, and society is not an organism with a central thinking organ. But the social purposes are not the purpose of an isolated individual, but rather of a collectivity of united individuals. They do not confront the individual as commandments of his own will, but of an overwhelming will that stands above him. Often it is clearly evident how this will comes to be, for example, in the case of laws passed by a legislative assembly. . . . Often, however, these commandments originate unconsciously or they stem from a remote time, of which there is no record. Thus the commandments of the society often take on a mystical appearance, and the same thing is true of the authority from which they originate. Not only ethics, but also the state offers numerous occasions for and inducements to mystical transfiguration.

Like the purposes of the individual, the laws of the state and moral precepts run the danger of contradicting each other when their number increases and the areas regulated by them become more varied with the progress of society. This danger becomes all the greater, as the conservative nature of the mind manifests itself especially strongly in these areas. Society and the state outlast the individual. . . . Certain commandments of society can maintain themselves even for centuries, for millennia—one need think only of the ten commandments of the Bible. . . . The old commandments that have not been annulled are joined by new ones, since new circumstances require consideration, and the work of legislation does not stand still.

Detailed scientific work is required in order to integrate without contradiction this infinite wealth of very different kinds of obligation. The sciences of this kind, jurisprudence and ethics, do not search for causal but rather for teleological relations. . . . Their usefulness can become questionable when they isolate themselves from the other sciences and from life and believe that they can create new knowledge out of themselves, apart from all experience. . . . Only when the sciences of what ought to be in society seek their foundation in the social sciences that search for causal relations, such as political economy and ethnology, and when they consider their own area as the origins and changes of what ought to be, only then will they be capable of enriching our knowledge. The starting point of all knowledge remains experience. And once, in a given state of affairs, the ordering of hitherto acquired experiences in a complex free of contradictions has been successfully achieved, any progress to new knowledge is possible only when a change of the environment or of the organism's cognitive means brings new experiences in its train.

[*The appendix to Part I, Kautsky's "Draft of a Developmental History of Mankind" of 1876, is omitted here.*]

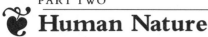
Human Nature

Section One
Heredity

Acquired Characteristics

We have seen what the nature of the dialectical process is that manifests itself in the movement and evolution of living beings. It is the antagonism . . . between the organism and its environment that moves and develops the former. . . . But the manner in which the organism reacts to these impulses, the manner of its movements called forth by them, depends on its peculiar nature, on the "a priori" contained in it. . . . If we want to understand this process, then we must take as our starting point the a priori of the individual, the organism with its inherited forms and capacities. If one already knows these, then one may forgo an investigationof them, . . . and need only take into consideration, one-sidedly, the influences of the environment. That has heretofore always been done in the expositions of the materialist conception of history. . . . Research into the factors of heredity does not fall within the field of historical science, but of natural science, where we historians are, one and all, laymen.

However, it is a peculiarity of the most recent development of the sciences that the more their individual areas become specialized, the more significant do the border areas become where two sciences come into contact with one another. . . . Thus biology, the science of life, and sociology, the science of society, cannot be separated quite so rigorously today. . . . It therefore seems to me appropriate, in spite of all the modesty incumbent upon a layman in the area of natural science, to touch here upon some questions of heredity and adaptation in the animal world, questions capable of casting light on the evolution of the human race, before we consider the latter itself. Unfortunately, the question of heredity is among the most controversial in biology today. It is closely connected with the question of evolution. . . .

The principal point of controversy is the question of the heredity of acquired characteristics. There is general recognition of what experience has shown for a long time, that organisms are influenced in their characteristics by their environment. Can characteristics thus altered be transmitted by heredity or not? If such transmission is possible, then there is no longer anything mysterious about the evolution of organisms per se. . . . But a number of natural scientists refuse to admit the heritability of acquired characteristics. Without it, however, the evolution of organisms becomes a very mysterious process, not just for every individual species, but in general. For a time it was a sign of good breeding in natural science to deny this kind of heritability. Now, however, the balance is tilting again in favor of the assumption of a hereditary transmission of acquired characteristics. . . . [Kautsky then quotes at great length from Tschulok, Deszendenzlehre, pp. 228–30, and summarizes the principal point he quotes as follows:] Thus there is basically no more argument about the transmission of acquired characteristics in general, but only about whether new characteristics have to be acquired by the somatic cells and transferred to the germ cells, or whether they have to be directly acquired by the latter, if they are to be transmitted by heredity. The absolute distinction between somatic and germ cells, too, has recently been called into question by some. . . . For the problem we have to solve here, what has been set forth as the unanimously accepted position of present-day natural science suffices completely.[1] . . .

CHAPTER TWO

Crossbreeding

In addition to the acquisition and the hereditary transmission of new characteristics through the influence of new conditions, a second factor in the evolution of organisms must also be considered: the acquisition of new characteristics through crossbreeding of individuals of different species or different varieties. [Kautsky rejects an explanation of the evolution of organisms by crossbreeding for three reasons summarized as follows:] . . . it has been established that crossbreeding can achieve new attributes, which occur neither in the parents nor in their forebears. Still, these attributes can be only new groupings of elements that were already present in the fore-

---

1. Kautsky had already in 1914 dealt with the same subject, relying heavily on Tschulok's *Entwicklungstheorie* of 1912 and reaching the conclusion that "we, therefore, see no reason that would oblige us to assume that acquired characteristics cannot be inherited." *Are the Jews a Race?*, pp. 37–39. See also II:6:3, below.

bears. . . . Crossbreeding is possible only between organisms of two sexes. The simpler ones, which multiply by cell division, can clearly never develop new forms by crossbreeding. . . . Crossbreeding, especially of animals, occurs extremely rarely in nature. . . . Change of the environment, then, remains always the most important factor in the evolution of organisms. . . .

Individual and Species

The question that the theory of evolution must answer is . . . not merely how individuals have evolved, but primarily how species of exactly similar individuals have evolved and how this evolution is to be reconciled with the constancy of species, based upon heritability, observed in the present time. . . .

[Darwin] does not take as his point of departure that which constitutes the species, the *agreement* of the essential characteristics in all individuals belonging to the species by virtue of this agreement. Rather, he starts from the *differences* that particular individuals of the same species display in spite of all their agreement. . . . Darwin assumed that things happened in nature similarly as they do in the breeding stable, only the selection of the individuals chosen to reproduce themselves is made, not by the breeder, but by the struggle for existence, through which all the less fit are eradicated and excluded from reproduction. . . . Quite soon, Darwin was confronted with the objection that variations are, as a rule, of an extremely trifling nature and in practical terms must be completely insignificant for the prospects of the individual.[2] . . .

Darwin did not know of the saltations, the mutations, which were not discovered by de Vries until long after his death. The nature of these changes is still very mysterious. We do not even know if they bring about new forms or only represent atavisms, throwbacks to old, superseded ones. Since it was so long before they were discovered, it is reasonable to assume that they are not a regularly occurring phenomenon, characteristic of all organisms, but rather only occasional exceptions, the causes of which are still entirely enveloped in darkness. At best, however, adduction of the mutations, which effect considerable changes at one blow, could rebut the objection that variations are too insignificant to be . . . of practical advantage for certain individuals in comparison with others of the same species. But this defeat of one objection to the Darwinian theory would be bought at the price of endangering the theory as a whole. For mutation appears to be a miracle that takes us back to the time of Cuvier, who still believed in a

---

2. See also p. 114, below.

new creation of every new species, if mutations are not atavisms or called forth by one of the two factors of evolution heretofore accepted by the theory of evolution. These are crossbreeding or a change in the conditions of life, for example, a chemical change of the soil in which the plant that is subject to the mutation grows.

Leaving that aside, mutation also does not eliminate a further objection to the Darwinian view. Even if the variations or mutations are pronounced enough to accord to the individual a decided advantage in the struggle for existence, they will lead to the formation of a new species only with difficulty if they are confined in their beginning only to a single individual or to a few individuals. . . . When some individuals within a species exhibit alterations, whether imperceptible or saltational ons, then the probability is very slight that precisely these individuals and their progeny will mate among themselves, completely excluding the immense majority of the normal fellow species-members. . . .

In yet another way artificial selection is different from natural selection. In the animals he is breeding, usually only a single attribute is of interest to the breeder. . . . It is only with regard to this one attribute that he selects his breeding material. . . . The selective struggle for existence is by no means so one-sided, though. The more various the organs of the organism, the more diverse their uses and the situations in which each organ, either alone or in association with others, has to act and to prove itself in the struggle for existence, the less it will depend on the form or the functioning of a single organ whether the organism is the "fittest" for the struggle for existence. For the same individual, very different forms of its organs can appear as the fittest in different situations. . . . *[Kautsky contrasts the explanations of the shape of the giraffe offered by Lamarck,* Zoological Philosophy, *p. 122, and Darwin,* The Origin of Species, *pp. 160–61.]* Lamarck thus places his principal emphasis on the character of the environment. . . . According to the Darwinian conception, each variation, if it is advantageous for the individual in certain cases, would have to lead to the individual's improved prospect of outliving the average member of the species and of propagating its peculiarity. Instead of a new species, we would get numerous individuals of the most diverse kinds. . . . These different individuals would mate among themselves in the most diverse relationships. The final result would not be the formation of new species, but only the dissolution of the existing species into a chaos of very different individuals. Or rather, if the varying of single individuals were the decisive driving force of the evolution of organisms, then it would be incomprehensible how species ever came to be formed[3]. . . .

3. Kautsky had developed the same argument with Darwin in *Are the Jews a Race?*, pp. 25–31. See also p. 114, below.

Environment and Species

The *commonality* of the characteristics of the *species* cannot possibly be explained from the *difference* of the *individuals*. . . . It can only stem from the influence of a factor that has affected and may still affect all individuals of a species in the same way. . . .

We must assume that, as soon as the conditions for its formation were given in particular sites, the primordial life-form on the earth, regardless of how it was fashioned, appeared from the outset in all these places in large numbers and within a short time in as large a number as the conditions permitted. . . . We must assume that the later forms of organisms, too, which evolved from the first ones, always developed not merely in a single specimen, later in a set of parents, but rather in quite a large number from numerous forebears, each time as many as the living conditions permitted and brought about. Only a change of these conditions can cause a change in the number of the mature individual members of the various species living at any given time. That is nature's true law of population, also for man, who, to be sure, occupies a special position inasmuch as he, in contrast to the animal, is capable within certain limits of artificially changing his living conditions and of increasing the supply of food available to him[4]. . . .

Only *one* factor remains to explain the commonality of the characteristics of a species: the *commonality of the living conditions* in which the individual members lived in the period of the species' formation. To be sure, not only this commonality of the environment must have existed, but also the commonality of the inherited physical characteristics (among which are also the mental ones) of the individuals forming the species. The same stimulus engenders the same reaction only when it affects objects that are the same. . . . The innunerable primordial life-forms of life's beginnings on the earth, the product of common conditions, must have already attained their common species-character through this commonality. The modification of the living conditions in one place or another, for example, through the slow elevation of the ocean floor, will have had the effect that in these regions new influences affected the identically similar characteristics of all their primitive inhabitants that were inherited and retained through heredity. Through these influences those characteristics were altered in the same way for all individuals of the species living there. In that way there originated a new species. . . .

---

4. Demography was Kautsky's first scientific interest and the subject of his first book, *Der Einfluss der Volksvermehrung auf den Fortschritt der Gesellschaft* (1880). His mature treatment is *Vermehrung und Entwicklung* (1910).

If *[due to migrations]* two different species were found in the same region, then the newly immigrated one was influenced in a different way by the conditions there than the native one. . . . Further alterations of the living conditions in the region will have affected each of these species differently, according to their inherited characteristics. . . . For every individual species it is now not merely the way the inanimate environment is fashioned that is determinative. Alongside the latter there arises a new kind of environment, the animate one, which affects every species in a very decisive manner, either as fodder or as foe. Thus, with the diversity of the organisms there also grows the diversity of the environment for the individual organism in it. . . .

That species are preserved and evolve further as such is only possible when the individualizing tendency of variation is outweighed by the mass effect of the environment, the "material conditions," as the language of the materialist conception of history puts it, an effect working toward the realization of uniformity. In the final analysis, evolution is decided not through the particularities of individuals, but rather through mass effect;[5] the impulse to development is given not by an initiative spontaneously arising from individuals, but rather by a change of the environment. *[Here Kautsky quotes from Darwin's preface to the second (1874) edition of* The Descent of Man.*]* Thus, in contrast to many of his disciples, Darwin recognizes the significance of a change of the environment for the change of organisms. On the other hand, we by no means fail to recognize that changes of organisms can also occur through the varying of individuals. However, in this point, too, Darwin himself must make even the variability, the changeableness within a species dependent on changes in the living conditions. . . . *[Kautsky supports this point with quotations from the first paragraphs of the first and fifth chapters of* The Origin of Species, *pp. 15, 101.]*

For an organism to hold its own in the struggle for existence, two kinds of adaptation are required: not only its adaptation to its environment, but also the adaptation of every single organ of an individual to its other organs. . . . The first organisms were extremely simple, without any division of labor in their bodies. New living conditions perhaps then caused individual parts of the simple being to be affected more and differently by their environment than the other ones and therefore to develop special characteristics different from those of the other parts. If they were such as were useful to the organism as a whole, then it survived. Thus a division of labor gradually arose among the different parts of the organism, with the latter becoming ever more complicated. That was certainly a process that required long periods of time and in which the struggle for existence made its inexorable selection. . . .

5. Kautsky says the same of human history, V : 1 : 10–12, below.

. . . In every instance the point of time eventually had to be reached for *[each new]* species when it attained to the state of relative perfection. In it, all the separate organs of the individual accorded so well with one another that an alteration of one of them, assuming that the environment remained constant, necessarily meant a change for the worse for the total organism, even though the alteration might have represented a perfecting of the isolated organ. . . . *[Altered individuals now]* have to be eliminated by the struggle for existence. . . . Therefore, the species remains unchanged from that point on until an appreciable change of the living conditions occurs, whereby the once attained adaptation and harmony of the organism is reduced and new adaptations of some organs become necessary. . . .

Thus the struggle for existence operates in a twofold manner. If new living conditions appear, then the organisms subjected to them are changed. . . . But things are completely different when, after long persistence of a certain state of the environment, the relative perfection of a species . . . is attained. From a factor of *evolution*, selection through the struggle for existence becomes henceforth a *conservative* factor, a factor that does not perfect the race through the . . . selection of the best, but rather protects it against being debased through eradication of the worst. . . . *[Thus]* we are able to overcome the apparent contradiction between the observations of nature in historical time and the testimonies of geology. The former indicate the stability of the species, which immutably pass on their species–characteristics. The latter make it imperative to assume that there occurred a continuous evolution of organisms from one or a few simple primordial forms to the infinite wealth of the present-day world with its, in part, extremely diverse organisms. This contradiction is overcome if we assume that the environment of organisms changes, that, however, these changes in the character of the earth do not proceed continuously, but periods of stability follow upon periods of change. . . . We may, as I have already done in my book *Vermehrung und Entwicklung in Natur und Gesellschaft* [Propagation and Evolution in Nature and Society], refer to that as an alternation of revolutionary and conservative periods in the evolutionary history of organisms. *[Kautsky then quotes from pp. 55–56 of this earlier work to add that on the earth surface, just as in society, there are no periods of total change or of no change at all.]*

From whichever side we choose to approach the problem of evolution, we always come to the conclusion that the driving force of evolution does not emanate from single individuals different from the mass, but rather from changes of the external world that affect all individuals of a species in the same way and thereby change the mass. The movements of evolution are movements of masses. And . . . only for the movements of masses can laws be ascertained. Whoever wants to come to know the laws of evolution must investigate the movements of masses. That holds true for every evolution, for that of men as well as that of the other animals and the plants.

Thus, from the standpoint of natural science we come to the basis on which historical materialism rests.[6]

CHAPTER FIVE

Marx and Darwin

... Historical materialism shares the same basis as [the general theory of evolution]. That is not to say that a knowledge of laws of society of itself enables one also to know laws of nature ... or that we should even be obligated simply to apply to nature laws we have recognized to be valid for society in order to attain to complete uniformity in our thinking. Of course, the opposite is permitted just as little, and yet it strongly suggests itself, for nature is the general, society only a special case within it. Therefore some assume that any law of nature, just as it is, must also be valid for society. That would be true if there were in the universe only quantitative differences and not also qualitative ones. Perhaps it will someday be possible to trace all the latter back to the former. ... In any case, each quality has its own laws, which hold good only for its domain, along with such laws as it shares with other qualities. Thus life has its own laws, ... although it remains subject to the laws of the inanimate world of physics and chemistry. The same is true of the mental phenomena of living beings. In turn, within the world of life we find the various qualities of the plants and animals with common laws, but also with special laws, and thus human society, too, constitutes a special quality with special laws, in addition, however, also with laws that man has in common with other living beings. ... Within society itself every mode of production is governed by laws that obtain only for it, in addition to others that it shares with every kind of production. ...

It does not yet constitute proof of the correctness of historical materialism that its fundamental principle is in agreement with that of the theory of evolution. ... Laws of society can be arrived at only through the study of society, laws of nature only through the study of nature. But when, while studying society, one discovers laws that agree with the laws of nature, then we may note this agreement with satisfaction and regard it as a confirmation of these laws in each of the two areas. This is true for the relationship of the materialist conception of history to the theory of evolution of organic beings, in which theory this evolution is accounted for by changes of the environment. ... *[Kautsky adds a number of quotations from Marx and Engels commenting, both favorably and unfavorably, on Darwin.]*

6. Some of the points made in this chapter already occur in *Are the Jews a Race?*, pp. 31–37.

The Transformation of the Animal into Man

In his book on the descent of man, Darwin furnished proof that our primal ancestors must have been apelike animals. . . . What interests us now is the other side of the coin: those facets of man that elevate him above the rest of the animal world. . . . Since the other animals have no development that we could call historical, the historical development of man must be grounded in his peculiar nature, which separates him from the animal world. *[Kautsky here quotes Darwin's* The Descent of Man, *p. 431, who ascribes early man's]* "immense superiority to his intellectual faculties, to his social habits . . . and to his corporeal structure." As for intellectual faculties and social habits, we lack any indication that would justify the assumption that the ancestor of man, whom we shall call an apeman, was superior in intelligence and strength of social cohesion to all the anthropoid apes. . . . What, in any case, however, distinguished the apeman from the other apes is his bodily structure. . . . What sets man apart is *his erect posture*. . . . The cause of the transition *[to this posture can only have been]* a change in the character of the environment.

Today we can still only conjecture about how the apeman's transition to an upright carriage took place. Perhaps the development was as follows: Just like the anthropoid apes, the apeman probably lived in a region of tropical primeval forest. If the climate of the region became dry . . . , then the forest might have been transformed into grassland. . . . Under these conditions, the previous tree-dwellers were increasingly forced to move about on the ground. . . . That could influence quadrumanes in three different ways. Some were unable to adapt to the new conditions; they perished. Other quadrumanous species gradually . . . transformed their hands into feet; from quadrumanes they became quadrupeds again. . . . But there was yet a third possibility: The arboreal animals became accustomed to walking erect; only two of their hands, those of the posterior extremities, were transformed into feet. The anterior ones remained hands. This last change presupposed an inclination to locomotion solely upon the rear extremities, such as we see in gorillas and chimpanzees. Perhaps this inclination is linked to their body weight . . . *[which]* can often cause an arboreal animal to move about on the ground. . . .

Man's body size was, then, in all likelihood one of the factors that prepared him for walking upright and for the far-reaching division of labor between hand and foot. This division of labor is even more important than his erect carriage. [*Kautsky quotes Darwin,* The Descent of Man, *p. 434, to support this point.*] The complete liberation of the hand from the labor of locomotion constitutes the beginning of the apeman's transformation into man. [*On the importance of the apeman's erect posture, Kautsky then quotes Engels'*

incomplete essay "The Part Played by Labour in the Transition from Ape to Man"
(p. 66). He notes again their different conceptions of the dialectic, which made
Engels find the impulse to the erect posture not, like Kautsky, in a change in the
environment, but in the apeman's climbing "mode of life." This, Kautsky argues,
fails to explain why not all apes came to adopt the erect posture.]

The Human Psyche

... The apeman's intelligence was necessarily raised above the level [*of that*
of the anthropoid apes] as soon as he was transposed into new circumstances,
while the apes remained in the old ones. With this change, new problems
arose for him that called for new solutions. . . . Along with his hand, his
brain also became more refined, and both of them together lifted the apeman
over the threshold of what the apes had attained up to that point. Some of
the anthropoid apes . . . used objects they found in nature as tools and weapons. They did not, however, go so far as to confer on the raw material
they found new, more appropriate forms, to turn it into tools and weapons. . . . With his superior intelligence, superior manual skill, and the ability
to produce tools suited to different purposes, the apeman who had become
primitive man acquired an additional ability, the ability to adapt more easily
and consciously to new circumstances. . . . This ability was perhaps simply
imposed on him. For it is quite possible that his habitat . . . ultimately assumed a character that compelled his emigration. It is possible, too, that
under the new conditions the equilibrium between births and deaths (both
natural and violent) was disturbed, an equilibrium that otherwise prevails
among every animal species during conservative periods of the earth's history. The new abilities may have reduced the number of fatalities caused
by powerful enemies or natural forces, while the food sources did not
increase. This must have generated a surplus population that was pressed
to emigrate.

Be that as it may, primitive man in any case possessed the capacity of
conscious, rapid adaptation to new circumstances to a quite different degree
than the anthropoid apes. That is evidenced by the fact that these apes
inhabit relatively limited areas with uniform living conditions, whereas we
have discovered traces of primitive man on all continents, in the most diverse
climates and altitudes with the most varied food sources. . . . This points to
a further difference between man and the animal. The evolution of the latter
is brought about by new conditions intruding into its habitat. In contrast,
man reaches the point where he himself seeks out new conditions. Thereby
the development of his intelligence is, in turn, given a very strong impetus. . . . To this is added the adaptation of his hand and of his tools and
weapons to very diverse kinds of activities. . . .

Men could reach this advanced stage only as social animals, among whom every experience, discovery, and invention of the individual was communicated to his comrades and passed on to posterity, so that the observations and achievements of individuals did not perish with them but were preserved and gradually accumulated. Upon this accumulation rests the entire progress of culture. . . .

In modern art, science, and politics, there are, to be sure, circles of people to whom it seems radical to feel themselves so superior to all that has been handed down that they do not consider it necessary to lose time studying it. Such people like to drape themselves in Marxist colors, but Marx did not at all subscribe to this method. He did not go beyond bourgeois economics by ignoring it, but rather by studying it more thoroughly than the great majority of the bourgeois economists themselves. Socialism, too, can only be developed out of capitalism, and it will be built up the more easily the better capitalism, which must provide its basis and starting point, is functioning.[7] There is no cliché more senseless than that everything that exists must be destroyed so that the social edifice can be rebuilt completely anew. Such a destruction of the old does not mean anything other than the elimination of the indispensable preconditions of the new; it does not make room for the latter but forces us to begin once again with the old. It does not carry us forward but backward. . . .

It would be wrong to explain man's progress solely by his social nature. This he shares with many animals, including some that are at a quite low level of development. However, the driving force issuing from society became peculiar to man alone through the emergence of *articulated speech*. The urge to communicate reciprocally among individuals of the same species is common to all animals that are developed mentally to some degree. . . . However, it was only man's phonic language that achieved the ability to designate certain things and processes, not only those that can be pointed to, . . . but also such as are not visible, as are past or are only expected. . . . *[This language]* becomes then the most powerful instrument of man's intellectual progress. The brain and language must have developed one another in close interaction. . . .

It is incorrect to believe that animals are not capable of forming concepts, that thinking without articulated language is impossible. . . . The animal is also able to recognize some regularly occurring relations and to draw conclusions from them. But pursuing complicated lines of reasoning, joining individual relations together into a coherent complex and drawing from it conclusions that are retained in memory and thereby become starting points for the discovery of more and more relations no longer obvious to the senses, that is impossible without language. . . . Even for shaping tools and

7. See also IV : 8 : 13, below.

words, an intelligence was required that went beyond the level previously reached by the highest animals. In their effects, technology and language then developed man's intelligence and society ever higher and lifted them ever more above animality. . . .

This whole development necessarily had the result that the power of the inherited instincts in man became ever smaller and that even the inherited drives became guided more and more by intelligence. *[Kautsky distinguishes between drives, which produce desires for particular goals, like sociability, mating, or self-preservation, without pointing the way to them, and instincts, which comprise desires not only for goals but for particular methods of reaching them.]* Only the specialized instincts increasingly lose their importance for man as stimulants of his volition and action, precisely because of their specialization. . . . The more various and complex the circumstances of the external world are that the organism has to master, the more rapidly they change, the less does instinctual action suffice, the more likely it is to change from a help into a hindrance, the more it must, from case to case, be modified and corrected and finally completely replaced by the intellect, by knowledge of the external world. . . . However, . . . we ought to admit that the innate drives of self-preservation, of propagation, of social cohesion still govern our activity with full force. *[Kautsky here quotes William MacDougall,* An Introduction to Social Psychology, *p. 38, whom he had criticized in a footnote on the preceding page for not distinguishing between drives and instincts.]*

When his living conditions change, man also modifies the expressions of his drives, his needs and wants.[8] But in spite of all changes, "inherited human nature" displays a strong ability to persist, and the character of these changes itself only becomes intelligible when we regard them as alterations of the inherited species–characteristics. That which is inherited, that which is a priori, determines the whole character of world history. . . . Those are quite wrong who assume that the materialist conception of history makes the character of every single historical phenomenon dependent only on the character of the environment of the men involved in it, on the "material conditions." It is no less dependent on the innate characteristics of the men themselves. . . . This fact was not overlooked by the materialist historians. But their task was only the investigation of the flux of history, not of what remains unchanged in it. The analysis of human nature is not the task of history but of anthropology. History presupposes that analysis.[9] . . .

For our purposes, human nature is relevant only as the starting point, as the thesis of the dialectical process that takes place between man and his environment and constitutes the historical process. No result, no synthesis of this process can be relevant as such a thesis, not the nature of man as he

8. See pp. 79–80 and II: 5 : 5, below.
9. See also II: 5 : 5, below.

has become historically, but only the nature inherited from his animal forebears, the nature with which man began the historical process. We can no longer observe this nature, for man in a state of nature in that sense does not exist any more. We have to attempt to reconstruct it from indications. As regards the anatomy and physiology of the human body, we historians must leave this task entirely to the specialized sciences. . . . The dialectical process between man and his environment, to the extent that it becomes a historical process, primarily takes on the character of an interaction between psyche and environment. . . . We must be satisfied if we succeed in establishing some of the most important mental features of primitive man and in thus obtaining a reasonably trustworthy starting point for the investigation of historical development.

Doing this will be very easy where general fundamental features are involved that every human being shares in common with the higher animals. However, the task becomes the more difficult the more we attempt to determine in detail what the psyche of primitive man was like, that is, the psyche of man who has not yet gone through a historical development. . . . The mere observation of backward men still living today does not help us much. It is not quite precise to refer to them as primitive men or as men in a state of nature, for even the most backward of human tribes we are able to observe have already developed far beyond the state of primitive man.[10] . . . If we want to make a sketch of primitive man's mental nature, then there remains to us only the following procedure: we must investigate the psyche, the ideas, and institutions of the most backward present-day human races and compare them with the behavior of the highest mammals, especially the social anthropoid apes, who are closest to human beings. The line connecting these two points is most likely to show us the direction of development taken in the transition from the animal to man. This procedure is difficult and does not always provide unequivocal results. They will always be of a more or less hypothetical nature. But it is the only procedure that allows us, in considering this question, to base our reasoning on definite facts and does not force us to speculate wildly.

A peculiar method of studying the mental nature of extinct primitive man was discovered by the inventor of psychoanalysis, Sigmund Freud. This method is expressed in the very title of one of his latest works: *Totem and Taboo. Some Points of Agreement between the Mental Lives of Savages and Neurotics.* . . . On the very first page of the book we read: " . . . In a certain sense *[prehistoric man]* is still our contemporary. There are men still living

---

10. As the German original of this sentence indicates, Kautsky used the terms "primitiver Mensch," "Naturmensch," and "Urmensch" almost interchangeably and without clear distinction. They are variously translated here as "primitive man," "prehistoric man," "early man," and, where necessary, "man in a state of nature."

who, as we believe, stand very near to primitive man, far nearer than we do, and whom we therefore regard as his direct heirs and representatives." As these representatives of primitive man living among us, Freud considers, of all people, the neurotics, the half and wholly insane. *[Kautsky then quotes and comments on a passage on the "omnipotence of thoughts" from* Totem and Taboo, *p. 87, and concludes:]* Truly, the notion is absurd that the nature of primitive man, as he was prior to all culture, could be studied by examining the waste-products of civilization in Professor Freud's office.

That is not to say anything against the importance of the Freudian hypotheses for medical science. They may stimulate it in a very fruitful manner. On that question I cannot pass judgment. But the object to which they refer, the unconscious, demands for its study, more than any other, the acutest self-criticism, sobriety, and precision. And it is just this object that most easily tempts one to arbitrary construction, exaggerations, and premature hypotheses. Unfortunately, Freud is very much inclined to such excesses, and many of his disciples have taken over from their master not his genius but his excesses. *[Kautsky here quotes two passages from Freud's* Group Psychology and the Analysis of the Ego, *pp. 137, 121, and comments:]* When one reads Freud, one could believe that all of man is only an appendage of his genitals. . . .

I have repeatedly been called on to incorporate results of psychoanalysis into my conception of history. However, I have not yet found any that would cast a new light on the historical process. I therefore see no reason to move onto this, for the present, at least for me as a layman, still very insecure territory. Should others who are more familiar with the nature of psychoanalysis want to draw upon it for the solution of historical problems, there is no objection to that; only it must be demanded that they understand something not only about psychoanalysis, but also about history and political economy. Without these, a conception of history is impossible.

Section Two
Man—An Egotistical Being

CHAPTER ONE

The Drive for Self-Preservation and Pleasure

. . . Relatively complex organisms in complex circumstances can emerge as freely moving ones only when their nerve center acquires the capacity to become aware of the environment to a certain degree and to guide the organism's movements in accordance with the conditions of the environment. That requires the capacities for *sensing* external stimuli and for *con-*

sciousness, for consciously distinguishing certain things and processes from others, and the capacity for *memory*. . . . With the *freedom of choice* among a number of motions, the will must also appear. Freedom of *choice,* however, does not at all mean freedom of the *will.* It requires a quite specific will, the *will to live.* . . . As soon as the capacity for conscious motion appears in the animal and motions of this kind become important for its existence, then its survival is linked to the presence of a strong will to live, of a drive for self-preservation. This is the primal basis of all drives. It is held in common by man with all animals, as far as they are capable of volition. . . . The more sensitive the organism and the greater the difficulties that must be overcome if it is to maintain itself in a hostile environment, the more intense must be its drive for self-preservation. . . . One may assume that in the most highly evolved living being, man, the drive for self-preservation must have attained an especially great intensity. . . .

Many philosophers are of the opinion that the primal drive of man (and of the animals, as well) is not that for self-preservation, but instead the striving after sensations of pleasure, the fending off of sensations of unpleasantness. . . . The activities and strong emotions that serve the preservation of organisms (of individuals and of species) are by no means always bound to feelings of pleasure. Fear is anything but a feeling of happiness, and for the preservation of its own life the individual accepts many a burden and pain that it would avoid if . . . "hedonism" were its strongest motivation. . . .

The drive for self-preservation is the most primordial, but not the only drive of animals and men. They are moved by many drives, which not seldom contradict one another, as we shall see. But the satisfaction of each of them evokes a feeling of pleasure, the frustration of its satisfaction a feeling of unpleasantness. This, however, is the *result* of the satisfaction or nonsatisfaction of the drive, not the cause of the drive. It can issue from very different drives and presupposes them. . . . The striving after pleasure or the fending off of unpleasantness is certainly a powerful motive in the life of organisms endowed with sensation and consciousness, a motivation that causes many of their actions. The most powerful, the primal drive is that for self-preservation, alongside which and out of which yet other, secondary drives come into being. . . .

CHAPTER TWO

The Drive for Self-
Preservation and Egoism

. . . Another philosophical school assumes that we act exclusively as a result of egoism, of selfishness. . . . *[Kautsky here quotes Schopenhauer,* The Basis of Morality, *pp. 150–51.]* . . . Is *[this]* not the necessary consequence of the

view that the drive for self-preservation is the most primordial of all drives?
. . . Matters are not so simple, however. In different circumstances, the drive
for self-preservation can have very different meanings, depending on the
living conditions of the "self". . . . *[Kautsky discusses at length how herbivorous
animals are generally peaceable, though the strong ones, when they feel threatened,
can furiously attack their enemies, while carnivores develop a joy of killing, and
the character of omnivores varies depending on their living conditions.]*[1] . . . Here
we find even in the animal world a striking example of the extent to which
the way food is obtained—the mode of production, as it were—conditions
psychic nature.

We do not know with certainty how the apeman obtained his food. . . .
His principal food was most likely vegetable in nature, with small, lower-
order animals, such as snails, shell-fish, insect larvae, etc., as garnishing.
. . . The anthropoid apes are herbivorous. . . . *[Therefore]* we may assume
that the psyche of the apeman . . . was that of a herbivore, although probably
of a herbivore of the stronger kind, who, at the approach of a dangerous
creature, was stimulated by his drive for self-preservation not to flight but
to resolute resistance. Strangely enough, there are a number of scholars
according to whom man is descended from a predatory animal, for example,
the school of Lombroso, in which the theory of the "born criminal" originated. According to this theory, crime is an atavism, a throwback to phenomena exhibited by our animal ancestors[2]. . . .

Another view . . . sees . . . in egoism the necessary result of the struggle
for existence in nature, which is said to be a struggle of all against all that
thus forces every individual to turn against all others and to maintain himself
at their expense. On this view, then, egoism is intimately linked with the
drive for self-preservation and, like the latter, is universal in animate nature. . . . This conception of the struggle for existence was not that of Darwin. However, he furthered it, if only because he called the dialectical
process of the interaction in nature between the thesis (the organism) and
the antithesis (the environment) merely a struggle, and not a struggle with
the environment. Even scholars who have studied and understood Darwin
think of the struggle for existence above all as a brawl of one individual
with other individuals, and not also as a struggle against the inanimate
environment, against wind and weather and the like. And when they think
of a quarrel with other individuals, they do not think first of a fight against
individuals of other species, but of a struggle with individuals of the same
species. . . .

1. Here and elsewhere in this and the next chapter, Kautsky draws zoological data from
the first two volumes of Brehm, *Tierleben.*
2. Kautsky had attacked Lombroso on other grounds in "Eine Naturgeschichte des politischen Verbrechers" and in "Lombroso und sein Vertheidiger."

Malthus and Darwin

For Darwin, the struggle for existence is due to the fact that far more organisms of a species always come into the world than can be nourished within the limits of the food supply available to them. . . . They are compelled to fight with one another for a place at the table, the strongest or best adapted emerge victorious, reproduce themselves, and so on, so that ever-stronger, better-adapted individuals are present in the species. Through this process the evolution of the species proceeds. This conception is still generally held today, and yet it is completely wrong. In my book *Vermehrung und Entwicklung in Natur und Gesellschaft [pp. 25–29, 45–47]*, I pointed out that a tendency of animals to increase their numbers up to the limit of their food supply would necessarily have as a consequence, not their higher evolution, but the destruction of their sources of food.[3] . . .

It is not the limits of the food supply that keeps the numbers of the individuals in the animal world within certain boundaries, but rather the unfavorableness of other kinds of circumstances. Every species, it is true, brings more progeny into the world than could be nourished by the available supply of food. However, the surplus annually exceeding the existing population is destroyed before it reaches the point of entering into struggle with the other members of the species for the common food supply. This surplus is destroyed through the vicissitudes of inanimate nature as well as through the predations of other kinds of animals. What appears as surplus increase among the plants is food for the herbivores. And the surplus increase of the latter is food for the carnivores.

. . . For the herbivores, the table is, as a rule, abundantly laden throughout the greatest part of the year, so that they need not fight with one another for fodder. But even in times of dearth, we do not observe such behavior among them. . . . Under these conditions, then, how should egoism come about as a universal phenomenon? . . . As to the carnivores, . . . in spite of their terrible teeth, there is no killing or even chasing away of the weaker by the stronger. . . . It may well be their sociability, their comradeship, that prevents this. . . . In the case of the predators that hunt alone, there is . . . frequently observance of definite territories. Under these conditions, it will happen very seldom that two predators encounter each other over a victim and begin a fight for it. . . . But should instances of this kind occur, they would in any case be so rare that they could play no decisive role in the evolution of the species by means of "the struggle for existence."

There are, certainly, fights of individuals of the same species among

---

3. Kautsky had also attacked the concept of the struggle for existence under pressure of overpopulation in *Are the Jews a Race?*, pp. 35–37.

themselves, often very bitter fights, and not merely among carnivores but also among the otherwise so peaceable herbivores, . . . : fights among males for the favor of a female, but that is something that has nothing at all to do with the struggle for existence motivated along Malthusian lines. . . . In addition to mating combat, there are also fights for feeding grounds, but usually not between members of the same species. Some predators harbor bitter hostility against members of other species. . . . However, fights of this kind, too, probably do not occur so often that they palpably affect evolution as "the struggle for existence." . . .

The earth would not have room for all the plants that germinate, if the herbivores did not eradicate the equivalent of the annual increase, and it would not have room for all the herbivores that are born, if the carnivores did not in their turn eliminate the increase of the herbivores. Now, what curbs the number of the carnivores, so that they do not continually threaten to exceed the limits of their food supply? . . . The greatest obstacle to the rapid increase of these animals is probably . . . the mortality of their young. . . .

Many a Darwinist will object that here it is, after all, limitation of the food supply that produces the struggle for existence and the selection of the best adapted. That is by no means the case, however. The limitation of the food supply that Malthus and Darwin have in mind is an uninterrupted phenomenon that continuously affects all individuals and thereby allows only the best adapted among them to survive, at the expense of the less well adapted. . . . The temporary conditions of dearth have a very different effect. They affect all the young that are alive at that time and destroy them all, the stronger as well as the weaker, although the former perhaps not to such a great extent as the latter. In contrast, the offspring of animals that come into the world in times of abundance all have excellent prospects of growing up, the weaker as well as the stronger. And the few that escape with their lives in times of famine will be so weakened that they will hardly prove to be the equal of the offspring from the time of abundance. A selection that proceeds in this way can hardly be considered as a selection in Darwin's sense. . . . Thus we do not find in the world of predators perpetual pressure to exceed the limits of the food supply, and hence we find there, as little as among the herbivores, ruthless competition of all against all.

One could expect to find, with the greatest likelihood, such a competition in the plant world. . . . Of the immense quantity of seeds . . . only a tiny fraction can grow to maturity and propagate itself. . . . Of those seeds that are not eaten beforehand or destroyed in some other way, one part will be driven by the accidents of wind and other influences onto suitable soil, the others onto unsuitable soil. The former will thrive, even if they are weaker; the others will become stunted, even if they are stronger. . . . One can speak of a competitive struggle of plants among themselves only when a quite large number of seeds of the same species alight next to one another on a limited expanse of soil of uniform quality.... Only the strongest... succeed in growing up into the light. The weaker ones waste away and perish. This is the way one usually imagines the competitive struggle of individuals of the same species in the plant world. This struggle is... only one among many possible ways in which plants grow to maturity. It is, moreover, questionable whether this possibility occurs in nature to a degree at all worth mentioning.

The great mistake of Darwin and his disciples was that, when investigating the mechanism of evolution, they did not sufficiently distinguish the state of nature from the state created through human intervention and too often imagined the former according to the model of the latter. That is the case with regard to their views on the establishment of a set of traits through a process of selection and also with regard to their views on the competition with one another of an excessively large number of maturing organisms of the same species. We regularly find such competition where man has, through his intervention, disturbed the equilibrium of species in nature....

Even if the Darwinian assumption were completely valid for plants, their struggle would take place between unconscious organisms entirely unsuited to the waging of war and could therefore not produce any psychic effects that would be transmitted to their progeny through heredity. However, in the world of conscious organisms actually and not merely figuratively engaging in combat with other individuals, the struggle with other individuals of the same species for a grazing ground or a quarry is such a rare phenomenon that it cannot bring about psychic effects that influence the character of the whole species and become established through continual repetition from generation to generation in such a way that the characteristics thus acquired become hereditary ones.

Thus we find no bases for the claim that in the animal world the drive for self-preservation takes the form of egoism, ... the striving to preserve and to promote one's own personality at the expense of fellow species-members by placing them at a disadvantage or oppressing them.... Egoism, crime, war against one's fellow species-members are not a universal natural necessity.[4] It is ridiculous to want to prove that they are such with Darwinist phrases, as even many serious scientists do. These phenomena are chiefly proper to humanity.... *[They]* cannot simply be explained by the drive for self-preservation of the solitary human *individual*, but only through the nature of his *society*. Only through it can man's peculiarity be

---

4. See also "Die Fabel von der Naturnotwendigkeit des Krieges," attacking Rudolf Steinmetz, Oswald Spengler, and, more briefly, Sigmund Freud, who held war to be inevitable because of man's aggressive nature.

fully understood. Hence we must, in some detail, consider man as a social being.

Section Three
Man—A Social Being

CHAPTER ONE

Egoism and Sympathy

The drive for self-preservation in man appears as something too obvious, too natural to seem mysterious. But it certainly does appear mysterious that man is guided not only by this drive, but also by another one, contradicting the first. Namely, by a feeling of obligation toward other men that drives him to cooperate with them, to support them, and to champion them, sometimes at risk to his own person. Where does this phenomenon come from? *[Kautsky describes theories, especially of the eighteenth century, explaining the development of society and the state as a result of growing human intelligence and of the social contract.]*

Ethnology has taught us . . . that men, even in the most primal state we can have knowledge of, always were united in societies. Furthermore, we find that nowhere among the anthropoid apes can there be found a struggle of all against all, even when, as is occasionally true of the gorilla, they live in isolation and not sociably. . . . The development of intelligence beyond the animal stage already presupposes society and, together with it, language. It was believed that single individuals might have surpassed the others in intelligence to such a degree that they recognized the usefulness of social unification. . . . However, when the general living conditions do not prepare the masses for new views, no outstanding individual is able to win them over to those views.[1] . . . And in the state of nature living conditions are so very much the same for all members of a society that the far-reaching differences in intelligence that make their appearance at a higher level of culture are absolutely impossible. Above all, the leap from isolation to society is such an enormous one that even the greatest prehistorical genius would not have been able to make it. *[Kautsky refers to Spencer,* The Principles of Sociology, *I, 71, and quotes from ibid., II, 246, 271, and from Stammler,* Wirtschaft und Recht, *pp. 91–111, passages suggesting that society is created by the intelligent and deliberate action of individuals.]*

[Kautsky then turns to another conception] that appeared in the eighteenth century. It assumed that two drives are naturally inherent in man, not merely

---

1. See III:2:13, V:1:12, below.

the drive for self-preservation, but also the drive for sympathy with his fellow men, or, as Comte later called it, altruism. According to this view, both drives are in continuous conflict with one another. This conception accords very well with the facts, but did not advance us much since it could not tell us where this sympathy, in fact, came from. . . . Sympathy or altruism remained something incomprehensible because the consideration of social circumstances still almost universally . . . took the individual as its starting point and did not go beyond him.[2] . . . No attention was given to the fact that society exerted influence on the individual. . . .

[Kautsky quotes Kant, "Idea of a Universal History," pp. 9–11, at length on culture being the result of the antagonism between the individual's social and egotistical drives.] Kant, like the other thinkers of his time and many still today, committed the great mistake of regarding the human beings he saw about himself as the type of man per se, of regarding their character as "human nature." In reality primitive man is . . . not at all inclined to expect and to elicit resistance to his action from the members of his society. . . . Social development through the division of labor and the rise of antagonistic interests within the community had to have reached a significant level before the individual became capable of severing the umbilical cord that bound him to the community, and to develop thought and volition different from those of his comrades. The capitalist mode of production has pushed individualism to its limit and, wherever it led to a competitive struggle, it placed the individual in very distinct opposition to his fellow men. . . . But this form of society encompasses only a very small period of time in comparison with the age of the human race. *[Kautsky now devotes over three pages to an attack on an article by the Kantian Marxist Max Adler in the Vienna* Arbeiter-Zeitung *seeking to explain man's social nature.]* We must descend to the animal world if we want to become acquainted with the origins of society and morality.

CHAPTER TWO

Darwin's Discovery of Animal Morality

. . . Although Darwin did not yet explicitly declare it in his first fundamental work on the origin of species, it was nevertheless clear from the outset that this theory implied the recognition of the animal origin of the human race. To this it was objected, among other things, that the fact of human morality, which was said to have no equivalent in the

---

2. In a footnote, Kautsky quotes as an exception Adam Ferguson, *An Essay in the History of Civil Society*, pp. 4, 6.

animal world, was enough to constitute an insurmountable chasm between man and the animal. The response to this objection was given by
Darwin's book on the *Descent of Man*, which gave a detailed demonstration of man's animal origin and, in doing so, also discussed the question of morality. Darwin showed that social animals exhibit psychic
phenomena completely analogous with those of human morality, that
both the former and the latter phenomena rest upon drives and instincts
that were acquired with social life and through it. Sociability, however,
developed in animals, as did every other of their characteristics, as a
weapon in the struggle for existence when living conditions made social
cooperation advantageous for the preservation of the species. With that,
the last barrier fell that had until then seemed to exist between man and
the animal, and the metaphysical fog was dispersed, in which human
morality had until then as a supernatural phenomenon awakened a rev-
erential shudder. In the last decades, many a Darwinian conception has
had to yield to more recent research, but his exposition of the relation
between morality and sociability seems to me not only unshaken but
indeed confirmed by the research done since his time.

Darwin's discovery of the nature of morality had no great influence
on the materialist conception of history, as Marx and Engels developed
it. . . . This conception had already been completely elaborated long before Darwin's work on the descent of man appeared in 1871. . . . Engels,
and Marx, too, took Darwin's standpoint with regard to the question
of the descent of man, and, like the latter, they considered man to be a
naturally sociable animal. But they did not pursue further the explanation of morality by this sociable nature. In contrast, it made a very
strong impression on me. I became acquainted with Darwin's *Descent of
Man* in the winter of 1874/75, earlier than with Marx's *Capital*, indeed,
even earlier than with the *Communist Manifesto*, and much earlier than
with Engel's *Anti-Dühring,* which appeared in 1878 and which first
made the materialist conception of history entirely accessible to me. In
the conception of history I formed at that time and sketched out in
1876 . . . the social drives, or, as I said then, the communistic instincts,
play a large role.[3]

The central idea of my sketch is the following: The prospering, the
growth, the perishing of peoples and of individual classes depends on
whether a particular form of society fosters or weakens in them the social drives, for ultimately that nation or that class is victorious which is

3. Kautsky critically summarizes this sketch of 1876 in *Erinnerungen und Erörterungen*,
pp. 214–16. He had already, at age twenty-one, identified morality with social drives in one
of his very first publications, an article on "Darwin und der Sozialismus."

held together by stronger social drives than its opponent. This sketch was never printed. When I became editor of *Die Neue Zeit* in 1883, . . . I was better able to appreciate the development of modes of production and their influence on society than in 1876. But I still saw in the social drives a decisive factor of social life. The first essay I published in *Die Neue Zeit* in 1883 treated of the "social drives in the animal world." One year later I published there another essay on the "social drives in the world of man."[4] . . . When the revisionist movement, at the turn of the century, in part opposed Kantian ethics to the materialist conception of history, in part tried to fuse them, I undertook to fill the gap with respect to ethics in Marx's and Engels' discussions of their conception of history. In 1906 I published my treatise *Ethics and the Materialist Conception of History*, in which I called attention to Darwin's explanation of ethical phenomena and which follows basically the same line of reasoning as the present book, of which it is the precursor.

Already before then, from 1890 to 1896, Peter Kropotkin had published a series of essays in *Nineteenth Century*, which then appeared in book form under the title *Mutual Aid a Factor of Evolution* and which have much in common with my writings on the "social drives" published in 1883 and 1884. It is not probable, however, that Kropotkin knew of my publications. His conception of the significance of the social drives also differs substantially from mine. He exaggerates exorbitantly the factor of "mutual aid," of "sociability," of which he considers himself the discoverer. . . . *[Kautsky quotes Kropotkin*, Mutual Aid, *pp. 260, 68–69.]* No less false than the claim that "sociability and intelligence always go hand in hand" is the other claim that "under *any* circumstances sociability is the greatest advantage in the struggle for life." . . . Only under certain living conditions is sociability a weapon in the struggle for existence; under others it is not. And the conditions that drive to sociability as well as those that induce isolation operate on both intelligent and less intelligent animal species. Higher intelligence is a privilege neither of the sociable nor of the unsociable animals. . . . According to Kropotkin, one would have to assume that sociability is the rule in nature and that animals living in isolation are exceptions. That is by no means the case, however. *[Kautsky quotes from Doflein*, Das Tier, *pp. 699–704, and then again refers to his two articles on social drives, of which he says:]* I may refer to them as illustrations and supports of what I have set forth, as I still consider even today what I said then to be in its essence correct.

---

4. The two articles, "Die sozialen Triebe in der Tierwelt" and "Die sozialen Triebe in der Menschenwelt," are reprinted in *Die materialistische Geschichtsauffassung* (1929), I, 424–75, but are omitted from the present edition.

Drives and Morality

. . . Thanks to its drive like character, our moral volition and behavior gushes forth out of our inmost being and dominates us as an inner voice, a demon, of which we do not know from whence it comes.[5] . . . That drivelike character makes our moral behavior and judgment so impulsive and makes the commandments of morality into categorical imperatives that require no reasoning. . . .

To be sure, different impulses to behavior can collide within an individual, especially in more highly developed, differentiated states of society. In such a case, rational reflection has to decide, unless one of the impulses proves to be stronger than the others. But such reflection will only make a selection among the motive forces of màn's behavior that are already present in him; it will not be able to create such a motive force. Even in the case of simple circumstances, however, when there is no question of a collision of drives, a mere drive does not always suffice to produce a particular behavior. Certain cases require, in the interest of society, that society not trust the discretion of the individual alone, but itself make certain demands of the individual. Is that possible in any other way than through a law that society decrees . . . ?

Only the individual has a consciousness and a will, not society. When we speak of a social consciousness or volition, then that is a fiction, for which there are, to be sure, good reasons. But if we want to explain it, we have to begin with the individual. . . . In the simple social conditions . . . of primitive society, all its members, who by nature possess almost the same bodily constitution, will also be shaped in the same way intellectually and be animated by the same interests. Hence they will all react to the same stimulus in the same way, think in the same way about the same object. . . . Therefore, what the individual demands from the others is that which he in turn encounters as the demand made by the others on himself, as a social demand that, due to his social drives, he cannot escape from. Thus a social consciousness comes into being, a social volition and behavior. . . . This agreement of consciousness is not the cause of the formation of society, but rather presupposes a society. It only results in a society acting with unanimity in cases where mere instinct or drive does not suffice to produce behavior advantageous for the society. . . .

Like moral behavior, moral judgment is also impulsive in the manner of the drives. Involuntarily, without lengthy rumination, one thing appears

---

5. A number of points in this chapter and the next one already appear more briefly in *Ethics*, pp. 89–98.

attractive, indeed venerable, to us as good; the other thing, in contrast, appears loathsome, as evil. Moral outrage is not engendered by theoretical reflections; it issues from the practice of social life. . . . He is morally evil or unethical who seeks his own advantage at the expense of others; he is morally good and ethical who defends the others when they are in danger, even when he is himself thereby endangered. Depending on the strength or weakness of his social drives, man will incline more to good or to evil. Yet this is no less dependent on his living conditions in society. When the individual's interest coincides with that of society, even men with weak social drives will be good. But when the social conditions are such that the interest of an individual is constantly in conflict with the social interest, even the strongest social drives will, given the appropriate circumstances, be incapable of preventing this individual from doing evil. . . .

Evil as a noteworthy social phenomenon makes its appearance only in complex societies with differentiated interests of individuals and of whole classes. It does not precede culture, is not characteristic of man without culture, but is a product of cultural evolution. The appearance that lack of culture produces evil is due to the fact that in more advanced societies the lower classes, those who are excluded from culture, are most likely to live under conditions that bring them into conflict with the commandments of those who profit from the society and are therefore in a position to be at a higher level culturally. It was not the lack of culture, however, that engendered crimes; rather, it was the living conditions of those without culture in hitherto existing societies of higher culture from which crime sprung. . . .

Conceptions of good and evil do not depend on what is actually good or harmful for a society, but rather on what one *considers* to be good and harmful. That is no proof against the claim that the *urge* to act for the good is a drive in us. The manner in which this urge expresses itself is determined to a high degree by the extent and the nature of our insight. . . . It is the same with our moral judgments and behavior. It depends, in every individual, on the one hand, on the drives inherent in him and, on the other hand, on his own insight into the given conditions as well as, lastly, on the traditions of his forebears that have been passed on to him, which he observes and uses as his guidelines. . . . To that extent morality is *autonomous*. But the individual cannot elaborate a morality for himself. . . . Morality is determined by his living together and his cooperation with others. The demands of morality are . . . essentially the demands of the others, which the individual is urged to meet by his social drive. Only to the extent that his individual morality is in agreement with that of his comrades does it become a social bond and a motive force of society. To that extent morality is *heteronomous*, . . . that is, the individual receives his moral law from the outside, from society. But this law can bring forth moral effects on him only when it is felt by him to be his own drive, not an alien law, obedience to which is imposed by coercion or bought with the granting of advantages.

CHAPTER FOUR

Society as an Organization

. . . We must not, following Spencer and Schäffle, call the organization of society an organism. . . . *[Unlike]* the animal organism, . . . the organization of society is composed of individuals, each of whom possesses his own consciousness. There is no other kind of consciousness in society. What appears as social consciousness is the agreement of the individual consciousness of the members of a society, as we have already seen. This agreement has its origin in the fact that all individuals of the same society are organized in the same way, that they enter life, grow up, are reared, sustain their lives under the same conditions. The agreement is still enormous among primitive men. Among many animals it suffices to bring about a unified cooperation for those purposes of sustaining life which their social union is to serve. . . .

Common behavior brought about through mere agreement of thought, of knowledge, of interests does not cease to play a significant role even in the most highly evolved human societies. Think, for example, of the spontaneous outbreaks of rage and the unified action of a crowd driven onto the streets by a powerful event . . . and there accidentally thrown together, without any organization whatsoever and without leaders. . . . In the simplest forms of society, mere agreement of consciousness alone determines social activity, while this agreement as a determinative factor of such activity becomes increasingly less significant the more a society becomes complex and organized, that is, the more it develops a division of labor among its members and causes some individuals among them to function as particular social organs, who have certain social tasks to fulfill. . . .

However, even the beginnings of the division of labor . . . are determined by nature. There is, above all, the division of the sexes, which is to be found among all higher animals, whether social or nonsocial . . . *[and]* also a division according to generations. . . . Among the social animals, [the young] can remain united with the adults, and in this case the members of the older generations will still serve as models that the young follow, even when the latter are already grown. . . . The division of labor between leaders and led then appears of itself . . . No matter how the organization of the animal or primitive human society might be constituted, nowhere is the position of leader a sinecure. Rather, it involves extremely strenuous and dangerous duties. And everywhere it can be retained only so long as the outstanding powers and abilities of the leader continue to be effective. . . .

Regardless of how superior in strength and courage and intelligence the leading animal might be to every individual member of its herd, it must always be much weaker than the whole of the associated group. It may be brutal to an individual member, so long as the herd as a whole has trust in it. It is not capable of imposing anything on the latter.... It is provided with no other organs and weapons than those possessed by every adult member of its species or, at any rate, by every adult individual of the same sex. Unlike the despot in human society, it does not have at its disposal an armed force confronting a mass of unarmed subjects without means of resistance. Thus, to the extent that the difference between democracy and despotism is relevant at all with regard to animal and primitive human societies, one must describe their original state as one not of despotism but of democracy.... Even today the success of a leader in a social group depends more on his prestige than on the material means of power he has at his disposal....

Very often the society needs other organs in addition to the leader, who sometimes alternate in their functions. Thus, most social animals post special sentries.... Mere prestige, which of itself confers the role of leader, does not suffice to explain this procedure.... Where there are several leaders who alternate with one another, we must assume an understanding among them, which may, to be sure, require only a few signals. We must presuppose a more detailed understanding among the members of a society when the cooperation of various kinds of activities occurs according to a plan, as for example, in the case of wolves hunting. *[Kautsky quotes at some length Brehm,* Tierleben, *II, 319–20, and Espinas,* Des Sociétés Animales, *p. 493, on the complex building activities of beavers.]* There is no doubt that unity of consciousness plays a great role in such construction enterprises.... In addition, one would at least have to assume that the practice of the older and experienced beavers provides a model. But even that will not always suffice as an explanation. *[Their building activities]* cannot be accomplished entirely without consultation and decision-making, which presupposes a language, unfortunately, incomprehensible to us, that is, a means of communication. It does not need to be a phonic language.... Lastly, we must assume language and communication and, finally, the making of a decision when migratory animals send scouts ahead into the region they want to turn to, wait until they return, and make the continuation of the migration dependent on their report....

Decision making is not a distinctive characteristic of human societies. We find it... even among some animals. And nowhere, not even among the most highly developed human beings, does it constitute the only foundation of social cooperation. Lastly, these decisions are still not what one can call a *norm,* a *rule,* for they are always valid only for one particular case. For the conscious formulation and prescription of rules, the intelligence of the animal does not suffice. But neither does that of primitive man. To be sure, decisions made from case to case . . . can with time become norms, if they refer to doubtful or controversial cases that recur in the same fashion from time to time in such short intervals that the memory of the oldest members of the band . . . still recalls the precedent-setting case. . . . Precedents that had worked well could in this way become norms, . . . a customary law, long before there was legislation in the proper sense of the word. . . .

The heeding of precedents, their elevation to norms, presupposes a highly developed language such as only men possess. Only in human society are such rules possible. Their existence elevates human society above that of animals. But far from creating this society, they are formed only in a higher stage of its existence. And, like every later kind of legislation, they always regulate only a part of social relations. In simple primitive societies, the number of such precedents remains small and without significance. In complex societies and in periods of innovations called forth by new living conditions their number finally increases so much that they become a quite immense, impenetrable jungle. . . . It then becomes necessary to sift through the regulations to eliminate the outmoded ones, to eradicate contradictions in the remaining ones, to make it all systematic and orderly. This process constitutes the beginnings of jurisprudence. . . .

Regardless of how law is established and how far its validity might extend in a society, it is a prejudice of lawyers' mentality to suppose that society is created and held together solely by public law. The most important bonds holding society together were from the start the social drives and the agreement in the interests, in the thought and volition of the members of the society. To these were also added in particular cases the example given by the elder or more gifted members as well as an occasional communication and agreement in doubtful situations. And to this day, these factors hold society together more than does the activity of the guild of lawyers, which has grown in size so very much in the last millennia, no matter how important, how indispensable they have become in some areas. . . .

CHAPTER FIVE

The Closed Society

. . . Language . . . makes possible kinds of social cooperation that could not be attained with the animals' simpler means of communication; it thus advances human intelligence and technology and makes social cohesion ever tighter. And yet it becomes at the same time also a means . . . of separating men from one another.

It is not yet possible to say when, where, and how human language originated. But one thing is certain: its formation and development is determined by certain laws. Men who were the product of particular conditions and lived under particular conditions will therefore have formed a particular language. . . . Human language perhaps arose only and will in any case have developed to a higher level only when primitive man was already so widely diffused that he *[came]* under the influence of very different living conditions. . . . The great language families existing today are so different that they can all scarcely have been derived from one single primal language. . . . We may assume that every horde living by itself originally formed its own language, which was, to be sure, related to those of neighboring hordes, but still at least as different from them as one dialect is from another of the same language today. The fact that the further we look back in culture, the more we encounter a variety of language argues for this assumption. . . .

The more articulated language developed, the more multifarious did the social activities and functions become that it made possible, but the more difficult did it become for an individual to participate in the life of a society, the language of which he did not understand. A condition was thereby created that sharply distinguished human society from animal society. The language of the latter was very simple . . . but it . . . formed a social bond that embraced all members of the same species, regardless of which herd they might belong to. Under these conditions, the herd itself did not need to be a rigorously closed association. . . . Far more closed are human tribes, because each of these tribes speaks its own particular language and therefore confronts all other men, to the extent that it comes into contact with them, without familiarity or understanding, often with hostility, most of the time with arrogance, since one despises what one does not understand. Diversity increases still more when, thanks to language, every tribe preserves its own special tradition of legends and customs, something that makes it even more difficult for the outsider to make himself at home in the life of an alien society. . . . Thus language made human societies, in contrast to animal societies, into permanently closed ones. . . . In the world of insects we also find rigorously closed societies, . . . *[but]* here and in what follows, when we treat of animals, we have only those in mind whose nature helps us understand man's original nature.

In yet another way articulated language contributes to making every society into a closed one. It makes it possible that each individual receives a particular name that he keeps permanently and that distinguishes him from the other individuals of the community. But it also makes it possible to hold fast, to fix, a relationship that occurs between two individuals. This fixing of things, relationships, events, that is implicit in language, and even more so in the writing that arises later, makes of it a conservative factor. To be sure, at the same time, language is one of the motive forces by which human society is brought into the flux of a development never reached by any of the animal societies. . . . In animal society, the individual merges indistinguishably with the other members of the herd as soon as it no longer needs its mother. . . . In contrast, language . . . makes it possible not only to retain relations, but even to establish the existence of some relations, of which animals do not even have an inkling, such as that between grandfather and grandchild. . . .

With the development of language there thus originates a permanent structuring of society, in which every individual now receives his particular place. The organization of society according to lineage makes its appearance, . . . an organization on the basis of kinship. It is based on blood-ties, but it is not the "voice of nature" that creates this organization—otherwise it would be curious that this voice remains completely mute in the animals' state of nature, at least with regard to the relations of adult animals with one another. . . . Even more than the community of language within a tribe the community of lineage, held fast by means of language, contributes to the closeness and the closing off of individual human societies. One can learn a foreign language, . . . but one can never have more than one mother, and it is impossible to exchange her for another later in life. . . . The extent of every single kinship-organization is now fixed with complete exactitude. It . . . also forms in its fixation a conservative element vis-à-vis other, progressing ones.

To this effect of language is added that of technical progress, which also distinguishes man from the animal. It brings about an increasing variety of human occupations, mounting dependence of every individual on the activity of others, and steady growth of the areas of social cooperation. . . . That has the effect of bringing about, for a long time, a growing intensity of the social drives, which are weakened again by countertendencies only at an advanced state of social evolution. The closed nature of the individual society, however, also has the effect of narrowing the operative scope of these drives. Among animals they apply to the whole species. . . . Human societies isolate themselves from each other, do not understand each other, and often confront one another with hostility. Under these circumstances, the social drives are limited to the individual's own tribe. Only to one's fellow tribe members does one owe assistance, loyalty, and veracity. One may lie to, deceive, take advantage of the others whenever one can. Under certain circumstances such deeds are declared to be the individual's patriotic duty. . . . In war the attitude toward the enemies of one's tribe . . . can lead to the worst brutality, wild blood-frenzy, and diabolical cruelty.[6]

CHAPTER SIX

War

. . . [War] is alien to animal societies. It presupposes, on the one hand, the closing off of individual societies from one another through the effects of

6. Kautsky had first made some of the points developed in this chapter in *Terrorism and Communism*, pp. 123–27.

the development of language, on the other, the effects of advancing technology.[7] The latter creates weapons and only thereby enables man to kill large animals and his own kind. It transforms man from a herbivore into a predatory animal that is accustomed to obtain his livelihood by killing other animals, to whom he ascribes the same psychic life that he observes in himself. Men whose language he does not understand are also mere animals to him. . . .

To the results of human evolution we have considered up to this point is added the disruption of the equilibrium that obtains in nature under external conditions remaining constant for a long time.[8] . . . In my book *Vermehrung und Entwicklung [pp. 29–47, 99–109]*, I have demonstrated that in the long run every species can maintain itself only if its fertility and the forces of annihilation threatening it keep each other in balance. . . . This principle is generally recognized today. *[Kautsky quotes Doflein, Das Tier, pp. 13–14, 914.]* The equilibrium of the organisms of a region is disturbed as soon as their living conditions change, for example, through . . . epochs of unrest of the earth's surface. . . . A new element of unrest is introduced into nature by man's technology. . . . It enables him, at first to a slight extent, but ever more as culture progresses, to destroy plants and animals harmful to him and to create space and living conditions for animals and plants useful to him. Shortsightedness and ruthless greed can even lead him to extirpate plants and animals from which he derives benefits. . . . An example of this is the constantly advancing destruction of forests. *[Kautsky quotes at length Engels, "The Part Played by Labour," pp. 70, 72–73, who said that this type of destruction was a general law of nature and one of the driving forces of the development of species, including that of man. Quoting Doflein, Das Tier, pp. 16–17, Kautsky contradicts Engels by stressing that only man, of all animals, is capable of destroying the balance of nature.]*

When technology reduces the factors destroying men and perhaps raises their fertility *[and]* also increases the sources of food, this has the result that the number of human inhabitants of the region in question increases, that their individual hordes grow into great tribes, and that these become ever more numerous. But the limitation of destructive factors, that is, of the rate of mortality, and the multiplication of the sources of food by technology need not always go hand in hand. The claim of the Malthusians that population growth always tends to occur more rapidly than the growth of the food supply is certainly wrong. This alleged law is wrong if only for the reason that it is supposed to apply to animals as much as to men, even

---

7. Kautsky made the same point in "Kriegssitten," pp. 68–69. Others made in the present chapter are already hinted at in *Ethics*, pp. 144–49, and are further elaborated in *Krieg und Demokratie*, pp. 3–11.

8. See II:1:4, II:2:3, above.

though the former live for long periods of time in a state of equilibrium, exhibiting a growth neither of the species nor of its food supply. It is, however, also wrong with respect to men if it is construed as a general law that is supposed to be valid under all circumstances.

But no less false is the opposed assertion, often advanced by socialists and other anti-Malthusians, according to which there exists a mysterious teleological relation between population growth and the expansion of the food sources, so that there can never be too many people. I have dealt with this question in detail in my book on propagation and evolution. Certainly, there can be no doubt that privation and misery in present-day society do not stem from overpopulation and that present-day technology makes possible a further expansion of the available food supply even on land that is densely populated and has long been cultivated. However, that does not always have to be the case and was not always so. Very often the population of a region increased faster than the augmentation of food rendered possible by the then available technology. In such cases there was only the choice between growing deterioration of the standard of living, resulting in an increased rate of mortality, and hence the limitation or complete cessation of population growth, or the emigration of the surplus population, or the extension of the area occupied by a tribe. . . .

The migrations brought about by overpopulation were, in the beginning of humanity, perhaps the most important cause of its expansion over the earth, to the most varied climates and topographies, and hand in hand with that expansion went the acquisition of new experiences and an increase of intelligence, skill, and technical knowledge. Such migrations could often lead to regions not yet inhabited by men. Then there awaited the newcomers hard struggles against an unknown nature that frequently presented conditions under which men had not lived up to that time and to which they had to adapt themselves. Difficulties of this kind were less serious when the migrations were directed into areas already inhabited by men. But . . . areas of this kind often did not provide space for both groups— under the given technological conditions. The original inhabitants attempted to fend off the intruders, and thus *wars* started.

The same result necessarily occurred when a tribe, growing in size, sought to augment its food sources through expansion of the territory it inhabited. . . . The territories of hunting peoples were originally . . . hunting grounds, which, without fixed boundaries, were defended by their possessors against intruders just as the territories of predatory animals are. However, since among men the natural equilibrium is sometimes disturbed, the intruders are not merely, as is the case with isolated predatory animals, young, inexperienced, still relatively timid animals, whose occasional intrusion can be fended off without a hard fight; rather, it is very experienced adults who invade the territory, and not single individuals but entire tribes. . . .

The development of technology bestows on man death-dealing weapons and makes him into a predatory animal. It causes the disruption of the natural equilibrium in the regions he inhabits and compels him to expand his hunting ground or to emigrate. Last, the development of language separates the individual tribes from one another, makes communication between them difficult, and produces a feeling of alienness, indeed, of hostility among them: All of that engenders war between tribes which has nothing to do with the struggle for existence in nature, but is a specifically human phenomenon—in spite of its inhumanity, a product of cultural development, despite its destructive effects on culture.

That is not intended as an accusation against culture. To accuse, to condemn, or even only to regret it because of its consequences is just as ridiculous as to praise it. We must understand it as the product of a necessary historical process. However, . . . instead of saying that war is caused only by the progress of culture, we can say that it is not naturally given, that it is not necessarily linked to the innate natural disposition of man.[9] . . . Then we may conclude from this that war is only the product of *certain phases of culture* and can disappear after these phases have been overcome.

Once war has made its appearance, it tends in turn to produce further reasons for new wars. It did so even in primitive times by often compelling the defeated tribes, if they were not annihilated, to leave the area where they had been living and to seek a new home for themselves, which often meant that they caused new wars to begin. Or the defeated tribe remained, but felt itself confined and robbed of valuable territories and contemplated revenge. Since that time the progress of culture has changed the causes of war in various ways. . . . But up to now the fact has remained that at its conclusion every war carries a new war in its womb. From the very outset, men have waged war in the belief that they will thereby improve their situation or out of fear that without war they will see their situation worsened. In particular cases that might be correct. In general, however, war has proved to be a terrible obstacle to technological and economic advancement, to be sure, not the advancement of every belligerent nation in particular, but certainly of humanity in general. . . .

The solidarity of the species, which still existed in the animal stage, now disappears completely. . . . Now everyone who does not belong to one's own people is regarded not only as an alien but also as an enemy. Both become one and the same thing. The range of morality is thus narrowly restricted for every person. . . . Within this limited range, the social drives can greatly increase in intensity. War itself, with the new dangers with which it now menaces every tribe, forces the members of each to stick together as tightly as possible. When the relations of strength are otherwise

9. See "Die Fabel von der Naturnotwendigkeit des Krieges."

equal, that tribe is most likely to succeed in war whose members risk their lives unreservedly in battle for the community. This is probably what those people have in mind who declare that war is a "bath of steel," a means of moral renewal. Well, this renewal happens to involve grave concomitant phenomena, an increase of brutality and cruelty. . . . These can become worse in man than in the most bloodthirsty predatory animal. . . . We may see in the special bloodthirstiness of men a consequence of war, of the killing of fellow species-members, which does not occur in nature and engenders a cruelty not characteristic of animals. . . .

Moreover, one may speak of the strengthening of the social drives by war only when, as in the primitive state of humanity, it is waged with complete equality of the comrades-in-arms. Morality is no longer raised by war when a nation is divided into different classes, and one is slaughtered for the interests of the other. . . .

Internal Differentiation of Society

The further progress of social evolution results in the appearance of divisions within the individual communities. Originally every horde was probably also an organization based on kinship. However, when the horde grows in size to become a relatively large tribe, different kinship-organizations are formed in it, which are called septs, clans, or gentes. These are generally based on much more intimate, personal contact among their members than is the tribe with its numerous members. Some of the functions of the tribe pass over to the gentes; in addition, new social functions are formed, which devolve on the gens. As a rule, the latter become more important for the existence of individuals than the tribe; it raises the social drives to a greater intensity, but also concentrates their effects more on itself, the gens, than on the tribe. Everyone feels closely attached to his gens, his sept; there then arises the possibility of conflicts, even of blood feuds between the individual gentes within a tribe. On the other hand, the kinship-organization is extended beyond the domain of the tribe through the introduction of women from outside the tribe. Social organization becomes still more complicated as soon as the division of labor creates occupations with their organizations, the guilds, as soon as various religious associations form within the community, and finally classes arise with their sharp antagonisms.

In the course of the growing extension of the human race, there appears, in addition to the division of labor within the polity, the division of labor among the polities, which is based on the different configuration of natural living conditions to be found in different regions. . . . The more this sort of international division of labor develops, the more does the temptation grow to acquire what one's neighbor has and what one does not possess oneself but would like to have. There originates a new source of wars, which thus become wars of depredation. But war does not always promise success. Alongside depredation there emerge the peaceful methods of exchange. In this way individual communities enter more and more into economic relations with and various kinds of dependence on others. An international commerce is established, through which a new kind of social unification is brought about that stands above the individual communities even when these attain the extent of major states. . . .

Thus we return, in a certain sense, to the starting point of evolution. Now the social drives are once again operative with regard to the entire human species, a fact that increasingly stamps war between individual nations within the species as an immoral act, to be sure, up to now only in the consciousness of individual thinkers and classes. Yet the movement in the direction of eternal peace through world commerce must finally become irresistible, all the more so as at the same time technological development is intensifying the devastations of every war to the level of diabolical insanity.

In the course of this development the social drives go through the most varied transformations. There are forms of society in which they grow weak, at least for certain social strata benefiting more from egoism than from mutual assistance, for whom the social drives change from a weapon in the struggle for existence into something that makes this struggle harder. This is chiefly the case where the individual obtains his livelihood not from labor shared with his comrades, but from exploitation of his fellow men.[10] But the social drives are so deeply rooted in man that they do not completely disappear from anyone. . . . The more varied society becomes and the more it is divided into different and diverse societies, the more frequently collisions among his social drives occur in the individual, drives that are now aimed at different and sometimes antagonistic kinds of socialization, the more easily does man find himself in an internal conflict among his social or moral duties. . . . Here the social drive, moral sentiment alone will not be capable of deciding. Here conscious reflection must in every particular case tip the wavering scales. . . .

CHAPTER EIGHT

Collective Thinking

Even in the animal world, unconscious impulses, instincts, and habits alone are not always able to effect appropriate behavior. . . . The more complicated

---

10. See also III: 3:3, below.

are the organism and its living conditions, the more will the particular assert itself alongside the universal in the various situations in which the organism finds itself, the more will conscious deliberation play a role alongside the unconscious impulses. . . . The more the particular, that which is new in a situation, preponderates, the greater are the demands made of the intelligence. . . . Man is not merely a consciously acting being. For even today, in the age of highly developed civilization, with its grandiose development of science, a large part, perhaps the preponderant part of our behavior is still based on unconscious instincts, drives, and habits. . . . But regardless of everything unconscious that slumbers and acts in us, individual conscious reflection and its restriction of the drives are playing an ever-greater role in man.[11] This progress, though, must be bought by man at the expense of many side effects that hinder and disturb him. These side effects spring from his nature as a social animal.

The higher animal has to maintain itself in living conditions similar to those of primitive man. That alone argues for the fact, even before observation confirms it, that at first both had to possess similar abilities. The animal must be as able as man to observe and to grasp causal relations and to draw conclusions from them. Without these abilities it could not survive the struggle for existence. But this capability is limited to a small area. Only its practice induces the animal to observe causal relations. . . . And only its practice provides the animal with confirmation or correction of its conclusions. . . .

It is no different with man. He does not differ from the animal with respect to greater correctness of his observations and conclusions, but rather with respect to the greater area over which they extend. . . . As in the case of the animal, man's thinking for a long time concerns only his practice; it has its origin in and serves this practice; its correctness is confirmed or its incorrectness shown by this practice. But thanks to man's technology, this practice is, even in its beginnings, greatly enlarged in comparison with that of the animal, and man's intellectual horizon is thereby widened. A host of new problems now confronts him. And they occupy not only the single individual. After all, he has in his language a means of communication such as no animal possesses. . . . Every new observation and new experience of any one person is immediately communicated to his comrades; their significance and the conclusions to be drawn from them are discussed with them and observed by each of them in practice. It now becomes necessary to bring many more causal relations into a higher relation with each other than previously and for this purpose to pursue longer trains of thought than the animal, which is, in turn, possible only with the help of language. From

---

11. See also II : 1 : 7, above, and II : 5 : 5, below.

this point on, higher abstractions take up ever more space in human thought. . . .

At the same time, naive man . . . wants to have an answer immediately to every question, and he wants it all the faster since at first these questions, just as for the animal, only spring from momentary practical needs. Under these conditions, he is readily inclined to premature hypotheses, and they are the more likely to assume a fantastical character the longer the trains of thought are from which they sprout, the more they distance themselves from their starting point of practical observation and ascend to become abstractions, and the more complicated the processes are, from which they originate or on which they want to exercise an influence. To the same degree, however, the great regulator of thought that gives to the animal's thinking its certainty becomes more faltering, namely, its immediate testing by the practical success or failure of its application. . . . Human thinking . . . becomes, for a long period of time, stifled more and more by lack of discrimination and by wild fantasies. Of course, even the most extravagant products of the imagination are rooted in concrete reality. We cannot imagine anything other than what our senses have shown us. But we can combine in our thoughts the individual elements of our sense impressions in the most diverse ways and exaggerate them to the utmost. . . .

[In] primal society, everyone grows up under the same living conditions. . . . Since the brain reacts under the same conditions to the same stimuli in the same manner, every individual will, on the whole, think just like the others in a primitive human society. Thus, in a certain state of development, every member of society will arrive at the same products of imagination as the others. There are, to be sure, differences among the individual brains, but these differences cannot be very great in the very simple circumstances of primeval times. And since wild fantasies are by their nature very vague, the individual differences will not prevent all from following approximately the same train of thought and from expressing it in the same way. . . . But what all consider to be true, must be true. After all, not everyone is a fool. . . .

The assumption that religion is the work of deceit presupposes that there already exist differences in knowledge within the community that are quite alien to primitive society, are quite impossible in it. And there must already be significant possibilities of exploiting men before it is worth the effort for the knowledgeable priest to use his great intellectual superiority over the ignorant crowd to his advantage through deceptions. . . .

If a view shared by all is easily considered correct without further ado, that holds all the more for a view that is communicated as the truth to the individual already in his childhood by his family. It then seems to him as something to be taken for granted. Once he is an adult, it already constitutes a part of his nature. [Kautsky quotes Lévy-Bruhl, How Natives Think, p. 63, at some length on what the latter calls the "collective representations" of primitive peoples and argues that these are "metalogical" rather than, as Lévy-Bruhl called them, "prélogical."] The power that these often quite absurd notions acquire over individuals can become quite enormous, corresponding to the overwhelmingly superior economic and intellectual power of the total society vis-à-vis the isolated individual. But it is nonetheless not so enormous as Lévy-Bruhl sometimes depicts it. . . . [Lévy- Bruhl, ibid., pp. 207–208, 236– 39, is quoted as saying that primitive hunters rely not on their skill nor physicians on physical symptoms but on magic.] Primitive hunters do not by any means rely exclusively on their religious dances and magic spells. . . . In the same way, when primitives have developed agriculture to some extent, they do not rely for its prosperity exclusively on the successes of their rainmaking procedures. . . . Matters are similar with respect to medicine. . . .

In reality, there takes place in human society a continuous increase of intelligence. However, it does not take place *through* collectively held ideas, but rather *in spite* of them. They have not rendered social progress impossible, but they have retarded it by inducing mankind to engage in much useless activity, often in harmful activity, and by causing humanity many detours and losses of strength. . . . Here we become acquainted with a second factor, which [like war] issues from the development of human society, is specifically human, distinguishes man from the animal, and yet plays an inhibiting role in humanity's development: *religion* or, if you prefer, *faith*.[12]

One may well say that collective ideas form the root of religious doctrines. . . . Frequently one seeks to make religion out to be a higher phenomenon standing above the naive collective ideas; this is done by distinguishing the latter from the former as superstition or magic. But where is the boundary between the two supposed to be located? . . . Magic is distinguished from religion neither with regard to content nor with respect to the method of thinking. If one must seek a difference, one can do so in the following: Magic concerns itself with the application of magical, mystical forces for private purposes, for the advantage of the individual user. In contrast, religious thinking wants to make the same magical forces serviceable for the purposes of mutual assistance. Accordingly, magic is predominantly thought to be associated with egotism, religion with social endeavor. . . . The content of faith is the same in the one as in the other; only its application is different.

The intimate amalgamation of morality and religion . . . is promoted by the fact that the demands of morality themselves become collective ideas, which mingle with the other notions of this kind. So close did the connection between the two of them become that many have arrived at the conviction

---

12. Kautsky had dealt with the origin and development of religion in "Religion" and on pp. 182, 354, and 355 of that article touched on several points made in the following paragraphs.

that without religion morality is impossible. In reality it was rather the existence of morality that gave rise to many conceptions of God, immortality, etc., which played a great role in more highly developed religious thinking. . . . The *force* of morality in society does not depend on the existence of collective ideas, but on the existence of social drives that can, certainly, be strengthened or weakened by particular social institutions, but not by collective ideas. The *certainty* of moral sentiment and judgment, however, is considerably diminished where they must operate in a complicated society, without having as their basis collective ideas that give to every moral demand the character of one that is taken for granted, from which it is, without question, heinously unnatural to deviate. Where morality rests upon collective ideas, it does not give men cause to rack their brains, there is a rule governing every case from the start. . . .

The extent of the domain of collective ideas grows. For a long time their power also grows and at the same time they have the tendency to become ever more absurd, the more they distance themselves from their starting point. In their origin, most of them are probably based on correctly observed, even if wrongly interpreted phenomena. Most of the time, though, only the interpretation is passed on; the interpreted phenomenon itself is forgotten. What was at first only a sudden idea, to be sure, not of a single individual, but of many, a hasty hypothesis of an entire society, becomes a mystical dogma that is passed on uncomprehendingly, combined with other dogmas of a similar kind. Since it has lost all meaning, it is now capable of being construed ever more senselessly. . . .

Much as the power, extent, and absurdity of collective ideas may grow, they are not unlimited. Factors arise that counteract and ultimately overcome them. The development of technology does not cease, and with it there also multiply man's experiences, his understanding of causal relations based on sober observations rather than fantastical imagining. Collective ideas cannot remain unaffected by this development. They have a different character among more highly developed peoples than among primitive peoples, a different one among hunters than among cattle-raisers or agriculturalists. But, still, the traditional moment and the rigidity of their formulae is so great that they adapt themselves to new experiences only with difficulty and more and more come to contradict these experiences. That contradiction needs either Talmudist tricks to be overcome or the subjection of dispassionate, profane thought to the exalted mysticism of the received collective ideas, if these latter are to maintain themselves.

An additional factor is the development of international communication. It brings a people into contact . . . with the most diverse collective ideas hitherto unknown to it. To be sure, the dominance of such ideas does not at first need to be weakened and can even be further extended thereby. . . . It is not difficult either to equate similar collective ideas of foreign nations with one's own or to reconcile them with each other. . . . There also occurs an appropriation of foreign collective ideas that cannot be identified with already dominant ones . . . as was customary in the Roman empire. . . . The internal contradictions of the various outlooks were not then overcome but merely ignored. . . . As a religious doctrine (not as an ecclesiastical organization), Christianity, too, is in large measure only a product of the highly developed syncretism of its time and therefore full of contradictions.

However, collective thinking . . . could not, after all, overlook all contradictions. In addition to foreign views one incorporated into one's own, there also occurred those . . . that were critically judged and rejected. Christianity is an example of this, too. . . . However, the critique of collective ideas was advanced most of all by the dissolution of those social formations that had created them. . . . *[Historical]* development has expanded society and has caused new social formations to emerge within its sphere, each of which has its particular interests and living conditions. Through the division of labor and later even more through the division *[of society]* into classes, this development has differentiated the members of society ever more, set great knowledge beside deepest ignorance, broad horizons beside narrow-mindedness, the greatest wealth beside the bitterest poverty, etc. How could collective thinking still be possible in such circumstances? Collective ideas, it is true, are characterized by an incredible persistence. Thanks to the strength of tradition, they maintain their influence for a long time, but confronting them there arises, ever more powerful, criticism increasingly based on profane, nonmystical knowledge.

The defeat of collective ideas is sealed once the free personality emerges, once the individual succeeds in liberating himself from the intellectual tutelage of the society in which he lives. . . . This intellectual emancipation occurs most readily where an economic emancipation is taking place. The wealthy, the rulers, the exploiters easily believe that they stand above society, which they do not serve, but which rather serves them. This often leads to traditional morality being undermined in their ranks, but also to the traditional collective ideas being gravely weakened.

In another way the personality is also freed from below in highly developed civilizations through the dissolution of the received social institutions and ways of thinking that formerly protected the mass of the population. The individual now has to rely on himself. . . . This development threatens the laboring masses with increasing ruination and ultimately with complete destruction, if they do not know how to join together in new social organizations and, struggling for and through these, to strengthen their weakened social drives once again and to establish a new morality. But these are no longer organizations like the primitive societies that arose of themselves, with no external regulation whatsoever, and developed of themselves collective ideas that the individual encountered in finished form and that he grew into. The new social formations and their intellectual content are the result of the individual's clear, conscious volition.

They do not hamper the independence of the personality; [*rather,*] they protect the conditions of its free unfolding.

This development undermining collective thinking occurs most readily in the large cities, where the individual can be kept track of to the least extent and must rely on himself to the greatest extent. There mass misery, immorality, and crime most readily take on horrifying proportions; there, however, bold criticism of the status quo and freedom of thought also flourish. In contrast, the village remains the most solid pillar of collective ideas.

Collective thinking has been strongly driven back in the course of social progress, but its results have not yet been completely eradicated by a long sight. The religious yearning, the metaphysical desire that lives in many of us—it is a lingering reverberation of the collective ideas of our primeval ancestors. This longing makes itself felt most keenly in times like the present, when the old is obviously collapsing, while the new has not yet assumed palpable form, and so many are losing their inner steadiness that their own thinking and reflection have not been able to provide for them. Then there arises the need for that inner certainty that was provided for man by his collective ideas, without his having to struggle for it by his own intellectual labor; the need for the reanimation of the mystical ideas, of which no one knew where they came from, which required no proof and yet bore in themselves such certainty. Once one began to reflect on where these ideas came from, they appeared to be an inner revelation of a divinity. . . . Modern man means the same thing when he says that the most profound wisdom cannot be gained through investigation and cannot be proved, but can only be experienced, drawn from his own soul. . . .

Section Four
Man—A Sexual Being

CHAPTER ONE

Preservation of the Species

. . . In a certain sense, one can understand the social drives as a particular kind of drive for self-preservation. They are formed under certain conditions that make it advantageous for the individual to be socially integrated with other individuals for purposes of his preservation. . . . They have a second, powerful source in the drives that serve the preservation of the *species* and that are very different from those for the *individual's* self-preservation. . . .

The lower, unicellular animals that propagate themselves, without mating, through budding or fission do not require a reproductive drive. . . . But as soon as the processes of reproduction become more complex and especially when the separation of the sexes emerges and reproduction can proceed only through the joining of a bearer of male sperm cells with a bearer of female ova, then the success of reproduction becomes dependent in most cases on many conditions. There are each time so many difficulties to be overcome that fertilization and propagation are not even possible without a certain degree of consciousness and volition, a degree that in the case of the higher animals must already be very considerable. . . .

It is therefore by no means surprising that in man we find not only a high level of intelligence, but also strong erotic urges and a great tenderness for his children, which require more effort before they become independent than in the case of any animal. Eroticism and mind are not at all opposed to each other as animal filth and divine purity. . . . The reproductive drives belong to the most powerful factors of human volition, and we cannot understand the latter and its operation in history if we ignore this factor. For the particular structure of a society, too, the prevailing relationship of the two sexes is of the greatest importance. Investigation into the beginnings of human development is, then, also very closely linked with investigation into the beginnings of the family and marriage. Unfortunately, this encounters very great difficulties.

CHAPTER TWO

The Care of Offspring and the Forms of Marriage

As a substitute, one could perhaps attempt to deduce speculatively a natural form of human marriage from the conditions of the rearing of primitive man's children. For the relationship between the animal male and female, the conditions of the care of their offspring do indeed play a crucial role. The reproduction of the species is assured only if the drives serving this end lead not merely to the union of the sexes, but also to adequate care for the progeny.

[Kautsky reviews the number of eggs produced and the care given to them by fish, amphibians, reptiles, and birds.] The intensification of the care of the offspring, which goes hand in hand with the diminution of the number of eggs and of the young, usually reaches a degree in the case of the birds that makes it very difficult, indeed impossible, for the female to carry it out satisfactorily alone. The male must collaborate. The relationship of the two endures beyond the act of copulation. The forms it assumes can be of the most varied kinds. They will depend on the living conditions of the animals, above all, however, on the manner in which the young must be cared for. *[This is illustrated at length with reference to various kinds of birds and mammals.]*

We find, then, also in mammals a natural basis of both monogamy and polygamy. Is there such a basis in the case of man, too? . . . Reference to the necessity of care of the offspring does not help us at all here. . . . The rearing and protection of the infant ape and even more so of the human child certainly make great demands on the mother that she alone would not be equal to. She needs help. But this help need not necessarily come from a spouse, if she is living in society. . . . In these circumstances it is hardly possible to decide which form of marriage is the natural one for man. . . . *[Kautsky quotes Doflein, Das Tier, pp. 693–94, and Alverdes, Social Life in the Animal World, pp. 43, 48–51, on the family life of the great apes. Of the social apes, like baboons, he says:]* Either there is indiscriminate sexual intercourse, . . . or every male associates himself with one or more females of the troop, which appear to him especially attractive or accommodating. Among the apes, however, this pairing is a response only to sexual need, not to the necessities of care of the offspring, which are taken care of by life in society. The pairing is, therefore, not tied to a definite period of time; it can be entered into and dissolved again at will.

Accordingly, for the sexual relationships of primitive men, too, only these two possibilities need be considered. One can assume neither strict monogamy nor polygamy in their case. It is only a question of whether there existed among them promiscuity, indiscriminate sexual intercourse, "community of women," or, on the other hand, loose pairings. The first view was represented chiefly by Bachofen in his *Mutterrecht*,[1] as well as by Morgan in his *Ancient Society*. Engels joined company with them in his work on *The Origin of the Family*. *[Kautsky also lists Alexis Giraud-Teulon, Herbert Spencer, A. Hermann Post, Sir John Lubbock, and Franz Müller-Lyer as sharing this view. He states his disagreements with Bachofen and Morgan and then quotes from his own early article, "Die Entstehung der Ehe und Familie," p. 207, written two years before Engels' monograph on the subject:]* "Within the tribe, complete sexual freedom obtained. In consequence of the feeling of jealousy and, on the other hand, as a result of the fact that the woman, being free and equal, stood under the protection of the community just as much as the man and that oppression of the weak by the strong was out of the question within the tribe, this freedom did not lead to communal marriage where every man had marital rights with regard to all women of the tribe, but rather to . . . monogamous, easily dissoluble, more or less loose alliances." I still hold this view today.

One may assume as certain that for the animal ancestors of man, as for primitive man himself, there were no necessary rules in the relationship of the sexes to each other that issued from the *way* they cared for their offspring. There were not yet any possibilities and reasons for a regulation of this relationship arising for the *sake of society*. I agree with Engels that in the primeval period man existed in a state in which sexual matters were not

1. Selections appear in English translation in *Myth, Religion and Mother Right*, pp. 69–207.

governed by rules. Whether this state expressed itself in indiscriminate sexual intercourse or in loose pairings, that is a point on which one can, at the present time, still argue. Perhaps one will never be able to ascertain it beyond any doubt.

The Original Forms of Marriage

That the relationship of the sexes was entirely unregulated in the primeval period is argued for by the fact, among others, that among primitive peoples the intercourse of unmarried women with men is not, as a rule, subjected to the slightest restrictions. . . . *[Kautsky cites half a dozen examples from different primitive peoples by quoting from pp. 332–33 of his own article of 1882.]* The condition of complete sexual liberty for unmarried women is in curious contrast to the situation of married women, whose relationship to their spouses takes very different forms among various primitive peoples, but is always governed by more or less strict social rules.

Why was sexual liberty annulled for one portion of the women? The emergence of marriage alongside unregulated sexual intercourse cannot be explained through recourse to a natural disposition of man. For a natural disposition, even assuming that it created rules, could only bring forth such that hold good for all adult women in the same manner. I see the ultimate cause of the emergence of regulated marriage not in *natural* conditions, but in *economic* ones, in the division of labor between man and woman.[2] To be sure, this division of labor also has its deepest basis in natural circumstances . . . the different capacities, strengths, and peculiarities of character of the two sexes. . . .

Thus, when the first tools were invented, it was a matter of course that man used them in a different way from women. Man used them as weapons, woman as means of production. . . . Human technology begins with the extension of the division of labor of the sexes, which as a rule had previously been limited to the sphere of procreation, to include the area of obtaining food. An economic moment was thus introduced into the relationship of the two sexes, which in the case of the animal had been determined only by the necessity of reproduction, by the needs of copulation, and the tending of offspring. . . . The further development of technology increases more and more the division of labor between the sexes. The more perfect the weapons and the greater the skill with which they are wielded as well as the knowledge of the wild game's habits, the more important does hunting become

2. See also III:3:2, below.

as a source of food, the greater is the role played by the eating of meat. All the more, however, is the man's behavior also determined by hunting and war. He becomes more brutal, bloodthirstier, but also more enterprising. . . . The women, burdened by the children whom they must carry or who are still unable to walk well, . . . cannot participate in hunting expeditions and, even less, in military expeditions. They, too, must travel on foot in the first stages of culture. . . . But searching for vegetable food sources does not require such rapid locomotion as does hunting.

In comparison with the restless hunter, the women became the more settled element, with the result that at first technology develops more rapidly in their domain of labor. Tending the fire, which was in the beginnings so difficult to ignite, falls chiefly to them.[3] They invent the arts of cooking. . . . They perfect the art of fashioning means of protection against the inclemency of the weather out of vegetable and animal materials: tents, coats, etc. They learn to plait and weave. . . . The fabrication of clay vessels, too, . . . is first carried on by them.[4] All of this presupposes that the nomadic way of life has already been restricted to a certain extent. On the other hand, every technical progress on the part of woman makes every new migration more and more difficult. . . . The last great technical progress made by woman ties her especially strongly to the soil: the cultivation of plants. . . .

The further the division of labor between man and woman advanced, the less was one part able to manage without the other. . . . Man and woman had to come together, not merely for the purposes of copulation, but for obtaining their livelihood. The horde now disintegrated into subdivisions. . . . Each campfire, each tent formed a household . . . *[composed minimally of]* an adult woman experienced in the household arts *[and]* a hunter who supplied the household with meat. . . . The union of man and woman in a household was the necessary consequence of the division of labor in obtaining food between the two sexes. It was a matter of course that the intimate partnership a man entered into with a woman in this way should also lead to their sexual partnership. Yet the latter was not the reason for the union of the two in a household. We have already made reference to the sexual freedom of the unmarried. It enabled every individual to satisfy his sexual needs without entering into a household.

[Kautsky quotes Müller-Lyer, The Family, *p. 106, who wrote that man, being armed, ". . . enslaved his unarmed mate and founded the family: his domain. . . ." Kautsky also quotes ibid., pp. 114–15, 141.]* The power of women grew in proportion to the development of agriculture. . . . It is not physical, brutal force, by which the position of man relative to woman is determined, but

---

3. See also III:2:8, below.
4. See also III:2:4, below.

rather the economic importance of each of the two for the common household. . . . The appearance of animal husbandry, too, raises still further woman's position in the household vis-à-vis man, insofar as it involves the breeding of small livestock like chickens. . . . It is a different matter in the case of larger livestock, which does not find its fodder in the household but requires extensive pasturage. The woman, bound to the household, cannot look after it. Pastoralism, which also involves protecting the cattle from predatory animals, becomes the man's affair. . . . Now the well-being of the household depends once again more on the man's work than on woman's. This state of affairs is further reinforced where the pulling power of cattle is placed at the service of agriculture, so that the latter ceases to be an affair of the woman and instead devolves on the man. Now he becomes the master of the house. It is not our intention to present here a history of marriage and the family. The facts we refer to are only meant to show that the relationship of the two sexes to each other in the household does not depend on physical force but on economic factors.

The position of the sexes in the household ultimately reacts back on their position in society. But the relationship between society and household is not thereby exhausted. The former is intensely concerned with the latter and intervenes with rules in the domestic rights and duties of man and woman. . . . Why did society for a long time not trouble itself about how men and women who had not united in a household behaved toward each other? Why does the household, in contrast, become a matter of public concern? That is certainly a question of the economic significance acquired by the household. The greater it is, the more does the well-being of society depend on the well-being of its households. . . . The household must be protected against arbitrary ruin. That becomes especially necessary due to concern for the children. . . . The household becomes an institution for the rearing of children. As such it forms the family. . . .

The less society itself does for the feeding and education of the children and the more it leaves these important functions exclusively to the family, the more rigorously will it, as a rule, be concerned to superintend and to regulate these functions. That it is not initially a matter of regulating sexual mating, but of safeguarding the children, is made evident by the fact that alongside often very strict rules for the members of a common household there can be found far-reaching sexual freedom for unmarried women. . . .

The regulation of marital relations is effected at first not by means of well-considered laws, but through collective ideas and their consequences. The expression "the sacredness of marriage," that is, its divine character beyond time and space, suffices of itself to point to a collective idea. . . . And since, with changing modes of production, the forms of the household as well as the significance of each of the two sexes for it also change, the forms of marriage and the family, too, must change from time to time. In this, however, inherited collective ideas, which always introduce an element of superstition into these institutions, invariably play a role. It is quite incredible how many forms of marriage and the family can be found among the peoples of the earth, and how many were to be found among them in the remote past. . . . Now which one of these should be "sacred" or "natural" for us, that is to say, immutably valid throughout history? Evidently that one in which we happen to be living at the moment. For the relationship of the sexes among men, only concern for the tending of the offspring, the rearing of the children, is given by nature. . . . But the forms to carry out this task vary with society and its resources; they change with historical development.

CHAPTER FOUR

The Prohibition of Incest

. . . Even under the most primitive circumstances still other restrictions of the original sexual freedom appear among men. We assume that they arise out of the concern . . . to exclude from procreation all influences that threaten to result in . . . quantitative or qualitative damage to their progeny. Among the restrictions of this kind is perhaps the prohibition against marrying outside of one's age-group. . . . Not only are sexual unions between persons of very unequal ages very often childless, but, what is even worse, the few children who issue from such unions are frequently weakly. If human intelligence and capacity for observation were highly developed enough to be able to apprehend this after segregation of the age-groups had taken place, then this offered a good reason for the prohibition. . . . We do not mean to say that clear knowledge of the laws of heredity was decisive here. There can be no question of that in primeval time. It is possible that some correct observations became intermingled with quite fantastical collective ideas, in order to bring about the result *[under discussion here]*.

Another restriction of sexual liberty appeared along with kinship-based organizations. It was . . . forbidden to the members of a kinship-organization to marry within it. The men of a gens were compelled to take their women from outside it. *[Kautsky mentions and rejects hypotheses explaining exogamy by John Ferguson McLennan, who saw it as resulting from a shortage of women due to the killing of female children, and by Friedrich von Hellwald, Edward Westermarck, and Franz Müller-Lyer, who regard the avoidance of mating among relatives as natural.]*

CHAPTER FIVE

The Freudian Hypothesis

. . . Here we are concerned only with the question: How did a prohibition of incest, a prohibition of consanguineous marriage, come about? . . . Freud invokes Darwin as a support for his assertion that primitive man was by nature polygamous. . . . Every horde of primitive human beings, says Freud, consisted solely of women with only one adult man as its leader. In reality, Darwin never maintained such a thing. . . . *[He]* left undecided whether the marriage-forms of primitive human beings were instituted in the manner of the social apes, among whom several males with their females are always joined together in a troop, or the manner of the gorillas, of whom he then still assumed that they were nonsocial, that they lived in isolation. But he inclines toward the first assumption. He stresses that human beings are social animals *[Kautsky quotes* The Descent of Man, *pp. 895 and 480]*. We may add that *[they]* belong to the social animals among whom not merely the females, but also the males of the social group stick firmly together. How are they supposed ever to have attained to that state, if every adult male was by nature animated by the most intense hatred of every other mature male? . . .

[Freud] assumes that the patriarch of every horde regularly drove away all his sons as soon as they reached sexual maturity, and goes on to report: "One day the brothers who had been driven out came together, killed and devoured their father and so made an end of the patriarchal horde. . . . This memorable and criminal deed was the beginning of so many things—of social organization, of moral restrictions and of religion" *(Totem and Taboo,* pp. 141–42). All of that resulted from the murder of the father, for which the sons had joined together, in order to be able to copulate with his women, their mothers and sisters. . . .

The psyche of savages . . . accords with that of Freud's patients in a quite remarkable manner: "In order that these latter consequences may seem plausible, leaving their premises on one side, we need only suppose that the tumultuous mob of brothers were filled with the same contradictory feelings which we can see at work in the ambivalent father-complexes of our children and of our neurotic patients. . . . They thus created out of their filial sense of guilt the two fundamental taboos of totemism" (Ibid., p. 143). These two fundamental prohibitions are the prohibition of consanguineous marriage and that of slaying the totem animal, which . . . was linked with various collective ideas. . . .

As Freud imagined them, primitive men are a bizarre hybridization of robust stallions snorting with rage and decadent weaklings from the literary circles and demimonde of Vienna. Primitive men, according to Freud's assumption, were sexually aroused to the utmost and lusted after women so strongly that they murdered their father in order to get them. And at the same time they were so jealous that no man tolerated another in the horde, that each engaged with every other in a life-or-death combat. And these same men, after having killed their primal father for the sake of the women, are supposed not to have hurled themselves upon the women and joined in a raging battle over them, which burst the horde asunder. Rather, seized by a moral hangover, they are to have sat down together calmly and peacefully in order to establish a new religion and a new social order, through which they forbade themselves to touch the women of the tribe and to consume animals of a certain species, proclaimed to be the father-surrogate, even when they were tormented by the gnawing pangs of hunger.

Freud demands even more from us, however, than the acceptance of this plethora of improbabilities, which are not made plausible by a single fact observed in the behavior of savages or animals. He also demands that we consider it possible that the moral hangover that followed upon the *singular* deed of primitive patricides has made itself felt in the horror of incest, undiminished *through hundreds of thousands of years* in all their descendants down to the present day, even though the wish to kill the father and sexually to possess the mother are to this day supposed to be powerfully alive in man. . . . *[Kautsky then ridicules Freud's statements " . . . that the beginnings of religion, morals, society and art converge in the Oedipus complex" (ibid., p. 156) and that in agriculture the son expressed " . . . his incestuous libido, which found symbolic satisfaction in the cultivation of Mother Earth" (ibid., p. 152).]*

Whether *[Freudian psychoanalysis in medical practice]* wreaks more mischief than it produces curative effects is something I cannot judge. As far as sociology is concerned, it certainly does not involve an enrichment of our knowledge. Only because it has become so very fashionable did we have to concern ourselves with it in such detail.

CHAPTER SIX

The Harmful Effects of Inbreeding

[Kautsky rejects a hypothesis, similar to McLennan's explanation of exogamy, by Cunow, Die Marxsche Geschichts . . . theorie, II, 118.*]* A prohibition of such rigor as that against consanguineous marriage can only be explained if society fears harm for itself from the forbidden practice. The only harm that such marriages can cause, though, is the damage from inbreeding. . . . But how did it come about that consanguineous marriages were forbidden? . . . In my article of 1882 on the genesis of marriage and the family, I still rejected the assumption that the prohibition of consanguineous marriages was to be explained by the endeavor to prevent the damage caused by inbreeding. *[Kautsky quotes at length from his article, p. 272.]* I explained the custom of exogamy in a way similar to Lubbock and Spencer as arising out of the everlasting feuds among savages, in which the defeated men were killed, while the women of the vanquished were appropriated by the victors. . . . But this explanation did not satisfy me permanently. The custom of men fetching foreign women for themselves could not, after all, explain the passionate prohibition against entering into a sexual union with women

of one's own tribe. Again and again, inbreeding urged itself upon me as the explanatory reason. And I believe that I have succeeded in overcoming the reservations that argue against it.[5] . . .

The more closed the organization of human society became, the more did the conditions for the emergence of the harmful effects of inbreeding arise that had not existed earlier in the animal state. . . . The appearance of inbreeding and its harmful effects was the first precondition . . . that had to be fulfilled if it was to lead to the prohibition of consanguineous marriage. The second precondition could only be fulfilled when men were capable of grasping the connection with their cause of those phenomena we know today as the results of inbreeding. . . .

Let us consider a tribe that has suffered to a high degree from the consequence of inbreeding continued through many generations. Its women are either infertile or the few children they bear are sickly. Primitive people do not, of course, have the slightest notion of the real causes of this sad state of affairs. . . . Then, by some stroke of luck, the men of the tribe take some female prisoners of war . . . [who] prove to be fertile and whose children turn out to be vigorous and completely healthy. Is it any wonder if a horror of the women of their own tribe seizes the men when they become convinced that union with them has been cursed, while union with the foreign women has been blessed by the gods?

Once this thought has been arrived at, and if continued mating with foreign women has confirmed the superiority of such marriages over those with members of the tribe, then the intensity of the prohibition against marriages within one's own tribe and the scrupulousness of its enforcement are easily explained: it is after all a matter of warding off great harm from the tribe. . . . Precisely because the prohibition of such unions is founded not on scientific understanding but on observations, which, like so many others made by primitive people, are intermingled with fantastical and mystical collective ideas, it assumes a religious and ethical form. Our hypothesis regarding the origin of the prohibition of marriage within the tribe thus does not at all presuppose a knowledge of physiology, such as savages do not possess; rather, it fits their way of thinking very well.

It is possible that hundreds and thousands of tribes perished from the results of inbreeding without grasping the cause of their ruin. However, once a tribe that suffered from inbreeding had forbidden it, then it necessarily rapidly flourished again. If there were other tribes in its vicinity that were also weakened by inbreeding, then it was natural that they . . . learned from the first tribe. When they did not, then they must have been pushed back

5. Kautsky had more briefly advanced the hypothesis presented here in "Kannibalische Ethik," pp. 866–68, *Vermehrung und Entwicklung*, p. 165.

by the tribe that rapidly increased in size. Thus the prohibition against marriage within the tribe or in the gens gradually became more and more general. . . .

. . . In human society there appeared, in contrast with animal society, new conditions for the procreation and rearing of children, for example, inbreeding, as well as the family consisting of female and male workers. These new conditions require social regulations of the sexual association, as the inherited drives no longer suffice to assure the most suitable unions of the two sexes in the interest of posterity. . . . The sexual relationships are among the first human relations that are subjected to social regulation, either by means of ethical demands or laws.

The Valuation of Sexual Drives

. . . The sexual drives are not of uniform nature. Some are related to the social, others to the egotistical drives. On the one side we find concern for the child, first on the part of the mother, then also of the father, and finally of the members of the tribe, the gens, the family. . . . In contrast, the drives that result in sexual love and that reach their climax in copulation are of a completely different kind. They engender among the members of the same sex not mutually supportive cohesiveness, but often bitter discord, indeed even bloody combat. . . . Human beings perform the sex act only in complete secrecy. . . . And this modesty is to be found even among backward peoples. . . . Should this not be due to the fact that [sexuality] acquires a nonsocial character because of the jealousy that arises when many men and women live together? Sexuality does not burst society apart, but it does impel the individual to step outside society during the time it is activated. . . .

. . . It cannot be our task here to offer a history of love and marriage. Whatever forms their phases assumed, the distinction was always maintained between the valuation of the functions that serve the rearing of children beginning with their procreation and the valuation of those activities that are directed to copulation and culminate in it. While the former are considered as lofty by the entire society under all circumstances and are treated with the greatest reverence, judgment of the latter vacillates. . . . This distinction assumes especially extreme forms when philosophizing about morality begins and the point is reached where the social drives are praised to the skies, venerated as an emanation of the divine essence, and in contrast with them all behavior from motives of egoism or lust are despised as the remnant of animality in man. . . .

The Origin of Sexual Modesty

It is likely that another phenomenon is closely connected with the differing valuation of the sexual drives of mating, on the one hand, and of tending the offspring, on the other, and with the impulse to remove sexuality into seclusion, namely the modesty that recoils from any uncovering of the genitals. This question is only loosely linked with the topic that concerns us here: ascertaining the peculiarity of man at the beginning of his historical development. But the question has often aroused our interest and, since we believe that we can make a few new observations about it, we ask to be allowed to discuss it here. . . .

. . . The habit of clothing *[the body]* had to precede the emergence of modesty. Man becomes embarrassed when, without intending it, he offers to the people around him an unaccustomed sight and thereby draws their attention to himself. . . . Sexual modesty . . . can only have developed from the sex organs in particular being permanently withdrawn from general view. . . . Why this endeavor to protect specifically the genitals, long before anyone gave thought to a garment of any kind? I believe that can be explained only with reference to man's erect posture. In his beginnings, man was already a much too differentiated being for his organs to be able to adapt themselves completely to his erect posture. . . . Among the organs much less well suited functionally in the case of man than in the case of the animal are the sex organs. . . . One of the first tasks of his technology . . . had to be that of making protective coverings for these parts. Such coverings were needed only for adults, not for children, who were not exposed to dangers. . . .

When it had become the custom to protect the genitals, there finally had to come a point where their uncovering attracted attention and caused embarrassment. This was made even more intense by the following circumstance: The genitals could always remain covered; however, for two different functions they had to be uncovered: for discharging excrements and for the loving embrace. . . . Thus the genitals were uncovered only for activities that came to be regarded as not belonging with society, as being such that it was indecent to perform them in society. Thereby the mere uncovering became itself an indecent act. And since the uncovering of the one sex in front of the other was now necessary only for the purposes of sexual pleasure, it easily gave rise to erotic feelings even when it took place for other reasons. . . .

Section Five
Other Characteristics of the Human Psyche

The Animal and Beauty

Before we conclude our overview of the drives that man receives from the animal world as inherited possessions and with which he begins his historical career, we must consider one more drive. It admittedly does not have a determining influence on man in such a high degree as the drives for the preservation and reproduction of the individual and for the preservation of society, but it nevertheless plays a great role in human behavior: *the craving for beauty*. . . . Aesthetics, like ethics, was used to lift man out of the context of nature and to elevate him above it. . . . The divine spark . . . in us is said to be attested to unmistakably by our yearning for the beautiful just as much as by our yearning for the good. . . .

Whether we may say that even the animal craves beauty depends above all on how we define beauty. *[Kautsky cites Plato's* Phaedrus, *250B (p. 170), and quotes several definitions from Kant's* The Critique of Judgment, *pp. 50, 60, 80 and 85. Of Kant's first one, he says that it]* suffices fully for our purposes. It says that we regard as beautiful every phenomenon that evokes in us a completely disinterested feeling of pleasure. . . . When we speak of beauty, we think almost always of visual or auditory impressions. . . . Disinterested enjoyment of or displeasure in such impressions is not confined to man, but can likewise be found among animals. *[Kautsky quotes and discusses at some length Darwin's views of animals' sense of beauty as stated in* The Descent of Man, *pp. 467 and 877.]*

How the nervous system acquired the ability to feel delight and repugnance, pleasure and displeasure in response to certain stimuli is still as little understood today as are the roots of mental life and of life in general. This aesthetic capacity probably developed, like the other capacities of the animal organs, as a weapon in the struggle for existence. But even though no organ may function in a manner that is incompatible with the continued existence of the organism, that is not to say that each and every function of an animal organ has to serve a definite purpose. Once the organ has been formed, it will always react to certain impulses or stimuli from the outside in a certain manner. That need not always happen in a way advantageous to the organism; it is even possible that it be disadvantageous. No organism is fashioned so teleologically that its organs always react in the most appropriate manner to external impulses. Appropriateness in the organism is not the work of a Providence that foresaw everything, but the work of a selection among many variations. . . .

The abilities of tasting and smelling, of hearing and seeing are indispensable for the organism's cognition of its environment. Agreeable and disagreeable impressions they call forth in us can serve to attract and to warn us. But the way the nervous system is constituted can have the result that it reacts to some chemical or mechanical stimuli with pleasure or displeasure, without appropriateness or inappropriateness to a purpose being involved. If we perceive some combinations of sounds as horrible dissonances and others as beautiful harmonies, the proximity of complementary colors as beautiful and of noncomplementary ones as ugly, though none of these hurt us or help us, this must be due to the nature of our nervous system. To this extent our sense of beauty has a natural basis. *[Kautsky quotes Billroth,* Wer ist musikalisch? *pp. 16, 17, 24, 105, and refers to Helmholtz,* On the Sensations of Tone.*]* The majority of the sensations of pleasure and delight of which an organism becomes conscious are of the interested kind, connected with the satisfaction of a real need. However, not every element of complicated combinations of impressions must, per se, be linked to an interest. In its connection with other impressions, it has become one that awakens pleasure. It can retain this capacity when it is later perceived by itself apart from that connection. . . .

Darwin, in the passage we have already quoted, pointed to another source of the sense of beauty: *habit.* Perhaps habit produced the feeling of beauty indirectly, as the opposite of ugliness. It is not what one is accustomed to that becomes the beautiful, but rather what one is not accustomed to becomes the ugly. . . .

Thus the notion of what appears beautiful to an organism can arise from two sources: from the constitution of the organism, from its very nervous system, that is, from the ego; and second, from its environment, which provides us with interested impressions of an agreeable nature and with habits, out of which disinterested sentiments of beauty can gradually be distilled. . . . Hence we find in human sentiments of beauty two elements of very different kinds: a natural one, which man has in common with many animals and which remains the same in the most varied conditions, and a social one, which changes along with the social conditions.

CHAPTER TWO

Art in the Animal and in the Human World

A new factor is introduced into the realm of beauty by man: the capacity not only to perceive and enjoy beauty, but also artificially to *produce* it. Along with human technology, the conscious dominance over matter, *art* emerges, one of the characteristics that separates man from the animal.[1] To be sure, here, too, as elsewhere, the distinction is not a sharp one. In this area, too, we find transitions. There are animals that erect structures, that adorn themselves, and yet others that employ instruments to create sounds. *[Kautsky illustrates this with quotations from Doflein,* Das Tier, *p. 444; Alverdes,* Social Life in the Animal World, *p. 159; Espinas,* Sociétés animales, *p. 500; and especially from his own early article "Kunst und Kultur," which, in turn, relied heavily on Darwin's* Descent of Man, *quoting from pp. 744, 841, and 876.]* Regardless of how highly we might assess the germs of artistic production in the animal world, they do not go beyond mere expressionism, beyond the striving to excite lively sentiments in us through the combination of certain colors, forms, and sounds, without making the least demand on the intellect either of the artist or of the public.

Human ability, however, passed beyond this animal babbling at an early stage. . . . The plastic and the graphic arts, which at first borrowed only single spots of color and lines from nature and imitated them, learned to go beyond the ornament and to join together lines and colors to fashion entire figures and combinations of figures copied from nature. And the development of language also allowed men to go beyond mere music in their use of rhythm and to employ it for the artistic presentation of events that they had experienced. . . . As soon as the ability to produce artistically appeared in man, he made abundant use of it. *[Kautsky quotes Bücher,* Arbeit und Rhythmus, *p. 13, who stresses the great efforts primitive people devote to decorating themselves and their implements.]* They also tend to accompany every activity with singing. That accords very well with the view that speech was originally singing and that the beginnings of language grew out of the necessity to communicate with one another when working together.[2]

In the beginning, everyone was just as much a productive artist as an enjoyer of the beauty of art products. However, despite the sameness of living conditions, certain differences in individual endowment nevertheless occur among animals and surely even more among men. They grow as men's pursuits become more complex, as their activities become more multifarious. . . . There develops the distinction between the creative artist and his appreciative public. . . .

In contrast to the enjoyment of what is beautiful, the production of it is an eminently social process, insofar as it takes place only for society, even

---

1. Some of the points made in this and the following chapter had already appeared in *Vermehrung und Entwicklung,* pp. 133–48.

2. This sentence refers to two conceptions mentioned earlier by Kautsky in passages omitted in the present edition, Darwin's suggestion that language developed from song (*The Descent of Man,* p. 463) and the view of Noiré that language developed in connection with jointly performed labor (*Das Werkzeug,* pp. 4–5).

though the artist as a rule requires solitude during the creation itself. . . . The concept of the beautiful, too, is not exclusively conditioned by social circumstances, but the artist is completely dependent on them. . . . The particular society supplies the artist with the artistic technique of his time; social taste makes a selection among artists and art works. It condemns some of them to being forgotten forever, while judging others worthy of preservation and thus also of being passed on to posterity, which for its part selects anew with a changed taste. . . . However, the particular society also sets certain ends for the artist, which he must serve. . . . It is true that we love beauty for its own sake, but the artist is a man like all others and as such he pursues in his activity certain ends that need not consist solely in the production of beauty for its own sake. He can place the powers that mastery of artistic technique confers on him at the service of very different ends that command his allegiance at any given moment.

CHAPTER THREE

Art and Economy

With the character of society, the ends also change that it sets for the artist and for itself. The primary purpose of art, however, remains in all circumstances the reduction of the monotony of life, which is to be made richer in color and variety by it; the reduction of the monotony of work or of the monotony of idleness. . . .

The extent to which art is developed in a society is closely connected with the amount of leisure time in that society. That can be seen even under primitive conditions. . . . Technical progress at first advances more rapidly in the sphere of women's work than in the sphere of men's work. That, however, means an increase of the woman's burden of labor. In early times, only man gains more leisure time through progress. He thus lives at the expense of woman, whom he exploits. The nature of the progress of art corresponds to that fact. To the degree that it is linked with work, it is advanced chiefly by woman. . . . Work songs are for the most part woman's songs. In addition to work, the most important occurrences in her life are marriages, births, and deaths. The wedding song, the lullaby, and the dirge are, in addition to the work song, among her specialties. In comparison, the men's songs are of very little importance. . . . Like music and poetry, the woman's plastic and graphic arts of that period are also connected with her labors, insofar as she creates anything enduring. With everything that she fabricates, she pays attention not only to its practicality but also to its beauty, whether it is a product of weaving, of clothes making, of wood-carving, or of pottery. Above all, of course, she decorates herself. . . .

The art . . . that as plastic or graphic art naturalistically reproduces living beings, animals and men, and as rhythmical art of language presents conflicts among men . . . is man's art as early as the Stone Age. . . . Only hunters could observe and reproduce what painting and sculpture depicted. And the most ancient of the epic poems, they tell of the works of men, describe war and the hunt with the greatest expertise. Art undergoes a further development through the introduction of the division of labor into the male world, while among the women such a division does not take place until the last century. . . . *[It]* ultimately has the result that the exercise of an art becomes a specific profession. . . .

The splitting of society into exploiters and exploited, its division into classes, then made the professional artist dependent on the exploiters. The greater the extent of the exploitation and the more extensive the exploiters' luxury, the more considerable are the resources they can expend for artistic purposes. . . . It is only the division of society into classes that provides the resources to maintain a body of professional artists to a significant extent in all fields of art.

Folk art still continues to live alongside professional art. . . . The great mass among the exploited consists of peasants, and in agriculture *[there are]* periods . . . of prolonged leisure. . . . The possibility of a folk art . . . disappears for the peasants as soon as they are compelled to fill the intervals between their agricultural activities with gainful industrial labor, cottage industry, woodcutting, etc. The workers of the cities, where labor knows no breaks, are from the outset not in a position to develop a folk art. But up to the emergence of capitalism, they are still capable of artistic enjoyment and of cultivating their taste, since until that time the exploiters invest the fruits of their exploitation only to a small degree in means of production, much more in luxuries, including also artistic works, buildings, resplendent garments, and so forth, which they display in public.

Capitalism impels the exploiters to accumulate a large part of the fruits of their exploitation as capital, to expend a relatively smaller part for luxuries. And in these they indulge little in public. At the same time, capital strives to transform into working time the entire lifetime of the masses that does not have to be devoted to the renewal of their strength through eating and sleeping. Thus the laboring masses under capitalism are robbed not only of any possibility of artistic production, but also of almost any possibility of artistic enjoyment. To be sure, from a certain point of its development onward, the proletarist knows how to obtain again more leisure time for itself, but its extent has so far not been very considerable. It has to be used by the proletariat almost entirely for the task of arming itself intellectually and organizationally for the class struggle against capital, which untiringly seeks to push the proletariat down again and again. Under such circumstances, only little time is left for the enjoyment of art, virtually none for the creation of art.

Not out of the proletariat, as some believe, but only out of the abolition of the proletariat under socialism can a new, high folk art again arise. And this folk art will probably be as closely linked to work as in the dim foretime. [*Kautsky quotes Bücher,* Arbeit und Rhythmus, *pp. 455–56, who speaks of "the world of cheerful work" of primitive people.*] The origin of *classes* and their antagonisms . . . are the factor that increasingly puts an end to the cheerful labor of primeval times. . . .

CHAPTER FOUR
Man's Urge to Inquire

Man's volition, which he takes over from his animal forebears and with which he begins his historical career, includes, along with the drive for self-preservation, for preservation of the species (reproduction), and for preservation of society (ethics), and along with the need of and desire for what is beautiful, the striving after knowledge. . . . Even the animal has urgent need of knowledge of its environment in order to succeed in the struggle for existence. . . . No less, however, [does it need] knowledge of itself, of its own strengths and abilities, which it must know before it sets itself a problem and undertakes its solution. . . . In this craving for truth there is nothing at all meritorious, nothing that elevates man above the animal; it is necessary for life. . . .

. . . The ego's active behavior vis-à-vis the external world is the first source of knowledge of its environment as well as of the ego, which cannot be understood by itself but only in its activity vis-à-vis its environment. To be sure, practice merely provides experiences. . . . In order that real knowledge might arise from them, the experiences have to be tested, compared with one another, ordered in a total complex free of contradiction. . . . but it is always practice that constitutes the starting point of knowledge, the struggle of the ego with its environment to advance the ego's various ends, which have their source in its innate nature and the demands of the environment. For its part, the result of the processing of practical experiences through thought then in turn renders practice more fruitful, so that, as a rule, the older, more experienced individual acts more appropriately than the younger, more inexperienced one.

In this regard a distinction must be made between the individual's learning from his own personal experience and learning from the experience of others. . . . This holds good for the animal as well as for man. However, as in the other areas of mental phenomena, a great difference between the animal and man is brought about also in this area by technological development. . . . It is only man's articulated speech that allows the individual . . . to describe phenomena in detail and to repeat the descriptions he has heard from others accurately in all details, to reproduce them from generation to generation, from tribe to tribe. This manner of propagating experiences is greatly facilitated and furthered by the invention of writing.

These developments suffice of themselves to expand enormously the

scope of the experiences of others at the individual's disposal as instructional
material, so that in comparison the scope of the single individual's personal
experiences becomes ever tinier, as it is not at all or only slightly extended. . . . At the same time, the means of communication develop, the
spatial scope of the experiences accessible to the individual is extended. . . .
Technology provides him not only with greater, stronger, faster organs of
movement; it also renders more acute his sense organs to a huge degree
and thus tremendously expands the extent of the world accessible to our
senses. It made it possible for man to establish the occurrence of a certain
gas (helium) on the surface of the sun before it was found on the Earth and
to weigh and to split atoms that are imperceptible.

The quality of men's experiences grew so enormously, and the forms
they assumed were so varied, that it became quite impossible for a single
brain to comprehend them all. . . . With the progress of technology, as its
consequence and then in turn as a means of developing it further, there
emerges the division of labor of the occupations and professions, so
that . . . only society as a whole still encompasses the totality of human
knowledge. And to that is added the great division of labor between practitioners and theoreticians. . . .

But not only the collection of already available knowledge and its combination into a complex free of contradiction becomes the task of science,
but also the search after new knowledge. . . . The more rapidly technology
advances and reshapes the environment, *[the more]* does it solve again and
again not only existing problems, but is also, in so doing, confronted with
new ones that require new solutions. . . . To be sure, the solution of particular problems need not always raise up new ones immediately. In such
cases men are glad to content themselves with solutions found in the
past . . . Nothing is more erroneous than to believe that the search for what
is new . . . is inborn in the human spirit. . . . But however long a . . . stage
might last that appears to us as stagnation . . . , sooner or later every solution
calls forth somewhere phenomena incompatible with the existing kind of
knowledge that impel men to strive after a new, higher knowledge. . . . New
problems can arise . . . more rapidly than solutions, so that the process of
inquiry is never concluded but always goes on, the activity of the researcher
becomes a habit, indeed a passion, which can become no less strongly
determinative of the behavior of some men than the passions of eroticism,
of self-preservation, of ethics, of aesthetics.

For no age is that more true than for the one we live in. So it seems
natural to consider the craving for what is new as one that is innate in the
human mind. . . . Yet it is always called forth by new phenomena in the
environment, never by an inner craving of the mind for what is new,
which . . . would be entirely without sense and purpose from the standpoint
of the preservation and the success of the organism, but otherwise, too,
completely incomprehensible. For one can always inquire only into what
has come within the scope of our cognitive capacity. Whence should there

come the urgent desire in man to investigate something of whose existence he has no inkling? . . .

The pure passion for inquiry has certainly become a motivation that is extremely important for human behavior. Just as little as ethics or aesthetics or eroticism does it constitute an economic motivation, even though it can, just like these, in certain circumstances, be amalgamated with such a motive. Like those motivations, however, the urge to inquire is also determined in its particular historical character by the formation of the environment at any given time. And like those motivations it, too, has its deepest roots in animality, for even the animal feels in itself the craving for knowledge of the world, that is of the small piece of the world that it is able to apprehend with its senses. Without such knowledge, the more highly developed animal cannot succeed in the struggle for existence.

CHAPTER FIVE

Man with his Contradictions

We have now achieved an overview of the mental constitution with which the human ego begins the process of historical development; an overview of man's drives and needs inherited from his animal forebears. . . . It is not in investigating man's a priori, but in investigating his further social development that we find ourselves dealing with economic relations.

Even now we can say this much: The economic moment is not that which is universally human. It belongs to what is historically particular, at least when we understand by the economic moment more than mere seeking after food. The materialist conception of history has been criticized for not recognizing what is universally human but only what is historically particular. That is an error. It has merely presupposed that which is universally human and has not concerned itself with it, precisely because it is only a conception of *history* and as such has only the task of investigating the historically particular.[3] However, since this has frequently been misunderstood, I felt impelled here to treat more thoroughly the universally human that is the basis of all that happens historically, . . . the sum total of those characteristics that man had acquired prior to the beginning of his historical career and that he developed further in that career without surrendering his essential nature. . . . For us that which is universally human . . . is basically nothing other than what is animal in man—everything that is not animal in him is historically particular. . . .

Nothing is more erroneous than the assertion that the materialist con-

3. See also p. 56, above.

ception of history rests upon the assumption that man is guided only by egoistical motives.... Human nature encompasses not just the drive for self-preservation, but also sexual love, ethics, joy in what is beautiful, as well as the yearning for knowledge. And since man as a whole enters into the historical process with all his capacities, drives, and needs, all of these intervene in the historical development, although not all to the same degree. What a powerful role the *[drive for]* taking care of offspring has played in history! The law of inheritance is one of its results in more highly developed society. How greatly it has determined the policies of dynasties! But... for all classes ... far-reaching political and social goals, "ideals," signify after all fundamentally nothing other than particular forms of care for offspring. Not for one's own sake does one fight for ... goals, the attainment of which one does not expect to see, but rather for posterity.... And even the sexual drive in the narrower sense of the word, as mere mating drive, has played its role in history. *[Kautsky mentions a few examples from the Trojan War to Henry VIII.]*

Joy in what is beautiful has also now and then had historical effects. *[An exploiting class may use the labor available to it to erect massive artistic buildings. To continue this process and to increase the number of exploited may require further conquests—one motive for Rome's constant warfare. The Renaissance popes imposed heavy taxes in Germany in order to beautify Rome with great art—which provided the impulse for the German Reformation. The passion of Louis XIV for building helped empty the treasury—one reason for the conflicts of the late eighteenth century assuming the form of the French Revolution.]* In another manner, joy in what is beautiful affected history and the economy through the origin of money.... Silver or gold ... could acquire this function only because they were generally desired on account of their use-value. This use-value, however, had its source only in man's aesthetic needs for glistening adornment. Thus the entire developed commodity production in the enormous proportions of present-day capitalism grew up on an aesthetic basis and perhaps could grow up only upon such a basis. For the use-value of even the most useful things is quantitatively limited.... Only of what is superfluous, what serves beauty, luxury, does one not easily have too much, especially when it is durable.... In the case of a precious metal there is the additional consideration of its great rarity....

We adherents of the materialist conception of history ... do indeed recognize the infinite diversity of human drives. But also the large measure of conflict among those drives.... The *individual's* drive for self-preservation can come into conflict with the drives that serve the preservation of the *species*, that is, reproduction, as well as preservation of *society*. Even the beautiful can be in conflict with what is appropriate, for the individual as well as for society or the species. And even within each of these kinds of drives conflicts can occur.... In the course of development, there appear within the horde, which grows to be a tribe and then a people, more and more separate social organizations. . . . Each of these social formations takes on certain functions, certain interests, which can well come into conflict with those of other social formations. How are the social drives supposed to guide the individual in such circumstances? And think of the many kinds of conflicts that can arise out of the craving for knowledge, out of different conceptions of what is considered to be truth!

It is often said that only the laws and conventions of societies create all human torment. That men should simply be entrusted to their drives, that these would by themselves point out to them the right path, that man is by nature good. . . . All anarchism is based upon this belief. But unfortunately man is by nature not merely good, that is, social, but also evil, that is, full of strong drives for self-preservation and for mating, which can easily bring him into conflict with many a fellow man in society. . . . And if man is always led upon the right path by his . . . drive, then we must ask which of his many drives indicates the correct path? With the exception of the aesthetic drives, they are all indispensable for his preservation and that of his kind. However, they are not all equally important. Depending on the particular situation, now the one, now the other can prove to be the stronger in their conflicts. . . . But once the situation is past that gave a certain drive the upper hand, then the opposed drives can be stronger, and repentance and pangs of conscience are the consequence. . . .

Not always, however, can one drive keep down the others in a conflict among them. In this case, the final decision devolves on a factor which, along with the drives and instincts, at an early stage acquires influence on animals' behavior: *knowledge of the environment.* The eighteenth century overestimated the influence of thought, of reason, on the behavior of man. . . . All social insufficiency was attributed to ignorance and irrationality. . . . The only motivations that move men were considered to be those of which they were conscious. Even today, one still frequently finds this overestimation of reason and of conscious motivations in views of society and its historical development.

The Marxist conception of history opposed this viewpoint: It drew a distinction between the motivations that actually move men and those of which they become conscious and which they express. It is the task of social science to uncover the real motivations behind the conscious, admitted, expressed motivations. That alone would suffice to point out that the unconscious plays a big role in society and history. . . . But *[science]* must not itself plunge into the unconscious, into "pure inner experiencing," as a means of cognition. The drives have no place in science, except as an object of investigation. Among those who have recently stressed the unconscious and have attempted to study it, Sigmund Freud, whom we have already discussed, has surely aroused the greatest interest. The attempt has often been made to reconcile the Marxist conception with the Freudian. . . . I have already explained above why I cannot participate in this synthesis.[4] Yet I gladly acknowledge that psychoanalysis, also in its Freudian version, is important for Marxism insofar as it opposes the hitherto common under-estimation of drives in man.

On the other hand, the animal has been sinned against, inasmuch as its cognitive capacity has been underrated. . . . Already at an early stage, there must have appeared in the animal the ability to form mental images from sense impressions, to connect them in thoughts and to draw conclusions from them, in other words, the cognitive capacity as an impetus of action. . . . The more complicated and changing the conditions are in which the organism finds itself, . . . the more must *[the instincts]* lose importance in comparison with cognitive thinking, until in man they play no more than a minor role. However, the drives, which are not directed to specific activities, still maintain themselves very strongly in man in the form of certain ethical, aesthetic, erotic, and "material" needs, which they engender. But because of man's very complicated and changeable conditions, these needs cannot be satisfied without a high development of his intelligence.[5]

The drives and many of the needs and goals that have their origin in the drives are innate, but are for that reason not unchangeable. Having in the final analysis sprung from the organism's living conditions, they can change along with it. However, no matter how much they may change, they can always bring forth only immediate goals and needs that recur anew again and again, that proceed from everyday life. In contrast, man's cognitive capacity attains to a level that provides him with a broader horizon. . . . From a servant of the drives it thus becomes, to a certain, constantly increasing degree, their master. It now no longer has the task of merely investigating the means that are the most appropriate for the satisfaction of the instincts and the drives in particular cases; it is able to set goals for man which are higher, more distant than those given just by the drives.

But regardless of how closely our ideals seem to approach to the clouds, their base nonetheless remains on earth. They become powerless, if they are not rooted in strong drives and are not in accord with them. The strongest intelligence cannot liberate us from our drives. And if it were able to do so, that would mean the downfall of mankind. How could we exist without the strong drives of self-preservation, of sociability, of reproduction! Our highest goals can only strive consciously on a very large scale for the same thing that our drives unconsciously press toward within a narrow compass.

In relation to our drives, however, the role of intelligence is the same

4. See II: 1: 7, II: 4:5, above.
5. See also I: 4:1, II: 1:7, and p. 80, above.

one we have come to know in other connections: When these drives come to contradict one another, our reason has the task of overcoming these contradictions. Eliminating conflicts—that is the special function of reason! The conflict between the ego and the external world, the conflicts that can arise among our individual thoughts, and lastly also the conflicts among our individual drives. Consistency of our activity, consistency of our view of the world, consistency in our surroundings—striving for this is its mission.

Section Six
Adaptation in Nature

CHAPTER ONE

Progress and Adaptation

Now that we have become acquainted with the "ego," "human nature," the "universally human" as the a priori, the thesis, with which the historical process begins, we turn to the antithesis and the synthesis resulting from the interaction of thesis and antithesis. The antithesis is the environment of the individual; the synthesis is adaptation.

Individual and environment are engaged in an unceasing struggle. That is true even of those parts of the world that are of use to the individual, for example as food. He cannot acquire food, which often conceals itself from him, without searching for it, without overcoming its resistance or reshaping its resistant forms. The individual as subject is confronted by the various parts of the environment as object. . . . Its particular properties are in every instance as important for the peculiarity of a given historical process as are those of the individual who is involved in that process. Nevertheless, we do not need to treat further of them here, since to begin with we are focusing our attention only on what is universal. Important as the universal, inherited nature of the individual is for our understanding of historical development, consideration of the totality of nature in general does not furnish us the least insight into this development. What becomes important for this development is the peculiarity of the *particular* milieu, which we are not yet considering here.

In general, we shall here point out only the following. By the individual's environment is often understood merely inanimate nature: climate, features and composition of the soil, etc. . . . Here we use the word in a broader sense, in which it refers also to animate nature, to all of the organisms around the individual, even the individuals of the same species who are distinct from the "ego." In the case of the individual human being, especially, one often understands by the milieu that determines him the society of those human beings with whom he has social intercourse. That is too narrow a limitation for our conception of history, however.

The synthesis, more than the antithesis, shall concern us here, the overcoming of the antagonism between the individual and his environment. As in the preceding discussion, we shall here, too, first consider the process among animals, in order to illuminate it more clearly as it occurs among men. . . . With regard to the effect of the environment on the individual, we must distinguish between . . . an unchanged and a changed environment. In the first case, the same stimuli to the individual are repeated over and over again and call forth again and again the same reactions. . . . When modified life-forms newly appear under these conditions, they will not maintain themselves more easily in the struggle for existence than the traditional life-forms, but rather perish more easily. In this stage, the struggle for existence has a conservative, rather than a revolutionary effect.[1] . . . Once a certain kind of organism has adapted to a certain milieu, then it no longer changes, as long as the milieu does not change. Its inherited character can still maintain itself for a period of time in a changed environment.

Darwinism is to be emphatically rejected, if one understands it to mean that, thanks to variation of species, the struggle for existence brings about a continuous further development of life-forms, even when living conditions remain constant, and that this further development consists in the organisms becoming ever more perfect and better adapted. According to this view, man is then the best adapted of all organisms, and the primeval organisms, however one might imagine them, were the least well adapted. If that were the case, then it would be surprising that the course of development does not lead to the supplanting of the older species of organisms by the younger, better adapted ones, so that ultimately only man still survives. . . . The first organism that achieved enduring life must already have been well adapted; otherwise it would not have been able to maintain itself.[2] . . .

As soon, however, as some of these primitive life-forms entered into another milieu, . . . innumerable creatures not adapted to the new milieu perished, until conditions appeared either in the milieu or in the organism or in both, which brought the former and the latter into harmony. . . . The growing complexity of living conditions then gradually brought into being, alongside the simple organisms, also more complex ones. . . . Even the simplest organisms known to us today prove to be complex structures under the microscope. . . . The progress of evolution is not one from less well adapted to better adapted organisms, but one from simpler to more complex living conditions and thus from simple to more complex organisms. . . . What appears as progress in evolution is in reality not progress

1. See II:1:4, above.
2. See I:5:3, above.

to a higher degree of adaptation, but instead mere adaptation to *new* living conditions.

Passive Adaptation

... Now let us assume that the milieu changes. Even the constantly advancing cooling off and shrinking of the earth periodically bring about such changes. . . . The organisms must adapt themselves to such changes, if they are not to perish. . . . At first every organism seeks to pass on hereditarily the characteristics it has, in whatever manner, acquired, as soon as they have also been acquired by its germ plasm. . . . A number of species will remain unchanged in the new circumstances. If they are thereby brought into conflict with these circumstances, . . . then they will die out, more or less quickly or slowly. Many extinct life-forms, of which petrified remains give evidence, demonstrate to us that adaptation is by no means a general law.

But even in the case of species, for which hereditary factors are not insurmountable, which vary more easily under the influence of new circumstances, an adaptation does not take place without difficulty, but rather at first only a change. This change, too, finds in the inheritance of the old characteristics certain limits and determining conditions. The change will not extend to all organs. After all, not all elements of the milieu are changed, and not all organs are capable of modification to the same degree. . . .

Now, the changes in the organism *[brought about]* through the new environment can be twofold in kind, either passive or active. Let us first consider the former. They occur without the least assistance from the organism. *[Kautsky cites examples of the effect of changes in temperature on the color or density of feathers or fur and, quoting Doflein, Das Tier, pp. 847–48, of changes in nutrition on the color of caterpillars.]* These changes are not per se adaptations. For individuals undergoing them, they can be useful in quite varying degrees. Some changes must even have a harmful effect. . . . Then again, other modifications can be very inconsequential, neither useful nor harmful. . . . Everything in the organism has its cause and is in this sense necessary, that is, an inevitable effect. Not everything in the organism has a purpose and is necessary as an indispensable condition for its preservation. For each phenomenon we must ask: Why? Where does it come from? But not for each one: To what end? . . .

We have seen that the modifications of organisms ensuing from a change of the environment do not necessarily constitute an adaptation because of that fact. Adaptations are only the final result of the selection that the struggle for existence makes among the plethora of modifications called forth by the change of the milieu. In turn, the modifications ultimately left

as adaptations are, for their part, not necessarily higher developments. . . . Now, the process of adaptation need not necessarily produce an
organism that has a greater variety of characteristics than its predecessor
. . . , if the new milieu . . . is as simple as the old one. . . . It is even possible
that an organism comes into a milieu that is simpler. . . . Then there can
even occur a simplification of its organization, a backward development,
degeneration. . . .

The entire higher evolution of the world of organisms is only a result
of the fact that, since the beginning of life on the earth, conditions on it
assumed ever more varied forms, due to progressive cooling and shrinking
with their consequences. We require no other factor to explain the fact that
we encounter in the world of petrified fossils organisms with increasingly
complex structure, the more recent the geological strata are in which they
occur, until finally man appears as the most complex of all life-forms, and
his principal organ, the brain, constitutes the most complicated of all
organs. . . .

CHAPTER THREE

Active Adaptation

The kind of adaptation just treated can be called passive, since the modifications from which it results are brought about directly through the
changed effects of the environment without any active role whatsoever on
the part of the organism. . . . There are also modifications which represent
indirect effects of the changed environment. This environment can take on
such a form that it does not directly change the organism affected by it,
but does impose altered functions on its organs. This change of function
then has a modifying effect on the organism. . . .

The complete transformation of an organ, which is different from its
merely being strengthened or weakened, cannot occur as a consequence of
the fact that it functions more or less intensely in its hitherto usual manner.
Rather, this occurs only because it is induced to function in a manner in
which it was, up to that point, put into action not at all or at most only
rarely. *[Kautsky refers as examples to terrestrial mammals becoming maritime ones,
like seals and dolphins.]* This kind of adaptation is the result of a changed
activity on the part of the animal; therefore it may well be contrasted as
active adaptation to passive adaptation.

The two kinds of adaptation are very different, but they also have much
in common. At first glance it might seem as though active adaptation, in
contrast to the passive, always achieved only results appropriate *[to the goal
of survival]*, but it need not be so. . . . If the environment changes, and
consequently, to begin with, some organ also changed, then *[the]* whole
body is brought out of its state of equilibrium. . . . There begins in it a

struggle for existence of its parts with one another, the outcome of which decides whether ultimately a new harmony comes about or the downfall of the organism or at least an impairment of its capacity for action. . . .

With regard to the changes achieved through the altered functioning of the organs, matters stand exactly as they do with the changes called forth by chemical or physical stimuli: they need by no means be adaptive. Many will be neutral, not a few inappropriate, but some will be adaptive. And the individuals who undergo such changes have the best prospect of surviving in the course of the selection effected by the struggle for existence. In this respect, therefore, passive does not differ from active adaptation.

In other respects, however, there are important differences between them. To be sure, I would not want to include among these the repeatedly accepted assumption that characteristics acquired through active adaptation cannot become hereditary, but only those acquired through passive adaptation. If not all of them, then many. Doflein says . . . on this point: " . . . All attempts to demonstrate experimentally a transmission by heredity of a characteristic acquired or heightened through practice have heretofore been unsuccessful. Their results cannot stand up to a rigorous critique" [Das Tier, *p. 906*]. That was written in 1914. Should it still hold completely true today, then it would, of course, still fall far short of proving that transmission by inheritance of active adaptations does not occur, but only that not *all* adaptations of this kind are passed on by heredity, which is true, after all, for passive adaptations, too. . . . [3]

It is, to begin with, not comprehensible why precisely those alterations of the body that proceed from an alteration of its functions should leave the germ cells unaffected. . . . Everything that influences the whole body also has an effect on the gonads; indeed, these prove to be especially sensitive. *[To support this point, Kautsky quotes at some length Stieve, "Ueber den Einfluss der Umwelt auf die Lebewesen," pp. 1154–55.]* Should one assume that the body in its entirety undergoes a change only in the case of passive adaptation, but not in the case of active adaptation? That would surely be absurd. But then it is incomprehensible why the germ cells should be modified only in the former case and not in the latter. *[Kautsky here refers back to an experiment he had cited in the unabridged* Materialistische Geschichtsauffassung *(1929), I, 172, from Tschulok,* Deszendenzlehre.] The required experimental example of transmission by heredity of a characteristic acquired through active adaptation is thus available. That such examples are not more frequent is doubtless due above all to the great difference between

3. See also II:1:1, above.

active and passive adaptation: the latter can proceed by leaps, whereas the former is, under all circumstances, a slow process.

Most of the natural scientists who are adherents of the theory of evolution are fond of interpreting the Aristotelian principle that nature does not make leaps, as meaning that in nature every development and change proceeds slowly and imperceptibly, that therefore revolutions are acts of folly invented by men, of which a thinker trained in natural science must not make himself guilty. . . . The theorists of evolution were certainly justified in invoking the *[Aristotelian]* dictum as against those natural scientist who assumed that the organisms of every geological period ended by perishing in terrible catastrophes and that those of the next geological period were the result of a new creation. Leaps of this sort do not occur in nature—nor in society. But that is by no means to say that the transformation of old into new forms must always be a process that appears to be slow and imperceptible to us, that the formation of something new can never advance so rapidly that it impresses us as constituting a leap. Mutations, leaplike, suddenly appearing variations,[4] . . . are perhaps instances of passive modification, in the case of plants due maybe to a sudden change in the conditions of the soil from which they draw their nourishment. . . . Whatever may be true of mutations, even disregarding them, instances of passive adaptation are known that constitute in such a short time such striking changes that they are easy to observe, and many of them can also be produced experimentally. . . .

In contrast, the transformation of an organ through its increased or altered use presupposes from the outset a frequent repetition of this use. . . . *[It]* often proceeds so slowly that at the end of the individual's life it has not yet become perceptible *[to man]*. Doubtless every nonrecurring activity leaves its traces in the cells. If the activity is repeated, then this trace becomes enlarged through the accumulation of the results of the same influence. If, however, the organism dies before the accumulation has reached a degree significant for the struggle for existence and it does not pass on this accumulation to its descendants, then an adaptive modification would never be achieved in this manner. If that is to be attained, then it is necessary that the modifications once attained, no matter how imperceptible they might be, be transmitted by heredity, so that the next generation starts out already having an increased stock *[of modifications],* to which it adds further modifications through further increased or changed use of the organ in the same direction until its transformation has reached a degree in which it becomes effective for the struggle for existence. Finally, a state of equilibrium among the organs within the organism will be restored as soon as they have changed

4. See II : 1 : 3, above.

to the point where the organism no longer requires a further intensification or change of the employment of its organ and therefore no longer intensifies or changes it; the organ's strength and its employment will now correspond to each other.

Such a process can require many hundreds of generations before it is concluded. It is primarily such a process that the evolutionary theorists have in mind when they say that nature makes no leaps, that every development proceeds slowly and imperceptibly, accompanied by the gradual accumulation of minute modifications. They forget that as a rule this applies only to instances of active adaptation. Passive adaptation can, under certain conditions, proceed in a way that appears very much like a leap to us. Moreover, . . . the process of adaptation does not advance without interruption, but only in certain stages of the history of the earth, in conjunction with profound changes in the environment of organisms.

Lastly, the Darwinians are caught in an irresolvable contradiction if they assume that the variations of individuals are at first quite imperceptible, yet effect the survival of the best adapted in the struggle for existence, so that these transmit their modifications to a progeny which further strengthens the new characteristics through accumulation *[of modifications]*. According to our view, the modifications that appear to be imperceptible exercise no influence on the struggle for existence.[5] The reason for the preservation of the adaptive ones among them is not that they equip the organisms furnished with them better for that struggle than the others. . . . At their inception the modifications are too trifling to be able to function as adaptive or nonadaptive ones. They appear as the result of the occurrence of a change in the milieu that influences in the same way all individuals of the same species and of the same time and locality. The change in the milieu therefore produces in all of them the same modification, although not in the same degree in all of them and with some rather small individual differences.

The accumulation of these modifications then occurs when they are transmitted by heredity and the influence of the new milieu persists. That is not a result of the survival of the fittest. Only when in the course of time the new, acquired characteristics have, through accumulation, reached a certain strength, do they achieve the capacity to influence the struggle for existence. . . . The species and the individual with adaptive new properties now gain ground; the others are pushed back, confined to a few protected localities or completely annihilated. If this is the process, then it is understandably very difficult, in cases of active adaptation, to demonstrate experimentally that they, too, can become hereditary. . . . Modifications going so far as to transform an entire relatively large organ, together with

5. See also II:1:3, above.

its skeleton, usually require many generations in order to reach an extent perceptible to human scientists. . . .

. . . Another distinction between passive and active adaptation *[is the following]*. The former occurs without any action by the organism, through direct chemical or physical influences of the environment on its body. In this process, mind, cognition, logical reasoning, and volition play absolutely no role. For active adaptation, however, the mind is of importance even at a low level of the animal world as director and adaptor of the body's movements, insofar as they are of the voluntary kind, not mere reflex movements. . . . The mind is capable of adapting the *movements* of an animal body to its particular milieu . . . , but it cannot give the *organs* themselves adaptive forms. To the extent that their structure becomes adaptive, that is a result of their use and of the selection among the organisms, not the result of planned volition.

. . . The human mind, however, is able to go beyond the limits set for the animal. . . . Man is able to succeed, when new situations arise, in creating new organs suitable to them, the purposive structuring of which is in large part the consequence of his reasoning, not the mere result of a new employment of old organs that is not grasped in its further consequences and of blind selection among its effects. And with that we set foot on the threshold to the historical development of mankind.

[The appendix to Part II, consisting of Kautsky's two early articles on social drives, "Die sozialen Triebe in der Tierwelt" (1883) and "Die sozialen Triebe in der Menschenwelt" (1884), is omitted here.]

PART THREE

❦ Human Society

Section One
Race

Man's Original Home

The laws of adaptation to changed circumstances hold good for every organism and hence also for . . . man. . . . On him, too, . . . passive and active adaptation operates, which adapts the *activity* of the congenital organs to new conditions and thereby changes the organs, but which does not consciously seek directly to create new, better-suited organs. Of these we shall treat only later. First we must examine the effects of natural adaptation in human beings.

If a species of organisms is spread out over several qualitatively different areas, then the species will exhibit in each of these areas peculiarities that . . . are found in all individuals of the species in the given region. . . . They are peculiarities called forth by the special nature of the living conditions in that region. If these special conditions affect the organism for a long time and so intensely that they modify not merely the somatic cells, but also the germ cells, then the peculiar character becomes hereditary, and the totality of the individuals who pass on the peculiar character forms a race unto itself within the species. It can even form a new species in its own right if the modifications go very far. An exact boundary line between race and species can scarcely be determined. . . . Humanity is generally considered as a single species divided into a number of races. . . .

How did the racial differences in man originate? On that question it is only possible to conjecture, as long as we do not know the animal ancestors of mankind. Nevertheless, we can already reject various assumptions as impossible or as at least improbable. The assumption is quite impossible that humanity issued from a single pair. . . . It is inconceivable that a new species developed out of an old one through mere variation of two individuals, both of whom varied in the same way, found each other, and mated, and whose descendants then continued to inbreed in the most rigorous manner, refusing any mating with members of the same species who did not vary in the same way. Diametrically opposed to this assertion is the position that humanity did not originate from a single animal species, the as yet unknown apeman, but that the different human races sprang from different species of apes. [Kautsky quotes Luschan, Völker, Rassen, Sprachen, pp. 23 and 370–71, as opposing this view.] Today we do not yet know the primeval ancestor of man. . . . Yet we may assume that among the animals living today the anthropoid apes are the ones closest to our apish forebears.

No less great is our uncertainty about the region in which we must seek the forebears of man, the apemen. Since we assume that they are very close to the anthropoid apes, it is reasonable to assume that they, like these, were at home in the tropics and . . . in the Old world. [Kautsky then reviews at some length various views on this question, referring to Darwin, Alfred Russell Wallace, Ernst Häckel, Moritz Wagner, Othenio Abel, and Henri Sanielevici, and quoting Luschan, Völker, Rassen, Sprachen, p. 11, and Peschel, The Races of Man, p. 32.] Much as Häckel and Moritz Wagner differ in this regard, they are in agreement in another: they assume that a profound transformation of the earth's surface forced the apemen to abandon their original home and induced them to live in new conditions. Perhaps they were only thereby induced to move about on the ground instead of in trees, to walk upright, to develop their hand and their faculty of speech, and, in association with these, their mental capacities, and thus to approach the state we today designate as human. . . .

CHAPTER TWO

The Migrations

As diverse as these hypotheses [on the apemen's original home] are, they agree insofar as each assumes that man's primeval ancestors migrated . . . in different directions, each of which placed them in different living conditions, so that they had to change in different ways. If men were descended from different species of apes, then this process of emigration into different areas would have had to make the differences between them even greater. It would be impossible that from those circumstances there should ultimately emerge the unity of mankind we can see today in spite of all the divergences. . . .

. . . When external circumstances remain constant, . . . the factors of propagation and destruction balance each other for every species. . . . Only great upheavals in the surface or in the atmosphere of the crust of the earth interrupt this state of equilibrium from time to time in some places or everywhere and produce changes of living conditions that cause some species to die out and induce some or all members of others to emigrate. Such revolutions can have occurred repeatedly in succession. In the case of the ice ages, it has been ascertained that several followed each other. . . . Each one of such revolutions had to induce man again and again to undertake migrations and thereby to increase his division into different races. . . .

Under the pressure of circumstances, he developed so far that he became capable of a new kind of adaptation to changed conditions: adaptation that was not just *active* but also *conscious* and was effected through goal-directed and, to that extent, artificial production of things and circumstances that made the struggle for existence easier for him under the new living conditions. . . . Through his inventions and discoveries and creations, man enters upon a path, on which he himself revolutionizes his living conditions from time to time and disturbs again and again the equilibrium with the environment that had been attained. Compared with the intervals between the various revolutionary changes of the earth, the intervals between technical and other advances of humanity are trifling. In comparison with nature, therefore, human society is constantly in a state of transformation.

Thanks to his technical advances, man is often in a position to diminish the factors of destruction threatening him or enhance those of his propagation, so that he increases in number. The area he inhabits becomes too constricting for him. . . . Technical progress, however, brings not only the necessity but also more possibilities of emigration. It makes it possible for man to live under conditions in which the apeman would have perished. . . .

The emigration of organisms of one area into another does not necessarily have to mean that the immigrants destroy the native species of the latter area and take their place. In most cases a number of the old inhabitants can survive and the immigrants are added to them. . . . Many native life-forms will have to become modified, if they are to be able to cope with the circumstances that have been changed by the immigration. . . . In the course of this process of adaptation, the native forms not equal to it, as well as some of the immigrant forms, will disappear. However, the result will be a nature enriched by new life-forms, that is more diverse than was the earlier nature of the area of emigration as well as of the area of immigration.

And only by this means is a higher evolution of organisms achieved, which is indeed nothing else than an increase of the diversity of life-forms. An increase, on the one hand, of different kinds of organisms within an area, and on the other hand an increase of different kinds of organs within an organism. . . . Today there still exist numerous extremely simple and low-order primitive life-forms, for example, amoebae and bacteria, and they show no signs of dying out. . . . Progress does not consist in the supplanting of lower forms by higher ones, but rather in the fact that the latter are added to the former. Without the lower ones, the higher ones would not be able to live at all.

Much the same holds also for the progress of human society and human knowledge. It, too, does not consist in new institutions or new knowledge supplanting everything that has heretofore existed or been known and in humanity beginning anew each time on a higher level. Progress consists, rather, in the fact that new institutions or knowledge are added to the old ones and thus increase the diversity of society or science. To be sure, this addition means a temporary disruption of the equilibrium in society and in science. Certain institutions or views no longer fit into the new total complex of relationships; they disturb it and have to be transformed and adapted to it or they disappear. Just as higher evolution in the animal world is indicated by petrified skeletons or shells of numerous extinct species, so the development of society or of knowledge is indicated by the remnants of extinct social institutions or views passed on to us.

Yet, as almost all more simple species of animals, from the most primitive on, nevertheless are still represented today and are indispensable for nature's present complex of interrelations, so too there continue to survive in the society and the knowledge of our day forms that have their origin in the primeval era, indeed in our earliest animal ancestors. Those who believe that everything that exists deserves to perish are just as wrong as those who assume that nothing at all changes in the world, that every revolution is mere appearance, that in the history of the world only the actors and the costumes are changed, while the tragedy or comedy they are supposed to perform remains everlastingly the same. In history as in nature, new things and beings are constantly being created, or rather old things and beings are being transformed into new ones, in nature in geological time periods. . . . In the synthesis of the old and the new into a higher unity, some things have to be eliminated, old things as well as new ones, until, united, they yield a harmonious formation that is more diverse and therefore stands at a higher level than the preceding one.

This law must also have held good for man's migrations. But it must have operated differently where he, together with the entire animal world around him was forced to migrate by revolutionary changes of the earth than where only his own progress, such as population growth, made life difficult for him in the district where he had been born and forced some groups of people to migrate. In the first case, all of nature had to change along with man. In the second, it is man alone who enters into new circumstances and changes under their influence. Since, however, the surface of the earth is extremely diverse, man, by spreading out, enters into very different living conditions, which influence his way of life, the way he obtains food, etc., in the most diverse fashion. In the beginning of culture, man is able to protect himself only to a small extent against influences of the environment. . . . He displays, however, a capacity for adaptation that is astonishing. . . .

It may well be assumed that the less human technology is developed, the greater is the effect of the natural milieu on the human organism, but also the slower is technical progress and the greater are the intervals between the individual advances and between the migrations. *[Kautsky quotes Morgan,* Ancient Society, *pp. 39–40, on geometrically accelerating human progress and refers to him and Hauser,* Der Mensch vor 100,000 Jahren, *p. 123, on the age of mankind.]* We have to assume that in early times it must, as a rule, have taken several tens of thousands of years before a human horde came to change its natural milieu and its technology. In this primitive stage, the natural environment could with all its power, as yet almost entirely un-mitigated by technology, operate upon the human organism through long periods of time in every area inhabited by men. At the same time, however, this environment assumed very different forms for the various parts of humanity. Each of these parts remained exposed to its particular environment long enough so that the peculiarity that imprinted itself on it could become firmly established, to such a degree that the special features of this peculiarity were passed on by heredity. Thus were the original races of mankind formed in this primitive stage.

CHAPTER THREE

The Separation of the Races

The distinguishing feature of a race is that it has the tendency to transmit its characteristics unchanged to its descendants even when the milieu in which it lives changes. . . . This unchanged transmission . . . can last through several generations; finally, though, the influences of the new environment have to have a modifying effect on the inherited characteristics, when that environment differs considerably from the earlier one and influences the life of the organism in a palpably different way. . . .

The manner in which a particular milieu affects a race, destroys it, causes it to degenerate or to become more highly developed, does not depend solely on the milieu, but also on the a priori of the racial character. Therefore, two different races can be influenced very differently by the same milieu. That holds good not just for different races, but also for individuals of the same race with different inborn capacities and drives. It is just as wrong to look for the determining cause of a certain behavior of a man exclusively in his environment as it is to look for it exclusively in his physical (including psychic) predisposition. . . . The environment is only one of the factors that determine the form of each organism. The second is the form with all its organs and capacities that the organism has inherited. Inheritance is the conservative factor of evolution, adaptation to changed living conditions the revolutionary factor. The milieu influences every organism, but it influences the different types in different ways. . . .

At first, differences of the races of man were produced by the fact that they had come to live under different conditions. Once different racial types had become established in this way, then each one reacted in a different manner to the same milieu. . . . Thus the migrations finally produced a situation in which there was a greater diversity among the human races than among men's living conditions. Very different races could live under the same conditions.

CHAPTER FOUR
The Mixing of the Races

Up to now . . . we have assumed that men were led by their migrations only into areas not yet inhabited by other men. But that . . . had to occur all the more rarely, the further humanity spread out over the earth. . . .

Due especially to the emergence of articulated language, but also of linguistic differences, and through the influence of kinship terms, common property, etc., the individual hordes turned from loose-knit associations into rigorously closed societies.[1] The migration of some individuals from one horde and their joining of another horde now had to become ever more difficult. . . . Along with the horde becoming closed off, there also emerged its custom of regarding the district it inhabited as a closed one, entry into which was, as a rule, forbidden to strangers. At the same time, there developed the technology not only of tools, but also of weapons, which initially were identical in many cases. For the hunter, the weapon was his preeminent tool. To the mere consumption of fruits, roots, eggs, worms, etc., man now added also that of flesh from mammals, birds, fish, etc. He got used to killing animals in order to feed himself, but also for his protection. . . . Then he finally reached the point where he killed men, too, who did not belong to his horde and who had entered its area without authorization. . . .

But often a horde could not avoid invading the neighboring area when its own area became too confining for it. This must have resulted in a bitter fight between the invaders and the hereditary possessors, which became all the bloodier the further the technology of weapons was developed. Thus war arose from progress in human "civilization," from progress in technology, language, social cohesiveness, from a progress unknown to the apeman as long as he was a "brute beast." Although war is not a universal law of nature, but is confined, in the world of vertebrate animals, to man,

1. On the points made in this and the next paragraph, see also II:3:5–6, above.

and then only to certain phases of his evolution, it is nonetheless a result, in its origins, not of malicious wantonness, but . . . merely of a lack of food or of overpopulation, whatever the causes of these phenomena might be. To them is added the obligation of solidarity, the duty of the community to protect each of its members or, if it is too late for that, to avenge him.

The migrations of early men were always accompanied by wars. At first by wars against their neighbors, who lived under the same conditions and were of the same origin and who hence belonged to the same race in every regard. If the migration continued, though, then it could happen that two tribes of different races encountered each other. That could result in one of the two tribes being annihilated or put to flight. But it could also turn out differently and as a rule it did. . . .

Only rarely does the victor slay all of the vanquished. The ones who wage war are always men. They do not fear women as belligerents, but rather consider them as welcome booty, partly on account of their labor power, partly, if they were young and pretty, because of the sexual pleasures expected from them. They are spared; the victors distribute them among their households. The conquered males are treated less leniently. Those among them capable of bearing arms are dangerous; the others are a burden. As long as the tribes are nomadic, it is also difficult to employ male prisoners of war productively without giving them the opportunity to escape. Nevertheless, in this stage it sometimes also happens that the male prisoners of war are spared. When one's own tribe has . . . lost too many men in battle, then it can seem desirable to fill the gaps with prisoners of war. The widows of the slain may choose from among the prisoners those who are to their liking. These are pardoned, adopted and allotted to the households of their saviors. Both women and men of other races can thus enter into a tribe and produce with it racially mixed offspring.

If the introduction of blood of another race occurs extensively and if the tribe then remains for quite some time in the same conditions and is protected from invasion by other races, then a new race will result from the mixture that at first is based on heredity, not on adaptation, but will, of course, survive only if its capacities are adapted, or are adaptable, to the demands of the environment. The extent to which the peculiar features we observe in the races existing today rest on characteristics acquired through the influence of the environment or such characteristics as sprang from racial mixtures will not always be ascertainable. Certainly the influence of the environment in the formation of races is very great. . . .

If new races arise through the effects of changed living conditions and races become the more diverse the more varied are the living conditions of the individual parts of the human species, the mingling of the races has, on the other hand, also attained an enormous extent. . . .

The races of men are formed in a manner completely different from the races of domestic animals. There are hardly any longer pure human races, neither in the sense of geographical races of animals in their natural state nor in the sense of races of domestic animals created through purposive selection by man and anxiously preserved by him in their purity. *[Kautsky quotes and ridicules a passionate statement by a German "race theoretician" culminating in the question: "If there are noble pigs, why should there not be noble men?" Haiser,* Freimaurer und Gegenmaurer, *p. 72.]*

The more a race has migrated and the more it then, at a higher level of culture, has absorbed racially alien elements into itself through commerce and social intercourse, through assimilation of prisoners of war and slaves, the greater is the racial mixture prevailing in its particular communities, the further removed is that race from racial purity.[2] . . . As a consequence of migrations, of the influence of very different kinds of natural environment, as well as, finally, of the most far-reaching intermingling of races, from one or a few races of apemen there ultimately emerged an immense diversity in the human species. This species is today divided into hundreds of different groups with different congenital features and capacities, each of which reacts to the same stimulus from the environment in particular, sometimes quite different ways. . . . To be sure, these peculiar features of the races and their role in history must not be exaggerated. Essentially, what is common in human nature prevails again and again. But by no means are racial differences entirely without significance for history.

CHAPTER FIVE

The Struggle of the Races as the Driving Force of History

That humanity is divided into different races, each of them different and each intervening in humanity's social development in a different way, was already recognized in early times. More recent theories . . . go far beyond this knowledge. They want to explain the entire history of humanity with reference to the differences and the antagonisms of the races. *[Kautsky then devotes two pages to a critique of Gumplowicz,* Der Rassenkampf, *quoting from pp. 185–86 and 195–96.]* We must reject the theory advanced by Gumplowicz, because it constitutes an inadmissible generalization of individual partial phenomena. However, it is nonetheless to be taken seriously, as it is based upon careful study of these phenomena.[3] . . .

Another race theory is to be taken less seriously, one that, in contrast to

2. Kautsky had dealt with the effects of migration and the intermingling of races in *Are the Jews a Race?*, pp. 51–56.

3. Kautsky had reviewed *Der Rassenkampf* in the year of its publication. "Ein materialistischer Historiker."

Gumplowicz's, has become widespread today. It is older than that of Gumplowicz, but bears all the signs of great juvenility. *[There follow Kautsky's comments, full of irony, on Gobineau,* Essai sur l'inégalité des races humaines, *and H. S. Chamberlain,* Foundations of the Nineteenth Century.*]* Chamberlain saw to the modernization of Gobineau's race theory and clothed it in the necessary Darwinian finery. Naturally, he hastened to take from Darwinism its weakest side, its equation of the races of domestic animals bred by man with the races of wild animals in nature. It did not for one moment dawn on him—nor on others who wrote about human races—that man . . . is neither a domestic animal, whose procreation is directed by a super-animal, nor a wild animal, which is dependent solely on the natural conditions in which it lives.[4] . . .

. . . The superiority of the artificially bred races over the natural races is of a peculiar kind. The former are superior to the latter in the characteristics that make them an object of exploitation for man. Should that also hold true for man? Should in this case, too, those races be the most noble who allow themselves to be exploited most easily, who create the most surplus products for their exploiters? Oh no, where man is concerned, just the reverse is supposed to be the case. Then the most noble races are supposed to be those who understand best the craft of ruling and exploiting; those individuals who are the subjugated and the proletarians thereby demonstrate that they come from inferior races. That our race-theorists are completely sure of. . . .

In the case of men, it becomes the more difficult to ascertain with exactness the membership of individuals in a particular race, the higher the level of their culture is, that is, the more numerous were the migrations and the changes of environment and the mingling of different races that their ancestors went through. A valuation of the various human races would require that not only a precise distinction be made among the races and their characteristics, but also that one know exactly the ends mankind has to serve, for a valuation, that is, a determination of appropriateness to an end presupposes an end by which it is measured.

All of these considerations do not exist for the race-theorists and the politicians, who today fill Germany and its neighboring countries and who influence especially its educated to understand and make history in their way. To solve one of the most difficult problems of modern science, the identification of the different races, their peculiar characteristics and capacities, mere instinct is sufficient for them. And they also find it sufficient for solving, with the greatest possible definiteness, an insoluble problem in the twinkling of an eye: the establishment of a scale of the greater eminence or

4. Some of the points directed at Chamberlain here had already appeared in *Are the Jews a Race?*, pp. 221–25.

meanness of the individual races. . . . The root of this "instinct" . . . is simply the arrogance of the race-theorist's own little self. All of these ladies and gentlemen are told by their "instinct" that the race they themselves belong to is the most eminent in the world, destined to enslave and to exploit the others. . . . This "instinct" is not even something original, but . . . from time immemorial, every people large and small has regarded itself as the crown of creation. . . .

We need not spend more time on this type of conception of history. But we still do have to devote a few words to another conception of history, which is defended by great experts on race and has some things in common with the theory of Professor Gumplowicz mentioned above: the conception that the races of man have always been at war with each other, that these racial struggles constitute the content of history and are inevitable. *[Kautsky names Luschan as holding this view and quotes from his "Anthropological View of Race."]*[5] What he said is still mild in comparison with what others of his colleagues permitted themselves. There is, for example, Professor Sombart. He glorifies war in yet another fashion . . . : " . . . But because all the virtues on which militarism places a high value are fully developed only in war . . . therefore war itself seems to us, who are inspired by militarism, something sacred, *the most sacred thing on earth.*" *[Sombart,* Händler und Helden, *p. 88].* Of course, Sombart also champions the idea of "master races":" . . . the chosen people of these centuries is the German people . . . because it believes in the heroic worldview which alone in this age comprises in itself the divine idea on earth. . . . Just as the bird of the Germans, the eagle, soars high above all the common animals of this earth, so should the German feel himself elevated above all the common peoples that surround him and that he glimpses infinitely far below himself." *[Ibid., pp. 142–43].*

. . . We need not tarry any longer today over the question whether war is something sacred, a blessing for humanity. However, the question must still be considered whether wars have a natural foundation in unavoidable racial antagonisms.

CHAPTER SIX
Racial Antagonisms

As far as we can look back into history, it has always been *organizations* that make war—hordes, tribes, later states. . . . The appearance of language turned the individual hordes of primitive men into closed societies. However, it also increased the possibilities of conscious, systematic cooperation among men, that is, the possibility of organizing them. Organization be-

5. Kautsky had quoted several pages from this paper in *Are the Jews a Race?*, pp. 66–74.

came necessary for production and especially necessary for the fight against menacing opponents, be they predatory animals or organizations of other men with hostile intentions.

It probably hardly ever happened that a belligerent organization coincided with a race. The original hordes were of necessity very small. Each comprised perhaps one to two hundred persons. . . . They probably never consisted of more than five hundred members. The more the means of acquiring food and also the means of transportation were improved, the larger could a tribe become. It is safe to assume, however, that its numbers always remained limited by the necessities of primitive democracy, which knew of no representative constitution. As a rule, a tribe probably did not include more males than a popular assembly under the open sky could encompass.[6] No horde, no tribe could encompass an entire race. Each race was divided into innumerable hordes or tribes. Only when primitive democracy has been overcome by the state are the boundaries of the polity expanded. From that point on, its expansion was restricted only by the limits on the power of the ruling class.[7] If this class was extremely powerful, then it was able to encompass an enormous empire. But even the greatest empire never completely comprehended a race, was never fully coextensive with it. . . . Never, at any time, was a race organized as a polity. For that reason alone a race, as such, was never able to wage war. . . .

All causes of war[8] give rise to hostilities between *neighbors*. Fighting against one's neighbor is the usual form war takes. . . . Seafaring navigation does not invalidate this principle. . . . It only expands, in comparison with landlocked countries, the notion of neighbor, which depends on the shape of the sea and the level of naval technology. . . . Until the present day, it has as a rule been one's neighbor against whom war has been waged. And until the emergence of the gigantic empires and oceanic navigation, he usually belonged to the same race . . . as his opponent. . . . But even in all the instances *[where people of different races fought each other]*, never did two races fight against one another en bloc;[9] and, even in these circumstances, a tribe belonging to the one race did not always fight only against tribes of the other race, but sometimes also, indeed here and there just as often and just as bitterly, against tribes of its own race. . . .

Why should different races have to make war against each other? Wherein does their "natural" antagonism consist? Admittedly, some races have features repugnant to others. The ideal of physical beauty of people of one

---

6. See also IV:3:5, below.

7. See the section entitled "The First States," below, esp. IV:3:7–8.

8. See II:3:6, above, and III:2:14, IV:2:4 and IV:3:7–8, below.

9. The same point is made, using illustrations similar to those omitted in the present edition, in *Are the Jews a Race?*, pp. 82–88.

race is always formed on the model of these people themselves. What we are unaccustomed to easily strikes us as odd, indeed as repulsive. . . . No doubt, there are racial antagonisms based on inborn characteristics. But they all reduce to *aesthetic* antagonisms. . . . From them, however, wars have never yet arisen. Regardless of how the technology of war might change, war has been from the outset something frightfully serious, always a matter of life and death. . . . How are such conflicts of interests supposed to spring from the inborn aesthetic peculiarities of the races? And yet that would have to be the case if the struggle among the races were to be a natural necessity and, more than that, a general, constant natural necessity, the motive force of history. That would only be possible if the various races were naturally divided into superior and inferior races, into those who were born to rule and those who were born to serve. Then, to be sure, the efforts of the former to subjugate the latter, and the endeavor of the latter to fight off the former, hence the struggle among the races, would be given by nature.

CHAPTER SEVEN

Superior and Inferior Races

Even if we assume, as the great majority of ethnologists does today, that mankind is descended from only a single species, it nevertheless can easily be assumed that the different races into which the species split developed their cognitive faculty, their intelligence, in different ways under the different conditions of their evolution they happened to come into. Thus we could distinguish between races that are by nature capable of accomplishing more mentally and others that display lower mental abilities. The question of whether or not this is true must not be confused with the question of whether the knowledge individual races have achieved is of a higher level than that of other races. It is self-evident that this is the case. . . . Only it would be more correct to speak in this connection of *peoples*, not of *races*. For within one and the same race there are different peoples with very different degrees of knowledge; in the same way, there are different individuals with varying knowledge within one and the same people if the latter is relatively highly developed. Here, where we are treating of *race* and thus of *inborn* characteristics and capacities, we do not speak of this knowledge that can be acquired and therefore can be very different in individuals of the same ability.

Now, it is in keeping with the theory of evolution that we assume that there are by nature intellectually lower and intellectually higher races. Not in the sense of the race-theorists discussed above, who assume higher intellectual talents in the ones and lower ones in the others from the beginning, but rather in the sense of evolutionary theory. In addition to the hand, the most important organ through which man rose above his animal ancestors was the brain. The development of man must have had as a consequence a higher development of his brain, just as this then must in turn have promoted his further development in other respects. Races less advanced in their evolution, one should then think, must therefore also have a less developed brain. To be sure, one would then have to assume that their backwardness was due solely to unfavorable conditions of development. If the backward races were placed in better conditions, then their brain would also develop better and finally become the equal of the brain of the best-developed peoples.

Now this conception ran into a number of remarkable facts. *[Kautsky quotes reports of members of primitive tribes achieving high educational attainments from Luschan,* Völker, Rassen, Sprachen, *pp. 42 and 374; Peschel,* The Races of Man, *pp. 152–53; and Myers, "On the Permanence of Racial Mental Differences," p. 77; and he concludes with these words by Preuss,* Die geistige Kultur der Naturvölker, *p. 3:]*

> In point of fact, the apparently meager advances (of the primitive peoples) already contain the application of almost all the capacities of thinking and feeling our culture has brought forth. The best proof for that is the fact that, given the same education in the same environment, accompanied by complete separation from their native land at an early age, the educability of individuals from the primitive peoples does not appear to be less on the average than that of whites.[10]

But how is this fact to be reconciled with the theory of evolution? Do not the primitive peoples represent the lowest, the civilized peoples the highest level of man's development, not merely as a social being, but also as a natural being? It appears that this is not the case, after all. We are led to this conclusion by another phenomenon, in addition to the facts just mentioned: the evolution of language.

We must assume that human language developed from a few natural sounds, in part sounds connected with sensation, in part imperatives.... The vocabulary can have grown only slowly, and the different forms of the same word used to designate different circumstances of the same object or process can have emerged only slowly. From the outset, therefore, one would have to assume that the languages of the most highly developed peoples are the richest in words and forms, that they become increasingly poorer the further back in culture we go. In reality, the exact opposite is the case. The wealth of words and forms that is exhibited by the languages of the most primitive peoples is nothing short of incredible. *[Kautsky quotes illustrations from Geiger,* Ursprung und Entwicklung, *I, 376, 385, and Müller,* Lectures on the Science of Language, *p. 400, and then rejects their explanation*

---

10. Preuss supports this statement with a reference to Boas, *The Mind of Primitive Man*, pp. 120–23.

*of the progressive impoverishment of languages (Geiger, I, 377, Müller, I, 400).
Referring to Lévy-Bruhl,* How Natives Think, *pp. 138–39, 146, he asks:]*
Where does this apparent retrogression come from? It comes about because
the function of language has changed.

Primitive man is an acute observer. He sees all the details, all of their
connections, as far as they can be recognized with his primitive means. But
the art of abstraction is as yet little developed. He sees only the particular,
not the general. He has words for every detail, none for more general
concepts. . . . *[The]* change in the function of language is evidently connected with a change in the nature of mental life, which is in turn conditioned
by the advances of technology. Each of these broadens man's horizon, makes
accessible to him new relationships that . . . call for causal explanation. When
such explanations cannot be immediately found in a sober manner, then
the imagination, powerfully stimulated by every new phenomenon, is called
on for help. Art and mysticism are strongly developed; they flourish
together.

Alongside these, however, positive knowledge nevertheless increases,
and on the other hand the material that is the object of knowledge grows
so much that it requires ordering even more urgently, and the contradictions
between the world as it is thought to be and the world as it really is and
the contradictions between different mental constructs become ever more
blatant. The felt need for classification and abstraction as well as for discovering and overcoming the contradictions in thought . . . becomes increasingly keen; the apparatuses of criticism and of abstraction become ever
more perfect. On the other hand, technical progress makes men less dependent on nature, especially in cities, so that they find it less and less
necessary to observe nature for the purposes of their everyday life. The
simple observation of nature through the senses by the ordinary man recedes
more and more; it is increasingly replaced by the observation of individual
specialists for scientific purposes, with apparatuses that strengthen the senses. All of that has the effect that the progress of civilization promotes sober
and scientific thinking more than artistic feeling and observation. . . . This
change in the process of thought seems to us to be the most plausible
explanation of the impoverishment or simplification of language as civilization advances. . . .

No matter how one might explain the course of linguistic development,
. . . there is no doubt about the surprising abundance of forms in the languages of primitive peoples in comparison with the written languages of
the civilized peoples. Still, it is not possible that language could have originated in any other way than out of a very few primitive sounds and slowly
grew to its richness in the course of its development. The length of this
evolutionary process must have been enormous; it might have gone on for
millions of years. . . .

Nothing could be more mistaken than the belief that the difference between low-level peoples and those at the highest level among the present-day civilized peoples encompasses the whole range of human evolution, from its starting point onward to the highest pinnacle it has reached hitherto. The high degree of development of language among even the most backward of the peoples still existing today proves that they all have behind them an enormous labor of cultural growth. This labor developed their mental powers so highly that what the further development of civilization might have added in the way of intellectual dispositions that become hereditary remained insignificant and was insufficient to establish in the civilized peoples a lasting superiority of their mental powers vis-à-vis the primitive peoples.

Class and the Faculty of Thought

Now, there is a serious reservation about the assumption that civilized peoples do not exhibit any inborn higher aptitudes in comparison with primitive peoples. The mode of thinking in the stage of higher-level civilization is . . . a different one than in the preceding stages. . . . A change of the function of an organ must, however, also modify this organ itself. How should it be possible, then, that the organ of thought in civilized peoples is not significantly different from that in primitive peoples? . . . This seemingly reasonable consideration is invalidated by several moments: the brevity of the period of time in which a people has hitherto been able to live as a civilized one and the separation of the classes and of the social functions of the sexes within the civilized peoples.

The high degree of perfection of language we find among savages bears witness to the immense span of time that must have passed before these people arrived at their present state from the stage of their original lack of language. . . . In this tremendously long period, man's languages, and along with them his organ of thought, developed to the high level we can observe today. . . . The time span . . . encompassing what we today consider the history of humanity was, in contrast, a quite short one. If humanity needed hundreds of thousands, perhaps millions of years to reach the level of present-day savages, the state of higher-level culture we call civilization . . . can be measured up to now, at most, in thousands of years for a single people. . . . That is a short span of time for the modification of an organ through its altered use, a modification that goes so deep as to affect the germ plasm and to become hereditary. For that reason alone it should not be surprising at all if a more advanced hereditary faculty of thought cannot be ascertained in civilized peoples than in backward peoples.

In this connection the following appears to be even more important,

however. What we call higher-level culture or civilization is formed simultaneously with the state and . . . classes. Under these conditions, every
people is divided into an exploiting minority and an exploited majority.
The latter has to supply the livelihood for the former; it must therefore
apply a much greater portion of its lifetime to mechanical work than it
would have to if it labored only for itself. At the same time, however, the
progress of technology has the effect of giving an increasingly monotonous
form to the individual's work.

The savage must know how to make everything that is required for his
and his society's preservation. A division of labor is unknown to him, except
for that between man and woman. That fact makes his work productive
only to a small degree, but makes it infinitely varied and provides his mind
at every moment with a different problem on which he must reflect. The
division of labor that already begins at an early time has the tendency . . .
to give a more monotonous form to the tasks set for the individual. However, this is made up for, on the one hand, by the fact that, along with the
growth of the productivity of labor, man's wants grow and become more
diverse, the horizon of the individual societies expands, and knowledge
becomes more varied; on the other hand, by the fact that, as the productivity
of labor increases, man may, if he forgoes a corresponding increase of his
wants, limit the necessary labor time, that is, the time he must expend for
the satisfaction of his wants. He thereby gains leisure time and the possibility
of occupying his mind with the most varied, freely chosen problems and
in that way to develop it.

This process is interrupted by the formation of classes. As soon as the
possibility arises for one part of a people to live by forcing the other part
to surrender to it the excess of the product of its labor beyond what it needs
for its bare subsistence, there then also arises the strong urge to increase
this excess, that is, to extend the labor time of the working classes. From
that point on, the progress of technology becomes ever more disastrous for
the intellectual life of the working classes. . . . That was already true for the
peasants, especially for the serfs among them, and for many urban artisans.
This tendency reaches its culmination in the proletariat of capitalist industry.

This also expresses itself in language. We have seen that the progress of
abstract thinking leads to the impoverishment of language. However, this
effect is brought about to an even greater degree by the constriction of the
horizon of the working population in a society divided into classes. . . .
Civilization reduces the working classes to the possession of a small fragment of the national language. . . .

Monotony is not confined to the process of production; it also affects
the products. Technical progress means mass production; its consummation
is production by machines. In the case of primitive production, the individual works with a few tools, alone or with some comrades, in his own
way, according to his own needs, for himself, for his family, for his working

comrades. And every horde, every tribe, every community works for itself in its own manner. Under these circumstances, there is a plethora of distinctive costumes, ornaments, and architectural styles. Every utensil, every tool, every piece of furniture is uniquely fashioned. Advancing civilization brings mass production, the production of fewer types for the whole world.

This impoverishment of the forms of industrial production, too, goes . . . hand in hand with the impoverishment of language. Each of these simplifications means an increasing economization of time and power. The civilized languages, with their abstract terms, permit more rapid communication and are also easier to learn than the complicated forms of the primitive languages that take every detail into consideration. The economic significance of the production of fewer types instead of individualizing production is well known. But the mind is certainly less stimulated by the monotony of mass production . . . than by the immense diversity of the products of handicraft. For the exploiting classes, this mind-paralyzing effect of mass production can be undone through artistic luxury, which is not governed by economic motives, and also by journeys to foreign regions. This compensation is not available to the working classes. . . .

Fortunately, the most pronounced phenomena of this kind are too recent to have been able to become hereditary features and to form a new race of subhumans. The intellectual power of the proletariat has remained undamaged. To be sure, it could develop only little under the conditions of existence of capitalism. Nonetheless, the working class has already begun to conquer new possibilities of mental activity for itself. *[It has done so]* not through change of the technology of production—that will continue to be monotonous and may become even more monotonous—but, through the shortening of the working day and through efficient utilization of the newly gained free time. *[It can use that time,]* on the one hand, for a return to nature, that is, to recover many of the stimuli that shaped the mind of the savage; . . . on the other hand, for participation in the intellectually elevating effects of culture that have until now been denied to the working masses. Primitive democracy was restricted to the tribe or the community. Modern democracy compels the working classes to concern themselves with the problems of an extensive state, indeed, with those of the world. . . .

The fighting proletariat is on the verge of conquering, for itself and for the working classes in general, the possibility of participation in this elevation of intellectual life. That is one of its most important historical tasks, just as important as the transformation of the process of production through its socialization. The two tasks are intimately linked with one another.

It has been a great mistake on the part of the majority of socialists concerned with agrarian policy up to now that they have paid no attention to this circumstance. They always investigate only which form and size of the enterprise yields the most product per hectare of ground; they do not consider what expenditure of labor this product requires and do not ask which kind of enterprise permits the greatest freedom of the agricultural worker from his drudgery and allows him to take part in intellectual labor of a higher level. . . . Only when this question has been successfully answered will it be possible to retain substantial masses of workers in agriculture and to assure its most efficient, most intensive operation and thus sufficient food for the whole nation. Then it will be recognized what a barbarous institution the small family farm is, which transforms the agriculturalist's every waking hour into working time, and that only large-scale agricultural operation permits a diminution of the agricultural workers' working time, without impairing production.[11] . . .

If the proletarian movement takes hold of the entire mass of the people, the more intense and more diverse activity of the mind that must then become universal may well ultimately cause the mental capacity of the whole of civilized humanity to reach a higher level, as it has happened up to now only in exceptional cases. The result could seem to be a race of supermen. But they would be supermen only in comparison with humanity as it has been hitherto. They will not constitute a race superior to other human races. For the proletariat of one country cannot permanently assume a privileged position. Each of its advances is endangered in its continued existence if it is confined only to one country and does not ultimately benefit the working classes of all countries.

The mental qualities of supermen can become hereditary ones only when civilized humanity based on socialism has become identical with mankind in general. . . . It will be quite a while before that happens. Even if we see the coming of socialist production in particular areas ever so close at hand, its general diffusion and the resulting endowment of mankind with new hereditary characteristics will necessarily take many generations. . . .

As we shall see, the state and class rule were formed and maintained by martial power. Freed from care about obtaining their livelihood through productive work, the greatest part of the ruling classes devoted themselves for a long time almost exclusively to warfare and to hunting. These activities they had in common with the savages. They were, in any case, not only more exciting but also more stimulating, richer in diverse incidents, than were the labors of a peasant or a shoemaker or a tailor. But they made no greater demands on the aristocrat's mental powers than the activity of the savages did on their mental powers. Indeed, hunting made mostly smaller demands, for it was carried on merely for the sake of pleasure, not for gaining a livelihood; hence it was engaged in only when and where the conditions were favorable for it. It was conducted with better weapons than among the savages and

---

11. See III:3:5, below, and the accompanying footnote 10 on agrarian policy.

was directed to only a very few kinds of animals considered worthy of the honor of being hunted by noble lords.

Warfare had a different effect! The development of weapons technology made the composition of armies more diverse. The development of transportation made them more extensive. Both required of the commander greater intellectual qualities and posed more varied tasks for him. But this same development often transformed the mass of warriors into mere machines directed by the commander at will. And the system of standing armies placed the soldiers in peace time in a state of mind-deadening boredom. These circumstances, too, did not advance the life of the mind.

In addition to hunting and warfare, there were, to be sure, other activities of the ruling and exploiting classes that did more to develop the mind. They had to administer quite large areas with a numerous population and to maintain relations of various kinds with foreign countries. Above all, though, they gained leisure time they could employ for the purpose of devoting themselves exclusively to mental labor, be it artistic or scientific. However, this leisure time could also be made use of by them in another way, for excesses *in Baccho et Venere*, in "wine and love," and everywhere the majority of the rulers ultimately preferred the life of pleasure to intellectual labor. From this state of affairs, too, there could not come an elevation of mental abilities.

Under certain circumstances, however, there arises a special stratum of intellectuals who are devoted exclusively to mental labor. Either it belongs to the ruling classes and is privileged; then it seeks artificially to preserve its privileged position for itself and its descendants. It closes itself off from the rest of the population as a special caste or a special estate: as a priesthood. In this case, its entire legitimate progeny belongs to the priesthood, whether it is intellectually qualified for it or not. Fending off all competition from the outside and retaining the less gifted, it easily rigidfies in mindless outward appearances, in anxiously preserved formulaic rubbish, which even an intellectual pauper can master and by which he can set himself off from the profane multitude. There, too, dullness of mind is finally triumphant. . . .

Intellectuals represent an enduring, higher life of the mind only when they do not constitute a privileged class, when they are recruited from the most talented individuals of all classes, who have to train and to prove their mental powers in the keen struggle for existence of ideas. This condition does not yet exist anywhere in complete purity. Everywhere the power of the state and other influences strive, at least within the stratum of intellectuals, to privilege certain professions or kinds of activity and to reserve these privileged positions even for the less gifted members of some families, to make them hereditary in these families.

The more this is achieved in a particular domain of intellectual work, the more does it become mired down in formalism and dogmatism. . . .

CHAPTER NINE

Sex and the Faculty of Thought

Among the factors that prevent the higher-level intellectual powers in class society from becoming universal hereditary racial characteristics and from thereby raising, with respect to natural endowment, the civilized peoples in their entirety above the primitive peoples, the most effective one is . . . the *intellectual abasement of women* by technical progress. The division of labor between men and women began at an early time, . . . as soon as the development of technology made of men hunters and warriors who set out on various undertakings, while women stay in the camp or in its vicinity. . . . The further technology advances, the more are women, until recently, reduced to household labors. In the nomadic age, they must still take part in the horde's migrations and thus often in its battles, too, even if mostly only as spectators. As soon as human beings become sedentary, the women, at least the great majority of them, never get beyond the limits of the village.[12]

They would certainly be mistaken who believe that the unremitting confinement of women in straitened circumstances must make of them creatures who are by "nature," that is, on account of inherited qualities, mentally inferior. . . . Where, as a result of social conditions, men's intelligence is more developed than women's, the high level of male intelligence, insofar as it is transmitted by heredity, must benefit the daughters just as much as the sons and at least have the consequence that the female progeny suffers no diminution of mental powers. But the deficient development of these powers in women under the given circumstances will, in turn, see to it that the male progeny do not enter the world all too gifted. The result will be that, in the course of the development of civilization, the innate powers of intelligence are not markedly changed either in women or in men.

Only in our own day is a development beginning, as with regard to the working classes so with regard to women, that promises a fundamental transformation. The development of technology is now finally so advanced that it no longer chains women to the house, but opens up to them occupational activities outside the home. On the other hand, it

---

12. See also II:4:3, above.

is so advanced that it can reduce work in the home to a minimum. In a class society, this has the result, of course, that the women of the laboring classes must take on work to earn money, in addition to their household work, so that they are doubly burdened, whereas the women of the exploiting classes can more than ever devote their entire time to a vacuous life of pleasure.

There are already indications, however, that the struggle of the proletariat for more leisure time finally benefits its women, too. Only thereby will that intellectually elevating development we see growing out of this struggle become universal and only thereby will it become possible that a race of men will emerge, equipped from birth with higher mental endowment—through the emancipation of the proletariat and of women. For the time being, though, we can only have a presentiment of this advance. . . .

We have seen how questionable the conception of history is that sees the motor force of history in the struggle of superior against inferior races. The conception of history has proved to be no less false that holds that the course of history is conditioned by the progress of the cognitive capacity, of innate reason. This view assumes that earlier, men were irrational; therefore they were contented with extremely irrational social institutions. But reason is said to have the property of growing, and the greater it is, the better must men recognize what is advantageous to them and the more easily must they institute a reasonable society.

There is no doubt that man's high mental position in nature is founded for the greatest part on the superiority of his mental abilities over those of animals. But this superiority arose in eras from which we know absolutely nothing about man's development. The peoples that are at a low level today are, like those at the highest level, products of the same course of development. Their cultural backwardness is neither due to an inborn mental inferiority nor need it have such an inferiority as its consequence.

What lifts civilized man above so-called primitive men is not higher *mental endowment*, but rather his *technology*. His technology of *production*, which increases enormously what he knows, as well as his technology of *thought*, which has grown no less astonishingly than that of production. One need consider only the tremendous advances of mathematics, the most powerful aid for the ordering of phenomena, whose affinity with the technology of the means of production is sufficiently demonstrated by the fact that quite a large number of mathematical operations are performed with more certainty and more rapidly by machines than in the human brain. And, in addition, there is the technique of recording information in writing, the infinite wealth of methods and of implements for research in the most diverse areas. Here, and not in the capability of our reason, is the cause of the immense intellectual gulf between us and the primitive peoples. . . .

Special Endowments of the Races

The cultural backwardness of a people thus does not at all mean that it is by nature less gifted than the peoples at a higher level of development. However, one may certainly assume that the different races are endowed in different ways. It would be odd if races differed from one another merely in external physical features and not also in mental abilities and proclivities. It is impossible to measure such qualitatively different features against each other, to assess them as being higher or lower. . . . Thus one cannot, for example, determine if musical ability is of a higher order than the ability to paint artistically or if mathematical gifts are superior to linguistic ones, etc. . . . The hereditary differences that may exist between the mental natures of different races do not at all mean that some are superior to others. . . .

Even though one cannot establish a hierarchy among the races according to their endowments, however, they are nevertheless different not only as regards skin color, skull shape, etc., but also with respect to mental abilities and to character. As a consequence, different races can react to the same stimulus or impetus with very different behavior. We observed above that the same milieu can influence the *forms* of different species of organisms in very different ways. The same is of course also true for the *behavior* of individuals of different races. . . . Naturally, that must necessarily influence very strongly the course of history and confer on the historical development of each race a particular character.

Theory compels us to make this assumption. But up to now the practice of historical research has been able to derive only scant profit from it. Even the distinction of the races according to physical features is not always easy, in view of the great variability of the human species. This variability is, however, especially great with respect to mental features, which are, furthermore, far more difficult to establish than the physical ones. The more highly developed a people is, the more migrations and miscegenations it has gone through and the further advanced are the division of labor in it and its breakdown into different occupations and classes, all the more difficult will it be to ascertain its national character, the greater are the differences of its individual members among themselves, the more strongly is innate character concealed by social traditions and conventions. . . .

What we know about the mental nature of an individual, we conclude only from his reaction to external stimuli. Our judgment of a particular person thus does not depend solely on his or her nature but also on the conditions in which we encounter that person. The same holds true for peoples as for individuals. *[Kautsky quotes with approval Goldstein,* Rasse und

Politik, *pp. 81–82, on the impossibility of identifying racial characteristics with any precision.]* The decisiveness with which judgments about racial psychology are still being made today even by very learned gentlemen is therefore nothing less than lofty wisdom. The World War brought this madness to its peak. *[Kautsky refers to and quotes from Sombart,* Händler und Helden, *p. 18, who, in 1915, had argued that]* any Englishman of any significance was not truly English. *[Carlyle was spiritually German, and Ruskin, Wilde, and Shaw were Irish.]*

The formation of a man's character by his environment must not be lumped together with the *manifestation* of his character in its reaction to the influences of the environment. The character will be recognized the more completely in its manifestation, the more the often fleeting situations vary that provoke its activation. In all of these diverse and sometimes contradictory activities, it is always the same already formed character that reveals itself. The formation of the character by the living conditions, in which the individual must maintain himself, is quite a different matter. Here we find that those factors of the external world are determinative to the greatest degree for the formation of the character that continuously exert influence on it in the same manner and thereby modify it so that it emerges from the process different from when it entered into it. Characteristics acquired in this way need not by any means necessarily become hereditary and thus constitutive of races. Only under certain conditions will this happen.

A clear distinction must be drawn between the acquired and the inherited character, in the case of peoples as well as of individuals. It is only the inherited character that appears as an a priori at the beginning of their historical development and becomes determinative of its particular nature. The acquired character, on the other hand, is the result of that development. Its particular nature presupposes a certain historical process. It cannot explain this process. However, both kinds of character in combination constitute in a people what is called its national character. If it is enormously difficult precisely to establish the national character even of a civilized people at a given time, the attempt has not even been made to investigate for any people how much of its national character during a certain period of time must be attributed to the influence of race and how much to the living conditions obtained then. Therefore, even if we must theoretically acknowledge that race is important for the course of history, we are today not yet able to ascertain this importance in concrete cases. For that reason, race has been of hardly any use to historiography, as has national character, too.[13]

---

13. Kautsky had made this point with reference to national character in *Nationalität und Internationalität*, pp. 4–6.

"National Character" in Historiography

Nevertheless, there are few historians who do not operate with national character as if it were the simplest, most obvious fact in the world, from which the deepest historical insights were to be drawn with the greatest certainty. The method used is certainly astonishingly convenient. You examine what a nation has accomplished and what it has not accomplished. From that you conclude that it accomplished the one because it had a gift for it and that it failed with regard to the other because it lacked the natural talent for it.

Now, it must be granted, as a matter of course, that a nation could accomplish only a particular thing if it had a gift for it. Without the necessary juridical talent, the jurists of the Roman nation, for instance, would not have been able to create the Roman law. But that fact is far from being sufficient to explain the creation of Roman law. That would be the case only if it were certain that no other people ever exhibited a similar talent, something that no one has yet undertaken to establish.

If other nations had had the same juridical talent without creating a Roman law, then that could be due only to the fact that the historical conditions in which they lived were different from those of the Romans. Thus one would first have to investigate the conditions from which that law sprang. Only if it should clearly prove to be the case that Roman law cannot be explained by them, would one be justified in assuming that it is a matter here of a special, inherited talent, proper only to the Roman nation. Of course, then the embarrassing question would arise of who had passed on this talent, which race had succeeded, even in the state of savagery, in acquiring that peculiar talent for the creation of a law that is suitable only for civilized nations. Yet it is not even known for certain which nations and races took part in the creation of Roman law. *[Kautsky then shows at some length that men of many different nationalities and races contributed to the formulation of Roman law, quoting Niebuhr,* Lectures on the History of Rome, *pp. 725–26, and Seeck,* Geschichte des Untergangs der antiken Welt, *VI, 131.]*

If special accomplishments are supposed to be the result of a people's outstanding talents, then the accomplishments would have to appear with that particular nation and disappear again only when it itself does. That, however, is not always the case by any means. *[Kautsky points out that the flowering of Arab culture—to which non-Arabs, like Jews, Greeks, and Persians contributed—lasted only a few centuries and that the great achievements of the Athenians were attained in a single century.]* In light of this fact, it is surely impossible to ascribe their accomplishments in that one century to an innate genius of the race, which was the same before and afterwards, and not to particular conditions of existence, which were created in the time of the Persian Wars and destroyed by the Peloponnesian War.

Oddest of all seems that conception which attributes to a special national endowment not merely progress but also its absence at a certain stage of development. *[Partly by quoting with approval Robertson,* The Evolution of States, *pp. 59–60, Kautsky attacks Friedrich Ratzel for stating that "Nature has given the Chinese the organs for discovering all that is useful to them but not for going any further" and that this "is the sole cause of the rigidity in their social system." Ratzel,* The History of Mankind, *I, 26.]* If it is already odd to explain the historical achievements of a certain people by recourse to a special inborn talent for them, then it is nothing short of ridiculous to trace everything that a people has not accomplished without further ado back to a lack of endowment for it, without asking whether the preconditions were at all given, without which the achievement in question is completely impossible. . . .

Almost at the same time in which Ratzel's *History of Mankind* appeared (1885), I published an article, "Die chinesischen Eisenbahnen und das europäische Proletariat," in *Die Neue Zeit. [Kautsky quotes from p. 542.]* As the materialist conception of history led me to investigate the Chinese mode of production and made it possible for me to uncover in the economic conditions the foundation of Chinese conservatism, it also enabled me to see in this conservatism not a law of nature but a transitory phase that would be overcome through a change of the mode of production. It seemed to me that the penetration of the railway system into China was inevitable. As a consequence, the enormous realm would necessarily be opened up to progress: "It is the tools of European civilization, above all the railways, that are setting in motion and revolutionizing the gigantic, inert masses of the Chinese people that have long lain immobile" (p. 547). At the same time when the great anthropogeographer Ratzel attempted to establish scientifically the natural disposition of the Chinese people to immobility, I was already able, thanks to the materialist conception of history, to see the Chinese revolution coming and to establish its inevitability. That is one of the successful Marxist prophecies from which I deduce the superiority of the materialist conception of history over conceptions of the struggle between races and of the innate "national soul." . . .

All the theories of race that explained the alleged rigidity *[of the entire Orient]* by innate endowments or deficiencies have dissolved into smoke, a fate that must necessarily sooner or later overtake every theory that considers a given momentary state as a permanent one and, instead of investigating its transient causes, simply presupposes as a given immutable cause that which must be investigated.

No people has developed all by itself. Early on, the different polities enter into relations of very diverse kinds with one another. Not all of these polities have undergone the same development. . . . So some can learn from others. . . . Frequently, though, that occurs unconsciously. . . . It is not always easy, often not at all possible, to ascertain exactly what one nation owes to another. In these circumstances, drawing conclusions from the achievements of a people as to its natural endowment can lead to the worst acts of arbitrariness; national rancor can run wild without hindrance. That, in addition to the great convenience of this method, which from the outset contains all answers to all historical problems, is doubtless an important reason why many historians are so glad to apply it.

For the German *[historians]* there are two objects in particular, two "races," as they assume, that are especially loathsome to them, the Semites and the Celts, whom they regard as the ancestors of the French. The less one knows about the peoples of these two language families, the greater is the certitude with which one condemns them. Spiegel, in his *Eranische Alterthumskunde*, denies to the Semites any and all capacity for art (except music), science, and politics. . . . Only for religion are the Semites supposed to be especially gifted. Chamberlain, on the other hand, denies to the Jews any religious talent. According to him, they are inferior in this regard even to some Negroes and Australians. The Celts are judged with the same arbitrariness as the Semites. *[Kautsky quotes Mommsen, The History of Rome, I, 419–20, 422, who wrote of the "Celtic nation":]* "With various solid qualities and still more that were brilliant, it was deficient in those deeper moral and political qualifications which lie at the root of all that is good and great in human development." Explanation: "Nowhere did they create a great state or develop a distinctive culture of their own."[14] Therefore they must have lacked the natural gift to do so. Is that not clear? *[Kautsky then argues that the Germanic tribes, too, could not create lasting states until they, especially the Franks, learned to ally themselves with the "Roman-Celtic" clergy of the Catholic church.]*

CHAPTER TWELVE

"National Character"—A Mystery

It is quite remarkable how disastrously the view that history can be explained by the particular endowment of the different nations has affected even extremely acute scholars. *[After returning to the attack on Mommsen for not even trying to explain how the Celts acquired their peculiar undesirable characteristics, Kautsky turns on Meyer, Geschichte des Altertums, I/1, 82–85, and*

---

14. See also a different translation in the abridged edition, pp. 78, 79. Both editions render "staatlich" as "political," but Mommsen's term "staatliche Anlage" suggests an inborn talent to create states.

Troeltsch, Der Historismus, *p. 38, who had stated that national character must be accepted as given and not subject to explanation by the historian.]*

Where the traditional conception of history believes that it has found something inexplicable, which nevertheless is supposed to explain all historical processes, there the materialist conception of history sees a problem, but not an insoluble one, rather a problem for the solution of which it urgently calls and points out the ways. While the preponderant part of the traditional conceptions of history diverts the researcher from this labor, discourages him and spurs him on to seek the basis of his science in airy fantasies, the materialist conception of history calls him to industrious, positive labor, to work to lay bare all external conditions that had an influence on the particular historical development with which the historian is concerned.

To be sure, as regards this development, it is not merely a matter of the external conditions in which the particular people being studied lived during the period of time under investigation. . . . They are one side of the historical process. The other side is the mental makeup, the sum total of the endowments and the knowledge with which the people enters into the process. This sum total is far from being a mystery, however; it is rather a product of the same people's living conditions in earlier ages, conditions that continue to exert an influence, partly as traditions, partly as racial characteristics that have become hereditary, and that, in combination with the conditions of a particular present, constitute that which is called the national character, insofar as the latter is something more than a fiction. Inherited character, then traditions that are passed down from the past, as well as, lastly, the influences of the present—those are the sources out of whose confluence there emerges the character of an individual and, in the same way, the character of a nation, to the extent that each of these three factors affects its individual members equally.

The easiest one among them to establish is that of the external conditions of the present, especially if it is the present of the historian himself, so that he does not have to reconstruct it out of material from the past, but can examine it through direct observation. It is more difficult to distinguish between the influences of tradition and those of race and to investigate the development of each of these two factors separately. It is usually extremely difficult to establish the mental racial character of a people in the present. It is quite impossible most of the time to determine the external conditions of the misty remote past in which it took form. Not, however, because the evolution of the race and of its characteristics is an impenetrable mystery, but rather because all of the required evidence for doing so is lacking. However, . . . scientific research may yet develop methods and reveal facts that afford us quite unexpected insights.

For the time being, though, the historical process will already be elucidated in a high degree when we have shed light on how it is influenced by the external conditions of the particular present and by the precipitate that the external conditions of the past have produced in the form of outlooks and institutions that were handed down to that present and can be ascertained in it. The unity of the human species is so very pronounced and the variability and adaptive capacity of the human psyche is so great that the portion of the historical process will be relatively insignificant that might still remain in the dark after this labor of illumination—remain there because it can only be explained by a racial peculiarity, the development of which could not yet be explained. In those cases where we do not yet know anything, however, we should openly admit our ignorance, in order thereby to stimulate further research. We should not, on the one hand, in order to deter research, declare that the limits of our knowledge at any particular time cannot be transcended and, on the other hand, elevate what has been represented as unresearched and unresearchable to a basis for the boldest assertions. And least of all should we proclaim these fictitious constructions to be the decisive moments of our science.

CHAPTER THIRTEEN

Racial Ties of Blood

For the sake of completeness, not because we have something new to say in this regard, let us, before we take leave of race, turn our attention briefly to another of the many inanities in which the application of racial theoretics in historiography is so rich.

This theoretics assumes a priori, and without further investigation and justification, not only that the different races as such are and must be hostile to each other, but also that the members of a race all feel themselves from the first closely attached to each other; closely attached by "natural ties," those of blood. This assumption is based on two presuppositions: first, that all members of a race are related by blood, even if only very distantly; and second, that relatives naturally constitute a community of thought, feeling, and volition. We have already demonstrated in other connections that both presuppositions are untrue. . . .

Even if a race of primeval origin were really descended only from a single individual,[15] and not from numerous individuals living alongside one another in the same conditions, and if all present-day human races were pure and not mixed to a high degree, as is mostly the case, even then having the same blood in common would still be insufficient by far to result in bonds of quite close intimacy. A natural intimate attachment due to sharing the same blood only results, as a rule, between mother and child; rarely

---

15. Kautsky had dealt with this "naive conception" in *Are the Jews a Race?*, pp. 44–46.

between father and child. In the case of man and presumably also of his animal forebears, we find no such natural tie. The indifference of most men toward their illegitimate children bears sufficient witness to that. . . . But even the often very close relationship between mother and child lasts only a short while in nature. Among animals, the mother does not distinguish between her grown children, who are able to make their own way in the world, and other members of the same species. The assumption that a natural impulse links the members of the same race with one another is therefore a completely unfounded assertion. . . .

CHAPTER FOURTEEN

Race and Language

We have already observed that cohesion of groups due to kinship, to be found among men in contrast to animals, is to be attributed to language, which records the genealogical relationships among men, makes them into enduringly conscious ones, and thereby creates organizations that arise naturally and cohere permanently as associations for mutual protection and for work.[16] From language, and not from the voice of the blood, spring those close bonds of kinship that unite individuals of the same lineage in societies composed of gentes.

In yet another regard language results in individual groups of men staying together permanently. Language is just as much a *product* of men's social intercourse with each other as a *means* for their intercourse. Men of a particular area, who are continually in contact with one another, will develop a common language. Men in another region that is separated from the former one will form another language. Once their languages have evolved to a certain level, however, the difference of the languages will be an obstacle to intercourse and a cause of separation, even if men from the one and the other region should happen to encounter each other. Men who speak a particular language ultimately develop also a common culture through their continual, intimate contact among themselves, one that is different from the cultures of other language communities. This sharing of a common linguistic culture in collective ideas, rituals, poetry, laws, etc. within a linguistic community contributes to binding its members even more closely to one another and to close them off even more from the members of other language communities.

16. See II:3:5, above.

Thus a particular character of its members, a "national character," can take shape for each such language and cultural community, at least when this community is very close-knit, lives for a long time unchanged in the same conditions, and does not yet exhibit great social differentiation in its midst. It would in all likelihood be a futile undertaking to attempt to establish a national character for modern civilized nations in their entirety. In these nations, every province, every larger city, every occupation engenders a particular character, and this character changes with the historical situations. Under these circumstances, the national character proves to be a Proteus that slips out of the researcher's grasp and assumes in rapid succession the most varied shapes. In contrast to these vague, unintelligible configurations, language is quite univocal and determinate. Among the mental characteristics of men that differ from one nation to the other, language is the only tangible one. . . .

The richer the history of a people is, the more diverse its vicissitudes are, the more numerous its hostile or amicable contacts with other peoples, which result in miscegenation, the higher its civilization is developed in consequence of these varied contacts and relationships, all the less will language and race be coextensive.[17] Even in its beginnings, language coincided with race in all probability only insofar as all those who spoke the same language belonged to the same race. But the reverse could hardly have been the case, that is, that all members of the same race spoke the same language. One may only assume that their languages all exhibited a certain agreement, more in their grammars than in their vocabularies. These languages were to that extent all related to one another, all belonged to the same family, if one can use this term for a relationship not involving descent from a common ancestor.

This linguistic kinship did not, however, by any means constitute a link holding the race together. A language is a common bond among men only when it is understood by all of them. Different languages can belong to the same family, though, and yet be so different that someone who has a command of one of them need not understand anything at all of the others. Whoever speaks one of the Indo-European languages does not, by virtue of that fact alone, understand all other languages of this group. . . . Indeed, the speaker of Low German does not even understand the Swiss when both command only their native dialects. . . . The mere relatedness of different languages is not obviously apparent; it had to be laboriously discovered by philologists. . . . The commonality of speakers of Germanic, Slavic, or Romance languages is just so much claptrap. Such commonalities had not the slightest influence on the course of history. They neither engendered rela-

17. A number of points made in this chapter on the relation of language to race had already appeared in *Are the Jews a Race?*, pp. 65–68.

tionships among peoples nor did they call forth common antagonisms of peoples speaking languages of the same family toward the entirety of the peoples belonging to another language family.

Whether we attribute the historical role that race is supposed to play to alleged natural feelings of physical kinship or to community of language, when we look more closely we find that neither for the one nor for the other can the least solid foundation be found. They are mere chimeras, mostly of professorial origin, which doubtless can, for their part, acquire historical importance, but only as agitational slogans when powerful interests take them into their service. They do not advance our knowledge of reality in the least, but rather seriously obfuscate it. No matter from what side we choose to approach the present-day application of race theories in politics and history, we always come to the conclusion that they originate from lack of reflection, even in the case of great scholars, for even they are subject to collective ideas, and that these theories in turn generate further thoughtlessness.

Therefore, although we theoretically acknowledge that the influence of race might have conferred a special character on some historical phenomena, we must nevertheless state that, as long as anthropology in the narrower sense still provides such uncertain results in the field of racial research and as long as the process of physiological transmission of characteristics still remains so much in the dark, historians as well as politicians should refrain from introducing theories of race into their fields of activity. For the time being, they can only cause mischief by doing so. And frequently that is the sole purpose of these theories.

Section Two
Technology

CHAPTER ONE

Anthropogeography

Up to now we have considered only those kinds of adaptation to the environment that the human organism shares with the animal organism. How the different kinds of natural environment influence the human organism, and especially the human psyche, has, since the eighteenth century, been thoroughly investigated in all its aspects by a number of brilliant researchers. Our understanding of history was thereby greatly enhanced, in a completely different way than through the theories of race. Yet we must enter a caveat here. Even if the study of the natural conditions in which a people lives allows us to gain more profound insight into the nature of its history than has until now been possible through the study of its race, one must nevertheless not exaggerate the benefit to historiography that such research can yield us.

Buckle, for example, is guilty of such exaggeration, great scholar and thinker [that he was] who today is undeservedly forgotten but who for a period of time was just as undeservedly reputed to have developed a conception of history that was in agreement with that of Marx. *[Kautsky quotes at great length Buckle,* History of Civilization in England, *I, 29–30, 109–10, who argued that in Europe nature was weaker than elsewhere and consequently men there could more easily free themselves from superstition and more nearly approach a just distribution of wealth.]* "The tendency has been, in Europe, to subordinate nature to man; out of Europe, to subordinate man to nature" (ibid., p. 109). *[Kautsky also quotes Hegel as saying that the mind cannot]* "build a world for itself" *[in the hot and cold zones;]* "the true theatre of History if therefore the temperate zone; or, rather, its northern half..." (Hegel, *The Philosophy of History*, p. 80). *[And Kautsky also refers to Gobineau's book on the inequality of human races where, on the contrary, it is claimed that the obstacles to civilization were greatest in Europe— which proved the excellence of its races.]*

The same natural conditions in the same area can, under different circumstances, exercise different influences on men. Thus, for example, their location on the Atlantic Ocean had a completely different significance for the West Europeans after the discovery of America and of the sea route to India than before. Similarly, the possession of coal mines conferred on England great economic power after the invention of the steam engine, while up to that time the coal there had been of little importance. Whether, therefore, certain natural conditions promote or impede economic and other social development can be ascertained only for limited areas and times and by no means as generally as is done by Gobineau and Buckle, if in opposed ways. Both were still children of an era that knew neither Darwin nor Marx nor Morgan; of an era in which the evolution of organisms as well as prehistory and economic history were unknown. *[There follow more quotations from Buckle,* History of Civilization, *I, 38–39; II, 287–90, 464, relating climate to the presence or absence of capitalism and of superstitions, and Kautsky's objections to them. Kautsky then refers to Ratzel,* Anthropogeographie, *as the most comprehensive statement of the results of anthropogeographic research and wishes Ratzel had better understood the differences among modes of production.]*

Anyone who wants to write history must be familiar with the results of anthropogeography.... Studies of the influences of climate, topography, and soil composition, natural irrigation, geographical location, and other natural conditions on the fate of humanity in particular areas and in certain stages of development have already taught us much about human history....

CHAPTER TWO

The Impetus to Historical
Development

Anthropogeography has acquired more importance for historical research than the theories of race. But the former is able to explain the historical process just as little as the latter are. Anthropogeography presupposes the historical process; it can only explain to us why it sometimes takes on this form and sometimes that one, but not why it takes place at all.

The influence of the natural environment on man is at first no different than its influence on animals and plants. Man changes due to the influence of nature only when his natural environment itself changes.... The historical process, however, takes place even when, on the one hand, the environment and, on the other hand, the races of the men participating in that process do not change. In comparison with history, race and nature are constant factors. They cannot explain why historical changes occur.

The Darwinizing philosophers of history see the motive factor of history in the struggle for existence of men with one another, whether as individuals, tribes, or "races." ... Struggles among different groups of the same species are something specifically human. They presuppose that a number of institutions already exist that elevate man above the animal. They are results of the historical process; they cannot have given the first impetus to it. Closely connected with the idea of supposedly natural struggles between hordes and races, which can be taken for granted and require no explanation, is the idea that it is the growth of population that sets the historical process in motion. Even Darwin accounts for the struggle for existence in Malthusian terms, through the supposed tendency to overpopulation that obtains in the whole of nature.[1] ...

Underlying this view is the notion, generally abandoned but unconsciously still effective, that the human race is descended from a single couple that has given rise to a posterity growing in size from generation to generation.... But, to the contrary, we must assume [that] ... the result of every process of adaptation tends to have the effect in nature that every species increases as much as its available food supply allows and that the forces of propagation and destruction operating in it hold each other in equilibrium.[2] Recent natural science, then, also assumes that the sum total of the organisms in an area exist together in a state of equilibrium among themselves and that none moves ahead at the expense of the others or is forced back by others. Upheavals of the earth of various kinds can period-

<hr/>

1. See II:2:3, above.
2. The concepts of equilibrium in nature and of the available food supply (*Nahrungsspielraum*) are central in Kautsky's *Vermehrung und Entwicklung*, esp. pp. 29–47.

ically disrupt this equilibrium, which, however, ... always reestablishes itself in calmer times. In such times, no species has the tendency to go beyond the limits of its food supply, and this is also true of man as long as he is an animal.

Accordingly, the pressure of a growing population cannot have been what occasioned those accomplishments that raised him above the animal and made his development more rapid than that of other organisms. The pressure of population certainly caused many historical actions, but only after the historical process was under way that disrupted the organisms' natural state of equilibrium. Here, however, it is a matter of discovering what gave to man in the animal state that first impetus that separated his development from that of the other organisms and gave it a special rate and a special character, so that it proceeds rapidly and without interruption, even in times in which the rest of the organic world undergoes no change. This cannot possibly have been brought about by factors decisive for the development of the totality of animal as well as vegetable organisms.

But what elevates man above the other organisms? Surely, only *his mind*. It seems reasonable to seek here the solution of the riddle and in fact it is, as a rule, sought here, even by materialists. The argument runs thus: His mind confers on man the ability to collect experiences, to learn from them, to broaden his knowledge. In doing that, he leaves the pathway of unconscious development, on which alone the other organisms advance, and enters upon the path of his historical development.... Does not our everyday experience suffice to demonstrate that at every moment we acquire new knowledge and that we strive again and again for further new knowledge?

That is true. In order to remove our difficulty, though, we must not take the present as our starting point, but rather we have to place ourselves in that stage where man still stood at the border of animality.... Our knowledge ... represents a relationship between the external world and our cognitive capacity. If neither the one nor the other of these two factors changes, then in our knowledge, too, nothing can change. In this regard, it is of no consequence whether our cognitive capacity is great or small. New experiences will basically again and again be of the same kind as the previous ones. They will not expand our knowledge, but only confirm it, make it more conservative and less accessible to innovations.

Only a change of the environment or of our cognitive capacity can lead to really new experiences and knowledge. However, for its part, a change of our cognitive capacity presupposes an alteration of our environment. A new environment causes the mental powers to engage in new kinds of activity. The cognitive capacity is thereby restructured. Under certain circumstances, it can become more effective, which ability becomes hereditary, becomes a racial characteristic, when the new conditions exert an influence that is intense and remains the same over many generations. At the conclusion of the process, the species will possess not merely a new and greater store of knowledge, but also a new and perhaps higher cognitive capacity. But this process takes place among animals just as much as among men. It presupposes a change of the environment independent of man. . . . It thus appears that the human mind, too, does not offer us the key that gives us access to the path of historical development. At least not when the mind remains in the context of nature, the context of causally determined necessities.

Thus, nothing seems to be left but to ascribe to the human mind the capacity for spontaneity, freedom of the will, which possesses the ability to produce impulses without itself having received any, to become cause without being effect.[3] This is a mystery and one of a quite different kind than that of life or mind in general. . . . It occurs to no one to want to take everything that is alive as well as every mental activity of the animal out of the total context of nature. Even for the mental activities of man insofar as they are in conformity with those of the animal, causal necessity is acknowledged. One has recourse to the mystery of the freedom of the will, of spontaneity, only where the human mind rises above that of the animal, in historical development.

A glance from the present back into the past shows us, however, that this development . . . takes place by and large in the same direction, traverses the same stages for all [peoples]. How is that to be reconciled with freedom, with spontaneity? This uniformity of development would become understandable if the same causes always produced the same effects. However, if man's will, at least to the extent that he goes beyond the animal, is not causally determined, is free, must not men's action then be a complete chaos, in which it is quite impossible to discover order and regularity? Indeed, the assumption of freedom of the will becomes nonsensical if it is not supplemented by a further mystery. Not only the attribute of *freedom* is supposed to be inherent in the human mind, but also that of *purposefulness*, which, to be sure, for its part also constitutes a necessity, although not a causal one. It is the necessity of striving toward a particular goal that is set for humanity as an ideal of highest reason. Thus, not only does the human mind begin the historical process out of itself, without an impetus from the outside; it also gives this process, out of itself, a necessary direction.

This assumption fits very well into the framework of idealist philosophy, which from the very start places the mental functions of the human organism as "mind" [or "spirit"] in general in opposition to the world. Philosophy of history becomes one of the strongest pillars of idealist philosophy. . . . But how can the historical process be explained other than idealistically, other than through recourse to the special spontaneity and purposefulness

3. See also III:4:1 and V:2:1–2, below.

of the human spirit? . . . Now, there can be no doubt that it is a special capacity of the human mind that set the historical process in motion and gave it its direction. . . . Yet the motive force of human history was a capacity of a completely different kind than that of freedom of the will. It was a capacity that in no way removed man from the total complex of causal connections. And its germs can be found even among the animal. Even in man's most intellectual activity, in his historical evolution, the remnants of the umbilical cord can still be discovered through which he was linked to his animal ancestors.

CHAPTER THREE

The Intelligence of the Inhabitants of the Forest and of the Grassland

The mental ability that elevates man above the animal, yet is to be found already in the latter as a natural predisposition, is . . . the capacity consciously to adapt to changes in the external world by making and employing *artificial organs*, which serve to strengthen or to supplement his natural organs or to increase their number through the addition of new organs. . . .

We must presuppose that the apeman, who had already become the mentally highest developed among the creatures of our world, raised his mental abilities still higher in the course of the development of his thinking apparatus driven onward by changes of the earth and by migrations. Like the apeman's other transformations, like his assumption of an erect posture and his development of the hand, this change was doubtless connected with a change of his environment that turned him from an arboreal animal into a ground–dweller. Perhaps this was caused by the fact that the dense jungle the apeman inhabited became increasingly thinner due to dessication of the climate and was finally transformed into a steppe. . . . Through living on open ground, the apeman then, in all likelihood, added to his already significant mental abilities the last and most important one: the capability of keeping pace with the new requirements of new conditions not just through a purposive adaptation of the *activity* of his natural organs, but by assisting and strengthening these organs of his own body with *implements* taken from the external world.

He did not come into possession of this new endowment through a sudden leap, but through the development of abilities he brought from what we still call his animal stage. This fact is attested to by some of the things we have learned of the lives of higher animals, especially those that are most closely related to us, the anthropoid apes. . . . *[Kautsky cites some examples of chimpanzees in captivity using and even fashioning certain implements.]* Thus the anthropoid apes already have at their disposal the intelligence necessary for some technical inventions. What distinguishes them from primitive man is the fact that in their natural state they have no occasion or motive to make such inventions. Their natural organs are sufficient for their usual natural environment. What initially elevates man above the animal is merely the fact that he happen to enter into a new environment. . . . However, even in the case of animals, one can observe that they employ implements found in nature to reach their goals, indeed, that they produce some implements themselves, even though they do not yet attain the creation of real tools.

One of the organs of evolving man that had need of artificial strengthening must have been his coat of hair. . . . Protecting himself against the coolness of the night, against wind and rain, *[all of which are]* felt more strongly on the open plain than in the thicket of the forest, becomes a matter of importance for man from the beginning of his existence. . . . Caves are not available everywhere. Therefore, it became urgently necessary to make protective contrivances that took the place of the lost coat of fur at least temporarily. . . .

CHAPTER FOUR

Plaiting

In order to make protective contrivances, primitive man had no need of divine inspiration. The art of plaiting bedding or lodging places is widespread even in the animal world, most of all among the birds, to an often astonishing degree. But some mammals, too, have developed it to a very high level. *[Kautsky quotes from Abt, in* Die Wunder der Natur, *II, 146 ff., a detailed description of the complex nest-building activities of the harvest mouse and refers to a similar description of construction work by beavers—see, II:3:4 above—stressing that these cannot be accounted for by "instinct" alone.]*

Man begins his career with a skill in plaiting inherited from his animal ancestors. We can deduce that from the fact that his closest relatives are among the few mammals that build nests for themselves. . . . *[There follow three pages of reports on the nest-building activities of orangutans, gorillas, and chimpanzees, respectively, from Wallace,* The Malay Archipelago, *pp. 39, 45 (whom Kautsky denounces for shooting the apes) from Alverdes,* Social Life in the Animal World, *pp. 48–49, 51, and from Espinas,* Des Sociétés Animales, *p. 502.]* Our animal forebears obviously already possessed the ability to plait and to weave. As soon as they made the transition from living in trees to living on steppes, they were faced with the task of adapting this ability to new circumstances. . . . here the art of plaiting must take on other forms. It no longer serves for the fabrication of nests but instead of windbreaks. *[Kautsky quotes Peschel,* The Races of Man, *p. 179, and Lewin-Dorsch,* Die Technik der Urzeit, *I, 26, on the use of such structures by primitive people.]*

The fabrication of such a windbreak requires hardly greater skill than the construction of an orangutan's or a gorilla's nest. Here we find one of the bridges leading from apish production to human production.

. . . I compare the behavior of the anthropoid apes with that of the lowest-level human beings of the present day. I know very well that man is not descended from the anthropoid apes, that the latter are merely a collateral line of his forebears. On the other hand, I do not forget that even the lowest-level human beings do not represent man's original state, but rather already have behind them an immensely long development, as the richness of their languages proves.[4] Nonetheless, it may be assumed that with these lowest-level men the remains of prehistoric times have not yet been so completely left behind as in the case of the more highly developed groups of men. And on the other hand, we may assume that, of all the animals, the anthropoid apes most resemble man's forebears, the apemen, not only physically, but also in their mental functions. What is shared by the anthropoid apes and low-level peoples we may, then, very well regard as a common possession of the apeman and of primitive man. . . .

What distinguishes *[man]* from his animal ancestors and raises him above them is the fact that he has to exercise his skill in a more diverse and more inconstant environment than the anthropoid apes. These only had to build their nests in trees, always with the same material, tree branches. . . . In grassland, *[man]* found different material in long, strong grasses. On the banks of waters, reeds and rushes were available to him. Once his intelligence had developed so far that it permitted him to go beyond the half-instinctive, because inherited, choice of plaiting material and in so doing to adapt himself consciously to the new environment, then he had thereby made a great stride from animality to humanness, a stride that necessarily resulted in further strides and thus initiated technological development, at least in the area of the textile industry. . . .

A mat made of reeds or grass was . . . easy to transport. . . . Also, the mat became usable for many different purposes. To begin with, it was smaller than the screen made of branches; each individual needed one for himself. He could cover himself with it when he slept; he could use it as a pad when the ground was rough or damp. . . . Finally, as soon as one had learned how to make it strong, the mat could also be used for carrying supplies and tools. With that the starting point of basket weaving was reached. . . . Then all that was necessary for the transition to pottery was the smearing of some baskets with clay so that they would be less pervious. Pottery, to be sure, also presupposed a knowledge of fire, to be treated below, as well as greater sedentariness, for clay pots break easily and are difficult to transport.

As soon as man knew how to employ material of different kinds and

4. See III:1:7, above.

above all of different colors for fabricating a particular thing, for example, a mat, then he was also not far away from ordering these materials in such a way that they appeared in forms pleasing to the eye. We have already seen that joy in what is beautiful is to be found even in the animal world,[5] a joy that can sometimes go so far that it leads to the creation of something beautiful. The development of plaiting by man soon leads far beyond these beginnings. . . . As the plaiting hand becomes progressively more perfect and as the diversity of raw materials for plaiting grows, there also takes place an improvement of [man's] habitations. The windbreaks are changed into roofed bowers with closed sides or round, beehive-shaped lodges. That opens the path for a new art, for architecture. Lastly, the development of plaiting also makes possible an expansion of the limits of man's food supply . . . as soon as he has reached the point where he catches [fish] with the help of meshwork, to which, with growing experience, he learns to give the form of nets or wirebaskets.

Thus we see in the ability to plait, inherited from [man's] animal ancestor, the germs of the development of a great part of what today constitutes human culture. By culture we mean the totality of all attainments of man that raise him above the animal. As with the explanation of any development, in the case of this one, too, the greatest difficulties lie in its beginnings. They remain insurmountable if we insist upon taking the human mind out of the total relational complex of nature and regarding it as something fundamentally different from nature. We can get past this obstacle only if we observe the relatives of our animal ancestors, the anthropoid apes, and reflect on how the transition from arboreal life to life on the steppes must have affected the apeman. If both of these factors are taken into consideration, then man's animal ancestry, already generally recognized for his physical structure, will, without any mystery, become comprehensible also for his mental nature. This is true for the areas of technology we have mentioned here. It is true for others, too.

CHAPTER FIVE

Digging

. . . Tearing open the ground [by apes] when they seized and pulled out the plants rooted in it was probably the stage preceding scratching and grubbing in the earth. As the apeman was then compelled to live predominantly on the ground and as, with the diminution of the trees in his environment, the food he could gather from the trees more and more decreased in quantity, the incentive to dig in the earth for food must have grown. In addition to

5. See II: 5: 1, above.

roots, bulbs, and tubers, it also offered him animal organisms that could serve to still his hunger. From a herbivore man changed into an omnivore. . . . In these circumstances, digging beneath the earth became an important activity for him. . . .

The apeman's front extremities were freed from the labor of locomotion. Thereby, and through the exclusive employment of these extremities for grasping movements, the evolving human beings were enabled to perfect the hand and its use, thus to increase the quantity of what they knew, and to develop their brain beyond the ape-stage. . . .

The human hand was badly suited to the activity of digging, but man succeeded in . . . adapting it to this work, which was required by his new living conditions, by strengthening it with implements he found in his environment. Even in the ape-stage, he knew how to tear branches from trees and to use them in different ways. . . . As soon as he made the transition from arboreal life to living on the ground . . . , he was also driven to stick branches into the ground in order to secure his windbreaks. The use of branches for tearing open the earth was then only a small additional step. [There follows a discussion of digging sticks as used by Australian aborigines and Bushmen, Kautsky quoting Ratzel, The History of Mankind, I, 357 and II, 271.] In its beginnings, the digging stick cannot have been anything other than a branch torn from a tree. But even in this unimpressive form, it constituted the germ of an immense development, the highest results of which are today the steam-plow and the motor-plow as means to tear open the ground.

In the digging up of the earth, we see the first activity preparing the way for agriculture, which, of course, required yet many other preconditions before it could begin to develop. Above all, it can appear only where and only when an area is available that is very rich in food sources, and man has learned to master these sources to such an extent that he is able to remain in the same encampment for several months, from planting to harvest. Until this situation obtains, all technical implements and knowledge that would make agriculture possible are of no use to him.

We assume that branches torn from trees were man's first implements when he dug up the earth. In addition, however, another implement had to offer itself to his attention at an early time. Not always and everywhere did man have branches at his disposal on a grassy plain with few trees. . . . For digging . . . rigid, stiff materials were needed. Such materials were found in stones. . . . Once the practice of using stones for digging had become general, then, as a matter of course, different ways of using the stones were found, corresponding to the nature of the soil in a given case. One had to make now boring, now scraping, now cutting motions with the stones. . . . In the course of this activity, the recognition arose of itself that not every stone was suitable for each of these activities. . . . But once the hand was armed with a stone and knew how to wield it, then it could not fail to happen that the hand occasionally also used the stone for purposes other than those of digging. *[Darwin's* Descent of Man, *p. 458, is quoted here on chimpanzees cracking nuts with rocks.]*

CHAPTER SIX

Defense and Attack

For herbivores threatened by carnivores, protection against these, their enemies, is no less important than obtaining food. . . . Herbivores join together not merely because they locate food sources more easily when they are united under the leadership of more experienced, older members *[of the group].* United they also discover dangers more easily, for example by posting sentinels, or they ward off an enemy more easily through their combined strength. The need for safety is perhaps an even stronger bond of cohesion for them than that of feeding themselves.

In this regard, too, . . . being forced out of the primeval forest into more open regions confronted man with new problems, which . . . impelled him consciously to seek adaptation through the artificial creation of new organs. . . . The transition to the new method of adaptation was made easier for him by the achievements his animal ancestors had already made. . . . *[There follow four pages of reports of baboons, orangutans, and monkeys throwing stones or branches and fruits to defend themselves, which Kautsky cites to counter Noiré's view that throwing was a skill acquired only by man and only after he had acquired the skills of hitting and stabbing.* Das Werkzeug, *pp. 370, 375, 387,390–392.]* Hurling things can of itself be effective for the animal's defense if it thereby only succeeds in *intimidating* its adversary, without striking him. . . . Simply throwing something in a certain direction can be a purely instinctive movement. It requires no preparation and practice, no aiming. . . . Throwing of this sort does not at all presuppose such a high-level intellect as is possessed only by man. . . .

As soon as he was deprived of the protection of the dense wood, the situation became entirely different for the apeman than it is for the anthropoid ape in the primeval forest. . . . *[Beasts of prey]* became dangerous for the apeman. . . . Much more often than in the forest, he found that he had to keep dangerous attackers away from himself by means of projectiles. He probably used as such what he found at hand; rarely branches, more seldom still fruits, like the tree-dwelling apes; but, far more often than these, the stones that lay closer to hand for him. Under these circumstances, the manner of his throwing changed. As a rule, apes throw only downward from above. . . . In contrast, the apeman—or man—is placed in a completely new situation as soon as he is transplanted out of the forest . . . onto a plain without steep elevations.

... Should an enemy now appear, he will generally be on a level with the thrower.... Gravity no longer aids the throw, but causes it to end prematurely if it is not given a trajectory of the proper height, which must be in accord with the distance that the missile is to traverse.

The primitive men who hurled missiles must soon have learned this fact from experience. It imposed on them some reflection when they threw things, which they had previously done almost purely instinctively.... thus, that fact alone sufficed to introduce into man's act of throwing an intellectual moment, which it lacks for the ape living under natural conditions. In addition, primitive man had occasion in his new environment far more often than earlier to hurl projectiles. The more frequently this was the case, the greater his practice and his skill in this activity became, the more often did throwing in the *direction* of an enemy result in *striking* the enemy....

The more it was recognized, after copious practice, that striking an enemy was even more effective than the rapidity of a hail of missiles, the more likely it was that each thrower paid attention to the trajectory of his projectile and gathered information about which of his missiles struck home and which did not. Being possessed of language, he must have exchanged his experiences with those of his comrades. He must have practiced, half in play, half seriously, throwing at a target.... All of that ultimately led to the substitution of the practiced, methodical throwing of stones to strike and injure an aggressor, for the rapid barrage intended to frighten off an opponent....

In close combat with a large predatory animal... even primitive man could have made use of weapons.... We may well assume that for man as well as for the anthropoid ape the first weapons used in close combat were tools. Because of the way they obtained food, they were familiar with wielding them and they changed their function in case of an emergency.... The digging stick forms the transition from tool to weapon. ... But with regard to all the most simple tools of man, of which alone we are still treating here, it can be said that... man could use them now for this purpose, now for that purpose, as soon as he had acquired great skill in wielding them. Not until a higher level of civilization, when technology offers more complex implements, does a permanent separation of tool and weapon begin....

As soon as man had reached the point of throwing at a target and striking it, a major change occurred in his living conditions. Only now could he hunt... larger vertebrates, indeed even warm-blooded animals closely related to him, with an intelligence that had much in common with his.... Once this skill had been acquired, however, hunting became not merely possible, but soon also necessary. For tools and weapons serve to disrupt the state of equilibrium in which man finds himself within animate nature ... the forces of destruction are weakened; those of propagation strengthened.[6] The result is an increase of the population, which calls for new sources of food, for either emigration or expansion of the food supply in the already inhabited area. Hunting, which contributes so much to the disruption of the natural equilibrium of population growth, now becomes in turn a powerful means for solving the problems that arise from this disruption of the equilibrium. If hunting compels emigration, it also makes emigration possible. It permits men to penetrate into areas that, while rich in game, are poor in those foodstuffs to which man was limited before he began to hunt. . . . On the other hand, hunting made it possible for the already inhabited area to feed a denser population.

Both migration into new conditions and increase in population density, the growth in size of the individual tribes and increased communication among them, all had to have a stimulating influence on [man's] intelligence, to offer new experiences, to pose new problems, and to provide new means for their solution.

There now also began the great division of labor between man and woman we already mentioned,[7] which goes beyond the natural division of labor among the animals that concerns only the sexual functions. With the latter as its point of departure, the division of labor in obtaining food now begins. Woman remains faithful to the old manner of obtaining food; in so doing, to be sure, she enters into conditions that make very great technical advances possible for her. From grubbing up the earth to look for roots and worms, she progresses to cultivating the soil; from plaiting, she progresses to making pottery, etc. More and more, man devotes himself almost exclusively ... to hunting. This field is much more uniform than the one that falls to the woman's lot; for a long time man's contribution to technical progress is much smaller than that of woman.

Along with his way of life, however, the human being's psyche also undergoes a complete change, especially that of the male, who at first is much more affected by the change than the female. . . . He accustoms himself to killing living beings that are close to him psychically. Not only does he overcome the abhorrence of spilling blood characteristic of the herbivore; he ends up acquiring a regular yearning for it. For a long time he murders, like the predatory animal, in order to obtain food or to safeguard his life. But the habit of murder and of taking pleasure in it is preserved in many men, perhaps in part as an inclination that has become hereditary, in part as a tradition that is passed down and

6. See III:1:2, above.
7. See II:4:3, above.

learned. This habit then continues to be effective even after hunting has ceased to be an important way of obtaining food. Murdering now becomes a pastime of the idle. . . .

At first, killing was confined to animals of other species. . . . Among the apes, we never find between individuals of the same species . . . murder and killing of fellow species-members. A development of weapons technology to a high level, a long habituation to the killing of warm-blooded animals with a psyche similar to ours had to have taken place before man attained the "maturity" necessary for attacking and killing his fellow human beings. We have already seen that, in addition to the technology of weapons and hunting, still other preconditions were required for war to make its appearance, above all the differentiation of languages. . . . Also, there arose causes of conflicts among the tribes that were becoming closed entities, something effectuated especially by the disruption of the equilibrium of population as a consequence of growing technology and population increase due to it.[8]

Man must have already developed all the distinctive features of culture: language, tools, weapons, the division of labor at least between male and female as a result of hunting, before the conditions for war were given. Ultimately the same development occurred with regard to war as in the case of hunting. The spilling of human blood, too, could become a pleasure. . . . This mentality, as a rule, remains confined to the men. . . . As we have observed several times already, war is not a natural phenomenon, but rather a historical category.[9] For many historians, it is the most important event in history. The advances in the means for obtaining food, clothing, lodging do not interest them. Only when men kill one another are they making "history" in the eyes of these historians.

The Production of Tools

So far, we have considered as tools only objects primitive man came upon in nature. . . . The mere use of them did not yet distinguish him, in the simplest cases, from his animal forebears. . . . As soon as his frequent employment of tools had conferred on man great skill in their use that allowed him to employ them as weapons and to kill animals . . . , he found in some animal organs new tools in finished form, which often fulfilled the functions of those already known to him better than these and sometimes made new

---

8. See II: 3 : 5–6, above.
9. See pp. 63 and 77, above.

functions possible and brought them about when living conditions required them. Such new tools or weapons were, for example, deer antlers or the jawbones of large mammals or fish. . . . Hunting . . . also enabled man to acquire the skin of animals and thereby to obtain a material for shelter and covering the body that is more durable, much warmer, and protects better than the primitive plaitings made out of vegetable material. Equipped with animal pelts, man could now venture forth into more inclement regions, . . . the diversity of the areas he inhabited thus grew and likewise the scope of his experiences.

The more skill and practice man acquires in the manipulation of his tools and weapons, all the more numerous and varied become the animals he knows how to kill, the more diverse become those of their parts he can add as new ones to the tools and weapons already known to him, the more abundant is his bill of fare. But also the conditions in which he knows how to live become more varied and again and again pose new problems for him and offer him new means for solving them. Thus, it is the mere practice of the employment of tools and weapons that of itself, as soon as it has been carried on long enough, results from time to time in technical advances.

But another effect on human technology of the continuing use of certain implements becomes even more important. . . . As he accumulated more experience, man learned to recognize with ever more certainty which properties the implement he used had to have, if it was to serve his purposes; he also acquired an increasingly comprehensive knowledge of the sources where he could, with the greatest probability, find the implements best suited to his purposes. . . . The more often man uses a particular implement, tool, or weapon, or raw material, the better does he know how it behaves under very different conditions and how it reacts to different stimuli. From this knowledge, there first accrues to him a growing understanding of how purposively to employ tools or weapons; ultimately, however, also an understanding of the possibilities for acting on the tool or the weapon itself in a purposive manner.

After long experience, man had, we can assume, progressed to the point of being able to identify among the pieces of sticks or stones, later also of bones, teeth, etc., that he found in nature, certain forms as the ones best suited for different purposes, which he especially favored. . . . Flintstones, in particular, yield many such forms. . . . As soon as further experiences gained from handling flintstones had shown primitive man how such stones react to being struck with other stones, it was only a small step to utilizing such knowledge for correcting somewhat the deficiencies of "eoliths" that had been found and that were not quite suitably formed, in order to improve their shape.

The first and most important step was thereby taken to the stupendous innovation: *the conscious and systematic production of a tool.* Such behavior by any animal under natural conditions is unknown. . . . Here we find one of the most important features of inchoate hominization. . . . But we must not imagine this first step as a leap. Its beginning consisted in the employment of sticks and stones for certain occasional activities man still shared with the ape. The *constant* utilization of such implements, whereby knowledge was acquired leading to the selection of certain kinds and pieces of the materials furnished by nature, already went beyond that beginning. The third and decisive step was then taken when continual utilization of certain kinds and pieces *[of natural materials]* brought recognition of the possibilities for acting on the imperfect pieces . . . in order to make their shapes more like those recognized as suited to man's aims.

We must assume, though, that, initially, . . . man's goal as he worked on the material for a tool or weapon . . . did not spring forth from the human mind. If man had immediately drawn forth from himself the idea of the most suitable form of a tool, in order then to realize it, that would really be a leap, which could be explained or, rather, not explained only by a mysterious "divine spark," for the divinity is always resorted to where no explanation can be found. When an explanation is possible other than the intervention of a god, then it is preferred. . . .

When he first artificially fashioned tools and weapons, man certainly did not act as a *creator of things wholly new*, but rather as the *imitator* of phenomena he met with in nature and he had learned to use. . . . Indeed, the next great step in the development of technology, the production of composite tools, surely also ensued from the imitation of natural forms. *[Kautsky here quotes Noiré, Das Werkzeug, pp. 358–59, on the origin of the ax—a handle with a pointed stone affixed to one end—as an imitation of the jawbone of a bear with its pointed tusk.]*

CHAPTER EIGHT
Fire

When we speak of the implements primitive man took from nature in order to assist, to strengthen, and to supplement the activity of his own organs with them, we must not omit to mention *fire*. . . . As with tools, so also with fire, the utilization of what nature offered preceded artificial production, and in this case, too, no Prometheus was required who brought the divine spark to men. Nature itself sometimes generates conflagrations, on the one hand, by volcanic eruptions, on the other hand, through lightning. That glowing lava ever attracted simple primitive people to come to it and to warm themselves at it, seems doubtful to me. . . . Also, volcanic eruptions are too rare a phenomenon to have been able to engender any practice and habit of everyday life. And only to such practice and habit, not to a unique occurrence, may we trace back one of the great technical advances, especially in the primeval period. . . . Where *[lightning bolts and resulting blazes]* occurred quite often and did not do much damage and where the fire was confined just to isolated dry spots and stumps, in which it long continued to smolder, there primitive men had the opportunity often to observe a fire unhurriedly and without danger.

What was it about fire that could interest primitive man? ... We may assume that it was the need for warmth that drew man first to slowly burning tree trunks set afire by lightning. ... With time *[he]* inevitably learned from experience that accidental fires could be fed by putting dry wood on them and finally also that single dry billets of wood could be carried elsewhere as they burned. ... Fire could become his daily companion, and thus experience with fire grew. ... Similarly, through their dealings with fire in their everyday life, men now gradually found out how it affected some of their foodstuffs. In this way. ... primitive man acquired the arts of roasting and cooking, to which were later added the beginnings of pottery, thanks to experience with clay-smeared baskets, and finally the beginnings of smelting and annealing metals, which initiated the triumphant advances of more recent technology.

It can today no longer be determined when man succeeded in achieving everyday familiarity with fire, in "taming" it, but it is certain that even those at the lowest level of development among men living now ... are familiar with the use of fire. I am not, however, of the opinion that hominization begins only with fire. Man must have already existed a long time and have passed through a significant development before he had advanced far enough to become conversant with fire. We deduce this from the fact that even the lowest-level peoples already possess a richly developed language, but that not all of them know how to make fire. *[Kautsky quotes reports to this effect on Australian and Tasmanian aborigines by Lubbock (Lord Avebury), Pre-Historic Times, 425, 431–32.]*

But, after he had learned to make use of fire and to preserve it, how did man acquire the ability to produce it himself? *[Kautsky quotes at length von den Steinen, Unter den Naturvölkern Zentralbrasiliens, pp. 224–27, who hypothesized that primitive man carried fire in the form of tinder in wood splinters or wood dust obtained by boring into wood with stones or animal teeth. Fire was then produced when, at one time and by accident, a few individuals, lacking stones and teeth, bored into wood with wood. Kautsky finds the first assumption suggestive but rejects the second one.]*

If we want to discover the path man followed in learning how to make fire himself, we must not seek the final step in this direction in a unique, accidental event; rather we must look for it in an everyday practice. We must ask, therefore, what could have led men, in the course of their daily activity, to bore wood into wood or to rub wood against wood. ... That probably happened when tribes that had already learned to bore into wood were forced to migrate into a new environment where they lacked their previous implements for boring or scraping, in particular sharp, pointed stones. Now they had to look for new implements and finally found that hard, pointed pieces of wood bored into soft wood offered a substitute, albeit a poor one, for their earlier boring instruments. . . . When boring generally, over and over again, caused wood to become hot and to begin smoldering, it is reasonable to assume that the correct cause of these effects was identified. . . . In any case, we must assume that once the necessary preconditions, ample experience in handling and fanning fire, were given, then the last step to generating fire, boring wood into wood, . . . was the result of a new environment that brought along new problems and new means for their solution.

CHAPTER NINE
Of Invention

. . . The question of how the use and the fabrication of primitive man's first implements in his struggle for existence arose has always occupied the minds of thoughtful men since they recognized that humanity had not all along been as it presented itself to a subsequent observer at a particular time. . . . To begin with, the first inventions could be explained only as resulting from isolated accidents. *[Kautsky cites* The Natural History of Pliny, *VI, 379 (Book 36, Chapter 65) on the supposed invention of glass and a similar story of an alchemist accidentally producing gunpowder.]* No invention, the history of which is known, can be traced back to a single accident. Each one is the result of a long history of development. . . .

Nor is the assumption much more tenable that the first inventions were the product of extraordinary geniuses, who recognized what implements men needed to make progress and who then set about discovering how these implements could be fashioned. To explain occurrences among primitive men, quite modern conditions are presupposed, differences in the ability and knowledge of individual men such as can be brought about only by a very advanced division of labor and class division. Even for the greatest genius, accomplishments such as those presupposed *[by this explanation]* would be inconceivable; even present-day science could not match them with anything comparable. *[Kautsky quotes Morgan,* Ancient Society, *pp. 38–39, on the inevitable "slowness of this mental growth . . . in the period of savagery."]*

The idea of evolution, which revolutionized all of the natural sciences in the last century, did not stop short of man. And as we can account for the evolution of organisms by their practice, their everyday activity, and a change of this practice in consequence of a change of their environment, so too does the number of areas grow more and more in which we are able to account for man's accomplishments by his practice and a change of his practice as a result of an alteration of his environment, without having recourse to geniuses who spontaneously invent higher goals and the means for achieving them. . . .

To the present, the language of even the highest-level civilized people is not definitively completed, but continues to evolve. It develops ever further through daily practice, adopts new terms and forms and consigns old ones to disuse, changes the meaning of words remaining in use, etc. No genius and no dictator can direct this development as he sees fit. The same is true with regard to the first inventions. They did not originate out of goals outstanding individuals set themselves and for the attainment of which they looked for means and ways; rather, they arose out of the everyday practice of many thousands of people in particular circumstances, into which they happened to come and to which they had to adapt their activity. . . .

Along with technical progress, the quantity of experiences men have and of the knowledge gained from these experiences increases, and the methods for organizing and integrating this knowledge are improved. Without these methods, the wealth of experiential knowledge would be merely confusing and chaotic, and further progress in the acquisition of knowledge would be impossible. Thus, the application of experience to the solution of new problems confronting us also requires ever more knowledge and reflection, . . . in order to recognize the problems, to pose them correctly, and to discover the means for solving them.

At the same time, division of labor develops and differentiation in human society sets in. From then on, . . . each individual is conversant with only a piece of the polity's total knowledge and skills. And this piece becomes increasingly smaller in proportion to the ultimately immense abundance of that total knowledge, even though in absolute terms, the knowledge of each individual can grow significantly. . . . In a relatively highly developed society, every solution of a technical problem becomes the business of relatively few specialists, who are enabled, by their special knowledge and the particular circumstances in which they grow up and work, to discover a particular problem, to formulate the question necessary for its solution, and then to find the appropriate means for the solution itself. . . . Thus, single individuals stand out more and more above the social process of invention as successful inventors, alongside numerous other workers who struggle with the same task with less success.

Complete uniformity of abilities does not exist even in the animal world. . . . Under natural conditions, differences in endowment are probably less strikingly apparent because it is, as a rule, not a matter then of adaptation to completely new circumstances, of new inventions, but mostly a matter of traditional, often instinctive actions. With regard to the process of invention, however, the differences in natural endowment weigh heavily in the balance. We must assume that, with increasing diversity of living conditions and of crossbreeding, variability among men grows and that the differences in natural endowment therefore also increase. In all likelihood, though, they could not have become even nearly as extensive as the differences resulting from the social difference of occupations and classes in a highly developed class society. Under the influence of these circumstances, the present-day kind of technical progress is certainly very different from that of the primeval period. But its fundamental elements have remained the same: everyday practice and change of the environment.

CHAPTER TEN

The Development of the Steam Engine

As an illustration of what has been said, let us consider the antecedents of one of the great inventions of modern time, the railways moved by steam-powered locomotives.[10] Usually we are told that James Watt once observed a tea kettle and immediately drew from this accidental observation the idea of the steam engine. . . . The reality of the matter, however, was entirely different from what this foolish anecdote reports. . . . If for a long time no one gave any thought to the *[well-known phenomenon that]* the steam raised the lid *[of a kettle]*, that must be ascribed to the fact that, under the given conditions, it was not possible to draw even the smallest benefit from the force lifting the lid and that it did not occur to anyone to think about impractical problems.

That changed only when, in the course of social evolution, there arose a class freed from the labor of production as well as of trading or of administration of the polity and therefore in a position to gather the knowledge gained from the experiences of the numerous practitioners in the very diverse fields of human activity and to integrate and to order it in a manner free of contradictions. A task that became ever more necessary due to the continuous growth of the body of that knowledge. . . . Only now, after a class of this kind had appeared, was research conducted, at least by that class if not yet by the others, merely for the purpose of eliminating the intellectual unease caused by every unresolved problem or contradiction. Thus began the scientific collecting and ordering of knowledge gained from experience, in the area of society as well as that of nature; invention, too, acquired thereby a different character.

Now one also began systematically to observe and to test the power of

10. This and the following chapter, comprising some fifteen pages mostly on the history of inventions, are drastically abridged here. Some of the points made in this chapter had already appeared in *The Economic Doctrines of Karl Marx*, p. 142. However, as Kautsky notes in his preface to the first edition of that work, the relevant chapter was almost entirely the work of Eduard Bernstein.

steam that had been noticed long before. This gave rise to varied experiments and apparatuses. . . . *[Kautsky refers to some of these appearing among the Greeks as early as 250 BC]* But everything learned about the motive force of confined steam led only to experiments and childish amusements as long as no need for utilizing this force arose out of everyday practice. That happened only in the seventeenth century. . . . Using steam power to move a machine did not become a practical task until the need emerged for an engine that was stronger than men or draft animals and also worked with greater regularity than water and wind. . . .

At the turn from the seventeenth to the eighteenth century, the wealth of experiential knowledge about the motive power of steam and the means of utilizing it to advantage had reached the point where several true steam engines were invented simultaneously and independently of each other. *[Relying on Matschoss,* Die Entwicklung der Dampfmaschine, *Kautsky relates such inventions by the Frenchman Denis Papin and the Englishman Thomas Savery.]* For the success of an invention, more is required than the necessary theoretical knowledge, the necessary practical need and the necessary concomitant interest in repeated experiments that alone provide the requisite experience. The requisite technical implements must also be available. . . .

Long before James Watt, the steam engine had already become a wide-spread device that was studied in many circles, not just in Britain. . . . He did not first invent the steam engine, but he did improve it to a great extent. In the meantime, however, a new field had sprung up for its employment under new conditions and for new purposes. . . . Now, in addition to mining, large-scale industry also had need of the steam engine. In Watt's engine it found the motor it needed, the one adapted to its conditions. . . . This is not to disparage Watt's achievement, but only to show that even the greatest genius does not create something new spontaneously, so to speak from nothing, but only develops further what already exists, adapting it to new needs and conditions on the basis of new experience. As he does this, he very often sees only the most immediate consequences of his own accomplishment; almost never is he able to grasp its future potential. . . .

CHAPTER ELEVEN

The Steamship and the Locomotive

[This chapter opens with a long discussion of galleys propelled by rowers and of sailboats.] Attempts to build a steamship, the operation of which would be reliable and effective without involving excessive costs, . . . were not undertaken with the necessary seriousness and perseverance until conditions had come into being that promised to make the new invention extremely

advantageous. These new conditions were given by the development of large-scale industry, which needed to be supplied with large, constantly growing quantities of raw materials, for example, cotton, from across the sea. . . . The steam engine became important as a motor not only for oceanic but also for river navigation. . . . Matschoss names six American engineers who occupied themselves with the problem of the steamship in the period from 1763 to 1804 and who in part produced "ingenious constructions." On the accomplishments of these and others were based the efforts of the American Fulton, who finally, in 1807, succeeded in building a steamship that was more than an experiment and was capable of regularly carrying out its task. . . . The innovation now swiftly spread on the rivers of America and Europe. Making continuous progress, it also conquered the ocean for itself in 1819.

It would have been strange if the attempt had not been made to use the new motor also for locomotion on land. In this connection . . . the lead was taken by Britain, whose mining industry had first prepared the ground for the practical employment of the steam engine. . . . Practical results were not attained until, with large-scale industry, the need for mass transportation arose, not only on the sea and on rivers and canals, but also on the highways; not until it was recognized that steam power could be used to advantage only for mass transportation; finally, also not until the form of road had been found on which alone the steam engine could manage such transportation.

Here, too, the inventor did not have to create something absolutely new relying solely on his own brain; he only had to adapt what existed already to new conditions and needs. *[There follows a lengthy discussion of Roman roads, where flat stones were laid only in two parallel rows for the carriage wheels, and of the use of wooden rails in mining in the sixteenth century, replaced by iron ones in England in the eighteenth to move carriages pulled by men and horses and even steam engines.]*

The man who is usually considered the inventor of the locomotive, George Stephenson, drew upon this experience. When he made his appearance, the infantile disorders of the locomotive had already been overcome. *[Kautsky refers to attempts by Richard Trevithik in 1804 and William Hedley in 1812 to resolve various problems before Stephenson built his first successful steam locomotive in 1817.]* In addition to the individuals just mentioned, others, too, were already occupied with building locomotives and succeeded in doing so. Stephenson was by no means the only one. What brought his name into the foreground was the energy he applied to transforming the locomotive from an aid to mining, which it had been up to that time, into an implement for the general conveyance of goods and people. That was connected with the development of mass production, which had been enormously advanced by the penetration of the steam engine into industry and which called for new means of transportation both on land and on water responding to the new needs. *[American cotton had to be moved from the port of Liverpool to the textile mills of Manchester.]*

CHAPTER TWELVE

Novelty in Technical Progress

Although of necessity very brief, our sketch has surely sufficed to show that technical progress is not the work of individual geniuses, who, stimulated by some accident or other or perhaps due only to stirrings in the depths of their spirit, suddenly conceive the idea of something new, with which they propose to benefit mankind. Every inventor stands on the shoulders of his predecessors; none creates anything completely new. . . .

In the twentieth century, even the single steps in the process of invention are ceasing more and more to be made by individuals. The concentration of industrial enterprises in giant firms makes it possible for these to establish and equip their own laboratories and workshops and to employ in them appropriately selected personnel who serve no purposes other than those of inventing technical improvements. Here this process is socially organized in a conscious and planned fashion.

And an invention is as little the result of an *accident* as it is the work of a single *individual*, if by accident one understands a chance, unique event. Only in the sense of something unforeseen, something not taken into account beforehand, does accident play a role in the history of inventions. *[Kautsky quotes Mach,* Kultur und Mechanik, *pp. 56, 67, to support this point with reference to the invention of glass.]* Our knowledge and consequently also our technical advances arise out of occurrences that repeat themselves, out of experiences of everyday life, or out of systematic experiments that must be tirelessly repeated over and over again, before they yield the desired result. . . .

Of course, the methods of technical progress are of a different kind at the higher stages of civilization than among primitive men. With them, technical progress arises predominantly from instinctive groping, in which all adult members of the society take part because they all . . . know the same things and share the same interest. Under these conditions, technology simply *comes into being* just as language *comes into being*. This mere becoming of technology ceases more and more, the more complicated men's tools and other implements become and the more advanced the division of labor is among them. . . . Concomitantly, it becomes ever more necessary that the goal the inventor of an innovation is striving to attain is clear in his mind before he sets about producing it in reality. Without an *idea* of what he wants to create, he achieves nothing.

But he does not generate this idea out of nothing. It presupposes a clear grasp of the actually existing needs that have to be satisfied, of the implements that are available for solving the problem, as well as of the manner in which this problem had hitherto been solved. It is always that which already exists that supplies the elements of what is new; always the new contrivance must take already existing ones as a point of departure. The further one traces the history of inventions, the less do the results brought forth by the individual inventor seem like leaps, the more do we see that the new . . . is completely contained . . . in the preceding elements and is only put together differently by the inventor to satisfy new demands made by the external world; that the new does not, then, originate from the psyche, but from a change in the external world, which affects the psyche and gives it new impressions.

The idea of the new is obtained from existing reality. The idea will be all the more perfect, that is, more useful and more useable, the more profoundly its originator has understood reality, its problems and its implements. Since, however, all-encompassing, exhaustive knowledge of reality is granted to no mortal, even the most ingenious, most knowledgeable, and practically most experienced inventor will hardly ever provide with his idea the image of what ultimately emerges as the result of his labors. The idea does not become important for the inventor because it prescribes for him from the very start what *forms* he must realize, but because it indicates to him the *direction* in which his efforts have to move. . . .

The activity of individual inventors who are guided by ideas drawn from the scientific mastery over reality—that is, at bottom from everyday practice—that is what distinguishes the technical progress of civilization from prehistoric one. Nevertheless, it is fundamentally the same forces that are active in the former as in the latter. What is new in the ideas is merely the reaction to the impulses a changed environment gives to the individuals living in it. . . . The mind only has to solve problems the environment sets for it; it does not spontaneously produce problems of its own accord.[11] And the means for solving them, too, it finds only in the environment. We see that the same principle is effective in the case of the evolution of human technology as in the case of the evolution of organisms in nature: in both, evolution is nothing but adaptation to a changed environment. Only it takes place unconsciously in the one case, consciously in the other.

To be sure, this conception is very different from that of the philosophy of history now dominant in Germany. For it, the bearers of progress are great individuals, who are such because they create something wholly new all by themselves and enrich mankind with it. The most important representative of this philosophy today *[is]* Ernst Troeltsch, who died at an all too early age. *[There follows a page of quotations from Troeltsch,* Der Histo-

---

11. See also I:5:1 and 4, above, and V:1:9 and 12, below.

rismus, *pp. 48–50.]* As far as the essential content of history, the origin of the new, is concerned, "no further insight is possible," according to this conception of history. No wonder that it comes down to an obscure mysticism that shoves everything off onto God, who, to be sure, is also unknowable. . . .

Troeltsch's exposition is one of the arguments advanced to justify the separation of the so-called human sciences *[Geisteswissenschaften]* from the natural sciences, of which we shall speak later.[12] Let me say just this much here. There can be no doubt that society is an area sui generis that has its special laws, and that for attaining an understanding of it the laws of the natural sciences, properly speaking, suffice as little as, say, the laws of mechanics do for biology. But the view that has found one of its most distinguished proponents in Troeltsch goes further. It maintains that society and its historical evolution are determined by factors completely irreconcilable with the laws governing all other processes in the world.

This is supposed to be explained by the fact that, in contrast to nature, only history is capable of bringing forth something new. . . . That means that the human mind *[or spirit]* has been granted the ability to violate the physical law of the conservation of energy, according to which the quantity of energy present in the world can neither be diminished nor increased. It can only be transformed from one form into another. . . . If we held to that point of view we would, in point of fact, find ourselves in the dubious situation of assuming with regard to man, at least historical man, that he stands . . . above nature. We will then hardly be able to avoid the supernatural. However, we avoid this questionable consequence of history if the study of the history of inventions . . . shows us that what is new in that history has its origin in the environment, not in man. . . . Now the objection may well be made that that applies only to profane inventions; that Troeltsch, however, had the most sublime social ideas in mind, which are far above plebeian, everyday technology.

CHAPTER THIRTEEN

Novelty in Social Ideas

When we followed the Stone Age immediately with the history of the development of steam engines and railways, we were getting ahead of ourselves. It may appear to be an even greater anticipation that in this chapter we are already scaling the highest peaks of the "superstructure" before we have properly laid down the "base." Of course, we will still

12. See V:2:2–3, below.

have to discuss the relationship between base and superstructure, . . . but in order to make the character of technical progress in the beginning of mankind completely clear, it was necessary to show both how its methods differed from those of the more or less scientifically educated inventors of later times and also what they have in common. Thus, it seems to us, already at this point, necessary also to investigate to what extent what is new in men's social ideas differs from what is new in their technical inventions. Later in this work, we will have no further occasion to treat again of the latter. So we must discuss the difference here, at the risk of anticipating some analyses that have their proper place later in the organization of our work.

When we speak here of social ideas, we are using the word in its broadest sense, in which it comprehends all elevated human goals, all ideals, whether of political, economic, ethical, sexual, aesthetic, or religious nature. . . . Between new ideas of this kind and new inventions there is certainly an enormous difference. It can be seen above all in the fact that technical inventions are of a very tangible nature. Their connection with the needs of and the implements offered by the environment is palpably obvious. With regard to social ideas, that is the less true the more sublime they are. Their object—the relations of men with one another, which are always of a mental *[geistig]* nature—is enough to have this effect. . . . The scientific exactness that is so important in technology for new inventions has up to now been attainable in only a few limited areas in the domain of the mind. New social ideas thus simply come into existence just like language came into existence, like the primitive inventions came into existence, without conscious recognition of the factors bringing them about. This difference between their objects also causes a path to be closed to social ideas that every technical innovation must follow and on which alone it can become serviceable: the path of *experimentation.* . . .

The author of a new idea wants to regenerate with it all of mankind or at least an entire polity, to free it from defects he has perceived in it. Without an awareness of such defects in his environment, without such an impetus from the outside, his new ideas would be quite pointless. No one will look for something new, if he is content with what exists or if it seems unassailable to him. And a new idea can find acceptance and become effective only when it has taken hold of considerable, decisive masses of people in the polity. Whoever conceives a new idea is therefore compelled to seek adherents for it, to take it to the public, to make propaganda for it.

His success in doing so will depend in large measure on whether the defects he is combating are felt by others as much as by himself. And whether the means he wants to employ seem as appropriate to them as to him. In other words, the founder of a new idea will find adherents for it only if he does not merely draw the idea from his own head but is led to it by circumstances that affect others as they affect him.[13] His propaganda will be successful only if he stands above the mass of people merely because he recognizes sooner and feels more strongly than the others the defects that are oppressing the others, too. . . . Since he knows just as little as the others how the new ideas have evolved in himself, he may, if the times make this appropriate, imagine that a divinity inspired him with them, and his followers may be of the same opinion. But they will certainly not accept his ideas for that reason. . . . Rather, the reverse is true. Because his ideas are in agreement with their own, because he expresses more impressively and more boldly what is alive in them, they are inclined to see something divine in him.

But under all circumstances . . . the embarrassing fact will remain that a new social idea is forced to appear before the public without having been tested in practice. . . . The social innovator will never find a society that lends itself to being experimented with on the basis of his proposals as long as is necessary for something satisfactory to come of it. Society wants to be convinced of the perfection of his proposals before they have been tested in reality. . . . A simple psychological procedure helps to surmount this difficulty. The reservations about the new idea disappear if it can be shown that the idea is not new at all, but was already operative and proved itself at some time in the past. The deficiencies of the present would then be due to the fact that it turned away from this tried and proved past. Since the past is always known only imperfectly, the proponents of the new often find in it, in the form of superficial similarities, precedents with which they can justify themselves, which give them the requisite self-confidence and provide their propaganda with an apparently realistic and often extremely effective foundation.

In his search for precedents in the past, the innovator is aided by the fact that no one can create something completely new. Everything new must draw on what already exists; it cannot be anything other than the further development and transformation of what already exists to adapt it to new circumstances. . . . The idea of radically destroying what exists in order to create something completely new is no less senseless in social than in technical matters. . . . Indeed, as long as the knowledge and the social conditions did not yet exist for scientifically deriving from the new, given environment the necessity of a new idea and the possibility of its acceptance, disguising the new as something old provided the only chance for a social idea of overcoming the mistrust, innate in the human mind, of all that is new and untested.

[Troeltsch, Der Historismus, *pp. 59–60, is quoted as explaining new ideas*

---

13. Some thoughts expressed here and in the rest of this chapter had already appeared in "Die materialistische Geschichtsauffassung und der psychologische Antrieb," p. 656.

as a result, not of the environment or earlier ideas, but of "illumination" or "in-spiration," as in the cases of Jesus, the Buddha, and Luther. Kautsky, to refute Troeltsch, quotes his own Foundations of Christianity, *p. 388, and Matthew 5:17, 18, with respect to Jesus, and Davids,* Buddhism, *pp. 179–80, with respect to the Buddha, to show that both denied being innovators.]* Luther is anything but unique. . . . The number of his precursors is great, and no less great is the number of his contemporaries who were active to the same end as he was. The agreement among them becomes explicable if it is traced back to the new impulses and conditions of the environment they all lived in. But it becomes even more incomprehensible than "illumination" itself if the new is sought in a purely personal inspiration. . . .

In connection with the question we are now concerned with, it is worthy of note that all the innovators of Luther's period regarded the new they strove to attain as something old. From the present, which oppressed them, they wanted to escape to a better future. But they saw its ideals in the past: in antiquity or in the Gospels. The Humanists turned to the former; Luther and all the religious reformers turned primarily to the latter. They believed that what the conditions of the age urged on them led them back into the past, that it reestablished this past, primitive Christianity, the "pure teachings of Christ." . . .

Even less than the Reformation can the English bourgeois revolution of the seventeenth century be considered as the product of the "inspiration" of a single individual favored by divine grace. On this subject we are already well enough informed to see clearly the connection of the new, which the revolutionaries strove for, with the new social milieu that had taken shape in England. Yet the Puritans and the other representatives of the new did not by any means see it clearly. Like the religious reformers, the revolutionaries of bourgeois England of the middle of the seventeenth century appealed not to the circumstances of the present, but to the Bible for their justification . . . *[and especially to the Old Testament, in which the Jewish priesthood attacks kingship, while the New Testament preached submission to secular princes—which had suited Luther's political needs].*

The eighteenth century then brought a brilliant flowering of the sciences and reduction of religious thought. . . . And yet even the boldest innovators of this epoch could not do without the support of the old. . . . Edification was found in the examples of the republicans of ancient Greece and above all in the Brutuses and the Catos of Rome, who had chased out kings and fought against and slain despots. *[Montesquieu sought his ideal of moderate progress not in the future of France but in the present and recent past of England, while the more revolutionary Rousseau found his ideal all the way back in the state of nature.]*

When it appeared in the nineteenth century, born out of the evils of the age, socialism, too, at first sought its backing in the past. Either also in natural law or in Christianity, though, of course, not in the contemporary one, but in primitive Christianity, not in its servility with regard to authority, but rather in its communism. *[Kautsky quotes Saint-Simon's "New Christianity" of 1825, p. 110, and a passage written in 1853 by Cabet as quoted in Lux,* Etienne Cabet, *p. 158.]* In addition to the justification of socialism by means of natural law or of Christianity, it was supported by references to earlier forms of communism, sought after or realized, from Sparta and Plato onward to the communal ownership of land in Russian villages.

The socialist movement of the nineteenth century had to have ceased being something totally new, it had to have become an acknowledged part of existing reality before the task was undertaken of deriving its content from the needs of the present and not from the forms of the past. That was done most completely by Marx and Engels, who showed that the socialist ideal necessarily arises out of the development of capitalism and that this development provides the conditions of its realization. . . . When something new has been recognized as *necessary* or *inevitable*, there is no longer any need to show that it proved itself in the past. Such proof even becomes senseless when the new is shown to be the necessary product of present-day circumstances that have no equivalents in the past.

If, however, a new social idea is something quite new, something that has never and nowhere proved itself, then it must . . . confine itself to merely serving us as a guideline, not as a presentation of the form the new will ultimately assume. This can arise only out of everyday practice and what is learned from it, and that practice must take as its basis that which is well known, the practice of today. The better we come to know the latter, its laws and its means, the more effectively will we be able to adapt it to the new needs, which we have likewise already clearly grasped, the less will the era of transition from the old to the new be characterized by institutions and attempts that have miscarried. . . . Not without reason did Marx apply all of his energy to studying present-day capitalism and always refused to think up "recipes for the cook-shop of the future." . . . Not through alluring pictures of the new that was to come did Marx and Engels contribute so much to the strengthening of the socialist movement, but through their recognition of the elements of the new already in existence, to the furthering and strengthening of which they directed the socialists' attention.

Nonetheless, no matter how great the self-restraint was that Marx and Engels imposed on themselves in their analyses of the forms of the future, all of their thinking and striving was still devoted to that future, whose already existing elements they had recognized better than anyone else before them. And they had to develop definite ideas about the forms of the path leading to the goal, though not about the forms of the goal itself. And in this regard we find that, as long as a great deal of new experience was not available, it was impossible for them, too, to envisage the coming new differently than as a return to something old. At the time when the *Com-*

munist Manifesto was written, they still imagined the coming revolution on the model of the bygone great French Revolution. . . .

Even for many a decade after the composition of the *Communist Manifesto*, we socialists imagined the path of the proletarian revolution, which we expected, according to the example of the bourgeois revolutions. Democracy had to be reasonably firmly established in the most important states of Europe and to have some effects; the proletariat had to have achieved intellectual and organizational independence, and we had to have accumulated much new experience . . . , before we reached the point where we recognized that the path of the proletariat to political power and economic emancipation was different from that of the bourgeois revolutions. Here, too, we came to recognize the new only when its elements already existed in abundance and were sufficiently obvious.

Even among Marxists, the tendency can still be found, not to account for what is new by means of new, already existent elements of the environment and thereby to justify it, but to make it out to be something old, something long since acknowledged by us, and thus to justify it. *[Kautsky quotes from the first page of Marx's* Eighteenth Brumaire of Louis Bonaparte *(p. 146; MESW, I, 398) the passage saying, in part, that just when men]* "appear to be engaged in revolutionizing themselves and things, in creating something that has never yet existed . . . they timidly conjure up the spirits of the past to help them, they borrow from them names, battle cries and costumes. . . . "

In spite of this ridicule, the Bolsheviks and their adherents in many different countries are proceeding in the very same manner in our own time. . . . They justify their completely new doctrine not with the quite unusual conditions in which it has arisen. Rather, as Luther and his followers supposed that what they were striving for was the return to primitive Christianity, which later generations had adulterated, Lenin and his followers claimed that what they taught and practiced was nothing else than the pure primitive communism of the *Communist Manifesto . . . [which]* had been adulterated by Social Democracy. Some of Lenin's disciples even maintain that Marx and Engels themselves had later added water to the wine of the *Communist Manifesto* and thereby diluted it. That, of course, is nothing but the fact that Marx and Engels did not remain stuck in their beginnings, but later derived new insights from what they learned from new experiences.

Present-day communists oppose the tactics Marx and Engels approved of when they were employed by the Social Democratic movement of their time. But the Bolsheviks are of the opinion that the doctrine they have preached since 1917 is not a bold innovation, but rather the return to the good old days of the Marxism of 1847. In addition, they also invoke the Paris commune of 1871 and the even older Jacobinism of 1793. On the other hand, to be sure, they feel hurt when traces of the spirit of Blanqui, Weitling, Bakunin, Nechayev are also discovered in their ideas.

All these examples from very remote and very recent times surely show quite clearly how innovators in the social sphere differ from those in the technical sphere. They are at the beginning little aware of what is new in their views and are inclined to let the new appear as something old, either something that has already proved itself in practice or something that was at least advocated by a recognized authority in the past.

We quite disregard here the fact that, like their action, men's thinking, too, has to begin with what already exists; that an innovation can consist only in the modification of what already exists; that there exists nothing new, even in thought, the elements of which do not already exist. But where, then, does that which is new in human development come from? What is new in the evolution of vegetable and animal organisms comes from the transformations of their environment, of nature. The beginnings of human technology, too, must be explained through transformations of the climate and of vegetation, which in turn can be traced back to alterations of the Earth's surface or of its position in planetary space, to the ground subsiding or rising, to ice ages and similar phenomena.

But how is the further development of technology to be explained, which has been taking place in historical time, a period in which, as we know quite definitely, the natural environment has on the whole not changed? Of what help to us is it to assume that the development of technology even in its higher stages, and ultimately even the development of social ideas, is also nothing else than a progressive adaptation of men to a constantly changing environment? Can a transformation of the environment that ensues neither from transformations of nature nor from spontaneous transformations of the mind be anything else than something supernatural? . . . As long as we are not able to show how, without a change of nature, something new that has not previously appeared in his head as an idea can enter into man's environment, we are faced with an unsolved mystery.

CHAPTER FOURTEEN

Advantages Due to Fertility and Mineral Wealth

We have moved forward from the Stone Age to Bolshevism in a few rapid leaps. Now we must return to the Stone Age and, in fact, to its beginnings.

Man entered upon the path of his higher development out of the ape-stage when a new environment further developed in him the ability to use natural objects . . . as implements in his struggle for existence and when the same new environment impelled him to employ his acquired abilities in such a manner. Two factors were therefore necessary to this development. First, the necessary abilities, above all, those of the mind and of the hand, and the availability of the necessary implements. Without these, the former were useless.

Now, the nature of the ground on the Earth's surface varies greatly. It does not bear the same plants and the same minerals everywhere. Among the first implements man learned to use were stones of particular shapes. These are by no means to be found everywhere. . . . It is clear that in regions where flintstone occurred frequently, men could much more readily come to use tools and weapons and thereby facilitate their struggle for existence and also to accumulate new experiences than men in other regions, even when the latter were not backward either with regard to mental ability or to manual skill. . . .

According to the different characteristics of the regions inhabited by men, not only the materials from which their tools were made and these tools themselves, but also the ways in which they were used necessarily had to assume different forms. Humanity became more and more differentiated, at first into hunters, agriculturalists, fishermen, cattle-raisers. . . . From the beginning, man lived from vegetables, from the fruits of the soil, which he rooted up and finally also learned to cultivate. There is hardly a people that lives without vegetable fare. It then depends on the environment man happens to enter whether, in addition, he develops hunting or fishing more. The one does not by any means preclude the other, however. Lastly, we find that the keeping of tame animals is very widespread even in early stages of civilization, alongside agriculture, hunting, and fishing. . . .

Often one meets with . . . all four ways of making a living side by side, but combined in very different degrees. . . . Which of the branches of obtaining foodstuffs predominates in a given instance . . . depends far less on the level of civilization of a people than on the nature of the region it inhabits. Thus the latter conditions not just the character of the tools being employed, but also the ends to which they are employed—and therewith the way of life of a people, its habits, character, skills, and experiences, and hence its knowledge and its views. In this manner, a differentiation among the various peoples becomes noticeable quite early.

And already when tools are first used, we find that some peoples enjoy a monopoly in the possession of materials that are indispensable for the technology corresponding to a given state of knowledge and of skills. . . . Thus, even at the beginning of civilization, there is a distinction between privileged peoples and those who are disadvantaged, who are excluded from the enjoyment of the assets of civilization. It was not capitalism that first created these differences. It was initially nature with its differences that created such monopolies. . . .

Just as today, monopoly engendered a striving to overcome it even in its beginnings. To be sure, every tribe was self-sufficient in the beginnings of civilization. . . . And each tribe spoke its own language. Still, we must not imagine that the individual communities were hermetically closed off from each other. . . . Men were then not tied to the soil. If the conditions in their own area became unbearable, . . . it was possible . . . to migrate into the neighboring area and to establish oneself there, peaceably or by force, permanently or temporarily. . . . The dialects were . . . after all not so different as to preclude all communication, especially when the more international language of gestures was used to help out. . . . Thus the individual tribes of mankind's remote past were in all likelihood never . . . completely without some relationship with their neighbors. These were relationships of very diverse kinds, hostile and amicable, but the latter kind were, most probably, as a rule, preferred, since they did not demand sacrifices. . . .

The result of these relationships must have been that the knowledge of tools and the methods both of production and of combat did not by any means remain the monopoly of the tribes in whose areas the preconditions for these tools and methods were solely to be found. As soon as the neighbors learned of their existence and became acquainted with their advantages, . . . they felt impelled likewise to acquire possession of these implements, . . . either through theft and conquest or through amicable exchange. Here, too, the first method was probably mostly the rarer one. . . . Although wars were very numerous even in prehistory, nevertheless we also find, even at an early time, indications of regularly occurring barter, although only between communities. The development of mankind must have attained a quite high level before the individual merchant made his appearance.

What objects were likely to have been given in exchange for the materials and tools of the tribes favored by nature? . . . Luxury objects were best suited for exchange, for example, articles of adornment, which frequently were small and weighed little relative to their value, did not easily decay, and of which one could never have too much, precisely because they were luxury objects, that is, they were superfluous, whereas one always needs only a definite quantity of what is necessary. . . . In addition, sundry luxury foods that could not be found everywhere, above all, salt, but also some spices. Later, products of special craftsmanship were added to these items. . . .

The sites where materials for luxury objects are to be found, which can be given in exchange for useful technical implements, become just as important for technical progress as the places where materials for tools are found. Peoples who dispose of neither the one nor the other are badly off and, in the development of technology, they fall far behind the possessors of more richly endowed ground. . . .

Advantages Due to
Geographical Location

Geographical location can become even more important than possession of sites where useful materials can be found. For having a certain material at one's disposal only makes possible, after all, the production and the employment of implements made from this one material. Through barter, on the other hand, one can establish relations with very different sites yielding very different materials and can thus achieve a considerable diversity in the implements one uses. A geographical location favorable to commerce in several directions can thus extraordinarily promote a people's development. On the other hand, it is condemned to a backwardness that can become hopeless if its location cuts it off from international trade. . . .

Proof that barter-trade must have begun already in the early stages of technology is given by the fact that tools and weapons made of certain kinds of stone have been found in regions where there is not the least occurrence of the material. *[Kautsky cites numerous examples from Peschel,* The Races of Man, *p. 209; von den Steinen,* Unter den Naturvölkern Zentral-brasiliens, *p. 203; Somló,* Der Güterverkehr, *pp. 18, 22; and Mach,* Kultur und Mechanik, *p. 62.]* At the sites where good stone material was to be found, there developed a lively production of tools and weapons. Extensive workplaces of this kind have been discovered. *[Examples are cited from Lubbock (Lord Avebury),* Prehistoric Times, *pp. 80–81; Hauser,* Der Mensch vor 100,000 Jahren, *pp. 38 ff.; and Somló,* Der Güterverkehr, *pp. 23–24.]*

The commerce between tribes did not merely serve the purpose of exchange of tools, weapons, and ornaments, however. It could become even more important through the exchange of knowledge and of methods, not just those of producing things, but also those of producing ideas, of combining complexes of relations that had been observed and handed down into higher-order internally coherent relational complexes. Just as much as the communication of foreign technology, the communication of foreign experiences and of the ideas stimulated by them is a means for the development of mankind. This is one of the points in which man rises above the animal. Among animals, only the younger, less experienced individual can learn from the older, more experienced ones. The adult, experienced individual, however, *[cannot learn]* from another animal of the same species. For they all live in the same conditions, are all provided with the same organs, and therefore have the same experiences.

In the beginning of civilization, as long as there is no division of labor among the adults of the same sex within a community, the adult, fully experienced human being can learn nothing new from his fellows. But the differentiation of their modes of production among the polities begins early and therewith the differentiation of their experiences and their knowledge.

The possibility thereby arises of learning things from foreigners that cannot be learned from the other members of one's own tribe and of thus going beyond the stage of knowledge and of culture given by one's own living conditions. . . . *[Kautsky refers at length to the example of ancient Greece, linked by numerous islands to the Middle East and its culture and itself subdivided into small areas with different cultures.]* To these great contrasts of the shape and resources of the land there corresponded far-reaching contrasts of economic and political organization. . . . In view of these contrasts, how much each of the Hellenic districts could learn from the other, how much intellectual stimulation, how much knowledge beyond the limits of its own experience reached it!

[Similarly, Palestine was located on important trade routes and surrounded by peoples of different cultures.] Intellectually, the Jews derived very great advantage from this situation. Not, however, economically or politically. Their land was poor in products that would have been suitable for exchange. And the little nation was too small and too weak to be able to exploit the transit-trade in the manner of brigands. . . .

CHAPTER SIXTEEN

Changing Advantages Due to Natural Factors

. . . The plant and mineral wealth of a country can be exhausted in the course of time by continuous demands upon it. In the case of mineral deposits, this . . . must occur sooner or later. . . . Plant life can renew itself again and again, but even some of it can be exhausted. That is especially true of forests. . . . Deforestation made it more difficult for the seafaring peoples of *[Phoenicia, Greece, and Venice]* to obtain wood for shipbuilding; it also, however, changed the climate for the worse, made the land infertile, and thereby diminished its population. . . . *[It]* is an important cause of the decay of old centers of civilization and of their decline into barbarous conditions.

The mere progress of technology alone, however, without the least diminution of the wealth of the soil in the products that make it superior to the soil of other areas, can also suffice to deprive a region of the advantages it gave to its inhabitants. . . . *[Once metals come into use, the availability of flint loses its significance.]* On the other hand, as a consequence of technological progress, a region can acquire a value it did not previously possess. As soon as it is possible to construct a profitably functioning solar machine that permits the conversion of solar heat into motive power, then the Sahara, today an unpopulated desert, may become the site of prosperous industry. That the advantage of a location with respect to commerce can change as technology changes hardly needs further illustration. . . . The adaptation of the technology of shipbuilding to the conditions of the ocean transformed

Britain's insular position at the edge of the ocean and yet also off the coast of Europe from a disadvantage into a very great advantage. It ceased to be at the outermost edge of world trade and came to be at its center. . . .

From the beginning of the human race and its diffusion in the world, some regions have proven themselves to be naturally favorable to its development, others to be unfavorable, so that differences have appeared among the various groups of peoples in the pace and the manner of their development. However, it is not always the same natural conditions that are favorable or unfavorable for development. Their effect changes with the state of technology. Nowhere on earth, therefore, do we find the same region always at the forefront of the development of civilization. . . .

From the decline of earlier civilized nations, the conclusion has been drawn that human societies are organisms similar to animal or vegetable individuals. As for the latter, so for the former it is said to be a law of nature that they go through stages of childhood, of growth, and of maturity, finally to fall prey to old age and death. This conception is widespread and yet it is quite absurd. . . . The human race has always been mature, just as its animal ancestors, too, were always mature in every stage of the development of their species; that is, they were capable of preserving themselves without outside help. It makes no sense at all to extend the concept of childhood from the individual to a species. . . . Nor does it make more sense to speak of the old age and the dying of nations. . . . When someone languishes under the effects of unfavorable external circumstances and finally perishes, no one will want to maintain that he died of old age. . . . Moreover, the so-called aging of nations is often nothing other than either their remaining at a state they have already attained to, . . . or it is a regression from a stage that has been reached to earlier ones, thus, according to the conception we are discussing, to younger stages. Consequently, this aging involves becoming younger! . . .

And then to speak of the death of a people! If it is to be a parallel to the death of the individual, then it must mean that all the members of a people perish, without leaving descendants. . . . In most cases when a people seems to disappear from history, in reality it only changes its name or becomes intermingled with another people whose name it assumes. Neither the one nor the other is a symptom of old age. . . . However, most cases of the aging and dying of a people that have supposedly been found in history have nothing at all to do with peoples, but rather with states. . . . A state is nothing but a particular organizational form of human beings. An organization can become inappropriate, it can fail, disintegrate, cease to exist, without its members therefore having to languish or even disappear. . . .

We are living in an age when there are already early indications of those circumstances being overcome on which the differences among the various peoples in their levels of civilization have been based and in consequence of which the leading role among them changed from one to the other.

Advances in the technology of transportation have been so immense that they are beginning to level out all those differences. They are bringing peoples and states into such close contact with one another that the monopoly of certain ones among them over some indispensable raw materials and sources of power will necessarily disappear in order to make way for an international communal ownership, just as today, in the most highly developed countries, the abolition of the monopoly enjoyed by a small number of landowners and capitalists over the most important sources of life already constitutes a goal that a constantly growing class and party is striving with all its might to attain.

Further, the development of transportation technology must ultimately have the result that every particular disadvantage of a location with respect to transport can also be more and more overcome. If the maritime location of a territory was decisive into the nineteenth century for the extent of its participation in world trade, since that time railways have increasingly served to make the interiors of countries accessible. The sphere of world commerce is thereby being rapidly expanded from year to year.... And what possibilities aeronautic technology holds for the future!... However, none of the technical advances needs any longer to cause the peoples who are now the most highly developed to be pushed back by others. That was, to be sure, the inevitable course of history as long as there was no real world trade, but only individual areas with relatively intense commerce with one another and numerous other areas whose trade with the outside world was almost nil.

The constant change in the ranking of the peoples involving very different races and climates cannot be explained by permanent differences among the races or climates, which are supposed to confer forever on a certain race or on men living in a certain climate the aptitude for leadership in world history. But where does this change come from? We have traced it back to changes in technology. Where do these changes come from? The advantage of some regions due to their fertility and mineral wealth and to their location with regard to transportation explains why their inhabitants advanced more rapidly with respect to technological development and its consequences than the inhabitants of other areas. However, that still does not by any means explain the process of technological development itself. We have seen what conditions foster it and which ones hinder it, but not what the force is that keeps it going once it has begun, so that it continues on without interruption. We have still not shown where that which is new in men's ideas, first of all in their technical ideas, comes from, the new that impels human society onward again and again and never permits the historical process to come permanently to a halt.

We have accounted for the beginnings of technology by changes in man's natural environment, for example, the subsidence of an area or ice ages, which played a large role in the very period when men raised themselves above the animal world. But the closer we come to the stage in which man's proper history, his written history, begins, the less it becomes possible to explain technical advances by changes of nature. Within the domain of written history, changes of the natural environment that could be explained by natural causes take place only rarely. In just this period of time, though, technical progress assumes an ever faster tempo.

We consider it impossible for the human mind to bring forth out of itself and at will the impetus for this progress. Rather, we must assume that it has its origin in the external world. But where does this something that is new in the external world come from, which again and again poses new problems for the human mind and provides it with new means for solving them; which does not allow it to rest content with its accomplishments, but compels it continuously to seek new solutions by new means? As long as we are unable to give an answer to this question, history will remain a field from which mysticism cannot be eradicated.

Section Three
The Economy

CHAPTER ONE

Natural and Artificial Organs

Once again we must put ourselves back in the Stone Age, in order to obtain a new point of departure for the solution of our problem.

The implements of primitive man . . . serve to extend his natural organs . . . or to strengthen, replace, or supplement them. . . . In order to function correctly, they must have become almost as familiar to man through their constant use as his natural organs, so that they obey his wishes just as these do and become, so to speak, a part of his own self. . . . The tool must . . . be adapted just as much to his own nature as to the nature surrounding him, on which it is to have an effect. The artificial organ has to enter into an intimate partnership with his natural organs. Even then, there nevertheless persists the great difference that the latter are permanently joined to the human body, while the former can be laid down as soon as they are not needed. *They become man's organs yet constitute at the same time parts of his environment.* It is their twofold character that becomes extremely important as it provides the basis of a new kind of evolution that goes beyond the kinds of evolution proper to natural organisms. In what follows, this point shall be examined more closely.

In the case of the natural organs of an organism, their differentiation and division of labor soon find, in any particular instance, definite limits. Of course, only what already exists can be adapted to new conditions; never can something completely new be created. . . . The differentiation of the natural limbs cannot go any further than it has in man, in whom the anterior extremities serve solely for grasping and striking, the posterior ones exclusively for locomotion, and in whose hands a further differentiation occurs between the right and the left one. . . . Even more far-reaching than the differentiation of man's limbs is that of his nervous system, especially that of the different sections of the brain. . . . Man's organic development beyond the animal has taken place to the greatest degree in the structure of his brain. . . . But even the development of the brain can merely effect a re-shaping of its already existing parts. . . .

The fact that all organs of an organism must serve the whole, that they must all be in a certain harmony among themselves, suffices of itself to set definite and very narrowly drawn limits to the development of every organ. The one-sided development of a single part that disrupts the functioning of other parts damages the organism as a whole, is detrimental to it in its struggle for existence and eliminates it. . . .

Since the organism cannot put down its organs and switch from one to another, it has to employ most of them successively for very different functions. Here, too, it is evident that the whole is more important than the part. The one-sided adaptation to a single function of an organ that is supposed to serve in succession a variety of functions is detrimental to the performance of the other functions and is thereby detrimental also to the entire organism; it does not permit such individuals to emerge and to propagate themselves. . . .

In addition to all that, every organism has at its disposal only a certain amount of strength that is conditioned by the amount of food it is able to obtain and assimilate. With this limited amount of strength all its organs must be set in motion. Once a harmony among the individual organs is also attained in this regard, then a shift of this relationship in favor of one organ that is now better nourished and more capable than before means that the other organs become stunted. And in no case can the enlargement or strengthening of an organ go beyond a definite limit.

The artificial organs of man are completely free of these limitations. As they are not parts of his organism, he is able to make use of powers other than those of his own body to move them: the powers of other men, which join with his own; those of animals; later the powers of water, of wind, of steam, etc., as soon as he learns to tame them and to make them serviceable for his purposes. The more he succeeds in doing this, the more gigantic his artificial organs can become. . . .

Thus the growth of man's artificial organs finds no limits in the natural limitation of his body. And the same holds true for the differentiation of these organs. . . . He can now fabricate tools that are adapted only to a single function. . . . The more diverse the experiences and the knowledge he thereby obtains, the more extensive the commerce engaged in by his polity, the more numerous and various the tools and the raw materials brought to him by that commerce, the more multifarious are the ways of making use of his tools, the greater are the impulses to and the possibilities for their progressive differentiation. The differentiation of tools and raw materials then also results in a greater differentiation in the uses of the hand and the brain and sometimes of other natural organs, too. . . . But even then the differentiations of the natural organs still remain confined within narrow limits, while the differentiation of artificial organs is practically unlimited.

Or, to put it more correctly, their limits are more broadly drawn. They are not determined by the need for harmony and the strength of a single individual, but rather by the extent of this need and the strength in the *society*, in which the artificial implements are put to use. A tool or a utensil that does not fit in with the life-process of a society and would disrupt it, cannot arise in it. . . . Like the individual animal organism and its natural organs, society and technology are very closely interrelated and interact with one another.

CHAPTER TWO

Working Together

The fact that man's artificial organs are not an integral part of him, but are separate from him, offers two possibilities, both of which become extraordinarily important. . . . First, the possibility that several men can work together to jointly set an organ into motion, when the strength of a single individual is insufficient to do so. Second, the possibility that different men can simultaneously or successively set into motion different artificial organs, all of which serve a common end. Thus human technology engenders two kinds of working on the part of man: *working with one another* and *working for one another*.[1] These kinds of work are almost entirely unique to man. . . . Even in the case of man, technology must have already attained a certain level before he reaches the point of fabricating implements that require the cooperation of several men for their use, like, for example, moving a relatively large boat. . . .

Only the emergence of artificial organs makes it possible that working together and working for one another are not something exceptional *[as among animals]*, but become something that occurs regularly and extends to very different areas, facilitated by the evolution of language, which is in turn powerfully promoted by these different kinds of cooperative labor.

The simplest kinds of working together and for one another among some

---

1. Kautsky had already touched on the distinction between these two types of work in *The Economic Doctrines of Karl Marx*, pp. 129–31.

animals that always recur in the same manner can finally become habits, which are either taught by the adults or are even transmitted by heredity, like the proclivity to nest building among birds. The purposive adaptation of the general habit or of the inherited instinct to the peculiarities of the particular case doubtless requires communication of the participants among themselves. . . . However, the means of communication are in any case so meager that they would lead only with difficulty to some agreement on more diverse or even novel behavior, should the animals' living conditions require such activity. At least as a rule, this does not occur in the conservative states of nature, when its equilibrium has not been disturbed. What keeps most social animals together is the need for protection and for guidance of the less experienced by the more experienced. On the other hand, even among the social animals, each individual sees to obtaining food for itself once the pasture or the location of fruit has been reached.

Only among men does the acquisition of food become a social process. It expands ever more to include the satisfaction of very different needs unknown to the animal, like those for clothing, lodging, adornment, knowledge, etc. As this occurs, the individual becomes increasingly dependent on society for the satisfaction of his needs; the relations inherent in working with and for one another become increasingly diverse and ever more close.

The far-reaching division of labor among men, which follows the lines of the division of labor among his tools and other implements, becomes particularly important. At first the division of labor among the tools—understood in the broadest sense of the word so that it also comprehends weapons and utensils—permits the same man successively to put into operation different artificial organs with one and the same natural organ. Soon, however, the point is reached where there also arises a division of labor among men: some constantly use certain tools for certain purposes and become familiar with them, while the others do not know how to use them, as they are accustomed to employ quite different tools for quite different ends. It is as though the single human species were divided into different species with different organs. But these artificially created, different species of man are distinguished from the natural animal species by the fact that none of them can permanently make do without the other species of man, that it needs the others either in order to be able to live at all, or at least in order to be able to live well, adequately to satisfy its needs and wants.

The first great division of labor of this kind, brought about by the development of technology, . . . is the one called forth by the emergence of artificial weapons, which become exclusively organs of males. These become hunters and warriors; the women remain faithful to the manner of obtaining food originally practiced by the entire species: the gathering of vegetable food stuffs and of lower-order small animals of various species. After fire has been tamed, the women also becomes its guardian; the domestic hearth becomes her domain, as does the processing of all the raw materials hunting man delivers to her, meat for cooking, skins for making clothes and tents, to which she also adds plaiting of many vegetable materials familiar to her. Both men and women now work for one another, for the common household of a smaller or a larger family; they are dependent upon one another and are bound to each other by economic ties.[2]

The next stage of the division of labor . . . is brought about by the differing availability of raw materials in different regions. Thus, there arises at a very early time an international division of labor in which the inhabitants of different regions develop specialties they exchange with one another.[3] . . . As dissimilar and apparently alien to one another as the individual polities might be, whose products thus come to be exchanged, they do in fact work for one another, they are dependent on one another.

It takes a long time until the division of labor moves beyond its first two stages, until particular occupations are formed within the ranks of the adults of each sex. For women, division into occupations made its appearance as a mass phenomenon only in the course of the last century. . . .

All human beings who are directly or indirectly dependent on one another by virtue of the division of labor stand in a social relationship with each other. At an early time, this relationship extends beyond the sphere of the polity to which the individual belongs. In contrast to the polity, this general social relationship is not produced by a stable organization with rules and boundaries laid down by the members of the organization themselves, but only by the more or less strongly felt need of all those who live in and through this relationship. This relationship constitutes what is called *"the"* society, as distinct from the individual, and for the most part firmly delimited, social formations, the individual societies that exist within the society.

"The" society is proper only to man. . . . Within a species of social animals, more or less loose animal societies are formed. In the case of man, these societies become closed. Each one is permanently separated from the other societies of the members of the species by characteristics that are different in different historical periods, such as, for example, a particular language, a particular (presupposed common) ancestor in the case of organizations based on consanguinity, a particular territory, particular common organs, e.g., chieftains, judges, etc., common traditions, etc.

If one of these societies is firmly organized and sovereign, then it constitutes a polity [Gemeinwesen], a concept not to be equated with the state. The latter is a particular kind of polity, of which we shall treat in Part Four. Within the polity, smaller organizations of many different kinds can take

2. See also II:4:3, above.
3. See III:2:14–15, above.

form. Above all of them stands "the" society, also called "civil" society, as distinct from the smaller societies in it.[4] *[Kautsky quotes a passage from his Die Marxsche Staatsauffassung, p. 39.]*

"The" society has so far never comprehended all of mankind. The latter has always been divided into several circles of men. Each of these circles constituted that which we call "the" society. That is, each of these circles was held together by the fact that its members, often without knowing it, worked for one another and were therefore constantly dependent on each other. Each such circle had an economic life of its own and had no relationship whatsoever with other circles of this kind. Its extent was dependent on the conditions of commerce at any given time. . . .

Only in our day is modern European society, which has taken hold of all continents, beginning to become identical with mankind, a fact that unfortunately expresses itself not only in world trade but also in world wars. . . . And while the scope of world trade has rapidly expanded in the last centuries, its intensity has also increased enormously. In the beginnings of exchange, only a very few tools, . . . or the materials for them, as well as luxury articles and luxury foods were exchanged. Since that time, the division of labor among nations and within nations has increased so much that for none of them can productive as well as personal consumption any longer proceed to the accustomed extent if world trade is disrupted.

CHAPTER THREE

Working for One Another

This growing dependence of nations and of individuals within every nation is the basis of a theory of the continuous moral perfection that is supposed to be brought about by industrial progress. *[Kautsky quotes Spencer,* The Principles of Sociology, *I, 63]* According to this theory, men begin to understand that every individual lives better, the better off his neighbors are, those for whom he works, and those who work for him, his suppliers or his customers. Thus social sensibility increases more and more; the antagonisms among men, those among individuals, classes, and nations, dwindle. We need only develop industry, and the most perfect morality and the most peaceable society, with peace among the classes and world peace, comes to pass of its own accord. *[There follow half a dozen passages quoted from Spencer,* The Data of Ethics, *pp. 225, 241, 244–48, and 259–60, which argue that "egoism comes before altruism," but that growing altruism brings advantages to each individual.]* Therefore, a reasonable egoist will act altruisti-

---

4. See also *Krieg und Demokratie*, pp. 12–14.

cally and see to it that justice is done, that the state punctually pays the interest on its debts, that workers work hard, and that no one's bill is left unpaid. . . .

We have examined these lines of reasoning more closely here because they are still very effective, even in socialist circles, especially in those influenced by British thought. Many pacifists, too, still think entirely like Spencer. His whole argumentation is founded on the assumption that men's working for one another calls forth a community of interests, a solidarity among them, and thus an intensity of morality, of social sensibility that grows with the intensity of commerce.

However, when a man works for me, I certainly have an interest in his accomplishing as much as possible for me, but not at all in my working as much as possible for him. The more he works for me, and the less I work for him, the better for me. . . . The relationship between buyers and sellers by no means causes a commonality, but rather an antagonism of interests. Each individual seeks to give as few products of his own labor as possible in exchange for as many products of others' labor as possible. . . . Only after a long development, which makes commodity production the universal form of production, does the law of value, *[the law of the exchange of equal values, that is, of equal amounts of labor,]* finally prevail, but even then only when there is free competition and buyers and sellers have equal power.

To begin with, everyone who needs a commodity he does not possess seeks to obtain it as far beneath its value as possible. This is achieved most radically when the commodity is taken with no compensation, when it is stolen. It is well known that in his beginnings, the trader is a pirate or a highwayman whenever the opportunity arises. Other methods used by one of superior strength against a weaker one in order to make the latter work for the former without corresponding compensation are: enslaving him; imposing a payment of rent on him; or employing him as a wage-laborer, who is paid as a wage only part of the value created by him.

If some of these methods of making others work for oneself have fallen into disuse in the course of historical development, that is not due to the ever-increasing elevation of morality brought about by the growing extent to which men work for one another. Rather, it is due in part to the fact that the plundered and the exploited acquire the strength to defend themselves. . . . Even the more peaceful methods by which the seller takes advantage of the buyer undergo a curtailment through the buyers' resistance where trade in commodities becomes a regularly occurring phenomenon, where the same buyers and sellers encounter each other again and again in the same marketplace. . . .

In this way, to be sure, the development of commodity trade does produce a certain "business morality," which under normal circumstances—not, therefore, in times of war or inflation, for example—distinguishes business life in highly industrialized states from that of backward ones. Now honesty really becomes the best policy. Now the law of value, too, prevails in commodity trade.

This morality, however, is of a very negative nature. . . . It does not contain the least impetus to helpfulness, to sacrifice of money, property, and strength, and possibly even to risking one's life, in order to mitigate the suffering of others and to rescue people whose prosperity or existence is threatened. This business morality is not erected upon an inner need, but upon a commercial calculation of what the most profitable way of proceeding is. It fails immediately as soon as new conditions arise in which deception and violence can be practiced without punishment and without loss of credit and the ability to sell one's goods. Businessmen, who are so rigorously respectable and honest in a highly industrialized country, do not scruple in the least to plunder and cheat defenseless and ignorant natives in the colonies. And the abnormal exigency of the state in wartime immediately causes a class of fraudulent suppliers to flourish, which for years sends all business morality to the devil.

Something similar is true also of the exploitation of workers. The masters of big industry set no value on slavery and serfdom or on the servitude of rent-paying tenants because the fine machines they employ would only be badly operated by workers obtained in such a manner. However, where it is a matter of labor-processes with cruder work methods, these same gentlemen find nothing to object to in slavery. The liberal British spinners were opposed to slavery at home, but it seemed very agreeable to them in the cotton-growing areas of the United States.

The higher morality that is supposed to ensue from the higher development of commerce and industry . . . was compatible with the most cruel mistreatment of women and children in capitalist industry. . . . Here, too, it was not the influence of growing economic dependence of men on one another, but the growing resistance of the wage-laborers that gradually taught the capitalists better manners and a kind of "social sensibility." The workers have to educate their masters to this end, a troublesome task that up to now has achieved significant results only in a few countries. And even there the exploiter's brutal basic attitude again comes to the fore as soon as the classes' relative power changes. . . . There is no doubt that the entrepreneurs themselves have an interest in the productivity of their workers and that this productivity increases with good wages and moderate working hours. Not even this calculation, however, can prevail against the general antagonism of interests that exists between the buyers and the sellers of the commodity labor power, if it is not helped along by an energetic resistance on the part of the latter. . . .

That is not to say that no morality at all can be found among entrepreneurs and vendors. We only maintain that such a morality does not arise from men's *working for one another*. But this is just one side of men's social work. The other consists in their *cooperation*. . . . Thanks to his technology, man adds to the motives of social coherence taken over from the animal world collective labor with common means for common goals and thereby creates a new and powerful source of solidarity and morality. . . .

Morality develops in yet another way along with human society, its commerce, and its division of labor. The more the scope of what is called "the" society is broadened, and the more the states, churches, and classes attain to an ever-greater expansion in it, the more does the extent of moral feelings that the individual harbors within himself grow also for him, until finally there appears the idea that they apply to the whole species, to all of humanity. That, however, has hitherto always proved to be an illusion. . . . To this day, one of the sources of morality is found in the struggle of one community or society of men against other men. We socialists are no exception. The nature and the intensity of proletarian morality are very closely connected with the nature and intensity of the proletarian class struggle, with the struggle, therefore, between proletarian and other men.[5] In any case, morality originates from a commonality of struggle or of work for a common goal striven for with common or concordant means.

On the other hand, working for one another has completely different effects from working together. It strengthens not morality but egoism, for at bottom it is nothing other than a roundabout way of working for oneself.

Even in the first association formed on the basis of the division of labor in society, the marital union, the contrast between working together and working for one another becomes apparent. As an association of two human beings who work for one another, marriage develops the tendency of each of the two spouses to make the other work as much as possible for him or herself, something which, given certain relations of power, leads to the dear wife being completely reduced to a slave. . . . Here, again, equality of the sexes in marriage is not brought about by the increase of the dependence of each of the two partners on the work of the other, but rather by a sufficient capacity for resistance on the part of the hitherto oppressed and exploited spouse, which grows out of new circumstances. Marriage shows also another side, however. It is an association in which the spouses work not merely *for one another* but also *with one another* for a common end: raising their children and making them into capable persons. . . . The resulting moral cohesion . . . is increased further when common activity for other common goals is added to this. . . .

But where will the moral cohesion of a socialist society come from when the class struggle, which produces morality, ceases with the elimination of classes? . . . Only socially organized, common action on the part of the workers—and then all people will be workers—for common ends with

5. See IV:8:13, below.

common means is able to eliminate the class struggle. There will thus develop for the first time in the history of the world a morality that no longer has its origin in a struggle of men against men, that in fact is able to encompass the entire human race in its full extent and that arises exclusively from the common struggle against the natural environment.

CHAPTER FOUR

Technology, Economy, and Obtaining Food

The nature of the implements . . . men utilize in order to satisfy their needs and to maintain themselves in the struggle for existence is very closely connected with the manner in which men work with one another and for one another when they employ these implements. But these two factors must be rigorously distinguished as *technology* and *economy*. . . . Nevertheless, economic theory is fond of confusing these two, even today.

And yet, Marxist economic theory has, for more than a half century, been developed in *Capital*, where the distinction between the two factors is explained with great clarity—one of the greatest achievements of Marxist economic thought. This is just as significant as the discovery of the fetish character of commodities, of the fact that the exchange of commodities is nothing else than a particular kind of men's working for one another. This distinction between the commodity as a product of social labor and its material character as an object of use is closely linked with the distinction between the material, technical character and the social, economic character of labor. *[Kautsky quotes Marx*, Capital, *I, 290–91.]*

Often the most diverse kinds of social labor are compatible with one and the same technology. Let us consider a modern factory. It can be run in a capitalistic manner. . . . The products are sent to market. The proceeds from them belong to the capitalist. But the same factory can also be run cooperatively by a producers' cooperative association made up of workers who own it in common. . . . A producers' cooperative association, too, produces for the market. Finally, the factory can also be owned by the consumers of its products—a consumers' cooperative association, a local community, or a state. It produces not for the market but for the needs of the social entity that owns it and regulates its operation. In the last case, the organization of this factory can, furthermore, take different forms. The workers employed in it can constitute a self-administering producer's cooperative association, that leases the factory from the given social owner. . . . *[They]* can, however, also be engaged as wage laborers under a management appointed by their representatives in conjunction with representatives of the consumers. . . .

It is evident that the same technology, the same material labor-process, makes possible the most varied kinds of social working with and for one another. Which kind of social labor appears at any given time depends, to be sure, on technology, but by no means on it alone. That is an extremely important viewpoint for research into social evolution. *[To show that, unlike Marx, many economists do not distinguish between technology and economy, Kautsky quotes definitions of the economy by Weber,* Wirschaftsgeschichte, *p. 1;[6] Bücher, "Volkswirtschaftliche Entwicklungsstufen," p. 2; and Grosse,* Die Formen der Familie und die Formen der Wirtschaft, *pp. 25–26; and he then quotes a full page from Rosa Luxemburg,* Einführung in die Nationalökonomie, *pp. 619–20, criticizing Grosse and pointing out that there are many kinds of hunting, pastoral, and agricultural economies.]*

CHAPTER FIVE

Agriculture and Industry

... If our hypothesis is correct, man's first productive activity, the first one creating a product, was the textile industry, the plaiting of windbreaks.... Hunting became possible only after man understood how to use artificial implements that could serve as weapons. Thus we may designate *industry*, with more justification than *hunting*, as man's first productive activity. The advances represented by hunting, as well as the transition to agriculture, are very closely connected with the development of industry and its technology. The same is true of the development of cattle raising by nomads. How important for the latter, for example, does the invention of the wheel, the development of wagon building become. We find no people, beginning with the most primitive hunters, without industry. It is determinative for *[a people's]* level of development and the type of its production....

Within one and the same mode of production, a distinction can be made between industrial and agricultural states, depending on the predominance of some branches of production or of others. This distinction can, in part, rest upon differences in the level of industrial development. In part, however, it is based on differences in the availability of natural resources and in location with respect to trade, just like the distinction between hunters and fishermen, between cattle-raisers and agriculturalists....

The importance of the right location for production is ... as old as production itself.... The evolution of the modern state engenders tendencies that seek to act counter to this law. The more economically dependent a state becomes on other states, ... the more can it be damaged in war.... Therefore, modern statesmen in military states try to see to it that their

---

6. Weber's "preliminary conceptual remarks," from which Kautsky quotes, are omitted in the English translation, *General Economic History*.

own state produces, as far as possible, everything itself. . . . To that is added a second consideration. War has become a predominantly industrial undertaking. . . . In particular, heavy industry is becoming important for waging war. This results in heavy industry and militarism being closely connected and promoting each other in all the major states and in heavy industry and the policies it pursues being pervaded by all the brutality, narrow-mindedness, and hostility toward foreign countries characteristic of militarism.

Finally, industry frees man from the soil, to which agriculture binds him. It permits the concentration of huge masses in cities, under the most varied conditions and engaged in the most diverse kinds of work whereby they intensely stimulate each other. Agriculture scatters people over wide areas and isolates them from one another; and even their occasional meetings offer them no stimulation, because each is engaged in the same activity, each knows the same things. . . . The urban, industrial population is therefore more intelligent and alert than the rural one. Since in war greater intelligence, . . . also plays a decisive role, statesmen, for that reason, too, seek to develop in their countries as much industry as possible regardless of whether the local conditions are favorable or not. Protective tariffs, especially, are regarded as an effective means to this end.

Accordingly, it could appear that historical development were moving in the direction of every state becoming an industrial state, the agricultural nations representing a backward stage, and every state attempting to become "autarkic," sufficient unto itself. . . . It can therefore appear that our future is not leading to a unified and uniform humanity, but rather to its permanent fragmentation into polities that are independent from one another and appear tiny in comparison with the totality of mankind. Each of them does not shrink from the greatest economic costs in order . . . to produce itself, with great waste, everything for which it lacks the natural preconditions and which it could obtain, with far less expenditure of labor, from its better situated neighbors through trade. This tendency is actually regarded as a law of the modern mode of production by various economists. [Kautsky quotes Sombart, Die deutsche Volkswirtschaft, pp. 369 and 387, to this effect.]

The World War and its consequences have demonstrated to all the world in the most persuasive manner how very greatly all countries are today economically dependent on one another, . . . [even] the United States of America. . . . Nationalistic politicians themselves, quite apart from the consequences of the continuous technical development of transportation, act counter to their own policies of national exclusiveness. For they are all in favor of the most rapid possible population growth in their own country. The more people, the more soldiers. . . . Everywhere the nationalists foster the increase of the population to such a degree that finally the country's agriculture is no longer sufficient to feed all its people. That, too, becomes a reason for developing industry, not, however, for the needs of one's own nation but for export, in order to obtain food from agrarian nations. This is one of the reasons driving industrial nations to try incessantly to open up to world trade, especially through colonial acquisitions[7] and the construction of railways,[8] agrarian regions that were self-sufficient and had little to do with world trade.

The extent of industry and agriculture, including cattle raising (and hunting, too, if one wants to add it), must always be in a certain relation with each other. If the proportionality of the different branches of the economy within a polity is violated, if the surplus products of agriculture do not supply enough food and raw materials for the industrial population or the surplus production of industry does not supply enough tools and other implements for agriculture, then the economic process can go on without disruption only if the proportionality is upset in the opposite sense in other polities. That is, industrial states can exist only if there exist alongside them sufficiently many and sufficiently extensive agrarian states.

The one-sided development of the industrial branch of production in the world, to such a degree that agricultural production cannot keep up with its needs, is certainly a source of great economic dangers. They are especially great under capitalist production because, not only for the aforementioned reasons of military policy, but also out of economic motives, capital flows more easily to industry than to agriculture, which is more conservative in its technology and mode of operation.[9]

But the danger would be no less great in a socialist society if in it the workers continued likewise to prefer industry to agriculture. It will be an urgent task of every socialist regime to make the living and working conditions in agriculture such that it attracts the workers as much as industry. Development of communications, increasing the number of intellectual stimuli and resources in the countryside, the transfer of industry to the countryside, combining industrial with rural work, large-scale agricultural operations will be indispensable for achieving that end.[10] Just as indispen-

7. This sentence summarizes a major theme of Kautsky's article "Der Imperialismus," sections of which appear in English translation in *Selected Political Writings*, pp. 82–89.

8. On the importance of railroads in this context, see IV : 8 : 9, below, and also "Finanzkapital und Krisen," pp. 843–46.

9. The importance of the proportionality of industry and agriculture alluded to here is elaborated on more fully in IV : 8 : 8 and 9, below, especially with respect to the causes of crises under capitalism. Kautsky had first dealt with the subject in this context in "Finanzkapital und Krisen," pp. 838–46.

10. Kautsky had elaborated on some of these benefits that would accrue to the agricultural population under socialism in *Vermehrung und Entwicklung*, pp. 225–40. This chapter is reprinted in *Die Sozialisierung der Landwirtschaft*, pp. 70–84. For Kautsky's thoughts of 1922 on the socialization of agriculture and the union of agriculture and industry, see *The Labour Revolution*, pp. 226–52. Kautsky had dealt much more fully with Social-Democratic agrarian policy in 1899 in his major work *Die Agrarfrage*. While this book has appeared in several languages (an

sable, however, will be universal peace, which will eliminate the martial motivations to develop industry in locations unsuitable for it. Then the most perfect proportionality among the branches of production will become possible for the whole of humanity. It will be based on the economic principle of the greatest productivity, the highest output, achieved with the least expenditure of effort.

But regardless of how economic conditions have changed heretofore and of how they might change henceforth, there has been, since the beginning of the economy, industrial labor alongside agricultural labor, if one includes in the latter the gathering of berries and roots as well as the capturing and killing of animals. And it is not to be expected that this juxtaposition will ever end. Both branches of labor are inseparably dependent on each other.

Their association is not torn apart by the fact that in the course of the progressive division of labor, some of their subdivisions fall to the lot of certain groups as special branches of production. Nor is it disrupted by the fact that in some regions the one or the other branch of production comes especially strongly to the fore and becomes dominant, depending on the favorableness of particular geographical circumstances, which change with historically changing conditions. In the beginning, it was almost always hunting (or in some cases fishing) that predominated. To that extent, one may regard it not merely as a particular branch, but as a particular stage of the economy. From that point on, though, a higher or lower stage of the economy can only be distinguished by whether the number of its branches of production is more numerous and more diverse in it or not, not by whether or not the one or the other large branch of production predominates, be it agriculture, cattle raising, or industry.

CHAPTER SIX

The Mode of Production

. . . The material and the social sides of labor condition each other; they determine each other in constant reciprocal interaction. A factory is not possible without extensive discipline among its workers. But in its very functioning, the factory produces this discipline. The psychological factor of discipline belongs just as much to the conditions of the operation of a factory as do certain machines and motors. Of the two sides of labor, the social one is by far the more important. Through it, each individual material

---

English translation is forthcoming), no revised German edition was ever published because Kautsky felt, as he wrote in 1919 in *Die Sozialisierung der Landwirtschaft*, pp. 8–9, that it would have required revisions resulting in "a wholly new work," as agricultural conditions had "completely changed."

labor-process is related to many others, all of which are intrinsically linked to the one great end of the preservation of society, that is, the preservation of all its members, the satisfaction of their needs.

It is only this intrinsic connectedness that gives the individual labor-processes their economic character going beyond their merely technical character. A totality of thus intrinsically connected labor-processes constitutes a certain social process of production, the particular nature of which appears as a certain *mode of production*. It comprehends first of all, the totality of the labor-processes required for the fabrication of the material products of a particular society, not only in their sum but also in their reciprocal relations, which are simply reciprocal relations among men. It is just these reciprocal relations that are most characteristic of a given mode of production and make possible different modes of production on the basis of one and the same technology and of the mode of labor conditioned by that technology. . . .

The production of material products is the basis of each mode of production, or, if you prefer, its skeleton. On this foundation there arises a production of nonmaterial products or effects or "services." They serve the satisfaction of social needs just as much as material products. . . . The difference between material products and services is of material nature; it tells us nothing about their social significance. . . . And the economic position of a producer of nonmaterial products can be quite the same as that of a producer of material products. . . . Here, too, it is evident how very much the technical side of the labor-process has to be distinguished from its economic side. But we all live on material products; we cannot exist without them, without food, clothing, lodging. The extent of labor-time society must expend on material products determines the quantity of labor-time that remains available for services. . . .

When we consider the process of production from the social, the economic side, not from the technical one, then it is not enough to regard it as the totality of all labor-processes that are linked at a given time for the preservation of society. To the comprehension of the tasks taking place in *spatial juxtaposition*, there must also be added the comprehension of those that take place *successively* and that are linked *with one another* for the purpose of preserving society. We must consider the process of production as a continuous, ever-self-renewing process in the service of a continuing, ever-self-renewing society.

Accordingly, in order to come to know a mode of production it does not suffice to regard the process of production as nonrecurring. Only through study of the *process of reproduction* do we succeed in recognizing its entire character, all its laws. In Marxist economics, therefore, the examination of the process of reproduction plays a major role. If Marx had succeeded in finishing his *Capital*, in presenting fully the total process of the capitalist mode of production as a process of reproduction, then there would surely have emerged from it a new corroboration of his theory of value. In my opinion, the necessity of that theory can be compellingly demonstrated only from the process of reproduction, not from a single round of production. At the beginning of *Capital*, Marx shows, it is true, that the exchange of commodities is regulated by the law of value and logically grounds the latter; he did not, however, demonstrate the mechanism that causes that law to prevail. This mechanism, in my view, is manifest only in the process of reproduction.

If, however, we consider the process of production not as nonrecurring, but rather as a process that is continuously being repeated, as a process of reproduction, then we find that the "economic principle," the striving "to achieve the greatest possible benefit with the smallest possible sacrifices"[11] is not the only principle governing that process. Another principle becomes at least as important: the striving to carry out the process of production anew, again and again, on the same or on an expanded scale, the striving to safeguard it as a process of reproduction. For the individual labor-process, for technology, only the "economic principle" is determinative. The employment of technology by socialized men joins to the "economic principle" also the need for the lasting existence of society.

Indeed, one can say that the endeavor to safeguard reproduction appears as an economic law even earlier than those of the saving of labor. The first tools and weapons certainly did not serve to save labor, but to make the work done for the preservation of society more effective, indeed, even to make some tasks possible at all. The need to save labor can become the strongest economic force only when work has a disagreeable, repulsive character, as when men do not work directly for themselves, but each lives from the labors of others, whom he must pay, or whose products he must pay for, with his own labor or the exploited labor of others or with its products.

But woe betide any mode of production in which the need for economical production alone is recognized and the need for ensuring reproduction is, for whatever reason, ignored, in which the "economic principle" alone is operative. Such a mode of production leads to ruinously exploitative economic practices, which always produce as cheaply as possible, which achieve the greatest returns with the least expenditure, but in so doing ruin the very sources of life. They exhaust the soil, destroy the forests, smother the maturing young, and lead the adult workers into premature old age and death. The capitalist mode of production would already have perished in misery and filth, if it did not spontaneously generate elements powerful enough to keep the "economic principle" in check and to stress the need

11. The quotation is taken from a longer passage by Bücher, "Volkswirtschaftliche Entwicklungsstufen," p. 2, quoted earlier by Kautsky but omitted from this edition. See III:3: 4, above.

for the continued existence of society, for safeguarding and promoting the process of reproduction. For the character of a mode of production, the conditions of reproduction are just as determinative as are those of a single round of production.

Of course, the relationship of men among themselves in the process of production can never become solely determinative of this process. Their relationship to nature, technology, will always be of great, decisive importance for the character of a mode of production. A certain technology is not compatible with every form of social labor. When the requirements of a certain technology come into conflict with certain social conditions, these will sooner or later have to give way and disappear, if in the long term the particular technology offers markedly great advantages and procures for neighboring peoples—or for domestic competitors—who employ it such great superiority that one's own country or one's own sphere of work is at too great a disadvantage if it refuses to have anything to do with this progress.

A certain technology, however, is not always tied to certain forms of social labor. A particular kind of labor-process can be carried on under very different modes of production. . . . Technical development constitutes the foundation for economic development. It is not identical with that development. For the formation of the various modes of production, other factors, in addition to the different kinds of technology, are also determinative.

CHAPTER SEVEN

Property

Among the factors that, in addition to technology and the particular characteristics of the nature of a region—climate, natural resources, geographical features, situation with regard to trade—exercise a determinative effect on the mode of production at any given time, the most important is the *property system* obtaining in the region at the time of this mode of production.

Property is something specifically human. To be sure, this view encounters great opposition. Property, we are solemnly told, is deeply rooted in the nature of living beings. *[Kautsky cites Petrucci,* Les Origines Naturelles de la Propriété, *who refers to plants claiming some soil as their own and insects and vertebrates defending their dwellings and food reserves.]* This fact is undeniably true. It would prove that there is property among the animals and even among the plants, if we take the words "possession" and "property" to be synonymous. However, the fact that someone appropriates an object and attempts to keep everyone else away from it does not suffice to make the object the property of its appropriator. Otherwise, although not all property would be theft, all theft would be property.

The possession of, or laying claim to, a thing is doubtless the precondition of property. . . . But *[it]* alone is not enough to make a thing into property, if there is not added to it another moment: *social sanction.* Only in society and through society does what is possessed become property. . . . Only society begets property and the system of property. . . . The cause for the absence of property among social animals is doubtless to be found in part in the fact that they have no articulated language, without which definitions and regulations of property are possible only with difficulty. . . . Another reason is probably much more important, indeed decisive: the fact that definitions and regulations of property are not necessary for the maintenance and the prosperity of animal societies. *[Kautsky then responds to Petrucci,* Les Origines Naturelles de la Propriété, *p. 175, who refers to the lodges of beavers as their family property.]* The relations of possession within *[animal]* society simply result from the nature of things, from the way of living of the individual families; none of the other families has an interest in disrupting them or an opportunity to do so, so that for the society, too, no occasion arises to intervene in the families' relations of possession to order and to regulate them. In all likelihood that was at first also the case for primitive man, who, in his beginnings, had even less need of a property system than the beaver, because he disposed of neither enduring structures nor stores of supplies. . . .

The ape uses sticks and stones only occasionally. After using them, it casts them heedlessly aside. Man becomes man under conditions that induce him to utilize sticks and stones quite frequently and repeatedly to protect himself and to obtain food. . . . Some of these prove to be more suitable than others. . . . At the same time he gradually learns to employ them for procedures in which only certain forms and materials achieve any success at all. Stones and sticks become tools, . . . which he must search for, often with difficulty, and which he finally must shape, if they are to serve his purposes. Now labor is contained in each of them.

. . . He saves implements of this kind, carries them about, in order to have them at hand again and again. In this way he becomes very intimately familiar with them; they become a part of himself; they become permanent, artificial organs that he adds to his natural ones. But they are not, like the latter, an integral part of his body. They can be taken away from him, separated from him, and yet they have become just as indispensable for his success in the struggle for existence as his natural organs. It is now in his interest that his artificial organs be safeguarded for him just as much as his natural organs. The society, to which the individual belongs, has the same interest. Its prosperity is entirely dependent on the prospering of its members' productivity and mettle and ability in combat. . . .

Among most social animals that do not lay in stores and have no permanent quarters, we find that their social interests are confined to the protection and the advantages the younger and less experienced members have in a society when they are led by older, more experienced members. . . .

Once the source of food has been made available, then it is left to each individual to appropriate as much of it as it can. . . . Society has no interest in intervening to regulate the appropriation of food. Consequently, we find here nothing that could remind us of proprietary rights; instead every individual seizes what he can catch hold of. . . .

In contrast, the implements of the members of society in their common struggles for existence are of a completely different order of importance for man. . . . Initially, as long as the *[artificial organs]* were simple and easily obtainable for everyone and the advantages of using them were not extraordinary, as long as each individual gathered his livelihood alone in a given district, without being dependent on others in doing so, . . . we can assume that no one disturbed another as he used the tool or the weapon he had at hand at just that moment. There arose no necessity for the social regulation of the prevailing relations of possession. But this necessity probably occurred ever more frequently, the more complicated the artificial organs became; the more men were compelled by them to work with and for one another; and the greater the advantages of technology became, the less society could continue to exist without it.

Of course, one should not imagine that primitive men now elaborated a code of property rights. . . . As is the case for some peoples up to the present time, it is likely that the judicial function was also the legislative one. Whenever quarrels or uncertainties occurred with respect to the use of artificial implements, the representatives of the society, the chieftain, the council of elders, or the popular assembly probably made a decision. When circumstances did not change, cases of the same kind, under the same kind of conditions, are likely again and again to have come before judges who had the same information and were like-minded and who therefore decided the matter in question again and again in the same way. Thus, it may be assumed, a certain customary law of property was gradually formed, which was the same for the same objects, but by no means laid down the same property rights for all objects. This law applied to all artificial implements, but the appropriation of objects of personal consumption that were obtained or fabricated with tools and weapons also had to be socially regulated more and more.

[Kautsky quotes at some length von den Steinen, Unter den Naturvölkern Zentralbrasiliens, *p. 491, and Nansen,* Eskimo Life, *pp. 113–16, on rules governing the distribution of food among the natives of Brazil and Greenland.]* This manner of regulating the distribution of game is diametrically opposed to our conceptions of property rights according to which man "by nature" has a right to everything that he obtains through his labor or that is created by the "labor," that is, the employment of his means of production. Bourgeois economics is, after all, of the opinion that it is not just man who works, but his means of production work as well, for example, machines and arable land; and profit and ground-rent are accordingly the results of

the "labor" of the soil and the other means of production referred to as capital. . . .

In view of the great uncertainty of the yields of hunting and fishing, it is of the greatest importance for the preservation of society that the differences among individuals in success at hunting and fishing be offset when the game is distributed, because otherwise now one, now another part of society would be condemned to hunger and starvation. Here, too, the interest in the continued existence of society, in the unhindered continuation of the process of reproduction, proves to be an important economic moment. . . . Like the property right to the objects of consumption, the same right to the means of production is not reduced to a simple pattern among primitive peoples; it is, rather, just as varied as their language. *[Kautsky quotes Nansen,* Eskimo Life, *pp. 108–109, 111, and Letourneau,* Sociology Based Upon Ethnography, *p. 408, for examples from Greenland.]*

. . . The *law of inheritance* is connected with property law. The artificial organs are not attached bodily to man. The length of their life is, therefore, not tied to the length of his life, as is that of his natural organs. . . . That is, of course, also true of the products of the employment of these organs. In part, these artificial organs are considered to be almost as closely connected with the individual as his natural organs. They are buried or burned along with the individual. Others are too important for society to be able to forgo them. Insofar as a man's implements are possessed by an organization, the proprietary right to them is not affected by an individual's death. Insofar as they are of a purely personal kind, who is to inherit the dead person's belongings is determined, in the beginning of civilization and also for a long time thereafter, by society or rather by the most comprehensive organization in society, the polity. That the testator can personally make this decision at his own discretion is a relatively very new institution. . . .

The provisions of inheritance law were for a long time just as complicated as those regarding property. *[Kautsky quotes Morgan,* Ancient Society, *p. 449, on the rules of inheritance among the Iroquois and concludes:]* What was in the interest of the gens, not the individual's personal inclinations, determined the way a dead person's belongings were passed on to others.

CHAPTER EIGHT

Landed Property

Landed property, that is, the social regulation of the use of land, develops relatively late. There had been no reason for such regulation as long as land had been available in abundance and no man disturbed another as it was used. That was certainly the case as long as food was obtained merely by gathering. . . . Every horde doubtless had its district, in which it roved about and from which it repelled intruders as well as it could. This common possession, however, did not constitute property; it was not sanctioned by any higher social power.

Within this district, it was probably not population growth that gave the first impetus to regulation of the use of land. . . . The same technical development from which the increase in men's numbers sprang also gave man the ability to migrate and to move to regions where he would not have been able to maintain himself as a mere creature of nature, without artificial implements. Thus it is likely that population growth expressed itself in the extension of the parts of the earth inhabited by men, rather than in the growth of the population within a region having definite boundaries.[12] Other factors must, as a consequence of technical progress, have caused society to regulate the use of the land much earlier than its crowding did.

The most important branch of production after gathering became hunting. . . . The solitary nature of hunting resulted in the dispersal of the hunters of the horde to different regions of the common district so that one would not interfere with the other, would not drive the game away from him. The allocation of individual districts within the tribal area to different hunters can take place on a case by case basis, but the same district can also customarily be assigned again and again to an individual hunter, or more probably to the hunters of a family, of a household. This is regarded as private landed property by sociologists who only know how to think in the modern European manner. *[Kautsky quotes—and argues with—such interpretations of hunting territories of Eskimos by Petrucci,* Les Origines Naturelles de la Propriété, *p. 189, and of Australian aborigines by Lubbock (Lord Avebury),* The Origin of Civilization, *p. 309, and by Letourneau,* Sociology, *p. 403.]*

Alongside hunting, agriculture developed. To an even higher degree than the former, it conditions a social regulation of the use of the land. . . . When men learned to fabricate implements and utensils, in which they could keep and transport some durable fruits, . . . there arose the possibility of conserving for later consumption what was not consumed immediately. Thus it became in men's interest to store up, rather than to squander heedlessly, the fruits they could not consume immediately as they plucked them from tree or stalk. Society now began to forbid senseless destruction of useful plants, just as a certain protection of game animals emerged at an early time in some circumstances. . . . This illustrates the thesis that the safeguarding of reproduction becomes one of the earliest and most important economic commandments. . . . Concern with plant growth becomes more intense, the

12. On the expansion of space providing food for man, see *Vermehrung und Entwicklung,* pp. 79–99. Kautsky had already dealt with the problem of population growth in his first book, *Der Einfluss der Volksvermehrung.*

higher the level of technology is in a tribe, the longer it can continuously stay in the same campsite, the greater its prospect is of harvesting the fruits of maturing plants. . . .

Once people begin to protect some plants, they soon take the step of also placing under protection the regions in which they occur in large numbers. Entry into these regions is then permitted only at certain times and only to those working in them. In this way there originates the first restriction of the initially quite unrestricted utilization of the vegetable wealth in the district of the horde. As soon as the technical power of the horde grows, it is a matter of course for it also to begin keeping ravaging animals away from these useful localities. They are fenced in to ward off deer, pigs, and other larger herbivores.

Once society's interest had been concentrated in this way on the plant growth of a limited locality, there then, with time, necessarily arose increasing understanding of the conditions of this growth. Man now began to promote the thriving of the useful plants growing there by artificial interventions, by eliminating underbrush and weeds. . . . When he finally recognized the importance of the seed as the means of propagation . . . and learned to place the seeds of plants in prepared soil . . . , man could then cultivate his useful plants wherever the natural conditions for them were given. Now he no longer had to travel to them; they traveled with him, until the total amount of the products he obtained from their cultivation became so great that he was able to stay in the same place permanently.

This is the way we imagine the origin of the cultivation of plants. Even more than some kinds of hunting, that cultivation required the segregation of certain plots of ground from the general area of the tribe. While the latter was open to unregulated use by all, these plots of ground were reserved for certain purposes, and their use was subject to certain rules. These rules were just as diverse in kind as the regulations of proprietary rights to belongings. . . . Within a polity, as the differentiation of the branches of production increases, precise distinctions are made in the regulation of landed property. . . . The particular nature of this law as it applies to each plot of land is closely connected with the manner in which it is utilized. *[Kautsky illustrates this by a report on property in the Congo by Frobenius,* Vom Schreibtisch zum Aequator, *p. 188.]*

[According to] the constitution of the German mark of the early Middle Ages, forest, pasture, and water were undivided common property. Arable land was likewise common property, but for each planting particular strips of ground were allotted even then to the individual families. The ground on which a house and its courtyard are located becomes private property. Thus, undivided common property is most suitable for hunting, cutting and gathering wood, fishing, and animal husbandry. For farming, a temporary division is more suitable. Construction of family houses and the cultivation of fruit trees seems to proceed best when the land is completely privately owned.

Whatever the forms landed property might assume, never are they the result of the individual's discretion. It is always the views of the majority that decide on those forms that are, according to its experience and conviction, best adapted for society and its continued existence.

CHAPTER NINE

The Development of Property

With speculation on the origin of society there also emerged speculation on the origin of property. Thoughts on this subject were arrived at in a world of developed commodity production, ... the simplest form of which was the single-handed operation of a business by its proprietor. This form was imagined to be the original form of economy. ... Solitary men wandered through the forests ... until it occurred to one of them to settle down permanently on a patch of land, to fence it in, and to declare it his property. Thus landed property was created. *[Kautsky quotes Rousseau saying this in his* Discourse on Inequality, *pp. 141–42.]* At the beginning of the nineteenth century, after the great French Revolution, romanticism arose, the interest in early times. ... A child of the reaction, romanticism was fond of showing up the past in the best light. However, this romantic mood soon dissipated; it was followed by researchers who were able to distance themselves as much from the new fashion of uncritical glorification of the past as from the preceding uncomprehending condemnation of it. They sought not to judge, but to come to know and to understand.

At that time, there arose legal, economic, and linguistic history. Among other things, people became acquainted with the constitution of the German mark, especially through the comprehensive studies of G. L. von Maurer, published in a series of books from 1854 to 1871; also with village communism in Russia, to which A. von Haxthausen was the first in Germany to call attention. At the same time, British and Dutch rule in the East Indies acquainted us with the forms of village communism to be found there. Acquaintance with these forms led to the view that common property in land preceded private property. This Laveleye attempted to prove in a synoptic treatise published in 1874 with the title *De la propriété et de ses formes primitives [and translated as* Primitive Property]. Marx and Engels, too, accepted the view that in village communism we had before us the original form of landed property. *[Kautsky quotes Engels saying this in his footnote on the first page of the* Communist Manifesto *(p. 67; MESW, I, 108–109)]*

More recently, on the basis of many facts, the view that village communism represents the oldest form of property in land has been challenged. Rather, it is said to be, at least in some of its forms, a relatively recent phenomenon, the result of tax legislation by governments, of the joint liability of the village community for payment of the amount of taxes imposed on it. . . . *[Kautsky then argues at length with this view as it was advanced by Hildebrand,* Recht und Sitte, *especially p. 185.]*[13] This is not to deny that some instances of village communism can have a certain connection with governmental tax policies. In the East Indies this connection is clearly evident. . . . But *[had they not encountered it on their arrival there,]* it would never have occurred to *[the British and the Dutch]* to invent such a communism for purposes of taxation, and they would never have succeeded in artificially creating it and imposing it on the masses of peasants. Once there exists a tax system founded upon communal ownership of land, however, then, to be sure, it exerts a strongly conservative force. Without the tax liability of the local community in Russia, communal ownership of land would hardly have survived there into the present time.[14] . . .

It is significant that, when the *Communist Manifesto* was written, it could still be assumed that the development of humanity recorded in the written history of a few millennia constitutes the character of humanity's entire development. Since then, advances in research compel us, from one decade to the next, to lengthen the age of mankind ever more. Today it is no longer counted in thousands, but in hundreds of thousands of years. Even the least evolved of the so-called primitive peoples of the present day have gone through an extensive and diverse development, as the complexity of their languages proves.[15] All occurrences of common property in land that our era could still observe certainly did not date from the primeval period, but are, rather, the result of a long development. That is true most of all of the village communism of the Indians, the Russians and the Germans.

Far less primeval still, though, are the methods of individual settlement that can be observed today, for example, in Siberia and North America. . . . We must assume that primitive man was even less able by far to live in isolation than contemporary man. All the more, then, must he have been unable in isolation, with inadequate technology, to find the strength necessary for cultivating the soil and for becoming sedentary. . . . The isolated settlement, which is possible today because of a highly developed technology, extensive eradication of wild animals, and a high degree of protection of the individual settler by the forces of the state against any

---

13. Kautsky discusses early Russian village communism further in *Die materialistische Geschichtsauffassung* (1929), II, 155, a page not included in the present edition.

14. See also *Nationalstaat, imperialistischer Staat und Staatenbund*, p. 25.

15. See III: 1: 7, above.

roaming robbers, was necessarily impossible in the beginnings of civilization.

Everywhere we find common property in land at the beginnings of agriculture as well as of hunting and pastoralism. . . . From the very outset, however, we find, in addition to common property, private property in some objects. But at first to a very modest extent. Strictly speaking, private property must be understood to be only personal property, but usually family property is also reckoned as such. . . . The extent of a particular household and thus of a particular family is dependent on technical economic circumstances. . . . Like the household of the extended family, the gens, too, could dispose over common property, especially common property in land. Our age has then often considered the leader of the household of the extended family as well as the chief of the gens as the private owner of the landed property administered by him. . . . Like personal property, all these different forms of common property, above which there is yet tribal property, do not constitute various stages of a developmental series, just as that is not the case with regard to the basic forms of the individual large branches of production. . . . Different ways of using man's artificially made organs and their products arise alongside each other and therewith different forms of possession, which are sanctioned by society and elevated to forms of property, if they appear to be compatible with the continued existence of society and suitable to promote its prosperity.

There are things that, from the start, cannot be used in any other way than personally, for example, adornment, clothing, some weapons and tools. . . . Initially, every adult human being of the same sex in a polity knew how to do the same things; thus, each knew how to fabricate the things he wanted to use personally. The objects of this kind that each individual produced accordingly became his personal property. Other objects, for example, dwellings, a tent, or a relatively large boat, were by the nature of things from the start not meant for the use of a single person. As soon as they emerged, they were from the very first the property of a larger community. . . .

About how land was originally used, there are, to be sure, slight differences of opinion. There are greater ones about how this original utilization of the land should be designated: whether as common property in land or as a complete absence of property. It is certain that, at first and for a long time, there was no private property in land. Rather, there was only a common hunting–ground of the polity, which in its very beginning we may call a horde. . . . It disposed over the land in sovereign fashion. How can that be called anything other than common property in land? . . . Regardless of the differences of opinion there might be about how those forms of common property in land came to be that existed in historical time and in part still exist today, there can be no doubt at all that for a long time, for hundreds of thousands of years, men used the land in common with no one at all having individual property in it. Communism in land is as old as the use of the land. Equally old, to be sure, is private property in tools, weapons, and ornaments.

Every form of property evolves, personal property as well as property of the various social organizations existing at any given time, the household, the kinship group, the tribe. It does so partly with technical progress, which incessantly changes the technical foundations of property, partly with the development of other forms of property, as they all, severally and together, serve in the same society the ends of that society and therefore also influence each other. Thus it is not always the same forms of property that predominate; depending on the configuration of the totality of technology and of the process of production, at one time personal property can predominate in social importance, at another time one of the forms of common property. . . .

Until the emergence of the capitalist mode of production, personal property always plays a modest role in society. It extends almost solely to objects of personal use. What appears as the dominance of private property in earlier circumstances turns out on closer inspection to be the dominance of family property. The latter, it is true, acquires great social importance, as does the property of the gens and the mark. In comparison, the proprietary rights of the tribe and later, at least so far, of the state take on less significance. The importance at a given time of particular forms of property is very closely linked with the nature of the individual owners' economic activity, be they physical or legal persons.

Always, however, it is the society that is the source of property rights. It sanctions the different forms of possession, which, usually without its express assistance, arise out of mere economic practice. Society elevates them to forms of property initially only on the basis of considerations of their social usefulness. It does not tolerate appropriations that seem to it to be harmful to its prosperity. It denies to such appropriations its sanction and thereby prevents them from becoming property and acquiring permanence.

Property is most dependent on society in the beginnings of the latter, as long as society is still homogeneous and other factors have not yet become operative that, in addition to social and technical practicality, exercise a determinative influence on the forms of property. We shall presently become acquainted with such factors. In the beginnings of society, personal property still plays a small role, and common property in the most important source of foodstuffs, in the land, is dominant. And the social drives, which impel every member of a polity to be helpful to his fellows, are very strong. In light of that, surely one may designate the starting point of the development of property as primitive communism, even though private property is just as old as common property.

[The chapter concludes with four pages of arguments with Cunow, Allgemeine Wirtschaftsgeschichte, I, especially pp. 15, 72, and 78, over the meaning of the word "communism" and the question whether what Cunow calls "communism of consumption" among primitive hunters was, as he believed, the result of hungry members of the horde forcing successful hunters to share their quarry or, as Kautsky holds, a consequence of the "social drives" that are conditioned by and in turn condition social life.]

CHAPTER TEN

The Conservative Character of Property

At first social usefulness, that is, what the decisive elements of society, originally the majority of its members, consider to be such, determines the law of property at a given time. But only at first. In addition, other factors important for property law take shape with the passage of time.

The saying that property is sacred is initially true only in the sense that the will of the society must always be determinative for the individual who belongs to it. . . . Today, however, the saying about the sacredness of property has taken on yet another meaning. According to it, the property acquired by the individual is supposed to constitute a right, which, not society, but a higher, sacred system of law standing above society conferred on him. A right, . . . before which even society must reverently come to a halt, no matter how inappropriate for its continued existence that right might appear to it. We are speaking here only of society in general; we must still leave classes out of consideration, although the phenomenon we now have in mind can be observed in class society. . . .

It will be pointed out that many socialists, too, today demand that the nationalization of capitalist enterprises should proceed only with compensation. I must confess that I myself am guilty of this view. But we call for indemnification not out of regard for the sacredness of property, but for reasons of social *practicality*, because we cannot socialize the entire capitalist apparatus with one blow, because a large part of it can be expropriated only gradually and until that time capitalists must continue to function if the whole process of production is not to come to a standstill.[16] . . .

But how is it possible that under certain conditions property, which has been created by society, can raise itself above society and confront it as an independent power? To a great degree that is to be attributed to the conservative character of the mind, which we have already spoken of.[17] Every

---

16. See also IV:7:10 and IV:8:13, below.
17. See I:5:4, above.

solution of a problem, not only in thought, also in practice, provides such satisfaction, that the individual does not throw it overboard without cause. . . . It becomes a custom, . . . to which subsequent generations are introduced at a very tender age. The greater the number of generations to which this custom is successively passed on, the more does the disposition to accept the solution—be it a view or an institution—become hereditary, and the solution itself is maintained ever more tenaciously. . . . A social organization is the more difficult to set in motion, the more extensive its membership and the more ramified its sphere of action. And existing views, too, are the more difficult to overturn, the more they are interwoven with others in a coherent whole. Bringing down an entire system requires an enormous expenditure of strength. Only the most urgent necessity, only the most obvious failure of what exists, can effectuate this.

Now, there are among men's ideas, and just as much among their artificial organs and their organizations, great differences with respect to their age and importance. . . . These differences make themselves felt as soon as new experiences occur or new problems. . . . Some existing ideas, some technologies, some social institutions are easily sacrificed to innovations that are a consequence of new conditions. On the other hand, men resist some other innovations very stubbornly and, when they are not able to ward them off, they try to preserve as much as possible for these innovations the appearance of that which is old. *[Kautsky notes that the French Revolution successfully introduced a new system of measurements, but that its new calendar failed to be retained. And he quotes Morgan,* Ancient Society, *pp. 329 and 336–37, on the persistence of systems of consanguinity.]*

. . . In comparison with other social institutions, systems of property are especially hard to move even to a greater degree than systems of consanguinity. An organization based on kinship is more extensive than a family . . . and sometimes the larger circle of kinship is more important for the protection and the existence of the individual than the narrower circle of the family. But the domain of a system of property is greater yet, and the regulations of such a system can become even more important for the existence of the individual than the nature of the kinship organizations. At the same time, with increasing division of labor and growing complexity of the ways in which men work with and for one another, the relations of possession and property also become increasingly diverse. Contradictions occur more and more easily between the various regulations regarding property. . . . It becomes ever more necessary . . . to shape the whole of the property regulations into a coherent system, which soon becomes much bigger than a system of consanguinity, not only by virtue of its operative scope but also through the quantity of its regulations.

Many regulations of the property system in a particular mode of production arise out of circumstances that already existed in earlier modes of production and stretch far into the past. Tradition and extent thus make of the system of property one of the most conservative, if not absolutely the most conservative, of human institutions. . . . The process of inventing particular technical advances can proceed rapidly in some circumstances, while the system of property remains unchanged. But, the way in which each technical innovation is employed, how it affects the processes of men working with and for one another, what social relations men enter in the course and as a result of these processes, all these things depend on the particular system of property.

If the system of property was originally determined by society, now the reverse happens—at least to a certain degree. For if the new becomes too incompatible with the existing order and if the new is too much in the interest of society, while the old comes ever more to conflict with it, then the interests of society finally triumph. The more coherent, free of contradictions, and comprehensive the old system of property was and the greater the force required for its transformation, the more comprehensive and vigorous the process of transformation will be, the more it will assume the character of a revolution. But it often takes a long time before that point is reached. It is incredible how conservative a system of property can be, how deeply rooted in men's minds, so that they disdain even great economic advantages and reject fruitful innovations if these are incompatible with the existing order. *[Kautsky devotes a page and a half to the example of German peasants stubbornly adhering to old patterns of common property or of distribution of privately held parcels of land when changes in crops had turned these patterns to their disadvantage.]*

In our discussion of property, we have so far dealt only with society as a whole. But it does not always remain a homogeneous entity. Not even the individual polities do so. We have seen that the division of labor between man and woman is formed at a quite early stage.[18] . . . Even there we find differences of property interests that sometimes become antagonisms. . . . But with time, the division of labor within the sexes also develops, at first at least within the male sex. And finally to the very diverse and sometimes antagonistic interests of the occupations are also added differences in the distribution of possessions and finally the interests of the social classes, which are antagonistic from the very start and under all circumstances.

In the case of the animal, all individuals belonging to the same sex and the same age-group possess the same organs. None has more or less of such organs than the others. . . . In contrast, artificial organs . . . can be distributed in such a manner that one individual disposes of more of them than another, indeed in such a way that some dispose of many and others over none at all. There arise antagonisms between the poor and the rich, and ultimately the point is reached where the men who employ an artificial organ are

18. See II:4:3, above.

completely different from those who dispose of it—something quite inconceivable in the animal world.

And yet eminent scholars can still be found who assure us, with earnest expression, that inequality among individuals has its root-cause deep in nature. That poverty and wealth have their origin in the difference in natural talents. They maintain in all seriousness that it is due to men's natural qualities that their artificial organs are not possessed by those who employ them, but by those who do not employ them, and that those who do not themselves employ these organs live better from their employment by others than do those who expend all their strengths and capabilities in the employment of these organs.

All these differences and antagonisms engender intense conflicts of individual groups of the society against each other, conflicts that principally concern the system of property. Due to them, the struggle over a particular system of property is not just one for greater effectiveness of social labor and of the other social relations linked with it, nor just a struggle between reason, which recognizes the importance of the new, and unreasonableness, which clings uncomprehendingly to the old. Rather, it is a struggle of social groups with different interests, each of which represents only its particular interest, but, of course, of two opposed interests one is always most likely to coincide with the general social interest of the adaptation of property to the new conditions, while the opposed one inhibits this adaptation and thus injures society as a whole.

Thus we find that the form taken by a system of property depends on three very different factors. First, on what is regarded at a given time as *socially effective or practical*. Under simple, primitive conditions, which are easily understood, that will usually coincide with what is really effective or practical, which often prevails of itself given the existing technologically conditioned methods of working with and for one another. As soon as a certain technology and a certain system of property have existed for a rather long time, there is added *the power of tradition*. When technical and economic innovations occur, it causes the system of property related to them to be no longer regulated solely according to the criterion of social effectiveness, but also according to whether it can be fitted into the traditional definitions and regulations. This leads not infrequently to great ineffectiveness, inconvenience, and abuses. Finally in the course of social development and differentiation, there are also added to the foregoing the differences among the interests of the sexes, the occupations, and the classes. . . . In addition to social effectiveness and tradition, there are also the *relations of power among the various social groups*. . . . If in these group conflicts, that group is victorious whose interest coincides with that of society, then the prosperity of society is secured. When the reverse occurs, society is injured, sometimes to such an extent that it perishes.

The system of property is thus dependent on very different moments that can undergo modification and combine with one another in a multitude of ways in the course of historical development. The mode of production at a given time, however, is determined just as much by the system of property as by technology. Were the system of property determined by social effectiveness alone, then for a given technology and given geographical conditions there would be only a single, determinate mode of production. As a result of the traditions and the relations of power among individual groups within society, different modes of production become possible for the same branches of production under the same technical and geographical conditions and hence under the same modes of labor.

CHAPTER ELEVEN

Organ and Environment

It seems to be nothing other than a shallow commonplace . . . that the artificial organs man creates for himself differ from his natural organs in that they are not parts of his body. . . . We have already seen, however, that this circumstance is responsible for the peculiarity of technical and economic development in contrast to the natural evolution of species.[19] And on that circumstance also rests the mechanism of the dialectic in social evolution.

. . . Man's artificial organs . . . merely supplement his natural organs and increase their strength, but at the same time they exist outside of man, . . . and to that extent they belong . . . to the environment . . . which poses problems for him. . . . He invents something in order to maintain himself in *[new]* conditions, . . . but once it has been created and employed, the innovation becomes a part of the environment. . . . As such, it was neither planned nor instituted and it develops properties man did not foresee, indeed, properties that often run directly counter to his intentions and needs and bring about conditions . . . that in part benefit him, in part harm him. In any case, these new conditions compel him to adapt himself to them, thus again to create new organs in order to take advantage of the useful aspect of the new conditions and to protect himself against their harmful one. . . .

The spinning machine was an invention intended to provide more product with less labor . . . *[and it]* fulfilled the purpose of higher profit. But that was not its only effect. . . . The advantages of machine-spinning became a privilege of big capitalists. But more important by far were the repercussions for the working class. . . . The dissolution of the proletarian family, unending torture inflicted on women and children by their work, dreadful ignorance of youth, the extensive spread of prostitution—those were the

19. See III:3:1–4, above.

effects of the machine that at first served in industry only as the organ of the capitalists, but even then functioned as the wage-laborers' environment. *[As further effects of the new industry, Kautsky, quoting Marx, Capital, I, 571, cites the rapid increase of cotton growing in the United States and, with it, the promotion of the slave trade and of slave breeding. And he also refers to American expansionism in the quest for more cotton land—the purchase of the Louisiana territory and Florida and the war with Mexico—as well as growing antagonism to slavery and the Civil War.]*

Overproduction, a falling of prices and profits, periodic commercial crises occurred as soon as the spinning machine became generally used.... The impulse to exploit the defenseless workers ... in the most inhumane fashion and thus to bring them rapidly to physical ruin, ... was intensified beyond measure by the growing competition of the factory owners among themselves.... The machine ... threatened completely to destroy the working class of the country, and with it the source of its strength and industrial prosperity, and thus to endanger the country itself. That fact awakened great misgivings even in the propertied classes and even more in the educated ones, on the part of all those ... for whom the question of reproduction ... in the future was important. They were joined by those propertied and educated people in whom there still survived the social sensibility toward his fellowman innate in man from his beginnings, and finally by some groups among them whose interests were opposed to those of the factory owners, for example, the big landowners of that period. Through them, the industrial proletariat, in its beginning still weak, dependent, and uncertain, acquired the courage to an opposition that ultimately became strong and independent enough to ward off the oppressors with its own strength. There developed the struggle for the protection of labor; unions and a labor party were formed; socialist goals were formulated....

As mere organs, the spinning and weaving machines corresponded completely to the purposes they were supposed to serve and were adapted to. As part of the spinners' and weavers' environment, the machines developed consequences that were very troublesome to their owners and to those who used them. Only as an organ did the machine originate in the minds of its inventors and first users. Once employed and put into general use, it formed a new environment that surprised its creators themselves....

In the Nile Valley or in Mesopotamia ... the dams and canals functioned as organs of the peasants. But simultaneously they became their environment. The peasants' entire existence depended on them and hence on the central power that had created them ... and maintained them.... The central power had created the conditions for improved agriculture and also drew from that fact the power that made it possible for it to monopolize for itself the advantages of this improvement.... As the peasant's environment, the dams and canals had completely different effects than as his organs.

Let no one object... that sufficient scientific training will make men capable of foreseeing all the consequences of their acts.... It is true that our scientific understanding is growing, but society is becoming proportionally more extensive and more complex. To be able to foresee everything, one would have to know everything.... Every solution confronts us with new problems.... We have no reason to assume that the growth of our knowledge could ever have any other effect. And... that is true also of the problems of our practice with regard to nature and in society. I do not in the least doubt that the victorious proletariat will succeed... in creating social institutions as organs of an adaptation of the present-day forces of production to its interests and to those of society. However, I am just as confident that as soon as these institutions have become... not mere organs of the workers but also parts of their environment, new problems will result from them, of which we do not even dream today....

Here we have finally come to the root of the truly new in history. The invention of an organ, by which we understand here... also methods, social organizations, and rules, ... means the adaptation of existent, well-known implements to existent, well-known conditions and needs.... Certainly, an image of what is to be created must be in our mind beforehand.... but this image is not conjured up out of nothing; rather, it presupposes in our mind very clear ideas of the materials and the forces at our disposal, of the requirements the invention must satisfy.... But much of what a new organ results in, once it has become part of our environment, will be something wholly new, something that has never yet existed, something hitherto completely unknown. *This something new is the new in history*, which has preoccupied our idealist philosophers of history so much. It is certainly a result of the human mind, but not one that was in the mind earlier than in reality. As a rule, it is... often not even noticed and recognized as new as soon as it appears.... Its origins..., being initially ignored, are often so obscure that later it is quite impossible to clarify them....

Here we find the possibility of explaining novelty without having to assume a supernatural ability of the human mind, a violation of the laws of causality and the conservation of energy. It thereby becomes possible for us to comprehend the history of humanity in harmony with the laws of nature. But the history of society nevertheless retains its peculiarity vis-à-vis the history of species of organisms in nature.

The evolution of the latter depends on changes of the natural environment that appear accidental in relation to the organisms living in it. They are, of course, not accidental when viewed from the standpoint of the total complex of relationships, ... but they are conditioned by completely different factors than the activity of the organisms...; they do not stand in any necessary relation with the latter; as regards the latter, they are accidental.

Quite different are those parts of man's environment that occur not as given by nature, but as social in character. To be sure, the beginnings of technical and thus also of economic and generally social development, we must, like modifications of organisms, trace back to changes in nature that, in this context, appear to be accidental. These also include . . . changes of nature *for man* while natural conditions remain the same, for example, when a people migrates into an area, the character of which differs from that of the region it had previously inhabited. . . .

Even in his beginnings, man is distinguished from the animal by the fact that changes of nature . . . do not just cause some physical and psychic modifications of his organism, which can become adaptational phenomena, but that they also lead to conscious adaptation through the creation of artificial organs. . . . The more often man goes through changes of his natural environment, the further does the development of his technology advance, since every alteration of the outer world impels him to add new achievements to already acquired artificial implements. Thus, with time, man's technical and social apparatus attains an extension and an importance such that it becomes almost more important for him as an environment than his natural environment. This apparatus now begins significantly and increasingly to change the received social relations, above all through the emergence of the division of labor, through the introduction of changing and continuously more varied ways in which men work for and with one another.

The artificial environment man himself has created now confronts him increasingly as a power standing above him and dominating him, a power that, to an ever-greater extent lays claim to all his thoughts and endeavors and changes his entire intellectual nature through its innovations. This artificial environment . . . begins to concern him at times more than the natural environment, if only because it repeatedly changes, while in comparison with it nature seems to stand still. In the past few centuries, man's artificial environment has not ever come to rest at all any more for a single moment. . . .

Every social innovation, which in the last analysis is to be traced back to a new kind of social labor that, for its part, originates in the last analysis from a new technology, becomes a new environment once it has been carried through. This new environment poses new problems for men and impels them to solve these problems with new means. This, in turn, leads to the creation of new organs and organizations that, for their part, again become parts of the social environment and give it a new form. In this manner, the process of social development continues ever onward, once transformations of man's natural environment have got it going, even when nature remains completely constant. It is a mechanism that generates its own motive force, after it has once been set in motion by an impulse coming from nature.

The Dialectic and Evolution

Here we find a dialectical process similar in many respects to that of Hegel. In both processes, it is ultimately mind that effects the development of society by itself, positing its own antithesis, then seeking the synthesis between thesis and antithesis, and, after it has found the synthesis, forming a new antithesis from the synthesis, etc.[20] . . .

Of course, there is nevertheless a great difference between Hegel's dialectic and the one I have set forth. As with every genuine idealist, with Hegel mind stands above nature and its causality—the law of the conservation of energy had not yet been discovered in Hegel's time. From the very outset, Hegelian mind or spirit creates its own antithesis spontaneously. To do so, it has no need of an impulse from without. . . . We, on the other hand, assume that from the start, ever since there have been thinking beings, thesis and antithesis, mind and nature, man (and animal, too) and environment have existed simultaneously, and man, like every other organism, is impelled to seek the synthesis between the ego and the environment, the adaptation to the latter.

That is true for the animal as well as for man. The difference between them is merely that the apeman . . . , through the creation of artificial organs finally brings about a special kind of synthesis with the antithesis, *[that is,]* nature, which did not proceed out of him. It is only these *[artificial]* organs and the forms in which men work with and for one another, finally their social relations in general growing out of these forms, which, from being a synthesis, become in their turn a new antithesis vis-à-vis the thesis, which is always . . . constituted by the human individual.

All these processes are effectuated by mental activity, but it is never mind alone that is effective in them. . . . For us, it is never the idea alone, but rather the interaction between the thinking man and his environment that causes the dialectical process. This is what makes our conception of history a materialist one. . . . We are aware of the fact that there is no mind in itself, existing independently of determinate bodies, and that it is nothing other than a particular kind of function of certain bodies. . . . On the other hand, we also are aware of the fact that social, hence mental relations between thinking men also are part of the individual's environment. . . .

We consider the designation "materialist" as the most appropriate one for our dialectic as well as for that of Marx and Engels. In any case, it would be absurd to call it an "economic" dialectic. It is then necessary to designate the conception of history erected upon this dialectic as a materialist and not an economic one. . . .

20. See also I: 5 : 1, above.

... Like Hegel, we assume that the dialectic in which the thesis itself generates its own antithesis holds good only for human development in society, whereas Engels regards it as a general law of nature, as a law of every evolution in nature.[21] ...

We must clearly distinguish three kinds of evolution.... That of the individual organism does not proceed at all dialectically. It repeats itself in the same way for each individual of the same species. The way it runs its course is already given for each individual with its germ. The environment can foster or hamper, disrupt or even prematurely break off this course of development.... But it can never change the sequence of its stages or its goal....

The two other forms of evolution, that of the individual species of organisms and that of human society, ... proceed in a dialectical manner. In both something new ... is generated by the antagonism between individual and environment. This antagonism alters the individual and adapts it to changed conditions as soon as the environment exhibits new elements.... In the world of organisms, of plants and animals, though, the individual has no influence on the change of the environment. Here the antithesis does not originate from the thesis; it always remains different from the thesis. The synthesis becomes a new thesis, but it does not produce a new antithesis. Dialectical evolution in the form that is properly Hegelian is ... confined solely to the human race, whose mental capacities are so superior to those of the animal that it is able to respond to the demands of a new environment for adaptation ... with the creation of new organs. These are intentionally invented and employed as implements; unintentionally, though, they produce a new environment, by changing in part the natural environment, and, above all, by transforming the social environment.

With regard to neither of the two kinds of dialectical evolution is there any movement in the development of animals and men toward a goal set by them from the outset. We find such a goal-oriented movement only in the development of the individual organism from its germ.... The kind and the direction of the evolution of species as well as of human society depend on changes in the environment, which in nature are accidental relative to the organisms living in it, not causally determined by their actions. In society, social changes stand in a causal relationship with human action and are to that extent necessary.

Therefore, once a certain scientific knowledge of society has been attained, the advent of some social changes can to a certain extent be known in advance. But regardless of how greatly our methods of social research might be improved, it will never be able to determine in advance the totality of coming social transformations and it will always be able to foresee only

---

21. For Kautsky's other disagreements with Engels on the dialectic, see I:5:2–3, above.

those transformations closest in time. As for organic evolution, so too is it impossible to make out a final goal for social evolution.

When one speaks today of the final goal of socialism, what is meant is not the final goal of humanity, but rather the final goal the proletarians and the proponents of their cause have set themselves in our time. No one can say definitely how far the coming reality will correspond to the goal, the ideal, set in the present. That will be the case to a greater degree, the better our intellectual leaders have grasped present-day reality, its needs and its resources, both material and intellectual. To none of those now living is it granted to see beyond this final goal of today. . . . In the course of the ages, mankind's history has taken very diverse directions. It is a hopeless enter-prise to want to establish today what direction it will follow in all of the future. It will probably, as heretofore, move in extremely varied zigzags.

CHAPTER THIRTEEN

Mode of Production and Mental Character

. . . The new technology by no means annuls for man the laws of the mod-ification by a changed environment of the organism's natural organs and functions. Certainly, the influences of the natural environment on the human organism are attenuated in many ways by technology. But, for their part, the new living and working conditions created by technology and the mode of production resulting from it exert particular influences on the organism, which modify some of its organs or some of their functions. . . . Even more than the muscles, the nervous system and especially its center are modified by external influences. Men's mental character is dependent to an enormous degree on their living conditions. . . .

No definite direction of development can be ascertained in the formation of different characteristics. The view is widely held that the human race evolves from bestiality to humanity. . . . Man's ancestors were not, as some researchers believe, tigers or buffaloes, but apes averse to all bloodshed. Men became tigers and buffaloes only through the development of tech-nology, which bestowed on them weapons sharper and stronger even than horns and claws. Since then, men's character changes very much with their technology, their mode of production, and their form of society. At one time, it becomes more cruel and bloodthirsty with increasing civilization, at another time ever more gentle. *[Kautsky refers here to his* Terrorism and Communism, *chapter 7, "The Effects of Civilization on Human Customs."]*

. . . Men's knowledge, too, changes with their environment. Every al-teration of the environment brings new experiences that are added to the old ones. Either they confirm and strengthen their combination into a coherent system or they disturb it and prove it to be incorrect, thereby making a new kind of combination necessary. Like men's character, their knowledge of the world and thus their whole outlook on the world also changes with a new mode of production.

Their innate tendencies and abilities are also transformed under the influence of a new world, even those having nothing to do with the requirements and activities of self-preservation: the relationship between man and woman in love; the relationship between parents and children and between the older and the younger in general; the conception and the creation of what is beautiful; the need to come to know the environment, . . . even when no practical need requires such knowledge. All these noneconomic factors of an ethical, aesthetic, and scientific nature are very profoundly influenced by a transformation of the environment that is in the final analysis conditioned by a transformation of technology. These factors, too, receive the impetus for everything new that they produce from the external world, not from themselves.

Thus not only man's antithesis changes with technology, but also the thesis: innate human nature itself. . . . In order to understand a particular age, it is not enough to be acquainted just with its mode of production. One must also have investigated the peculiar nature of the people of that age in all its various needs, wants, abilities, and properties of character. . . . Men's peculiarity in a given time is, however, once again nothing but the nature of primitive man, carried over from his animal stage and modified by innumerable changing living conditions. . . . Each of these conditions, which affected his ancestors and determined their character, their customs, and their views, lives on more or less concealed in their descendants, partly as oral tradition, partly inherited drive or other peculiarity of the organism. . . .

The living conditions of a people within a given period do not alone suffice to make its activity . . . comprehensible. In order to understand it fully, one really would have to know its entire prior history, something that is of course unattainable. But the farther and the more penetratingly one traces it back, the closer does one approach an understanding of the events of the period one initially wants to shed light on. . . .

It is precisely that which makes it so difficult to investigate history according to the materialist method, and here is perhaps one of the most important reasons why that method has hitherto been so little applied. In order to make a particular historical period understandable, this method cannot be content to elucidate the events of that time, which must of course be the starting point, and moreover to relate them to the then-prevailing mode of production, its problems, conditions, and solutions. It must also ascertain the mental disposition of the people when it was confronted with these problems. . . . A materialist historian must, therefore, always be oriented toward and knowledgeable in universal history. That is expecting a great deal. A mere specialist will not be able to do much with the method of our conception of history.

A people's various characteristics do not all stem from the same living conditions, from the same period of time. Some are perhaps only a century old; others may have their origin in the Stone Age. Every side of a people's mental nature is, however, the result of definite conditions of the environment, hence, if you will, of definite material conditions. And therefore, *in the final analysis*—Marx and Engels always stressed this word—man's entire mental nature is, certainly, to be accounted for by his material conditions of life. But not in its entirety by *those material conditions in which he happens to be living.*

We must, then, distinguish between two factors if we want to write the history of an era. On the one hand, there is mental nature, the complex of needs, wants, ideas, etc., with which man enters into the period. The understanding of this nature requires knowledge of the preceding modes of production and their effects. Then there is, on the other hand, the knowledge of the mode of production proper to the era itself. What is new in the latter mode of production in comparison with its predecessors will explain the new needs and desires, means, problems and goals that appear in that era. These new factors will enter into a conflict with the old factors of that kind; this conflict constitutes the historical process of the period.

This does not at all mean that the same mode of production must affect every people in exactly the same way. Every people has not just its particular environment, its particular geographical situation, topography, and natural resources, which . . . are very important for the peculiar character of its historical process. It also has in its background its own historical development; it has . . . been subjected to other influences than the other peoples of its time.

CHAPTER FOURTEEN

Individual and Society

Not just the peoples, however, have their peculiar characters, but also every individual within a people. . . . Even among the simplest organisms, no two are exactly the same. How then should that be true of the most complex of all organisms, human beings, and of the most complex of their organs, the brain, which moreover in each individual experiences widely varied and different impressions. The same environment never affects two individuals in precisely the same way. . . .

If one considers only what is personal, individual in men, then one would have to expect to find, instead of a society moving along determinate paths, a chaos of the most diverse strivings, directly contradicting, thwarting, impeding one another, and often canceling one another out. . . . But men are . . . also all members of the same species. In each one of them, what he has in common with his fellow men predominates over what differentiates him from them. And what he has in common with them causes him, in the main, to react to the same external stimulus in the same way as his fellows after all. Only thus does it become possible for him to join with them for the purpose of social activity. And only what is shared, not what is purely personal, exerts a social influence; only it can call forth social evolution. . . . In the case of men in our surroundings only what is personal to them and distinguishes them from others interests and concerns us. . . . And yet what each of them has in common with all the others is socially most significant, it is what, in addition to the particular technology and natural environment, has a determinative effect on the character of society. It conditions the manner in which a society or a people reacts to a given environment and develops it further. . . .

An idea, an innovation, an invention, acquires historical significance only when it becomes a mass phenomenon. . . . Nevertheless, the personality, too, certainly has its functions in history. Not all men are equally intelligent, bold, or strong. The differences of their natural endowment are given even more diverse forms through the differences of their social position, which, even with equal intelligence, boldness, and strength, confers on some individuals a privileged position, gives them the opportunity to acquire more knowledge than others, to dispose over the powers of others and thereby to increase their own; or accords to them a position in which they are more protected and may dare to do more than others.

Such privileged men will be better able to react to what is new in the environment, better able to grasp new problems, . . . to find the means for solving them and to propagate these despite all resistance. They are regarded as the creators of new ideas, although they have only discerned earlier than the others the new already existing around them. . . . Such personalities are historically important as pioneers of new ideas. But they will have historical success only when the new environment has already made great masses of people receptive to these ideas, when the leaders and those who bring enlightenment to the people only clearly express what the mass, already searching and groping, longs for.[22]

Up to now we have always treated only of the interaction between environment and individual. It now turns out that the individual's environment is at one pole, at least in large part, society, hence the mass. At the opposite pole, however, we no longer find the individual, but again the mass as the force set in motion by the environment and in turn moving the environment. Does the mass constitute its own environment, then? And is it set in motion by itself? We would then have the same mystery, the same

22. See also V : 1 : 9–12, below.

violation of causality and of the conservation of energy that we rejected earlier in the case of the mind. It would not become more acceptable by being translated now from the language of idealism into that of materialism.

Fortunately, it is not necessary that we make this assumption. On the one hand, the environment in its totality will always comprise more than a particular mass of men, . . . even when this mass becomes synonymous with all of society or all of humanity. For the environment that exercises a determinative influence on us also comprises . . . all technical implements . . . and the entire natural environment. . . . On the other, . . . it is always nature and society in their totality that have an effect on individuals. What manifests itself in the mass as discernment and volition is only a totality, resulting from summation and interaction of the discernment and volition of numerous individuals working with and for one another. It is only these individuals' agreement with respect to their natural disposition, their historical development, their traditions, as well as, finally, their momentary living conditions that produces the agreement of the individuals' discernment and volition, out of which arises the mass movement with its historical force.

Incidentally, a mass of people appearing in history has hardly ever become coextensive with society. For at an early time society ceased to be a homogeneous formation, in which all members occupy the same position and have the same living conditions, interests, and authority. . . . We find the division of labor between man and woman . . . as well as the division of society into age-classes with different rights and obligations. . . . Since then, differentiation in society, and thus the formation of groups, has increased enormously with growing division of labor and transportation technology. On the one hand, society has grown beyond the sphere of the individual polity. It encompasses a number of such polities. On the other hand, today every polity has grown so much that within its sphere the formation of numerous strong groups has become possible, at first kinship-organizations, then territorial groups, . . . and, within these, again occupational organizations. . . .

Each of these groups has its particular knowledge, its particular interests; each is affected in a particular way by an environment common to all of them and reacts in a particular way to it. To be sure, the common social interest pushes them all in approximately the same direction, but very different deviations are still possible. The final outcome has often been referred to as the resultant of a parallelogram of forces.

The formation of groups in society, however, advances ever further. Working for one another can attain forms in which only some work, and the fruits of their labor, minus the costs of maintaining the workers, go to others. The groups formed on this basis become groups of exploiters and exploited, of *classes*. Their interests are not just different but downright antagonistic. In spite of the common interest in the prosperity of society, their antagonism can become so deep that the endeavors of the different classes diverge in opposite directions, so that a parallelogram of forces with a common resultant becomes quite impossible, and the movement of society assumes the form of the subjection and the repression of one class by another.

The struggle of the classes appears here to be the only motive force of social evolution. And yet here, too, we find in the last analysis the development of technology and of the mode of production proceeding from it to be the decisive factor. For from that development result the transformations in the power relations of the classes, without which social development in a class society seems hardly possible.

In the periods of written history, society's development often takes the form of class struggles. These, therefore, must chiefly engage the historian's attention. But this period occupies only a small span of time within mankind's evolution.[23] We have, therefore, up to now not treated classes and class struggles, even though we could not entirely avoid occasionally touching upon them. A theory of humanity's development must also be possible without reference to the class struggle, which will constitute only a relatively brief and, as we expect, soon to be transcended episode in it. But our theory would be incomplete if that episode were to be excluded from it, if we took no notice of it at all. Practically, it is exactly the stage of class society that is of greatest significance for us, since we are still caught up in it and must function in it. . . .

We have, however, entered into a stage of society in which the conditions seem to us to be given that make an abolition of classes possible, indeed necessary, and press toward bringing the episode of class society to an end. It may lay claim to eternal duration just as little as eternal permanence was granted, say, to gentile society or to the mark community before it. The theory of the historical development of class society must not be synonymous for us with the theory of social development in general.

Section Four
Marx's Preface

CHAPTER ONE

Will and Mode of Production

The path on which I came to the materialist conception of history set forth here is very different from the one taken by Marx and Engels, although I

---

23. See IV:1:1, below.

was, early on, decisively influenced by them. But, as different as my conception of history might be from that of Marx and Engels in its grounding, in the method it employs it is in complete agreement with theirs and also in its results, with subjective deviations, of course, resulting from differences in talent, working conditions, and contemporary circumstances under which each of us worked. Marx and Engels were far superior to me as geniuses, as well as by virtue of the favorable circumstance that these intellectual giants . . . came together in joint research and activity unique in the history of the human intellect. On the other hand, I benefit from the fact that I have survived our masters by more than a generation—Marx even by almost half a century—and thus have acquired from numerous experiences knowledge that necessarily remained hidden from them.

If, in spite of this difference in the path we followed, in our talents, and in our experiences, my conception of history is so much in agreement with that of Marx and Engels, I find that to be a confirmation of the method I have applied in my historical labors for a half-century and have, as I hope, perfected in doing so. Even today, I am still in agreement with Marx and Engels as regards the method and its application both in investigations of the past and in practical participation in the struggles of the present as well as in discerning the tendencies determining our future. That is true although I diverge from the philosophical basis of that method, insofar as I conceive of the dialectic of evolution in the world of the species of organisms and of human society partly in a different way from them.[1]

[Kautsky reprints in full Marx's classical summary paragraph on the materialist conception of history in his "Preface to A Contribution to the Critique of Political Economy.*"]* When considering those statements in Marx's preface with which we must concern ourselves now,[2] it is necessary above all to turn against some misunderstandings. Marx states: "In the social production of their life, men enter into definite relations that are necessary and *independent of their will*, relations of production which correspond to a definite stage of development of their material productive forces" (p. 425; *MESW*, I, 503). This sentence is sometimes understood as meaning that particular relations of production arise spontaneously out of the given technology, without any volition whatever on the part of men. Construed in this way, the statement would, of course, be nonsense. Marx himself says that a relation of production is a relation men enter into with one another for the purpose of production. . . . No one will want to maintain that Marx was thinking of reflex movements that happen "independently of the will" of men. Relations of production presuppose conscious, purposive cooperation

1. See I: 5 : 2–3 and III : 3 : 12, above.
2. Kautsky discusses the rest of Marx's summary on IV : 9 : 1, below.

of men, which is not possible at all without conscious volition directed toward definite ends.

But the particular nature of this volition is independent of men's preferences. It is partially determined by their inborn needs. . . . Moreover, every man grows up in a specific social setting with given traditions, institutions, and views, which also engender specific needs and wants. . . . These traditions exist prior to him, wholly independent of his will. And the same is true of the level of his knowledge of the environment. . . . Our cognitive faculty is also an acquired, inherited characteristic with which we must make do, which cannot be improved by our mere will. To be sure, men succeed in inventing aids to their acquisition of knowledge, which enlarge its range and reliability. But these inventions, too, are dependent on certain conditions that are independent of our will. The subjective factor that is relevant for men entering into relations of production, their needs and their knowledge, is thus independent of their will.

Of course, that holds true all the more for the objective factor, the configuration of the environment, which for its part also calls forth certain needs and wants. . . . On the other hand, the implements man has at his disposal for the satisfaction of his needs and wants are also dependent on the nature of his environment. . . . The manner in which any given environment influences man also depends . . . on his specific character, above all on his knowledge. . . .

However, entry into relations of production is independent of man's will in still another sense. . . . Technical progress . . . certainly does not occur without men's volition, within the . . . work of inventors. But not only are their problems and the means for their solution given to them independently of their will by the conditions existing at a particular time; the relations of production resulting from the new technology have been foreseen by the inventors of this technology only to a very slight extent and are completely independent of their volition. . . . It is certainly true that these relations of production, too, have usually not been created without a certain volition on the part of the persons entering into them. Factory-hells would never have been built and put into operation without capitalists who wanted to extract profit from them. But . . . their volition is directed only to the exploitation of the given technological and social circumstances. Much the same is true of the proletarians, . . . [who] want to sell their own labor-power, as well as that of their wives and children, at any price, driven as they are by the will to live. But that this will had to express itself in just this way certainly did not depend on the will of the workers concerned. . . .

What the particular nature of men's needs at any given time is and what means are at their disposal for satisfying them, that is independent of their will. It is determined by the given, specific level of development of their material productive forces. These "material forces of production" must be defined in more detail. They are derived from nature's wealth, out of the substances and the forces at our disposal in the external world, and they are material in nature insofar as we designate the totality of the external world as matter. But in comparison with the evolution of society, nature does not appear to be developing.... The stages of development of the material productive forces originate, therefore, from the development of knowledge of nature and from the technical application of this knowledge.

No technology can be successfully applied unless men join together for definite actions. The relations of production thereby arrived at are prescribed for men by their own technology. They are not prescribed for them by a higher power standing above them and independent of their own will, but rather by their own will, which is, in the final analysis, nothing but the will to live and to preserve its species that is innate in every organism endowed with will. The same will that creates technology also creates the corresponding relations of production. But the particular nature of these relations of production depends just as little on men's preferences, on their mere will, as does the state of their material forces of production.

Incidentally, the relations of production at any given time are not, strictly speaking, determined by the material conditions of production alone, but also by other moments, for example, by the given system of property. But the latter consists, in its turn, of two elements: first, property relations that are brought into being by the nature of the material conditions of production themselves; and second, property relations that newly appearing conditions of production find already existing. Either these forms of property must be adapted to the new circumstances or the latter are adapted to the received forms of property. In the long run, therefore, the forms of property cannot be in contradiction to the material conditions of production. In the last analysis, it is always the latter that determine the relations of production.

The materialist conception of history does not by any means make men's entry into relations of production, nor the historical development occurring upon the foundation of those relations, independent of men's volition and knowledge, hence independent of men's mind. Rather, it presupposes such volition and knowledge as indispensable, but it determines the limits of their efficacy and points up the consequences that necessarily ensue from a particular volition and knowledge under certain conditions, as well as how such volition and knowledge necessarily appear as the consequence of certain conditions.

CHAPTER TWO

Base and Superstructure

Marx... continues: "The totality of these relations of production constitutes the economic structure of society, the real foundation, on which rises a legal and political superstructure and to which correspond definite forms of social consciousness" (p. 425; *MESW*, I, 503).... This characterization of the relationship of economy and consciousness with the terms economic foundation and ideological superstructure is, among the tenets in which the materialist conception of history is formulated, probably the one . . . that has made the deepest impression and is considered to be the central point of this conception. And yet it is precisely this sentence that has occasioned the strangest misunderstandings and interpretations. . . .

Marx here compares society with a building. . . . A building is erected according to a certain plan drafted by a master builder. . . . That is the very opposite of the Marxist view that rests upon the realization that society cannot be erected, but that it simply becomes, simply develops. . . . The comparison of society with a building is attended by yet another danger, if we think about it uncritically: the danger of considering social conditions in a state of rest, not in a state of motion. According to the conception of dialectics accepted by Marx and Engels, isolated things in themselves in a state of rest cannot be known at all. . . . The passage about the ideological superstructure contrasted to the economic structure as material foundation is, then, not to be taken literally.

Also, one must not, as frequently happens, conceive of the matter in a crudely materialistic manner, as if the base consisted merely of material things, machines, tools, raw materials, railways, etc., and the superstructure merely of nonmaterial ideas. . . . The "material forces of production" contain not only substances (as well as forces) supplied by nature, but also mental labor that discovers those material riches in nature and ways of rendering them useful. The whole of social wealth disposed of by mankind and all the productive forces at its command beyond what it had already mastered in its animal state, must be ascribed to the development of man's knowledge. And in any given moment, the wealth of society is determined much more by the level of its knowledge, of its mental qualities, than by the quantity of things available for its use. [Kautsky quotes at some length Thomas Hodgskin's work of 1825, Labour Defended against the Claims of Capital, pp. 44, 49, 63–65, expressing similar thoughts also referred to with approval by Marx, Theories of Surplus Value, III, 266–67, 294–95, 297–98.]

If it is true even of the material forces of production that they are in large part mental or intellectual in character, then that is all the more true of the relations of production men enter into among themselves, corresponding to the specific nature of their productive forces at the time in question. . . . The totality of these relations of production, the "real foundation" or base, on which a legal and political superstructure and definite forms of social consciousness are built up, is therefore by no means . . . constituted merely of material things of the external world, but rather determined very strongly by mental factors, by men's needs and wants and by their knowledge, . . . and by a great variety of interests, not only egoistic, but also the social, sexual, aesthetic ones, and those striving for knowledge, to the extent that they require certain relations of production for their satisfaction.

... On the other hand, the ideological superstructure is not at all of a purely mental nature. This superstructure is not a matter of intellectual needs or wants and outlooks the individual develops in isolation in his head. Such needs and outlooks can never acquire historical significance. Marx, then, speaks explicitly of "definite forms of *social* consciousness." ... Only by means of reciprocal communications and mutual understanding do views shared *[by numerous people]* receive a social character and thereby the power to shape history. This communication and understanding becomes the more necessary, the more society becomes differentiated according to social conditions and possibilities of education and the more the forms of consciousness of different men consequently diverge from each other.... But *[communication and understanding also become]* increasingly difficult, for the development of technology and of the economy extends more and more the circle of men who are socially linked with one another and expands even more rapidly the scope of the knowledge, newly found as well as that received from earlier generations, which is accumulated in society....

Even when it is a question only of linguistic communication, ... this communication to a broader circle of people is impossible without the aid of material things, paper, pens, type, printer's ink, the printing press, etc. ... Even more dependent on material things are those intellectual productions ... that operate in part or entirely through sense impressions of another kind. Where would the natural sciences be without observatories and laboratories, etc., with their growing technical implements; where would music be without instruments; drama ..., painting ..., the plastic arts ..., architecture, how many materials do they require in order to give form to their ideas! ... Even the religious forms of ideology cannot attain to social significance without the mediation of material things. ...

Thus one cannot simply say that only material things are to be found in the base, and only ideas and feelings in the superstructure. ... And there is more. It also cannot be said that base and superstructure always stand in a relation of cause and effect to one another. They influence each other in constant interaction. Certain legal, political, and religious views are conditioned by certain economic circumstances, but the reverse is equally true. Legal and political conditions also affect economic life to determine it. And the same is true even of religion. ...

Does all this not demonstrate the insufficiency of the materialist conception of history and the invalidity of the distinction between the real foundation and the ideological superstructure? It would certainly demonstrate this if the materialist conception of history had as its goal the explanation of individual social *states* in isolation, without their connection to the *movement* of society. Our conception, however, is characterized precisely by the fact that it is *dialectical*, that it considers only movement as knowable and inquires into it. When we do that, then the metaphor of base and superstructure takes on a completely different appearance. What the materialist conception of history has to accomplish is the explanation of the formation of what is new in history. It has to explain, in every state of society, the *new* ideology that arises in it. We have already had occasion to discuss the emergence of the new in society and need not add much here.[3]

If we consider in a particular society the new ideas struggling to become influential, then we can note that they are preceded by new technical and economic conditions. These do not immediately engender new ideas. Men are conservative and seek to adapt the new technology and economy to the old ideas. Only insofar as these factors are not compatible with one another does there arise a stage of uncertainty, of searching and groping for new forms of ideas and of social institutions determined by them. The new ideas corresponding to the new economy take form much later than the latter does. This stage of searching and groping and of the realization of new ideas lasts until a state of equilibrium between ideas and economy is brought about, until the former correspond to the latter. . . .

Thus, if we consider only the *new* ideas of a particular period, they always form a superstructure rising on a previously constructed new economic base. Now, there is no idea that was not new at some time. . . . All that have developed in the course of history . . . can, in *the final analysis*, be explained materialistically. But, of course, only in the final analysis, as Marx and Engels stressed repeatedly.

It will not do at all to attempt to explain *all* the ideas we find present in a state of society by the economic conditions existing at the same time. Among the ideas of an age, a distinction must be drawn between the old ones it inherits from its predecessors and the new ones it brings forth itself.[4] . . . Many old ideas are preserved, but, to be sure, only those that are compatible at least to some degree with the new state. Otherwise . . . they would be abandoned, either explicitly or in point of fact, that is, they would cease to practically determine men's behavior. . . .

The emergence of new ideas under the influence of new material conditions, the adaptation of old ideas to new circumstances, the struggle against those old ideas that prove to be incompatible with the new ones and their ultimate eradication: such is the content of the intellectual struggle of every era in which a new technology or economy appears. The impulse for this movement is provided solely by the economy. Ideology follows the economy only hesitantly.

But in order to understand the ideas a particular era has inherited from an earlier time, I must not investigate this era alone, but also the preceding

3. See III:2:12–13, above.

4. Beginning with this sentence, some paragraphs in this and the next two chapters, including some omitted from the present edition, appear in another translation in Hook, *Marx and the Marxists*, pp. 163–65.

epoch. I must ascertain what was new then in that epoch's ideas and what was not. Again we will find that only a part were newly developed; only this part can be explained by the economic conditions of the time. For an explanation of the others, I must refer to an even earlier period. Thus, in order to understand the total ideology of our time we must go back into the remote past. Only then will we succeed in laying bare all its economic origins. But we will always find, if we dig deep enough, that all ideas are rooted in economic conditions.

That is the meaning of the image of base and superstructure. The relations between the two factors are not so simple as they appear at first glance.

CHAPTER THREE
Christianity and Revolution

As an illustration of what has been said, let us take Christianity. Among the ideas determining the intellectual and spiritual life of our time, it is still of great significance.... How deeply rooted belief in the Bible is was just recently shown by the wonderful "monkey trial" in Dayton *[Tennessee]*, the attempt to forbid, in the name of the Bible, the teaching of Darwin's theory in the American democracy. The ideology of our time cannot be described without according a large place to Christianity. Yet it would be quite futile to attempt to derive the ideas of Christianity from the economic conditions existing today. If we want to understand it, we have to go back to the time when it appeared as a new phenomenon in world history.... *[Kautsky briefly describes the economic and political conditions of the Roman empire and points to novel Christian ideas as a reaction to them.]*[5]

In addition to these features, however, Christianity contains many other ideas, which it ... encountered as already long dominant.... These were traits of the Jewish, the Egyptian, the Assyrian, the Persian, and even of the Greek way of thinking, which had developed hundreds and thousands of years earlier and had become deeply rooted.... These pre-Christian elements in Christianity cannot be explained "materialistically" by the economic conditions of the era of its beginnings. For many of them it is *[not]* possible to uncover the time and the conditions of their origin.... We are today not yet by any means in a position to give an economic, materialist explanation of all elements of a given world of ideas. Many gaps still await being filled by future researchers. That is not, of course, proof that the materialist conception of history is invalid any more than than lack of a connecting link between ape and man disproves the theory of evolution. There would be evidence against its validity only if it could be established

---

5. Kautsky had done this at great length in Part II of his *Foundations of Christianity*.

that an idea was new, and the economic conditions of the time of its origin were well known, but investigation of both elements led to the conclusion that a relation of that idea to these conditions was out of the question.

Like every phenomenon, Christianity, too, can be grasped only in its movement, in its becoming and its transformations. . . . If we want to understand the Christian elements still effective in present-day intellectual life, then it is not sufficient to describe the emergence of primitive Christianity and to investigate how it evolved. Since that time, great economic changes have occurred, and each of them changed the form of Christianity that existed when it happened and gave to Christianity a particular character. *[There follows an eight-page sketch of the changing role in Western Europe of the Christian religion and church from the days of the Roman Empire to the beginnings of socialism.]*[6] . . . In spite of all these economic, social, and intellectual changes, Christianity has maintained itself for almost twenty centuries. . . . The letter has always remained the same, but the spirit that breathes life into the letter has been very different in different ages and countries and, at the same time in the same country, among the various classes and parties that have adhered to Christianity.

CHAPTER FOUR

The Base in the Last Analysis

We have seen that the degree to which new and old elements are intermingled in the political, philosophical, religious, and artistic ideology of an era, of a class, or of a party can be very different depending on the particular circumstances. . . . A history of the ideas of an era, written from the standpoint of the materialist conception of history, must not confine itself to relating these ideas to the given economic conditions. The attempt to explain completely the entire spiritual and intellectual content of an era by its economy will never succeed. In another way, Engels already stressed repeatedly that the economic conditions are the decisive factor in world history only

---

6. Kautsky had a long-standing interest in applying the materialist conception of history to the explanation of the history of Christianity. Apart from his best-known *Foundations of Christianity* of 1908 and two early articles on the same subject, "Die Entstehung der biblischen Urgeschichte," and "Die Entstehung des Christenthums," he wrote *Thomas More and His Utopia* (1888) and *Vorläufer des neueren Sozialismus*, first published in 1895 and partially translated as *Communism in Central Europe in the Time of the Reformation*. Volume I of *Vorläufer* deals with a number of medieval sects and Volume II is devoted to Thomas Münzer and the Anabaptists. Kautsky returned to the latter and also deals with the Quakers in his last completed major work, *Sozialisten und Krieg*, pp. 3–20. See also his pamphlet of 1903, *Die Sozialdemokratie und die katholische Kirche*, where Kautsky discusses some aspects of the history of the Church since Roman times. The third edition of this pamphlet includes the German text of the present chapter on "Christianity and Revolution" as an appendix.

in the *last analysis. [Kautsky quotes from Engels' letters on historical materialism to J. Bloch of September 21–22, 1890, and to W. Borgius[7] on January 25, 1894; pp. 487, 502–503.]*

The intellectual forms transmitted *[from earlier periods]* do not belong to the results, to the superstructure, but to the conditions, to the base of the new economy as well as to the base of the new forms of consciousness corresponding to the new economy. Study of a historical epoch from the standpoint of the materialist conception of history must therefore always begin by separating the old and the new both in the economy and in the ideology of the era in question. What is new in the ideas can then, without doing violence *[to the facts]*, be traced back to what is new in the economic conditions.

Should one want to investigate the entire intellectual life of an age with reference to its economic sources, then it becomes necessary to undertake the *[following]* quite laborious task, which cannot always be carried out completely. One must trace back the various old elements of the dominant ideas to the time of their origin and relate each of them to the economic conditions that newly emerged at that time. And then one must also investigate how the change of these conditions, up to the age whose total ideology is to be studied, modified the intellectual element in question.

Critics of the materialist conception of history reproach it with unduly simplifying historical interrelationships by trying to explain the infinite variety of what occurs in history by referring it to a single factor. In reality, the presentation of history from the standpoint of the materialist conception of history is a far more complicated process than most of the traditional ways of writing history. The latter are either nothing but mere recounting of history, which can, after all, be only the starting point of research, not its conclusion. . . . Or traditional historiography seeks to explain the different ideas operative in society by the very thing that is to be explained; this is conceived of either as the result of the outstanding intellectual force of a hero or of the inherited spirit of a race or as the "spirit of the age." . . . All these ways of writing history do not go beyond the surface phenomena and investigate only individual phenomena in isolation, without attempting to integrate them into a total relational complex. The significance of the materialist conception of history lies not least in the fact that it compels *[the researcher]* to regard all historical phenomena of all ages in a coherent, total relational complex. That is not a simplistic, limited simplification, but, if the task is taken seriously, an immense complication of historical research.

[There follows a long argument with Rudolf Stammler who, in "Die materialistische Geschichtsauffassung," p. 530, had insisted that] legal forms belong

---

7. Kautsky thought, as was generally believed, that this letter had been addressed to Heinz Starkenburg, because it was the latter who had published it.

not to the superstructure, but to the base of the economy, which is not possible without them. . . .

As soon as we go beyond the simplest forms, social phenomena become ever more complex, and the influence of the given productive forces and of all the living conditions on the content and the direction of men's volition and their decisions becomes more and more complicated. This is due to the fact that to the inherited and individually acquired capacities and needs of men there are now increasingly added socially transmitted laws, religions, etc. These are very different for different regions and times and often shape in very different ways the influence of the same productive forces on the formation of the relations of production and their superstructure.

Let us therefore not forget: Only in the *last analysis* is the whole legal, political, ideological apparatus to be regarded as the superstructure to an economic base. For an individual phenomenon in history that does not hold true by any means. Whether it is of an economic, ideological, or other kind, it will function in some respects as base, in others as superstructure. Only for the phenomena in history that are *new* at a particular time does Marx's statement about base and superstructure hold good unconditionally.

CHAPTER FIVE

Production of Life as Production of Human Beings

One more passage of Marx's preface needs to be examined more closely here. . . . What is meant by the phrase: the social production of *life*? . . . We must not limit the social process of production to the means for preserving mere animal life. This process serves to satisfy all of man's needs and wants. And by his very nature man is a being moved not merely by hunger and thirst, but also by other needs of a social, sexual, aesthetic, and truth-seeking kind. Many a technical means, invented to satisfy existing needs, has an effect beyond this satisfaction, intensifies already existing needs or awakens new ones. . . . Production of life does not mean . . . merely obtaining *subsistence*, but also assuring a certain *standard of living*. We find here even at the starting point of the base a "moral" element in it, which is, to be sure, in its turn a product of technology. Examined more closely, the "natural" needs shrink down to a minimum. Among these, Marx numbers "clothing, fuel, and housing."[8] But these already presuppose a certain technology; they are historically conditioned.

Engels directs our attention to another side of the "production of life."

---

8. The terms "moral element," "natural needs," and "clothing, fuel, and housing" refer to a passage Kautsky had just quoted from Marx, *Capital*, I, 275.

In the preface to the first edition of his work *The Origin of the Family, Private Property and the State*, he writes.

> According to the materialistic conception, the determining factor in history is, in the last analysis, the production and reproduction of immediate life. This, again, is itself of a twofold character. On the one hand, the production of the means of subsistence, of food, clothing and shelter and the tools requisite therefor; on the other hand, the production of human beings themselves, the propagation of the species. The social institutions under which men of a particular historical epoch and a particular country live are conditioned by both kinds of production: by the stage of development of labour, on the one hand, and of the family, on the other. [p. 191]

[Kautsky then quotes a long passage from Marx and Engels, The German Ideology, *pp. 30—32, in which, much like Engels forty years later, they refer to "the production of life, both of one's own in labour and of fresh life in procreation."]*[9]

Not the procreative act, which remains identically the same, but the different forms of marriage and of the family are what Engels had in mind when he spoke of the production of human beings. . . . It is indisputable that the forms of marriage and the family change and that this change is of the greatest significance for man's development. But Engels claims more than that. His understanding of the two kinds of production that determine social evolution would be justified only if each of the two factors developed independently of the other. It would be meaningless if the changing forms of the family and marriage, like all other changes in society, could also be accounted for in the last analysis by alterations of the productive forces. Then the latter would remain the, in the last analysis, solely determinative moment of development.

Since Engels' proclamation of the family as an independent factor of social transformations, a number of relationships have been uncovered that indicate a dependence of the forms of the family on the forms of the economy. . . . Man develops his technology, he changes both his environment and the techniques of caring for his offspring through his technology, and thereby also changes the forms of marriage and of the relationship of spouses, not just to each other but also to their children, hence the forms of the family. . . .

As important as the sexual factor is, . . . as a factor remaining constant it can be disregarded when it is a matter of investigating *changes* in human society. Of course, . . . all sexual moments . . . bearing social character become, like the forms of the household, dependent on the nature of the social

9. Kautsky notes that *The German Ideology*, first published by the Marx-Engels Institute in Moscow in 1926, had become available to him only when this section of his present work was already written. The subsequent discussion therefore refers only to Engels's words in the preface to *The Origin of the Family*.

environment, which in the last analysis is to be accounted for by economic factors, in part those of the present, in part those of the past. . . . And even many purely animal sexual functions are influenced by the mode of production and the way of living dependent on it. The nature of work and of life in cities produces an earlier sexual maturity than do work and life in the countryside. There are modes of production that bring forth sexual frigidity. And there are others that have the opposite effect. . . . Finally, there are modes of production in which low fertility of women and others in which enormous fertility have been noted. . . .

It is only language that permits, first, establishing the simplest relations of descent, retaining them permanently in consciousness, and then progressively following an individual's genealogical tree into its more distant ramifications.[10] Only then does there emerge . . . the possibility of a kinship-organization. But kinship becomes a socially . . . recognized and effective organization only when and only insofar as social needs appear, for the satisfaction of which the circle of relatives seems to be best suited. That, too, is dependent once again on social conditions that are rooted in the development of productivity. Thus, the strength of the kinship-organization at any given time does not depend on natural bonds of blood, but on economic and technical conditions, as does the strength of every other social grouping. . . . Nor was the notion of kinship given by nature, as is usually assumed. At first, only the relatives of one lineage, the male or the female, were considered to be related by blood. Here again, then, the fixation of kinship depended on definite economic conditions. What is true of the family and marriage, then, is also true of kinship-organization, the clan or the gens. None of them is a social organization that takes form independently of the relations of production and exists alongside them. Rather, they are brought forth by definite relations of production and change with them. . . .

If we assume that the social relations connected with sexual intercourse are determined in their emergence and transformations not by the changes of technology and the economy, but by another, as yet unknown factor, then we thereby violate the unity of the materialist conception of history. . . . There are no facts that could be taken as evidence that social development is determined as much by the changes in the production of human beings as by the production of the means of subsistence. All the facts known to us argue against it. The broadening of the concept of the mode of production through inclusion in it of the production of human beings has hence remained completely unfruitful for the further development of Marxist theory. It has not enticed anyone to apply it in research and has not led to any new insights.

10. See II:3:5, above.

Production of Life as
Preservation of Life

. . . If we hold fast to the expression "the social production of life," we would constrict the materialist conception of history and omit from it an important factor of history, if we did not class with the social production of life the safeguarding of the individual and of the polity to which he belongs through armed combat against enemies. Even animal societies are not just organizations for obtaining subsistence, but also for common defense and resistance. As regards the relations that men enter into in war, however, exactly the same thing holds true as Marx said of relations of production properly speaking. They, too, are "relations that are necessary and independent of their (men's) will, which correspond to a definite stage of development of their material productive forces." . . .

The character and the extent of the individual closed societies that settle their conflicts with one another by fighting change with economic conditions. The concept of the human enemy is also changed thereby. . . . The nature of the conflicts leading to war also changes with economic conditions. They arise at first out of the need for hunting grounds, for pasturage, later out of the desire to enlarge an area of exploitation or to obtain or keep possession of a position that dominates trade better geographically, etc. The way war is conducted at a particular time also depends entirely on the given material conditions. . . . The technology and the strategy of the commander depend on the nature of the expected theater of war, which is conditioned partly by natural, partly by economic circumstances. . . . It depends, further, on the given weapons technology, on the wealth of the state, . . . also on the size of the country and the number of its inhabitants.

Lastly, the prospects of victory are also dependent on a factor not at all material, the spirit animating the armies. . . . If an entire large mass of people, a nation, say, or perhaps a whole class, is cowardly or brave, peace-loving or eager for battle, devoted to their leader or disdainful of him, that cannot be explained by individual accidents, but by circumstances that exercise a similar and lasting determinative influence on all members of the mass. Thus, that fact is to be explained by their living conditions, their occupations—circumstances conditioned by the mode of production. These circumstances, on which the whole national character depends, can be modified in an army by the particular circumstances of the military system; for example, by the regularity and ampleness of the troops' provisioning and payment, the treatment of the men by the officers, etc., circumstances that for their part are also to be accounted for directly or in the last analysis by economic conditions, the wealth of the state, the level of taxation, and the way the working classes are treated by the higher classes.

Thus everything having to do with war, the armament and organization of the troops, strategy and tactics, victory and defeat, is determined ultimately by the development of the forces of production and the relations of production.

At the same time, a traditional way of conducting war can also react on the structuring of new economic conditions. The organization of military forces and the social system are often closely linked with one another. *[Referring to the Germanic gens—on which he quotes Delbrück,* History of the Art of War, *II, 39–40—and to medieval feudalism, Kautsky then shows that their]* organization serves war quite as much as the economy. *[He then points out that armies of peasants, like the Swiss, and of townspeople, like the Athenians, tend to fight in tight mass formations, with each individual relying on his comrades, while big landowners, economically and politically largely independent and isolated from each other, like Homeric heroes and medieval knights, rely on their individual courage and training and on their weapons rather than on mass discipline. On the knights, he quotes Delbrück,* History of the Art of War, *III, 233, 243–45.]* Thus, the spiritual element in the conduct of war, the spirit animating the warrior, also is not a matter of his choice, but depends rather on the conditions of the surroundings in which he grows up and fights.

Martial superiority, too, is economically conditioned. . . . Very often the backward people is the stronger one. That is true, for example, of the fifteenth-century Swiss whom I just mentioned. . . . Since the emergence of capitalist industry, though, it can generally be said that higher economic development also means military superiority. . . .

War is always economically disastrous for the vanquished and not infrequently for the victor, too. *[Kautsky cites nomads' raids on agriculturalists, British trade and colonial wars of the eighteenth century, French revolutionary wars, and the Franco-Prussian war of 1870–71 as examples of wars bringing economic benefits to the victors, while the victorious wars of Louis XIV brought economic ruin to his regime.]* In our century, the technical and economic conditions of warfare have become such that a large war can no longer end any other way than with very serious economic damage to all participants, to the victors as well as to the vanquished. . . . Thus the effects of war can be very different under different economic conditions.

If mankind is taken in general, then war has certainly only hindered, not promoted its development, for in all circumstances war has meant destruction of workers and means of production and artistic treasurers. . . . If humanity is nevertheless becoming richer, that is happening only because up to now warfare has proved to be weaker than the process of production. . . . But war . . . has influenced a certain kind of social development to a very high degree. If humanity has not developed uniformly, if parts of it have remained in complete ignorance and have even sunk from affluence into misery, while other parts rose brilliantly to . . . opulence, knowledge, and power—if social development at times becomes a movement toward the aggravation of all antagonisms, both . . . between the individual peoples and in some peoples between their classes, then that is due above all to war. War has in part created these antagonisms, in part immeasurably intensified them. They will not be successfully overcome unless the conditions for abolishing war arise simultaneously.

It is, however, equally impossible fully to understand the development of human society without investigating the nature of war. The materialist conception of history is incomplete if we do not understand "the social production of life," which is its starting point, in a sense that makes it possible to include in this production war and preparation for war. . . . We do not have to ask ourselves here whether war was a suitable method of preserving life in society, but whether it was considered and employed as such and what the conditions were for doing that.

CHAPTER SEVEN

Economy and Natural Science

a. Knowledge of Nature and Technology

Before we conclude our commentary on the opening sentences of the passage in Marx's preface on the materialist conception of history, we must discuss one more idea, . . . because it is absent from the preface and because, without clarity regarding it, a gap is left in our conception of history. Nowhere in his preface . . . does Marx speak of gaining *knowledge of nature*, although he speaks of the fact that "the mode of production of material life conditions the general *process* of social, political and *intellectual life*" (p. 425; *MESW*, I, 503). Now, the "general process of intellectual life" certainly encompasses gaining knowledge of nature, natural science, from a certain stage of development on. What is the role of natural science in social development? . . .

There can be no doubt . . . that knowledge of nature is among the "productive forces." . . . To what extent at any given time man makes use of his own abilities and the forces of the environment, hence transforms them into productive forces (understood in the broadest sense) for himself, depends on the degree of his knowledge of his own nature as well as of the nature of his surroundings, thus on the level of his knowledge of nature. And this knowledge is the changeable factor in the sum total of the available productive forces. Man's innate abilities and the forces of his natural surroundings do not in the main change in the course of social development. . . . The development of the "material productive forces" is therefore basically just another name for the development of knowledge of nature. Accordingly, an intellectual process, that of gaining knowledge of nature, appears as the bottom base of the "real foundation," the "material substructure," of human ideology. On the other hand, however, we also find knowledge of nature in the "superstructure." A particular religion or philosophy is founded just as much on certain views of nature as on certain social outlooks. And art, too, has always been based on contemplation and knowledge of nature. . . .

Clearly, from the perspective of the materialist conception of history, the role played in history by knowledge of nature is a very complicated matter. These difficulties have led some Marxists to assume that the development of the natural sciences is independent, at least in part, of the general social development and proceeds according to its own intrinsic laws.
. . . The acquisition of knowledge of nature, the adaptation of thought to the facts of nature, has made gigantic forward strides in the course of human history, at an increasingly rapid pace, but the object of this adaptation, nature, has remained unchanged during this period of time. How is this possible? The change of another object, of the economy, cannot explain the changes in the adaptation of thoughts to the immutable facts of nature. [Kautsky quotes Friedrich Adler who, in his Ernst Machs Überwindung des mechanischen Materialismus, p. 174, had argued that in many branches of natural science thoughts are "never functionally tied to changes in their object," and Conrad Schmidt who, in a review of Bogdanoff, Die Entwicklungsformen der Gesellschaft und die Wissenschaft, had insisted that natural science proceeds through a logical process. Schmidt and Adler] see progress in man's understanding of his environment, at least in some areas, exclusively in the movement of thought, in logical activity.

But where does this movement come from? The individual's cognitive faculty does not change, nor do his surroundings. But the law of logic do not change either. It is not clear why it should be possible that the same brain confronting the same facts with the same logic arrives today at this view and tomorrow at another view of the same facts. On the other hand, it is undeniable that knowledge of nature is to be obtained only from the facts of nature, not from those of the economy. Where, then, do the changes in our views of nature come from? The difficulty is solved very simply as soon as we consider that the facts to which our thoughts must adapt themselves at any given time . . . are only those facts of our environment of which we become *aware*. . . . In comparison with society, nature does not change; however, the range of the facts of nature that are *known* to us does change. . . . Every expansion of this range requires new adaptations of men's thoughts to facts that might have existed from time immemorial, but that are new for the knowing individual.

But what leads to the extension of this range? . . . Logic is extraordinarily important as a means of ordering in coherent interrelational complexes the

plethora of the facts of our environment confronting us. . . . Yet it is absolutely incapable of helping us to apprehend new facts. What helps us to
apprehend new facts is . . . *technology.* Every technical innovation has the
task of solving a definite practical problem. It can, however, do more than
that and result in consequences the authors of the innovation did not and
could not think of.[11] Among the most important of these is the consequence
that the innovation acquaints us with facts of our environment that were
previously concealed from us. Technology often offers man . . . organs that
make new sense impressions directly or indirectly accessible to him. *[Kaut-
sky quotes from his own 1896 article, "Was will und kann die materialistische
Geschichtsauffassung leisten," pp. 233–34:]*

> Telescopes and microscopes, instruments for weighing and measuring, lab-
> oratories and observatories, etc. . . . provide not only the means for solving
> the problems of natural science; they also supply these very problems.
> These means, however, are the results of economic development— results
> that in turn become, through the agency of man, the causes of new prog-
> ress. The development of the natural sciences goes hand in hand with the
> development of technology, understood in the broadest sense of the word
> . . . [to include] not merely tools and machines. . . . The present state of
> mathematics belongs just as much to the economic conditions of existing
> society as the present state of machine technology or of world trade. . . .

But it is not just technology . . . that increases the range of the facts of
nature man becomes aware of. The economy, too, works in the same
sense. . . . In the beginnings of the economy, each of the small primitive
tribes lived in a limited area in complete isolation from the others. Only
the facts that the nature of this area offered to his senses, existed for man.
. . . With technological development, a division of labor emerges among the
tribes. . . . *[It]* forces *[them]* into communication, either peaceable or warlike
in character, . . . which also involves an exchange of what has been learned
from experience. . . . The invention of writing, . . . the progressive improvement of the means of transportation, especially of oceanic navigation, expands the field of the facts of nature that become known to the individual,
at times enormously. . . .

The range of the facts of nature known to us is very much extended . . .
not only spatially, but also temporally, especially through writing, but also
through graphic and plastic art. . . . Evidence of facts of nature has also been
discovered that existed long before man appeared. Here, too, technology
and the economy were effective. . . . Mines as well as the cuts and tunnels
of railways have given us knowledge of the successive strata of the earth's
crust and have also let us become acquainted with numerous remains of
organisms peculiar to the various strata. Thus we were informed of the

11. See also III:3:11, above.

facts of nature that led to the theory of evolution as an adaptation of men's thoughts to those facts.

As unchanging as nature is in comparison with society, the range of natural facts accessible to our consciousness is quite changeable, and the expansion of this range, like the development of society, is effected in the last analysis by the changes of human technology and economy. Along with the abundance and diversity of the observed facts and their interrelations, however, the methods of collecting and ordering them also develop: logic, mathematics, and critical epistemology, which appear to dwell solely in the realm of mind. Technology, economy, and understanding of nature are intimately interrelated. Every advance on one side effects an advance on the other. The expansion of man's knowledge of nature makes possible technical advances and improvement of human practice with regard to the production of life. Every advance of this practice makes us aware of new facts of nature and thereby brings us . . . the possibility and necessity of new adaptations of our thinking to the facts. And, on the other hand, men's practice in applying their newly gained knowledge provides the best touchstone for the correctness of the new adaptations of their thoughts.

From a certain degree of social division of labor onward, the activity of investigating the environment is separated, to be sure, from the everyday practice of the production of life. If science is then no longer determined merely by practical motives, the range of the material it processes, the range of the facts at its disposal nevertheless remains dependent on the level of technical and economic development in the society. It is true that the more science advances, the less does the technology of everyday life suffice for the solution of its problems. . . . And to a high degree the further progress of some sciences is no longer determined directly by the technology and economy of everyday life, but by special scientific technology. But that, too, is not a development effected by mere logical thought. . . . It remains progress in the adaptation of thoughts to new facts, of which we are made aware by new technical instruments and methods. And, moreover, the development of scientific technology always remains dependent on the general state of practical technology, on the raw materials, tools, and labor-power that it has at its disposal as well as on the state of the social wealth. . . .

Thus we find . . . in all respects that the development of our knowledge of nature as well as of our views of society is dependent on society and on the factors moving and changing it. Our views of nature at any given time are of course always determined by the facts of nature we know, not by the society we live in. One must not conceive of the close connection of the understanding of nature with the conditions of production in such a primitive, crude manner, as if new views of nature were the reflection of new economic conditions. Rather, the new technology and economy have a revolutionizing effect on natural science by supplying the latter with new facts from the realm of nature, which men would not have become aware of without the new technology and economy. . . .

Merely becoming acquainted with facts, with the empirical, does not of itself provide understanding. It is merely the starting point. True understanding is attained only when the individual facts are brought together in a coherent complex of interrelations. Understanding is the greater, the more all known facts have successfully been brought together into a single coherent totality of interrelations. That cannot be achieved by the mere empiricist, but only by the philosophical mind. But woe betide that mind if it goes beyond the foundation of the empirical, of experience, and seeks to attain new insights by means of mere logical thinking. . . . In that effort it will always fail.

Least of all today does the philosophical investigator of nature have reason for such border-crossings. The number of new facts of nature made accessible to us almost every day is so enormous that they again and again race ahead of any adaptation of our thoughts to them. These facts would bring us not new understanding, but uncertainty and confusion, if we did not succeed in arranging them together with the old facts in a coherent totality of interrelations. . . . There is no doubt that without the philosophical mind we would make no headway in science. But it is the environment that supplies that mind with problems and with the means for solving them. It finds neither the ones nor the others in itself.

b. Views of Nature and of Society in Ideology

The question: What is the motive force of the development of our understanding of nature, . . . must not be confused with another question, which also points to a connection between men's view of nature and the economy. This second question arises from the fact that man lives simultaneously in nature and in society, that he receives from the one and from the other various impressions that he attempts to fashion in his brain into a coherent image of the world. Which of the two factors proves to be paramount . . . in this process?

It might seem that the impressions of immutable nature were far stronger than those of inconstant, mutable society and of its foundation, the economy. Does not political economy itself search for natural laws of the economy? And are not extremely important social processes and demands often explained in terms of natural sciences, war and competition, anti-Semitism and contempt for Negroes, colonial policies as well as many policies of alliance? . . . This mannerism means the exploitation of natural-scientific views for social ends. References to natural laws for the solution of social problems do not originate from desires for knowledge, but from needs to advance particular interests. . . . To invoke natural science arguments is nothing other than a modernization of the mannerisms of the age of belief in God, when the individual raised his own wishes and goals to be the will of his God and believed that he thereby justified and sanctified them. . . . Endeavors of this kind . . . do not prove that knowledge of nature influences knowledge of society. Rather, they constitute one of the various forms of the reverse process of our views of nature being influenced by our social being. . . .

[Kautsky quotes Otto Bauer's essay "Das Weltbild des Kapitalismus,"pp 889–90, an attempt at what Bauer called a "transcendent history of ideas."] The transcendent history of the natural sciences . . . is influenced not by new *facts* of nature, revealed by new technology and economy, but by new *ways of thinking* that arise from new economic and social conditions and influence man's thinking in its entirety, his whole way of adapting his thoughts to the facts, not just his thoughts about society but also those about nature, hence his whole worldview.

[Kautsky then quotes his own book of 1902 on The Social Revolution, *pp. 12–14:]*

> As long as the bourgeoisie was revolutionary, *catastrophe theories* were dominant in natural science (geology and biology). They started out from the premise that the evolution of nature proceeds in sudden large leaps. When the bourgeois revolution was completed, catastrophe theories were replaced by the conception of gradual, imperceptible evolution resulting from the accumulation of innumerable, very minute advances and adaptations in the competitive struggle. To the revolutionary bourgeoisie, the thought of catastrophes occurring also in nature seemed very reasonable; to the conservative bourgeoisie, this notion appeared to be unreasonable and unnatural. That is not to maintain, of course, that the natural scientists were in their particular theories directly determined by the political and social needs of the bourgeoisie. . . . But everyone is involuntarily influenced by the mentality and the experiences of the class in which he lives, and everyone brings something from that class into his scientific views. . . . The conditioning of a view by the attitude of the classes from which it emerges, of course, proves nothing as to its correctness or incorrectness. Its historical success, though, is dependent on this attitude. . . .

One more circumstance must be taken into consideration in this context. . . . The period of economic individualism, of free private enterprise, although it does not create them, certainly increases and expands the conditions for an individualism of the mind, for the physical liberation of the individual from the bonds of convention and collective thought. These conditions, which arose already in antiquity for specific small strata in the large cities on the Mediterranean, acquire an extraordinary extension and intensity in the capitalist mode of production. This kind of individualism must not be equated with economic individualism. The strata combating the latter most vigorously belong to the most energetic champions of the intellectual freedom of the individual. In the examination of all relationships involving individuals, this individualistic thinking misleads the investigator to start out from the individual, to try to explain mass phenomena by the nature of the individual. Thus, for example, philosophy, in these circumstances, seeks the explanation of ethics, . . . not in the conditions of social cooperation, but in an a priori characteristic of the individual. In the same way, Darwin took the individual as the starting point in his investigation of the motive forces of the evolution of species. *[Kautsky here summarizes briefly what he had written in II: 1:3, above.]* . . .

Ways of thinking that proceed from man's social life erected upon his technology can, as they influence his views of nature, become a serious source of errors for the formation of a conception of nature and of a world-view. In no case do they promote the clarity of natural-scientific thinking, founded upon the observation of the facts of nature. Every area of human thought has its particular sources of error. The social sciences are greatly hindered by the fact that we live in a society of class antagonisms. Since the individual investigator of social matters belongs to a certain class or has an interest in a certain class, he is also interested in certain results of his research. . . . It can be an extremely selfless interest in the well-being of others that motivates him. But his impartiality is nevertheless diminished. And to that is added the difficulty of entering into the mentality of men who live under completely different conditions than the researcher. And yet such an understanding is indispensable when it is a matter of social investigations pertaining to different classes.

Fortunately, such sources of error are not insurmountable. Other conditions being equal, they will make themselves felt the less disruptively, the more comprehensive, the less one-sided the researcher's activity is. The social researcher will be the more impartial and understanding, the more he is able to weave what lies closest to hand for him—the present, his country, his class—into the great interrelational totality of the evolution of the whole of humanity from its beginnings. On the other hand, the natural scientist will be the better able to keep himself free of the influence of his views of nature of ways of thinking originating in his social milieu, the less he confines himself to a specialty, the more he seeks to relate his special knowledge to the totality of the views of nature and the more he also grasps the peculiar character of the society and of the ideas arising from it. To be sure, this must happen in a way that makes it possible to unite the facts of nature and the facts of society with one another without contradiction, to combine both in a common worldview. . . .

If we want to understand the development of natural science and philosophy, the influence on them of dispositions and mentalities originating from social conditions absolutely must be taken into consideration. . . . This influence, however, is by no means indispensable for the development of the understanding of nature. Rather, it falsifies that understanding. The more it can be excluded, the more the history of natural science becomes one drawn solely from the facts of nature, the better. In contrast to the influence on men's conception of nature of social dispositions and ways of thinking, an influence of technology and of the economy on the natural sciences through the discovery of new facts of nature not only does not constitute a source of error, but constitutes rather in the final analysis the only motive force of the progress of men's knowledge of nature. This progress in turn results in further progress of technology and the economy. The two ways in which the natural sciences are shaped by technology and the economy are therefore fundamentally different from each other and must be kept rigorously distinct. . . .

And so we conclude our commentary on those statements of Marx's preface that concerned us here. . . . Examination of the antagonistic forms of the process of production shall be our next task in this work.

The State and the
Development of Mankind

PART FOUR

🍒 Class and State

Section One
Definitions

How Long Have There Been Classes?

[Kautsky quotes the opening sentence of the Communist Manifesto *of 1847 that "the history of all hitherto existing society is the history of class struggles" and notes the absence of any reference in Marx's preface of 1859 to* A Contribution to the Critique of Political Economy *to preclass modes of production and its statement that the entire "prehistory of human society" down to the present rested on "antagonistic" forms of the social process of production. But he concludes from Engels' footnote of 1888 to the opening sentence of the* Manifesto *limiting it to "all written history;" from Engels' preface to the German edition of 1883 of the* Manifesto *(MESW, I, 101); and, above all, from Engels,* The Origin of the Family, *which relies heavily on Marx's notes on Morgan's* Ancient Society, *that]* our masters later significantly limited their original opinion that all of previous history had been a history of class struggles, when they became more closely acquainted with the results of research in primitive history and in ethnology, and these results themselves provided ever-deeper insight into the nature of primitive societies.[1] . . . The dichotomy of social development until now into two phases, a classless and an "antagonistic" one, was therefore ultimately recognized and emphasized by both Marx and Engels. Nonetheless, it is asserted again and again that the materialist conception of history teaches that all history up to now has been the history of class struggles. *[Kautsky*

---

1. See also IV:9:1a, below.

quotes Bukharin, Historical Materialism, *p. 177, and Max Adler,* Die Staats-auffassung des Marxismus, *pp. 305–306, to this effect.]*

The period of time prior to the emergence of classes encompasses by far the greatest part of the history of mankind's development until now.... We will not go wrong if we say that before domestic animals were tamed and food-plants were cultivated, there were no classes. *[Seeking to bring up to date Morgan's estimates of the relative length of his "ethnical periods"* (Ancient Society, *pp. 39–40), Kautsky assumes that the period of primitive communism lasted eight hundred thousand years or more, that of fully developed class societies perhaps ten to fifteen thousand years.]* Measured solely according to its temporal duration, it is then not classless society, but rather society divided into classes that presents itself to us as the exception, a mere episode in the history of human society....

Now, these distinctions are certainly dependent on what one understands by class. *[Kautsky quotes Bukharin,* Historical Materialism, *pp. 143–44, and notes that Bukharin regards salaried employees as a distinct class, while]* we assign salaried employees to the class of wage-laborers. According to Bukharin, the classes and their antagonisms originate in the fact that social cooperation requires leadership.... There is no social cooperation without leadership... whose instructions are followed by the others... We have seen that even in the animal realm societies often cannot do without leaders.[2] ... And on the other hand, if we go beyond capitalism, will the process of production be able to take place in a socialist society in an anarchistic manner, with no leadership at all?...

CHAPTER TWO

The Concept of Class

... If we want to comprehend the class struggle, we must take the word "class" in the sense in which the founders of the theory of class struggle understood it. *[Kautsky quotes the brief unfinished final chapter of* Capital, *III, 1025–26, in which Marx says that "wage-labourers, capitalists and landowners form the three great classes of modern society" due "at first sight [to] the identity of revenues and revenue sources" of each. Kautsky then quotes a page from his own article of 1903, "Klasseninteresse—Sonderinteresse—Gemeininteresse," in which he sought to complete what Marx began in his fragment. The passage concludes (on p. 241):]*

> Now we see what constitutes the individual classes. It is not just the fact that they have the same revenue sources, but also that they conse-quently have the same interests and the same *antagonism* toward the other

2. See II:3:4, above.

classes, each of which endeavors to constrict the sources of revenue of the others in order to make its own flow more abundantly.

. . . We Marxists are surely all in agreement that the labor of the workers is the wellspring from which not merely wages, but also the profit on capital (together with interest) as well as ground-rent are drawn. But how does it happen that the worker does not receive the whole product of his labor, but that part of it remains in the hands of the landowners and capitalists? . . . Superfluity of means of production on one side, lack of them on the other, that is, definite property relations constitute the basis for the division of classes. Not, however, the distinction between organs that lead and organs that execute in the process of production [as Bukharin had held]. . . . Whoever owns the means of production decides how they shall be employed. If he loves the idle life of a rentier, he can . . . lend his means of production or his money in return for interest. But he can also hire workers, in order that they put his means of production into operation, and can himself organize and manage them. This role [of the capitalist] in the production process, however, does not explain but rather masks the exploitative character of capital. . . . It is not just the capitalist and landowner active in the process of production, but the idle rentier, too, who pockets surplus value, the product of unpaid labor.

That is, to be sure, not to say that there is no difference between the idle and the functioning exploiter. The former can be expropriated at a single blow with a stroke of the pen, without the least disruption of the production process. All that is required is the necessary power on the part of the exploited. The functions of the exploiter who is active in the process of production [need] . . . not always . . . be performed by a capitalist. The functions themselves, however, are indispensable, and therefore also the functioning capitalist as long as the persons and institutions do not exist that are capable of replacing him. Thus, the functioning capitalists cannot by any means . . . in all circumstances and with one blow be dispossessed of their capital, but only under certain conditions and therefore not all of them at the same time.[3] . . .

From the fact that the prosperity of a capitalist enterprise makes it possible not only for its capitalist owners but also for its workers to improve their situation, many bourgeois economists drew the conclusion that there is an agreement, a harmony of interests between capital and labor, and that the antagonism between them is merely a misunderstanding. Remarkably enough, though, this misunderstanding is the more in evidence among workers, the more intelligent they become, the more their intellectual horizon is broadened. Only completely ignorant workers believe in the harmony of interests. Common interest in the flourishing of the enterprise . . .

3. See also III:3:10, above.

certainly exists between capitalists and workers, but it cannot overcome the antagonism arising from the fact that no business can maintain itself under the conditions of capitalism, which does not generate a profit, and that profits are created only by the unpaid surplus labor of the workers. The fact that . . . the situation of the workers depends to a high degree on whether the capitalist is capable or incompetent, kind or severe, generous or miserly, can only serve to aggravate further the already existing antagonism.

Wherever men (or animals) consciously cooperate for a common end, there leadership is necessary. The success of the common enterprise is to a great extent dependent on the nature of this leadership . . . . The more men's destiny is dependent on the nature of their leadership, the more intolerable does it become for them not to have any influence on the appointment of their leaders. That becomes completely intolerable when the leader is installed by a power whose interest is opposed to that of those who are led. The fact that his capital property puts the capitalist in a position to take on necessary directive functions in the process of production does not, then, diminish in any way the antagonism between capital and labor. . . .

Up to now we have assumed the most favorable case for the exploited class, namely that it consists of free workers. *[After briefly considering slavery and serfdom, Kautsky repeats:]* Thus we find again and again as the basis of exploitation and of the class antagonism arising from it the fact of property in the means of production or of the right to dispose of them on the one side, and on the other the lack of such means or of disposition over them on the part of men who could not exist without employing those means of production. The concept of class is thus a polar one. A class by itself alone is inconceivable; it always needs its polar opposite: exploiters and exploited, masters and serfs.

But is this definition compatible with the existence of classes where the producer, either as an individual or as a member of a cooperative, disposes over his means of production and lives solely from his labor, not from the labor of others, such as small peasants or artisans who do not employ wage-laborers, or members of the liberal professions like physicians or self-employed writers? . . . As soon as the formation of class antagonisms in society occurs, . . . the groups of such workers, at least peasants and artisans, can assume the character of classes. The strata of intellectuals are of too heterogeneous a nature to permit them to become more than isolated professions without a common class character. Yet they, too, cannot avoid taking part in the class struggles of their time.[4] Peasants and artisans can now acquire class consciousness. But in contrast to that of the true classes, it is of an ambiguous nature. As owners of means of production, they believe they have interests in common with the large-scale exploiters. As workers,

4. See also IV:5:5 and IV:7:16, below.

they have sympathy with the exploited. Depending on the historical situation, now the one, now the other point of view predominates among them.

Moreover, these strata can seldom exist for a long time in a class society without many of their members entering actively or passively into a relationship of exploitation. When free peasants live alongside serfs, the manorial lords will always endeavor to force the former down into the position of the latter or to drive them off their holdings. On the other hand, the peasants always run the danger of getting into the hands of usurers and of thereby falling victim to capitalist exploitation. Or the reverse may happen: they prosper, become well-to-do, enlarge their holdings. Then they hire farm laborers and maidservants and so ascend into the ranks of the exploiters. Thus, in a class society, those groups are also drawn into class antagonisms and class struggles that initially are not true classes but mere occupations outside class society.

Class antagonisms can be abolished only through abolition of the property relations on which they rest. . . . But by no means are all antagonisms in society thereby done away with. . . . A great conflict of interests exists . . . between producers and consumers. . . . This antagonism can at times cause fierce social struggles, but it is not a class antagonism. Sellers and producers are not a different class from buyers and consumers. Everyone who sells does so for the purpose of being able to buy again. And no one can produce without consuming, though the reverse does occur. As a consumer, everyone has an interest in low prices of all products, as a producer, on the other hand, in a high price only of the products of his own branch of production, not of the other branches. . . . The producers' interest is therefore at bottom only the particular interest of individual occupations, whereas the interest of the consumers is the common interest of the whole society. . . .

Every stratum of producers strives to raise the prices of its products, when possible by means of artificial monopolization, such as protective tariffs or the establishment of cartels. If all producers simultaneously and uniformly employ such means, then the prices of all commodities rise simultaneously and uniformly. That appears to be a senseless procedure. . . .

[But] the owners of the means of production can still gain an advantage as producers of commodities if wages do not rise or do not rise correspondingly. In this way, the antagonism of interests between producers and consumers can become a class antagonism between capitalists (urban and rural) and wage-laborers. Nevertheless, one must not simply equate the struggles between producers and consumers . . . with class struggles. . . .

The antagonism between buyers and sellers will disappear only when commodity production is abolished, and production for the market or for the customer is replaced by production to meet the needs of society. The path will be cleared for those changes by the same means that will abolish classes, by the conversion of the means of production into the property of society, which is thus given the possibility of organizing production for its own needs.

In any case, one must take care not to construe every antagonism between individual groups in society as a class antagonism. Only a group that stands in a relationship of exploiter or exploited with another group or class, or seeks to ward off or to attain such a relationship, may be called a class. Only in this sense will we speak of class in the following pages.

CHAPTER THREE

Occupations

a. The Division of Labor

... Class must not be confused with occupation, which is a natural consequence of the division of labor in society. This division appears in continuous interaction with technological progress and increases proportionately as the scope of society grows as a result of this progress. *[Kautsky quotes Adam Smith who, in* The Wealth of Nations, *I, 12, explains the division of labor as a "consequence of a certain propensity in human nature . . . to truck, barter and exchange one thing for another," a propensity he cannot explain.]* We have already indicated how the division of labor came into the world. *[Kautsky repeats briefly what he said on p. 186, above.]* As we have seen, the division of labor between man and woman constituted the beginning.[5] . . . The division of labor in the family appears without any exchange of commodities and prior to it. This exchange itself . . . takes place at first between polities; it is a result of a division of labor among them.[6] . . . Only later does an appreciable division of labor develop within the polity and within the same sex, which goes so far that it produces lasting differences in the abilities and the knowledge of different groups of individuals and thereby engenders different occupations.

b. Intellectuals

The first occupation to emerge within a polity appears not to be based on the exchange of products at all. . . . *[It is]* that of the intellectuals. *[The*

5. See II:4:3, above.
6. See III:2:14–15, above.

following discussion is developed as an argument with a long quotation from Meyer, Geschichte des Altertums, *I/1, 93–95, who says that some of the early intellectuals or "magicians" were madmen, some cheats, and some ruminators. Kautsky rejects all three possibilities and remarks with reference to the last one:]* Not only in the case of *[the animal]*, but also for primitive man, indeed even for the majority of men in present-day society, reflection is concerned only with such causal relationships as are important for practice. A large number of technological and social conditions must be fulfilled before some men are in a position . . . to undertake solving problems that do not directly have anything to do with practice. . . . The philosophical spirit is alien to primitive man. . . .

Primitive man's knowledge is of two kinds. On the one hand, there is positive knowledge that has its origin in the experiences of his practice and becomes ever greater as his technology progresses. . . . Arising from the general, public practice of small tribes, known to all of its members, it is a knowledge belonging to all. On the other hand, we find among primitive men a knowledge of a fantastical kind, a merely imaginary knowledge, premature hypotheses drawn from isolated observations, often based only on superficial consistency. . . . This knowledge acquires power in society only by virtue of the fact that it rests on collective ideas. Because they are ideas shared by all, they are accepted by every individual unexamined, without inspection.[7] . . .

What is essential for intellectuals . . . *[is]* a particular disposition and acquired knowledge. The inherited dispositions are the constant, the acquired knowledge the variable element we are dealing with at this point in our investigation. It is in the latter, therefore, that the explanation must be found why, from a certain stage of society on, certain inherited dispositions that were always to be found permitted a special occupational stratum of intellectuals to arise.

The knowledge men have at their disposal grows steadily with the development of their technology. Every new discovery or invention brings new experiences, new knowledge in its train. Similarly, every migration. For a long time, the only division of labor remains one between the two sexes. . . . Everyone knows and can do the same things that the others of the same sex know and can do. The more the diversity of the tasks grows, the more does that of knowledge grow too, whether it is real, positive knowledge or only imaginary knowledge. Its extent finally becomes so great that it is difficult to master it completely. Everyday knowledge is still general, but knowledge of the treatment of unusual phenomena, such as diseases, droughts, the dying of cattle, etc., is ultimately acquired, culti-

7. See II:3:8, above.

vated, and passed onto posterity more and more only by those who have a special inclination and opportunity, perhaps also an ability, to devote a considerable portion of their time to this pursuit.

It would not be possible for an individual by himself to cultivate the old traditions pertaining to the unusual, to supplement and to develop them further through addition of new experiences, and to maintain the esteem and respect for this knowledge in the general public. Where medicine men occur, we find that it is quite a number of people in a tribe, not single individuals, who make it their business to preserve and develop this knowledge. They form organizations for this purpose, clubs or guilds, in which each member communicates to his comrades everything he knows and learns and instructs the younger ones in it. I attribute the emergence of an occupation of intellectuals not to the occasional presence of fools, tricksters, or daydreaming brooders, but to the growth of the body of knowledge, which the average individual can no longer master, but which must be preserved and further developed by organizations established especially for that purpose. . . .

At first, the medicine men and shamans have to participate just as much in the labors of everyday life . . . as the others. However, the more the surpluses of society increase, the more copious can the gifts become that the "magicians" receive for their good offices, the less do they have to rely on their gainful labor and the more time can they devote to their "science." Here we find once again technical progress and not natural talent as the explanation for the development of an occupation of intellectuals.

Finally, though, the extent of the knowledge of society becomes so great that no brain is capable of taking it in and mastering it in its entirety. . . . A division of labor among the intellectuals according to definite areas of knowledge then becomes necessary. . . . Even then each of the new branches of intellectual activity, whether that of physicians, astronomers, or geometers, remains directly useful for practical ends, and the positive knowledge in each of these branches remains mixed with collective ideas. These do not have their origin in recent experiences, but have been passed down from early times when the total knowledge of society was still the common property of all. The mysticism and the wild fantasies that many consider the products of the imagination and the trickeries of individual sorcerers are the result of the age prior to the emergence of an occupation of intellectuals and are in part taken over by the latter unchanged, in part adapted to new experiential knowledge, but are not invented by the intellectuals.

The amount of knowledge continues to grow so enormously in the course of the millennia that the division of the sciences into different fields of activity no longer suffices. It now becomes necessary to make a further division in most branches of science between applied . . . and pure science.[8] . . . Simultaneously, the development of society also takes a turn that makes it possible for the individual thinker to be active as an individual personage without the support of his guild and to leave his mark on a certain area of knowledge. Here, the thinker's native abilities certainly play a large role. But the division of labor in the sciences does not depend on them. It is determined solely by the extention of the field of knowledge, that is, of the material for knowledge, as the division of labor in the economy is determined by the extension of the market it has to supply. That the science of Assyriology appeared in the last century is to be ascribed to the fact that excavations in Assyria brought to light the material for this science. It is not due, say, to the fact that suddenly professors were born who had a native talent for Assyriology.

CHAPTER FOUR

Occupational Antagonisms

Long before there arises an occupational division within the stratum of intellectuals, the progress of the division of labor in material production resulting from the growing range of knowledge and skills and the growing extent of society also brings about divisions among occupations. About them, nothing special is to be said in our context. Important as they are, we shall content ourselves here with noting their existence.

The number of occupations in society grows, and with it there develops more and more, alongside the process of men working together, that of men working for one another. We have already seen . . . that this working for one another, in contrast to their working together, need by no means bring forth solidarity, that in certain circumstances it can even engender antagonisms, especially when there is private property in the means of production and exchange of commodities.[9]

When a division into different occupations occurs, the individual cannot live from the products of his own labor. He produces things of which he needs only a small fraction or no part at all for himself; the greatest part is intended for others. The same is true of the services he performs. On the other hand, he is dependent on the products and services of others.

When there is communal ownership of the means of production, the provisioning of every individual is effected by everyone working for the community and receiving from it what he needs. An example of that is given by the village community of ancient India. . . . *[There]* in addition to the peasants, there were also various occupations, intellectuals, and artis-

8. See also V:2:3, below.
9. See III:3:3, above.

ans. . . . Each of them is also a peasant, has a share in the communal land. For his work in his occupation, he is compensated either with agricultural work done for him on his share of the land by the members of the community or by gifts in kind.

When there is private property in the means of production, accounts are settled in a different way: either through the exchange of products for products or of products for services or of services for services. Under these circumstances, antagonisms among the individual occupations can arise, for each seeks to give as little labor or as few products of labor as possible and to receive in exchange as much as possible. When force is not used, the exchange relations are determined by the play of supply and demand. . . . Now if the product of one occupation is regularly exchanged for that of another in such a manner that one always gives more labor for less labor, then, with freedom of movement in the economy, the first occupation will be less attractive than the other. In the former, the number of its members and of the products it brings to market will decrease; in the latter it will increase. The relationship between supply and demand will continue to shift in this way until the quantities of labor exchanged are equal to each other.

Thus, even under commodity production, the demand for protection against any exploitation is realized, that is, the demand for avoiding doing any work for others, for strangers, without receiving an equivalent in return. Here is to be found the psychological basis of the law that value is determined by labor, which law exists only as a tendency and only to the extent that all occupations are accessible with equal ease to every member of the society. It is completely wrong to regard labor-value as a fixed magnitude that can be calculated for every commodity. And the law of value becomes operative only when free and equal men work for each other, each of whom is able to defend himself against forcible exploitation. When particular occupations enjoy monopolies, the law of value becomes ineffective to a certain degree. Such an occupation . . . becomes an exploiter of other occupations. Nevertheless, it does not become a class in the proper sense of the word, as we are using it here. . . . Even a monopolist who is such to the greatest extent possible will not succeed in doing what some exploiting classes do: pocketing the labor of others (or the product of their labor) without itself giving labor in return.

To be sure, the exploiting class, too, can and often must perform labor. But it performs that labor for itself, not for the exploited class. When a feudal lord goes to war in order to repel an enemy from the territory he rules, he is performing labor, military labor. And the peasants in bondage to him can benefit from this labor if he succeeds in keeping away the enemy and protecting them from devastation and pillaging. But he performs this labor not for them, but for himself: he wants to keep his area of exploitation productive. In this manner, the owner of a horse also works for himself and not for the horse when he supplies it with fodder or builds a stable for it. No exchange of labors takes place here. No more does such an exchange occur between the worker and the capitalist by virtue of the fact that the latter is active in his own firm. If he keeps his firm going, he does so for himself, not for his workers. That becomes obvious when he throws the workers out onto the street to replace them with a machine, when his profits will thereby be raised.

In the case of classes, their antagonism and hence also, where conditions allow it, their struggle are necessarily given along with their existence itself. Between occupations, too, antagonisms and conflicts can arise, but they are inevitable only under certain conditions, such as those of commodity production. And they are always of a different kind from class antagonisms and hardly ever so intense, because they do not divide the whole society into great, hostile camps. We have already called attention to the fact that every seller in turn becomes a buyer. And the occupations can very well exist alongside one another as groups of free and equal men, with no exploitation of any kind. For the ruling classes, however, exploitation is a question of their existence. The antagonisms and struggles among the occupations, for example, the quarrels between guilds in the cities of the Middle Ages or the jurisdictional disputes between labor unions imbued with the guild spirit, do not by a long shot take on such significance for the development of society as do the class struggles.

CHAPTER FIVE

Abolition of Classes and Abolition of Occupations

Class and occupation must be rigorously distinguished from each other. Their difference in kind is already evident in the fact that the abolition of a class can, if the historical conditions for it are given, very well take place with no damage to society, in fact to its great benefit. And we have every reason to assume that we are heading toward a situation in which any and all exploitation will be eliminated and thus all classes abolished. . . . Abolishing the division of labor would mean extinguishing all the knowledge and skill that society has acquired, a senseless and hopeless beginning. Even the effort to reduce the number of occupations would be as reactionary as it would be unsuccessful. To be sure, some occupations become superfluous in the course of technical progress, but only because others take their place. . . . We have no reason to assume that the number of occupations will decrease, let alone disappear, as social development proceeds further; rather, we have every reason to expect that this number will become even greater still.

In this connection reference is, admittedly, made to Frederick Engels, who is supposed to have expressed the opposite opinion. *[Kautsky quotes from* Anti-Dühring, *p. 320:]* "The old mode of production must... be revolutionised from top to bottom, and in particular the former division of labour must disappear.... Productive labour, instead of being a means to the subjection of men, will become a means to their emancipation, by giving each individual the opportunity to develop and exercise all his faculties, physical and mental, in all directions; in which, therefore, productive labour will become a pleasure instead of a burden." *[And Kautsky adds in a footnote:]* Already around 1845, in the manuscript on *The German Ideology*, Marx and Engels developed their rejection of the old division of labor. There they write: "... in communist society, where nobody has one exclusive sphere of activity but each can become accomplished in any branch he wishes, society regulates the general production and thus makes it possible for me to do one thing today and another tomorrow, to hunt in the morning, fish in the afternoon, rear cattle in the evening, criticise after dinner, just as I have a mind, without ever becoming hunter, fisherman, shepherd or critic..." (p. 36). That is approximately the same notion as that set forth by Engels in his *Anti-Dühring*, only with a more incomplete presentation of the division of labor and strongly influenced by the utopians with respect to the ideas about the coming communist society. *[Here the footnote ends.]*

But Engles... calls only for the disappearance of the *old* division of labor. Socialists do, indeed, take a different position on the division of labor than do the bourgeois economists. In the capitalist mode of production, the wage-laborer and ultimately the laboring man in general is considered only an accessory of the apparatus of production, as a special kind of means of production. He exists only for the sake of production. Everything that promotes the productivity of labor, or even only appears to do so for the moment, is to be put resolutely into effect, with no regard for the way in which it affects the workers. The division of labor is developed accordingly.... The socialists' goal is the emancipation of the laboring man and thereby of all men. Socialists, too, strive for the highest productivity of labor and hence a far-reaching division of labor, but only under conditions where the laboring man does not suffer but benefits because of it.

... The different and increasingly diversified activities of manual labor underwent a division once cities arose with different handicrafts. These killed the home industry of the peasant, so that his activities, too, became one-sided and more and more served only agriculture.... But the general and far-reaching degradation of manual labor begins only with large-scale industry, which in its capitalist form made rapid advances from the eighteenth century on. To the division of labor in society according to occupations, it added the division of labor within the factory, the decomposition of the process of production into ever-simpler manual operations.... This decomposition is the precondition for the appearance of the machine, which requires two kinds of workers: highly skilled, independently thinking workers with quite extensive knowledge, who know how to build, control, and guide the machines, and completely ignorant ones, who serve the machine blindly, who are its helpers.

The further this development advances, the more work loses all appeal for many workers. . . . As long as the diversity of tasks to be performed by the individual worker grew with the progress of the division of labor, technical progress developed not merely the productive forces existing externally to man, which were at his command, but also the mental and physical forces inherent in man himself. But once the diversity of tasks leads to men's specialization in individual occupations, the danger arises that only a fraction of the individual's strengths and capacities is developed, that he will become one-sided and limited if he remains tied entirely to a single specialty. That is what happens, though, as soon as classes arise and the exploiters cannot squeeze enough out of the exploited. Now the tendency emerges to transform into labor-time in the service of the exploiter all of the worker's time that does not serve for the minimal restoration of the energy expended by him. This makes work a burden . . . all the worse the more specialized and monotonous it becomes. This reaches its high point under industrial capitalism.

With industrial capitalism, however, the reaction begins, already among the socialist utopians, whose tendencies in this respect were taken over by Marx and Engels. As a practical matter, this reaction of the proletariat has so far been confined to the reduction of labor-time. But it must not stop at that. The reduction of labor-time has its definite limits beyond which it cannot go without diminishing the quantity of the manufactured products and therewith the prosperity of society. . . . It is possible, though not probable, that the general reduction of the working day to less than eight hours would today depress the welfare of society. But where is it written that these eight hours of work must all be performed in the same factory and in the same activity? How much fresher and more joyful the workers in factories and mines would be if they only had to work four hours there, and each of them could spend the other four hours he owes to society doing something completely different, depending on his inclinations and abilities, for example, in agriculture, as a construction worker, as a chauffeur, or in an art or a science? . . .

The most recent development of technology increasingly creates the preconditions for this way of organizing the division of labor. Thus, for example, the linkage of agriculture with industry is increasingly facilitated, on the one hand, by the transmission of electrical power and, on the other, by advances of the transportation system. . . . To be sure, the introduction of an appropriate reorganization of the process of production will encounter some difficulties. These will not be insurmountable, but . . . the proletariat must first obtain a decisive voice in the process of production before one can undertake to allot the labor-time of the individual worker to different occupations in such a manner that the social division of labor does not cause him to become stunted.

That is what Engels meant. He was by no means of the opinion that the division into occupations had to be abolished. He knew very well that without thorough preparatory vocational training and resolute concentration on a definite area of labor nothing can be accomplished in many occupations, especially not in intellectual ones. . . . But the shackling of the individual to a single specialty, that he certainly wanted to abolish. It ruins a man even when it is a matter of the most elevated activities, of art and science. How much more so then when his activity consists of a few monotonous manual operations.

. . . The participation of the individual in different occupations will also have the effect that he ceases to develop a special occupational interest of his own and thus to diminish his interest in matters of general social interest. We may thus expect that, with the class struggles, the conflicts of individual occupations with one another will also approach their end and that society will again become, on a higher level, just as harmonious a formation as it was in its beginnings, as long as there were no classes and the division into occupations was not yet far advanced.

CHAPTER SIX

Class, Occupation and Estate[10]

The concept of *estate* is related to the concepts of class and occupation but is not identical with either of them. By an estate we understand a group of members of a community who are set apart from the other members by explicit regulations of this community. This happens through the conferral of special rights or the imposition of obligations on the group and through the linking of membership in the group to specific conditions, for example, heritability or the demonstration of special knowledge and the like.

In order not to become lost in too many details, let us disregard caste, which like an estate is a group of men especially privileged or burdened and especially closed off, not through regulations decreed by the community, however, but by old, rigidified customs that have taken on the character of something sacred and inviolable. Originally they might have been nothing more than estates . . . but this origin has been forgotten. . . . Castes can be abolished only by overcoming the power of the old customs. . . . The caste is a particular kind of estate. . . .

The closing off, in estates, of certain parts of a people from the others

---

10. This chapter, of which less than half has been retained in this edition, is translated almost in its entirety in Bottomore and Goode, eds., *Readings in Marxist Sociology*, pp. 103–107. There, "Stand" is translated as "status" or "status group" rather than as "estate."

can be imposed on them in part by the polity or its ruling classes in order to preserve an existing social order. It can, however, also be imposed on the polity by the elements who have joined together and closed themselves off in the estate, in order to consolidate their victory over other parts of the polity. Beyond that, the different estates have very different character- istics, depending on whether they correspond to a class or to an occupation. The estate of physicians or of government officials is something entirely different from that of the nobility. To be sure, the conferral of estate- character on an occupation usually means that it is also provided with certain privileges and monopolies that make its position similar to that of a class. . . . The privileged position of the officers' estate in many states up to the present day often bestows on it the character of a ruling and exploiting class. The same holds true for the clergy of many religions. . . .

In its origins, an estate coincides with a certain class (or with a set of classes) or with a certain occupation, but that seldom remains the case. . . . Technology and production change incessantly and with them also occu- pations and classes. But the privileges, obligations, and conditions of mem- bership in the individual estates do not change in the same measure. The result is, on the one hand, that the institutions of an estate can become ever more of a fetter on the process of production and increasingly oppressive for society. On the other hand, the original identity between an estate and the corresponding class or occupation disappears more and more.

Thus, the feudal aristocracy, for example, was originally equivalent to the class of large landowners. But in the course of time, even before the collapse of feudalism, the point was finally reached when non–noble ele- ments acquired extensive landholdings, while not only individual nobles but entire aristocratic families lost their landholdings. . . . On the other hand, from [the beginnings] of the Middle Ages until well into them, the estate of the Catholic clergy was to a high degree equivalent to the occu- pation of the intellectuals. But the more cities and commerce with the Orient developed beginning with the crusades, the more numerous did the intel- lectuals become who did not belong to the clergy, until finally the functions of intellectuals in the modern sense have come to be carried on almost exclusively outside the Catholic clergy. . . .

In precapitalist society, which developed extremely slowly in every re- spect, classes could assume the rigidity of an estate and preserve it for a long time. Capitalist society, which undergoes constant technical, eco- nomic, political, and scientific transformation, becomes incompatible with the rigidity of any estatelike constitution. It dissolves all bonds characteristic of estates. . . . Capitalist society tolerates only classes without the disguise and constraint of estates. This is the characteristic feature of capitalism, as that of socialism will be the abolition of all classes. . . .

Where there are estates or occupations, their existence is clearly evident. The same is not true of classes, which are not clearly demarcated by reg- ulations of the polity. Thus, when the bourgeois revolutions abolished the

system of estates, the champions and ideologues of those revolutions believed that the realm of liberty, equality, and fraternity had begun. . . . A
scientific accomplishment was needed to discover and to lay bare the classes,
their antagonisms and economic foundations. That was one of Engels' and
Marx's greatest achievements. . . .

The Concept of the State

The concept of the state is intimately linked with the concept of
class. . . . To begin with, we can take care of the definition of the state very
briefly, not because everyone is in agreement about it and the concept is a
very simple one. Rather, because we will later concern ourselves in some
detail with the development and transformations of the state and only then
will it become clear how we are to understand the Marxist definition of the
state. . . .

Many do not distinguish between state and society. *[For example, Max
Adler,* Die Staatsauffassung des Marxismus, *pp. 33–34, 53, whom Kautsky
quotes and argues with.]*[11] If state and society were equivalent, then there
would always have been states, as long as the human race has existed, and
then it would be impossible even to think of dissolving the state. The same
thing can also be pointed out in reply to those who see a state in every
sovereign polity, because each has leaders, is subject to certain rules governing living and working together, and because in every such polity a
definite authority decides what is just in conflicts and in doubtful cases.
Lastly, because there is a coercive power that enforces the decisions of the
leaders and judges. . . . Every researcher certainly has the right to create a
special terminology for himself. But when every organization that has the
purpose of preserving and protecting a particular kind of socialization is
designated a state, then the distinction among the various kinds of organizations that serve such purposes is not facilitated but made more difficult.

As a rule, it is assumed today that all these sovereign organizations, all
these polities, constitute a developmental series. The state is considered the
last one in this series so far. Since the idea is often still held that men
originally lived in isolation, that is, in couples, the family, as a rule, is
considered to be the first member of this series. *[Kautsky quotes* Hegel's
Philosophy of Right, *§349, p. 218, and Mommsen,* The History of Rome,
I, 80–83, as examples of this view.] In reality, however, the polity with its
leaders is an older phenomenon than the family. The state grew out of the

---

11. Kautsky had written at greater length on the distinction between state and society and
also on that between *Gesellschaft* and *Gemeinschaft* in *Die Marxsche Staatsauffassung*, pp. 31–40.

tribe, not out of the family. . . . But we, too, regard the state as the highest form of the development of the polity up to the present time. . . .

We are treating here of the state as it actually appeared in history, not of the state as it is "supposed" to be or of the idea of the state, conceived of as something completely different from the reality. The philosophers who derive the concept of the state not from observation of states that really exist or existed, but seek to arrive at it through speculation or epistemology have made of the state the most magnificent and sublime thing man is able to bring forth. Hegel's effusions on this subject are well known. *[Kautsky quotes from Hegel,* The Philosophy of History, *pp. 38–39—"The State is the Divine Idea as it exists on earth"—and the* Philosophy of Right, *§§ 257 and 258, p. 155; § 260, p. 160; § 272, pp. 174–75, and from Lassalle, "Arbeiter-Programm," pp. 196–99, who said:]* . . . "The purpose of the state is the education and development of the human race toward freedom."

The idea of the state in Hegel and Lassalle . . . makes it possible to abstract from so many features of the actual state, which are considered undesirable, and mysteriously to smuggle into it so many features one would like to see in it that the final result of the idea becomes the opposite of the reality. Still, even the idealist philosopher remains the prisoner of reality, that is, of the external world surrounding him. Even if the idea of the state detaches itself in his consciousness from the mental image of the real state he is dealing with, the notion of the one state unconsciously affects the notion of the other one and falsifies it. Thus both Hegel and Lassalle come to discover in the Prussian state in which they lived more features of the idea of the state that filled them with enthusiasm than the facts justified. . . .

CHAPTER EIGHT

The Marxist Conception of
the State

[Kautsky traces, with many quotations, the development of Marx's and Engels' conception of the state from their Hegelian beginnings—"The Leading Article in No. 179 of the Kölnische Zeitung," p. 202—via The Holy Family *of 1845, pp. 116, 121, to* The Eighteenth Brumaire *of 1852, in which Marx denounces the "frightful parasitic body" of the French "executive power [with its] immense bureaucratic and military organization" (p. 237; MESW, I, 477), which originated under the absolute monarchy and grew under each subsequent regime, and Marx's letter to Kugelmann of April 12, 1871, in which he declares the smashing of this "bureaucratic-military machine" the prerequisite of "every real people's revolution on the Continent" (p. 420).]*

. . . Not the abolition of the state, but the establishment of the democratic republic without the domination of the bureaucracy and the military was what Marx regarded as the task of the next revolution in France when he wrote the *Eighteenth Brumaire* in 1852 and also later. . . . Marx and Engels

considered the most important task of the working class, after the democratic republic had been achieved, to gain control of governmental power
in it as the means of economic emancipation of the proletariat.

[Kautsky also quotes from Marx's Critique of the Gotha Program *of 1875
(p. 354; MESW, III, 25):]* "Freedom consists in converting the state from
an organ superimposed on society into one thoroughly subordinate to it."
That and not the abolition of the state appears as the task of the proletariat
as soon as it has acquired political power. . . . But Marx and Engels remained free of Hegel's and Lassalle's adulation of the state. They came to
regard it as a power apparatus in the service of the ruling and exploiting
classes for the repression of the ruled and exploited, as an organization . . .
serving only a minority that by means of the state apparatus places the
powers of the collectivity at its own service and increases thereby its own
forces tenfold. . . .

[Kautsky quotes from Marx's Civil War in France *of 1871 (pp. 206–207,
208–209, 212; MESW, II, 217–18, 219–20, 222–23), where he once again
denounces "the centralized state power, with its ubiquitous organs of standing army,
police, bureaucracy, clergy and judicature" and said that by destroying them the
Paris Commune "supplied the republic with the basis of really democratic institutions."]* As one can see, Marx stresses again and again that the proletariat's
immediate practical task is not the abolition of the state but replacing the
bureaucratic military monarchy with a truly democratic republic. But he
always emphasizes the character of the state as a means of class
domination. . . .

[Kautsky then quotes Engels, "Introduction" of 1891 to Marx, The Civil War
in France, *MESW, II, 189:]* "In reality, . . . the state is nothing but a machine
for the oppression of one class by another, and indeed in the democratic
republic no less than in the monarchy; and at best an evil inherited by the
proletariat after its victorious struggle for class supremacy, whose worst
sides the victorious proletariat, just like the Commune, cannot avoid having
to lop off at once[12] as much as possible until such a time as a generation
reared in new, free social conditions is able to throw the entire lumber of
the state on the scrap heap." Here, too, there is no question of the victorious
proletariat having to abolish the state at once. Rather, it is merely "to cut
down as far as possible" the omnipotence of the organs of the state. It is
true that Engels speaks of getting rid of "the entire lumber of the state,"
but he considers that to be a task of later generations who have been reared
in "new, free social conditions."

The conception of the state presented here by Engels, which is in agreement with that of Marx, is also my conception. It is the basis of the following

12. This phrase, on which Kautsky comments, is mistranslated here. Instead of "having
to lop off at once," it should read "immediately cutting down as far as possible."

analyses of the state. One thing needs to be noted, however. This conception was not derived from the "idea" of the state, but obtained through observation of states that have hitherto appeared in history. It is thus not an eternal conception, but is dependent on the form the state assumes at any given time. Since the last pronouncements by Engels on the state more than a generation has passed that has not left the character of modern states untouched. The question whether or not Marx's and Engels' characterization of the state, which was still completely accurate for their time, also holds true without qualification today, will have to be especially examined. But that can be done successfully only after we have become sufficiently acquainted with the state as it has been heretofore. Only an understanding of the state as it has been will allow us to comprehend fully the modern state, both in its conformities and in its deviations from the old state. But we are not yet treating of that here. I call attention to it now only so that, as he reads the following discussions of the state, the reader will always keep only the old state in mind, will measure my remarks against it, and will leave the modern state out of consideration until I explicitly begin to speak of it. . . .

The existence of a coercive power does not of itself suffice to make of a polity a state in Marx's sense. In the prestate polity, this coercive power is formed by the predominance of the majority over the minority, which has a crushing effect when it is a predominance of the collectivity vis-à-vis a single individual. . . . The chieftain or judge has no other coercive means at his disposal to enforce his decisions than the agreement of the mass of the tribe. In contrast, the state has heretofore meant the dominion of the minority over the majority. Its coercive power did not rest on the moral predominance of the majority, of the great mass, but on the predominance of a minority over a great majority—a predominance that could result from a superiority of weapons, knowledge, wealth, or of economic or some other indispensability. One can certainly recognize that a policy cannot exist without a certain coercive power of its organs vis- à-vis the individual and still resolutely combat the coercive power of the state as it has existed up to now.

Section Two
The Origin of the State and of Classes

CHAPTER ONE

Engels' Hypothesis

Written history is a history of states and of class struggles. At the beginning of this history, we find both, state and class, already intimately linked with one another. In order to grasp a phenomenon completely . . . one must know how it has evolved. . . . Unfortunately, we know nothing at all about the very beginnings of states and classes. . . . We do possess sufficient reports about the founding of numerous states, . . . but all these states . . . constituted basically only transformed existing states. . . . Numerous hypotheses have been advanced about the origin of the first classes and states. Some of them are based on mere speculations, others on indicators inferred from observed facts. The more the latter is the case and the more a hypothesis is compatible with the course of later history, handed down in written form, the more readily may we accept it.

For the purely speculative examination of the question, the matter is very simple: no one voluntarily submits to exploitation and domination. Without coercion—no classes and no state. Coercion is exercised by those who are stronger (physically or intellectually) upon the weaker. . . . Human beings are different by nature. . . . Accordingly, the elements of classes and of the state should already be given by nature. . . .

Certainly, every social being strives for respect and influence . . . but the outstanding individual in a tribe would not acquire [them] among his fellows if he were to set about enslaving and exploiting them. . . . Under prestate conditions, the outstanding individual knows very well that there is only one means to attain influence and respect in his tribe: championing the tribe's interests more strongly and effectively than the others. . . . Even if the exploitation of classes and the coercive power of the state could result from the physical superiority of some individuals over their surroundings, it would still be necessary to explain why this superiority produced such effects only after hundreds of thousands of years of human development. That alone points to the necessity of investigating the particular conditions under which the formation of classes and states became possible.

For that reason, Marx and Engels rejected the mere force theory, which, to be sure, is very simple and appears to be very persuasive, but does not explain anything at all. In their investigations, they arrived at the conclusion that the formation of classes proceeded from economic development and that the exploiting and ruling classes then established the state. In their view, then, classes existed earlier than the state. That was completely in harmony with the conception of history, according to which in every social change the economic factor is the primary one, the political (and the ideological) factor the consequence of the former. *[Kautsky then quotes several pages from Engels,* Anti- Dühring, *pp. 197–99, and* The Origin of the Family, *pp. 272–73, 275.]* In addition to the two factors of the formation of classes that Engels listed as early as 1877, the heritability of social functions and slavery, yet a third one is named in 1884 and thrust into the foreground: the emergence of private property and of differences in wealth. As the fundamental motive force of this development, however, there always appears the division of labor "...between the masses discharging simple manual labour and the few privileged persons.... The simplest and most natural form of this division of labour was in fact slavery" (*Anti-Dühring*, pp. 200–201).

Critique of Engels' Hypothesis

What we designate here as Engels' hypothesis was a view shared by Marx. It is a conception that is not confined to Marxist circles but is widespread, though with some differences in details. In the work of Morgan, Engels found an account of the transition from the gens to "political society," which in the main agreed with and confirmed his own views. Nevertheless, serious reservations can be advanced against them.

The hypothesis of Engels, Marx, and Morgan has its point of departure in the gens, in which complete democracy and extensive equality of social conditions prevailed. Three factors are supposed to have undermined this equality and thus to have created class antagonisms and to have made the state possible and necessary. As the first of these causes, it is noted that in every polity the regulation of social relations requires functionaries... *[who]* in the course of the time make themselves independent of the polity and, instead of being its servants, become its masters.

[According to Engels, Anti-Dühring, *p. 198,]* it could appear that heredity of offices occurs "almost as a matter of course," "in a natural way." But then, as always when a claim is made for "naturalness" in history, one must ask again and again: If the phenomenon is so natural, why does it not make its appearance already in the state of nature? Every herd of social animals has its leaders; but nowhere is this function hereditary.... In the case of objects the individual uses personally... the question does indeed arise of what is to happen with them when their owner dies.... But the law of inheritance that is established for such cases by the polity is by no means "natural" or "a matter of course." It turns out quite different under matriarchy than under patriarchy. And this law of inheritance holds good... only for personal possessions. The great sources of life that are used communally or are at least used under the supervision of the collectivity, above all the land, remain in the hands of the collectivity.[1] ...

Even when the bequeathing of weapons or ornaments to one's children or other relatives has become so general that it is taken for granted and seems to be "natural," that does not by any means have to be true for

1. See III:3:7–9, above.

offices. In order that they be regarded as private property and hence as heritable, they must have first become independent of society. Instead of explaining the fact that social functions become independent, the heritability of offices rather presupposes this independence. What Engels refers to as the beginnings of heritability of offices is in reality nothing else than the custom of preferentially choosing only members of a particular family for a particular office. It is not always clear where such customs come from. In no case did they give anyone . . . within the gens a right to be chosen. . . .

If the social functions became increasingly indispensable [— *another explanation Engels had offered for their growing independence*—], then that must have had a downright negative effect on the heritability of offices, for the more important an office is, the more is freedom required in the selection of the one who is to fill it. . . . In all of this, it is not clear why the bequeathing [*of offices*], if it should in fact have occurred, and indispensability . . . of competent administration should have had the result not only of making officials independent of those who elected them, but also of conferring on them a coercive power over the latter, without which a state is inconceivable. The democratically elected officials of the gens are supposed to have . . . raised themselves as a nobility above their fellow gens members and pushed them down to be ruled and exploited. . . .

Whence came, then, the coercive power of the oppressors vis-à-vis the mass of the gens members? Neither in *Anti-Dühring* nor in *Origin of the Family* does Engels give an answer to this question. . . . To be sure, he reports that "simultaneously with their state, the Athenians established a police force . . . " (*Origin of the Family*, pp. 282–84), [*but, in fact,*] the Athenian state had already been in existence for a long time and had undergone many transformations . . . before this police force was instituted in the fifth century, at the time of the Persian Wars. [*Kautsky cites Beloch,* Griechische Geschichte, *II/1, 113.*] . . . Thus we are not dealing here with a power that the officials of the gens had at their disposal before there was a state and that permitted them at that time successfully to assert their usurpations in opposition to the mass of the gens members. . . . The gendarmerie, as Engels correctly designates the police force of slaves, constituted in Athens a power only as against the individual, not as against the army of citizens. . . .

Engels speaks of the "independence of social functions in relation to society"[2] as a process that introduces the emergence of the state. In actuality, we find such a growth of independence only in very developed states and

2. The rendering in the English translation of *Anti-Dühring* (p. 198) of "Verselbständigung" as "independence" fails to convey that the term refers to the *process* of *becoming* independent. Also, "gegenüber der Gesellschaft" implies "as against society" as much as "in relation to society."

even then only occasionally, under special conditions and only approaching, never achieving, completeness. We find an independence of state authority in relation to its social surroundings where a monarchy disposes of a strong mercenary army and bureaucracy in its pay and where the different classes in society balance one another to some extent. Otherwise there is no independent state authority. The difference between the social functions of the state offices and those of the public offices of the prestate era does not consist in the fact that the ones are independent and the others are dependent, but rather in the fact that the ones are dependent on certain classes and, in the service of those classes, suppress other classes, whereas in the prestate era the leaders, judges, and legislators of the polity were in the service of a classless, undivided society. That the social functions become independent in the polity, to the extent that this occurs, presupposes the existence of classes. It cannot account for their origin.

In addition to the independence of social offices resulting from heritability and indispensability, . . . Engels adduces as an element of the division into classes the differences in wealth that appeared within the individual polities even before the emergence of the state. It is certainly true that there were such differences. The more technology developed, the more did the number of objects grow that were possessed by individuals and families and formed their private wealth. . . . Regardless of all the original equality of social conditions, one family could enjoy good fortune, another one could suffer bad fortune. . . . Only one must not imagine that these differences were very extensive. For after all, the most important sources of life, especially the soil, still remained under the control of the polity.

Above all, though, it was the use that was made of private wealth that was decisive. As long as there was no state power, wealth enjoyed no other protection than that provided by the collectivity of the citizens of the polity. . . . They would immediately withdraw this protection from the individual if he used his wealth to suppress and exploit his fellows. On the contrary, according to the morality of primitive democracy, the dictum applies to wealth that was later coined about the nobility: it obligates. . . . *[In]* primitive democracy . . . the appearance of differences in wealth could therefore not produce differences of class and class antagonisms.

Certainly, even then wealth conferred power and influence. But not because it scourged poorer fellow citizens with the whip of hunger, but rather because it helped them. The more helpful and generous the rich man was, the greater was the respect he enjoyed. . . . Therefore, wealthier persons were often . . . given preference in the election of officials, . . . if only because greater demands could be made on their material resources . . . — an important consideration in the election of officials in Athens or ancient Rome. From this preference for the rich, there might also have resulted the special phenomenon that appears as the heritability of offices, the traditional

preference for some families in the election of officials. A genuine dependence of the mass of the people, let alone their exploitation, can never have
developed out of all this. . . .

[In Anti-Dühring, p. 307, Engels had said:] "It is . . . the law of the division
of labour which lies at the root of the division into classes." Up to now,
Engels' arguments have demonstrated nothing of the kind, even if we consider the division of functions between leaders and led as a division of labor.
It does not lead to a division into classes. Just as little is this the case with
regard to the division into richer and poorer, which does not have anything
at all to do with the division of labor.

CHAPTER THREE
Slavery

As the third factor of the emergent division into classes, Engels adduces
slavery. It is undeniably a relationship of exploitation and oppression. . . . Slavery is based on the forcible integration of foreigners into the
process of production, without their concomitant integration into the polity
itself as its members. . . . To that extent, they do not constitute a true class
of the people in the polity. Slavery does not arise out of a division of labor
in the polity, but out of *war* against foreign polities, hence out of force,
though, to be sure, force that is economically conditioned. . . .

. . . In many nations that waged war successfully, wealth in general was
a result of pillage and theft. . . . Differences in wealth . . . [can] result from
different shares of the spoils of war. . . . But in order to explain this differentiation in society, too, we must go beyond the sphere of the isolated
polity. Only in this way do we succeed in finding the first beginnings of
class divisions. Confining ourselves to investigation of the division of labor
within the framework of the individual polity does not take us very far.

Even these new conditions, based on the differences between slave owners and slaves and between citizens who own slaves and those who live
only from their own labor, do not suffice to explain why the officials of
the polity turn from servants of the mass of the people into servants of a
minority as against the mass.

The number of slaves in a prestate polity cannot have been very great.
. . . The largest number . . . must originally have been of the female sex.
. . . In the prestate era—and in most instances even later—every slave was
integrated into a family. . . . Coming from different nations, speaking different languages, the slaves were, additionally, split up among different
families, without being brought together by common labor within the

common polity. The result of all that was that the slaves were powerless and did not constitute a danger in society. Not until the era of states did conditions arise, above all the accumulation of large fortunes, that led to the assemblage of extensive masses of slaves. *[Kautsky cites various estimates of the number of slaves in fourth century* B.C. *Athens and in Italy under the late Roman republic.]* A large number of slaves constitutes a serious danger to the society that subjugates them, all the more so since, in this stage of advanced state and economic development, to original domestic slavery there is added more and more the employment of slaves for purposes of profit, accompanied by their concentration in large multitudes, in large-scale enterprises, in mines, . . . on plantations. . . .

The slaves, who worked together in large groups and as a rule were male and who were worked to death for the sake of insatiable profit, certainly constituted a danger of a completely different order than the family's mostly female house slaves. The uprisings of the first kind of slaves became more frequent. And when the slave could not rebel openly, he took advantage of every opportunity to get by as a brigand. Under these circumstances, the slave owners urgently needed a repressive force in order to avoid being swallowed up by the growing mass of their slaves. . . .

The slaves stood outside of the polity; they remained alien to it. For defense of the polity against external enemies, however, there was no better protection in the prestate democracy then the people's army. It was more numerous than an army that was recruited only from a single class or represented merely a single occupation in the polity. . . . Thus the members of the gentile democracy had no reason to invent a state authority in order to safeguard themselves against the slaves, an authority that would have stood not just above the slaves but also above the freemen.

Even the appearance of distinctions in wealth made no difference in this regard. It would be a great mistake to assume that the poorer freemen made common cause with the slaves against the richer . . . and that an armed force independent of the people's army became necessary. . . . As long as primitive democracy existed, relatively great wealth did not become a means to exploit one's poorer fellow citizens. Rather, it offered to the latter the possibility of living parasitically off the rich. That was still true in the era of the state, where the state was organized democratically. The more slaves there were in a state, the more they were exploited, the greater were the revenues of the wealthy that they shared with their less well-off fellow citizens, either through donations to the poor or indirectly through duties paid to the state, which supported the poor.

In the democratic states of antiquity, the free proletarians and the slaves as a rule felt no sympathy with each other. *[Kautsky illustrates this by quoting Weber,* Economy and Society, *III, 1342; Bücher,* Die Aufstände der unfreien Arbeiter, *pp. 61, 118; Mommsen,* The History of Rome, *III, 367, 368; and his own* Foundations of Christianity *pp. 411–15.]* Even less could there be any question of solidarity between the free poor and the slaves in the times in which we must look for the beginnings of classes and states. . . . The free always formed a solid front against the slaves, and the organization of a special state power, independent of primitive democracy, for the repression of the slaves was completely superfluous.

Like the tendency to heritability of social functions and the emergence of differences in wealth, slavery cannot constitute a moment that could serve to explain the formation of classes within the polity and the development of the polity into the state.

CHAPTER FOUR

The Conquest State

The attempts to explain the formation of classes and of the state by factors arising within the primitive polity yield no satisfactory results. . . . Primitive democracy, common property in so many important means of production, the general readiness to help any of one's fellows form an insurmountable barrier that prevents any social development toward the formation of exploiting and exploited classes and of a state authority ruling over the polity and independent of the mass of the population. To be sure, rudimentary classes appear in some tribes prior to the emergence of the state. But these rudimentary beginnings do not grow from within the polity, but from its contact with other polities, from war. War supplies the slaves and thus the first laborers who do not work for themselves or their polity, but for a foreign master. War supplies the booty that makes it possible for particular individuals and families to accumulate fortunes they would never have been able to produce to the same extent by the labor of their own hands. It is in this direction that we must advance further if we want to arrive at the origin of classes and of the state.

In its further development beyond the stage of the mere capture of slaves and chattels, war now becomes war of conquest. A victorious tribe subjugates the vanquished tribe and appropriates its entire country and thereupon forces the vanquished to work regularly for the victor, to pay tribute or taxes. As is well known, this has happened time and again in history. Where it occurs, the division into classes appears, not through the splitting of a polity into different subdivisions, but through the union of two polities into one, of which one becomes the dominant, exploiting class, while the other becomes the dominated, exploited class. The coercive apparatus imposed on the vanquished by the victors develops into the state.

Those who have been subjugated do not as a result of this process become mere appendages of alien families. They remain in their own families, also in their local communities, whose self-government need not be abolished. Further, they are not aliens in the new polity, as are the slaves who are not necessary for the preservation of the polity, at least at the beginnings of slavery. From the outset, the new polity is based on the labor of the sub-jugated; it cannot exist without them. They form an integral part of the polity. Thus, they become one of its classes in the full sense of the word, a class for which slaves form only a first beginning. The same act that brings about the first classes also forms the first state. Classes and the state go together from the beginning of their existence.

[Kautsky quotes Herder, Outlines of a Philosophy of the History of Man, *pp. 244–46, on the origin of monarchies in war, and Gumplowicz,* Der Rassen-kampf, *pp. 211–13, the first]* coherent, systematic theory of the formation of classes as a result of the subjugation of one tribe by another *[as well as his own strikingly similar views expressed in 1876, seven years before Gumplowicz's book, in his then unpublished "Draft of a Developmental History of Mankind."]*[3]

That the materialist conception of history was far superior to any other, that it could best account for the facts of history, became my firm conviction at the beginning of the eighties under the influence of Engels' [Anti-Dühr-ing]. Since then nothing has shaken that conviction; everything has strength-ened it. But how was I to reconcile with it my assumption about the origin of classes and the state, which was too deeply rooted in my mind for me to be able simply to abandon it? It took a long time for me to discover the weaknesses of Engels' hypothesis. . . . I assumed that historical develop-ment did not follow the same paths everywhere. Under certain conditions it took place a Engels thought it had; under other conditions, as I imagined it. Historical research had to ascertain in every case which path had actually been followed.[4] . . . That was my conception for quite some time. Grad-ually, though, there arose in my mind reservations about *[Engels' views].* I entertained them all the more willingly, the more I succeeded in freeing my hypothesis, based on the formation of states through conquest, from the character of a mere force theory, to lay bare the economic conditioning of the force through which the state and classes are established, and thus to integrate my hypothesis into the materialist conception of history without contradiction.

Independently of this conception of history and in some cases even guided by anti-Marxist views, others, too, moved in the same direction in their

3. See I: 1 : 2, above.

4. For examples of this combination of Engels' and Kautsky's earlier interpretations, with emphasis on the former, see *Parlamentarismus und Demokratie,* pp. 26–32, first published in 1893, and also "Sklaverei und Kapitalismus," pp. 717–19.

research. I find very noteworthy in this regard Franz Oppenheimer's book *The State*,[5] which in the most important points arrived at the same views I advance here. I owe many valuable, stimulating ideas to him. . . . I found many references that proved very useful for grounding my conception in the writings of Friedrich Ratzel, especially in his book *The History of Mankind*. Max Weber's last works provided me with especially rich and profound illuminating insights into the subject that concerns us here. Surely no one has yet grasped so clearly as he did the difference between the states of Oriental despotism and the Mediterranean city-states of antiquity as well as the peculiar character of the medieval feudal state in continental Europe in contrast to these two kinds of states.[6] His study of the significance of Puritanism for the rise of industrial capitalism also provided me with a number of insights that had a very productive influence on my work.[7] Although Max Weber conceives of the origin of the state differently than I do, he contributed more than any other author to enriching and deepening the economic foundation of my conception of the formation of the state.

This economic foundation, on which I now base my hypothesis and which in its essentials is still that of 1876, has its starting point in the fact of a division of labor, . . . which, leaving aside the one between the sexes, appears earlier in society than does the division among the occupations: The division of labor *among different tribes living under different conditions of existence*.[8] . . . This division of labor has the result that, depending on the different nature of the areas they inhabit, tribes that have acquired different abilities, customs, and technical implements live next to each other. . . . That easily leads to the poor, martial, nomadic tribes attacking the well-off, peace-loving, settled tribes. Again it depends on the particular economic conditions and on the intellectual and emotional conditions ensuing from them whether the intruders merely plunder or settle down in the land as the ruling estate and establish a state. Just how that happens, we have yet to examine in greater detail.

Here I shall only make the additional observation that the explanation of the formation of states and classes through conquest need not belong to those force theories that Engels rightly decries. Our masters knew very well the importance of force in mankind's history *[Kautsky quotes Marx:]* "In actual history, it is a notorious fact that conquest, enslavement, robbery, murder, in short, force, play the greatest part" (*Capital*, I, 874; *MESW*, II, 101). *[Also on the subject of "primitive accumulation," Marx said:]* "These methods depend in part on brute force, for instance the colonial system.

5. Greatly expanded as *Der Staat*, vol. II of Oppenheimer, *System der Soziologie*.
6. See IV:5:7a, IV:6:2, below.
7. See IV:7:1, 3, 6–7, below.
8. See also III:2:14–15, above.

But they all employ the power of the state, the concentrated and organized force of society. . . . Force is the midwife of every old society which is pregnant with a new one. It is itself an economic power" (*Capital*, I, 915–16; *MESW*, II, 133–34).

Now, it is exactly the same methods Marx presents here as those of the primitive accumulation of capital that are employed in the original formation of state authority and classes. And there is no doubt that force is "an economie power," indeed a very vigorous one, which in certain circumstances can effect enormous economic transformations, for example, the appearance of new and the disappearance of old classes. Only it must not be supposed that the economic effects of force are always those which in a particular instance are planned and striven for by those who possess and employ force. . . . It depends in the last analysis on the given economic conditions what goals the men of an age, of a country, of a class, set themselves, what resistance they encounter, what forces they have at their disposal to overcome it, and finally what enduring result comes of it all.

As important as the role of force in history is, it helps us very little to comprehend the course of historical development if we confine ourselves to establishing that force intervenes in history. Force and its consequences become comprehensible only through investigation of the economic conditions under which it appears and is effective. . . .

Section Three
The First States[1]

CHAPTER ONE

Sedentary Agriculturalists

If we account for the emergence of the state and the appearance of classes by conquest, that does not mean that classes had to be formed in this manner everywhere and in all circumstances and that another origin of the state is not possible. . . . Quite a number of classes are not the direct product of conquests, but the result of economic development. In those areas, however, in which written history begins, the history of states and of class struggles, every origin of the first classes and states can be traced back to conquerors. . . . Incidentally, Cunow claims the same type of origin also for the states of the Incas and the Aztecs in America. . . . (Cunow, *Die soziale Verfassung des Inkareiches*; Cunow, *Die Marxsche Geschichts . . . theorie*, I, 298–300).

1. A number of points made in this Section are further elaborated in *Krieg und Demokratie*, pp. 19–30, 37–43.

The oldest states of concern to us here are all located in the regions of certain great rivers in North Africa and Asia. . . . The Nile, the Euphrates and the Tigris, the Indus . . . draw their abundance of water from high mountain ranges and then flow through a rainless plain, in which a luxurious vegetation is possible only in areas reached by their water. In contrast, the Ganges, the Yangtze, and the Hoangho all run through regions by no means lacking in rain. Close to the borders of these fluvial regions lie steppes that in places take on the character of sandy deserts. These extreme contrasts of living conditions have produced very great differences also in the way of life and the modes of production of the inhabitants of the different regions. . . .

Among the nomadic hunters we find cultivation of plants by the women and the taming of some animals already in advanced stages. . . . The more vegetable food moved into the foreground for the inhabitants of river valleys, the less necessary it became for the men to go hunting . . . The possibility of sedentary life was soon transformed into a necessity. The cultivator's house could be more massive than his tent. . . . Among the peasants, the number of the industrial products they fabricated, used, and accumulated grew and with them grew their industrial skill. To be sure, their industry remained principally cottage industry for their own use. . . . In the nomadic state, it is difficult to amass stores of food and supplies. . . .

As soon as a tribe has progressed to the point where it is able to stay permanently in one place the question of means of transportation becomes irrelevant. For the sedentary peasant, it is not difficult to store up grains of cereals. . . .

At first the cultivators of the soil probably settled close to the river. . . . But that was a dangerous position, most of all, of course, for the habitations, but also for the arable land. Any flood could sweep it away. On the other hand, the land next to the river must have become too narrow when the population grew. . . . The better the cultivators became acquainted with the river and its varying levels, the easier it became for them to hit upon contrivances that made it possible to convey water from the river to points situated higher up or to store up floodwaters: dams, reservoirs, canals, bucket-elevators. . . . These works became the country's most important sources of life so that it seemed quite impossible to neglect or to abandon them. The result of all that is that the cultivator, in contrast to his nomadic past, clings to the soil with extreme tenacity.

That, however, is not the only transformation he undergoes. . . . For the man, the whole nature of his activity is changed. Hunting now claims only little of his time or none at all. . . . The animal husbandry that developed allotted to him the taming and guarding of the large animals, primarily the cattle. . . . As soon as the point was reached where the digging stick or the spade was replaced by the ox-drawn plow, the cultivation of the soil, which had previously been the task of women, became man's work. . . . For the construction of the irrigation works [and the family's lodging] the men likewise became indispensable.... Thus the free hunter... turned into a laboriously toiling manual laborer.

The use of weapons, vital for the hunter, becomes for the agriculturalist an undesirable interruption of other activities that are more important for his existence. He finally no longer uses weapons... except for defense. For this purpose, he prefers other means if they lead to the same goal. The shedding of blood, a pleasure for the hunter, often becomes for the agriculturalist a repugnant activity from which he recoils in horror.... The inhabitants of the river valleys... have no cause for wars of aggression. Bound to the soil, which provides them with suitable food, they are the less inclined to want to acquire new land as they find nothing but desert and wilderness outside the river valley.... Poorly armed, ... unaccustomed to the use of weapons, they have always been and are still today extremely peaceful people....

The military weakness of the peasants is further accentuated (prior to the emergence of state power) by the isolation of the individual villages from each other.... Agriculture makes it difficult for the peasant to enter into close relations with other men, except for his neighbors.... Every village becomes a world unto itself.... This isolation of the villages from each other makes it difficult for them to cooperate in the defense against an overwhelmingly powerful enemy for whom the individual villages are no match.

Thus, the effect of agriculture in the river valleys is to raise the peasants' level of prosperity, but also thereby to increase the inducement to their poorer neighbors to pillage them. And at the same time it diminishes the [peasants'] capacities for defense and also the possibilities of saving themselves from destruction by flight....

CHAPTER TWO

Nomadic Herdsmen

When men in the higher stage of hunting culture were forced into the desert or when the climate of their environment became ever more arid, ... the consequences were necessarily completely different than when men at the same level of development happened to enter river valleys or relatively large oases with abundant vegetation.... The less hunting and the cultivation of plants suffice to meet the need for food, the more important does a third factor become, which among hunters is considered almost exclusively as a pastime, among agriculturalists only as a supplementary or secondary source of livelihood...: the taming and raising of *useful animals*.... Of the tameable and useful animals, only a few are fit to accompany men in the desert, ... sheep, some kinds of cattle, asses, horses, and camels....

Protecting these friends and riches becomes the most important task of the nomad. Numerous hungry predatory animals threaten them constantly. ... If hunting requires continual practice with weapons and keeping them in the best condition, then the same necessity arises from the protection of herds. The nomadic herdsman, unlike the agriculturalist, does not become disaccustomed to the use of weapons. ... He does not deal only with four-footed robbers. ... Under the nomad's living conditions, the number of animals he owns is highly unstable. ... *[It]* can swiftly be reduced in the extreme by unfavorable accidents. ... Then there is nothing left for the herdsman to do but to borrow animals from his more favored neighbors or, and this often seems more profitable, to steal them. ... That is, one does not steal from neighbors in one's own tribe; that would run counter to the primitive morality of solidarity among the members of the tribe. But ... robbing an alien tribe to the benefit of one's own is regarded as very praiseworthy.

Thus the nomadic herdsman must always be prepared for war, and he never lacks opportunities to use his weapons, sometimes to protect his own possessions, at other times to appropriate alien ones. ... The motive of revenge has the result that the raids originally arising out of an emergency situation are continued. ... Thus robbery becomes a permanent institution, a regularly employed method of obtaining a livelihood. The result is a breed of men who are extraordinarily bold, pugnacious, and rapacious. Nomadic herdsmen become all the more dangerous because their mobility makes it possible for them easily to assemble in large groups. ... How great is the disadvantage, vis-à-vis the herdsmen, of the peaceful but slow and dull farmer, who clings to the soil and isolates himself in separate, small villages!

In other respects, too, herdsmen and agriculturalists constitute extreme contrasts. One the one side, there is the peasant, who stores up his harvest and uses it frugally, for he must make do with it until the next harvest, and, moreover, must also set aside seeds and reserves. Further, the peasant, especially when he artificially irrigates his fields, can foresee the annual yield of his labor with a reasonably high degree of probability. One the other side, there is the herdsman, whose livelihood, whether gained from the breeding or the theft of cattle, is always extremely uncertain. His is the daring and recklessness of the gambler, and he looks down with disdain on the peasant's frugality and caution. Whatever he obtains is used for immediate enjoyment. And no less does he despise the peasant's industry. The latter has to toil and moil day in, day out, ... if his undertaking is to thrive. The herdsman roams about in the world free and without constraint, in continual struggles with it, which, however, are not felt to be a burden, but rather a pleasure. That is true, to be sure, only for the men. The women in the household always had their burdens; they always had to perform heavy labor, whether the men were hunters, herdsmen, or agriculturalists.

Much more than in the character of the women, the change of the modes of production brought about the greatest contrasts in the character of the men.

[Kautsky notes that the ancient Hebrews were aware of the antagonism between herdsmen and agriculturalists. To these descendants of nomad bedouins, the shepherd Abel is peaceable and the agriculturalist Cain murderous. In the Zoroastrianism of the Medes and Persians, who ruled over peasants, the realm of light under Ormuzd is identified with agriculture, the realm of darkness under Ahriman with the desert and the nomads.]

CHAPTER THREE

The Nomads' Capacity for Creating States

There is, then, a great contrast with respect to the mentality of peasants and of nomadic herdsmen, between the affluence, but also the dullness and slowness, the defenselessness and submissiveness of the former, and the poverty, skill and mettle in combat, venturesomeness, and often also the lively and adaptable intelligence of the latter. We see, then, that peasants and herdsmen constitute two factors, the coincidence and collision of which at a certain level of development necessarily resulted in the herdsmen rendering the peasants subject and tributary to them. Individual tribes of herdsmen combined numerous local communities or mark communities of peasants into a polity that was ruled and exploited by the herdsmen, who now ceased to be herdsmen. In this way the first states were created.

Again and again, Ratzel calls attention to the nomads' great capacity for creating states. *[Kautsky quotes Ratzel,* The History of Mankind, *III, 152.]* He does not notice that this capacity is not inherent in the nomads as such. Nothing of this capacity is to be seen when nomads stay by themselves, but only when they encounter agriculturalists. Each of the two elements is equally necessary for the state. . . . Indeed, the agriculturalists are more important in this connection than the herdsmen, for there can be no establishment of a state without sedentary agriculturalists. States can, however, be formed even under conditions where their antagonists consist not of nomadic herdsmen but of tribes possessing qualities similar to those of such herdsmen *[for example, hunters in the Americas]*. Nowhere, though, does the establishment of a state occur through the conquest of hunters or herdsmen. Only the agriculturalist can be easily subjugated and forced to labor for others. . . .

Cunow points out that the formation of the state presupposes a certain level of production technology on the part of the vanquished and of administrative technique on the part of the victors. *[Kautsky quotes Cunow,* Die Marxsche Geschichts . . . theorie, *I, 297.]* These technical preconditions must certainly be present if the founding of a state is to be possible, but a number of psychic preconditions are also required. Certain intellectual abilities and character traits, ways of feeling and thinking, give rise to the state. That would entail an idealistic conception of history, however, only if these psychic preconditions proceeded from a movement that moved itself, that is, from nothing. . . . But man's innate spirit, which was, after all, the same for the peasant as for the herdsman, [would have] to create the same psychic conditions in both cases. . . . Consideration of the conditions of production and of life of herdsmen and of agriculturalists suffices to comprehend the peculiarity of the mentality of the ones and of the others. The capacity of force, of war, for creating states is thereby completely explained by its economic conditions.

CHAPTER FOUR

The Founding of the State

. . . What is most likely to happen first when [peasants and a warlike tribe] encounter each other is not the founding of a state, but the occasional plundering of the peasants, which can go so far as to completely depopulate an area, [where slave raiding is involved, as in the Sudan]. . . . But the peasants were not always defenseless nor the nomads superior to them in matters of military technique. . . . If the nomads wanted to obtain the good things produced by the peasants, there was in such cases nothing else they could do but to engage in barter. . . . It accustoms the nomads to the possession of peasants' products and makes them even more covetous of them. But, of course, it also increases their understanding of the conditions under which they were produced and shows the foolishness of destroying these conditions of production. When the nomads have reached that point, they use the superior strength they might enjoy . . . to leave the conquered as peasants where they live and to impose on them a regular tribute by which the vanquished ransom themselves from threatening destruction. This arrangement was widespread in antiquity; even at the present time it can still be found in Arabia. [Kautsky quotes Meyer, Geschichte des Altertums, I/2, 379, 383.]

Here we encounter the second form of exploitation to appear in history. The first is slavery, where only isolated individuals are compelled to work for others; under this second form, this is true of whole tribes as collectivities. It is a common feature of both forms of exploitation, however, that the exploited does not belong to the exploiter's polity. The slave because he has no civil rights whatsoever; the payer of tribute because the polity to which he belongs has not yet lost its independence. Exploiters and exploited form two distinct polities. Thus they are not two classes. The two tribes become such only when they are fused into a single polity, with a common government and common laws, which are laid down by the exploiting tribe. This tribe thus becomes the ruling class, to which the exploited tribe is subordinate as the ruled class. . . . They are two tribes . . . that become a single polity, a state, by virtue of the fact that their prior spatial separation ceases. Since the settled tribe cannot abandon the land it inhabits and cultivates without losing the sources of its life, it is the nomad who must renounce the steppe and take up residence in the land of the agriculturalists.

That can be a process that takes place gradually, but it will never be one that occurs without the use of force. And it can very well happen all at once, by means of the invasion of a conquering tribe. From the beginning of the state up to the present time . . . when a sudden unheaval occurs in the life of states, it is, as a rule, a matter of a *political* revolution. This can bring in its train an *economic* revolution, but so far those who have supposed that they could also put a new mode of production in the place of the old one at one blow have always deceived themselves. The political revolution itself presupposes slow, gradual social changes that are to be explained in the last analysis by economic conditions. That is true even of the first political revolution in the history of the world, the founding of the first state by means of conquest.

If warfare against an agricultural tribe and its defeat by nomads . . . is to conclude with the victors remaining in the land of the vanquished and assuming the government of the latter, then two conditions must be fulfilled. The conquering tribe must have acquired an understanding of the nature and requirements of the mode of production of the subjugated people; otherwise the conquerors will soon have ruined it. . . . They could have attained this understanding only through lengthy intercourse with the tribe they were to subjugate later, partly . . . by way of trade, partly . . . through exacting regular payments of tribute. Both of these presuppose that the two tribes are neighbors of one another. When nomadic tribes from far away invaded areas whose culture was completely alien to them, they could only pillage and lay waste to them but not establish lasting states in them. . . . The subjugated, too, must have achieved a certain economic level. Their production must yield such fruits that not just the cultivators, but also their masters can live from them. . . .

In any case, the founding of states was based on the use of force. But the extent of the pressure exerted by the attackers and that of the resistance put up by the defenders was surely not the same everywhere. Accordingly, the relationship between the ruling and the ruled classes could take very different forms. . . . Thus the mere fact of conquest is sufficient to permit different kinds of dependence and exploitation to exist alongside one another within a single state. . . . A victorious tribe of nomads was, as a rule, not content to conquer and subjugate just one of the small agricultural polities. It annexed in succession a number of such polities and could allot to each of them a different position in the state they formed together.

Lastly, different class relations could be formed by further conquerors. . . . The new intruder could either exterminate the ruling class it met with and replaced, or degrade it and use it. . . . A division of labor between the old ruling class and the new one then easily developed. The old ruling class was superior in knowledge, and the new one reserved making war for itself and left to its predecessor the tasks of administering the state and cultural policies. . . . In this way, two higher classes take form alongside one another as the estates or castes of warriors and priests. The latter can thus acquire a special position as an estate that they did not have in the prestate stage.[2] . . . Where a priestly estate acquired power and respect it was, as a rule, able to maintain its privileged position in the face of all new conquerors. *[Kautsky cites the role of the Egyptian priesthood up to the Hellenistic period and of the Christian church in the period of the Germanic invasions of the Roman empire.]*

Among the victors, too, as a result of the different shares the individual strata among them had in battle and in victory, social differences could take shape, which in certain circumstances could attain the magnitude of class antagonisms. In all likelihood, it was not always a single tribe of nomads that descended upon an agricultural area by itself. . . . Nomad tribes easily joined together for common undertakings. Under certain conditions, too, several tribes could have been simultaneously forced to migrate by the same cause, for example by a general, widespread drought. . . . The leading tribe surpassed the others in might and booty and formed a kind of aristocracy within the alliance of victors.

On the other hand, within a tribe itself, not all of its members need have participated to the same extent in all raids and expeditions of conquest. Not all families find themselves in the same situation. Some have an excess of fighting men; others lack them. Some have at their disposal sites suitable for agriculture, others do not. . . . Around a leader who had made a name for himself through his successes gathered the able-bodied excess population as his retinue for adventurous expeditions of very diverse kinds. . . . Occasionally, the different tribes made peace with one another, and their entire excess of martial forces became available for a large-scale expedition against a neighboring civilized land. . . . Their victory could be such that the retinues of warriors remained in the conquered country and the rest of the tribe followed after them. When conquest proceeded in this manner, the elements *[of the conquering tribes]* devoted to agriculture received more and better land in the new area and perhaps in addition also a few slaves to work with them. But the functions of ruling and exploiting are seized by the retinues for themselves. These distribute among themselves large areas with numerous workers. . . .

2. See also IV:5:5, below.

As professional warriors and exploiters, these retinues elevate themselves
as a nobility of office above the mass of their former comrades, who continue
to live from their own labor. To be sure, the latter, too, are superior to
the subject population, those who are unfree. They pay no tribute and take
part in the political assemblies of the ruling class. They make up the stratum
of the common freemen. As a rule, however, this stratum does not exist
for very long. As we shall see, the formation of the state brings in its train
the condition of permanent war.[3] For a military expedition, all the freemen
can be mobilized in the general levy. In the nomadic stage that could be
done. However, it is not compatible in the long run with settled, intense
agriculture, and the free peasants are ruined in the process. Either they go
into debt or are bought out and replaced by latifundia worked by slaves,
as in ancient Italy, or they must seek refuge under the protection of a
powerful lord, who relieves them of the duties but also of the rights of
bearing arms.

We see that very diverse stratifications and class relationships can form
in the state even at its beginning, by virtue of mere conquest, leaving aside
those that come about later through purely economic development. These
we shall treat of later.[4] But no matter how diverse the divisions into classes
might become, class mentality does not change within agriculture.... On
one side, the peasant remains the industrious, frugal, peaceable, often fearful
and humble laborer and creator of a surplus product in excess of what he
needs for himself and his family. On the other side, the mentality of the
landed nobility has even until today remained the same as that which characterizes the men among nomadic herdsmen and, in part, also of nomadic
hunters. Even today the nobles despise strenuous gainful labor.... Only
the pursuits of the nomads seem to them appropriate to their rank: hunting,
war, pillaging (as long as no other classes appear that are strong enough to
prevent them from engaging in those pursuits). The aristocrat is as little
gifted with frugality as the nomad.... Hand in hand with contempt for
work and frugality goes contempt for the working and frugal man, hence
for the "common" people in the state.

Arrogance has always been part of the nature of any aristocracy....
[With it] goes concern for preserving the "purity of its blood." Since rulers
and ruled are two different tribes, if not always two different "races," that
confront each other with hostility, marital unions between them do not
take place easily from the beginning of the state. But it is because of the
arrogance of the aristocracy that, when the two tribes live together permanently, the barriers separating them tend to be made still higher.... Like
the rapacious nomad, the aristocrat, too, loves to condescend to the daugh-

3. See IV:3:7, below.
4. See IV:4:3–5, 7, 10, 12, IV:5:5–7a, below.

ters of the peasants, to put them at the service of his lust. But he regards these women and their children, should such eventuate, no differently than the nomad does the kidnapped slavewoman. . . . If we still discover, as soon as we scratch him, so many traits of the Tartars of yore in the true, status-conscious nobleman of today, . . . that is due to the fact that the living conditions of his class are even today in many states still very much in conformity with the living conditions of the nomads. . . . The aristocrat's functions as ruler and exploiter engender always anew in him some of the qualities that gave the nomad greater vigor than the agriculturalist. . . .

CHAPTER FIVE

The Expansion of the State and of the Tribe

The formation of the state is synonymous with the formation of classes and class antagonisms, as a result of which the state is, from the outset, an institution in the hands of a ruling and exploiting class for the repression and exploitation of another class that feeds not just itself but also its lords by its productive activity. . . . Yet another characteristic distinguishes the state from all the polities that preceded its formation. . . . Every individual tribe was a sovereign polity unto itself. The state, on the other hand, always rests upon the combination of several tribes into a single, relatively large polity. . . . That is likewise necessarily linked with the character of the state as an instrument of exploitation. . . .

A state appears only when the intruding tribe, wholly or in part, does not take up agriculture, . . . but becomes an exploiter. . . . Having settled down, however, this tribe can no longer engage in its old way of gaining a livelihood by nomadic cattle raising. . . . Exploitation . . . must suffice to sustain it completely. . . . Whereas, prior to the formation of the state, the slave is merely a helper with the work, and tribute offers only somewhat more amenities of life, we find in the state the third form of exploitation, its highest and most oppressive form: here the exploiter's existence becomes completely dependent on the yield of exploitation. . . .

In the periods of beginning state formation the productivity of labor is, however, very low. It provides only slight surpluses over and beyond what is required for the maintenance of the laborer's family. . . . The number of the ruled in the state therefore had to be far greater than the number of the rulers. The commands of the latter are no longer backed up by the superior strength of the majority, as were the commands of the leaders of prestate polities, but by the superior physical force of a minority. . . . Only if the conquering nomadic tribe succeeded in subduing quite a few settled tribes . . . could the victors devote themselves entirely to the work of forcibly repressing and holding together *[the conquered tribes]* and live completely from the fruits of their exploitation. . . . Only then had a genuine state been created.

By its greater extension, by its capability and necessity of expanding, the state distinguishes itself even at its inception from the polities that existed prior to it. . . . The question of what conditions the expansion of a tribe in a given instance has so far been little investigated. . . . It is nonsensical to assume that the size of a tribe is a result of the fact that people incessantly become more numerous. . . . In reality we know that among the organisms of the world there exists in normal times a condition of equilibrium.[5] . . . Man can certainly disrupt this equilibrium by means of his technology, but not to such an extent that a continuous population growth would result. . . . We do not find at all, then, that the tribes in the prestate stage . . . become ever more extensive. . . .

But . . . why does the population of an area split up into a certain number of tribes of a definite size? . . . If a tribe becomes so numerous that some of its members can obtain their livelihood only very far from its center, where the power of the tribe does not reach to protect them, where they must live beyond close personal contact with their fellows, then those living at a distance easily become alienated from the tribe. As they cannot live in isolation, they must under such conditions join together in a new tribe of their own. . . . Thus, the better the routes and means of transportation are, the more extensive can the tribe become. Tribes grow not as a result of natural population increase, but as a result of technological progress. But they nevertheless always remain limited to a small area. *[Kautsky mentions those Swiss cantons that maintained their tribal direct democracy and says they have populations of 14,000 to 33,800.]* Even under the most favorable conditions, the population of a tribe in the prestate period will not have exceeded by much the size of the population of one of the original cantons. The more primitive and unfavorable the conditions were, the further the average population of a tribe will have stayed below that of one of the original cantons. . . .

CHAPTER SIX

Association of Tribes

[For] tribes adjacent to one another, . . . common ends can arise, like the warding off of a common enemy or the necessity . . . of seeking new habitations, which an isolated tribe would not be strong enough to obtain and maintain. . . . Joint action . . . is undertaken most readily when the tribes speak similar languages, . . . have developed under the same conditions, or

5. See II:2:3, II:3:6, III:2:2, above.

have even detached themselves from a common mother-tribe, with which they still maintain relations, when they thus have customs, needs, and modes of thought that are in agreement with each other. In some circumstances, such tribes can ultimately achieve closer relations than occasional collaboration, namely, a permanent alliance. But this alliance never becomes so close and firm that a new polity results from it. Each of the individual tribes in the league always preserves its full sovereignty. *[Following Morgan's Ancient Society, Kautsky describes the Iroquois confederacy and quotes Seeck, Geschichte des Untergangs der antiken Welt, I, 209–10, on Germanic tribal federations.]* When the league brings success, it remains together. When it does not, it easily disintegrates. . . .

CHAPTER SEVEN
The Tendency of the State to Expand

The barriers to growth that restrict the tribe do not exist for the state. The members of each of the subjugated tribes are still compelled by the requirements of production and of democracy—to the extent that they are still allowed to govern themselves[6]—to live and to work close to the center of the tribe in any given instance. The obligation to perform military service need not keep them together, though. In the state, they are very often dispensed from military service by the ruling class. The members of the ruling tribe, however, now live from the labor of others. . . . The enterprises from the yield of which the individual exploiter lives continue to operate even when he stays away from them for a long time. He can take part in tribal assemblies . . . even when they take place at a great distance from the political center of the state, and the same is true of military . . . expeditions. That is, this independence from work for their livelihood ensues only for the *men* of the ruling class. The *women* remain tied to the household. . . .

We have seen that the formation of the state and of an exploiting class is only possible when several subjugated tribes are united into a polity by a single victorious tribe (or an association of tribes). Now we see that the state in turn creates the conditions that make possible its expansion beyond the domain of an individual tribe. The expansion of the state depends now almost solely on the military strength of the conquering tribe.[7] As far as

6. See IV:5:2, below.
7. See also *Nationalstaat, imperialistischer Staat und Staatenbund*, pp. 6–8, and *Die Befreiung der Nationen*, p. 14. Kautsky reprinted the relevant chapter from the latter work in his *Von der Demokratie zur Staats-Sklaverei*, pp. 22–23.

this strength is sufficient to keep the multitude of the subjugated people under control and to defend the borders of the state against intruders, that is as far as the state can grow.

With the growth of the state its military power can even increase.... The more extensive the state, the more diverse the elements of which it is composed, the easier does it become to treat these elements in different ways, to give to the one a better, to the other a lower position in the state. The first ones then easily feel privileged, even though they are not part of the ruling class, and they are therefore prepared to defend the existing order in opposition to the worse situated elements, to reinforce the armed forces of the ruling class. *[Referring to and quoting from Herodotus (Book IX, ch. 28 and Book VII, chs. 60–96) II, 497–506, 644, and from Delbrück, History of the Art of War, I, 63, 68, and citing Beloch, Griechische Geschichte, III/1, 284, Kautsky describes the Spartan state and the Persian empire at some length as examples. With reference to the latter, he adds:]* Here we become acquainted with a second method by which a dominant people can increase its military strength beyond what is given by its own numbers.... A portion of the tributes from the subjugated peoples was used to buy warlike nomads who menaced the civilized country with their pillagings, so that they would not just stay quiet, but would in addition use their excess strength to provide contingents that entered into the service of the ruling people.... The greater the empire, the more soldiers it needed in order to protect its extended borders and to hold down the mass of the subjugated people, but the more its means grew for mobilizing and maintaining, in addition to the ruling tribe, other troops loyal to it....

With the state there was given its capacity for continuous, and, under certain conditions, also rapid expansion and at the same time also the constant impulse to expand. As long as the state was still adjacent to cultivated land that held out a prospect of tribute, the rulers of the state felt the insatiable need to conquer it. A people living solely from the labor of its own hands never has need of more land than it can cultivate or use as pasture or as hunting grounds. A natural limit is thereby given to its polity....

The exploiter, however, who lives from the labor of others, can never possess enough land, assuming that he is able to reduce to servitude the men needed for cultivating it.... The mere possession of the land without peasants to cultivate it means so little to an exploiter that when cultivators are not available for him of their own accord, he forcibly ties them to himself as slaves or as serfs. However, when land along with cultivators belonging to it beckons to him as a prize of victory, he is always eager to acquire it.

The state can also, by the mere fact of its existence, be compelled to wage war against tribes and to annex their areas that produce nothing that could in any way arouse the greed of their exploiters.... In addition to threatening conquerors from without, brigands, who live in the country, must also be fended off. . . . The pastoral peoples of the highlands are poor and warlike and hence are no less rapacious than the herdsmen of the steppes. *[Kautsky refers to Highland Scots, Montenegrins, Albanians, Berbers, and Kurds as examples.]* In relation to nomads of the one and the other kind, a state on or in whose borders they live is on the defensive. . . . The state often shows its defensive attitude by building long walls, . . . but a powerful, warlike state is more inclined to another kind of defense, namely, defense by means of attack. . . . Yet that is only temporarily effective. Therefore, the attempt is finally made to obtain relief by permanently occupying the rapacious neighbor's territory and building fortifications in it. *[Roman expeditions into Germany and Darius' into southern Russia are cited as examples.]* When it is possible, the settlement of the land by sedentary agriculturalists must be fostered. . . . The advance of a state into the steppes is not always caused just by the need for protection against nomads; frequently the reason is also the desire for their territory as an area for agriculturalists and thus the desire to increase the number of the exploited. In the case of tsarist Russia, the latter motive was certainly the predominant one. . . .

Recruitment of warlike nomads to serve the masters of the state often goes hand in hand with attempts to repel the nomads. In addition to making war on them, their recruitment is another method of rendering them harmless and preparing the way for subduing them. . . . The process of their subjugation is also furthered by corrupting the nomads, by buying their chieftains and giving them the means to create a power position for themselves within the tribe and to transform a relationship of trust into one of domination. If the state also supports the presumptions of the rich vis-à-vis the poor, then the differences in wealth can become veritable class differences, whereas in the case of a tribe that is left to itself they necessarily remain insignificant and are never able to divide it.[8] . . .

To the two motives for expanding the state considered up to this point—the unlimited urge to expand the sphere of exploitation and the need to safeguard this exploitation against plundering invasions—is added at times yet a third motive. . . . The first states had at their disposal only the simple administrative apparatus that the conquering tribe brought along from its prestate period. They can therefore only have been small and have expanded only to the degree in which the administration of the state was successfully improved and perfected. It was not always the case that states bordered on one another, . . . but, the state's continuous impulse to expand had to have the consequence sooner or later that one state's borders encountered those of another state.

. . . Quarrels due to borders not being respected could not fail to occur between neighboring states. . . . And the perpetual greed for expansion of

8. See IV:2:2, above.

the sphere of exploitation leads the stronger state to attack the weaker one in order to take land away from it. Moreover, between the ruling classes of two states there is always mistrust. Each of them has achieved its dominant position through war and can maintain it only by constant readiness for war. Each fears its neighbor's readiness for war. . . . Thus not just the desire for more exploitation but also the desire for greater security impels *[a ruling class]* to use every opportunity offering a prospect of success to carry war into its neighbor's state, in order to weaken, to diminish, or to completely annihilate it, that is, to drive out, or reduce to servitude, or exterminate its ruling class, and to put its own ruling class in its place. To wars motivated by mere greed and those for defense are now added supposedly ethical wars of aggression for the safeguarding of the fatherland, preventive wars and wars of prestige.

. . . Almost every war, regardless of its origin, ends with a conquest by the victor. When evenly matched opponents confront each other, wars can repeat themselves over and over again, without resulting in such a weakening of one or the other party as to render it unable to fight. From time to time, though, it can also happen that a power comes into being that surpasses in strength all other states within its reach. If its level of civilization is high enough and if it encounters in these states the appropriate administrative apparatus, then it can rapidly subjugate them all and unite them into one empire. . . .

CHAPTER EIGHT

Imperialism

It might be thought that this constant striving for expansion is characteristic only of the states of the past. It is true that at the present time no drive to expand is apparent in Europe, at least not in Western Europe. . . . The same powers, however, that have restrained themselves in Europe, tend even now boundlessly to expand themselves outside of this continent. . . . The methods of colonial policy are to this day those used in the establishment of the first states. And in the exploitative colonies (to be distinguished from settlement colonies) the ruling and exploiting class is still formed by an invading foreign tribe standing above the native population that supplies the oppressed and exploited masses, as above an inferior race to which it is not linked by any common interest.

The striving to expand and to hold together ever more firmly the colonial empire has been given a name of its own in Britain during the last generation. It is called imperialism. This designation has been generalized, and today there is a predilection for calling thus any effort of a state to expand, . . . and this name is considered to be in itself a scientific explanation of the phenomenon. . . . However, since the word "imperialism" has gained currency only in the last few decades, the impression arises that the tendency designated by the word is no older than it. And that appears all the more to be the case as an economic theory has connected imperialism with the newest form assumed by capitalism, namely, finance capital.

This latter view is not foolish, but makes very good sense. Like the landed aristocracy, banking and commercial capital are usually imbued with the urge to expand the sphere of exploitation that is peculiar to the exploiting classes in a state. How many commercial wars have been produced by commercial jealousy! In contrast, industrial capitalism is, in its beginnings, exceedingly peaceably minded and averse to all wars of conquest. To the extent that industrial capital in Britain became stronger, British policy became more peaceable. Free trade and peace became the slogan of the leaders of industrial capital, of the Cobdens and the Brights. ... The development of both joint-stock companies and of employers' associations brought industry more and more into close connection with banking capital, and thus brought forth the new phenomenon that Hilferding, the first to investigate it systematically and thoroughly, named finance capital.[9] In this form, industrial capital develops the same spirit of violence toward the exploited and its competitors as has hitherto characterized all exploiting classes.

To that extent, certainly, finance capital is, then, responsible for imperialism and therefore constitutes a new phenomenon characteristic of the last decades. But that should not be understood as meaning that the striving of states to expand is a wholly new phenomenon. It is as old as the state itself and has, until now, been characteristic of every state. The new aspect introduced into this phenomenon by industrial capital consists merely in the fact that for a time it acted counter to and weakened this striving after new conquests, while, since the last decade of the past century, it has not only not counteracted the drive for expansion in all capitalist states, but has supplied it with new strength.

If we may nevertheless expect a progressive checking of this drive for expansion, it is because we are counting on the growing strength of the industrial proletariat in the countries of decisive importance for capitalism, and on the no less growing strength of the national rebellions and independence movements in the colonies themselves.[10] It is, however, also possible that finance capital, taught a lesson by the World War, finds this method of expanding its sphere of exploitation too risky. It might conclude

9. Hilferding, *Finance Capital.* On finance capital and imperialism, see also pp. 433–44, below, including n. 28.

10. See IV:8:5, below. On colonialism and anticolonialism, see also *Sozialisten and Krieg,* pp. 650–63.

that this way of trying to increase profits endangers its entire capital and that it would be more profitable to shift to an ultraimperialism, an international cartelization of the finance capitalists of all countries.[11]

But this is a topic that belongs in the chapter in which we will treat of the most recent tendencies in the state. Here it is sufficient to state that even up to the present day all states have exhibited a constant urge to expand. ... This urgent desire, the drive to wars of conquest, is necessarily linked with the nature of the state as it has been up to the present time. Its deepest root consists in the drive of every exploiting class to increase the yield of its exploitation, which is most easily achieved by increasing the number of those who are exploited. As the drive for expanding large-scale enterprise is immutably inherent in industrial capitalism, so too is the drive for expanding its territory unalterably inherent in the state, as long as it is an instrument for the class domination of an exploiting class.

Section Four
Effects of the State

CHAPTER ONE

Economic and Political Means

[This chapter is devoted almost entirely to an argument with the distinction drawn by Oppenheimer, The State, pp. 24–27, between the "economic means," that is, one's own labor, and the "political means," that is, the appropriation of the labor of others or robbery, to obtain "economic objects of consumption."]

If the state is itself the product of certain economic conditions, of the division of labor between herdsmen and peasants, its existence in turn brings about new economic formations of the most diverse kind. On the one hand, new classes come into being that are not directly created by the state. ... On the other hand, from new circumstances the state acquires new functions, by no means all of which are a further development of its original function, that of fostering the exploitation of the laboring masses by the ruling classes.

---

11. Kautsky had first, in a single, very cautious sentence in "Der Imperialismus," p. 921, advanced the concept of "ultraimperialism" as a possibility which "from a purely economic point of view could not be excluded." On imperialism, see also IV:8:9, below, and *Sozialisten und Krieg*, pp. 287–95, 650–63.

Communism and Private Property

The first and perhaps most important consequence of the formation of the state is the change of the function served by property. *[Kautsky summarizes what he said above about the various forms of property, especially on pp. 199–200; and in III:3:9–10.]* Until the state appeared, property, whether private or communal, always had the task of helping laboring man.... That is completely changed as soon as the state emerges and a small minority rules in the polity, which subjugates and exploits the mass of the people. Property law is now adapted to these ends, as a means for fostering exploitation. Once a servant of the laboring mass, that law now becomes its master, a hard-hearted and cruel tyrant. At the same time, traditions and technical considerations continue to play a role in determining the form of property. But the spirit that now pervades all forms of property is the opposite of that of the prestate period.

As a rule, the conditions of domination and exploitation are not favorable to communal property, but that is by no means always the case. Often, it was precisely the communal ownership of land that became a basis of exploitation, as in British India, on Java, and in the state of the Incas in Peru. *[Kautsky returns here to his argument in III:3:9, above, that Russian village communism was not just a product of tsarist tax policy, but that originally communal property of agricultural land was probably the rule.]* As soon as agriculture was carried on more intensively,... the individual peasant had to oppose, to an ever-greater extent, the periodic redistribution of the land.... And, on the other hand, as long as periodic redistribution took place, it was an enormous obstacle to a progressive intensification of agriculture.... Thus the progress of agriculture necessarily exerted pressure for complete private property in the land. That does not mean that this is for all times indispensable for agriculture. But it is difficult to overcome where agriculture is carried on in small peasant farms. Where these are not replaced by large-scale enterprises, agrarian development proceeds from communal property in the land to private property. *[There follows further discussion of early Russian village communism.]*

Trade

... A relatively unhampered exchange of commodities is made possible within a relatively large area by the formation of the state.... By counteracting brigandage, the ruling tribe makes it safer to transport precious goods. Lastly, the new state government has to improve the means of transportation from the center where it resides to the various sections of the state, . . . on the one hand, in order to facilitate the transport of tributes to the central government and, on the other hand, in order to make it possible rapidly to move large numbers of troops to a threatened location at any time. *[Kautsky refers to great imperial road systems, quoting descriptions by Mommsen,* The History of Rome, *II, 85; Heeren,* Historical Researches, *I, 20;* Herodotus *(Book V, ch. 52), II, 375; and* The Travels of Marco Polo *(Book II, ch. 20), pp. 221–22.]*

The level of development of the means of transportation among the Persians, the Romans, the Chinese, and the Mongols described here certainly came about only after a long evolution. Its first beginning, though, was given with the formation of the state. Only the resources at its disposal made these means of transportation possible, and only the expansion of the state made them necessary. . . . The more the state grew in strength and extent, the better did the means of transportation become within its domain, the more frequent and pervasive became exchange among the individual tribes and provinces in it. Trade beyond the borders of the state also became more brisk, if the ability of the state to protect its traders outside of its territory as well as inside it grew at the same time.

But . . . the state also expanded the exchange of commodities through the exploitation it brought about. . . . The ruling classes now live from the surpluses produced by the exploited. They are driven to increase their number by expanding the territory of the state, but also to increase the work load of each of those exploited and to reduce as much as possible his share of his own product. . . . By all of these methods, they increase the quantities of the surplus product . . . that are over and above what they need in order to live. They use this excess partly to expand their armaments, partly to increase their luxuries. . . . But they will also expend a constantly growing portion for the exchange of commodities. From the very beginning, the most prominent objects of exchange are metals and stones, materials for making tools and weapons as well as jewelry, by means of which one can attract the attention of one's fellows and set oneself apart from them. From the start, trade in commodities serves the purposes of war and luxury. War and luxury are enormously increased by the state and therewith also the resources and the requirements of trade.

The latter now assumes quite different dimensions from the prestate period. It . . . becomes a regularly recurring business and finally one that claims all of the time and attention of some men. The stratum of merchants appears as a lifelong occupation and also as a class. For the individual merchant lives by obtaining the commodities with which he trades where they are cheap and selling them where their price is high. He exploits either the producer or the consumer or both. . . . When the merchant sees to it that he is paid for the value-creating labor of transportation, he is not committing an act of exploitation. But he can leave his labor . . . to someone else and he does so, when the division of labor is more highly developed, and still makes a profit. . . . A new class is created and a new class antagonism. It rests on the basis of the state, but it is by no means identical with the class antagonism created by conquest, even though it results from the latter.

But in order that the merchant might appear, . . . a quite large quantity of commodities must be available, *[to him],* which he exchanges for other commodities. . . . At first, we find that only in the hands of the landowners and of the government are the quantities of products concentrated that are necessary for engaging in trade in commodities. . . . As soon as the state was established, the chieftain's function as trader for the entire polity was transferred to the state government. It became more extensive to the same degree that the state expanded, that the surplus in the hands of the ruling class and therewith the briskness of trade grew. Since at the same time the functions of perpetual warfare . . . *[and]* of more numerous and increasingly complicated administrative tasks . . . claimed plenty of the time and attention of the rulers, and since the functions of trade . . . required special knowledge, the masters of the state soon turned over the trade monopoly belonging to them to people especially charged with that task. These people they selected from the numerous host of servants placed at their disposal by the tributary population. *[Kautsky quotes Weber,* General Economic History, *pp. 55, 198, 202, on princely monopolies.]*

State monopoly of trade characterizes the state of the transition from communism to private property, of the transition from tribal trade to trade by private individuals, and is only compatible with a still quite primitive state of commerce, when it extends to just a few products and is conducted with just a few peoples. . . . With time, the exercise of the trade monopoly by state officials must have proven unprofitable and burdensome. . . . Trade assumed forms making it necessary that the trader be given full discretion with regard to the commodities he had to exchange. . . . The individual trader could achieve greater freedom of movement only be ceasing to be an official of the state or of the landowner and becoming instead its or his debtor. The state and the landowner made the commodities at their disposal over and beyond their needs available to people whom they had come to know as successful traders in their service. The latter were to trade freely with these commodities on the condition that they would return the value advanced to them and share the profit with the state or the landowners.

CHAPTER FOUR

Usury

Thus the free merchants were created with the help of loans. In this manner, two kinds of capital arose at the same time: *trading capital* and *lending capital*.

. . . These two kinds of capital must be clearly distinguished from *industrial capital*. The latter is a very recent phenomenon; in its developed form, it is only a few centuries old. . . . Trading and lending capital, however, are as old as written history itself. *[Kautsky quotes Marx,* Capital, *III, 728.]*

At first, it was the large landowners or the owners of great herds who lent money (or cattle or commodities), and not only to traders but also to peasants. . . . In the state, the peasants find themselves in distress more easily than before, while at the same time they lose the resources with which to remedy it. Even in normal times, the payments of tribute to the state and the landlords consume all their surpluses, and the peasants can accumulate reserves only with difficulty. Every misfortune . . . makes it impossible for the peasant to fulfill his obligations. . . . His neighbors . . . no longer dispose of any surplus resources to help him with. Such resources he now finds only in the hands of the state and the landowner. However, the new spirit of property has already entered into these, . . . the spirit of private property that seeks to transform all property, even that of the polity, into a means for exploiting the laboring strata. *[They]* part with their surplus to the needy only as loans. . . . Interest must be paid on the amount with which they help out— and in the first, very long-lasting stages of this new property system, the interest is extraordinarily high. *[Kautsky quotes Buckle,* History of Civilization in England, *I, 54, on interest rates in ancient India being set at 15–60 percent and Salvioli,* Der Kapitalismus im Altertum, *p. 193, on Brutus charging 48 percent in late republican Rome.]*

If the peasant was not able to pay back the capital with the interest on time, something that happened quite often, then he had to work off his debt in some way. Hence the increasing debt-peonage among the peasants, a new form of their exploitation. *[Kautsky refers to the struggle of the prophet Jeremiah against debt slavery in the seventh century* B.C. *and quotes a description of debt slavery in the fifth century* B.C. *in the Book of Nehemiah, 5, 1–7.]* In fact, the struggle against the peasants' debt-peonage was one of the first forms in which a class struggle manifested itself. This kind of slavery brought about by the peasants' indebtedness to the landlord or to the state appears again and again, however. . . . *[It]* becomes a sovereign means used by conquering exploiters to obtain forced laborers when the direct purchase of slaves is already forbidden, and a free, propertyless wage proletariat does not yet exist.

Throughout all of antiquity, the large landowner is glad to remain a usurer, even though special banking capitalists appear alongside him. . . . But his chief business remains war and the spoils of war. His usurious transactions do not hinder him in these pursuits. But engaging in trade, which in ancient times required long journeys, would prevent him from being always ready to take part in a military expedition. . . .

At first, creditors and debtors belong to different tribes. Only the ruling tribe has large surpluses at its disposal that it can lend out. Only the members of subjugated and exploited tribes find themselves in a plight forcing them to take out loans. Then, too, solidarity within a tribe continues to exist for a long time even after the state has appeared. It is only the members of another tribe, even within the same polity, who are aliens, indeed enemies, ... from whom one takes as much as one can. . . . In the state, the original tribal solidarity disappears in the course of time. At first in the ranks of the subjugated, who make up the great mass of the people in which differentiations of various kinds develop first, with different and often antagonistic interests. The aristocratic usurer is joined by the plebeian, and finally things go so far that the aristocrat and even the sovereign of the land are required to pay interest by plebeian owners of money. But that does not happen until money . . . has become a great power, and even then only where war has ceased being a profitable enterprise. . . .

CHAPTER FIVE

Trading Peoples

In the case of trade, tribal differences manifest themselves in a different manner than in the case of usury. Foreign trade is the first form of commerce. This means that the merchant is a foreigner in at least one of the two countries engaged in trade with one another, for at the beginning he must transport his commodities himself and also purchase them, take possession of them, and sell them himself. . . . Peoples whose geographical location makes them especially suited for transit trade between great and rich states and peoples among whom the technological conditions for the transport of commodities are especially well developed will easily produce more traders than those tied to the soil because they engage only in agriculture. *[Kautsky refers to nomadic Arabs and seafaring Phoenicians and Greeks and to Jews in Palestine, all located at the crossroads of trade.]* Thus there are certainly particular peoples who can be called trading peoples. But they have not become such as a result of a special racial character. Where is the commercial spirit a priori supposed to have come from in the hundred thousands of years of the existence of mankind, during which there was no trade by individuals and no regularly occurring trade at all? And in its homeland, each of the trading peoples was divided into the same classes and occupations as other peoples. In each of them, the great majority consisted of peasants. Only when individually dispersed among foreign peoples were they forced to take up trade, because that was, until recently, about the only occupation one could pursue as a foreigner among foreigners.

Writing

In the primitive small tribe, all the relations of men among themselves as well as with their environment and with the products they had made were simple, easy to understand, and subject to little change. Everyone knew these relations and participated in them. Oral communications sufficed to establish and regulate them. Individual memory was adequate for retaining them. Matters are completely different . . . for the ruling class in the state, which joins a large and constantly growing number of small communities and tribes together into an extensive polity. . . . Depending on the manner in which they were subdued, their obligations and rights took different forms. Great quantities of the most diverse natural products were gathered in and stored up by the state government; great masses of men were called together for forced labors of very different kinds. Extensive armies had to be equipped . . . ; great projects of fortification, road building, and irrigation had to be carried out. And these circumstances and activities did not repeat themselves regularly every year. Every victory, every defeat, every uprising could change them decisively. And swift messages from the center to the periphery and vice versa often became an urgent necessity in the interest of the state. The individual member of the ruling class was not capable of grasping all these factors at one time and of retaining them. . . . Oral communication and individual memory alone sufficed less and less for carrying out all the dealings that the state entailed for its rulers and exploiters. . . .

Where class antagonisms appear and there are forces in the state hostile to each other, each of which has an interest in interpreting and passing down established obligations from its own point of view, there interminable quarrels easily arise, if only oral traditions exist. . . . In addition to the duties and rights of the state, there also emerge those of private individuals, which it was advantageous to record and to make capable of serving as evidence. . . .

All of these circumstances make it ever more necessary that an objective means be added to the means of subjective communication and transmission, a system of writing that makes it possible lastingly to represent single words in such a manner that they can later be understood in the same way by all who have been made acquainted with the symbols of the system of writing. Pictorial representations, suggesting certain phenomena, usually processes, are already to be found among primitive peoples. . . . To the representation of processes is now added the indication of concepts, of words, which ultimately progresses to the formation of phonetic symbols out of which words can be composed. . . .

Like language, writing, too, cannot have been invented by individuals, but can only have arisen out of the social practice of many individuals, who agreed in their thinking, feeling, observations, and graphic ability. After a certain point in its development, writing follows the same course as language: from a confusing multiplicity of designations, it advances to increasing simplification, which, to be sure, goes much further in writing than in language. For a word must always designate a concept, whereas writing, as it evolves, reduces the symbols for concepts to symbols for syllables and finally to symbols for a few sounds.... As with language, in the case of writing the progressive simplification of the designations goes hand in hand with an enormous abundance of experiences and ideas, which acquire their social expression and their social effectiveness by means of these technical aids to communication. Born out of an extension of social relations and tasks, the development of writing promotes further extention of such relations and tasks. *[Kautsky quotes and comments critically on Meyer,* Geschichte des Altertums, *I/1, 216–19, and also quotes Dümichen,* Geschichte des alten Aegyptens, *pp. 319–20.]*

... Writing and its use in practice must have developed together with each other and by means of each other; that is true for every technical aid. ... First, the practical need for it has to arise, then the attempts begin to satisfy the need on the basis of what has been learned from experiences and of the available implements. These attempts lead to new practical experiences that make possible more successful technical contrivances, ... and thus the latter develop in constant interaction between practice and the instruments serving practice.... From the state emerged the new needs that made a perfected system of writing necessary, and, to the degree that this system was improved, the affairs of the state and the affairs of the upper classes could be conducted better, the state could expand, and both landowners and merchants were able to exploit more men.... Writing arose out of the needs of the rulers of the state, of the merchants, and of the usurers.

CHAPTER SEVEN

Science

Writing certainly did not arise out of the needs of poetry or science. At the time of its beginnings, it could not yet satisfy those needs at all. But gradually there grew out of writing the basis of science,[1] inasmuch as writing made it possible to collect an abundance of experiential knowledge going far beyond what the individual could learn from the personal communications of the people around him....

The laboring masses ... who work in the traditional confines of the vil-

---

1. The German word "Wissenschaft" means science in the broad sense of systematized knowledge.

lage have no need whatsoever of writing. They have no desire for it, and no one sees to it that knowledge of writing is imparted to them. The higher level of education that is based on knowledge of reading and writing and in the course of centuries gradually arises from them has remained, frequently down to the present time, a privilege of the exploiters and their creatures. That is not to say that every exploiter comes to share in it and has need of it. To the same extent as writing, there develops with the growing expansion and complexity of the state, the division of labor among the ruling classes and their creatures, above all that between military matters and civil administration. The latter has need of writing much sooner than the former. . . .

Between the development of the continuously growing state and the mass of knowledge being accumulated with the help of writing there is a certain parallelism. . . . While the development of the polity in the prestate stage often took place without conscious awareness, in the state work on the development of the polity increasingly becomes an activity directed to definite goals and resting on thorough knowledge of diverse circumstances. . . . Similarly with knowledge. In the prestate stage, without writing, knowledge is small in its extent, is accessible to all, and because of the equality of social conditions affects everybody in the same way. The conclusions drawn from everybody's experiences are collective ideas.[2] . . . That changes as soon as the expansion of commerce in and through the state and the retention of the new experiences flooding in because of that expansion result in a massive accumulation of knowledge. Its effect is overwhelming if the unordered mass is not successfully organized and the plethora of contradictions contained in the various conceptions received from the different peoples of the state is not eliminated, for at first the knowledge recorded by means of writing consists of the combination of those conceptions. . . .

In this way, science arises out of the incoherent knowledge of early times. The striving of science to produce a totality of interrelations in knowledge is, to be sure, prejudiced in the course of its progress by the fact that knowledge increases in a way that makes it impossible for even the greatest scholar to master it all. More and more specialization in particular subject areas manifests itself, which, to be sure, have to strive for coherence with one another again and again. Nevertheless, the so-called human sciences *[Geisteswissenschaften]* are at the present time again considered to be such that their fields have nothing in common with those of the natural sciences, so that the two kinds of science may contradict one another just as much as the different ideas of collective thinking.[3] . . .

2. See II:3:8, above.
3. See also V:2:2, below.

Of course, the totality of knowledge and hence science encompasses numerous areas that are a matter of indifference to the statesman as such. However, writing and, in its train, science develop in and through the state, and it is, above all, the state that most occupies the thoughts of scholars and savants.[4] . . . This was even more the case in the states of antiquity. To the extent that men reflect on inexorable nature, they search for causal, necessary relations. It does not occur to anyone to investigate how nature should be organized; in contrast, the obligations of men in the state and in society appear to be the most important question as soon as the unity of the prestate polity, in which the behavior of individuals toward the polity and its character are simply taken for granted, is dissolved.

The search for causal relations is inborn in man, as it is even in the animal.[5] But at first it extends only to individual cases of practical interest. The effort to bring the whole world into a totality of causal relations arises later than the seeking after a teleological totality of relations in the state and society. All of oriental philosophy has not gotten far beyond this latter state. . . . Still, . . . the need for causal explanation is so strong that one cannot concern oneself much with social and political matters without discovering causal relations in them, even if one only wants to conduct a teleological investigation. With the wealth of social and political experiences that the state supplies on an ever-greater scale and that accumulate more and more because they are recorded in writing, there arises a growing quantity of insights into the nature and the tasks of the state and the means at its disposal, insights that are accessible only to those with a literary education. . . .

Whoever does not possess these insights is incapable of participating in the administration of the state as well as in its shaping, in its legislation. . . . Where a laboring class began to rebel against the ruling classes, and, in order to be able to do so more effectively, attempted to learn to read and write, the rulers became aware of what a great protection the ignorance of the masses meant for them. They then did everything they could artificially to maintain this ignorance.

Thus, alongside the brutal violence of the warrior, the higher learning of the educated became a new means of class domination. And the struggle of the laboring masses against their exploiters must set itself the goal not merely of free disposition over the . . . means of production and of free activity in the state, but also of breaking the privilege of knowledge. To be sure, the exploited have up to now only rarely made this last goal their own. Only in the last few centuries have the conditions arisen permitting them to strive for and to attain to knowledge. Everyone readily feels the weight of political constraint and of the lack of means of production. But,

4. See IV : 5 : 5, below.
5. See II : 5 : 4, above.

in order to recognize the importance of higher learning, one must find oneself in new circumstances that reveal its importance and at the same time offer the possibility of acquiring it. The peasant who continues to live in old, traditional conditions regards the knowledge orally passed down from his forefathers and proven by the practice of centuries as completely sufficient for his purposes. The wisdom of books he despises. But his ignorance also leads him to the opposite extreme, to the overestimation of what is in books. He lets himself be convinced that some of them contain supernatural wisdom, divine revelations, accessible only to a favored few.

Today, in the age of the natural sciences, those who claim to be educated prefer to propagate the view that the ignorance of the laboring masses is the consequence of their innate lack of intelligence as members of an inferior race. . . . That is, of course, nonsense. But . . . some favored strata of the upper classes were able to rise to the heights of immense intellectual achievement, while the mass of the people remained on the level where they had stood at the beginning of the state. . . . Indeed, even absolute intellectual degradation of the laboring masses could occur, through their being overburdened with monotonous, mind-deadening, torturous labor and through the abuse of the intellectual superiority of those ruling strata, who . . . maintained their position as the exploiting class by means of their higher learning and counted on the crudest superstitions to frighten anyone who . . . wanted to reduce the tribute they demanded.

Like the state, writing and the science that arise out of the state are also glorified as the quintessence of all things lofty and magnificent brought forth by mankind. But owing to the close connection of their origin with the state, these achievements have not overcome the class character of the state, but rather aggravated it. All things lofty and magnificent to the upper classes. To the lower classes, increased misery, increased coarseness and ignorance, from which the conclusion is then drawn that the exploited classes are themselves at fault if they have not succeeded in accomplishing as much as their exploiters. The brighter the light of science shines, all the darker—in the state as it has existed so far—is the laboring masses' night of ignorance. . . .

CHAPTER EIGHT

Money

With trade, . . . there arises the need for a medium that facilitates the cumbersome exchange of commodities for one another, that, furthermore, possesses a value in its own right and that makes it possible to measure with greater exactness the value relation in which the commodities stand to each other. Finally, it must be a medium whose use value and exchange value change only slightly in the course of time, so that it is possible to store up the profits of trade in order to be able to achieve greater results with the accumulated sum, . . . or even just in order to be able to live a life of pleasure for a long time without having to work. The same need for the immutability of the value of this medium arose for the interest on loans. The medium that serves to satisfy these needs was a special commodity, which became money. Like language and writing, it grew out of men's social intercourse, but also out of the need to retain what had been gained, just as they did. Like language and writing, it had evolved and had not been invented, even though subject, in its higher forms, to various conscious controls by the state.

In his *Contribution to the Critique of Political Economy* and in *Capital*, Marx exhaustively treated the nature, the development, and the functioning of money. Drawing on him and his theory of value, which alone explains money satisfactorily, I, too, have a number of times written on that topic. *[For his own views on money, Kautsky refers to his* Sozialdemokratische Bemerkungen zur Uebergangswirtschaft, *pp. 106–56.]* In its origin, money is a commodity that everyone can use, that everyone accepts. As long as such a commodity had not appeared, it was necessary that everyone who brought a commodity to market found a taker for it who had a commodity that the other needed himself. The exchanges of commodities were greatly facilitated when everyone became accustomed to exchange his commodity for one that was accepted by all. . . . Whenever two commodities are exchanged for each other, the value of one is always measured by that of the other. The more the one commodity is accepted by everybody in an exchange, . . . the more it becomes customary that the value of every commodity is measured in definite quantities of this one generally accepted commodity, that this quantity is considered the price to be paid for it. The more highly trade in commodities is developed, . . . the more does the favored commodity become the universal medium of exchange. As it does so, it simultaneously develops its functions as measure of value and as medium of circulation. . . .

It is not enough, of course, that a commodity be generally readily accepted in order for it to become the money commodity. It must have other properties in addition, such as constancy of value, which requires a constancy not merely of the conditions of its production but also of the qualities determining its use value and, further, divisibility into small and very small pieces, each of which has the same use-value as the large pieces, so that they differ only in the quantities of labor represented by each of them. *[Kautsky quotes and comments critically on passages on the use of cattle as money by Luxemburg,* Einführung in die Nationalökonomie, *pp. 715, 722, 723–24.]*

. . . Precious metals . . . do not have to be fed, nor do they belong among the treasures consumed by rust and moths. They do not change in their physical properties and hardly in their value, even when they are kept stored up for decades. And precious metals can be not only stored up, but also easily concealed without suffering damage . . . *[and they]* can also generally be transported more easily than, for example, cattle. . . . It is only metallic money, indeed, strictly speaking, it is only the coin that becomes fully developed money. For one can call money fully developed only when its use-value consists exclusively in the fact that it serves as the medium of circulation, when it cannot be used as anything else. . . .

Whoever has money can acquire any commodity that is brought to market; he can buy services from men and even buy men themselves. Money becomes a . . . very potent source of power. The power of money becomes the foundation of military might itself. . . . The more trade in commodities and production of commodities develop, the less is the government of a state able to maintain itself without money, . . . the more eager it is to transform into payments of money the tribute and services to which it obligates its subjects. *[There follows a four-page critique of Max Weber's theory of the development of money, quoting from his* General Economic History, *pp. 236–40.]*

CHAPTER NINE
Accumulation of Treasures

[Kautsky quotes Weber, General Economic History, *pp. 237–38, on the accumulation of treasures and accuses him of not distinguishing between]* the accumulation of money . . . *[and]* the accumulation of jewelry and curiosities *[for display and prestige]*. . . .

Definite limits were set to the demands made by the mighty of a country on those subject to them, because the taxes paid in kind were not money, could be used only *in natura*. Of money, however, one can never have too much, once it has become indestructible metallic money that can be hoarded with no limit. The more money one has, the more of it one *can* spend in order to buy means of power or of pleasure. All the more, however, *must* one also spend for means of power, for the enemies who covet one's hoard become all the more numerous.

To the same extent that precious metals become the money-commodity, the craving of the states for the sources of these metals grows. . . . To conquer and retain such mines was a strong endeavor of states from early times. *[Kautsky cites examples, particularly the Second Punic War as a contest for the control of Spain with its silver and gold mines.]* The power of attraction that the gold and silver mines exercised on the rulers of states in the age of simple commodity production—prior to the development of capitalist industry—and the great power conferred on them by the mines constitute an important moment in the history of states, which, as a rule, receives too little attention. . . . The mine owners . . . spend *[the precious metal]* as money, in order to buy commodities or services with it. Thus metallic money finally comes most often into the hands of those who have surpluses of desired commodities they can part with or who trade with such surpluses. *[India is cited as an example.]*

As the profits from trade and industry became, in addition to the mines, immense sources of revenues in money for princes and lords, . . . these latter still, sooner or later, everywhere undertake to transform into money-taxes also the taxes paid in kind by the peasants, who everywhere formed the great mass of the population until well into the last century. . . . At first this process . . . had a murderous effect on the peasants everywhere. They had previously been accustomed to produce for their own use and for the use of their lords. . . . They had little to do with the market. Now they had . . . to have sold their surplus product in the market before they could pay their taxes. Unfamiliar with the tricks of the marketplace, they were confronted with traders who were very well acquainted with all its ruses. And they were now made dependent on the favorableness and the inclemency not only of the weather, but also of the market. Whereas earlier crop failures were ruinous to them, . . . now an abundant harvest could also become a curse, if it could be sold only at low prices or not at all, something that could easily happen under the bad transport conditions that confined the peasant to a single market.

The peasant's indebtedness, his being sucked dry by usurers, now assumed very large proportions and it accelerated all the more the ruin of the peasantry, inasmuch as now the usurious interest charges, too, became payable in money. At the same time, the transformation of taxes in kind into money-taxes also enormously strengthened the drive to raise taxes. . . . Unlike the taxing of merchants, this tendency does not plague strata that are able to defend themselves somewhat, but rather completely helpless elements. Like the slaves and the other forced laborers in the gold and silver mines, when money-taxes have been imposed, the peasants, too, belong for a long period of time to the most tormented and exploited creatures. *[Kautsky refers to Marx,* Capital, *I, 344–48.]*

Thus, as soon as it has assumed metallic forms, money is a means of aggravating the antagonisms between the classes and between states and peoples, of strengthening the drive to extend the territorial range and the degree of exploitation, and at the same time also of increasing the power of the exploiters and the belligerents, and of making the effects of war and of exploitation ever more horrible. . . . It was only to be expected that all the exploited and their advocates came to believe that social ills could not be cured unless money was eliminated. . . . Even today, there are still socialists who *[think in this way].* They do not know how to distinguish between technology and the economy and hold a technical instrument— money is nothing else—responsible for the deplorable circumstances associated with its use under certain economic conditions.

They forget that in a world of class antagonisms every technological advance, indeed any progress whatsoever, has the tendency to be monopolized by the exploiting and ruling classes and to be employed as a means for increasing exploitation and servitude. But the evil lies in the monopolization of the advance, not in the advance itself. That was true even of writing and of the science that arose out of it; it is still true in our time of the machine and it is true in the same way of money. Money is an indispensable means for overcoming the barriers that, in the primitive tribe, were placed in the way of extending the division of labor and the diversity of products. Money is indispensable, if the individual is to be able to obtain with peaceful means and in the freest possible manner just those products that his individuality requires. Without the aid of money, the whole division of labor must be undone, the state of the future must resemble a penitentiary or an army barracks, in which the same portions are allotted to each, each wears the same uniform, lives in an identical cell, and has no needs or wants beyond these, or where every organism of production is nothing but a self-sufficient family.

That is not to say that money will always be required if production has been expanded on a gigantic scale and the division of labor has been infinitely extended. . . . One can imagine circumstances in which the productivity of human labor has risen so very far or labor has become such a pleasure that all products will be available in abundance and everyone can be allowed to take as much of them as he wants. Unfortunately, this happy age is still far from being attained. We are not yet swimming in abundance; productive labors are still, in the majority, onerous affairs, so that everyone tries to go about obtaining products that he needs and cannot make himself in such a way that he receives for the work he performs products requiring at least the same amount of labor. As long as this is the case, extensive division of labor and extensive individualization of the satisfaction of needs will make money indispensable, especially when it is considered important that no one have to work for others without pay, that no one be exploited. The socialists' task is not to eliminate money, but to eliminate the class relations that cause the indispensable technical means for expanding the division of labor in society to function as a means of exploitation and repression.

CHAPTER TEN

Irrigation Works

The effects of the state we have treated up to now can be found more or less in all states. In addition, however, an effect must be taken into consideration that occurs predominantly in those states we must regard as the most ancient. . . . In the stage of settled agriculture, the population tends to grow rapidly. . . . On the banks of rivers in arid regions, population growth induces efforts to extend the arable land by making areas, in addition to those naturally irrigated, accessible to life-giving moisture through artificial arrangements. *[Kautsky elaborates on what he had written on p. 278, above, on canals, dams, reservoirs, etc.]* Thus, by means of a network of irrigation works an ever-greater area along the river is wrested from the desert and added to the cultivated land, and the population along the river is thereby significantly increased.

This activity, however, is limited by the independence of the small polities that form along the river. . . . Irrigation works along such a mighty river as the Nile, for example, require, if they are to go beyond the first minor beginnings, far more workers than a single little district, let alone a single village, is able to provide. Further, irrigation works constructed without plan, though they might benefit one area, can cause serious damage to another. . . . Once the management of the water supply in the individual districts of the mark communities along the river has reached a certain, not very high level, any further progress beyond that point requires the existence of a power that stands above the individual districts or communities, . . . and is strong enough to subordinate the various particular interests of the villages to the common interest of their agriculture in its totality and to concentrate all their workers for work at the critical places. This power was that of the state. Responsibility for adequate and extensive irrigation works in the interest of agriculture became one of the most important functions of the states of the Orient. *[Kautsky quotes Marx, Capital, I, 650, note 7, and Engels, Anti-Dühring, p. 199.]*

It is still an open question whether state power arose out of the functions of water management, with which we see it charged in historical times, or . . . whether these functions, to the extent they attained in the state, were made possible only by the state; whether the state is the prerequisite of extensive water management or its result. In their conception of the origin of the state, Marx and Engels assumed the latter. *[Kautsky quotes Engels, Anti-Dühring, p. 165, and Marx, Capital, I, 649, note 6, and also, at some length, Dümichen, Geschichte des alten Aegyptens, pp. 19–20, 23–24, as well as a page from an early article of his own, "Die moderne Nationalität," p. 395.]*

This conception of the origin of the state in the necessity of subordinating, both in the struggle against the river and against the external enemy, the different mark communities to a common central authority, which became an exploitative aristocracy, contradicted the point of view of my first conception of history, which I had already formulated in 1876, that the state was the product of conquest.[6] Both conceptions were based on well-attested facts. . . . I looked for a solution that . . . would make it possible to combine them without contradiction.

6. See IV:2:4, above.

In the article just cited I developed this solution. I assumed that both processes operated alongside one another and furthered one another. To be sure, the necessity of common defense against enemies and of common irrigation works produced the need for an association connecting the individual mark communities with each other, one of which... became a guiding central authority. However, this latter community had no executive power at its disposal; it could not be very strong. On the other hand, the invasions of nomadic herdsmen were able to unite the small agricultural communities into a state only when the herdsmen found such a central power already in existence and took over its functions. Only now, through the military might of the conquerors, did this central power acquire the strength for greater accomplishments. . . .

We may well admit that the necessity of taming rivers created the need for a central authority and perhaps even brought forth the beginnings of one, but that only the formation of the state by a conquering tribe gave to the central authority the strength that enabled it to satisfy the needs of extensive water management. Only now did it become possible to concentrate the workers of all the villages at a single point for common undertakings... and to overcome the particularism of the villages.... It thus became possible for irrigation works to be constructed according to a plan. Their direction naturally devolved upon the directors of the state or to individual officials appointed by them especially for that purpose. These officials, being exclusively occupied with overseeing the irrigation works, accumulated a wealth of experience and thus acquired knowledge far greater than that of the common people, knowledge stored up and passed on within their narrow circle. It was not by means of higher learning that the rulers and exploiters of the state achieved their superior position. Rather, this position first created the conditions enabling the rulers to acquire higher learning than the bondsmen. Once acquired, it did then become a new pillar of their power.

CHAPTER ELEVEN

Irrigation Systems and State Government

If the need for a central authority arising out of the battle against the river had sufficed for the primitive agriculturalists themselves to create a state government corresponding to their needs, then one should think that, also in later times, this same need would always have to bring the peasants together to create anew such an apparatus whenever the already existing government of the state failed and neglected the irrigation system. Joining together to preserve something already existing, . . . the existence of which has become a necessity, as the entire process of production has been adapted to it, must be easier, after all, than joining together to construct something that is as yet untested and that one has hitherto done without. . . .

[Quoting from Müller, Der Islam, I, 467; II, 71, 507; Wachsmuth, Europäische Sittengeschichte, II, 509; Gibbon, The Decline and Fall of the Roman Empire, III, 61; and Daniels, Geschichte des Kriegswesens, II, 131, Kautsky devotes several pages to the Arabic conquests of Mesopotamia and Spain and the establishment and reestablishment of irrigation works there and their neglect by subsequent conquerors, especially the Ottoman Turks in the Near East and the Christians in Spain. Quoting from a long chapter on India he had written for, but omitted from, his first book, Der Einfluss der Volksvermehrung, Kautsky then deals with early British neglect of irrigation works in that country.]

All of these examples demonstrate what an important material basis of the power of the state the irrigation works were in the states of the Orient. On them depended all of agriculture, the most important source of food. We have also seen how the concern shown for these works depended entirely on the character of the ruling tribe, which was determinatively influenced by very diverse conditions of its life. But nowhere do we find an example of the emergence out of the peasantry of the beginnings of the formation of a state government for the purpose of building irrigation works that fulfilled this purpose. Where the state government that imposes itself from without fails, no factor arises from within that would be able to take over its functions. . . .

The necessity of common irrigation works did not overcome the isolation of the villages; it only increased the peasants' dependence on the state government, which, under the given conditions, was alone capable of creating such structures. . . . But prosperity did not accrue to the peasant as a result. Where the irrigation systems functioned, the yield of the peasants' labor was increased. But the surplus product did not remain in the peasant's hands; it was taken from him as taxes. *[Kautsky quotes Müler, Der Islam, I, 281– 82.]* . . .

Thus the improvement of agriculture by artificial irrigation has the same results as do all other advances made in the state. The state calls forth the advances; it furthers them; without it, they are not possible. But the state develops them under conditions that result in their advantages benefiting only the rulers and exploiters. The situation of the exploited and oppressed is not improved, it is often made worse by these advances.

CHAPTER TWELVE

The City—Industry and Art

. . . It is probable that as a result of the success of the irrigation works and of what was learned from constructing them, there arose in the rulers both the desire to build further structures on dry ground and the understanding required to do so. It was not the rulers who had to bear the burden of these structures, but the great mass of the corvée-laborers. An important inducement to erect such structures resulted from the second great function that accrued to the state government in the Orient, namely, providing protection against rapacious nomads, a function that was no less important than the struggle with the river. . . .

After a state had been founded, . . . there arose alongside the peasants' villages on suitable sites the permanent encampments of the conquerors. From these they were able to keep the conquered in check. As a rule, the main force settled in the center of the territory of the state; individual garrisons were stationed closer to the borders. . . . The conquerors came with their women and children and slaves, to which were added the servants their subjects had to supply. . . . The more extensive and densely populated the empire was and the greater the payments of tribute and the better the means of transportation were, the greater could these encampments and the more numerous could their populations be. But also all the greater were the riches that were stored up in them. . . .

The variety of these riches was increased by trade, which preferred to seek out such permanent encampments where it was most likely to find surpluses of products for which it could exchange the products that it itself brought. These encampments were usually also favorably situated for trade, since care was taken to locate them . . . where several roads coming from different regions intersected. . . . Thus, as the state grew in extent, the permanent encampments . . . became centers where the riches of traders and *[warriors]* accumulated. . . . In consequence, however, the temptation also became greater for the poor nomads occasionally to assemble on the borders of the state in order to attack such an encampment at a favorable moment. . . . There thus arose sooner or later the necessity of enclosing every permanent encampment of the conquering tribe with a wall in order to protect its inhabitants. Only rarely did a conquering tribe forgo building such a wall. . . .

[The wall] made of the encampment a city. Like so much else we have already pointed out here, the city, too, is a product of the state. That is not to say that every city of more recent origin was initially a permanent encampment. We shall become acquainted with yet other kinds of cities.[7] But we may certainly assume that the first cities originated in this manner. *[Kautsky quotes Müller, Der Islam, I, 274–75.]* The older and more extensive a state was, the larger and richer were its cities, but also the greater, on account of the waterworks alone, was the experiential knowledge of the ruling classes or at any rate of their agents in the field of construction. And

7. See IV:6:1, IV:7:4, below.

lastly, the more numerous were the workers from among their subjects who were at their disposal. Thus very huge encircling walls could ultimately be erected. *[Kautsky quotes* Herodotus *(Book I, chs. 178–79), I, 89–90, on the walls of Babylon, and* Genesis, *II, 1–5, on the tower of Babel.]*

No less important for a ruling class than material power is moral power: prestige. The greater it is, . . . the less does the ruling class have to make use of material means of power. Demonstrating their power to their own people and to neighboring peoples becomes a task that occupies the rulers of every state to a very great degree. . . . In addition to fortifications, edifices built for the sake of prestige became an object of zealous concern for the kings and the mighty in the state: the erection of magnificent dwelling-places for the living and the dead, . . . above all, however, for the gods of the ruling tribe, not only in order to secure their favor—for they were thought to be as hungry for prestige as were the rulers themselves—but also to make manifest far and wide their superiority over the gods of other tribes. . . . At first these structures were supposed to arouse awe for the rulers of the country, the living and the dead, the mortals and the immortals. But to the degree that exploitation became more extensive, that its foundation became firmer and appeared to be less threatened, the desire for pleasure grew in addition to the desire for power. Then the original severity and gloominess of these edifices gave way. . . . Whether ominous or cheerful, though, they were always supposed . . . agreeably to affect the particular sense of beauty of the viewers. Not practicality but aesthetic effect became the most important consideration for structures of this kind.

The master builder, who organizes and directs the construction work according to plan, now becomes an architect, who not only has to achieve stability and usefulness of the building, but also an aesthetic effect. The problems of the builders now become increasingly complicated; the knowledge required for their solution becomes ever greater. . . . The workers must now also know how to shape columns and walls beautifully and adorn the spaces enclosed by them with works of painting or of plastic art, according to the architect's intentions. . . . A state government that has hundreds of thousands of corvée-laborers or slaves at its disposal can now introduce a division of labor among them. . . . The operations of handicraft and of the graphic and plastic arts, which were carried on amateurishly in the prestate period by every member of the tribe with more or less skill, in addition to other kinds of work, now, in the state, become the businesses of particular occupations, . . . although that is true . . . at first only of those who served the luxury of the powerful exploiters in the state. . . . Impressive pomp could also be developed in furniture, implements of the most diverse kinds, tableware, carpets, jewelry, and articles of clothing. . . .

Skilled workers could not be taken from among the corvée-laborers who had to render service for a few months a year and then returned to their villages to till the land. They came from among the bond-servants who were permanently integrated into the household of a magnate as bought slaves, as prisoners of war, or as tribute paid by the subjugated. . . . In order to make the number of available workers more adaptable to the changing demand, the lords hit upon the device of permitting some of their workers, when they did not need them just then, to work for others in return for compensation they had to share with their master. . . . In this way many bond-servants were able to acquire a little wealth and to buy themselves free. Others were set free as a reward for especially good accomplishments. . . . As soon as a demand for free craftsmen arose in the city, the sons of free peasants immigrated to it. As a rule, the peasantry produced a surplus population, while in the city crowding soon created such unhealthy conditions that the number of deaths surpassed the number of births there. Every city would soon have died out if the ranks of its population had not been filled again by constant immigration. . . . Finally, some few free handicrafts had already developed in the prestate period when circumstances were favorable. The rulers of the state gladly drafted people who had knowledge of particular arts. . . .

Thus the number of free craftsmen and artists in the city grew in very different ways. It reduced the number of those in bondage who finally in some instances disappeared completely. . . . At the same time, however, a new way of employing bond-servants developed: slaves who worked or produced not for the needs of their master but for others on orders of their master. . . . Or an entrepreneur could employ many slaves in a workshop producing commodities for the market. Slave workshops of this kind became dangerous competition for free workers. . . . Special trades [are] necessary for those elements of the city living outside of a large household that was provisioned by the peasants' payments in kind. Thus there arose the trades of baker, butcher, cookshop proprietor, and retail merchant as well as of those weavers and builders who did not produce for [the magnates'] luxury.

As a result of this whole development, there emerged, in addition to . . . foreign trade, a new kind of exchange of commodities among individual producers within the polity, and there originated commodity production in the strict sense. . . . The free worker in the city . . . sets out to produce what he does not want to consume himself in order to get in exchange for it that which he needs. He does not just bring surpluses to market, but rather his entire product. If he cannot sell it, he is threatened in his very existence. It becomes much more insecure than that of the peasant in the countryside. The city is the soil out of which grows commodity production.

Commerce itself also takes on another character now. . . . The objects of commerce now include, in addition to the products limited by nature to certain areas, the products of industries that achieve especially great productivity in certain cities. . . . Much as natural conditions affect the development of particular industries, it is social and political conditions brought about by the formation of the state and ... of the city that become decisive for them. ... Within the city, both commerce and industry are from the outset the business of private entrepreneurs. That also reacts back on foreign trade. Here, too, tribal trade and the princes' monopoly over trade yield more and more to private commerce. In both foreign and domestic trade, mere barter ultimately no longer suffices. Trade in commodities within the city requires money as much as does foreign trade. In turn, that intensifies the need of the mighty in the realm to transform the taxes paid in kind by their peasants into money-taxes, an undertaking that, to be sure, continues to encounter great difficulties for a long time.

As a result of all of that, life in the city, in contrast with the monotony and simplicity of village life, becomes increasingly more colorful, more diverse, more noisy. But it also becomes more stimulating due to the concentration of very varied occupations in a very narrow space. The arts and the sciences now take a rapid upturn in their development, in striking contrast to the immobility and unchangeability of the village. This rapid development became possible only through the state, which brought forth the city.

CHAPTER THIRTEEN

Rise and Decline

Ever since the city appeared, there is not just a glaring difference between it and the countryside, but also a sharp antagonism that becomes determinative for the forms of many class antagonisms. For the city lives completely from ... the products of the peasant's labor, without giving him in return corresponding quantities of its own products. That is to say, this is true for the Orient and for antiquity, but not for our own time. We are not yet speaking of the latter here, as we must point out again and again.

The fact that the city lives from the exploitation of the peasant by the ruling classes is obvious where the peasant delivers taxes in kind to his lord, who maintains with them his household and his craftsmen and artists in the city. The relationship ceases to be recognizable at first glance when it is mediated by money. Money has, generally speaking, the property of obscuring exploitative relationships. When the peasant must pay taxes in the form of money, he brings the natural products that represent his duties not directly to his lord, but to the market in the city. ... For his commodities he receives the proper value. All exploitation appears to be excluded. But ... he must surrender this value entirely or in large part as taxes and returns to his village empty-handed or with very few industrial products. The effect of the money-tax, then, is that the households of the lords of the state purchase agricultural products for their own consumption, they employ craftsmen and artists, and finally they buy foreign products from the merchants. In sum, its effect is to supply the city with sustenance. Thus the circuit of commodity production repeats itself, starting anew again and again, but always in such a way that the peasant only supplies products without receiving others in return for them. . . .

The learned men, the artists, and the many craftsmen of the city produced nothing that the peasant needed and yet they lived from his products. They found buyers for their own commodities and services only in the ruling family and the nobility, among the warriors and the priests, who paid them with the yield of the peasants' exploitation. . . . The workers of the cities therefore considered, at least in the Orient, the great lords not as their exploiters but as their patrons, to whom they owed gratitude and subservience. On the other hand, it would not have occurred to even the most servile peasant to see the king and lord to whom he paid taxes as the one to whom he owed his livelihood. All of urban civilization was built upon the exploitation of the peasant masses. The more extensive these masses and their exploitation were, the higher could civilization in the city rise.

But even in the city itself, this civilization was not distributed uniformly. The basis of urban civilization was the fact that it became possible to free numerous workers from the necessity of agricultural labor to make them available to perform other labors for their masters. The more such workers could be maintained and kept working with the same means, the more numerous and immense were the works they created. That means, then, that the lower the standard of living of the laboring masses in the city and the countryside and the lower the level of their civilization was, the higher was the level of the civilization that they produced for their rulers, the civilization of a few thousand exploiters, that grew up out of the lack of civilization of millions subject to servitude and exploitation. That numerous workers labored for some few who benefited from it explains why such rich resources and stimulants for civilizing advancement accumulated in the hands of those few, and why civilization could in the state, at least for its rulers, flourish with a rapidity and attain a level that were altogether inconceivable in the prestate stage of development.

But, on the other hand, the basis on which this upswing of civilization occurred also accounts for the fact that it was of a very uncertain nature and encountered limits it was unable to transcend. It was built on the foundation of the forced labor of bond-servants, serfs, and slaves. To be sure, alongside these a stratum of free workers came into existence, which could become very extensive, but which constantly had to compete with unfree labor, whose standard of living became determinative for all workers. Forced labor is reluctant labor. . . . Fine instruments of labor cannot be entrusted to unfree workers. . . . The free worker, who is in control of the product of his activity himself, has a far greater interest in his work. He works eagerly and with precision, and even in antiquity finally achieves the highest degree of what . . . can be achieved with simple tools. . . . Even the most skilled and experienced artist or craftsman of antiquity and of the Orient . . . does not seek to perfect the instruments of his labor. Only very rarely does he possess the means to do so. But when he has them, he uses them to buy slaves and to make the latter work for him. In this case, he himself ceases to be a worker. . . . The free worker of antiquity and of the Orient remains an impecunious solitary worker, a poor wretch at the edge of misery. . . .

Thus we find one barrier to technological development in antiquity and the Orient in the *servitude* of labor, which brings forth conditions and methods of thinking that force even free labor down to a level precluding a more highly developed technology. There is, in addition, another barrier consisting in the *enormous cheapness* of human labor in the city and the countryside, which allows its masters to squander it boundlessly. The peasants subject to the corvée, the slaves captured in war, and even the free workers in the cities were completely incapable of resisting their masters and employers. Everything that these workers put to their own use was regarded by the ruling class as an improper curtailment of the product of their labor. . . . All the artistic and technical greatness of antiquity and of the huge realms of the Orient up to the present time—to the extent that they are not the result of a highly developed division of labor among the occupations and of wonderful manual dexterity—is based on the employment of immense masses of men, minimally nourished and almost completely unclothed, and on the most ruthless squandering of their labor power.

In these circumstances, the rulers' inflexible intent, pursued with unbending energy, is to supply the state again and again with new workers who are incapable of resistance, unfree workers. Any effort to acquire labor-saving machines and thus to increase the productivity of labor is thereby precluded. All interest is concentrated on the one method that is most likely to secure an abundant supply of unresisting labor: *war*. War supplies sufficient new masses of workers, either through the acquisition of prisoners of war or of new tracts of land, the cultivators of which become serfs of the conquerors. Under these conditions, the interest of the ruling classes is directed to the technology of war, not that of production. The most important technical advances of antiquity were made in the area of war material, in addition to that of luxury articles. . . . In the area of production for the consumption of the masses, on the other hand, there is no technical progress worth mentioning in the period of the state we have been considering so far, unless it be a few scraps that fall from the table of the luxury and weapons industries. *[Kautsky quotes Beloch, Griechische Geschichte, II/1, 87, on the primitive agriculture of Greece in the Periclean age.]*

This wretched foundation of the magnificent civilization created directly or indirectly by the state does not, however, just set definite limits to that civilization, which it cannot transcend. Its existence is thereby also made very insecure. The unfree workers, especially the slaves, often live in conditions that strongly inhibit their natural propagation and frequently make it completely impossible. When this is the case, the level of production and civilization that has been reached . . . cannot be maintained at all, unless war constantly provides it with new masses of unfree workers. . . . Continuous war then becomes a condition of life of state civilizations, or, rather, continuous victory. For defeat, of course, brings no influx of new workers; it is more likely to result in the loss of already available ones. Thus civilization becomes dependent on the extent of the military strength of the ruling class. As the latter dwindles, so does the former also. *[Kautsky cites Periclean Athens and Rome as examples.]*

If the city-states of the Mediterranean perished from depopulation, due in large part to the fact that the peasantry, the reservoir of workers for the city and its civilization, was supplanted by slaves, the same is not true of the realms of the Orient located on the great rivers of that region. There peasant agriculture provided large surpluses and a slightly increasing population. . . . Production and civilization could maintain themselves even when the supply of slaves decreased or failed entirely. But the preservation of the irrigation works became all the more important there. . . . An oriental state could perish just because of its military strength, if the latter was strained to such an extent that the irrigation systems were neglected as a consequence. . . . Thus here, too, we find everywhere retrogression and decay of the civilization that was rapidly raised by the state to magnificent heights, until the same motive forces that created the state undermined its economic foundation and thereby the state itself.

The state follows a different path in [India and especially China]. . . . Hand in hand with their great natural wealth goes, as long as the irrigation works are kept in good repair, an exceedingly numerous peasant population, which produces considerable surpluses and with its taxes makes possible sumptuous wealth for the ruling classes. This wealth, in turn, provides work for a numerous urban population composed of very diverse occupations. . . . The enormously large numbers of very cheap workers in the city and the countryside makes it possible for these workers to be employed in a wasteful manner. Upon this wastefulness was built the entire process of production in the state in East Asia just as in western Asia (and Egypt) and in southern Europe, the differences in natural conditions notwithstanding. Thus nowhere did there arise an impetus to seek labor-saving machines and methods. In eastern Asia, too, the entire interest of those who controlled the process of production was directed to placing that process at the service of the rulers' luxury. The entire amazing progress of China's technology took place almost solely in the luxury industries.

Once China had attained such an extent that beyond its territory there was nothing worth having, once this state had created an administrative apparatus that functioned smoothly, and once its industry had reached the utmost of what could be achieved with simple tools, . . . then the limit had been reached up to which this kind of state was able to advance. For the poor wretches in the city and the countryside, all the preconditions for the attainment of any further technical advances were lacking. For the ruling classes, on the other hand, no new problems arose in connection with either foreign or domestic policy, which could have caused them to look for new means of solving them. They sank into a monotonous, mechanical repetition of traditional ways of acting and thinking.

This kind of state did not die from depopulation. Nor did it decay because of excessive strain on its military forces and of neglect of the tasks required of it by its civilization, the most important of which was the maintenance of the irrigation works. But it did petrify into the mindless conservatism that is often considered to be a racial characteristic of the Chinese. However, this conservatism, as well as the lack of martial inclination of the Chinese, which results from the same conditions, immediately comes to an end, as soon as a strong shock from without produces new problems. China and, to a lesser degree, also India have been able to maintain the civilization created by the state without interruption down to the present time. But they show us what the limits of this civilization were even where extraordinarily favorable circumstances saved them from downfall. These limits were in the last analysis based on the fact that . . . the growth of wealth and power and of knowledge, which resulted from the state, is confined only to its upper classes. . . .

CHAPTER FOURTEEN
Civilization and Its Decay

[Kautsky quotes Robertson, The Evolution of States, *p. 170, on the decline of all ancient civilizations.]* Of what kind is the civilization that must necessarily come to decay? Is every rise of civilization, every higher-level cultivated polity, necessarily destined from the outset to end in decay? . . . The law of necessary decay as the end result of development applies only to a particular stage, not to culture as such. By culture we understand the sum of all accomplishments that raise man above the natural condition and that in the last analysis are based on his technology. The division of the development of culture into three stages, savagery, barbarism, and civilization, is quite widespread today. . . . If we characterize these three stages . . . , we will have to give a summary of the foregoing discussions of social development. *[There follows such a summary of what Kautsky had said earlier about prestate social development of hunters (the stage of savagery) and pastoralists and agriculturalists (the stage of barbarism).]*

It is not cultural progress in the stage of savagery, nor that in barbarism, but only that in civilization that is condemned, or at least was heretofore condemned, to end in decay or stagnation. What is the cause of this phenomenon? Could it be that a more sophisticated understanding of the world, a higher degree of mastery over the world by means of advanced technology, as well as an advance in the development of art, finally lead to paralysis or corruption of the human spirit? That seems absurd on the face of it, and not the least proof for it can be found, Jean-Jacques Rousseau notwithstanding. No, if the cultural advance occurring in civilization has hitherto always ended differently than in savagery and in barbarism, then that is due not to the particular *fruits* of civilization, but to the particular *soil* from which these fruits grow, in contrast to the soil of savagery and barbarism. In the first two stages of culture, this soil was formed by homogeneous polities with free and equal members who lived from their own labor. Nor does that change in the more highly developed stages of barbarism. Slavery and pillage are, to be sure, prejudicial to general equality and freedom and to living from one's own labor, but they do not yet become the indispensable foundations of social existence.

The existence of the state, however, is erected from the outset on the exploitation of alien workers. . . . The great mass remains in the stage of barbarism even after civilization has developed to a high degree. This barbarism, however, now acquires a new countenance through its contrast with the results of civilization, even when it apparently remains unchanged. That is almost never the case, though. The laboring masses are often depressed below the standard of living of the free barbarians of the prestate stage. Broad strata of the laboring population now find themselves in distress and misery such as occur only occasionally in the stage of barbarism as a result of exceptionally occurring natural catastrophes but now become a permanent state of affairs even under the most favorable natural conditions. And the freedom, the strength, the self-confidence that are characteristic of free barbarians as well as savages are completely lost to the laboring masses in the state.

This contrast between barbarism and civilization within the polity and society and the progressive degradation of the barbarian basis accompanied by the progressive elevation of the civilized superstructure—that is the contradiction that as yet no civilization has been able to overcome and that causes it, at best, finally to become rigid, but generally to degenerate. Those who consider society and the state as organisms, like biological ones, see in this rigidification and degeneration a natural process that . . . is as inevitable as aging and death. Savagery and barbarism constitute the youth and the manhood of society; civilization, its old age.[8] . . .

But it is by no means a law of nature that the conditions of civilization

---

8. See also III:2:16, above.

must always remain the same. Civilization can finally reach a stage in which it is possible to let the masses who perform the work required by that civilization have the fruits of their labor in the fullest measure and to transform their activity from labor for a minority in the polity, and a minority, moreover, consisting of their class enemies, into work for themselves, that is, for their own class or for the whole society. Once civilization has reached this point, culture can again, without interruption, grow and thrive under it, just as under savagery and barbarism. No longer will it be exposed to aging, to decline, due to internal causes. External causes could, of course, still bring about its decay even then, for example, the coming of a new ice age. But a conception of history has to reckon not with geological, but with historical eras. For us, the only question to be considered is whether we have already reached the point of being able to transform civilization from an affair of the upper ten thousand into an affair of the totality of civilized nations. We socialists answer this question in the affirmative. As we shall see, we have every reason for doing so.

Section Five
The First Forms of the State

CHAPTER ONE

Aging of the State and Aging of Civilization

... If we have recognized the causes that have heretofore led again and again to an aging of civilizations, that does not free us from the necessity of also investigating the causes of the aging of states. Both are equally necessary for an understanding of the historical process. To this end, we must consider yet another kind of effect of the state, ... its *political* effects.

CHAPTER TWO

The Democracy of the Vanquished

When the state is formed, at first it seems that politically nothing of importance changes for the subjugated population, at least not when this process occurs in peaceful forms. . . . One must not believe, as do many even at the present time, for example, the Communists, that every antagonism among peoples and classes can only be fought out by bloody war. But, it is certainly just as foolish to believe that when two opponents reach a peaceable understanding, the persuasiveness of their arguments will be decisive and not the strength of the instruments of power at their disposal. Given sufficient knowledge of the situation and intelligence on both sides, however, these instruments of power need not be put to the test. . . . War is always a product of ignorance of the relations of forces on one side and the other. . . .

If the peasants had voluntarily accepted their new masters, then there was no reason to deprive the individual villages of their self-government. On the contrary, this self-government must have been desirable also to the ruling tribe, which, after all, at the beginning of the state had no administrative apparatus that would have been able to assume to a sufficient degree the tasks of this self-government. . . . And yet a fundamental change had to occur, if only because the peasants' mark community or village community ceased being a sovereign polity and henceforth formed only part of such a polity. . . . The more the state expanded, relatively the more insignificant did the affairs of the local community become, which alone could still be settled democratically by the laboring classes. . . . The laboring masses had nothing more to say when it was a matter of the relationship of their own local community to other such communities in the state, let alone when it was a matter of the relationship of their state to other states. . . . The conquering tribe that set up the state did not need to take away from the laboring masses any rights they had previously exercised; it simply denied them access to newly emerged functions. The more the state grew and the more extensive and complex these functions became, the more they also require knowledge and abilities that the peasants and craftsmen, given their class position, were not able to acquire. . . .

Since war is merely the continuation of foreign policy, with the monopolization of that policy by the ruling class the decision over war and peace is put exclusively into the hands of the latter. The same is true of the responsibility for military affairs. The state rests from the outset on the martial skills and powers of its ruling class. . . . Hence its primary attention is devoted to military matters, both to the preservation and greatest possible perfection of its own military strength and to the organization of the military strength of its subjects.[1] . . .

The dominance of the ruling class in military matters is made all the easier as, just as in savagery and barbarism, also for a long time in the state . . . every warrior must provide his equipment himself. . . . In the state, weapons technology, above all else, is developed to a high degree along with technical skill. Perfected weapons then become . . . quite unaffordable for the common man. Like his knowledge and his skill, his technology, too, mostly does not advance beyond the level of barbarism. The magnificent and terrible weapons of civilization remain re-

1. See IV:3:7, above.

served to the aristocrats, . . . who also alone have the time to practice their use. In battle they are at the forefront. . . . The aristocrats were also experts with regard to war, in comparison with the poorly armed contingents of peasants, who were mere dilettantes. Where warlike tribes were incorporated into the state as subjects, the attempt was made either to disarm them completely, sometimes even to wipe them out—at least their men—or, when it was possible to negotiate with them, to bribe them and to place them at the service of the ruling class and under its supreme command as mercenaries. . . .

The monopolization of foreign policy and of leadership in war by the aristocracy characterizes the state from its first beginnings onward. The aristocracy is so profoundly bound up with the nature of the state that even today the nobility in all modern states that still have one include the diplomatic and the officer corps among its particular domains, even though . . . since the emergence of capitalist industry, the character of the state has greatly changed.

. . . Another area that is administered without asking the subjects for their opinions . . . is the establishment of the amount of tribute. . . . The taxes paid to the state are at first imposed not on the individual subjects—in its beginnings the state lacks the bureaucratic apparatus for doing so—but on the local community. . . . How the latter shifts the taxes onto its members is a matter that at first is left up to it. . . . When nothing changes in the state for a long time, then the taxes, like many other ordinances, acquire the character of customary law. But apart from the force of custom, there is no other power that could prevent the state from squeezing out of its subjects as much as it can get from them. . . .

Very different degrees of combativeness and of love of freedom are possible among the various tribes, depending on the geographical conditions in which they live and work. . . . Hence in its attempts to establish or to expand a state, the conquering tribe very often encounters more or less stubborn resistance that is not easily broken. If its efforts are nevertheless successful, then the defeated tribe is of course not treated leniently. Heavy burdens are imposed on it; its weapons are taken from it; its self-government is restricted as much as the initial lack of a fully formed apparatus of domination allows. A bailiff from the ruling class, backed up by a sufficiently large armed force, is placed over the vanquished. The knowledge and regulations resulting from this arrangement then easily serve to restrict self-government even of the subjugated tribes that are better treated, should friction occur between them and the state government.

Still another factor works to this same end. . . . The chieftain, as the representative of his tribe, is now responsible not just to the latter, as before, but also to the ruling tribe. The more he becomes its servant, the more does he cease to be the servant of his own people, the more does he achieve the position of a lord vis-à-vis his own people, who leans for his support on a power independent of and standing above the people, the power of the conquerors. . . . The chieftains might still be elected by their tribe. The chieftain's superior power, however, can now also enable him to make his office hereditary in his family, at least when he secures the support of the state government for doing so. Under these conditions, the families of chieftains of the conquered tribes can become a new kind of nobility, lower in rank than the nobility formed by the tribe of the conquerors, but above their own tribe. . . .

Whether through the raising of the chieftains above the community of their own people or through the imposition of bailiffs from the ruling class, in any case the leading offices of the original self-government of the tribes and local communities sooner or later become independent of these, until finally the development of a bureaucracy more or less eliminates even the remnants of self-government. And, in addition, the entire policy of the state that stands above the tribes and the local communities, the organization of the state as a whole, its foreign policies, its military and financial systems, are in any case from the outset outside the domain of primitive democracy. Thus, with the formation of the state the death knell is sounded for the democratic rights of the subjects, of the great mass of the population.

CHAPTER THREE
The Democracy of the Victors

To a far greater degree than the subjugated tribes and villages, the conquering tribe or association of tribes is at first able to preserve its democracy within the state. . . . But the democracy of the victors, too, acquires from the start—although in a quite different sense than the democracy of their "subjects"—a new character that sullies the purity of that democracy and paves the way for its eventual downfall. From the beginnings of the state onward, democracy within the ruling tribe is a means of settling not only its own tribal affairs in the narrower sense, but also the affairs of the state, that is, the common affairs of all tribes incorporated into it. Without their participation, the ruling tribe runs the state for them and often also against them. . . . Thus in relation to the subjects, democracy within the ruling tribe becomes a means of ruling and exploiting them, hence precisely the opposite of the democracy that existed in the prestate tribe.

Even when its democracy continues to exist unchanged, the ruling tribe becomes, in the new state polity, an aristocracy with a privileged position, which jealously guards against the intrusion of any of its subjects into its ranks. . . . The victorious tribes . . . were based on kinship-organizations and only needed strictly to maintain these in order to safeguard their aristocratic position. The victorious tribe immediately constituted a hereditary nobility, which permitted marriages only with persons of equal rank and only recognized as nobles children from such marriages. Engels was of the opinion that "rule over subjugated people is incompatible with the gentile constitution" (*The Origin of the Family*, p. 311). In reality, we must, rather, assume that this constitution acquires a new source of strength through this rule. ... For the peasant who is tied to the soil, his neighbor, even when the latter is not related to him, becomes more important than a member of the same lineage living far away.... Thus the gentile constitution continues to be preserved for a long time among the aristocrats after it has disappeared in the mass of the people....

The isolation by marriage and by kinship of the ruling tribe from its subjects is accomplished most easily when both parties belong to different cultures, for example, religions, or to different races.... The superiority that helped the ruling tribe to gain its position is then usually attributed, not to the peculiarity of its mode of production that developed in it the abilities of the conqueror, but to its innate racial character.... Not concern for fending off intrusion by the plebeians into its privileged position, but only concern for preserving the purity of its noble blood is supposed to have led to the nobility's strict regulations governing marriage and inheritance.

The nobility does not, however, seek to maintain its position as a privileged minority solely through such concern. This position rests upon its military superiority.... Every activity not compatible with its martial strength, training, and readiness is rejected by the ruling tribe as not "appropriate to its status," as a humiliation. It remains reserved to the subjects. ... Among these activities is that of the merchant, which, ancient as international trade is, arises as the activity of a particular occupation only in the state.... One of the reasons for this is that trade... compelled the merchant to be absent from his home again and again.... That was hardly compatible with constant readiness for war against internal and external enemies....

Further, there was also the fact that the mentality of the warrior and ruler hardly agrees with that of the merchant. The warrior and ruler commands. He breaks the will of others with his superior means of power.... Courting good will is not appropriate to the status of the warrior and ruler. He is permitted to assume the role of usurer; ... for as such, he also dictates his conditions to someone dependent on him. But the aristocrat may not negotiate with "commoners" in order to gain their favor, as the merchant does. Even more despised, naturally, is all work done by poor wretches, by subordinates, hence every craft. *[Kautsky quotes Socrates' contemptuous view of craftsmen as summarized by Drumann,* Die Arbeiter und Communisten in Griechenland und Rom, *p. 26.]*

Aristocrats and Art

We know that man has, from his beginnings, possessed artistic proclivities, disinterested pleasure in certain forms, colors, tones, and rhythms. With the development of technology, he learns . . . also to produce what he perceives as beautiful. Under primitive conditions, every man is an art expert and an artist, although everyone does not have the same talent. The state and the division into classes tears asunder, like many another, also the aesthetic function into two parts. One man enjoys art; the other produces it, as his occupation, no longer for himself but for the one who enjoys it, from whom he receives commissions and the wherewithal so that he can practice art according to the ideas of his patrons.[2] This dependent position is incompatible with the spirit of the aristocracy. Much as it values the arts that furnish special attractions to their pleasurable life, that enhance their pomp and their prestige, the aristocracy nevertheless despises those whose occupation it is to produce art no less than the craftsmen from whose midst the former emerged. *[Kautsky quotes Aristotle's* Politics, *VIII, ch. 2, §§ 3, 5; ch. 3, §§ 7, 12; ch. 6, § 15 (pp. 230–32, 239), saying that young men should learn drawing and music but not well enough to please others, which is craftsmen's work and hence vulgar and unworthy of free men, and, similarly, Plutarch, "Pericles," 1, 2, in* Plutarch's Lives, *II, 2.]*

Nothing could be more mistaken than to assume that the character of the art of a country and a period is merely the product of the artists practicing there. They are themselves the product of their social environment. No less than by them is the character of artworks . . . determined by those who supply the artists with their commissions and the means for carrying them out or who buy their finished works from them. They are the ones who make a selection among artists and artworks as these engage in their struggle for survival. The orientation dominant in art at any given time is the artistic orientation of the ruling classes at that time. That remains true to this day. . . .

The Aristocracy and Science

The state also creates the conditions . . . for raising the study of the interrelations of things to the status of a special occupation, that of science.[3] Through the development of commerce and the elaboration of writing, the

---

2. See II : 5 : 1–3, above.
3. See also IV : 4 : 7, above.

state unites in some centers a rapidly growing wealth of knowledge that requires ordering and compilation into a coherent total complex of inter-relations. But the state also creates the men who are able to devote themselves to this task to a greater extent than would have been possible in the prestate stage. . . .

It now happens that members of the aristocracy devote themselves to science. To be sure, they engage in science as little as in art for purposes of economic gain. Although their living conditions allow them to occupy themselves with music and poetry, they forbid them to practice the plastic and graphic arts, which have too much of the craft about them. As for science, the study of nature interests them less. Conquering men, repressing and commanding men, that is what they consider to be their task. Nature cannot be commanded, and whoever wants to rule over nature must first patiently subordinate himself to it. That does not correspond to the kind of thinking of aristocrats, which their social functions develop in them. Certainly, their position in life raises them above the great multitude. In some circumstances—this was the case especially in trading cities—this position made much new knowledge accessible to them that could not be reconciled with the traditional collective ideas of the masses. Then the aristocrats' leisure and independence could give rise to speculations about the world in its totality, to a natural philosophy. . . .

Much more than in their natural philosophy, the thinkers among the aristocrats exhibited their contrast to the common people in their thoughts about the state. The state, which seemed to them to be synonymous with themselves, preoccupied them above all else. Most important to them are their own actions and aspirations in the state and through the state. . . . Above all, aristocrats are enabled by their position in life to write history. They are, after all, the ones who, in the stages of the state we are discussing here, make what is called history, the history of the states, of their governments, their wars, their upheavals. As soon as writing was invented, one of its first effects consisted in enabling the rulers of states to pass on to posterity reports about their successes (naturally, not about their defeats). . . . Of course, such accounts take on a scientific character only when they assemble a quite large number of facts, order them clearly, and establish coherence among them. . . .

Philosophizing about state activities was added to its *descriptions*. The scientific study of the state became much more important than natural philosophy, that is, the detachment of the man of rank from popular religion, when lower classes threatened to rise and to undermine . . . the rule of the aristocracy and at the same time caused very diverse circumstances to emerge, as was the case especially in some cities of Greece. A variety of speculations now arose about the best state, the best ethics to preserve the state, and the best training in these ethics. At the same time, however, the people of superior rank also became ever more free in the choice of their manner of living. This occasioned reflection about which way of conducting one's life resulted in the greatest personal satisfaction, the greatest personal happiness. . . .

Although the accomplishments of some individual aristocrats in some fields of knowledge were very important, nevertheless military matters and the activity of ruling remained the principal occupation of the great majority of them; and their class was incapable by far of supplying all the personnel required by the intellectual occupations to perform the tasks set them by the civilization that was growing in and through the state. The mass of intellectuals had to come from the classes beneath the aristocracy. . . . Some of them served the aristocrats or the state as slaves; many scraped by as free servants or as parasites of an aristocratic patron of the arts and sciences. Others lived in the position of free craftsmen. Yet others belonged to an aristocracy driven out of its position as ruler by a conqueror, an aristocracy barred from military service for whom intellectual pursuits were the only means of preserving for themselves a position above the great multitude.

From time to time, organizations of intellectuals succeeded, under favorable circumstances, in attaining a position of equal rank with the military aristocracy. In some cases they even succeeded in attaining supreme rule in the state, as did the Catholic Church in the medieval West or the organizations of Buddhist monks in Tibet. To be sure, such turns of events as a rule presupposed that these organizations became indispensable for the preservation of the state, that there either was no military aristocracy or it consumed itself in internal strife, and that those ruling organizations of intellectuals succeeded in acquiring extensive land holdings along with control over the labor cultivating them. . . .

Between the two extremes of slavery and magnificent dominion, we find innumerable shadings and variations in the situation of the intellectuals of different periods, and in the same period and the same country in the situation of the different occupations and organizations of intellectuals, and even among individual intellectuals. In their totality, they do not constitute a special class with special class interests. . . . They are divided into numerous occupations, whose interests and modes of thought bring them close now to one, now to another of the great classes of society, for whose class struggles they can often become important, indeed indispensable, by virtue of their superior knowledge.[4] But until the emergence of capitalist industry, they are almost never spokesmen and defenders of the laboring classes, but rather the often very willing, indeed enthusiastic servants of the aristocracy and of its state. . . . When the lower classes were for once sufficiently favored

4. See also IV:7:16, below.

by circumstances to be able to display stirrings of opposition, it is not surprising, then, that they regarded the sciences with hostility or at least with distrust, and branded them as inventions of the devil.

CHAPTER SIX

Monarchy

Like every animal organism, every social structure, too, must have a head, which effects the unity of its volition and its actions. And in a society of animals or men, this head can consist only of an individual of the species in question. A social will is an abstraction. Only the individual animal or the individual man can will. . . . To say that every social organization must have a leader or director does not yet tell us anything at all about how he is appointed to this function and what kind of powers he has. . . . Human societies become so complex . . . that a leadership founded on mere prestige rests on too uncertain a basis. And men are enabled by their language explicitly to designate individual persons as people whom they deem trustworthy and to demarcate precisely both their tasks and their powers, even if at first not on principle, not once and for all in advance but rather from case to case, whenever a new situation causes a doubt to arise. . . . The selection of the chieftain, his dependence on the trust and the approval of his tribe . . . belong to the most important characteristics of primitive democracy, as it existed in human polities prior to the formation of the state.

This situation undergoes a fundamental change in the state, even when the dependence of the chieftain on the tribe that chooses him at first continues to exist, both in the tribes of the vanquished and in those of the conquerors. . . . On the one hand, the defeated have their own chieftain, whom they have chosen themselves. He sometimes has . . . the might of the conquering tribe behind him vis-à-vis those who elected him. This diminishes his dependence of the latter and bestows on him a position superior to that of his fellows. On the other hand, the defeated are now also faced with the chieftain of their conquerors. Him they did not choose; he is not dependent on them. He represents for them the whole might of the victorious tribe. . . . Every single member of the ruling tribe is a higher being for the defeated, to whom they must submit, a demigod. But the chieftain of the conquerors appears to them as the lord of the demigods, even as a kind of supreme divinity. This chieftain might remain dependent on his own tribe, on the aristocracy, to a high degree; in relation to the mass of the people he becomes an absolute ruler.

Even in relation to his own tribe, however, his power grows. . . . Tribes distinguished early on between chieftains for peacetime and those for war. Like their functions, their powers, too, were different. . . . The peace-chieftain cannot do anything important without obtaining the advice of the elders or of the whole people. *[But]* in war... it is often necessary to decide rapidly, to act suddenly, ... [and] to follow the leader without hesitation, resolutely, and with unanimity.... Prior to the appearance of the state, democracy is preserved as long as peace is the normal condition and war is an exception. This situation changes considerably already for those nomads who... pillage weaker but richer neighboring tribes, ... *[and]* this change is further intensified in the state.... Even in peacetime, the ruling tribe must be constantly equipped and trained for war. War becomes its lifelong occupation; the nomadic tribe evolves into a warrior caste.... The war-chieftain is transformed form an occasional into a permanent functionary of the state; he becomes its permanent leader, its king....

When... conquering nomads were confronted with entire states to be overpowered, then certainly no single tribe was capable of playing the role of conqueror. Only a league of tribes had the strength to do so.... In such a league, not all tribes lived... in precisely the same geographic conditions, and therefore each one could develop particular inclinations, needs, and abilities.... The most warlike ones were most likely to provide the leader of the league, from a tribe and from a gens that had won special prestige in warfare. *[Kautsky quotes Herodotus, I, ch. 125, and III, ch. 97* (Herodotus, I, 66, 245) *on the various Persian tribes under Cyrus the Great.]*... The conquerors themselves... became aristocrats; the others remained free men... and paid no taxes.... To the nobility was allotted the tributary population and the leading positions in the military and in the state administration, which, instead of paying a salary, were also endowed with landholdings and tributary subjects. The tribe and that one of its gentes that had provided the league-chieftain and the commander-in-chief, the king, were accorded the highest rank....

Vis-à-vis the subjugated people, the king could find support in the tribes of the conquerors. Vis-à-vis these not entirely homogeneous tribes, who occupied the position in part of common freemen, in part of low-ranking nobles, he could mobilize the warlike masses of the privileged and wealthier tribes among the conquerors who were certainly better armed and trained in the use of weapons and had more to lose from a failure of the state apparatus. Most of all, however, the king could rely on his own tribe, which constituted the most unified organization within the aristocracy, had the greatest resources at its disposal, and to the greatest degree also defended its own preeminent position when it defended the ruling family.

... The more powerless the others became, the more likely was it that individual members of the great families, even the immediate relatives of the king, ... might be taken by the notion of rising up against the reigning king. The latter was thus led to employ for his personal protection elements who were personally dependent on him and did not come from the high-ranking nobility.... Finally, everywhere in the state, *mercenaries* come to be employed by the central government, mostly warlike nomads or adventurers from many different countries. . . . Intended for defense against external enemies or for new conquests, the mercenaries become the strongest force at the disposal of the king, who hires them, for use also against his enemies within the state, to whom they are not bound by ties of any kind. They constitute the culmination of the development of the ancient monarchy, which is freed through them from all tutelage on the part of its aristocrats. No one, it is true, escapes the moral influence of his surroundings. In the case of the king, that is an influence exercised not only by the lords of the court nobility, but also by the ladies of the harem, most of whom are slaves, by personal servants, and by eunuchs. But even when it is completely united, the aristocracy scarcely has any material means of coercion for imposing its will on the king, when mercenaries predominate in military affairs and are paid regularly, unless the king's opponents should be put in a position to enlist mercenaries, too, and in larger numbers than the king himself. . . .

In addition to mercenaries, there was also another factor that made monarchs independent of their aristocrats. . . . When the holder of a state office had to be recompensed for the troubles associated with that office and to be enabled to make the extravagant expenditures that would obtain for him the necessary prestige and the necessary means of power to be effective, then the method nearest at hand, and often the only possible one, was to endow the office with the appropriate landed property and the revenues connected with it. But the result of this was that the officeholder did not receive his pay and his means of power . . . from the king, but obtained them himself from his own property. There resulted a large degree of independence of the aristocratic officials vis-à-vis the monarchy as well as their endeavor to make the landed property, once it had been obtained, hereditary in their families. Since, however, the landed property belonged of right only to the one who held the office, the effort to make the property hereditary became the effort to make the office hereditary. If the landed property had at first been bestowed only as a bonus added to the office, now the office became an appurtenance of the landed property. This development is one of the most important causes of the tendency to make hereditary all state offices or all offices whatsoever that were linked to landed property. *[Kautsky refers to his discussion in* Vorläufer, *I, 51–52, of celibacy imposed on the Catholic priesthood, especially under Gregory VII, to prevent Church property from becoming hereditary.]* In fact, the monarchs, like the high officials appointed by them, usually succeeded in obtaining recognition of the hereditary character of their offices. . . .

The monarchs soon sought to fill state offices with persons who were not rewarded for their functions once and for all with landed property, but who received from the king only a certain salary that could be withheld from them immediately if they failed to fulfill the duties of their offices satisfactorily and that could not in any case confer a hereditary claim. The pay could consist of natural products. But . . . only officials at court, in the household of the king, could receive their pay in natural products directly from the royal storehouse. Officials outside the court had to rely on deliveries from their environs. That is, they often had to collect their salary themselves, which somewhat diminished their dependence on the monarch and, on the other hand, increased their dependence of the closest landowner. The officials became completely dependent on the monarchs . . . only when simple commodity production and with it the monetary system were far enough developed so that the king could impose money taxes and the officials were paid with money from the royal treasury.

The greater the number of officials in the state who were not invested with landed property, but were paid by the central government, the more independent did the latter become of the aristocracy. . . . The monarchs were fond of recruiting the instruments of their administration from the lower classes, in order to escape the tutelage of the nobility and to limit its power. They preferred most of all to take their officials from the ranks of the intellectuals, free or in bondage, organized (in priesthoods) or unorganized, who were most likely to possess the knowledge necessary for administering the state, above all, knowledge of reading and writing. *[Kautsky refers to the Chinese bureaucracy and quotes Preisigke,* Antikes Leben, *p. 24, on the ancient Egyptian bureaucracy.]* The development of such an apparatus of officials brought the absolute power of the ruler, who paid for it and on whom it was completely dependent, to its peak. Of course, there are always moral forces that influence him more or less. In all polities, in which nothing important changes for long periods of time, the power of tradition is a strong force which even the strongest individual does not like to oppose. Similarly, no one can avoid the influence of his everyday surroundings. . . . But in the stage that the state finally reaches everywhere in the Orient, there is, under normal circumstances, no material power that would be able to oppose the sovereign inside his country. . . .

This stage, however, is not only the high point but also the end point of the development of oriental states, to the extent that this development results from the internal antagonisms brought about by the formation of the state. . . . Oriental despotism could be accounted for by the nature of the countries in which it arose. But not by deducing it directly from that nature, so that as long as the soil remains the same, its product, too, cannot change. But rather by demonstrating that in certain countries under the same conditions particular modes of production arise, the collision of which does not just produce the state, but also ultimately brings forth its despotic form, which lasts as long as those modes of production last. That in the Orient the state has hitherto not gone beyond the despotic form, that the latter is apparently its last and highest form, is a consequence of the fact that the economic conditions on which it was founded did not permit a higher mode of production to result from them.

The First Class Struggles

a. The Exploited Are Weak and Divided

We have now become acquainted with the social and state basis on which the class antagonisms that are necessarily bound up with the state take form and are fought out—to the extent that they are fought out. Above all, we must note that even at an early period class antagonisms are no longer as simple as they often appear to be. It is still widely believed that always and everywhere there have been only two classes, whose struggle contains all of history within itself, whether they are called the rich and the poor, rulers and ruled, exploiters and exploited. In our preceding discussions, we were ourselves often compelled to use these expressions. But as indispensable as abstractions are for elucidating some relationships, one must not, when they are being applied, forget the multiplicity of phenomena from which they were drawn by concentrating on their common features.

We have already seen how even the ruling and exploiting class in the beginnings of the state, although consisting only of a league of a few tribes, is rapidly differentiated into free commoners and lower and higher nobility. Standing above these, the family of the monarch, together with his courtiers, becomes a class of its own; and alongside them competing classes and tribes arise, which are not directly created by the fact of conquest, but gradually grow out of its consequences: priests, bureaucrats, merchants, usurers, and bankers. They all participate in the exploitation of the mass of the common people, and yet (with the occasional exception of the priests under special conditions) they are underprivileged in relation to the military nobility and to the monarch, who originated from it, together with his court nobility. Below all of them, there are the laboring masses, who in turn are divided into the very diverse groups of slaves, serfs, peasants subject to paying rent or tribute but otherwise free, free craftsmen, artists, those knowledgeable about nature such as physicians, astronomers, etc.

In every village, men work side by side who belong to different occupations as well as those who have different social positions within the same occupation. Further, different villages, or at least different districts in the state, are governed by different laws. Even more numerous are the occupations and the social positions in the cities, the rights and obligations of the different cities, indeed even of the individual quarters in the cities. Even the individual streets differ among themselves according to the occupation or the tribe whose members prefer to live in them. Each of these groups leads a life of its own; each one maintains amicable or hostile relations with other groups. These relations are by no means brought about exclusively by class interests. Questions of prestige or of competition can cause members of the same class to quarrel most bitterly. . . .

To be sure, the state joins the individual small tribes together into a lasting community and promotes commerce and intercourse among them, but only certain occupations and especially the ruling class are strongly influenced thereby. The rural population still remains to a high degree in the isolation of the village. As for the big city, there the individual newly arrived worker remains for a long time isolated among the enormous mass of people who are strangers to him. And he finally enters into close contact only with his immediate neighbors. . . . There is no method of communication other than verbal, personal contact. Under such conditions, all antagonisms and conflicts among men express themselves only within the narrowest compass; they are experienced not as necessary, but as accidental; not as the result of general economic conditions, but of particular personal dispositions. What manifest themselves are not struggles between classes, but ethical fights against the wickedness of individual persons, of the peasants, say, against the hard-heartedness of their landlords and usurers or of the latter against the laziness and depravity of their laborers and debtors. Even up to the present time, this ethical conception of class antagonisms has not been gotten rid of.

In the ancient Orient, however, it usually does not lead to an ethical struggle, but to ethical indignation. For there the exploited classes have very little ability to fight. If the peasants had possessed that ability, a state would never have been established. Once a state has been founded, the peasants in it are made even more defenseless and deprived of all power to resist. If the oppression by their lords becomes too intolerable, then they may well be moved to rise up against it. But their uprisings are mere outbreaks of wild desperation, without any hope of victory. . . . The individual villages remain isolated, and it is never the total mass of the peasants in the state but always only individual villages that rebel, without preparation, without weapons, without leadership, against the lords, who are less numerous but well armed, organized, and led, and always ready to attack. Thus peasant uprisings are, as a rule, drowned in blood. They testify to strong class antagonisms, but also to the impossibility of a continuing class struggle and of raising the exploited through it.

Things are no better for the laboring masses in the cities than in the villages. . . . Politically and economically dependent on the central government of the state, this population also found itself constantly confronted with a formidable military force surrounding the king. The situation was similar in the capital cities of the provinces, in which the king's satraps had their seats, together with the garrisons under their command. Thus the cities of the Orient were as a rule incapable of gaining for themselves the self-government that the villages were able to preserve through long periods of time. *[Kautsky quotes Weber,* Economy and Society, *III, 1227–28, 1244–45, on the absence in Asian history of autonomous urban communities with corporate character and citizenship.]* It is of the greatest importance to recognize the difference between the oriental and the occidental city. On this difference rests to a great degree the difference in the character of oriental and occidental history. No one has elaborated this difference better than Max Weber. He thereby made a significant contribution to a materialist conception of history, which he, to be sure, rejected. . . . He did not clearly identify the motive forces that led to the differences between Occident and Orient.

It was impossible in the Orient for the inhabitants of a city, to the extent that they belonged to the same class, to unite and in tenacious, indefatigable struggle jointly to protect their interests, to expand their rights, and to improve their social situation. The inhabitants of a street or the members of a craft could sometimes join together, when a sudden grievance or an occasional ordinance by some low-level agency aroused them, in order to demonstrate or to give loud expression to their displeasure. But they did so only to call to themselves the attention of higher officials or even of the king himself, so that he would learn of things that would otherwise remain unknown to him, not in order to force him to make some concessions. To the extent that guilds were permitted, they remained without power and their authority was very restricted. The association of the guilds into a united body, a class organization, was out of the question. Indeed, the despots in general feared any independent organization of any large size as the greatest danger to the state, that is, to themselves. . . .

Whenever the masses of the city came together in public, whether on regularly occurring occasions, for example, fairs, or for unexpected reasons, especially great catastrophes, when curiosity or fear drove everyone into the streets, they then displayed all the features that Gustave Le Bon (in *The Crowd*) regarded as generally characteristic of the broad mass of the common people, who in his opinion were completely unpredictable, capricious, mindlessly active when they were joined together in a large group. He overlooked that this is true only of huge, unorganized masses of men who are strangers to each other and have been driven out into the streets and aroused only by mere rumors, by an accidental impulse. In the large city of the Orient, the conditions for huge mass movements were given, but at the same time all possibilities for purposive action by these masses were eliminated by oriental despotism. Like the occasional outbreaks of desperation of some villages, the occasional riots in the city, too, could hardly end otherwise than in their bloody suppression. If the mass of the common people did happen to win out, perhaps as a result of the authorities' being panic-stricken, then they were unable to make use of their victory for anything but looting and destruction. This necessarily led all the more to collapse of the victors. . . .

. . . In modern cities, too, there are still occasions when unorganized masses come together without political and social goals, for instance, for large sporting events. In some circumstances, such masses still exhibit even today the characteristic features of the earlier "rabble." . . . If something unforeseen provokes them, say the absence or the failure of a favorite on whom the betting has been heavy, then such masses are often seized by a wild fury that expresses itself in senseless destruction. . . . No one will claim that such outbreaks are expressions of conscious class antagonisms. For the lower classes, then, the conditions for conducting class struggles were very bad in the ancient Orient.

b. Vying for the Ruler's Favor

The exploiting classes were better off. Fewer in number, the members of each class could, for that reason alone, come together more easily. Moreover, they were often already tightly organized by kinship and by tribal membership, which in the state became membership in an estate, and the entire state apparatus worked for them, not against them. Others of the exploiting classes, which were not identical with the conquering tribe, . . . merchants, usurers, priests, formed occupational organizations having power of a completely different order from the craftsmen's guilds, since they monopolized factors of the life of the state—knowledge in the case of some, money in the case of others. And they could form supralocal, national alliances more easily than the guilds, since they possessed the arts of reading and writing. In most instances, the various classes of the exploiters were united in their rejection of the movements of the lower classes; often they were most bitterly hostile to them. After all, the laboring classes were the fertile soil they all shared, from which each of the upper classes drew its means of subsistence. . . . Nevertheless, most of the relations of exploitation assumed very fragmented forms, different for the different villages, for the different streets of the city, for the different local trades. This inhibited extensive class struggles also of the upper classes and among the upper classes. . . .

. . . As soon as the number of classes in the state grows and the central government of the state becomes more independent of the upper classes, it appears possible for one class to obtain an advantage relative to another, not by gaining new strength of its own, but by gaining the favor of the head of state. Competition for the ruler's favor now becomes the content of the politics of all classes, the content of all politics, even of the lower classes. . . . These politics, too, were in part a result of class antagonisms. . . . They could become a form of class struggle. Yet one had to look very carefully to find in *[them]* . . . any struggle and any class character. In the case of the lower classes, this contest in servility of course did not lose the character of petty local and local-guild desires and in the upper classes it took on entirely the character of personal place-hunting and climbing. . . . Whoever considers such goings on can easily conclude that here it is a matter only of the wholly subjective and usually unpredictable antagonisms of individual personalities.

The means of influencing the ruler . . . were naturally very different for the different classes depending on their specific character. All that was left to the lower classes was to petition or to demonstrate, to put their desperate situation on display. Even the various uprisings served no other purpose, to the extent that they had any purpose at all and did not quite spontaneously arise out of provocative situations. To the usurers and bankers, it seemed natural to buy the favor of the monarch, as they bought everything else. Often the monarch directly invited them to do so, when he happened to be in financial straits—not an exceptional occurrence. But only the richest among them had wealth at their disposal great enough to bribe the richest of the rich. . . . But in the state it was not a question only of the monarch's will. . . . A great deal depends on the zeal and the understanding of the lower-level officials. . . . The lower the official stands in the hierarchy, the worse he is paid and the smaller is the sum required to make him compliant to anyone who gives him money. On the other hand, it is also often possible to influence the monarch with less expense indirectly than directly, by buying the intercession of people in his entourage, of a favorite woman, a courtier, a personal servant, or a eunuch.

. . . The military nobility has less need of the method of *bribery*, and it is also less available to it. But, on the other hand, that nobility belongs to the same tribe as the king; some of its members are even relatives of the monarch, some belong to his permanent entourage, some are in any case related to members of this entourage or are their friends. Thus, every noble finds intercessors of whom he can hope that they will bring his requests to the sovereign's attention. That is all the more the case when entire large noble families or factions or parties have common wishes to advance. Under despotism, *intrigue* is the favorite political weapon of the nobility, as *bribery* is that of the bankers and usurers.

Rarely, however, is a sovereign capable of adequately satisfying the appetites of all his magnates, the more so as their appetites grow larger with eating. Furthermore, their interests are often too opposed to each other. . . . There are also princes who are miserly, or envious, suspicious, malicious, or simply stupid. Rather than being champions and instruments of the interests of the ruling classes, they can become a danger to them or at least to some of their members. A prince of this kind . . . always has at his disposal the means of doing away with particular individuals if they appear troublesome or dangerous to him. . . . The mass of the laboring classes is much less threatened by raging tyrants on the throne than the immediate associates of the head of state, his generals, his ministers, his relatives. It is just these who, for their part, are in the best position to forestall the destruction menacing them. It is not seldom that the initiative to replace a prince . . . by another, more compliant one originates in their circles. Sometimes the rebel himself becomes a usurper. Depending on the means the ruler's opponents have at their disposal, they turn to assassination or to an armed uprising. . . . Yet, even when they succeed, such upheavals change the character of the state just as little as the desperate rebellions of the exploited are able to. The person of the ruler, the personnel of his entourage change; despotism remains and, with it, its governmental apparatus.

Demonstrations and outbreaks of desperation on the one side, bribery, intrigue, assassination, coup d'état, civil war on the other—these are the methods of political activity in the despotic state. Rarely is this activity a pronounced class struggle. Nor can it always be traced back in the last instance to a class antagonism. The conflicting interests that grapple for influence over or for possession of governmental power are often of a merely local, occupational, or even solely personal nature. Although every class struggle is by its nature a political struggle, a struggle for political ends or at least with political consequences, that does not at all mean that every political struggle is a class struggle. It is true, however, that there are few political struggles that do not also influence the relations of classes. The state and the classes condition each other; they constantly interact with one another.

c. The Immobility of the Orient Despite All Disturbances

In the ancient Orient the goal of political struggle never becomes one of social revolution, aimed at bringing about a higher social order, not even when it is intensified to the utmost, to the point of becoming an armed uprising with the goal of toppling the existing government. . . . As a rule, such insurrections are successful in the Orient only when they are begun by the mighty of the realm, who do not rebel in order to put an end to an existing relationship of exploitation, but rather only in order to put themselves in the place of other beneficiaries of this relationship. These rebels are socially conservative. On the other hand, the lower exploited classes, which would have the greatest interest in casting off the yoke of servitude and exploitation, are much too weak even to attempt to do so. To the extent that their uprisings have any goals at all, these are as a rule petty in nature and are not such they they can in any way overturn the existing relationships among classes.

Occasionally, to be sure, there have been uprisings of the lower classes even in the Orient that succeeded and brought about a social revolution. But not for long. And they did not bring about a new mode of production. Soon the old state of affairs had been reestablished, for all the conditions for a reorganization of society were lacking. . . . All that happened was that some of the poor became rich and some of the rich, poor. . . . More often there occurs another kind of uprisings by oppressed elements in the oriental state, which in some circumstances can succeed permanently, but also do not constitute social progress. . . . In the course of their expansion, the states often find themselves compelled to annex areas that are difficult of access and of slight fertility, whose inhabitants are extremely warlike and liberty-loving. . . . Such tribes . . . take advantage of every difficulty of the state, into which they were incorporated, to rebel. . . . But uprisings of such a kind also do not set themselves goals that are revolutionary with respect to the economy. What they at best seek to achieve is the return to the past, to the prestate stage. Socially, these rebels cannot be anything other than reactionaries. They can destroy the state but not raise it to a higher level.

Despotism is the highest form that the state in the ancient Orient is able to attain, and the ancient Orient extends up to the present time. There is no power in the state that could lift it beyond despotism, just as there was no force in the old society that would have been able permanently to counteract the growing misery of the laboring masses. The social stagnation of oriental states, lasting into the nineteenth century, that is, until industrial capital also seized upon them, was noted by European observers long ago. . . . Marx saw the cause of this immobility in the immutability of the conditions of production in the village, that is, of the economic foundation of the state. *[Kautsky quotes* Capital, *I, 479.]* This social immobility of the states of the Orient . . . threatens each of them with ultimate decay. In addition, there is yet another moment that, after its glorious rise, accelerates its decline.

CHAPTER EIGHT
The Downfall of the State

The productive activities in a state can flourish, . . . and still the state will decay if its ruling classes lose the abilities to wage war and to govern. . . . Here, too, we must point out that we are not yet discussing the present-day state. That a ruling class loses these abilities in the course of time was heretofore almost a law of nature. A conquering tribe acquired its abilities to wage war . . . in the rigorous conditions of existence and combat in which it lived before it founded a state. By this act, it created new living conditions for itself, which were not always such that they strengthened in it the virtues of the warrior and the ruler and which increasingly had the opposite effect the more the state became consolidated and expanded. It is true that at first

these virtues were perhaps further strengthened in the conquering tribe, as
it (that is, its men) now had to devote itself quite exclusively to the activities
of waging war and of governing the state and no longer had to participate
in productive work. . . .

. . . No matter how great the pleasures that waging war and giving orders,
as well as hunting, the practice for war, might offer the aristocrats, they
did not suffice to fill their lives. They also desired pleasures in their rest-
breaks. . . . The lords who have rich tribute at their disposal . . . count abundant meals among the most important pleasures of their leisure time. The
less it is a question of hunger at these meals, the more important does the
titillation of the palate become that is associated with some foods. But
drinking becomes even more important than eating, especially for the men,
as soon as technology has reached the point of being able to produce, from
certain vegetable ingredients, beverages that not only taste good, but also
produce feelings of cheerfulness, strength, and exuberance. *[Kautsky cites
Plato who, in the* Republic, *II, § 363 (Plato's The Republic, p. 52), refers to
the just being rewarded by the gods by being "everlastingly drunk," and he notes
the heavy drinking of Alexander the Great and also of his father Philip of Macedon.]*

Women became perhaps even more ruinous than wine for the rulers of
the world. Regardless of what the primitive forms of marriage might have
been, the original economic equality in every polity was enough to prevent
a man from having, as a rule, more than one wife. . . . And the hardships
of life were so great that among hunting peoples their sexual coldness is
generally conspicuous. That changed when slavery made its appearance. In
addition to the women, for whom one had to ask their families and for
whose valuable labor-power their families had to be amply compensated,
the victorious warrior could now take into his household as slaves women
captured in war. . . . But in the case of the nomads, the difficulties of trans-
porting households were too great not to limit the number of slave women.
. . . These difficulties disappear in the case of warriors who settle down.
And at the same time the possession of governmental authority opens to
them new sources for the acquisition of slave women. One of the most
important *[forms of]* tribute imposed on the subjugated people is the annual
delivery of beautiful virgins. . . . The harems of the mighty in the realm and
above all the harem of the king or the sultan himself now assume enormous
dimensions. *[Kautsky refers to the Book of Esther, III, 3, 14.]*

To the harem system was added prostitution. . . . The first cause of prostitution I find in the appearance of foreigners in the city, of traders and
mercenaries. . . . They cannot take either wives or slave women with them
on their travels and may not allow themselves liberties with the free women
of the city . . . ; nor with the property, the slave women, of others. If they
want to satisfy their sexual needs, the most obvious thing for them to do
is to rent slave women from their owners for occasional use. Renting slaves
for specific purposes was by no means anything unusual. Free women of

the lower classes who found themselves in desperate straits could be brought to the point of hiring themselves out. In this area, too, as in so many others, we find in the Orient and in antiquity competition between slave workers and free ones. . . . The starting point of prostitution was probably always the demand on the part of foreigners. . . . Once it had appeared, though, it was also made use of by natives, to the extent that their social position made it possible for them to lead a life of pleasure. . . .

There was no aristocracy that could resist the seductions of the life of sensual pleasure. Their effects on it were the stronger, the more extensive the state and the greater its wealth was and the greater the number of the male and female servants, whose sole task was to refine the life of pleasure and to increase its enticements. Also, active participation in governing and waging war was reduced for the lords the more mercenaries and bureaucrats there were to take over these labors for them. In addition, the rulers promoted this development, mostly through their own example. . . . However, it happened not seldom that the nobility at the princely courts was consciously and intentionally corrupted, in order to break its craving for independence from the monarch. This development was irresistible, for there arose no social force that would have been able to put an end to exploitation and despotism. The lower classes lacked the fighting ability to do so. In the upper classes there was no one who was seriously willing to do so. . . . It was simply the fatal destiny of the ruling classes that the same factors on which their power rested also undermined that power. . . .

This "aging" and dying off of individual states, or, more correctly, of their ruling classes is a completely different process from the "aging" of a civilization.[5] The former is usually a process taking decades or centuries; the latter can last for millennia. . . . The decay or stagnation of a civilization results in the last analysis from the decline of its laboring classes; the decay of a state, on the other hand, from the decline of its ruling classes. . . . A state is incapable of surviving the downfall of a civilization on which it is erected. A civilization, however, can continue to live and flourish quite well, even if many a state perishes within its domain. Heretofore, though, it seemed that the state and civilization had in common with the biological organism at least the fact that the former, like the latter, must inevitably die off from internal causes. . . . That is certainly true for the states and the civilizations of the Orient up to the present time, which we have primarily had in mind. But under other conditions than those of the Orient, social development created other forms of the state and other civilizations. Does the gloomy prognosis of inevitable death hold good also for them?

5. See also III:2:16, and IV:4:14, IV:5:1, above.

CHAPTER ONE

The Origin of the City-State

Up to now we have principally discussed the state as it took form in the great plains traversed by rivers, . . . from North Africa to China, arising out of the proximity of peaceable agriculturalists and warlike and rapacious nomadic herdsmen. We have every reason to assume that this was the most primordial form of the state, the one that first produced that higher-level civilization we have recognized as a result of the state. But this kind of state did not remain its sole form. Under different geographic conditions, other kinds of states emerged, which are, however, all the same in their nature insofar as they are all based on the rule over sedentary agriculturalists of a tribe or an association of tribes coming from without. As for the formations of states by natives in the Americas, we know too little about them to be able to trace out how conquest and subjugation by hunters rather than herdsmen proceeded. Their influence on general human development is so slight that we disregard them here. . . .

. . . The states of Greece . . . were founded by immigrating nomads who came by land from the North, . . . nomads who met with an older, sedentary population having a not insignificant culture whom they subjugated. . . . The oldest picture of Greek society, as, for example, the Homeric poems present it, shows us a warlike landed nobility as the ruling class with peasants obligated to render services and to pay taxes. This nobility is under a chieftain, a king, whose power, however, is small vis-à-vis the aristocrats. But the natural conditions in Greece were of a quite different nature from those in the great river valleys of the Orient. . . . Traversed by many high and deeply rifted mountain ranges, the land is divided into a number of short and narrow valleys with, in most cases, infertile soil. . . . The farming population of each of these regions was small in size, and the food it produced was insignificant. Consequently, invading conquerors that subjugated this population could only be small in numbers, and their revenue from the exploitation of the peasants necessarily remained meager. . . .

The less prospect there was of improving the paltriness of the revenues from the indigenous agriculture by conquests of neighboring regions, the more did the exploiters find themselves inclined to seek new sources of revenue on the sea, which almost every one of the Greek states bordered on. Expansion onto the sea, that was something that did not occur to the despots of the Orient, who strove only to increase the number of peasants slaving for them. . . . The Greeks, too, became accomplished seafarers only when the infertility of the soil drove them to do so. . . . In the fertile Eurotas

Valley of Lacedaemon *[and]* . . . in Thessaly . . . agriculture remained the population's most important way by far of procuring a livelihood, and therefore the feudal character of society was preserved there in its purest form. . . . At first, fishing was probably the principal motive for venturing out to sea. . . . But the Greeks . . . used what they learned about navigation from this kind of work also for other, more profitable undertakings. . . . Piracy, trade on their own account, and transit trade ultimately brought the Greeks far greater gains than agriculture. Learning from the East, the trading states also soon developed their own export industries.

Of course, it was the country's rulers, the military nobility and its chieftain or king, who were most likely to seize upon these sources of wealth. They were the leaders in the raids they undertook with their retinues, they pocketed the lion's share of the booty. *[However, contrary to Max Weber's view, whose* General Economic History, *p. 202, is quoted here,]* in Greece, too, the position of power of the great families, of the nobles, rested not upon the ships they owned, but primarily and always upon their landed property. That was the grandest, truly noble form of property, and has remained so. . . . The great families already had high positions in the state before it turned to maritime navigation. . . . The noble despised commerce in the maritime state just as much as in the agrarian state. . . . He sought to obtain profits from trade by equipping ships and also contributing commodities or money for trading transactions, but leaving these in the hands of non-nobles appointed especially for this purpose. . . . In any case, a distinct merchants' estate arose in the course of time alongside the nobility, which, like the latter, grew in wealth and power.

With their growing wealth, the robbers were in danger of themselves being robbed. . . . They had every reason to protect themselves against pirates. . . . In order to achieve greater safety, the rich, mighty families, which had previously lived scattered on their properties, combined together. . . . This concentration permitted them to gather quickly to fend off invaders, and the narrow compass of the area allowed them to enclose it with a strong circuit wall. In this way the city arose in the state of the seafarers. . . .

As intimately bound up with the city as the aristocratic families were, . . . they still always remained landowners with an agricultural enterprise outside the city; they never became city-dwellers pure and simple. The prosperity of the city itself, however, depended less and less on the landed property of its aristocrats. In this respect, the city in the Greek states and in coastal areas of the Mediterranean generally, especially the eastern ones, was fundamentally different from the city of the great empires of the Orient. The latter city . . . is distant from the sea, while the cities of so-called *[classical]* antiquity were always coastal cities. The size and prosperity of the city of the Orient depends on the size of the territory exploited by the ruling classes. . . . The might and the wealth of the Greek city, however, depends almost not at all on the number of peasants exploited by the aristocrats living in it nor on the degree of their exploitation. . . . It is on the wealth of the coasts reached by their ships and on the martial strength they develop that the importance of the Greek city, its commerce, and its industry, and the extent of its population depend. . . .

For the Greek, the city becomes equivalent to the state. . . . Thus there arose the type of the city-state, which is different from that . . . of the oriental state.

CHAPTER TWO

Class Struggles in the City-State

To the peculiar character of the city-state there corresponds the peculiar character of its politics, in particular of its domestic politics. . . . In Greece, only small states with mostly quite infertile soil were possible. As long as it lives only from exploitation of the peasants, the master class . . . cannot raise itself far above the strata of the exploited either culturally or with regard to instruments of power. . . . On the other hand, a few thousand people in a limited area are able to communicate with one another more easily than millions of people living on a wide plain. It is to this that I primarily ascribe the fact that from the start we do not find in Greece that servile obsequiousness that in the Orient the peasant and the craftsman exhibit and also feel toward the ruling classes. . . . Men whose interests agree can act in common more easily when they are closely crowded together in a city than in the countryside. In Greece, in addition, there was also the fact that the city was not, as in the Orient, kept down by the weight of an overwhelming rural territory and its rulers; rather, the city surpassed the rural territory and its inhabitants more and more in importance and dominated them. Under these conditions, rebellion against the authorities in the polity was made significantly easier. . . .

As the absolute monarchy became the typical form of the state in the Orient, so did . . . the republic in the city-states. . . . As early as the seventh century B.C., the republic had the same effects that always recur in societies divided into classes down to the present day. Where the monarchy has consolidated itself reasonably well and has become hereditary, it seeks to become a power standing above the classes, not in order to abolish them, but rather to strengthen its own power by taking advantage of their antagonisms. . . . The class antagonisms are thereby masked and their intense aggravation is often prevented. In the republic, the class antagonisms appear in a much more unmediated fashion; and a ruling class can pursue its interests much more ruthlessly. The expectations of many a liberal who believes that the republic is an instrument for mitigating class antagonisms are thereby shown to be illusions. Rather, the republic is an instrument for aggravating them. But that is no reason for Marxist socialists to speak disdainfully of it.

In most of the Greek states, the aristocracy brought about the downfall of the monarchy. The republic at first served the aristocracy and its interests. The masses of the people were now mercilessly exploited by the nobility and depressed ever more. But under the given circumstances, as the pressure grew so too did the counterpressure. To the factors we have already mentioned as favoring the resistance and the rebellion of the lower classes in the Greek states were added two that operated to the same end.... The seafaring element of the common people is far more energetic and freer from traditions than the peasant or the urban petty bourgeois, since it is accustomed to find abroad very diverse political and economic conditions, quite different from those at home.... Maritime navigation also requires far more boldness and enterprise than does agriculture and urban handicraft. Peasants and craftsmen received from the sailors an impetus, a leadership, a strength, that they did not have in the inland cities....

The aristocracy was small in numbers in the little cities and it did not grow as rapidly as the city's wealth and also its size.... The more the wealth of the city grew, the more did it attract poorer states to plunder it. The greater the city was in size, the less did the nobility suffice for its protection... *[and]* the greater was the non-noble part of the free population that could call some property in the city and state its own, property that could be damaged by a foreign invasion. It became every more necessary and expedient to mobilize this part of the population for the defense of the city....

Thus it happened that more and more of the able-bodied among the peasants and the citizens armed themselves and practiced using their weapons. And this became increasingly possible the more the city's wealth grew, the more its wars yielded slaves, and the resources increased for buying slaves. Thus, the number of peasants and citizens grew who had their work done by slaves and found time for military service. But the number of those among them who had the means to acquire sufficient weapons to serve in the army as heavily armed soldiers (hoplites) also grew. That was facilitated further by the fact... that the advances made in metallurgy made it easier for the middle class to acquire metal armor, so that the knight lost his military superiority over the well-off among the simple citizens, whose solidly compact battle-formation now decided the outcome of wars. *[Kautsky refers to Beloch,* Griechische Geschichte, *I/1, 348.]* The whole population of the city thereby acquired a warlike character. *[Kautsky quotes Weber,* Economy and Society, *III, 1359–60, to this effect.]* Under such conditions, it was not possible in the trading and industrial cities for the noble families permanently to maintain their hegemony and the exploitation founded upon it, to the extent that it applied to the mass of the citizens.

For a time after the overthrow of the monarchy, the situation of the workers, especially of the peasants, probably became worse. In particular, participation in military service was injurious to them, as it compelled them to neglect their farms, for which they were not always compensated by the spoils of war. Their indebtedness grew, and cruel debt-laws decreed the enslavement of the debtor who was unable to pay what he owed. But the same ability to bear arms that ruined the peasant economically bestowed on him political power that with time permitted him not just to fend off the growing pressure from the aristocrats, but also . . . finally to eliminate the privileges of the nobility one by one, to burden the nobility with increasing contributions to the state, and on the other hand to increase contributions that the state had to provide for the benefit of the lower classes. In this way, the state was transformed to a certain degree into the opposite of what it had been originally, from a means of dominion for the aristocracy and the rich into a means of dominion for the relatively poor and from a means of exploiting the latter into a means of exploiting the former.

That the motive force of this development was constituted by the necessity of arming citizens and peasants is heavily emphasized by Max Weber. *[Kautsky quotes* General Economic History, *pp. 324–25, but stresses that]* for its part the military reorganization originated from new technical and economic conditions. And the importance of military innovations for democracy must not be overestimated. Like the Athenians, the Spartans, too, changed over to the armaments and the tactics of the hoplites. But these did not lead to democracy among them, because they lacked the city in which the largest part of the population was concentrated. . . . *[And since their country]* was very fertile, it could feed a larger number of aristocrats—especially if they lived very modestly—than could the rural territories of the trading cities. . . . Consequently, the aristocrats of Sparta did not find it necessary to mobilize the masses under their rule for fighting as hoplites to such a great extent as did the city-states. . . .

In the great states of the Orient, struggles of the laboring classes to improve their lot were, as a rule, out of the question. . . . Matters were quite different in the Greek republics. Here we find not only class antagonisms and occasional riots *[as under Oriental despotism]*, but also constant class struggles that are fought with the greatest tenacity and that . . . in general result in an irresistible, gradual advance of the lower classes, of democracy. . . .

When they wrote the *Communist Manifesto*, Marx and Engels presumably had, among the peoples of antiquity, primarily the Greeks and Romans in mind, when they stated that the history of all hitherto existing society is the history of class struggles. This corresponded to the state of historical knowledge at that time. . . . We have already seen, and Engels himself still came to recognize, that prior to the emergence of the state there were no classes and no class struggles.[1] We can now add that even after the emergence of the state and of classes, regular class struggles of the kind carried on in the modern states are to be found only in the city-states. . . .

CHAPTER THREE
Democracy and Exploitation in the City-State

As different as the city-state of the Mediterranean was from the oriental state extending over a wide territory, they both ultimately arrived at the same outcome, at despotism, at the suspension of all political life and at economic stagnation and thereby at the ruin of the state. It is true that under favorable circumstances ancient democracy succeeded in abolishing all privileges of the nobility, indeed the nobility itself as a separate estate, and in dissolving its gentile organization—as in Athens, but not in Rome; it succeeded in enforcing complete equality of political rights of all citizens in the state, also in imposing all burdens of the state on the rich, turning the poor into pensioners of the state. However, democracy did not succeed in destroying the roots of the problem, the very division of society into classes. And consequently it was unable to halt the resulting decline and the ultimate downfall of the state.

Much as the nobility lost, it was able to preserve its intellectual preponderance in the life of the state. . . . Democracy did not simply do away with the nobility, but rather preferred to entrust to it the chief offices. Indeed, the leaders of the democratic movement themselves originated predominantly from the nobility, . . . they were either at odds with the other members of their estate for personal reasons or they were farsighted enough to recognize the inevitability of the advance of democracy and thought it wise, or in the interest of the state, to take into their own hands the guidance of victoriously advancing democracy. [*Kautsky quotes* Aristotle's Constitution of Athens, *chs. 27, 28; pp. 97–99.*]

. . . Following the Persian Wars, corruptibility and in general the exploitation of office for purposes of personal enrichment rapidly increased in all the high offices of all the larger Greek states, in aristocracies as well as democracies. . . . This was not the least cause of the great wealth of the leading aristocrats. For that reason, they were willing to pay so much in order to gain votes. As their power in the state increased, the voters became,

1. See IV: 1:1, above.

by means of democracy, more and more the state's stipendiaries. For every public activity they came to receive payment. . . . Thus a poor citizen could live entirely from the state and the bribes with which the politically ambitious elements among the wealthy were not stingy.

Where did the state obtain the immense resources necessary for fulfilling this task? It could not take them from the poor citizens. . . . The rich had to pay through the nose. Less in the form of money taxes than in the form of payment in kind. . . . They had to build warships for the state; they had to organize festivals and spectacles and to make them as brilliant as possible. The strange state of affairs obtained that the wealthy were exploited by the poor. Was not a socialist ideal thereby attained, even if in a peculiar form? Not at all. All the great resources that the wealthy expended for the poor had to be created by human labor. But by whose labor? . . . The state could maintain itself and fulfill its obligations only through the emergence, in addition to the citizens, both poor and rich, of numerous laboring individuals, who worked for the citizenry and were exploited by it. Democracy was operative only within the citizenry; it only had the result that, in addition to original exploiters, another, broader stratum of exploiters was formed, which in part directly, in part indirectly through exploitation of the rich, led a parasitical existence at the cost of the true laborers. . . .

Piracy and wars provided innumerable slaves. . . . In the states extending over large territories, . . . agriculture was carried on by free peasants or by serfs, who were subject to taxes and to personal services, but were often exempt from military service and led a family life that frequently yielded a numerous offspring. There slavery was primarily household slavery for purposes of luxury. In the city-states, on the other hand, industry, construction, and mining were increasingly carried on with slaves. Finally, slavery also penetrated into agriculture there. For the peasant was called upon to do military service. . . . He must neglect his property, gets deeper and deeper into debt, and finally has to sell his land to a wealthy man. The latter can have the land cultivated by free wage-laborers. The proletarianized peasant himself became one such, if he did not prefer to go to the city. . . . But the carrying on of agriculture by slaves gains the upper hand, as does the concentration of landed property in a few hands. The slaves cannot have a family life; the size of the agricultural population is maintained only by constant and successful warfare. War, which in part pauperizes the peasants, in part wipes them out, now becomes indispensable as a means of maintaining the supply of slaves and thereby agricultural operations. . . .

The more war and politics became means of gaining a livelihood, not only for the nobility at first, but also for the common citizen, the more did the citizens seek to obtain time for this way of gaining a livelihood, both in the city and in the countryside. Some neglected their trades, . . . to live entirely from subventions by the state and wealthy politicians. That was, to be sure, a meager existence. Whoever was able to, preferred to buy himself one or a couple of slaves and have his trade carried on by them. It could then continue to function even while he himself was away at war. ... This way out became all the more possible for the citizen, the cheaper the slaves were, whose price depended wholly on the frequency and the success of wars. Thus the hitherto free workers were diverted more and more from labor ... and led to exploit unfree laborers as the source of their livelihood. They carried on the exploitation in part directly, by employing slaves themselves, in part indirectly, through taxation of the rich, who exploited numerous slaves.

The citizenry also knew how to make use of free workers, however, who are in part independent craftsmen, in part wage-laborers, especially in agriculture and in the construction of buildings. In a state whose industry and commerce were growing, there was continuous immigration of numerous workers from poorer states. ... These newcomers were joined by [freed] slaves. ... The more citizenship became, through democracy, a means of gaining a livelihood, and the more the citizenry felt itself powerful in relation to the nobility, in the numbers it had already attained, the more sparingly were newcomers admitted to citizenship. A large stratum of free workers was formed in the state, who had no civil rights and received subventions neither from the state nor from private individuals, for they had no vote to be bought. They were dependent entirely on their labor for their livelihood, insofar as they did not themselves employ slaves. Not only did they receive nothing from the state, they also had to pay taxes to it. Thus they were among the objects of exploitation from whom the poor citizens as well as the rich in the state lived. ...

In a powerful, militarily successful city-state, though, there was yet a third method of exploitation, through which an abundant income was made available to its citizens. It could become the most important of the sources of revenue of the city-state. This was the case of Athens, the most democratic of the larger city-states. [There follows a lengthy discussion, including a quotation from Aristotle's Constitution of Athens, ch. 24, p. 94, of the conflict between the Greek agrarian states governed by aristocrats, notably Sparta, and their sympathizers among the landowning aristocrats in the city-states on the one hand and, on the other hand, the mass of citizens in these democratic city-states dependent on the importation of grain. Athens, predominant among them, came to exploit its democratic allies by various means.] The more Attica's power and, in Attica, the power of the citizenry grew, the greater did the pressure exerted on its allies become, the more unbearable their exploitation of them. ... All Hellas turned against Athens, which collapsed miserably in the Peloponnesian War. ... The poorer strata of its citizenry were much more interested in the preservation and expansion of Athens' predominance and in the continuation of the war than were the landowners. ... The war brought them pay and spoils and was being fought to maintain the exploitation they were carrying on, thus for their existence, whereas the landowners had an interest in ending

the importation of grain from afar. In this regard, as well as in their aristocratic tendencies, they were in agreement with the Spartan enemy....

We see that the proletariat and the democracy of ancient Athens were
radically different from the modern proletariat and modern democracy....
In the ancient city-state, democracy was, just like aristocracy and monarchy,
merely an instrument of exploitation. It differed from the other constitutions
only with respect to the category of persons who took part in the exploitation. In relation to the mass of the exploited, this category constituted,
even in the freest democracy, only a small, privileged minority in the state.
And, as in the Orient, this minority ultimately lost its martial strength.
The ruling citizenry was corrupted in democracy by its power in the state
just as much as the nobility was in other states.[2] Through their parasitical
leisure, some lost their fitness for military service along with their interest
in and capacity for politics. Those who remained fit for combat had become
accustomed to find their means of livelihood in war. They became mercenaries.... Political leadership now came into the hands of successful generals, who knew how to obtain rich spoils. Democracy came to an end.
Greek freedom... went down to defeat before the Macedonian military
monarchy, which unified Greece and Persia into an empire that in its turn
disintegrated into a number of military monarchies set up as Oriental des-
potisms by successful generals with armies of mercenaries.

CHAPTER FOUR

Mixed Forms of the State

As the ancient democratic states could not overcome exploitation, but were,
rather, founded upon it, they ultimately had to decay and perish, in spite
of all their differences, just like the Oriental despotic states. We have characterized here the most extreme types of the different forms of the state.
We can consider, on the one hand, the Persian state and, on the other, the
Athenian one as the most important representatives of these. Each of these
two types of state is based on a particular character of the region in which
it appeared, as well as on a particular character of its neighbors and of the
level of its economic development. Between these two extremes, however,
there are numerous mixed forms, each of which is also dependent on particular natural and economic conditions. Only two will be mentioned here,
which acquired special importance for our history because of the traditions
they left to us: the Jewish and the Roman state.

---

2. Kautsky had dealt with "urban democracy in antiquity" in a brief chapter in an early
work, *Parlamentarismus und Demokratie*, pp. 32–36, where he argued that political power in
democratic city-states fell into the hands of the rich and of the lumpenproletarians corrupted
by the rich.

[There follows a summary of ancient Jewish history to the end of the Babylonian captivity and the restoration of the city of Jerusalem in 538 B.C.] It now formed a city-state with a small territory, but a city-state located on land, not on the coast. And it was not trade and industry nor piracy and naval warfare that its existence was based on. The conditions of its existence were of a completely different kind. . . . Since the state was incapable of conquering additional land, the Jews who constituted an excess population had to confine themselves to going abroad individually, something that was done most easily either as a mercenary or as a trader. . . . They turned to areas whose fertility bound their inhabitants to the soil. *[There]* they took over the function of trade, which was not performed by the natives. . . . The number of the emigrating Jews who settled abroad increased more and more . . . but they remained aliens where they lived, full of longing for a state in which they could govern and act as fully empowered citizens. As little as the small city-state of Jerusalem was able to satisfy this longing, . . . it nonetheless provided a center around which the millions of Jews of the Diaspora could gather in spirit. It identified them as a nation in their own right. . . .

What united the Jews was their own particular religion, their own particular form of worship, which had its center in the temple of Jerusalem. Renewing this cult over and over again by a pilgrimage to Jerusalem . . . became an important task of every nationally minded Jew. Like other places of pilgrimage, the city of Jerusalem lived only from the pilgrims. . . . Thus the Jewish city-state was based on . . . the strength of a religious cult. Not a military nobility, nor a monarch, also not a popular assembly became the ruler in this state, but rather a priesthood, which served the cult and jealously watched that it not lose its cohesion and its influence on the souls of the orthodox.[3]

. . . The priesthood of the Jews supplied the models and the arguments when, in the Roman empire, a new sect arose out of Judaism, but soon was in opposition to it. Originally, this new sect principally served charitable purposes with a bureaucracy of its own, which remained independent from that of the state and often competed with it and which assumed a priestly character, since it took over a form of worship of its own from the Jewish priesthood and adapted it to the social conditions of the Roman empire. It also took from this priesthood the presumption that it was called to rule over the state.[4]

. . . The state of Rome had in common with the city-states of Greece that it arose close to the coast at a place well suited for trade. But Rome had a

---

3. Kautsky had advanced explanations of the peculiarities of pre-Christian Jewish history, including the Diaspora, at much greater length in his *Foundations of Christianity*, pp. 187–320.

4. For Kautsky's explanation of the rise of a bureaucracy and especially of bishops in the Christian communities of the first three centuries, see *Foundations of Christianity*, pp. 433–49.

different hinterland than the Greek trading cities. . . . The Romans had no desire to become seafarers themselves. They preferred to let foreign seafarers come to them . . . and to carry on trade with them. Thus the ruling classes of Rome became rich through its commercial situation. But they did not use their wealth for naval armaments, but rather for becoming superior to their neighbors on land . . . until in Sicily, Rome encountered the Carthaginians. *[There follows a discussion of politics in Carthage and its conflict with Rome, especially over the Spanish silver mines.]* After the fall of Carthage, there was no longer any power in the sphere of the civilization of antiquity that would have been able to resist Rome. All the states of the East had been declining for a long time and now were fighting only with armies of mercenaries. Rome's superiority to them all was due primarily to the fact that it began its entry into the circle of the conquest-states of antiquity later than the others, when the morale of its citizens had not yet been undermined by the effects of exploitation. However, Rome's superiority also rested . . . on its geographical peculiarity that made it a land power for which it was possible, as in the case of Macedonia, to appropriate the advantages of a maritime state. . . .

. . . As an agrarian state, Rome, like Sparta, remained too much caught up in rural dullness and narrow-mindedness ever to be able to develop a Periclean Age. On the other hand, though, it was nonetheless too much a maritime city and a metropolis not to become acquainted with arts and sciences. . . . And even though its aristocracy maintained its political power longer than did the aristocracy of Athens and preserved its gentile organization into the imperial period and after all political life had perished, it was nevertheless still not able, like Sparta's aristocracy, to repress every democratic movement. The latter finally proved to be just as irresistible in Rome as it had been in Athens, but it prevailed only when the period of decline had already begun. This decline began after the Punic Wars. At first it was a moral decline, then a decline with respect to domestic politics, finally an economic decline and a decline in foreign political matters. That Rome subjugated all other states of antiquity and welded them together into an empire only boiled down to the fact that the downfall of the one city became tantamount to that of the civilization of antiquity.

CHAPTER FIVE

The Fall of the City-State

. . . Under the social conditions of antiquity, class struggle did not prove to be a means of keeping the development of society ceaselessly moving to ever-higher forms. Class struggle was incapable of preventing the final decline because it . . . could not lead to abolition of classes and put an end to all exploitation. . . . Thus the decline and downfall that every system of exploitation sooner or later brings in its train also became inevitable for the city-state. . . .

. . . In the city-state, the exploitation of the great majority of the population by a minority . . . assumed forms that under some circumstances brought about decline even more rapidly than under despotism. For in the city-state, more than under despotism, slavery became the basis of the process of production. . . . The massive extent and the enormous cheapness of slave labor eliminated . . . the peasant families from the process of production. That, however, also eliminated the reservoir from which the citizenry in general was drawn. In the cities of antiquity, there obtained such unhealthy conditions that their rates of mortality were much higher than their birthrates. . . . A constant influx from the countryside . . . presupposed numerous prolific peasant families. In the city-state, these were supplanted more and more by slaves. . . .

In the city, too, . . . the labor of slaves and of immigrating foreigners supplanted that of the citizens. The process was made easier by the growing strength of democracy, which made available to the citizens so many sources of livelihood in war and in politics that productive work became less and less necessary for them. On the other hand, the same process became to all intents and purposes a powerful motive force of democracy and of the intensification of exploitation by the state and the ruling classes. For the greater the competition from cheap slave labor, the more did the propertyless part of the citizenry feel itself impelled to broaden its political rights in order to be able to live from their sale.

This process . . . had to end with economic decline and ultimate ruin, once the acquisition of new slaves came to a standstill. For without them, it had become impossible to continue production. Obtaining slaves through war and abduction, however, is a process that necessarily undermines its own foundation. . . . A state requires continuous victorious expansion in order to be able to depopulate ever-new slave preserves. . . . The distance that the slaves have to travel to reach their "consumers" becomes greater and greater. This increases more and more the cost of the slave material, the employment of which, given the great unproductiveness of its labor, is only worthwhile when it is extremely cheap. When slaves began to become rarer and more expensive, the large landowners of the city-states attempted *[to transform]* them into serfs. . . . *[But]* they remained . . . instruments of exploitation by a state and by a landlord whose hunger for surplus product knew no bounds. . . . Depopulation and impoverishment in the realm grew irresistibly. *[Kautsky cites estimates of the population of the city of Rome of one million at the time of Augustus, of half a million two centuries later, and of at most thirty to forty thousand three centuries after that.]*

The entire existence of the state was founded on its military superiority. But how was that to be maintained when the population was constantly declining and wealth was constantly decreasing? . . . The citizen army begins to shrink in size very early. . . . Through the magnitude of the victories and the abundant exploitation made available to them in the extensive empire, the citizenry of the ruling city, poor and rich alike, became accustomed to lead an indolent life of gluttony and carousal, which smothered all sensitivity to social matters as well as all martial spirit. . . . The ruling citizenry had nothing else in mind but exploiting the state. The proletarians among the citizens sold their votes; the hereditary aristocracy and the aristocracy of wealth bought the votes in order to be elected to offices in which they were able to bleed and plunder the provinces. The provincials, of course, had not the slightest interest in the state, which oppressed them and reduced them to misery. Matters were . . . not improved when the emperors made themselves the highest-placed exploiters in the state and . . . the landowners carried on their exploitation more and more for the state, to which they had to pay taxes, rather than through the state for themselves. As a result, the interest of the ruling class in the state also was completely extinguished. . . .

Only by payment and the prospect of booty could some parts of the citizenry still be moved to serve in the army. . . . An ever-growing number of mercenaries had to be recruited among the warlike barbarians outside of the empire. . . . The Roman Empire had rested for two centuries on the work of barbarians, in particular that of the Germanic ones, in agriculture and on their service in the army, before it collapsed completely under their attack. But even before the end of the state was thus brought about externally, all political life within the state had stopped entirely. . . . The administration of the state, too, fell to the lot of the chief general; its principal activity consisted in keeping the more and more stagnating economic life going, in order to supply the resources required for the army of mercenaries. It is understandable . . . that under these circumstances general despair, disinclination to raise children . . . became ever more widespread. . . . The ultimate cause of this weariness of life is to be found . . . in social conditions that were the final result of the exploitation of the broad masses in the state carried on for a long time and completely undermining strength of the state.[5]

CHAPTER SIX

The Socialism of Antiquity

The state of antiquity was so intimately linked to exploitation and in particular to slavery that it was incapable of going beyond them even in

5. Kautsky had dealt with the declining economy, especially of slavery, and prevailing attitudes in imperial Rome in *Foundations of Christianity*, pp. 45–183.

thought. . . . Pondering the question of the best constitution was universal, at least in the democratic states, but among the boldest, the most acute, the most comprehensive thinkers of Greece, there was none who called for a state without any kind of exploitation in Greece. Such a state was simply impossible under the given technological conditions without giving up civilization. . . . To be sure, persisting in exploitation ultimately also led to the decay of civilization for every state. . . .

Aristotle, in his *Politics*, I, ch. 5, *[pp. 40–41]*, . . . explains . . . that by their nature some men are slaves, others are masters. . . . No doubt, Plato glorified communism in his book on the Republic, . . . but . . . in his state there is a class of rulers and a class of workers who are ruled. . . . He calls for communism only for the rulers, in the interest of preserving their rule, in order to strengthen their solidarity and to make impossible all conflicts of interest among them. He is interested only in the class of rulers; it is exclusively of their organization that he treats. He speaks of the peasants and the craftsmen merely in passing. . . . He does not object to the enslavement of barbarians and to the institution of slavery as such.[6]

[Kautsky then argues at some length against and quotes from Pöhlmann, Geschichte der sozialen Frage, *I, 241–42, 246, 286; II, 305–309, who, using the term "socialism," cites instances in Greek literature advocating]* the abolition of social conflicts within the citizenry that threatened to burst it and thus the state asunder. . . . What is called communism or socialism in antiquity has nothing to do with the abolition of slavery. And just as little with the idea of progress to a higher form of society. All its forms, not just the crudest ones of simple distribution of goods or even of the pillaging and the murdering of the rich, . . . but also the refined forms, like that of the Platonic state, were at bottom reactionary or conservative. They sought their models in the past, which had already known common property in the land. . . . The prototype of Platonic communism was the barracks-communism of Sparta's aristocracy, adapted, to be sure, to the requirements of an Attic aristocrat and philosopher.

Leaving aside the speculations of a few philosophers, which had no practical effect, we see only two social ideas active in the struggles of the lower classes: on the one hand, living at the expense of the state, that is, at the expense of the labor of slaves and subjugated peoples; on the other hand, a return to agriculture carried on by free peasants. Cancellation of debts or the creation of new farmsteads for peasants are the goals of the efforts of social reformers and social revolutionaries, who want to prevent the citizenry from languishing in a life of slothful parasitism and who strive to maintain it in a state of complete military fitness and political independence. Further than that Solon, the Gracchi, or the Jewish prophets, for example,

---

6. Kautsky had earlier dealt with Plato's communism in *Vorläufer*, I, 6–24.

did not go. . . . The state of the future, the prospect of which was held out by Christianity as the salvation from the afflictions of the present, had an enormous effect. It was, however, not expected as the result of class struggles and political upheavals, but rather as the creation of a miracle-working Messiah, who would conjure up a magnificent fairy-tale land. . . . But the more the movement of Christianity became a mass movement, the more did this ideal become sublimated from one expected on earth into a super-terrestrial one that will be granted to us only in a better hereafter.[7]

No more so than in the aristocratic and ultimately despotic state of the Orient were philosophy and class struggles able to create in the more or less democratic city-state of the Mediterranean basin a new social ideal that they fought for.

Section Seven
The Capitalist Industrial State

CHAPTER ONE

Industrial Capitalism

. . . As in the states of antiquity, in those of Christianity also the conquerors became a military nobility. . . . The new exploitation found the form adapted to its needs already existing in the Roman colonate *[a system involving tenant farmers bound to the soil]*. In the states of the Middle Ages, as in antiquity, trade and industry developed alongside the nobility and the priesthood; fierce class struggles occurred; but the freedom of movement of the classes also finally ended in their subjection to a despotism based on a bureaucracy and a mercenary army. Just as before, this decline of political life went hand in hand with an economic decline. . . . As early as the sixteenth century, however, *[factors]* appeared in some states . . . that in the nineteenth century completely overcame the tendencies to decline and brought about a completely new direction of historical development, radically different from that of antiquity, in spite of any external similarities of some class struggles of antiquity with modern ones. The great power that changed the course of human history so fundamentally is *industrial capital*. . . .

Only since Marx do we draw a sharp distinction between merchant capital, usury capital, and industrial capital. . . . We know that merchant capital and usury capital are very old, . . . whereas industrial capital plays a

---

7. The communism of consumption of the early Christians and also their chiliastic phantasies were discussed by Kautsky in *Foundations of Christianity*, pp. 323–61. For an earlier, briefer analysis of this subject, in the context of the decline of the Roman slave economy, and also of the reforms advocated by the Gracchi, see *Vorläufer*, I, 33–43.

role only in the modern period. . . . Trade and usury are compatible with quite diverse modes of production. Max Weber *[Kautsky quotes from* The Protestant Ethic, *pp. 20, 21]* also points out *[that]* . . . what Marx designates as industrial capitalism is the only kind of capitalism that is proper to the modern period alone. Only Weber emphasizes in his characterization of this capitalism a relatively insignificant feature: the rational character of the organization of labor; that is to say, he stresses the fact that the individual enterprise is based on a precise system of bookkeeping. *[Kautsky quotes* The Protestant Ethic, *p. 18.]*

What is new about modern capitalism is not its rationalization (only the perfection of this rationalization), but rather its organization of *free labor.* Weber rightly places the greatest emphasis on this point. And . . . he knows that modern socialism can only arise out of the free proletariat of industrial capitalism. *[A long paragraph on the latter point is quoted with approval from* The Protestant Ethic, *pp. 22–23.]* The nature of work employed by the merchant, the usurer, or the banker is determined by the kind of labor dominant in the particular process of production, not vice versa. He can employ slaves or serfs just as well as wage-laborers. Only by virtue of the fact that "the rational capitalistic organization of free labour" penetrates into the *process of production* does this kind of organization of free labor become the one that is dominant in society and that determines the character of society and the direction of its development, its internal conflicts and goals. . . . This important reference to the mode of production is lacking in Weber's definition of modern capitalism as "the rational capitalistic organization of (formally) free labour." [The Protestant Ethic, *p. 21*] The penetration of this form of organization of labor into *industry* is what is decisive and historically important. It is this, above all, that is the defining characteristic of modern capitalism. And we therefore consider it appropriate to contrast modern capitalism . . . as the capitalist *mode of production* to the Graeco-Roman and Oriental forms of capitalism, which comprised only trading capital and usury capital.

On the other hand, when Weber speaks of the organization of free labor, he leaves out of consideration a moment that alone identifies the whole process as a capitalist one. . . . The modern worker is really free, not just formally. What causes his freedom to appear as a merely formal one is his *lack of property*. . . . The fact that the free worker does not own his own means of production, which he needs in order to be able to work and subsist; that these means of production are owned by another, who thereby becomes a capitalist—this is what makes the worker dependent on the capitalist and makes it necessary for him to work for the capitalist. And to work for him so long that a surplus value, a profit, accrues to the capitalist. This creation of profit in the process of production becomes much more important and critical for the industrial capitalist than the "exact calculation" of the entire management of the business, from which the profit seems to result. And the methods of its *creation*, not just those of the mere *calculation* of the surplus value or profit, are what bestow on industrial capital its enormous historical significance and enable it to break out of the vicious circle in which the state and society had previously been trapped.

CHAPTER TWO

The Progressive Force of Industrial Capitalism

The methods of exploitation we have come to know up to now have all led to the ultimate economic decline and ruin of the state, even if for a time they brought for its ruling classes a sometimes very brilliant flourishing of its wealth, arts, and sciences. . . . The cause of this was, in the last analysis, that each of these methods of exploitation was based on waste and served waste. . . . The defeated were left as much as they needed in order to continue to live and to work. . . . That permitted an ongoing continuation of exploitation, but prevented any technical progress on the part of the exploited. . . . The corvée-laborers were much too poor to improve the technical apparatus with which they worked. The slaves were a much too unwilling labor force to be entrusted with delicate instruments. The exploiters whose riches could well have provided the means for employing appropriate tools and methods and whose science, fostered by them, would have been able to invent such implements, had not the slightest interest in such matters. . . . Under the conditions obtaining in the Oriental and the Graeco-Roman state, all economic activity, after all, served only consumption, only enjoyment. . . . Bankruptcy is the result of this as of every other wastefulness that is continued unceasingly and intensified beyond all measure. . . .

Completely different results are achieved by the capitalist mode of production. . . . The precapitalist exploiters of slaves and serfs knew of no other method for increasing the amount of exploitation and thus their welfare than the wasting of labor-power. In addition to this method, another is available to industrial capital. It becomes ever more important and is used more extensively, and it is this method that gives a completely new turn to history. The recognition of this fact we also owe to Marx, to his grandiose analysis . . . of the creation of surplus value. . . .

Extending working time and forcing down wages cannot go beyond certain limits. . . . Then there appears a new method of increasing surplus value—with the same number of workers and the same working time—that was not, or virtually not, available to antiquity and that is capable of being employed and extended without limit. This method consists in reducing the value of labor-power without diminishing its real wages. . . . It is the method to lower the prices of products and hence of the worker's living expenses by means of technical improvements . . . in production and in transport, so that, while real wages remain constant, the worker has to expend less labor for the production of his own livelihood and, despite the unchanged length of the working day, can devote more time to the production of surplus value. . . .

The capitalist who introduces such improvements has only his additional profit in mind. But through them he brings about great social changes. . . . Competition compels the other capitalists in the same branch of production to imitate his improvements and to make them universal. That brings about a lowering of prices; the extra profit of the entrepreneur who introduced the improvement ceases, and only new improvements can bring him new extra profits. The lowering of production costs and consequently of prices, however, remains in effect. To the extent that the products affected by this development are such that they are among those consumed by the workers, they lower the production costs also of the commodity labor-power. . . . For the first time in the history of the world, it now becomes possible to increase exploitation without an extension of the working time or a deterioration of the worker's standard of living. . . . For the first time, a system of exploitation appears that is not bent on the gradual destruction of the already existing productive forces it encounters, but rather, to an ever-more enormous degree, on their augmentation. Only now does the possibility of states emerge that need not decay in stagnation and misery and finally fall before the superior might of rapacious barbarians, but that bear within themselves the germ of steady perfection. With this, state and society enter into a wholly new epoch.

CHAPTER THREE

The Spirit of Capitalism

We have now seen . . . what a new element industrial capitalism introduces into the history of mankind. We still have to show, however, where this new element comes from, and what industrial capitalism itself originates from. It cannot be assumed, for example, that it is merely a further development of earlier forms of capitalism. Nowhere do merchant capital and usury capital oppose the methods of exploitation of the feudal lords and slaveowners, . . . but they place themselves at the service of those methods, draw their strength from them, and intensify their effects. . . . [They] often oppose industrial capital in its beginnings, hand in hand with the feudal lords and the warlike monarchs. Only to the extent that industrial capital prevails and makes trade and interest-bearing capital subservient to it, do the latter change their character and work jointly with industrial capital toward the development of the productive forces. . . .

In the period of primitive accumulation, from the fifteenth century on, a large part of the peasantry is cast onto the labor market as free laborers,

with no means of production whatsoever. . . . *[These]* propertyless workers,
. . . all of whom agriculture cannot employ and to whom the crafts, organized in guilds, are also closed, . . . throng to obtain work for wages from
the *[new]* industrial capitalists. . . . It is only the large-scale enterprise that
becomes the form in which industrial capital develops the forces of production. In cottage industry, the worker himself still owns his extremely
meager instruments of labor, which he is incapable of improving because
of his poverty. What he lacks is the raw material, which the capitalist
supplies to him. In large-scale enterprise, however, the worker and the
means of production are completely separated. The capitalist now controls
the instruments of labor as well as the raw material for this labor. And the
instruments of labor are now in the hands of wealthy people, who . . . have
an interest in improving them. Finally, the free worker can be entrusted
with refined tools, which the slave would ruin. . . .

At this point, a line of thought should be discussed that was intended to
serve either as a complement to or as a refutation of Marx's description *[of
primitive accumulation]*. . . . To lay hold of the material elements of industrial
capitalism, to connect them with each other and to set them in motion, a
new spirit was required on the part of the proletarians and even more on
the part of the capitalists. . . . That was pointed out by Max Weber in his
treatise on *The Protestant Ethic and the Spirit of Capitalism*, which is as scholarly as it is penetrating. . . . *[According to him,]* it is Calvinism that develops
the spirit of capitalism most strongly and most readily. . . . The capitalist
mode of production, says Weber, arises out of the capitalist spirit, and not
vice versa. . . . Traces of this spirit can be seen in New England as early as
the seventeenth century, and yet "the New England colonies were founded
. . . for *religious* reasons. In this case, the causal relation is certainly the reverse
of that suggested by the materialistic standpoint." (Weber, *The Protestant
Ethic*, pp. 55–56.)

Yet . . . the effect of this causal relation that threatens historical materialism with disaster, . . . is at once considerably reduced if we employ a
different terminology and regard what Weber calls the "spirit of capitalism"
as the spirit of a petty bourgeoisie striving to rise. As an expression of "the
spirit of capitalism," Weber quotes some passages from the works of Benjamin Franklin, in which the latter stresses that time is money, that credit
is money, that money is something extremely important, and that one must
be industrious, frugal, and respectable in order to obtain credit and money.
That is certainly a spirit that fosters the rise of the petty bourgeois to become
a capitalist. But can this spirit be explained only by recourse to religious
moments? Can it not be accounted for, without such moments, by definite
economic conditions in which the petty bourgeoisie can find itself? But once
we recognize the "spirit of capitalism" as the spirit of the petty bourgeoisie,
a spirit that fostered the rise of capitalism, . . . the causal relation collapses,
according to which the spirit of capitalism appears prior to capitalism and

only creates the latter. Weber did not make a happy choice when he cites Franklin. . . . On the one hand, his writings are pervaded by a spirit that is still very much that of the petty bourgeoisie; on the other hand, it is not at all true that they precede the emergence of industrial capitalism. . . .

It is certainly true that the Calvinist religion was very favorable to the emergence of industrial capitalism. But it must not be forgotten that this is only one among several aspects of Calvinism. . . . Calvin called upon all elements that opposed the rising absolutism of the ruling princes, not just the citizens of the cities, but also the noble landowners, to the extent that these were still fighting for their independence. . . . [*Their*] union conferred on Calvinism its great strength in many countries, as in France, in the Netherlands, in Scotland, in some Habsburg territories, Lower and Upper Austria, Bohemia, Hungary. . . . The same Calvinist doctrine was just as able to assume feudal features as capitalist ones, depending on the class position of its adherents. The religious root of the spirit of capital is, then, not of a very robust nature.

Weber stresses categorically that "religious ideas themselves . . . contain a law of development and a compelling force entirely their own" (*The Protestant Ethic*, pp. 277–78). It is remarkable that this law of development of religion takes so very much into consideration the class position of its faithful. That is not to deny that Puritanism strongly promoted the development of industrial capitalism in Britain as well as in Holland and later in English-speaking America. Weber offers a wealth of evidence for this. His arguments for it are of the greatest significance. But there is one thing they do not prove: that new economic outlooks arise out of religious thought according to its own law and that religious ideas are the new element that, in accordance with a law of development entirely their own, penetrated into medieval society and thus brought on industrial capitalism. . . . It was quite different moments that created the spirit of capitalism.

CHAPTER FOUR

State and Town in the Middle Ages

. . . In the states founded by Germanic barbarians in the western and northern parts of the Roman Empire and expanded beyond them, historical evolution proceeded under historical and geographical conditions that finally made it possible to transform the path of development of states from a circular or a spiral one into a path of continuous progress in a particular direction, at least for the foreseeable future.

The most important legacy the Germanic states received from the Roman Empire was the Christian church. . . . Such an international, powerful body, centrally directed in an absolutist manner, had not existed before. . . .

Thanks to it, the intelligentsia, which was then concentrated in the Church, acquired an influence on state affairs that it could not have even remotely approached if the military aristocracy had ruled alone. Through the intelligentsia, the various states of Christianity were also in much closer contact commercially and intellectually than would have been possible if the individual states had been completely independent. A further legacy of the Roman Empire was the disappearance of slavery.[1] . . . That made no great difference . . . for agriculture, where even in antiquity, especially in the Orient, the corvée-labor of peasant families had often preponderated over that of chattel slaves. But it did make an enormous difference for the medieval town in contrast to the city of antiquity. . . . From the outset, the medieval town organized its entire economic activity on the basis of free labor.[2] . . .

[*A second*] difference [*was*] . . . a necessary consequence of the impassable nature of the land, of the lack of means of transport, of the low productivity of agricultural labor, and of a barter economy. Under such conditions, the landlords could not gather in fortified encampments and from these rule and exploit the territory of the state. Each landlord had to live with his retinue among the peasants who paid taxes to him and performed corvée-labor for him. In order to protect himself and his villages against incursions of warlike nomads or by neighboring rapacious nobles, he fortified his dwelling-place, in which his subjects also took refuge in an emergency. With the growing productivity of agricultural labor, the number of workers the landlord could employ for his personal purposes increased. In this manner, he acquired the means for building his dwelling-place ever more solidly: it became a castle. Next to it, at the foot of the knoll on which it was erected, lay the village.

Some villages were situated in a favorable location, on trade routes. . . . Even in the darkest times after the fall of Rome, trade had never entirely ceased in Italy and from there it spread out to the East, on the one hand, and over the Alps on the other. At points where numerous merchants appeared periodically with their wares, . . . there soon also appeared a quite large population, which lived . . . from trade in commodities, from providing transportation and lodging, and finally also from the production of commodities. . . . The wealth in such places soon made them especially attractive to brigands, either private ones or those organized by a state. On the other hand, . . . the citadel next to the village was increasingly less adequate . . . to shelter all its inhabitants with their belongings. But the population, grown numerous and rich, was now able to protect itself by building

---

1. See IV:6:5, above. Kautsky had devoted a chapter to the disappearance of slavery in the Middle Ages in *Vorläufer*, I, 55–62.

2. The development of towns and free artisans in medieval Europe was the subject of a brief section of one of Kautsky's earliest books, *Thomas More*, pp. 7–9.

a circuit wall that surrounded the village next to the citadel or along with the citadel. This wall made the village into a town.

Thus the medieval town originated quite differently from the city on the great rivers of the Orient *[or]* the city of antiquity on the coasts of the Mediterranean. . . . *[In]* Italy . . . topography and transport conditions remained favorable to the formation of city-states of the Graeco-Roman type. . . . There, as they had often done even in antiquity, the nobles constructed citadels within the cities. . . . *[But]* beyond the Alps, the nobility remained outside the town throughout the Middle Ages. . . . To the extent that the citizenry was obligated to render services to the lord of the castle, it succeeded in buying itself free from these obligations or often in simply refusing them, without his being able to obtain them by force. . . . Thus every kind of compulsory labor now ceased in the town for its entire population. It was ruled out there on principle. That was something completely new in the state. Ultimately, the lord of the castle had no more say in the business of the town. In this way, the town gained its . . . self-government. . . . The class struggles between the nobility and the non-noble citizenry, which in antiquity took place within the city, assume in the Middle Ages the character of struggles of the towns against the knights living outside the town. To be sure, there are also class struggles within the town, for example, between craftsmen and merchants. There is also a patriciate, an urban nobility that had its origin in the original peasant landowners of the village, out of which the town grew. . . .

As in antiquity, in the Middle Ages, too, we see democracy generally advancing more and more in the towns. . . . The complete separation of the nobility and the town meant a large degree of independence for the citizenry. Yet, this separation diminished the strength of the town. In antiquity, when the nobility and the citizenry lived together in the city, both could work toward common goals with their united strength, and they found such goals in obtaining prisoners of war and in subjugating other cities and people.[3] . . . Such exploitation could take on dimensions for many a victorious city that made it possible and worthwhile for the citizenry to devote all its time and attention to warfare. . . . Thus those powerful city-states of antiquity could arise that culminated in the Roman empire. . . . In the Middle Ages, no town outside Italy could achieve such a position of power and dominion over such an extensive area.

Beyond the Alps, every town met with opposition from the nobility. . . . *[Towns]* were not concerned with the subjection of other towns, but rather with unity with them for joint defense of their liberties and for jointly fending off brigands. Or they gathered around the central authority in the state, around the monarchy, in order that it might defend them against the

3. See IV:6:3, above.

nobility. . . . *[Except in Switzerland,]* the monarchy everywhere maintained itself in the medieval and newer states of the Occident, in contrast to the states of antiquity. The monarchy drew most of its strength from playing the towns and the nobles off against each other. These are joined by a factor unknown in antiquity that appears as the fourth contending element, namely the Church. And the latter stands above the states in its orientation, while the towns and the nobility are guided mainly by local interests. . . . In the Middle Ages, the power of the monarchy does not rest on any disciplined state apparatus, . . . but chiefly on the size of its own landholdings, its "crownlands." . . . Under these circumstances, the conditions arose that brought the spirit of capitalism to maturity in the same period when primitive accumulation all at once supplied Western Europe with masses of riches and proletarians that needed only that spirit for them to give rise to industrial capitalism.

CHAPTER FIVE
Free Labor

. . . Generally speaking, the mentality of the ruling classes sets the tone for the lower classes in every age. Not only because the former surpass the masses in power and splendor and attract their attention, but also . . . because the ruling classes own everything that the oppressed and exploited yearn for. . . . In antiquity, contempt for work spread from the aristocracy to the other classes. . . . The craftsman . . . wanted to attain a life free of work by buying slaves, . . . or by selling his political power. . . . The position of the craftsman in the Middle Ages is completely different.[4] A free man, but with no prospect of ever becoming an exploiter of other men, he lives solely from his labor, but he is also capable of warding off any exploitation by others. . . .

Since the emergence of the state, work had, to an ever-higher degree, been held in low esteem, despised by the exploiters, hated by the exploited. . . . The medieval craftsman makes work once again honorable. His work is not forced upon him by anyone. The product of his labor is entirely his own. His work is the foundation of his social power, which permits him to strive, within the town, for freedom and equality vis-à-vis the classes standing above him, the merchants, the usurers, and the patricians. But it also enables the town, along with the nobility and the Church, to influence the state and to wrest ever more concessions from the monarchy.

The importance of handicraft in the Middle Ages was greater than in the

---

4. Kautsky had described the position of medieval craftsmen with special emphasis on conflicts between guildmasters, journeymen, and unorganized workers in *Vorläufer*, I, 63–112.

Graeco-Roman and the Oriental world, if only because now there were no slaves in the town whose competition held down free labor. But also because the market for the products of urban industries was now more extensive, and the demand for craftsmen was therefore greater. . . . In northern climates . . . the lower classes, too, frequently have need of the craftsmen *[for their clothing and housing]*. In addition, the peasant himself is better off than in the times when slavery predominated in the cities. He is now freed if he flees to the town: a warning to the landlords . . . not to place *[too heavy]* burdens on the peasants. . . . The medieval peasant generally has more interest in the products of handicraft and has a greater need of them.

. . . The craftsmen of a trade joined together in associations. . . . *[Whereas]* in the Orient and in antiquity, the craftsmen's guilds were usually just as weak as handicraft was, . . . *[the medieval guilds,]* made bold and defiant by their association, free and socially indispensable, developed a new spirit, . . . that of pride in work, of contempt for nonworkers, not only of the propertyless vagabonds, but also of the idlers among the lords, whether those at the sovereign's court, in the aristocracy's castles, or in the Church.

. . . Free labor made it possible to entrust the worker with more delicate tools. It made it advantageous to employ labor-saving devices. As a result of free labor, the achievements of natural science improved technology, and what was learned from the new technology in turn provided science with new knowledge. In all likelihood, this was first noticeable in the mining industry, which in antiquity and in the Orient had been carried on only with forced laborers, slaves, and convicts. . . . In the sphere of the slaveless economy of the West, mining *[was]* probably the first branch of production in which capitalist enterprise appeared on a relatively extensive scale.[5] But the miners were . . . free, defiant men, who could be persuaded to undertake the dangerous and forbidding work in the bowels of the earth only by the offer of even better conditions than those of the free workers in the towns. In these circumstances, it became both possible and advantageous for the entrepreneurs to procure devices for saving or facilitating labor. The very same mining industry that in antiquity had become the locus of the most brutal drudgery became, since the Middle Ages, the starting point of the most refined technology. . . .

The development of technology in the mining industry of necessity had to have an effect on the technology of the town. But the handicrafts of the latter on their own also produced reflective men of a higher level of learning who were able to perfect the existing technology. . . . By means of free labor, handicraft and natural science had developed so much that they were

5. Kautsky had dealt at some length with the development of mining in the medieval and early modern period in *Vorläufer*, I, 112–46. See also his earlier article on the role of miners in the German Peasant War, "Die Bergarbeiter und der Bauernkrieg."

able not merely to appropriate the achievements of the Arabs, but also to make them into the starting point for that grandiose development of natural science and of technology . . . which conferred on European society of the last centuries its enormous superiority over every other hitherto existing social formation.

This development was completely confined to the towns. That the military nobility, which ruled over and exploited the countryside, could not participate in it was obvious. But the Church, too, the representative of the intelligentsia in the Middle Ages, contributed as good as nothing to the course of this development. Rather, the Church hindered and crippled it to the best of its ability. . . . The Church had been a progressive element as long as the traditions of Graeco-Roman culture represented a higher level of development than predominantly Germanic barbarism.[6] Once the latter had been overcome, tradition became a fetter on the understanding of reality and on the utilization of its elements for human ends. But the Church could not escape from the influence of the tradition that had become its essential intellectual nature. It was all the less able to do so as it was an apparatus of domination and consequently, just like other centralized castes of priests before it, aimed at uniformity, not at freedom of thought.

This freedom of thought, which had brought forth such brilliant results in the city-states of antiquity, arose . . . anew in the towns of the Christian Occident, but now hand in hand with the freedom of labor, which antiquity had been lacking to such a great degree. . . . But it was not the craftsmen who became the pioneers and most distinguished agents *[of the new way of thinking]*, much as their work created its material basis. The objects of the new thought were so wide-ranging and so diverse . . . that soon a single individual could no longer completely master them. . . . Alongside the intelligentsia of the Church and the court, there now appeared a bourgeois one, which from the outset stood opposed to those two strata.[7]

CHAPTER SIX

Asceticism

We must discuss yet another side of the way of thinking that arose in the free handicrafts of the Middle Ages, in diametrical opposition to the way of thinking of the ruling classes, and that represented something entirely new.

. . . Like the brigand, the warrior and the military nobility, too, are bent

6. Kautsky had discussed this role of the Church as well as its political and economic power in the Middle Ages in his *Thomas More*, pp. 34–41.

7. See also IV:7:16, below.

on prodigality, on squandering products, workers, indeed often even means of production. . . . Their way of thinking becomes normative also for the other exploiting strata. . . . We find the same phenomena in the Middle Ages. The same passion for war on the part of the nobility, the same joy in boundless pleasure and ostentation among the aristocrats, the clergy, the urban patricians, merchants, and bankers, and the same satisfaction taken by the lower classes in the luxury and the extravagance of the upper classes. . . .

The lower classes were, however, not always unanimous in this satisfaction. . . . Exploitation was necessarily always endured with difficulty by the exploited. But where it was traditional and there was no prospect of throwing it off, it was usually borne submissively as divinely ordained dependence. Where . . . it became possible for the exploited to move more freely, there immediately arose among them a mood of opposition. . . . But when conditions . . . offered no prospect of attaining anything through struggle, then their opposition remained confined to mere thought. . . . Out of the misery of the poor and the exploited a virtue was made, to which the way of living of the wealthy was contrasted as depravity. Under these circumstances, asceticism, praised as the path to sanctity, came to be both preached and practiced. . . . Usually it was the poor themselves from whose ranks the ascetics originated, but sometimes it was also exploiters who had gotten indigestion from an unbridled life of pleasure.

Thus it was . . . at the time of the declining Roman Empire and of the emergence of Christianity; thus it was in the Orient . . . and . . . similar circumstances appeared when the Middle Ages were coming to an end. . . . The prodigality and also the indebtedness of the nobility and the princes grew rapidly. In general, the lower classes took delight in the extravagant display of the courts and the Church. . . . But . . . protest against the conduct of the exploiters did not fail to appear, and its first form was the condemnation of their life of pleasure and therefore of the life of pleasure in general, hence the preaching of asceticism. However, asceticism now assumed two different forms. On the one hand, it drew upon the forms of the old asceticism that were present in Christianity. . . . The Church had long before found forms that permitted it to recognize the tradition of renunciation and nevertheless to engage in the opposite practice. . . .

But, in addition, there arose another kind of asceticism . . . something quite new, an economically as well as politically revolutionary factor. The old asceticism had arisen out of the low esteem in which work was held. The fakirs . . . , the wandering dervishes, . . . the mendicant monks, they all . . . lived from charity, that is, they lived by letting others work for them. The asceticism . . . of free workers is of a quite different kind. Toward the end of the Middle Ages, this asceticism sprang forth from the way of thinking of the craftsmen opposed *[to the great exploiters]*. These new ascetics find the source of their strength and their pride in their work. Their asceticism must not go so far that it is detrimental to their ability to work and to fight. Thus no fasting and no mortification of the flesh, no doing without good solid food, without good clothing and lodging, without a healthy family life. . . .

Like the wage-laborer, the craftsman lives from his work, . . . but in contrast to him the craftsman controls *[his]* means of production and *[his]* products. . . . In the Age of Discovery and of the Reformation, the germs both of proletarian and industrial-capitalist class-consciousness were already contained in the craftsmen. Consequently, their opposition to the ruling classes assumed at a very early time two different forms, a communistic one and an individualistic one. . . . Each of these directions found expression in the most diverse anti-Catholic sects. I have treated of the communistic sects in my book *Die Vorläufer des neueren Sozialismus* [The Precursors of Modern Socialism]. . . . Heretical communism recruited its adherents chiefly among the miners, who at the time of the Reformation were already pure wage-laborers in the service of capital, as well as among the weavers, who also already exhibited many proletarian features. . . . Nonetheless, in the sixteenth century there was not yet a distinct and class-conscious proletariat. The petty-bourgeois basis of the Anabaptist movement was not strong enough to sustain a rebellious communism hostile to the state in a period of the most ferocious persecutions. . . .

The other direction of the oppositional new asceticism, the individualistic one, was more congenial to the spirit of the handicrafts and to their mode of production, which did not tend toward large-scale enterprises. . . . *[Its]* economic basis *[was]* the strongest possible promotion of individually owned and operated enterprises, the unification of their forces against the common enemy in mutual helpfulness. Given the separate operations of the individual enterprises, this helpfulness finally became nothing other than the obligation of the brother blessed with more than he needed to extend to the more needy brother credit, not charity, nor credit for purposes of extravagance but rather for productive expenditures. This presupposed a particular creditworthiness on the part of the borrower. This . . . form of ascetic opposition found . . . expression in numerous sects. Calvinism became the historically most important one among them or, more correctly, a particular current in Calvinism for its rebelliousness was just as open to aristocratic elements as to bourgeois ones.[8] . . .

The bourgeois current of Calvinism found its strongest expression in England, where the handicrafts, especially those of the giant city of London, jointly with peasant elements, were made strong by special circumstances. . . . The asceticism of English Calvinism conferred on it its particular name of Puritanism. . . . The long contest between revolution and counterrevo-

---

8. See IV:7:3, above.

lution in England during the seventeenth century ended . . . with a compromise that allowed the Puritan sects freedom of organization and agitation and the possibility of the freest economic development. From that time on until the present day, compromise has become the general form in which political and economic conflicts in Britain are settled. From that time on, the way was also cleared for industrial capitalism in Britain more than in any other country of Europe. The factors that brought this about [included] . . . those arising out of the geographical situation of the country . . . [and] its natural provision with minerals valuable for industry. . . . Puritanism . . . certainly fostered very much the emergence of industrial capitalism in Britain, but its effect must not be overestimated. And even less must Puritanism as a religious phenomenon be plucked out of the total historical context and considered a pure mystery that sprang forth from the soul of religious man just in the England of the seventeenth century through the spontaneous motion of religion without any impulse from without.

The way of thinking Max Weber calls the "spirit of capitalism" that according to him appeared prior to industrial capitalism and only made the latter possible and that is supposed to have its origin in Calvinism—we can find this way of thinking already in Anabaptist communism, which was by no means tending toward capitalism, and in its precursors, as well as among the Puritans. It is the spirit of the handicrafts rebelling against feudal, ecclesiastical, princely, and usurious exploitation and prodigality: the spirit of sobriety, of assiduous diligence, as well as of frugality and productive accumulation, that is, of the accumulation of goods and money, not in order to squander it later, but in order to increase one's productive forces and therewith one's own power. This spirit brought about the flourishing both of the communistic industry of the Baptists in Moravia and of the individualistic industry of the Puritans in England a century later.[9]

As we have seen, Weber cites Benjamin Franklin as an example of the capitalist spirit.[10] Now what does the latter preach? Industriousness, moderation, and frugality. . . . But . . . what is purely capitalistic about Franklin's recommendations? Are they not also characteristic of every good master of a craft since the Middle Ages? . . . Weber emphasizes particularly as a characteristic of the capitalist spirit the admonition always to be concerned with being deserving of credit. . . . In the demand for personal industriousness and personal moderation as the precondition of deserving credit, one could rather see a feature of the petty-bourgeois spirit than of the capitalist spirit, but, to be sure, a result of that side of the petty bourgeoisie that is akin to capital, in contrast to the side it shares with the proletariat.

9. Kautsky had described it in *Vorläufer*, I, 215–19.
10. See IV:7:3, above.

The Emergence of Industrial Capital

Like that of the Baptists, the industry of the Puritans also had to grow. In the one case as in the other, there prevailed diligence, moderation, abstinence from all pleasures that cost time and money. In the one as in the other, there was the same effort characteristic of the intelligent, well-off craftsman to make his production apparatus as effective as possible and also to develop his personal productive force as much as possible. . . . All of that yielded . . . large surplus products in the enterprises, among the Puritans as well as among the Baptists. . . . What appears as God's blessing to the religiously minded sectarians presents itself to us in the case of the individualist Puritans as nothing other than the accumulation of capital. *[Kautsky quotes Weber]* on the naive fusion of profit-making with piety [The Protestant Ethic, *p. 162*]. In a footnote, Weber correctly observes: "Possession in the feudal-seigneurial form of its use is what is odious, not possession in itself" (*The Protestant Ethic*, p. 267). That is evidence, however, that the Puritan ethic arises out of the class struggle of the self-confident and defiant petty bourgeois, especially of the craftsman against the feudal nobility, hence out of an economic basis, and that it is not the economy that results from the religion.

Weber himself was well aware of the economic foundation of the Puritan ethic that engendered the "spirit of capitalism." He . . . showed that the most pious Puritans were up-and-coming petty bourgeois. *[Kautsky quotes The Protestant Ethic, pp. 174–75, and a footnote on p. 279.]* The problem was to prevent the rich Puritans from deserting to the enemy . . . , from investing their wealth in large commercial enterprises or in financial transactions, in loans to the state or to feudal wastrels, in tax-farming, etc. They had to employ their money in a manner pleasing to God. But, to the craftsmen's God, industry, the production of commodities, was especially pleasing.

The same development . . . also created the conditions for carrying out this expansion of commodity production profitably, thus in accordance with God's intentions. The times of Puritanism were times of very rapid growth of the proletariat. The Puritan way of thinking of the rising petty bourgeois . . . necessarily fostered the industriousness of all workers who adopted it, whether they labored in their own enterprise or in that of another. And the free craftsman, who spurns as a humiliation any charity from the wealthy lord whom he is combatting, refuses to have anything at all to do with begging. . . . Just as he does for the *[Puritans']* condemnation of poor-relief, Weber also presents much evidence for the fact that Puritanism produced undemanding and docile workers. *[Kautsky quotes footnotes from The Prot-*

estant Ethic, *pp. 268 and 282, including the following:]* "Capitalism at the time of its development needed labourers who were available for economic exploitation for conscience' sake. Today it is in the saddle, and hence able to force people to labour without transcendental sanctions." There is much truth in these remarks, but they are one-sidedly exaggerated and pointed. Industrial capitalism would not have gotten very far if no other workers had been available to it than the pietistic wage-laborers from the ranks of the Puritans. In addition to the latter, it had available, even in its beginning, numerous propertyless people who were driven not by their religion but by their misery to place themselves at the service of capital. Also, . . . we find capitalist enterprise in the mining industry long before Puritanism, indeed even before Calvin. . . .

The religious-ethical spirit of Puritanism . . . is . . . not to be explained by a spontaneous movement of religion and ethics, but by the living conditions of a handicraft that was struggling to establish itself and that possessed the strength and the will to cast off the domination of the feudal nobility . . . in every respect: economic, political, as well as ethical. And the influence of the Puritan way of thinking on the evolution of industrial capitalism must not be overestimated. It constitutes just one of its roots. . . . Its most important root was the possibility of profitably employing industrial workers on a relatively large scale, at first as miners or as craftsmen, who . . . worked for a merchant who sold their products. . . . Traders and usurers, too, now began to invest their accumulated profits . . . in industry. And these wellsprings of accumulation were soon flowing more abundantly for rising industrial capitalism than the profits originating from the handicrafts. . . . This development occurs everywhere, among very diverse creeds where there is, on the one hand, accumulated capital and, on the other hand, masses of proletarians, who either are ashamed to beg or are prevented by force from doing so, and who are therefore compelled to live from the sale of their labor-power. Puritanism certainly contributed much to the development of industrial capitalism and to making England the country in which it assumed its classical form. Weber has said much about this subject that is profound and important. But what he has said refutes neither the materialist conception of history nor the account given by Marx in *Capital* of the evolution of industrial capitalism.

CHAPTER EIGHT

Progress and Social Revolution

. . . Industrial capitalism unites numerous free workers under a common command. It disposes of the means to increase the augmented strength of their cooperation still more by artificial devices and it arises in a time when science has reached the point of inventing such devices on a rapidly growing scale. . . . Competition forces the capitalist to employ the most advanced equipment. . . . It compels him incessantly to accumulate a portion of his profits, so that he can expand and improve his enterprise. . . . Where industrial capitalism makes its breakthrough, it overcomes the degrading effects of feudal exploitation and brings to society continuous increase of wealth, hence economic progress. Decaying society is no longer, as before, regenerated from without, by barbarians. . . . Now the regeneration of society takes place from within, through motive forces it develops itself. . . . Today this is also the only possible method of further development. . . .

The earlier methods of exploitation in the state revolutionized in the main only the production of luxuries.[11] They left the masses in the old conditions of production. . . . In contrast, capitalist production becomes mass production early on; it revolutionizes primarily the relations of production of goods for the masses. . . . Usury in the form of credit now becomes a means of supplying growing industry with increased funds. And commerce . . . now makes the sale of articles for the masses its chief task. It, too, enters into the service of mass production, for which it becomes indispensable under the conditions of capitalism. . . . An immense process of change now takes place, rapidly and irresistibly, that fundamentally reshapes also the conditions of the mass of the exploited. . . .

Only in severe conflicts of interest could the new tendencies of industrial capitalism prevail, only in class struggles of the most intense kind and on a scale such as the world had never seen before. Class struggle is not a new invention. Classes and their antagonisms are as old as the state, and when the classes have some freedom of movement in the state, these antagonisms discharge themselves in the form of class struggles. . . . However, when the conditions of production, above all, those of mass production, have not changed, then *[even changes in the power of classes]* do not lead to new forms of production, but only to a change of the persons or of the beneficiaries of these forms. In the most extreme case, they lead to the supplanting of an existing form of production by another coexisting with it, often by an older form. In such circumstances, class struggle, as intensely as it might rage, cannot become a means of higher social development. . . . Where the conditions for the creation of new forms of production do not exist, even the most violent and most thorough political revolution cannot become a social revolution. . . . That was the case in antiquity. . . .

The French Revolution and, before it, the English Revolution took place under entirely different preconditions. . . . *[There]* we find that the elements of industrial capitalism are given: an independent urban petty bourgeoisie struggling to rise, which already comprises the beginnings of industrial

11. See IV:4:13, above.

capital as well as those of the industrial proletariat and with which the peasantry allies itself. The new mode of production developing out of these elements feels itself cramped and paralyzed by the old feudal powers, which threaten the whole society with decay and death. Once these powers are defeated, the consequence is not a mere change in the persons composing the various classes, nor a reanimation of outmoded forms of production, but a swift and energetic advance to new forms that had not been able to unfold up to that time. Thus the change in the power relations of the classes becomes an upward shift to new, higher forms of economy and society.

If one does not regard the mere overthrow of the government, but the new formations resulting from it, as the essence of a social revolution, then the latter is something that appeared only with industrial capitalism, . . . but since then has become an indispensable means of further social development. No matter how many events of earlier revolutions might be superficially similar to those linked with the rise of industrial capitalism, they are not, like these, *social revolutions*.

CHAPTER NINE
Modern Democracy

. . . It is often thought that the idea of cooperation among classes contradicts the idea of class struggle. . . . But in a more highly developed state . . . numerous classes appear, having very diverse, in part antagonistic, in part harmonious interests, and each class is, moreover, extensively differentiated internally. It is a crudely simplistic conception of Marxism that sees in the present-day state only proletarians and capitalists, because in *Capital* Marx could operate only with these two classes for the purpose of laying bare the laws of the capitalist mode of production. As early as 1889, I devoted an essay, *Die Klassengegensätze im Zeitalter der Französischen Revolution* [Class Antagonisms in the Era of the French Revolution], solely to the refutation of this simplifying distortion of the notion of class struggle. There I showed that this revolution was, to be sure, a class struggle, but a struggle of extremely diverse classes that were often deeply divided internally. Under such conditions, it becomes unavoidable from time to time that different classes join forces against another class or several other classes in order to fight more effectively for some common interest. . . .

It is an error, though, to consider such alliances as enduring formations. . . . A policy would be mistaken that presupposed a lasting cooperation of different classes or that even went so far as to believe that such cooperation was the method by which one's own class (or political party, something that cannot be discussed further here) could come to power in the state and achieve its own particular ultimate goals. But, in the history of the world, cooperation of different classes has often taken place and achieved very great results. No political revolution has come about in any other way. This cooperation is always the first act of the revolution, while the second consists in the conflict of the victors among themselves. . . .

As a rule, the king and the citizens of the towns acted together against the haughty nobility. . . . Yet powerful, independent towns had to appear just as threatening to the king as a powerful, independent nobility and a powerful, independent Church. The Age of Discoveries and of the Reformation, which greatly expanded the sphere of commodity production, increased the power of those who had money at their disposal . . . *[and]* the hunger for money among the nonindustrial and noncapitalist exploiters: the aristocrats, the clerics, and the princes. . . . The same development of the monetary economy brought economic ruin to many an aristocrat, his indebtedness to the hated townspeople. . . . But there was . . . yet another path that led to money. . . . From haughty, high-handed knights, the nobles changed into smooth courtiers who plundered the state at the prince's court, or . . . officers of the hosts of mercenaries that henceforth took the place of the . . . feudal levies. Even in Catholic countries, but more so still in Protestant ones, the Church became to a certain degree a state-church. Its clerics were made into officials paid by the state. Thus the power of the monarchy was enormously increased. Once its most dangerous enemies, the nobility and the Church now became its most faithful supporters. The monarchy attained absolute power in the state.

The united power of these elements was now turned against the towns and the peasants, especially the former. . . . What the decaying nobility and the flagging Church were no longer able to take from the townspeople by themselves, the increasingly strong government of the state took from them, in order to pay the nobility and the Church from the loot and to turn them into its obedient servants. The absolute monarchs, it is true, attempted to feed as well as possible the goose that laid the golden eggs for them. They promoted commerce, . . . industry, and transport through the many diverse methods of so-called mercantilism. . . . With the growth of industry, the strength of the industrial classes increased; simultaneously, their antagonism to the ruling regime was heightened. . . . At the same time, the demands made on the state by parasitical, lazy clerics and idlers at court grew far more rapidly than did the ability of industry to pay taxes. These parasites threatened the very existence of the state. It became essential to cast them off. But since the absolute monarchy had tied itself to them for better or for worse, it had to fall along with them. . . . From these struggles against the feudal and clerical monarchy, there resulted a new form of democracy, nowhere perfect, everywhere driven back from time to time by setbacks, but still on the whole advancing victoriously, constantly growing in strength and in extent. . . .

The democracy of antiquity usually achieves its consummation at the high point of the economic development of the state. It ushers in the decline of the state. . . . Modern democracy, on the other hand, arises in a situation in which it must first clear the way for a technological and economic upswing that proceeds ever more powerfully and has no end in the foreseeable future. . . . It does not sink into despotism but arises in battle against it. And the democratic movement finally attains the strength to smash despotism completely. . . . Never before had the thinking of men been so far-reaching, so profound, and so boldly critical as in the age of modern absolutism, which is known as the Age of Enlightenment. . . . The democratic revolution carried forward the effort of absolutism to establish the equality of all before the law. But it alone had the strength to achieve it completely, to put an end to the legal privileges of the nobility and of the state-church. To the extent that this might not have succeeded yet, it will necessarily happen with the further strengthening of democracy, that is, of the democratic elements. . . .

The democracy of antiquity was always built on slavery and on the domination by the polity in question of tributary areas. Modern democracy grows out of the freedom of labor in the town. It necessarily strives for freedom of labor also in the countryside. . . . The democracy of antiquity was merely that of the city; modern democracy is democracy of the state. For the first time since the formation of the state, . . . modern democracy brings about complete equality of rights for . . . all adult members of the polity. That distinguishes the modern democratic state fundamentally from all earlier states. In this regard, it is like the prestate polity. But it is distinguished from the latter not only by the existence of a state apparatus, . . . but also by the existence of exploited and exploiting classes within itself. In this regard, . . . the modern democratic state is like the other earlier forms of the state. Political equality of rights does not of itself eliminate exploitation.

Socialists who fancy that they are radical, because they believe that only the necessary quantity of boldness and energy of will is required in order to leap forward into socialism with a single bound, speak disparagingly of democracy as merely "formal" or "bourgeois" democracy, because achieving it does not of itself bring about this leap into socialism. . . . The ridiculousness of the words "formal" and "bourgeois" in this context becomes immediately obvious as soon as we list the democratic freedoms one by one. Is it possible to speak of a formal or bourgeois universal, secret suffrage? Or, for example, of formal or bourgeois freedom of association, freedom of assembly, freedom of the press, etc.? Of course, . . . a merely formal democracy is also possible and, unfortunately, often enough actually occurs . . . when the democratic freedoms exist only on the paper of the constitution and are trampled underfoot in the practice of the state. But it is sheer mischief to speak of formal democracy also when the democratic freedoms are fully in force, just because the mere existence of democracy does not immediately abolish all class differences.

The question that is at issue here for socialists is whether democracy is necessary for the proletariat to accomplish its social advance. It would be a sleight of hand to replace it with the question whether democracy is equivalent to the abolition of all exploitation and triumphantly to declare the negative answer to this second question to be a negative answer to the first one.[12]

Capital in the Democratic State

. . . In Eastern Europe and the Orient, industry skips . . . the stage of medieval handicraft which . . . only made industrial capitalism possible in Western Europe. Brought to the East from Western Europe, the new industry immediately assumes there the hitherto most highly developed forms of capitalism. Thus a powerful petty bourgeoisie does not arise there to pave the way for the industrial proletariat for the achievement and maintenance of true democracy. Lacking all traditions of a "bourgeois" democratic movement, that is, one borne by a strong petty bourgeoisie, the industrial proletariat in Eastern Europe and even more in Asia immediately comes to the forefront of the struggle for democracy and sets its stamp upon the latter. That means that the course of history there will not be a mere repetition of the history of Western Europe since the Middle Ages.[13] For the industrial proletariat develops other abilities, inclinations, and needs than the petty bourgeoisie. And the struggle for democracy is never a struggle solely for the political rights comprised by democracy, but also a struggle for the improvement of the economic and social position of the democratic elements.

Much as obtaining and safeguarding democracy may require military superiority of the democratic classes, . . . there nevertheless appears with the

---

12. The themes of the last two paragraphs were repeatedly stressed by Kautsky in his anti-Communist writings. See *The Dictatorship of the Proletariat*, pp. 4–41 (where, on pp. 35–37, he could quote his earlier article, "Ein sozialdemokratischer Katechismus," pp. 402—403); *Terrorism and Communism*, pp. 229, 231; *Von der Demokratie zur Staats-Sklaverei*, pp. 27–28; *The Labour Revolution*, pp. 22–31; *Neue Programme*, p. 35 (this passage appears in English translation in *Social Democracy versus Communism*, pp. 120–21). See also pp. 393 and 405 below. Kautsky had emphasized the same points particularly with reference to parliamentarism already in his 1892 commentary on the Erfurt Program, *The Class Struggle*, p. 188, and especially a year later in *Parlamentarismus und Demokratie*, pp. 61–62, 95–122. See also "Republik und Sozialdemokratie in Frankreich," pp. 479–80; *Die Befreiung der Nationen*, pp. 16–17; *The Labour Revolution*, pp. 81–82.

13. See IV:8:5, below.

modern democratic state a completely new type of state. Within the democratic state—once democracy has become secure—there is no longer room for armed struggle as a way of carrying on class conflicts. These are decided in a peaceful manner by propaganda and by voting. Even the mass strike as a means by which the working class can exert pressure hardly seems applicable under democracy. It is certainly quite compatible with democracy, being nothing more than a comprehensive application of the freedom of association guaranteed by democracy. But it offers a prospect of success only vis-à-vis a government that is not anchored in the majority of the population. The attempt of a minority to impose, by bringing production to a halt, a measure on the majority that the latter resolutely rejects can never succeed in a democracy, and the ultimate failure of such a strike can result only in the serious diminution of the fighting strength of the defeated party and class for quite some time. It is another matter when a minority wants to impose its will on the majority and do violence to democracy. For protecting democracy, the mass strike can have a decisive effect.[14]

... Class conflicts are not precluded by democracy. They only cease being civil wars.... To that extent, democracy moderates class conflicts. The economic antagonisms, however, remain, and can even become more intense. But how is it possible that exploitation continues in a democracy, if there is no more military superiority on the part of the ruling and exploiting classes?... Industrial capitalism has no need of military force in order to exist.... It succeeded by producing more cheaply than the modes of production it encountered, thus by being economically more advantageous for society.... It advances society by developing the forces of production in the form of large-scale enterprise. But it does so only by employing numerous wage-laborers in its factories, whom it exploits just as the slave driver did earlier. And this exploitation, personal profit, not the profit of society, is the purpose of the capitalist firm.

Yet, it is not direct forced labor but free labor that the capitalist employs. ... It is his lack of property that drives the free laborer to hire himself out as a wage-laborer. This lack of property on the part of large masses of

14. Kautsky had been engaged in long polemics on the political mass strike and the role of unorganized workers in it with Rosa Luxemburg in 1910 and with Anton Pannekoek in 1911–12. His more important contributions to these polemics were the following: "Was nun?"; "Eine neue Strategie;" "Zwischen Baden und Luxemburg;" "Die Aktion der Masse;" "Die neue Taktik;" "Der jüngste Radikalismus." All but the third and the last of these articles have been collected in Grunenberg, ed., *Die Massenstreikdebatte* and all except the last one appear in French translation in Henri Weber, ed., *Kautsky, Luxemburg, Pannekoek: Socialisme.* Both of these volumes contain also major articles by Luxemburg and Pannekoek. The articles "Was nun?" and "Die Aktion der Masse" as well as earlier writings on the mass strike by Kautsky and by other German Socialists are reprinted in his *Der politische Massenstreik,* and long excerpts from "Was nun?" appear in English translated in *Selected Political Writings,* pp. 54–73. For a later statement on the subject, see *Sozialisten und Krieg,* pp. 330–35.

workers . . . is, like the primitive accumulation of capital, in its beginning as a mass phenomenon, a result of brutal force, of the expulsion of free peasants and tenant farmers from their farms, etc. However, this force was likewise not exercised by the industrial capitalists, even if its results benefited them just as did those of primitive accumulation. Later it was the competition of industrial capitalism itself that ruined numerous craftsmen and made them propertyless, but in the beginnings of capitalism that did not yet play a role. At first, the capitalist appeared as a benefactor, who gave employment to the propertyless. . . .

Once it had become quite widespread, industrial capitalism itself produced by purely economic means the hosts of propertyless workers it needed. . . . That happened in a completely peaceful manner, . . . through methods of cheapening products . . . at the expense of innumerable industrious and useful individuals. . . . It was the majority, the mass of consumers, who benefited from this. . . . Without any use of external force, the propertyless were compelled, by the existence of private property in the means of production, to sell their labor-power to capital. This private property was not created by capital. The free peasant and the craftsman have need of it. . . . Capital cannot be formed without security of property. Who would accumulate without it? Even the wage-laborer clings to it, partly because he continues to think like his peasant or craftsman ancestors, partly because he recognizes that without such security the entire process of production and hence also the existence of the workers themselves would necessarily go to ruin in wild chaos.

When rebellions of a more highly developed industrial working class occurred, the workers not only refrained from looting but also . . . prevented the lumpenproletariat from engaging in it. *[Kautsky contrasts the absence of plundering in revolutionary Paris in February 1848 and under the Commune of 1871 and in Germany in 1918 to its frequency in rebellions influenced by slavery and serfdom in antiquity and in Russia in 1917.]* The worker is opposed to arbitrary infringements of property for the benefit of single individuals; but for him society stands above property, and when the interest of society collides with a particular property, it is the latter that must give way. The capitalist, on the other hand, . . . asserts an absolute claim *[to his property]*, which both state and society must respect. . . .

Industrial capital . . . cannot simply be expropriated without economic damage to society and to the workers themselves. Capitalist concerns can be transformed into socialist ones only gradually. . . . There are certainly a number of capitalist enterprises that a socialist regime can, and indeed often must, socialize immediately, if they have assumed a monopolistic character that is oppressing the entire polity, . . . *[but]* the expropriated capitalists must be adequately compensated. If that is not done, then it is an injustice to the other capitalists whose firms are not yet ripe for being socialized; but it is also economically imprudent. For one then takes from the other capitalists any motivation to carry on with their firms, to continue to invest money in them, if they have to be prepared to have this money later simply confiscated.

Either the socialist regime would have to take over all capitalist concerns simultaneously, without any preparation, and to carry on with them, something that is entirely impossible, all the more so the higher the industrial development of the particular state. Or the socialist regime will bring about a general closing of all capitalist concerns and thus an industrial crisis of such an extent that in comparison with it all previous industrial crises would pale into insignificance. This would necessarily mean the bankruptcy of the socialist government. This crisis could not end with the construction of socialism, but only with the revival of the capitalists' rule.

In a socialist polity, the expropriation of capitalist enterprises without compensation could become appropriate and necessary as a punitive measure against those capitalists who seek to damage the socialist regime by shutting down their enterprises. But this measure, if it is to be effective, presupposes that to those capitalists who do not close their enterprises, the prospect of full compensation be held out for a later time when their branch of production attains socialist maturity.

Hence even a socialist regime, no matter how revolutionary it might be, will have to deal differently with capital than the bourgeois revolutions did with the property of precapitalist exploiters. When enterprises are socialized, their owners will have to be compensated—which, to be sure, does not preclude that the sums of money used for compensation be raised by taxing the entire capitalist class.[15]

As we see, capitalist exploitation rests on completely different foundations than the precapitalist methods. It rests . . . on the *economic necessity* of a property, the function of which can, certainly, be made superfluous by superior economic institutions, but which cannot be eliminated by the mere application of military force without severe economic damage to the country. Capitalist property must always return as long as the conditions for economic institutions superior to capital are not given, even when force succeeds for a time in smashing it. This, incidentally, could happen only in barbaric lands, the laboring population of which has not yet grasped the requirements of industry.

The property on which capitalist exploitation is based is therefore a

15. The question of compensation for socialized enterprises, including the point raised in the last sentence, was discussed by Kautsky at greater length in an article, "Expropriation und Konfiskation," published immediately after the outbreak of the German Revolution and reprinted as an appendix to the 2nd edition of *Was ist Sozialisierung?*, pp. 28–32, and in 1922 in *The Labour Revolution*, pp. 131–42. The gradual and "less painful" method of "confiscation through taxation" had already been suggested by Kautsky in a lecture in 1902, during the Revisionist controversy; *The Social Revolution*, pp. 118–23. See also p. 209, above.

temporary economic necessity. . . . As long as this is the case, it has no need
of military force for its protection against the entire working class. . . .
Industrial capital and modern democracy create a type of state such as was
previously quite impossible.

CHAPTER ELEVEN

The National State

Yet another very important point must be mentioned, with respect to which
the state of modern democracy differs from the earlier forms of the state.
. . . The state is formed by the joining together of several, often very numerous and necessarily small polities to make a large whole under the
dominion of a conquering tribe. . . . It is only the military might of the
ruling class that holds *[it]* together. . . .

Modern absolutism . . . grew in strength simultaneously with industrial
capitalism, in a period of rapid development of the productive forces and
of knowledge as well as of growing interest in matters of state, at least on
the part of the population of the large cities, and of a completely unprecedented boldness of thought. . . . The state bureaucracy oppressed . . . all
parts of the country to the same degree. Hence the struggle against it also
took hold of all parts of the state. The striving for democracy united them.
The centralization of the state apparatus resulted in a particular city becoming the center of the state. . . . Not only the king and a principal part of the
administration of the state and of the army together with their leaders made
their seat there, but also the court nobility. The capital city was linked with
all parts of the state through means of transport as perfect as possible. The
bulk of the surplus value obtained in the state converged in the seat of the
court and was expended there, which in turn attracted numerous elements
of the population to the capital. . . . The entire intelligentsia of the country
and also its lumpenproletariat now thronged to the capital. . . .

The language that was customary in the capital city became the language
of the royal court, of the state administration, of the judicial courts, and of
the schools in which the bureaucrats were educated; it became the language
of command in the army, but also the language of the educated not only
in the capital, but throughout the state. Other languages or dialects spoken
in the territory of the state developed no literature and education of their
own. They became the languages of the uneducated and were confined to
use within the family or disappeared altogether, so that ultimately everyone
in the state used the same language. . . . The representatives of the various
provinces who came together in the capital city merged there into a homogeneous community, a nation, which, proceeding outward from the
capital, came increasingly to include the whole population even of the
smaller towns and of the countryside. *[Kautsky devotes a long footnote here*

to Bauer, Die Nationalitätenfrage, *who had defined a nationality as "a community of character developed out of a common fate." Kautsky acknowledges that this definition usefully supplements his preferred one of a nationality as a community of language.]*[16] ...

Democracy ... does not merely continue with the centralized unified state it takes over from absolutism in more or less fully developed form; but it also turns it completely upside down. It is no longer the state that constitutes the nation, but the reverse. Under absolutism, very diverse areas with different languages were joined together through conquest, ... through inheritance, and through marriage, without consultation of their populations. Absolutism strove to impose on them the same language, the same laws, and the same economic policies. ... Democracy ... strives for the joining together in a common self-governing state of areas with populations that feel themselves united as a nation by the same language or by other common bonds. The government should issue from the people. In the administration, in the courts, in the schools, in the army, the language of the people should be spoken. Association through the state with tribes speaking other languages that seek to obtain a privileged position within the polity becomes intolerable. No less intolerable is the fragmentation of a nation into different small states condemned to both political and economic impotence. The striving for the national state arises out of the same conditions that lead to modern democracy. Like those conditions, it ... rests upon the principle of self-determination of peoples. Like the progress of industry, that of the self-determination of peoples is irresistible.[17] ...

The effort to establish national states has often led to military conflicts between states. ... War is always disadvantageous for democracy; it promotes military dictatorships, ... *[and it]* leads to the satisfaction of the self-determination of a nation through violation of the self-determination of other nations, hence through violation of their democracy. But, since in our era the latter always prevails in the end after all, a state cannot find rest and is repeatedly threatened from without as long as its borders are such as to do violence to parts of foreign peoples. *[Kautsky denounces Bismarck for excluding German Austria and including Alsace-Lorraine in the new German empire and fears that some of the new boundaries of 1919 might lead to further*

---

16. For earlier reviews by Kautsky of Bauer's book, see *Nationalität und Internationalität* and *Die Befreiung der Nationen*, pp. 32–39, 42–44. Much earlier, Kautsky had dealt with the development of trade, absolutism, and the national state in *Thomas More*, pp. 10–20.

17. During World War I, Kautsky had dealt with the relationship of democracy to the national, i.e., language-based, state in *Nationalstaat, imperialistischer Staat und Staatenbund*, pp. 5–14; *Die Vereinigten Staaten Mitteleuropas*, pp. 14, 36–56; and especially *Die Befreiung der Nationen*, particularly pp. 17–32. For his studies of nationality problems in specific countries, see also *Serbien und Belgien; Elsass-Lothringen;* and *Habsburgs Glück und Ende.*

wars, but he hopes that] the democratic elements in Europe will grow stronger economically and socially, and thus also politically, rapidly enough to bestow on the League of Nations the power and the impulse to implement the adaptation of state boundaries to the needs of the nations by means of democratic methods.[18] . . .

The inhabitants of a pure national state are attached to it. . . . Not the least military force is required to hold them together. Moreover, the borders of such a state are given from the very start and determined exactly by the nature of its inhabitants. As the inhabitants of a national state rise up against any conqueror, so too do they not seek after conquests at the expense of their neighbors, when the latter are likewise national states without irredentas.

We disregard here the policy of colonial conquest that has been a cause of conflict of considerable significance between some modern states. We do not need to discuss this policy further here. . . . It affects states without capitalist industry, without modern democracy, and without national consciousness (in the modern sense). But the world is already as good as divided up, and, thanks to the capacity for expansion of European and now also of American capitalism, a capitalist industry is rapidly developing in the colonial areas. Because of it, there arises in these areas not so much an indigenous capitalist class as an indigenous proletariat, capable of engaging in struggle and eager to do so, with strong democratic and national tendencies.[19] These will soon be capable of spoiling thoroughly any conqueror's pleasure in domination and exploitation. The masses join together more easily against a foreign exploiter than against a native of their own country.

The closer we approach the condition of universal democracy in all states with industry of any significance, the more superfluous do armies become for the protection of a country; the more securely is it protected by the strength of democracy on both sides of its borders. Certainly, without such democracy, the League of Nations and everlasting peace are only a utopia. . . . It is only in our own day that democracy, at least in the most influential states, is beginning to gain sufficient strength to make it possible that from the coexistence of the states of the modern democratic type, which is completely new in history, there can emerge also the completely new institution of the abolition of armies and of war by means of a league of these states. In this modern democratic state, neither the exploitation of the working classes within it nor its relationship with its neighbors rests upon the military might of its ruling class. Nevertheless, even under democracy the state

---

18. Kautsky returned to the relation between democracy and the League of Nations ten years later in *Sozialisten und Krieg*, pp. 633–43, 668–69.

19. See IV:8:5, below.

apparatus has so far remained in the hands of such a class and has served its exploitative ends.

CHAPTER TWELVE

The Growth of the State Apparatus

a. Army, Commerce, Customs

As the functions of repression of the lower classes increasingly recede in the democratic state, it might be supposed that as a consequence of democracy the state apparatus, which after all originally served principally such functions, would become increasingly smaller. . . . In reality, however, as democracy advanced, the state apparatus became . . . ever more extensive. This was in contradiction to the tendencies of democracy but was produced by the same industrial development that made the advance of democracy irresistible. *[Kautsky cites as another example of such a "contradictory development" the tendency of industrial evolution toward the expansion of territories without customs barriers and, on the other hand, the division of old, large European empires]* into small national states as a consequence of democratization. The dependence of politics on the economy is just not as simple as some adherents of the materialist conception of history think. This dependence can bring forth serious contradictions. It belongs to the tasks of historical development to resolve them in a higher synthesis—in Europe, to join together the various, self-governing states in an economic zone within which there is free trade. . . .

Democracy has been accompanied by universal compulsory military service, that is, by an enormous expansion of armies. Radical democracy is opposed to standing armies and is in favor of the militia system, but for political, not economic, reasons. . . . In the Anglo-Saxon states there lurks behind a small professional army of hired soldiers . . . the general levy of all the people in case of a war, which necessitates the provision of armaments for such a levy even in peacetime. And how greatly do these armaments grow as a result of technological progress, which occurs in the same measure as does the progress of democracy! Existing weapons are constantly improved, and again and again new, often quite monstrous ones are invented and added to the former. They do not just threaten us with the most terrible horrors in case of war. They also constitute an oppressive, constantly growing burden in peacetime. . . .

. . . Today, in the era of highly developed democracy, a state surrounded by democracies and pursuing no aggressive tendencies hardly requires an army for its protection any longer, if the institution of the League of Nations

Chapter 12. The Growth of the State Apparatus   *383*

is at all rationally constructed. Once Russia has acquired a democratic regime and has joined the League of Nations, then one of the greatest obstacles to general disarmament will have fallen. Until now, we have not come to this point. Consequently, the progress of democracy has up to now been accompanied by continuous . . . expansion of the military state apparatus. But we may expect that from now on every advance of democracy will have the opposite effect, if it . . . encompasses a relatively large area, possibly all of Europe, if not the entire, present-day capitalist (in part state-capitalist) world and thus makes universal disarmament possible.

Nonetheless, the state apparatus will be further expanded. The functions imposed on it by labors of peace are not reduced, they increase. . . . As the population of Europe became denser in the course of the Middle Ages . . . trade grew and required improved means of transportation, which in turn augmented trade and its needs. . . . Far more even than the needs of commerce and transportation, it was military considerations that compelled emerging absolutism to improve roads, so that its armies could move more rapidly. . . . The state now had to take responsibility for highways, as well as for canals, the construction of harbors, etc. Tasks of this kind . . . were tremendously expanded by the technological revolution of industrial capitalism. . . . Railways, like the postal system and the telegraph, are so important for the existence of the entire population that a governmental superintendence and regulation of the construction and operation of railways cannot be avoided even in Britain and the United States.

. . . To these were added numerous other tasks of an economic kind. . . . Production had always been socially regulated, but it was relatively small groups that did the regulating. . . . Monarchical absolutism paralyzed and killed the self-government of the towns, the guilds, and other independent organizations. It took over their functions and added to them new ones resulting from industrial capitalism. . . . Here we shall call attention to only one point, customs.

The institution of customs is ancient. It began with the tribute traveling merchants had to pay to rapacious tribes . . . in order to obtain safe-conduct. . . . Whoever had the power, exacted duties. . . . Emerging absolutism increasingly abolished these duties, which did not benefit it, and in their place introduced customs at the borders of the state. It was, not least of all, these customs that made the new state into a solidly unified formation. At the same time, however, customs increasingly acquired . . . a new function, that of promoting industrial capitalism. Alongside the tariff intended to provide the state with revenues, there arose the protective tariff. That alone sufficed to make economic activity dependent to a high degree on the policies of the state. Subsequent economic development required ever-stronger intervention by the state in economy. One need think only of the growing tasks of social welfare policies. . . .

b. Education, Justice, Health Services

In yet other numerous areas there fall to the state tasks that it previously did not have, for example, responsibility for *education*. In antiquity, it usually remained an affair of the family... *[and]* in the Middle Ages *[one of]* the Church.... The latter drew its strength from traditions passed on through writing.... Knowledge of reading and writing became indispensable for its functionaries.... The tendencies of the religious reformers sprang out of life itself, but they drew their arguments from the Bible.... Because the struggle was therefore carried on as a literary one, ... it became all the more necessary that all opponents of the papacy be the equal of its defenders at least in the art of reading. A concern for good elementary schools was characteristic of all the reformers. That is one of the factors that conferred on the Protestant countries an economic superiority over the Catholic ones and perhaps fostered industrial capitalism in the former even more than the Calvinist Puritanism to which Max Weber attaches such importance.

Improved and more widely distributed elementary schools had become necessary not only because of opposition to the monopoly of knowledge on the part of the Church but also owing directly to the new economic conditions in the towns.... With the abolition of the self-government of the towns by monarchical absolutism, responsibility for elementary education was transferred to the state.... It reserved for itself the regulation of the schools in order to be sure that they did not permit any free thought to arise. The quality of the elementary schools was kept as low as possible, restricted to reading, writing, arithmetic, and the catechism.... For emerging democracy, the elementary school then became one of the most important objects of governmental concern. This school now... had to educate thinking, knowledgeable men who were sufficiently well informed about nature, the economy, and the state to be able to educate themselves further in the areas in which they had to accomplish something in life. That meant a tremendous expansion of the functions of the state.

... In the towns of the late Middle Ages, there were also higher-level schools,... in which Latin, the language of science of that period, was taught and the way to science itself thereby opened. Such schools, too, were in the period of absolutism taken over by the state, which... founded additional Latin schools. In some towns there were also important scholars who gathered students about themselves and... in some towns... formed regular guilds with masters, journeymen, and apprentices, ... called universities.... As the centers of all higher learning, the universities came to have very great social importance.... *[With]* emerging absolutism... *[and]* the advance of industry and the sciences, ... they represent, in keeping with the course of their historical development, a peculiar amalgamation of fac-

tories producing officials and of research centers, which on the one hand
have to disseminate the most submissive sentiments toward the state and
on the other hand have to engage in very free research. Corresponding to
the expansion of the sciences and of their technical apparatus, they, as centers
of research, have to add on ever more and ever more extensive institutes,
clinics, laboratories, etc. Due to the development of technology and of the
economy, numerous new kinds of schools are added, . . . technical and commercial intermediate schools and advanced academies, for the maintenance
and administration of which the state, not the towns, was also predominantly responsible.

The development of medical knowledge also causes . . . an expansion of
health services in general, . . . so that they . . . also become the responsibility
of the state. . . . As democracy grows, there also increases concern for the
ill part of the poorer population, which the state had previously abandoned
to its misery.

On the other hand, not only does the number of jurists grow with the
development of capitalism, but also the number of jurists employed by the
state, for example, judges. Along with the cities, the number of criminals
grows, not just that of criminals who are such from necessity, but also of
those who are criminals from greed. . . . The growth in size of the organizations of wage-laborers, which gave their members strong economic and
moral support lacking to them if they are isolated, counteracts the increase
of crimes committed from need. However, it is only in very recent times
that this effect can begin to make itself felt. Until that point, there was a
constant tendency of criminality to grow even in democratic states. . . .

With the expansion of commerce brought about by industrial capitalism,
conditions, especially in the economy, become ever more complex and
gigantic in their extent. . . . Accordingly, legislation and the administration
of justice, too, become ever more complex, and the instances of conflicts,
or at least of uncertainties, about rights and obligations requiring judicial
decisions become more numerous. Thus there is also a continuous growth
in the size of the judicial system, which had become entirely an affair of
the state since the days of absolutism, whereas formerly justice had generally
been administered in relatively small circles, . . . as by the landlord, the
village mayor, or the town, etc.

c. Taxes

[With the expansion] of the state apparatus . . . also in democracies, . . . its
expenses grow, too, . . . and consequently so does the state apparatus for
collecting taxes. . . . In antiquity, . . . it was at first simple. At a few places
used as trade depots, customs were collected; in addition, tribute was imposed on subjugated cities and rural districts, which each of them had to

raise collectively. How the city or the district divided the tax among its members and collected it from them was a matter with which the state did not concern itself. Often the state did not collect duties and taxes through its own officials at all; rather, it leased them to private individuals, to wealthy people, who were able to pay a large sum . . . for the right to bleed to the utmost the population that had been delivered up to them.

In the Middle Ages, the power of the king was so small that he could not compel the payment of taxes. . . . When occasionally a quite large expenditure became necessary that the sovereign could not cover with his own means, then he had to beg for the money from his "subjects," from the lords of the nobility and the Church, as well as from the towns. For this purpose he called their representatives together from time to time, which gave rise to the establishment of assemblies of the different estates. . . . For rising absolutism, its bureaucrats and soldiers made it possible to compel the payment of taxes. . . . The imposition of taxes, of ever-higher taxes, of new taxes again and again, became one of the principal activities of the government. With that, however, came the construction of an apparatus for imposing and exacting taxes, which the absolutist state no longer collected through the mediation of the landlords and the towns, but directly from the peasants and townspeople. . . .

d. Change in the Character of the State

. . . While the state apparatus had arisen and been maintained through military might, the importance of the latter now diminished more and more in relation to other, economic and cultural functions. In part the state took them over from smaller social entities, especially the towns, but in part they arose as quite new ones out of previously unforeseen economic, technological, and political circumstances. With this development, the relationship of the lower, exploited classes to the state was also changed.[20] . . . The state now increasingly acquired functions that were of importance also for the exploited and that only the state apparatus could adequately perform. Now the exploited thought less and less of destroying the state . . . , but rather of gaining control of the government in order to make it serve their needs. And, at the same time, the hopeless resignation of the lower classes also disappeared more and more; they joined ever more energetically in the struggle for control of the government, at first in the struggle for democracy

20. Kautsky had already made this point in writing more than forty years earlier, in "Ein materialistischer Historiker," p. 547.

and then in the struggle for the utilization of democracy for the purpose of exercising growing influence on the state. . . .

Yet the state has hitherto remained in the hands of the exploiting class, and its apparatus serves as before to preserve exploitation. This exploitation, however, now rests less and less on the force of arms. Economically it is now the result of a legally grounded system of property that the free workers as craftsmen and peasants themselves need to safeguard their means of production and their products; and politically it is supported by a state apparatus that the free workers themselves must more and more claim. Thus, the laboring masses enter into a new kind of dependency on the state, which exists regardless of its military forces even in completely democratic countries. But democracy also makes it possible to wrest this whole immense state apparatus with its irresistible power out of the hands of the great exploiters that still hold it today and thus to turn the apparatus of domination into an apparatus of emancipation.

CHAPTER THIRTEEN

Politics as a Vocation

The more extensive and complex the state apparatus becomes, the more do those responsible for managing it and putting it to use have need of special knowledge. In all modern states these are the officials, the bureaucrats and, in the democratic state, also the politicians of the various parties, members of parliament and journalists. It is a mistake to suppose that democracy consists in the elimination of bureaucracy. In modern society, with its enormous, ever-changing activity, every large organization with a variety of tasks needs specialists, . . . usually with an extensive division of labor. . . . The joint-stock companies, too, need a bureaucracy, similarly trade unions, cooperative societies, even political parties, when they have attained a certain size, organizational coherence, and permanence. . . .

One of the most important sides of democracy, which by itself is enough to make the empty talk of "formal" democracy look ridiculous, is the freedom to form associations. Alongside the structure of the state, there arise under democracy numerous free organizations, independent of the state and serving the most diverse ends. Some are superfluous or of no significance; but many are extremely important. . . . Despite the absolute expansion of the state bureaucracy in the democratic state, its power diminishes relative to that of the free organizations. It can dictate to them less and less; more and more it must negotiate with them and call on them to help in the fulfillment of its tasks. It thereby increasingly loses the character it had during its absolutist period. It becomes more flexible, resilient, and worldly-wise. . . . The state official administers the state, but he does not dominate it or determine it. He is . . . the servant of the state government.

The latter, of course, is always constituted of individuals, it is basically only an abstraction.... The state has no will, no purposes, and no goals. Only men have them, men who rule in the state and through the state.

... In the absolutist state it is, in theory, the monarch who appoints and dismisses the officials, ... who sets the direction for all their activity, ... who controls them.... When absolutism is overthrown, these powers of sovereignty are passed on to democracy, that is, to the collectivity of the people. But ... a relatively large collectivity can act in a concerted manner only if it has organized itself and created for itself individual organs, that is, entrusted individual men with the task of carrying out the will of its majority.... Under democracy, the functions of sovereignty are transferred from the broad mass of the people, who assemble periodically, to representatives elected by them, to parliaments that in the people's name install, oversee, and depose governments and enact laws. There is often continuity between these parliaments and the old assemblies of estates in the feudal era,[21] but ... in the modern parliament the individual member represents the entire nation, the interests of which he has to safeguard.... In the beginnings of the modern parliaments, the individual representative often still had his eye on the special interests of his electoral district. Proportional representation has completely eradicated *[this type of]* politics....

... At first, it is easy in the election campaign for the candidate to entice the unorganized, naive mass of the voters with promises that are forgotten after the election. That changes once the voters and the politically interested parts of the general population make use of the democratic freedoms to join together in permanent organizations, which constantly follow parliamentary politics, permit only proven politicians to run for office, and rigorously monitor those elected.

... Behind the struggles of individual candidates ... during an election, and behind the conflicts ... in parliaments, there stand the interests of different, antagonistic classes. Not only of different classes, though, but also of different methods, for one can seek to reach the same goal in different ways.... Only in the beginnings of democratic life, when the masses of the people do not know how to use the democratic freedoms properly, ... can it happen that the struggles of the parties in parliament are nothing but a personal wrangling of individual politicians over the governmental feeding trough. The better the masses know how to make use of their rights, the more clearly do the parties become representative of certain interests and methods of classes. The expansion of the political parties to large, completely free mass organizations becomes an absolute requirement of modern, parliamentary democracy.

But it also has need of another institution: a free press read by the masses

21. Kautsky had described these in *Parlamentarismus und Demokratie*, pp. 39–42.

that informs them adequately about politics. The press, the political party, and the parliament—including the parliamentary government—are the great organs of modern democracy, which is incomplete if the necessary strength or freedom is lacking to any one of them. . . . If they have sufficient power, *[they]* are the organs through which the people, that is, its strongest class and political method at a given time, rules the state, controls the state apparatus, that is, the bureaucracy, and gives it direction. But just as in the modern, complex state its administrative personnel increasingly has to consist of specially trained experts, so is that also true for those who as the organs of the people confront the organs of the state. . . . More and more, all those who energetically participate in the politics of the state—and often even those who take part in local politics—come to constitute a special vocation, requiring special abilities and special knowledge and experience. This is true of parliamentary representatives, party functionaries, and journalists. . . .

In another way, the development of politics as a vocation is promoted by . . . industrial capitalism. The first of the ruling and exploiting classes, the military nobility, administered the state itself. . . . Where all political life was not strangled by despotism, the nobles always remained the real governors and rulers of states. . . . That was true even . . . in the democratic states of antiquity;[22] later it was also true in the cradle of industrial capitalism and democracy, in Britain, and has remained true down to the present day. . . . In contrast, the capitalists were able only exceptionally to become the governors of states. . . . *[They]* lead a life full of worry . . . about their survival in the ever more intense struggles for profit and power with competitors, suppliers, customers, and workers. . . . The field of business speculation was . . . enormously expanded by the appearance of shares of stock. To the ups and downs of the commodity market are now added those of the stock market. . . . The function of consuming the surplus value, insofar as it is not accumulated, falls chiefly to the capitalists' ladies and offspring. . . . Their businesses rob the active capitalists of the time, but also of the farsightedness necessary for fruitfully engaging in politics. . . .

Therefore, instead of descending himself into the arena of politics, the capitalist prefers to send into it combatants whom he has hired. Under absolutism, he bribes individual officials. If he is a financial magnate, he is able to influence even ministers, indeed monarchs themselves, by granting loans and similar means. Under democracy, he seeks to buy its organs, parliamentary representatives, parties, and the press. But, in the course of the development of democracy, of the growth of the political experience and power of the masses, this kind of political activity becomes increasingly difficult. . . . To be sure, the filling of the campaign chests of certain parties

22. See IV:6:3, above.

by individual capitalists is still carried on in a lively manner. . . . The main organ capitalists make use of today under democracy to see to it that their interests, general as well as personal, prevail in the state, has become the *press*, in particular, the daily press. A daily newspaper has become a colossal apparatus, requiring great sums of money. . . . In this area, the superior strength of big capital vis-à-vis the propertyless makes itself oppressively felt.

CHAPTER FOURTEEN
Force and Democracy

It is principally these facts that are marshaled by a number of socialists against democracy to prove that it fails as a means of the proletariat to emancipate itself. These socialists come for the most part from economically backward countries with an undeveloped proletariat. Their doubt about democracy is at bottom their doubt about the proletariat itself. In the place of its independent activity, which can fruitfully unfold only under democracy, they want to put a messiah or a Moses, who is supposed to lead the proletariat into the Promised Land.[23] They cite as their justification the term "dictatorship of the proletariat," which Marx used at one time, but only in passing, without explaining what kind of state constitution he had in mind for this political condition. In the same text (in *Critique of the Gotha Program*, pp. 355–56; *MESW*, III, 26–27), however, he spoke out in support of the demand for the democratic republic. Regardless of what Marx might have understood by the dictatorship of the proletariat, nowhere does he declare himself for dictatorship as the *form of the state* that is indispensable for the emancipation of the proletariat. To do so would have contradicted the principle that he put at the head of the rules of the First International: the emancipation of the working class must be accomplished by the working

23. A number of points made in this chapter had been more fully developed by Kautsky in *The Dictatorship of the Proletariat*, pp. 4–58, 140–41, for example, the view of dictatorship as an indicator of proletarian "immaturity" and especially the argument that the dictatorship of the proletariat was to Marx not a form of government but "a condition that necessarily arises out of pure democracy where the proletariat is preponderant" (ibid., p. 45; I have corrected the translation, as is frequently necessary in this book). Kautsky also advanced an interpretation of Marx's conception of the dictatorship of the proletariat in *Von der Demokratie zur Staats-Sklaverei*, pp. 38–43, 83–84; in a polemic with Lenin's *The State and Revolution* in *The Labour Revolution*, pp. 59–89; in *Die Marxsche Staatsauffassung*, p. 19; and in *Social Democracy versus Communism*, pp. 29–47. This latter book, published eight years after Kautsky's death, consists entirely of variously combined unidentified excerpts from Kautsky's writings of 1932–37. The chapter referred to consists of excerpts from "Marx und Marxismus," pp. 182–93; from "Die Diktatur des Proletariats," pp. 437–38; and from *Neue Programme*, pp. 20–25.

class itself,[24] thus not by an arbitrary government that directs the workers as it pleases. . . .

In the above-mentioned letter on the *[Gotha]* program, Marx declared that it was the "goal of the workers" to convert "the state from an organ superimposed on society into one thoroughly subordinate to it" [Critique of the Gotha Program, *p. 354;* MESW, *III, 25*]. A dictatorship, however, pushes the superimposition of the state on society to the extreme by taking control, not only of the state apparatus, but also of the organs intended to subordinate the state to society *[parliament, the political party, and the press]*, and transforming them into organs of the state apparatus. The subordination of society to the state becomes completely unbearable, if this state apparatus in addition subordinates to itself the entire process of production, something that no despot has ever done before. Only a state apparatus subordinate to society, not one ruling it absolutely and arbitrarily, can become a means for replacing the management of production by private capitalists with a socially determined management and thus a means for emancipating the proletariat.

The existence for an extended period of a dictatorship as the normal condition of the state points to a high degree of weakness of the proletariat in this state, hence also to its inability for the present to replace capitalism with socialist production. If such a regime does not want to renounce large-scale industrial production, which would be manifest bankruptcy, not just economic, but also military bankruptcy, then it has only the choice between state capitalism and private capitalism. But the more absolute the power of the state and the less developed democratic supervision and critique are, the more pedantic, fussy, but also corrupt does the state bureaucracy become; the less is it capable of acquiring the flexibility and adaptability required by the production and circulation process of the world of commodities; the farther does state-owned industry fall behind privately owned one—the privately owned industry abroad, if none is allowed within the country;[25] the more does the dictatorship see itself impelled to continue production at the expense of the laboring masses, of the peasants, for whom industrial products are made enormously more expensive, as well as the industrial workers. . . . As good as its intentions might have been originally, the dic-

24. The German text to which Kautsky here refers—"Provisorische Statuten der Internationalen Arbeiter-Assoziation," p. 14—speaks of the working class in the singular in contrast to the original English version which uses "working classes." "Provisional Rules of the First International," p. 82; *MESW;* II, 19.

25. These and similar passages in this chapter obviously alluding to the new Soviet regime were, a few years later, elaborated with explicit reference to it in *Bolshevism at a Deadlock*, especially pp. 72–87. See also "Die Aussichten des Sozialismus in Sowjetrussland," especially p. 427.

tatorship is thus brought by the force of economic laws into ever-stronger opposition to the workers, who confront it without any rights. . . .

. . . For the same reasons of economic necessity, the dictatorship sees itself increasingly compelled to appeal for aid to private capital, both within the country and abroad, and to expand more and more the range of capitalist influence in the state. . . . Therefore, in a dictatorship, even when it initially behaves like a dictatorship of the proletariat, the proletarians ultimately become completely powerless vis-à-vis an ever-stronger capital. The latter . . . can buy the state apparatus, that is, the individual officials, indeed finally the dictators themselves, if not by personal bribery, then by blackmail, by making the granting of monies to the state dependent on certain concessions. This method becomes the more effective, the more it is a matter of dealing with foreign capitalists, because domestic capital has been destroyed, driven out, or at least intimidated. A dictatorship, then, does not by any means eliminate the possibility that the capitalists might influence and, indeed, ultimately control the state apparatus through their wealth. . . .

. . . Democratic institutions . . . make it possible for large and constantly growing strata of the working classes . . . to create their own press, their own parties, a representation of their own in parliament, which are inaccessible to capitalist bribery and see as their most important task the struggle against capital. Whenever under a democracy the laboring masses have not yet succeeded in creating for themselves such organs of their political will, that is the case merely because they do not yet have a political will of their own. This is due to special living conditions that can be explained economically, geographically, and historically. Of itself, democracy can certainly not produce such a will. Democracy is only a means for making it, where it exists, effective in a state. And a glance at the development of society during the past century teaches us that this is something more than a mere possibility. . . . Under democracy, the working classes gain strength politically more and more, the richer their political experience becomes, the more extensive the means for their political education are, the more sizable and united their parties are.[26] . . . Some of the workers' parties already stand on the threshold of the conquest of political power through democratic means.

. . . But will the capitalists calmly accept that? This is the question asked by the opponents of democratic methods among the socialists, who see in armed civil war the only method of decisively fighting out class struggles. No doubt, the capitalists will strongly resist their political dispossession by

26. Another, virtually complete translation of the rest of this chapter (of which nearly half has been omitted in the present edition) appears in Beetham, ed., *Marxists in face of Fascism*, pp. 245–50.

democracy, which must ultimately bring in its train their economic dispossession, and they will employ all possible means to prevent the victory of democracy, even the means of armed power—if such means are available to them to a sufficient extent. . . . The capitalists do not rule . . . by virtue of their own military superiority over the masses, whom they fail by far to match in numbers. . . . Their economic indispensability, not their military superiority, is the weapon that the capitalists can use against a democratic regime of the working classes: the sabotage of the capitalists who bring their factories to a stop, as they did, to a considerable extent, for a time in Russia in the 1917 Revolution.

Whether this weapon of the capitalists achieves success, indeed whether it is employed at all, will depend above all on the political and economic sophistication of the workers coming to power. . . . When a workers' government does not understand how to socialize immediately some branches of production and in the others to induce the capitalists to continue production, the result will be either an outright capitulation of the workers to the capitalists—not forever, of course, but nevertheless for some time—or the use by the workers of senseless violence, the occupation by them of all the factories, the expulsion of their owners and managers, as happened in Russia in 1917. This state of affairs . . . must end in chaos that is . . . followed by a return to private capitalism. In certain circumstances, this return can take place by way of a detour through a kind of state capitalism. In no case can social production by free workers' organizations be successfully achieved in this manner. . . .

As a rule, . . . the antidemocratic socialists believe . . . that not economic but military resistance is to be expected from the capitalists as soon as democracy threatens them. Democracy would, in their opinion, then be forcibly eliminated, and thus civil war and a dictatorship based on military force would become inevitable. It might indeed come to something like this here and there. But the struggle that would then be conducted would in fact be nothing other than a struggle for democracy. . . . A socialist who expects from the capitalists a desperate attack of this kind against democracy demonstrates by that very expectation, even if often unwittingly and without wanting to, how ridiculous the empty talk about "formal" democracy is, which must remain ineffectual as long as socialism has not been established.[27] . . .

. . . When people . . . disparage "formal" democracy, they are doing their utmost seriously to paralyze in the working classes the willingness to fight for democracy. Socialists of this stripe can become a danger not just for democracy, but also for the proletariat. . . .

27. See IV:7:9, above.

The question of whether the capitalists will undertake an armed attack on democracy comes down . . . to the question of whether they will be able to find an adequate armed force that is available to them for this purpose. . . . The answer depends entirely on the conditions in which the workers' party takes over the helm. In a democracy, this will happen only if it has the support of a majority of the population. . . . It is not just the socialists who are devoted to democracy. . . . In a modern industrialized country, and here it is a question only of such a country, . . . the overwhelming majority of the people will favor the preservation of democratic rights. In these circumstances, an appeal by the capitalists to an army based upon universal compulsory military service to overthrow democracy would be dangerous to no one so much as to the very ones making the appeal. . . . An army recruited from volunteers . . . will be . . . too small to be able seriously to endanger democracy in opposition to the great mass of the nation. . . .

There is yet a third possibility: the capitalists hire venal individuals in order to arm them and to use them to combat stirrings within the working class that are troublesome to them. At first, the American capitalists made use . . . of the so-called Pinkertons, whose task was particularly to intervene in strikes. Today it is the Fascists who have become the paid executioners of the people's freedom. They are certainly dangerous, but fortunately only under certain conditions that the capitalists cannot conjure up as they choose. In order to be politically effective, the Fascists must appear in large numbers—in Italy, with its 39 million inhabitants, about half a million. In Germany, they would have to be almost one million strong in order to attain this proportion. In an industrialized country, it is impossible to get hold of such a large number of scoundrels in the prime of life for capitalistic purposes.[28] In Italy, the circumstances were especially favorable to Fascism.

First, for a long time, . . . the number of Italy's declassed has been exceptionally large. *[Kautsky mentions peasants and petty bourgeois turning to banditry and unemployed intellectuals to putsches throughout the nineteenth century as well as a revival of lumpenproletarian traditions due to the World War.]* In addition, Fascism occurred in a time when Communist influences had split the Italian proletariat, thoroughly disorganized it, and induced it to engage in senseless experiments, which on the one hand frightened the capitalists and drove them into the Fascists' arms, while on the other hand at the same time the failure of these experiments exhausted the proletariat and crippled its fighting capacity. These then are the conditions for the rise of Fascism. They are limited to a particular country and a particular point in time and will not be repeated very easily. . . .

The emergence of Fascism does not demonstrate that it will everywhere be the answer of capital to a victory by the working class under democracy.

28. See also *Wehrfrage und Sozialdemokratie*, pp. 8–9.

It merely shows that capital is already afraid today of this coming victory and that already today, in some states where the circumstances are favorable, reckless and shortsighted strata of capitalists are taking advantage of them to bring about suppression of democracy by force of arms. If this is not happening everywhere at the present time, that is due to the fact that the opportunity is not given everywhere and surely also to the fact that more farsighted statesmen of the ruling classes recognize that this manner of saving capitalism is tantamount to driving out Satan with Beelzebub.

There is no reason to expect that, at the time when the proletariat gains political power, the situation will be more favorable for attempts to over-throw democracy by force than it is today. On the contrary, with every year by which we distance ourselves from the World War and the mercenary mentality it created, with which the process of production returns more onto its normal track and the number of the unemployed and the desperate diminishes, there also dwindles more and more the prospect that the violence-prone among the capitalists will be able to halt the advance of the working class under democracy by unleashing a civil war, to remove de-mocracy itself. But even if that occurred in one state or another under special conditions, the victory would be Pyrrhic. For in the modern state the progress of democracy cannot be permanently prevented. And where it is temporarily brought to a halt, this success is due only to means that inflict profound damage on the economy and force the state that employs them down to a low level within the family of nations.[29]

Charisma

. . . In his book *Economy and Society*, Max Weber investigates the different types of authority, and he speaks of a kind of rule over the masses by individuals that they exercise by virtue of the trust and respect they have attained. The capability by which an individual achieves this Weber calls charisma. . . . By operating with the term "charisma," instead of using the simple, generally understandable expression "gift" or "talent," Weber in-troduces, in his entire discussion of the subject, a suggestion of mysticism into the subconscious that does not promote clarity. *[Kautsky quotes* Econ-omy and Society, *III, 1112, and I, 241–42.]* Here Weber is speaking only of "superhumans," who gain ascendancy over the masses through super-

---

29. For elaborations on this prediction, see IV:8:14, below, and "Einige Ursachen und Wirkungen des deutschen Nationalsozialismus," pp. 243–44. Most of this article appeared in English translation as part of "Hitlerism and Social-Democracy," pp. 53–73, and some excerpts from it appear in *Social Democracy versus Communism*, pp. 106–112. The first page of the article is translated in Beetham, ed., *Marxists in face of Fascism*, pp. 270–71.

natural accomplishments or accomplishments considered to be such, not of organs of ordinary democracy, but of extraordinary dictators, who are either demigods or swindlers. . . . The concept of "authority" arising from charisma is a very peculiar one. *[Kautsky quotes* Economy and Society, *I, 242, referring to the charisma of "berserks," epileptics, and swindlers.]* Indeed, where have berserks ever established their authority over others? And where are epileptic convulsions a means for ruling the masses? . . . It is also possible to gain the trust of the masses by other means, for example, by selflessness and enthusiasm and outstanding intelligence—and in a democracy that has existed for some time, it is possible only by such means. . . .

The whole question of charisma comes down to the following: In a democracy, in the primitive type as well as those of classical antiquity and of the modern period, one obtains positions of leadership only through the trust of one's fellow citizens, hence by surpassing the average in certain areas that are important for the polity. In special circumstances, that accomplishment might seem to be tinged with magic, but that is not of the essence of charisma. What is of that essence, however, is the possibility of individuals to act freely, so that each can develop and display his best abilities. That is not possible. . . . in a bureaucracy, . . . nor under any kind of despotism. In an aristocracy, this possibility is restricted to a small circle. The possibility for developing "charisma" is greatest in revolutionary times, when old authorities are collapsing and new ones must first prove themselves and when the opportunity for this exists. . . . Once the "bearer of charisma" has won the trust of the masses with his accomplishments (not by miracles), . . . then he can demand . . . obedience from an individual who is opposing him. But he will never succeed in ruling the masses against their will without an apparatus of domination, which does not enter into the present discussion. In this sense, no authority will ever arise out of charisma, nor has one ever arisen. . . .

. . . Weber . . . speaks of revelations and miracles, by which an individual becomes the recognized leader of a mass of people; he does not, however, speak of the greater experience and specialized knowledge that enable an individual to achieve greater successes and thereby to win the trust and the devotion of the mass. And precisely because of his inclination to magical explanations, Weber gives a quite wrong account of the process by which this trust is gained. . . . According to him, it is only after the leader has won the masses for himself that he has to demonstrate by his successes whether his charisma is genuine or not. *[Kautsky quotes* Economy and Society, *I, 242.]* In reality, matters are the reverse of this. No one will, merely by maintaining that he is favored by God, induce a mass of people in whose midst he lives to follow him blindly and to entrust to him their weal and woe. . . . Practical success has the effect after the event that people believe in the miracles and revelations. . . . In all ages, we find that certain individuals who are preeminent in the public sphere are distinguished by their strength

of character, their knowledge, and therefore by their successes. . . . In cred-
ulous times, . . . outstanding men might claim to have magical powers, but
many others among their contemporaries do that just as they themselves
do. That is not the basis of their superiority. . . . How could, of all people,
a man like Weber assess the influence of knowledge as being so slight! . . .

CHAPTER SIXTEEN

The Intellectuals

. . . Not every stratum of the population offers equally favorable conditions
for the formation of leading, farsighted politicians. The best conditions for
that are offered by some—not all—circles of intellectuals. *[Kautsky sketches
a history of the intellectuals, briefly repeating some of what he said in IV:1:3b,
IV:5:2, and especially IV:3:4, IV:7:5 and 12b, above.]*

The intellectuals are not a class, they have no special class interests; they
are divided into diverse vocations with very different professional interests.
They are not able to conduct a class struggle of their own. However, they
can certainly make the cause of another class their own, take part in its
struggles, and stimulate it intellectually to a high degree, especially since
the emergence of democracy, under which intellectual superiority becomes
more important than brute violence. . . . In such a complex society as the
modern one, class struggle and politics in general require special study, for
which certain strata of the intellectuals are especially well qualified by virtue
of their daily activities. More so than the members of the class whose cause
they make their own, such intellectuals are in a position, thanks to their
education and their financial disinterestedness, to rise above local, professional, and temporal narrow-mindedness and to recognize and champion
the lasting and general interests of the class in question in opposition to
narrow particular interests. . . .

The position of every single one of them in the class struggles is not
given a priori. Better than members of one of the classes, some intellectuals
are able impartially to recognize to what extent the conditions of social
development and of social prosperity are connected with the interests of
the various classes. And they can reach the point of deciding in favor of a
class from the standpoint of the interest of society as a whole—in addition,
also for ethical reasons, out of compassion for those who suffer and are
burdened. . . . Only the intellectuals of *[this]* kind will be a considerable gain
for the class they turn to. They will raise its class struggle to a higher level
and make it more successful and less costly in sacrifices. . . . This benefit . . .
can become quite enormous. . . .

[Kautsky quotes two pages from his Die Klassengegensätze im Zeitalter der
Französischen Revolution, *pp. 46–48, describing the role of the bourgeois intel-*

lectuals in the French Revolution in this light.] I wrote this in 1889. At that time, I still considered intellectuals to be a separate class. Since then, further studies have shown me that that was inexact. . . . Through the development of capitalism, society has become much more differentiated. The Third Estate, the apparently so homogeneous "people," has split. Above all, the chasm between capital and wage labor has opened up within it. Today, the most diverse and contradictory sympathies and tendencies take the place of the ones by which the mass of intellectuals of the eighteenth century were, despite all individual differences, animated in common. . . . What common interest could unite all [intellectuals] into a single *class*? . . .

. . . There are today strata of intellectuals who are, according to their working conditions and not seldom also according to their standard of living, nothing other than wage-workers. . . . More and more of them are finally coming to recognize their community with the proletariat. . . . They are now acquiring class consciousness, but not a special one as intellectuals. They now make socialism the goal of their efforts. Besides these, there are, to be sure, among the intellectuals those in whose activity the exercise of authority is much more strongly developed than are the points of contact with wage labor. . . . They acquire a different class consciousness, that of an exploiting and ruling class. This is the case with many factor managers, high civil servants, judges, etc. Between these two strata of the proletarian and the capitalistic intelligentsia there is a broad stratum of intellectuals who in their intermediate position recall the old petty bourgeoisie, which was also neither clearly capitalistic nor proletarian. *[Kautsky quotes* Bernstein und das sozialdemokratische Programm, *p. 130, stressing that]* "the intelligentsia is that stratum of the population which grows most rapidly" *[and also pp. 133, 135].*[30]

The intellectuals who are brought close to the proletariat by their working conditions constitute a valuable addition to the fighting forces in its class

---

30. The passages quoted by Kautsky appear in English translation in *Selected Political Writings*, pp. 21–22 and 23–24. The chapter on the new middle class in *Bernstein und das sozialdemokratische Programm* makes the points summarized here more fully. Kautsky had already dealt with the intellectuals and their rapid growth in a section of his commentary on the Erfurt Program on the "educated proletariat," *The Class Struggle*, pp. 36–42, and had devoted an article to the subject three years later, "Die Intelligenz und die Sozialdemokratie." Subsequently he wrote and often provided statistics on the growth of what he interchangeably called the intelligentsia or the new *Mittelstand* in *The Social Revolution*, pp. 45–49; *Die Vernichtung der Sozialdemokratie*, pp. 22–23; "Der neue Liberalismus und der neue Mittelstand," partially reprinted in *Der politische Massenstreik*, pp. 252–53; *Die proletarische Revolution*, pp. 32–40 (the English translation of this work, *The Labour Revolution*, omits the first sixty-three pages on the revision of the Erfurt Program, but these pages are reprinted in *Texte zu den Programmen*, pp. 181–274, the here relevant ones being pp. 228–41.) See also Kautsky's comments on the 1925 SPD program, "Grundsätzlicher Teil," in Kampffmeyer, ed., *Das Heidelberger Programm*, pp. 10–12, and in *Texte zu den Programmen*, pp. 290–94.

struggle. But for this struggle itself, they offer the proletariat no new insights. In this area, it is rather other strata of workers who, having already participated in the class struggle for some time, have the advantage of greater experience over the new organizations of white-collar workers, etc. In this regard, the latter can still learn from the former. From among the intellectuals standing between the proletariat and the capitalists, not entire professions, but only single individuals will cast their lot with one side or the other. Those intellectuals who join the proletariat will become important for it not through their numbers or their significance in the economy, but by virtue of the superior knowledge that they bring to it.

Under democracy, the various classes need a certain general political knowledge in order to be effective, in order to be able to select, with all the relevant knowledge, uninfluenced by demagogy and illusions, the democratic organs they elect and to indicate to them the political direction that seems most appropriate. Every class that engages in politics needs knowledge of the laws of economics, of the economic conditions in its own country and in the other countries taking part in world trade, and knowledge of political and social history at least of the last centuries. Individual members of the working classes can acquire this knowledge by themselves . . . , but . . . it can be brought to the great mass of the working classes only by intellectuals who . . . have special political and social knowledge. . . . The highly educated intellectual . . . [with] a theoretical understanding of the state and society . . . can most readily raise up the fighters in the class struggle to a higher viewpoint, show them more distant goals, and give a more unified and coherent form to their activity. . . .

. . . One must not include only the academically trained among the intellectuals. . . . The autodidact's knowledge is dependent on accident, but when it is sufficient, it easily produces more creative, more independent thinking than does the routine of the schools. And everyone, regardless of his original occupation, who in a democracy is placed in a post in which, as his vocation, he has to function as an organ of democracy, becomes thereby an intellectual. He does so whether he is a writer, a party or union official, or a parliamentary representative. . . . The intelligentsia only forms separate vocations, not a separate class. It is possible to be a member of the intelligentsia with proletarian class consciousness, and the factory worker or the craftsman who takes on intellectual functions changes only his vocation, not his class. Clearly, the distinction between a vocation and a class is not mere theoretical splitting of hairs but can assume great practical importance.

Although the intelligentsia is not a new class with its own class interests and a class consciousness of its own, nevertheless, in the forms and functions that it acquires in the capitalist mode of production and in the modern democratic state, the intelligentsia constitutes a factor of the greatest significance for the manner in which modern class struggles are fought out and in which these struggles determine the whole course of history. This is, to be sure, even more true of the industrial proletariat. It is only through its association with this proletariat that the intelligentsia acquires its full historical importance. . . .

Section Eight
Abolition of Classes and of the State[1]

CHAPTER ONE

The Decline of the Proletariat

Two tendencies are inherent in industrial capital, through which it . . . fundamentally alters the character both of society and of the state. Up to now, we have discussed chiefly . . . the tendency to steady and constantly more rapid growth of human productive forces. Now, however, we must also consider the other tendency. . . . Here . . . we enter upon an area that has already been treated extensively by Marxist literature, indeed, an area that forms the basis of all of socialist literature. . . .

In its demand for cheap raw materials and auxiliary materials, capital not only presses on to exhaust as rapidly as possible deposits of coal, petroleum, iron ore, etc. It lays waste wide areas by ruthlessly cutting down forests; it reduces in size great sources of food by indiscriminate fishing; it exterminates important fur-bearing animals, seals, and whales, etc. . . .

As disastrous as ruthless capitalist exploitation becomes for various areas of our life, nevertheless one can say, on the whole, that the destructive effects of industrial capitalism are more than compensated for by the advances in natural science and technology associated with it. But industrial capitalism threatens to become nothing short of disastrous with regard to the productive force that is for us the most important of them all: that of *man as worker*. Without him, all the means of production are only lifeless matter; he alone confers on them a soul and life. Man is, however, not only the supreme *means*, but also the supreme *end* of production. At least when viewed from the standpoint of society in general, which is synonymous here with that of the worker. Viewed from the capitalist standpoint, to be sure, the wage laborer is a mere means of production, just like a draft animal. And the purpose of production is the capitalist's profit. No matter

---

1. "Abolition" is used here to render the impossible-to-translate German "Aufhebung" only for lack of a better single term, especially as Engels, in a famous passage discussed by Kautsky in IV:8:15, below, had specifically emphasized that the state is not "abolished" but withers away. *Aufheben* can mean "to abolish" or "to supersede," "to preserve," and "to lift up," hence "to transcend."

how much lasting prosperity and lofty culture a mode of production might bring the workers, if it ... does not produce surpluses for the capitalists, then it seems to them and their theoreticians an abomination.

The capitalist per se does not care about the worker as the end of production, but he cannot be indifferent to the well-being of his workers as means of production. If workers are ruined faster than they can be replaced, then capitalist production, too, must ultimately go to wrack and ruin. . . . There is no substitute for the human force of production. It is, of course, possible to have various human activities carried out by machines, but these machines must themselves be set in operation, watched over, and fed with auxiliary substances and raw materials by men. . . . Thus, the method of exploitation of industrial capitalism, just like the methods of exploitation that preceded it, ultimately threatens to lead to the final decay of society, despite the enormous advances in the development of technology that accompany it. . . . This process must endanger the entire society all the more inasmuch as the capitalist mode of production, thanks to its superior technology, in part displaces, in part reduces to misery the precapitalist modes of production. *[Kautsky mentions as consequences hunger, overwork, unemployment, overcrowded slums, alcoholism, prostitution, and syphilis.]*

Moreover, the ruination of the masses by capitalist exploitation becomes far more dangerous than every earlier kind resulting from precapitalist methods of exploitation. For ... these methods remained restricted to certain regions, alongside which numerous barbarian peoples were still able to persist. . . . In the face of the weapons technology of industrial capital, . . . there is no possibility of serious resistance by barbarians or savages. And modern transportation technology is able to make its way to all of them. But the expansion of the area of capitalist exploitation does not have to rely on the force of arms. It has a means at its command that was lacking to earlier methods of exploitation: the greater cheapness of the commodities mass-produced by it, by means of which it pushes every other mode of production aside. . . . The industrial capitalism of our own day has already taken hold of almost the whole world. . . . That means that there are no barbarians left who are strong and knowledgeable enough to be able to enter into the heritage of the capitalist world, should the latter decay as, for example, the Roman Empire did before it. Profound degeneracy would then threaten all of mankind.

Bourgeois economists consolingly point out that the degradation of the working classes, . . . which comes with industrial capitalism, is only an infantile disorder that industrial capitalism will overcome, since it ... engenders itself the forces counteracting the increasing misery of the masses of the people. . . . Everywhere the capitalists seek, just as they did a hundred years ago, to depress wages, to extend hours of work, to force women and children into the factory, to raise rents for apartments, etc. Where they have a free hand, as in China, they are engaging at the present time in the same terribly destructive exploitation of human labor power and human life as took place in Britain in the childhood period of industrial capitalism there. The capitalists have not spontaneously reached a higher level of feeling and thinking concerning welfare. . . .

To the extent that a higher level of social awareness can be found today among the capitalists—taken as a class, not as individuals—than two or three generations ago, that is . . . a result of the resistance faced by this profiteering. The workers have taught their employers to be more socially aware men. When these encounter workers who are incapable of resistance, their newly acquired social conscience immediately ceases to function. The fact that it is possible to ward off successfully the tendencies of capitalism to increase the workers' misery, indeed, to take the offensive against capital from a certain point on and to limit more and more its power in relation to those whom it exploits—that is the most powerful social fact since the emergence of the state and of exploitation. Jointly with the expansion of the productive forces effected by industrial capital, this fact will ultimately make it possible to put an end to all exploitation of any kind, without abandonment of the general level of culture we have attained. In contrast, prior to the emergence of industrial capital, a general abolition of exploitation could only have resulted in a general rustication of society. . . .

CHAPTER TWO

The Rise of the Proletariat and the Struggle for Democracy

Resistance against the tendency of industrial capitalism to increase the misery of its wage-laborers and finally to destroy them can originate from two sides: from the exploited themselves and from nonproletarian circles who sympathize with the exploited. In its beginnings, the industrial proletariat is so weak that its resistance is hardly of any importance and that of the nonproletarian opponents of the capitalists is more evident. . . . Large land-owners, craftsmen, intellectuals were certainly able to recognize, without capitalistic bias, the devastating effects industrial capital inflicted on the workers and to see the dangers arising from this for the future of society. In militarist states, these critical observers were joined by military men who feared for the armed strength of the state if industry undermined the physical fitness of the workers. Ethical sentiments, pity for the tormented human creature, combined with economic insight to produce the effort to put a stop to the murderous tendencies of capitalism.

This effort itself could, in turn, assume two forms. Bolder, more far-sighted thinkers . . . formulated plans for social organizations that assured prosperity for all. In this way, the beginnings of modern socialism were formed. . . . The inventors of the various utopias were keenly intent on putting them into practice immediately. But the funds that were made available for the establishment of socialist colonies were too small. . . . The colonies had to be set up on the smallest scale conceivable, far from the sphere of civilization, under conditions in which toughened peasants would probably have been able to maintain themselves, but not city-dwellers and least of all intellectuals. . . . Their enthusiasm brought them together, but it was unable to persist in the face of the sober reality of everyday life. None of these colonies was successful. In this way, the proletariat could not be emancipated.

Somewhat more was achieved along the other path, not that of socialism but that of social [welfare] policy: appealing to the state to enact laws for the protection of workers, especially those among them least capable of resistance, women and children. . . . But . . . the capitalists, whose freedom to exploit was threatened, put up furious resistance against labor protective legislation. As paltry as its regulations were, they often remained a dead letter. The desire for profit proved to be stronger than pity and scientific insight. Pity can become a strong force, but it is effective only as long as . . . one is aware of the suffering of the others. For most property owners, though, that is always only temporarily the case, to the extent that it is a question of the suffering of the propertyless, about whom they are usually informed only indirectly, by reports, and only occasionally. . . . And scientific understanding, that is, dull theory, is all the more incapable of producing energies for a persistent struggle. . . .

The two paths, that of socialism and that of social legislation . . . became ways to the progressive limitation of capitalist power only when the proletariat became strong enough . . . successfully to defend its interests itself. . . . At first, though, these two paths meant nothing other than the salvation of capitalist society from early ruin. They preserved for it that which is indispensable for its existence: a working class permanently capable of intense labor. Through long decades, it seemed that the industrial proletariat was wholly incapable of successfully resisting its oppressors, that it could at most rise up in outbreaks of desperation, which achieved nothing or were even bloodily suppressed. . . . Like all beginnings, those of the modern labor movement are far more difficult to discern than is the course of its subsequent development, which is clearly evident. Less obvious than the latter are the factors that, despite all of the repressive forces of capitalism, nevertheless finally enabled the proletariat to fight back successfully against them.

Certainly very important for this was the fact that there were different strata in the proletariat, with very different capacities for resistance. Completely incapable of resistance were those whom capital treated most cruelly, women and children. Because of the whole manner of their upbringing and mode of life, the men were better able to offer resistance. They, too, were divided into two categories: skilled and unskilled workers. The latter came originally in part from the lumpenproletariat, in part from the rural pop-

ulation, both of which lacked all organizational experience and any coherence among themselves. . . . The skilled workers . . . came in many instances
from the crafts, whose journeymen had in earlier times formed very com-
bative associations. The traditions of these associations were still alive
among skilled workers in the period when industrial capitalism was emerging. The first resistance to capitalism came from them. . . . Their successes
spurred on the lower strata of workers and showed them the way. They
were promoted by the aggregation of great masses of workers in a few
industrial centers and, within these centers, in individual large-scale enterprises produced by industrial capitalism.

No less important for the rise of the proletariat, however, was the democratic movement that commenced in Britain in the last decades of the
eighteenth century and later in France. . . . As industrial capital grew
stronger, not only its economic antagonism to the proletariat became increasingly evident but also its political one in the question of democracy.
And it was, above all, this political antagonism that created a proletarian
class consciousness and proletarian class politics, much more than the economic antagonism . . . that was at first considered only as a personal one
against the evil capitalist or at most as a local or occupational matter. . . .
In our view, as has already been set forth here repeatedly and as was often
stressed by Engels, the economic moment is only the factor of historical
development that *[is determining]* in the *last analysis*, not the sole factor
appearing on the surface of events. . . .

In the course of the struggle for democracy, as soon as its achievements
have taken on palpable forms, considerable differences appear among the
various classes fighting for democracy. The "middle class," consisting
mainly of the propertied classes as well as the better off among the well
educated who did not belong to the nobility, . . . saw no other means of
gaining democratic rights for itself than summoning the entire laboring
mass to do battle for such rights, which of course were then supposed to
become rights of this entire mass. The very same capital that sought to
make its workers socially completely unfit for combat, itself spurred them
into struggles the successes of which necessarily gave them strength and
self-confidence. Yet the workers at first fought, in effect, not for themselves
but only for their exploiters. That showed itself clearly in the struggles for
the franchise. Almost nowhere was universal and equal suffrage obtained
as the immediate result of the democratic movements. If the democratic
movement becomes too strong, then the privileged classes seek to divide
it. They grant the franchise to the capitalists, sometimes also to the peasants
and the petty bourgeoisie. The proletarians are left out.

*[There follows a brief history of the suffrage limited by property qualifications
in nineteenth-century Britain and France and in Prussia and Bismarckian Germany.]*
Other countries of Europe followed a similar course. Liberalism, the kind
of democracy practiced by the bourgeoisie, which is of course not synon-

ymous with the idea of democracy, everywhere denied universal suffrage to the masses, in Austria, Belgium, and in the other smaller states of northern Europe. Since no Bonapartes appeared on the scene there seeking to exploit revolutionary ideas for their dynastic purposes, nowhere in those parts was the experiment made of granting universal suffrage by an upstart on the throne or by the adviser of an upstart on a new throne, as that of the German Emperor in 1871 undoubtedly was. . . . Universal suffrage and fully developed democracy in general are a result and an achievement of the proletarian class struggle. Even Marx was not yet in a position to be able to observe what forms the class struggle assumes in a highly developed democracy, for in his time such a democracy existed in Europe, if at all, only in Switzerland. . . .

We are thinking here of democracy in countries that for a time passed through the phase of monarchical absolutism and centralized state government with enormous bureaucracies and standing armies. . . . In *[these]* countries . . . the struggle for democracy became a powerful means for summoning the prostrate proletariat, which was almost incapable of fighting, to struggles in which it found allies in other classes. Strengthened by them, it intervened in struggles it would not have dared to undertake alone and acquired experience and self-confidence. Through these struggles, too, the barriers of locality and of occupation that had fragmented the proletariat in its beginnings were overcome; through them it acquired an interest in general questions affecting the entire working class, and it also learned to unite the energies of the whole class into a single force.[2]

Thus, in these political struggles the proletariat necessarily attained a strength and an understanding that impelled it everywhere sooner or later to make itself politically independent as a class and as such to go its own way and that enabled it to do so successfully. The fact that the proletariat sets out on its own paths does not mean that the actions of the other classes and parties become a matter of indifference to it, nor that it cannot act jointly with one or the other of them from time to time for certain common ends. . . . It does, however, mean that it must maintain its independence even in the case of such coalitions, that its occasional collaboration must never lead to its subjection to the leadership of others.

What significance the struggle for democracy had for . . . the proletariat . . . becomes evident if we compare the countries of Europe, where such struggles were necessary, with . . . the United States, where the workers encountered an already considerably developed democracy. It is due not

2. That, for such reasons, electoral and parliamentary conflicts "are among the most effective levers to raise the proletariat out of its economic, social and moral degradation" was already stressed by Kautsky in *The Class Struggle,* p. 188, and again in *Parlamentarismus und Demokratie,* pp. 110–15.

least of all to that fact that up to now a large workers' party has not been successfully formed there, in spite of the very energetic and self-sacrificing efforts of so many immigrant socialists from countries in which the proletariat had to fight strenuously for democratic rights. The counterpart to this is Russia. In the last half-century, its population, more so than that of any other modern country, has carried on extremely costly struggles for the most primitive of democratic rights. Through them, the proletariat there acquired a class consciousness, and the socialist parties have achieved an importance going far beyond the level that the Russian Empire reached in the economic sphere.[3] . . .

CHAPTER THREE

The Rise of the Proletariat and the Reduction of Working Time

. . . *[Isolation and lack of free time]* greatly hamper the petty bourgeois and the peasants in the attainment of adequate political knowledge. Like the capitalists, almost all of them find it difficult to function as organs of democracy—if, in addition, they want to continue to carry on their business. But they are inferior to the capitalists in that, as a rule, they do not even acquire the ability to grasp governmental affairs and to judge them independently, to form and to hold together their own parties whose orientation they determine. Like the capitalists, they must, as a rule, entrust particular professional politicians with the representation of their interests in the state and with the pursuit of the policies they consider desirable. The capitalists, though, have enough power and political understanding to keep the professional politicians whom they select dependent on themselves, at least intellectually, often also financially. The reverse is true in the case of the peasants and petty bourgeois. The professional politicians they select easily change from being their servants to being their masters. In these circumstances, it often happens under democracy that the laboring masses become a mere herd of voting sheep in the hands of professional politicians and of

3. Kautsky had developed this contrast between American and Russian workers, with emphasis on the former, in "Der amerikanische Arbeiter," pp. 740–44 and especially p. 751, an article in which he generally compared the development of American and Russian capitalism and labor; ibid., pp. 676–83, 720–27, 787. Kautsky also dealt with American history and society (especially as the basis of anti-imperialist policies) in *Die Wurzeln der Politik Wilsons,* pp. 11–26. He attacked Samuel Gompers as an enemy of the proletarian class struggle in "Samuel Gompers." Kautsky compared the historical position of the proletariat in Russia and Britain and the influence of Russian and British socialism in Germany in *Rosa Luxemburg, Karl Liebknecht, Leo Jogiches,* pp. 4–8.

the strata of powerful exploiters standing behind them. Democracy, conceived as the means for the people's domination over the state apparatus, then becomes a means for the political domination of capital or of property owners in general (including the great landowners). . . .

At first, the proletariat is even less able than the petty bourgeois and the peasants to follow systematically an independent political course. Overwork and miserable housing conditions depress it even more than the latter, . . . *[but it]* can raise itself above them intellectually in the course of its class struggle. . . . Two things distinguish the proletarian not only from the artisan and the peasant, but also from the capitalist: He . . . is able, when concerned with political matters, to free himself from the influence of the special interests of the business in which he works; he is able to view the conditions of the polity from a higher standpoint. . . . More so than the other classes mentioned here, he is open to broad points of view and can more readily acquire a theoretical interest in social questions. In this respect, he most resembles the intellectuals. Individual members of the proletariat can surpass many intellectuals in this regard.

. . . The worker . . . demands again and again further reduction of his working time and will continue to demand it until the limit is reached that is still possible without endangering the production process.[4] This limit . . . can be shifted again and again by technological advances, not only by new machines, but also by new methods and forms of organization. . . . That class . . . has the prospect of achieving the highest cultural and political level that has the most time to take part in cultural and political education and activities, in addition to engaging in gainful work. . . . *[Even if]* the reduction of working time . . . means only an increase of the workers' interest in the enjoyment of nature, in sports, or in diversified leisure-time work, . . . it lifts the worker out of the degradation into which unbridled capitalism plunges him. The reduction of working time always also results in increasing occupation with political activity and a striving for general education on the part of ever more strata of the class of wage-laborers. . . .

By virtue of the wage-laborers' economic situation, the best conditions are given for them—in addition to the intellectuals—to raise themselves to comprehensive points of view on social matters and to contemplate distant goals. The class of wage laborers is also, owing to its lack of property, least interested in the status quo and most inclined to be receptive to new ideas. Finally, the progressive reduction of working time is best suited to give this class the possibility of accumulating the knowledge and the experience required to develop the mere disposition to accept new and great ideas into genuine absorption, shaping, and energetic championing of such ideas.

Like the struggle for democracy, the struggle for the protection of labor,

4. See also IV:1:5 and IV:7:2, above.

in particular for the reduction of daily drudgery, also has the effect of raising the proletariat to a higher level. Hence the economic and the political struggles both tend toward this result. It was deeply rooted in *[the workers']* conditions that the first great labor movement, that of the Chartists, set itself two goals above all: universal suffrage and the ten-hour day. These two points everywhere constitute the starting point of every serious workers' party. The labor unions are, with different means, all striving for the same thing. Where fulfillment of these two demands is achieved, efforts are made to advance further in the same direction: the extension and consolidation of democracy and reduction of . . . working time. . . .

Like the struggle for democracy, so-called social *[welfare]* policy or social reform also tends to raise the proletariat, so that from the lowest class of society it becomes the most highly developed of the working classes. Indeed, it becomes the class to which the leadership of society increasingly falls, the class most interested and most likely to succeed in obtaining the establishment of new institutions that economic changes have made both possible and necessary in the interest of society. That is true even of those innovations that bear no specific class character and are compatible with the continued existence of bourgeois society.[5] Until the World War, there was only *one* republican party in Germany, the Social-Democratic Party. . . . Until the World War there was in Germany only *one* party that energetically advocated women's suffrage, the party of the proletariat. . . . No party in Germany fought energetically for universal disarmament and for methods of international understanding instead of an armaments race, except the Social-Democratic Party. . . . Not just in questions concerning only workers, but in all questions of further social and political development, the workers' parties have today become the leaders everywhere.

The most advanced strata of the proletariat, which grow more and more, have attained not only intellectual independence, but also intellectual superiority in relation to the mass of the rest of the population. At the same time, they also achieve growing unity in relation to it. The interests of the petty bourgeois and the peasants are ambivalent, . . . neither purely capitalistic nor purely proletarian. The interests of the proletariat are entirely consistent. And since it is capable, from a certain level of its development on, to make itself politically and intellectually independent, it is also able to form its own class party. It, to be sure, is capable of significant accomplishments only if intellectuals sympathetic to it supply it with knowledge that the proletarian, who has only his own resources, is not able to acquire. But this party does not by any means subordinate itself to the intellectuals who join it.

The bourgeois parties are also class parties, but only in the sense that

5. See also "Klasseninteresse—Sonderinteresse—Gemeininteresse," pp. 262–64.

each of them represents principally the interests of a particular class, not, however, in the sense that it consists only, or even only predominantly, of members of that class. Neither the great landowners nor the capitalists are numerous enough to be able to form a mass-party by themselves under democracy. The bourgeois parties have as their basis the fact that neither peasants nor petty bourgeois nor intellectuals have heretofore been able to join together permanently in relatively large separate class parties. . . . Peasants and petty bourgeois enter the political struggle, summoned and led by elements having some interests in common with them, who nevertheless only use them as followers for their own purposes. The bourgeois parties are not class parties as far as their composition is concerned. Each of them contains very diverse strata, classes, and parts of classes, including workers who have not yet achieved political independence. The bourgeois parties are thus less united, less homogeneous and consistent in their policies than the workers' parties.[6] To all these factors of intellectual and organizational superiority of the workers' parties in relation to the bourgeois parties is added a growing numerical preponderance. With the progress of industrial capital, the industrial proletariat also grows in size . . . *[that is, there is an]* absolute and a relative increase of the class of wage-laborers in society. *[Kautsky cites German and American statistics on the changing numbers of workers and self-employed in industry and agriculture.]*

As the mass, the economic importance, and the intelligence of the industrial population grow, so too does the attraction exerted by the proletariat on strata of the people that do not entirely belong to it but are close to it with respect to their standard of living and their economic relations. This attraction becomes the stronger, the greater the intellectual and organizational independence and unity of the proletariat are. . . . The classes in society are in reality not so rigorously distinct as they have to be in theory. . . . Thus, there are numerous intermediate grades between the class of wage-laborers and the other working classes, peasants, artisans, and petty traders, just as there are between them and the intellectuals. Vacillating between the proletariat and capital, individual members and even whole groups of these classes and strata decide more in favor of or against the proletariat, depending on particular personal influences, historical situations, and economic constellations. Thus, a part of the peasants, petty bourgeois, and intellectuals can become ever more bitterly antagonistic to the proletariat. A constantly growing part, especially of their poorer strata, will be drawn to the proletariat and make the proletarian cause its own. . . . In this way, too, the mass army grows that marches under the proletarian banner.

---

6. Kautsky had dealt with the relation of classes to parties in "Klassendiktatur und Parteidiktatur," pp. 273–79.

The Victory of the Proletariat

If one considers all the factors set forth above, which arise out of the struggles of the proletariat to ward off the tendencies of capital to increase its misery, as well as from the utilization of the results of these struggles, and lastly out of the growth of large-scale capitalist enterprise, then it becomes clear that the advance and progress of the proletariat in capitalist society is irresistible. Sooner or later the point is reached everywhere when the proletariat not only fights off the tendencies of capital to degrade it, but also goes on the offensive, at least in times of economic prosperity, which are the most favorable for the struggle of the proletariat. The stratum of the population that was once the most degenerate, the most ignorant, and the most uncouth has today already taken over the leadership of the development of society. The primitive struggles for higher wages and shorter hours expand to become struggles for the transformation of the state and of society. This development can end in no other way than with the victory of the proletariat in society, which will be ushered in by its victory in the state through democracy. This latter victory will lead to the conquest of the whole state apparatus, since the result of this victory is that the organs of the democratic state are selected by the proletariat and thus become its organs. . . .

. . . Today the chief question for the Social-Democratic Party is not how it is to come to power, but rather how it is to hold fast to power in order to accomplish so much with the available material means and the available men that from them forms of life emerge that are superior to those hitherto in existence both from the standpoint of the laboring masses and from the standpoint of the lasting prosperity of society as a whole so that they will be joyfully adopted and maintained by these masses. . . .

. . . Private property in the means of production . . . was, in combination with small-scale enterprise, an urgent need of the mass of the laboring population. No less a need for the mass of consumers, hence for society in general, is large-scale enterprise. Combined with private property in the means of production, however, it increasingly becomes an oppressive institution for the workers as well as for the consumers—for the latter when artificial monopolies are created through the establishment of cartels or trusts. There emerges the task of preserving the large-scale enterprise, but to transform it from private property into public, social property, to transform the functions of the capitalist in the enterprise, insofar as they are economically important, from private into public ones, to make the motive force of economic activity not the striving after private profit, but the striving to meet social demand. All socialist systems and programs are in agreement on this goal and that is hardly likely to change in any way. But the various socialist systems differ greatly from each other with regard to the form that is to be given to social ownership of the means of production and to the organization of social labor....

The forces of industrial capital and the dimensions of the complex of industrial interconnections have grown too enormously for anyone to be able to contemplate mastering them with a smaller and weaker organization than the most powerful one in society, the state. The conquest of the state apparatus is regarded more and more by socialists as the most important means for undertaking the necessary reorganization of the process of production, its transformation from a sum of private processes into a collective, consciously organized social process.... But the traditional state apparatus was not made for the purpose of developing a mode of production that is superior or even equal to the capitalist one. It is an apparatus of domination, intended to compel obedience. Adaptation to the needs of the producers and consumers is alien to it. The nationalization of industry can mean only that the enterprises of large-scale capitalist industry to be socialized, insofar as they could not be managed better as cooperative or communally owned enterprises, are to be converted into state *property*. It does not mean, though, that they are to be administered by the traditional state bureaucracy....

... The democratization of the state apparatus does not take care of everything. Special organizational forms still have to be created, which are adapted to the peculiarity of each of the branches of production and transportation that is to be socialized, in order best to look after the interests of its producers and consumers.[7] ... In this area there will still be much to learn, ... much experimenting will have to be done. We will be dealing here ... with a process of development that goes on gradually, similarly to the process of the growth of the capitalist mode of production, but which can, certainly, be carried out far more rapidly than the latter.

... One thing can already be said now: ... it is inevitable that the process of economic development in the direction of socialism ... will end with the abolition of all classes and class antagonisms, thus with the formation of an entirely new social organism.... That is not some kind of mystical categorical imperative, ... but rather simply the result of the class position of the proletariat, from whose class struggle against exploitation socialism emerges. With the industrial proletariat, there arises for the first time since the formation of the state and of social classes a working class that is capable of using the state for its emancipation.... Unlike other working classes, like peasants and artisans, it is a class that can never, through the increase of its means, become employers of wage laborers or slaves, hence exploiters.

---

7. Kautsky had said more on this point in 1919 in *Was ist Sozialisierung?*, pp. 16–17; the entire passage is quoted in translation in *The Labour Revolution*, pp. 205–07.

The proletariat can definitively free itself only through the abolition of all relationships of exploitation.[8]

One might perhaps think that a new relationship of exploitation could result from the policy of colonialism. . . . The white workers take control of the state government and socialize production. . . . They are, however, active only as superintendents. . . . Under their command, Chinese and Indian coolies, . . . Negroes, etc., work as oppressed and exploited wage-laborers. Such a possibility . . . is disposed of by the simple fact that the number of white workers is much too great for them to be able to achieve a higher level of affluence in any other way than by their own labor. . . . Exploitation is profitable only for a small minority that lives from the labor of quite large masses of people.

If in many Anglo-Saxon colonies the white workers are hostile to the colored workers, that is not due to their desire to exploit them, but to the fear of being ruinously outcompeted by them on account of their lower standard of living. This hostility will diminish to the extent that the colored proletariat obtains better living and working conditions through its struggles. Admittedly, in many cases the white workers do not understand that yet. . . . They seek to keep the colored workers from making advances by arrogant segregation from them . . . and guildlike monopolization of their spheres of work. Even today, this is true of American labor unions vis-à-vis Negroes who want to join them and of white mine workers in South Africa vis-à-vis black workers who are struggling for work methods that do not violate their human dignity. These white workers are thereby dividing the working class, instead of uniting it, and in that way they help capital, even if entirely unintentionally. In spite of everything, the same movement that raised the white workers also takes hold of the colored workers, and the advance of the latter is just as irresistible as that of the former. The model of the white workers necessarily promotes the advance of the colored workers the more, the more successful it becomes, the more the white workers obtain power and affluence. . . .

CHAPTER FIVE
Roads to Socialism

We must count on the advance and ultimate victory of the non-European proletariat as much as on that of the European one (in which are also to be included the North American and Australian). Here as well as there, this

---

8. On the special role of the proletariat in history, see also *Bolshevism at a Deadlock*, pp. 87–91.

process will take place on the basis of the same laws of industrial capital, which is more and more taking hold of the whole world. That is by no means to say, however, that the same process must everywhere assume the same forms.[9]

The European proletariat (and that of the British dominions and of the United States, as well) carries on its class struggles and accomplishes its rise on the foundation conquered and prepared by a vigorous and independent petty bourgeoisie in cities capable of struggle. Such a petty bourgeoisie and such cities are lacking in the areas of Oriental despotism.[10] When these areas are taken hold of by industrial capitalism and thereby filled with the need for modern democracy, only *one* class can be found there that takes up energetically the struggle for democracy: the proletariat, in addition to a stratum of numerous intellectuals who are the first to yearn for democracy but lack the strength to conquer it without allies. The peasant, who in Western Europe in the periods of the bourgeois revolutions is most likely to follow the leadership of the petty bourgeoisie and of the bourgeois-minded intelligentsia, as long as he is revolutionary, finds in the countries of oriental despotism only the proletariat and a proletarian-minded intelligentsia as a leader.

As we see in Russia, that confers on the proletariat a much greater power than in the West, given the same numerical relationship between the agrarian and the industrial population. This situation, however, also presses the proletariat, in addition to endeavoring to establish democracy, which under the given conditions surely becomes both attainable and inevitable, also to attack tasks presupposing a highly developed capitalist industry and an advanced proletariat; a proletariat that in long years of training through democracy and free mass organizations has raised itself to a level that the proletariat under despotism and with meager industrial development cannot attain. The situation is also complicated by other factors. On the one hand, the intelligentsia of the East, which is familiar with the history of the revolutions of the West, easily sees in its own revolution merely a continuation of the Western revolution, . . . which makes it less perceptive of the peculiar nature of its own revolution. On the other hand, however, this intelligentsia is influenced by the theories of Western European socialism.

If the proletariat comes to power in an Eastern state, the intellectuals of this kind feel obligated to use that power for the immediate establishment of socialist production, for which the economically advanced West has

9. The only non-European country Kautsky ever studied at first hand was Transcaucasian Georgia, which he visited September 1920–January 1921, when it was governed by Mensheviks, just before the Bolshevik invasion. In *Georgia*, he deals with, among other subjects, the problem of a socialist regime in an underdeveloped country and particularly its relation to the peasantry. See especially ibid., pp. 75–85.

10. See IV:5:7a, IV:7:4–6, above.

hardly yet created the rudimentary bases. These intellectuals then believe
that they are ahead of the West, serving as an example to it and showing
it the way. In making this attempt, which exceeds its strength, the proletariat
must of necessity fail and lose its hard-won democratic freedom to a new
despotism, a bureaucratic-military despotism under the leadership of a dictatorship of intellectuals with whom the proletariat feels itself allied. To
that extent, the dictatorship is of proletarian origin. But it does not mean
rule by the proletariat. . . .

No modern state, however, can do without a highly developed industry
today, if only because it has a need to be powerful. Russia, too, must develop
its industry further at any price. If it succeeds, then there will grow the
strength and independence of its proletariat and of democracy without
which the proletariat cannot prosper. If the efforts to invigorate industry
fail, then the regime bringing about the general decline of the state will
appear to be the author of all social evils. The country will head toward
catastrophes, which the dictatorial regime can survive only with great difficulty.[11] In this case, too, democracy must again triumph. So, to be sure,
will industrial capitalism. The industrial proletariat will have to struggle
with the latter not only for its own working conditions but also for the
leadership of the peasants. But finally, given progressive industrialization
of the country and developed democracy, the leadership of the popular
masses and with it growing power in the state will devolve more and more
on the industrial proletariat. This power can then be exploited all the more
readily for socialist ends, if at the same time socialist parties take over the
helm in Western Europe and clear the way for the economic development
to socialism.[12]

In the other two giant realms of the East, China and India, development
will proceed in a different manner. Here, too, there are no self-governing
cities with a vigorous, independent petty bourgeoisie that could smooth
the way for modern democracy. Industrial capitalism does not arise there
from such a petty bourgeoisie; it is introduced from without. As in Russia,
the industrial proletariat in alliance with the progressive parts of the intelligentsia will here, too, have to solve simultaneously the revolutionary
problems arising out of its own class position and those that in the West
fell to the lot of the petty bourgeoisie and the solution of which is the
precondition of the successful struggle of the proletariat for emancipation.
As in Russia, the proletariat will here, too, acquire greater power than in
Western Europe relative to the degree of development of industrial capi-

11. Kautsky is here briefly repeating what he had argued in 1925 in *Die Internationale und
Sowjetrussland*, p. 55.
12. See also *Socialism and Colonial Policy*, pp. 4–44, and *Georgia*, pp. 69–70. The latter
passage appears in a different translation in *Selected Political Writings*, pp. 135–36.

talism of these countries. But it will also find itself confronting more complicated situations.

In contrast to Russia, however, industrial capitalism is younger, the proletariat consequently still less developed and weaker in these two immense realms of East Asia. The influence of Western Europe on the intelligentsia of these states is smaller, and to the degree that there is such an influence, it comes more from Britain (in China also from America) than from France and Germany. Neither the French Revolution nor the Paris Commune nor Karl Marx have so far exerted influence on the struggles of the Chinese and the Indian proletariat. On the other hand, there is, in contrast to Russia, in China and in India an old, highly evolved culture of a quite distinctive nature, which confers on the thought of the intellectuals there a special character even when they take up the results of western science. Finally, the entire population of those realms, and not least of all the intellectuals and proletarians, are at the present time occupied to a high degree by the struggle against foreign domination. Now such a struggle always produces the tendency toward the union of all classes of the nation for collective action and toward the obfuscation of the antagonisms between them.

In China, the proletariat is still too weak to safeguard democracy, let alone to march forward in the direction of socialism. The penetration of industrial capitalism, to be sure, was able, since it appeared as foreign domination, to call forth a popular movement strong enough to topple the reigning dynasty, which did not prove to be a match for the foreigners. But on the fall of Manchus, as on the fall of the Romanovs in Russia, there followed at first, not a period of democracy, but, after a time of anarchy, a period of dictatorship. Corresponding to the condition of the country, this dictatorship was much more backward than the Russian one, which was, after all, at least at the outset and in its intentions, inspired by grand goals and borne by the most progressive class of the country, the proletariat. In China we have hitherto seen only dictatorships of competing generals, pursuing no other goal than that of personal power. . . . It remains to be seen whether the democratic forces in that country, in particular the proletarian organizations, are already vigorous and independent enough to found a lasting democratic regime, proceeding outward from southern China. Sooner or later, such a regime must certainly eventuate as well as a strong influence of the proletariat on China's democracy and through it.

In India, the struggle against the foreign domination of Britain is still in full swing. If it is thrown off within a short time, then it will probably be followed here also at first not by a democracy, but by a plurality of competing dictatorships of generals and princes. But it is quite possible that the liberation struggle will acquire a duration and assume forms, the effect of which will be that the self-determination of the Indian population advances at the same speed as the development of industrial capitalism and of the proletariat, and that the traditional absolutism of the Anglo-Saxons in British India will be followed immediately by a regime of lasting democracy, with no transition through a period of ephemeral native dictatorships. Democracy and proletarian class struggle are made difficult in India by the religious antagonisms between Hindus and Muslims, . . . as well as by the constriction of the Hindus' social life in castes.

Yet another kind of advance of the proletariat is about to take place in formerly Spanish America. . . . If in Spain itself its absolutism inhibited the rise of an urban bourgeoisie at an early date, there was in its colonies from the very outset no possibility of such a bourgeoisie. The Spanish conquerors did not come as peasants, . . . but as feudal landowners who drew their revenues from the work of forced laborers. . . . The masses of the common people remained in complete economic, political, and intellectual dependence. . . . Political life consisted in the brawling of individual generals or of wealthy landowners, who could buy a general along with his mercenaries, for control of the state apparatus in military uprisings, which were called "revolutions."

This situation is only changed by the penetration of industrial capitalism, which makes it entrance there, as is usual everywhere outside of Western Europe, with the construction of railways. Its rise is especially brisk in Mexico, which borders on the United States and is more influenced by them than any other state of Latin America and the resources of which, precious metals and petroleum, attract capitalists from very different countries, notably the United States. Thus, there develops here, too, an industrial proletariat whose rise pulls along the very numerous agricultural proletariat. . . . In Mexico, the proletariat in effect stands alone when it undertakes to act in accordance with democracy. It finds no self-confident petty bourgeoisie that would have politically paved the way for it in the utilization of democracy. Nor a self-confident peasantry with landholdings of its own, but only wretched tenant farmers with minuscule plots of land and peons of the owners of latifundias. Further, no intelligentsia of any significance. . . . The great mass of the people can neither read nor write. . . . More than in any other country, the proletariat there has to rely intellectually on itself alone. And what is more, its neighbor is a state that is, to be sure, economically highly developed, but whose working class stands in the last place among industrialized countries as far as class consciousness and class politics go.

Despite all difficulties, Mexico's proletariat has accomplished extraordinary things in the last two decades. The democratic movement that made a breakthrough in 1911 . . . has been able to prevail again and again in spite of repeated military revolts and setbacks, and the proletariat has become increasingly stronger and independent in this movement and through it, until today, under President Calles, it controls the state. It has known how to fill the democratic freedoms, which before were only empty forms, with a living content and to stem the rebellions of the generals. . . .

It cannot yet be said with certainty whether Mexico's proletarian organizations and the government of Calles supported by them are now already capable . . . of founding a lasting democratic regime and of forever putting an end to the era of putsches and dictatorships of generals, who are in the pay of the Church, of foreign capitalists, and of the great landowners. But it is hardly likely that the proletariat will ever lose the leading role it has attained in Mexico's democracy, unless the agricultural laborers were to make a complete about-face after they have been transformed into land-owning peasants. There can be no doubt that all further progress in Mexico can take place only under proletarian leadership. There is no other class in that country that would be able to take that role. The Mexican proletariat will be able to keep the leadership of the state the more easily in its hands, the more it is careful to refrain from setting itself tasks that are beyond its powers at a particular time and that could for some time wear it out.

Clearly, there are very different roads that the proletariat can take as it advances. These are determined not only by its general class position, but also by the particular geographical conditions and the social ones that have become historically significant, under which its class struggles take place. The extent of its political power in a country at a given time does not depend merely on the degree of development of industrial capitalism there, but also on those particular conditions. That does not constitute a refutation of the materialist conception of history, but it is indeed a warning not to construe it in too mechanical and too simplistic a manner.

. . . As the market of the capitalist mode of production increasingly becomes a world market, as the economic life of every country comes to be ever more closely dependent on the world market, as the capitalists establish international cartels and capitalist governments recognize the necessity of the League of Nations, so too will the proletariat of every country not be able to conduct its class struggles successfully without cooperating closely with the proletarians of other industrial countries. The socialist International has become a necessity for the proletarian class struggle. . . . Its reach is broadening more and more to include the whole earth. . . . But the more it expands, the more difficult it will be *[to make it capable of]* great and decisive actions . . . , that have to be carried out according to a common plan in all countries of the International by their socialist parties at the same time and in the same manner.[13] And it is not at all possible that a proletarian International be led dictatorially by the socialist party of a single country. The

---

13. See also *Die Internationale*, pp. 50–68, and also *Die Internationalität und der Krieg*.

more the International expands, the more will it have to place its main emphasis on being a means of mutual understanding and communication for the socialist parties of all countries. The more it grows, however, the more important and difficult will even this task become. . . .

Still, no matter how diverse the roads to power might become that the proletariat follows in the different regions taken over by industrial capitalism, the goal to which they lead is just as much the same everywhere as industrial capitalism and the economic laws of its motion are everywhere the same. The sentence in Marx's preface to the first edition of *Capital* remains valid, that "the country that is more developed industrially only shows, to the less developed, the image of its own future" (I, 91). And the following statement from the same preface likewise retains its validity, namely, that a society "can neither leap over the natural phases of its development nor remove them by decree. But it can shorten and lessen the birth pangs," that is, when it "has begun to track down the natural laws of its movement" (I, 92). If in the Christian society of the Middle Ages all roads led to Rome, today all roads of the proletariat lead to democracy and to democratic socialism.

The forms of production that socialism calls forth need not be the same everywhere. Like the road leading to them, their final form can also be very different under different natural and traditional conditions of social life. Even in the same country and at the same time, these forms will not be the same for all branches of economic activity. Advances in technology and in social experience will cause them to be further developed and . . . become ever better adapted to new conditions and requirements. Socialism does not mean a rigid, immutable formation of a perfect society; rather, it refers to the direction that the further development of society will take under proletarian leadership. . . . The goal of this new direction of the development of society will not be reached at one blow. But the proletarian movement, out of which this goal arises and which strives toward it, cannot and will not find rest until it has been reached. The proletarian masses will find no contentment until their exploitation and thus all exploitation has ceased, not just in a single country but in the whole world.

CHAPTER SIX

The Undermining of
Capitalism

. . . Before we conclude the examination of the developmental tendencies inherent in present-day class struggles, we must discuss yet another question: Will the capitalist mode of production come to an end in a way similar to the feudal one that preceded it and was supplanted by it? . . . This assumption . . . is still very widespread today in socialist circles. . . . Should capitalism not also finally assume forms in which it becomes an obstacle to further economic development, indeed, an obstacle to a prosperous economic life in general, so that the salvation of society from economic decay now makes the replacement of capitalism just as necessary as the replacement of feudalism was at an earlier time? In the first half of the last century, this assumption could appeal to the evidence of the frightful devastation inflicted on the working class by industrial capitalism wherever it was able to wreak its havoc without restraint. Under these conditions, socialism appeared to be a means of saving the proletariat from complete decay and thus society itself from ruin.

This line of reasoning is characteristic of utopian socialism. But even Marx and Engels, at least in their beginnings, were not able to stay entirely clear of it. *[Kautsky quotes a passage from the* Communist Manifesto, *including the statement that the bourgeoisie]* "is unfit to rule because it is incompetent to assure an existence to its slave within his slavery, . . . its existence is no longer compatible with society" (p. 79; *MESW*, I, 119)]. That was correct for British conditions at the time it was written. . . . But in his *Inaugural Address* of 1864 as well as in the first volume of *Capital* of 1867, Marx already expressed views very different from those he had held in 1847. . . . He . . . praised . . . legislation for the protection of labor as an effective means of countering the tendency to plunge the proletariat into ever-deeper misery. . . . Under the condition of growing democracy, the proletariat in large cities gains control more and more of their government and is able, even in the midst of capitalist production, to improve the living conditions, especially the housing conditions, of their population to such a degree that the level of its general health is noticeably raised. Like all of technology, that of health services likewise makes enormous advances, and, thanks to the improvements of transportation and the growth of the labor movement, intellectual life becomes more developed even among the agricultural workers.

We therefore can no longer say today that the capitalist mode of production . . . is bringing about its own end through its mere economic development. The inclination to undermine the physical health of the urban workers and the intellectual life of the agricultural worker is still very much in existence among the capitalists. They ruthlessly seek to suppress any and every organization of agricultural workers and, whenever they can, deny funds to any housing and social welfare policy favorable to the workers. But the proletariat is increasingly gaining the strength to overcome these obstacles.

CHAPTER SEVEN

Crises

In addition to those just discussed, however, the development of industrial capitalism brings still other facts to light that seem to indicate that it is digging its own grave. . . . It appeared that in a capitalist society, exploitation would have to lead to *overproduction*. . . . That would lead to crises caused by lack of demand, with enormous losses of capital and horrendous unemployment, which would of necessity become more intense and result in society ultimately drowning in its own juice. . . . Marx and Engels did not accept this theory. *[Kautsky quotes and discusses passages from the* Communist Manifesto, *pp. 72–73;* MESW, *I, 113; and* Capital, *I, 786, and refers to Marx's explanation in Volume 2 of* Capital *of crises as disturbances of the necessary]* proportionality . . . between the production of means of production and the production of consumer goods. . . . But nowhere is it shown that these crises finally have to assume a character that precludes the continuation of the production process in capitalist form.[14] In his work against Dühring (1878), . . . Engels attributed crises to the fact that, owing to modern technology, production has the tendency to expand more rapidly than the market. *[Kautsky quotes* Anti-Dühring, *p. 301.]* Here, too, it is not shown that the capitalist mode of production must at some time arrive at a limit, after which its further expansion is rendered increasingly difficult economically. That could occur only when the absorptive capacity of the market could no longer be adapted in any way to the capacity of industry for expansion. For that, however, there exists no theoretical necessity. . . .

[The extended crisis of 1873] could force upon Engels the idea that capitalism had entered a new phase, that of the chronic crisis. . . . Capitalism was destined to decay just as feudalism had before it, if the proletariat did not succeed in conquering political power and in replacing capitalist with social property in the means of production and in the products fabricated with them. At that time, we Marxists all accepted this view.[15] . . . But a new economic upturn began at the start of the nineties and was just as extensive and enduring as the preceding period of lasting depression. The pendulum then swung back in the other direction, not only in bourgeois economics, but also for many socialists. It seemed that a new era of capitalism had dawned. The cartels grew then to have great importance, and many people expected of them that they would succeed in organizing production and in eliminating crises. In the last two decades, though, the history of the capitalist mode of production has had so many and such painful crises to show, while at the same time the number, the extent, and the tightness of the cartels and trusts has grown more and more, so that surely not many

14. Already in his controversy with Bernstein, Kautsky had denied the charge of the latter that both Marx and the German Social-Democratic Party expected a breakdown of capitalism and the revolution as its result. *Bernstein und das sozialdemokratische Programm*, pp. 42–46. See also "Verelendung und Zusammenbruch," pp. 607–608.

15. See *The Class Struggle*, pp. 71–87. For Kautsky's 1922 proposed revision of the Erfurt Program's passage on crises, which he had drafted in the period referred to here, see *Die proletarische Revolution*, pp. 53–61 (in *Texte zu den Programmen*, pp. 259–71).

people still believe that crises will be overcome by associations of entrepreneurs.

It is true, however, that the crises have changed their character. Their danger for capital, that is, for industrial, not for speculative, capital has diminished somewhat, but not their destructiveness for the working class. Unemployment during periods of crisis is still the most frightful scourge of the proletariat. To the extent that it is moderated, that happens not on account of new institutions of capital, but because of new gains made by the proletariat under democracy, because of unemployment insurance provided by the state and the labor unions. There is, however, no longer any basis for the expectation that the crises caused by lack of demand will someday reach such an extent and duration that they render the continuation of the capitalist mode of production impossible and make its replacement with a socialist organization of production inevitable.[16]

CHAPTER EIGHT

The Limits of Capital Accumulation

[Kautsky devotes most of this chapter to critical remarks on Luxemburg, The Accumulation of Capital *as presenting]* . . . a theory . . . that attempts to show that an ultimate economic failure of capitalism is an inescapable necessity because of the conditions of its circulation process, despite or rather precisely because of the constant growth of the forces of production. This is in contrast to Marx, who demonstrated the opposite in the second volume of *Capital.* . . .

[Kautsky refers to his review of Hilferding's Finance Capital, *"Finanzkapital und Krisen," pp. 838–46; his* Vermehrung und Entwicklung, *pp. 196–224; and his article, "Der Imperialismus."]* In these articles and chapters, I developed a conception of the process of circulation based on the difference in the conditions of production in agriculture and in industry following Marx's theory of the proportionality of industry. In my opinion, this conception explains why crises . . . must of necessity occur periodically. In large part, they are caused by the fact that agricultural production cannot expand as rapidly as industrial production. . . . Consequently, a disproportion between the two must again and again occur from time to time.[17] That is not to say

---

16. For Kautsky on crises, see also *Bernstein und das sozialdemokratische Programm*, pp. 135–52; "Krisentheorien"; "Finanzkapital und Krisen," pp. 797–804, 874–83; and also "Nochmals unsere Illusionen," pp. 267–68; *Von der Demokratie zur Staats-Sklaverei*, pp. 101–102.

17. See also III:3:5, above.

that this is the sole cause of crises. . . . *[There are also]* causes of crises that arise out of special situations, political and military catastrophes and errors of legislation, not out of the nature of the capitalist mode of production in general.

The difference in the conditions of production between industry and agriculture . . . results in the markets for industry being unable to expand as easily and as rapidly as industry itself. . . . Industry cannot, within its domain, get rid of all the products it has fabricated, means of production and consumer goods, by selling them to industrial capitalists and workers. It always produces surpluses that it can dispose of only if a factor active outside its area takes them off its hands. Agriculture is such a factor. Industry has need of agriculture, however, not just as a market for a part of its products, but also as a supplier of foodstuffs and raw materials. . . .

CHAPTER NINE

Accumulation in Agriculture

In the studies cited above, I have discussed the question of why capital turns much more readily and much more intensely to industry than to agriculture: . . . Natural causes alone account for the fact that agriculture cannot develop as rapidly as industry, given a developed state of technology. That is compounded by the fact that heretofore capital has flowed to agriculture much less rapidly than to industry. Therefore, in order to increase the quantity of agricultural products required by a growing industry, so far the simplest and fastest way has always been preferred. That has been the inclusion of new, hitherto not opened up areas with agricultural populations in the commerce with the centers of industry. This procedure . . . is as much a consequence as a precondition of the expansion of industry beyond a certain limit. . . .

The most important means for expanding trade is not conquest, not "imperialism," but the improvement of the means of transport. Mostly, it pays to transport agricultural products only when inexpensive means of mass transport are used. Until well into the last century, only transportation by ship met that requirement. . . . Then railways appeared and provided a mighty means of mass transport on land. . . . There now began a period when agricultural regions were very rapidly opened up for industry, regions that were in part already densely populated, in part quickly settled with colonists.[18] There thus arose a powerful aid for the development of industry, which was, under the conditions then obtaining, synonymous with the development of the capitalist mode of production. The recurring periods

18. See also "Finanzkapital und Krisen," pp. 843–46.

of prosperity and crises were linked to the progress of railway construction; they were always periods of *industrial* prosperity and crises.

The construction of railways, not imperialism, was the all-powerful means for opening up to capitalism, that is, to industry, as customers and suppliers those agricultural . . . regions that industry needed. Imperialism, the conquest of agricultural regions by industrial states, is only an episode in this general process, an episode that became very important for some European states, but also disastrous. Imperialism does not by any means constitute an economically necessary condition of all capitalist accumulation.

The most important regions of European colonial policies since the end of the Middle Ages were conquered before there was a capitalist industry of any significance. These conquests were part of the primitive accumulation of capital, which preceded capitalist industry. They were carried out for purposes of pillage, not of industrial development. . . . The most important colonial areas had already been taken up when the expansion of West European, especially British, industry awakened the need to acquire agricultural markets. The construction of railways, which answered to this need in the greatest degree, was initially not linked to any "imperialism" on the part of the industrial states, not in America, not in Australia, nor in British and Dutch India, nor in Siberia or in Japan. Their expansion in China is not at all connected with European conquests.

The precapitalist areas that have had to be conquered by Europeans in the past century in order to be brought within the sphere of capitalist industry by means of railways are quite small in size and even more in economic importance in comparison with those mentioned here. They really comprise only Africa and the Near East. In our own day, the world is, in the main, divided up. And a new epoch, opposed to that of imperialism, is beginning: the revolt of the peoples conquered and exploited by Europeans against all European domination, indeed, against all European influence. . . . But this progressive restraint on imperialism does not at all mean a collapse of capitalism. It will merely foster a new form of capitalism, the Asiatic form. And with that, the construction of railways will continue. . . .

. . . Railway construction . . . can supply regions, if they are only thinly settled, with immigrants who, as farmers, increase their production. Or, if these regions already have a numerous population that has not yet gone through the separation of industry from agriculture, railways can rapidly carry through this process. In one way as in the other, railway construction can ensure for a long time to come that agricultural . . . production keeps pace with industrial . . . production, that growing industry is supplied with sufficiently increased quantities of foodstuffs and raw materials and that enough new markets for its products are opened up to it. To be sure, this process cannot go on indefinitely. And since today every agrarian state is very eagerly seeking to develop an industry of its own, . . . industry will always continue to have a tendency to develop more rapidly than agriculture, which must again and again cause new crises. And thus the time may after all not be as far away as it still seems now, when all available agricultural regions of the earth have been sufficiently settled and provided with railways and when additional railways will not add new suppliers or open up new markets of any consequence.

But even then the economic end of capitalism need not have arrived. That would only be the case if agriculture only in its precapitalist form were relevant for the further development of industry. . . . Accumulation of capital originating with industry need by no means involve the enlargement of industry; it can also mean expansion or intensification of agriculture. It would signify that all the more, should the time ever come when, due to industrial overproduction, industrial profits constantly fall, and in agriculture not only ground-rents but also profits rise.

Even at the present time, much capital is being invested in projects intended to increase agricultural production, for example, in gigantic irrigation works in America and Egypt (including the Sudan). The process of the separation of industry and agriculture goes on continuously and transforms more and more activities previously carried on by farmers into activities of industry. If, then, this process began with the destruction of the peasant's family industry, it is now also taking productive activities from the proper domain of agriculture. *[Kautsky mentions the production of butter, cheese, sugar, and fertilizers and the substitution of electrical and gasoline motors for draft animals.]* It is possible, of course, that the industrial population and with it the entire population of the earth will ultimately become so numerous that even the most extensive accumulation of capital and the most far-reaching progress of technology can no longer make agriculture capable of satisfying the growing needs for raw materials and foodstuffs. That, however, would mean the end of any further development, not only for the capitalist, but for any mode of production whatsoever.

A half-century ago, this Malthusian fear was still very strong in bourgeois circles. Today it has generally been abandoned, not because we have come to hold the opinion that the earth has unlimited space available for indefinitely many millions of people, but because the practice of artificially limiting the number of births has become widespread, so that now the opposite fear is beginning to take hold. . . . We have every reason to expect that men today are capable of adjusting the number of births in society to its economic conditions and requirements. Neither from depopulation nor from overpopulation, neither from a growing disproportion between industrial and agricultural accumulation and production nor from crises resulting from such a disproportion, do we have to expect a collapse or a failure of the capitalist economy, a catastrophe that would compel its replacement with another, higher one. . . .

. . . Capitalism . . . survived the ordeal of the war and is today, considered from the purely economic standpoint, more solidly established than ever. It has recovered, in spite of the greatest follies of governments and short-sighted capitalists and landed proprietors after the war, in spite of the insanity of the Treaty of Versailles and of its sanctions, in spite of inflations and obstacles to trade of all kinds. . . . The question *[now]* is whether Europe can arise again or whether it will decline. . . . Today the center of gravity of the economy and of culture can be shifted to the coasts of America—on both oceans. But that would by no means result in the downfall, indeed not even in a profound disturbance of capitalism on our globe. It has demonstrated in practice in the most impressive fashion its ability to survive and to adapt to the most diverse, even the most desperate, situations. There are no arguments of economic theory that could call its vitality into question.

Does that prove the hopelessness of socialism? *[Kautsky quotes Rosa Luxemburg saying so in* The Accumulation of Capital, *p. 325.]*

CHAPTER TEN

The Presuppositions of the Necessity of Socialism

The situation would really be hopeless for socialism if it based its expectations solely on the assumption that crises, as the *Communist Manifesto* states, will become ever "more extensive and more destructive" or on the assumption that the progressive accumulation of capital will spontaneously produce its own limits. But the *Communist Manifesto* already points also to another agent that is destined to become the "gravedigger" of capitalism, the *proletariat*. And this same *Manifesto* already shows that the rise and growth in strength and the final victory of this class is inevitable. We have already treated of that topic.[19] Must the victory of the proletariat lead to socialism, however, if capitalism proves itself to be economically vigorous?

Historical materialism must not be understood to mean that a mode of production cannot be overcome as long as it remains economically vigorous.[20] Let us recall our discussion of the original formation of the state and of classes.[21] . . . The peasant economy remained *technologically* at the same state of development, . . . but its *economic* position was changed. The free peasant . . . became a serf subject to taxation. . . . This new mode of production was not a consequence of the decline of the peasant economy that preceded it, nor was it a consequence of an economic superiority of the

---

19. See IV:8:2–4, above.
20. See IV:9:1c, below.
21. See pp. IV:3:1–4, above.

victorious nomad economy.... The new mode of production was a product of force, of the superiority of those who had an interest in it and enforced it. This superiority can, but need not be economic.... It can be a mere superiority of numbers—under democratic conditions—or of knowledge or of martial ability. But, to be sure, such a superiority will not be accidental but economically conditioned....

The advent of socialism is, then, surely dependent on certain economic conditions and a certain knowledge of these conditions, which make it possible for the victorious proletariat to replace the capitalist mode of production ... with another that satisfies it. Such a mode of production is precisely the kind we call a socialist one.... If the new mode of production should prove to be less effective than the present one, then the working classes would demand and bring about the return of the latter. It is said that in such a case the workers would just have to make sacrifices for their ideals. But with regard to the economy, their ideal is a mode of production that satisfies them better than the present one, that provides them, to be sure, not only with more material goods, but also with more knowledge and freedom. They can doubtless make sacrifices temporarily, in order later to reap a richer harvest.... But it would be nonsense, if they were continually to make sacrifices for a system of production that continually gave them poverty, ignorance, and lack of freedom....

The prospects of socialism do not depend on the possibility or necessity of a coming collapse or decline of capitalism, but on the expectations we may entertain that the proletariat will gain sufficiently in strength,[22] that the forces of production will grow sufficiently to supply an abundance of goods for the masses of the people, and that the forces of production, as they grow, will assume forms that facilitate the social organization of their employment; finally, that the necessary economic knowledge and conscience will develop in the working classes that guarantee a fruitful application of these productive forces by the working classes. Those are the preconditions of socialist production....

The opponents of socialism frequently maintain:.... The more the workers' prosperity increases already under capitalism, the more they will come to terms and reconcile themselves with it and refrain from all uncertain experiments. The increasing moderation of class antagonisms is said to push socialism even further into the distance to the same degree that the proletariat grows in strength. On this, not on the accumulation of capital or the growth

---

22. Kautsky stressed this repeatedly, from one of his early articles to his last book, in "Ein sozialdemokratischer Katechismus," pp. 366–67; *Bernstein und das sozialdemokratische Programm*, p. 54; "Verelendung und Zusammenbruch," pp. 609–10; "Zwei Schriften zum Umlernen," pp. 142–43; "Nochmals unsere Illusionen," p. 268; *Von der Demokratie zur Staats-Sklaverei*, pp. 101–103; "Marxism and Bolshevism" pp. 192–93; *Sozialisten und Krieg*, p. 253.

of crises, in fact, hinges the fate of socialism. That should not be taken to mean that we socialists should oppose all social reform, because it could mitigate class antagonisms. This view, as it was preached by so many anarchists . . . , could originate only in the brain of a professional revolutionary or a fanatic who was concerned not with raising the proletariat, but only with bringing about a civil war as rapidly as possible. Should a socialist really want to prevent social reforms that could have effects favorable to the workers, he would thereby succeed only in completely discrediting himself in the eyes of the laboring masses. If social reforms or, as some believe, democratic freedoms, hence the indispensable conditions of the advance of the working class, truly moderate class antagonisms, then the cause of socialism would be lost.[23]

I, for my part, must say: if I became convinced that the improvement of proletarian living conditions progressively mitigated class antagonisms, then I would feel obligated to give up the cause of socialism. It would pain me to do so, because I would have to acknowledge that my life's work had been misdirected. But I would also have a certain feeling of relief, for socialism is for us only a means to an end, to the final goal of the complete emancipation of the proletariat. Today, we see only *one* possibility of reaching this goal; that is the bringing about of socialism. If, however, the same end could be achieved within the framework of the present mode of production, then that would mean that our goal could be reached more easily, more simply, and with smaller sacrifices than we socialists had previously thought. . . . Should it prove to be the case that the advance of capitalism of necessity brings forth spontaneously a moderation of class antagonisms, so that the workers feel more and more content under capitalist leadership, then we would have to admit that openly and renounce our socialist goals; we could do so without thereby betraying the cause of the emancipation of labor.

CHAPTER ELEVEN

The Intensification of Class Antagonisms

Before we study the question of whether the antagonisms between the classes are becoming more moderate or not, we have to know what we are

23. Kautsky had made the same point thirty-five years earlier in "Der Entwurf des neuen Parteiprogramms," p. 753, and again in *Die proletarische Revolution*, p. 49 (in *Texte zu den Programmen*, pp. 253–54). That social reforms and democratization, though highly desirable, cannot remove class antagonism was repeatedly stated by Kautsky, as in *The Class Struggle*, pp. 89–90, 93; "Reform und Revolution," pp. 253–54; and "Positive Arbeit und Revolution," pp. 325–27.

to understand by them. If the expression "intensification of class antagonisms" means that the class struggles assume increasingly violent forms,
then the view implicit in that expression would certainly not be correct.
. . . The stronger the workers are, the better organized, the better educated
they are about economics, then the better planned and prepared do their
struggles become, the less are these struggles directed against single individuals and objects, the more are they directed against particular social
institutions harmful to the workers, institutions by which the level of wages,
the hours of work, the worker's dependence, etc., are determined. The
struggles of this kind are waged no less resolutely, but they can take place
without senseless fury, without insane destruction, and as a rule do occur
without such attendant phenomena, even when the entrepreneurs behave
in an extremely provocative fashion. This kind of behavior on their part,
however, is becoming increasingly rare, the more the workers' militant
organizations grow in strength.

To the foregoing is added a general tendency toward the moderation of
customary behavior that has appeared in the working classes and the intelligentsia since the eighteenth century, but not, certainly, without meeting
with strong countertendencies. *[Kautsky refers to his chapter on this subject is*
Terrorism and Communism, *pp. 121–57, quoting from pp. 131 and 142.]*
There I showed that the proletariat in particular can, by its class position,
easily be made receptive to the ideas of humanity *[that is, respect for the dignity*
of the individual]. . . . The more the proletariat grows in strength, the more
it becomes the leading class in society both on the road to humanity and
on the road to democracy. . . . A moderation of manners in the class struggle,
however, need not at all mean a moderation of class antagonisms, that is,
a drawing closer together of the social goals of proletarians and capitalists,
an increase in the number of interests they have in common. Only this will
be discussed in what follows.

A growing . . . harmony of interests is supposed to arise from the fact
that the progress of the productivity of labor, brought about by industrial
capital, benefits not only the latter but also the workers and that the workers
have just as much interest in the prosperity of the economy as do the
capitalists. That is correct, but only little community of interests is the
result. To the extent that the advances of productivity are due to the general
progress of natural science, they are an achievement of society in general.
The capitalist is merely their appropriator and beneficiary. And he promotes
and applies them chiefly for the purpose of saving himself wages. Together
with all other consumers, the workers, too, have as consumers a share in
the fruits of technological progress. But they are not merely consumers,
but also producers and as such the machine often confronts them as an
enemy. And in the capitalist economy, there is no period of prosperity that
is not necessarily followed by a crisis. The crises, however, [are] . . . factors
that aggravate class antagonisms. Even if one cannot maintain the position

that the crises are becoming continually more devastating, nevertheless Marx's demonstration of the inevitability of crises under capitalist conditions of production has not been refuted.

There can be no doubt that the situation of many, though far from all, strata of workers has improved in the course of the last half-century; for some, the improvement took place even earlier. But this would lead to a moderation of class antagonisms only if it resulted spontaneously from the development of capitalism. That, however, is by no means the case.... A number of strata of the working class have made considerable advances, but always only in struggle against capital.[24] They did not and could not succeed in completely smothering the capitalists' striving to impoverish the workers. Whenever an opportunity seemed to present itself for undoing a success the workers had achieved, capital took advantage of it to attack that success.

The progress of the proletariat since its deepest humiliation thus does not consist in the fact that its struggles with capital are becoming fewer, but in the fact that to the proletarians' struggle for the improvement of their situation there have been added their struggles for the defense of the positions they have already won. Such struggles, however, are usually the bitterest ones.... Class struggles thereby become ever more diverse, but class antagonisms are not thereby moderated, but rather become harsher, ... also because, even when the intensity of the antagonisms of interests remains the same, the attitudes of the opponents become the more embittered, the longer the conflict lasts, the oftener it recurs.

Further, as the forces of production and the general wealth of society grow, the workers' needs increase far more quickly than the improvements they succeed in obtaining, a circumstance that necessarily increases their discontent and aggravates class antagonisms. The exploitation of the workers grows, that is, the quantity of what is left to the working class from the product of their labor does not increase as rapidly as the product itself. Up to now, the achievements of the proletarian class struggle have not sufficed to overcome this tendency of the capitalist mode of production. The technological advance of the means of production of capital proceeds far more rapidly than the social advance of the proletariat. And the latter accelerates the former. The higher wages are, the greater is the incentive for introducing labor-saving machines and methods.

... Statistical proof of growing exploitation is not easy to obtain and remains a matter of dispute. But exploitation manifests itself in forms in which it is comprehensible to the broad masses of the people without any statistics and provokes and infuriates them. The manifestation that is nearest at hand is the growth of the personal consumption of the capitalist exploiters,

24. See also "Der Entwurf des neuen Parteiprogramms," p. 754.

which is proceeding far more rapidly than that of the consumption of the workers and of the lower classes in general. . . . From the material circumstances in which the propertied classes live, the working class becomes acquainted with elements that could be made generally available. Such elements. . . . develop in the working class to become needs, the satisfaction of which it strives for and the denial of which embitters it. The more rapidly the workers' exploitation and the capitalists' personal consumption rise, the more do the workers' needs grow, far more rapidly than their wages. That, too, heightens the workers' antagonism toward the ruling and exploiting classes.[25] The workers' "greediness" grows even among those in better circumstances; indeed, it grows more among those workers who feel strong enough to fight than among the impoverished ones who often content themselves with bemoaning their misery and begging for small alms. . . . The workers' demand for continually new improvement of their standard of living will never be satisfied, but will grow more and more as long as they see classes above themselves with wealth that, without being reduced, permits senseless extravagance and as long as they see in the possession of the propertied class elements of prosperity and the enjoyment of life that are denied to them and that, in view of the existing great wealth, could be made available to all. . . .

The ways in which surplus value is consumed . . . include also the consumption by the *government* that is controlled and used by the capitalists. Perhaps even more rapidly than the personal consumption of the exploiters, this consumption, especially that caused by armaments and wars, has increased. The rapid improvement of the means of transportation has increased the size of armies on a gigantic scale. And the enormous advances of the technology of production give an ever more monstrous form also to the instruments of the technology of destruction and to the havoc wrought by these. . . . We social democrats have always fought against the armaments race on ethical and also on economic grounds. We expected that this policy must ultimately exhaust the resources of the states. . . . We had underestimated the magnitude of the exploitation of the working classes. We assumed that it was increasing, but a growth so enormous that it became possible to squander the resources of the nations in the most insane manner, without crippling their economic growth—that exceeded our assumptions. In fact, that became possible only when the productive forces of the capitalist mode of production grew much more rapidly than did the quantity of the products allotted to the workers. Thus, this, too, is another proof of the increasing exploitation of the workers.

In the final analysis, the state expenditures are all paid from surplus value,

25. See also *The Social Revolution*, pp. 42–44.

if we understand by surplus value that part of the total product of the workers—wage-laborers and others—remaining after deduction of the costs of maintaining the workers and their families. Still, . . . it is by no means a matter of indifference who pays the taxes that cover the state expenditures, whether it is the workers or the exploiters. If the worker is taxed, that means that it is the state government itself that takes the tax from the worker's wages and thereby transforms it into surplus value, reducing his wages by this amount. If the tax is imposed on the capitalist or some other exploiter, like the landowner, then he must pay the tax from the surplus value he has already taken from the workers. In the second case, the worker, in his struggle over the level of his wages, has to deal with only one opponent, the individual capitalist who employs him. In the first case with two opponents, his employer and the state, and the power of the latter is as a rule even more terrible than that of the individual entrepreneur. Thus, the taxation of the worker becomes one of the most effective methods of holding wages down.

It might seem that the antagonism between capital and labor is diminished, or at least veiled, by the taxation of the workers, because then it is no longer the employer but the state that appears to be the most important cause of insufficient wages. But the antagonism is not diminished, only shifted onto another track. If the taxes rise that the capitalist has to pay, he at first tries to compensate himself by raising prices; that, however, is dependent on the state of the market, does not always succeed, and is detrimental to the sale of his products. He is more likely to help himself out by reducing wages. If, on the other hand, it is the workers who are obliged to pay the taxes, then they seek to obtain an increase of their wages as compensation. When capital is taxed, in which case the workers have to defend their wages, their situation is more favorable than when they themselves are taxed, in which case they are faced with the task of obtaining higher wages. The antagonism of these two classes is intensified, though, in each of these cases. That is all the more true as, at least in democratic states, to the economic struggle over wages, which taxation calls forth, is added the political struggle over taxes in the parliament that has to legislate them as well as in the elections, in which the members of parliament are chosen.

With the wastefulness of the capitalist-governed state, which arises out of growing exploitation, the social antagonisms become more and more intense in the struggles over taxes. These antagonisms are not moderated when the proletarians gain influence over the state apparatus. For they must use that apparatus to diminish as much as possible the unproductive expenditures for armaments and to avoid wars, but also to promote the improvement of the situation of the propertyless classes and strata as much as possible. That leads to new taxes and struggles over new taxes, struggles not only over the level of the taxes, but also over the purpose they serve. These struggles become an important moment in the class struggles of our time, a moment that makes them ever more bitter. . . .

Despite the growing . . . extravagance of the individual capitalists and . . . of the state they control, the exploitation of the workers is increasing so enormously that the wealth of the capitalist society is swelling in a staggering fashion. [Kautsky cites numerous statistics on pre–World War I German national income and government expenditures and then notes that coal miners' wages rose only 35 percent and the population increased by 31 percent, while in roughly the same period (1895–1910)] the expenditures of the German government and the amount of the annual accumulation doubled. . . . Clear proof of increasing exploitation.[26]

No less than the increase of consumption, which is difficult to grasp statistically, and, above all, the extravagance of the capitalist class and the struggle over shifting the burden of the growing taxes, it is the rapid growth of accumulation that more and more intensifies the class antagonism between labor and capital. Accumulation has that effect by the mere fact that it constantly alters in a fundamental way the relations of power between the two classes and thereby again and again creates new material for conflict. The capitalist class utilizes its growing wealth more and more for the purpose of repeatedly gaining new and stronger positions of power vis-à-vis the working class. The tremendous growth of capitalist accumulation makes possible the no less tremendous revolution of technology in the sphere of the capitalist mode of production, especially that of Western Europe and the United States. . . . Not only were the old branches of industry completely revolutionized, but whole large new ones were created: the electrical and chemical branches, those producing automobiles and airplanes, etc. At the same time, the transport system of the entire world was revolutionized, starting from the relatively tiny regions of the northern part of Western Europe and the northeastern part of the United States, [so that] enormous mines, textile factories, ironworks are arising in regions previously inhabited only by barbarians or savages.

The growing exploitation of the workers in the area occupied heretofore by capitalist production is accelerating more and more the rate of accumulation. In turn, the latter expands all the more rapidly the area of capitalist exploitation, so that the total yield of that exploitation grows with the force of a tidal wave. . . . At the same time, however, the number of proletarians is also increasing more and more. . . . In the capitalist states, the proletariat is increasingly becoming the mass of the nation. . . .

26. Kautsky had emphasized growing exploitation as a cause of class antagonism in "Der Entwurf des neuen Parteiprogramms," p. 754; *The Class Struggle*, pp. 200–201; *Bernstein und das sozialdemokratische Programm*, pp. 104–14; *The Social Revolution*, pp. 38–44.

[Among the] capitalists, it is an ever-smaller group of capital magnates on whom the management and exploitation of the growing masses of capital devolves. The great fortunes are increased ever more rapidly not only through the process of accumulation. The preponderance of these fortunes and of large-scale industry ruins the small capitalists and promotes the centralization of capital. The functioning of joint-stock companies and banks and the formation of cartels ultimately have the result that the capital of others increasingly falls under the control of the capital magnates. The system of joint-stock companies is supposed to "democratize" capitalism. In fact, it brings about something quite different. Numerous intermediate strata between the capitalists and the proletariat, and to a certain degree even some better paid strata of wage-laborers, can save sums of money that are too small to establish a capitalist enterprise with. In the form of stocks and deposits in banks, these funds belonging to the little people are placed at the disposal of the great capitalists and increase their economic power.[27]

The capital magnates increasingly unite in their own hands the capital of industry and of the banks. They thus form finance capital, as it is called by Hilferding, who has studied this process in an exemplary manner. Through this unification of capital, they become to a growing extent the masters of the entire society, and they dispose of its fate in a more and more autocratic manner. Not only the propertyless, but also many propertied workers, such as peasants and artisans, and even many owners of capital, are increasingly pressed hard and threatened by these magnates. Their domination becomes all the more oppressive, as these new monopolists, like all monopolists, strive more and more to protect their interests in domestic and foreign politics by means of brutal force. This is in fundamental opposition to the first industrial capitalists and even more to the farther-seeing among their earlier theoretical champions, whose ideals were unrestrained competition, free trade, democracy, and international peace. From the very beginning, this ideal was clouded by troublesome countertendencies, but it nonetheless constituted an antithesis to the tendencies of the banking capitalists, who always went hand in hand with the great landowners and with absolutism and inclined to the use of force.[28] In the

---

27. On this effect of stock ownership, see also *Bernstein und das sozialdemokratische Programm,* pp. 98–104; *The Social Revolution,* pp. 58–60; *The Road to Power,* p. 28; *Kriegsmarxismus,* pp. 20–24.

28. Kautsky had dealt at greater length with this difference between early industrial capital and banking capital in his first article on imperialism, "Ältere und neuere Kolonialpolitik," pp. 801–806, 809–12, and referred to it later in "Der imperialistische Krieg," pp. 475–76, and in *Sozialisten und Krieg,* pp. 289–90. The disappearance of this antagonism due to the growth of cartels, monopoly, and finance capital is noted in *Handelspolitik und Sozialdemokratie,* pp. 40–41; "Nochmals unsere Illusionen," pp. 231–32; *Nationalstaat, imperialistischer Staat und Staatenbund,* p. 23; and *Sozialisten und Krieg,* p. 291. See also IV:3:8, above.

last few decades, this policy of force has increasingly become the program of all who have at their disposal the power conferred by capital.

More and more, it is society as a whole that suffers from that policy. But only the proletariat is capable of waging a systematic and energetic struggle against the yoke of big capital, because it resists capital from the outset, while the other strata dominated by it are hindered in their struggle by various property interests and even capital interests. Nonetheless, it is becoming extremely important that the proletariat with its particular class interests also increasingly represents the interests of the great mass of society, in which it is itself coming more and more to constitute the majority. The proletariat is thereby becoming the champion of the interest of society as a whole,[29] and it is gathering around itself more and more of the numerous intermediate strata that are coming into being between itself and the capitalist class.

To the same degree, however, the antagonisms between the proletarians and capital are not moderated, but multiply, as capital feels itself increasingly menaced by them in very diverse areas, not merely in those of wages and hours of work. The growth of democracy and the improvement of the workers' standard of living do not diminish, but increase the fronts of attack and the material for conflict between the antagonistic classes. Thus the antagonisms between them become ever deeper.[30] . . . Today, these antagonisms appear nowhere harsher than in Britain. . . .

CHAPTER TWELVE

Economy and Politics

There can be no doubt about the increasing intensification of class antagonisms in capitalist society. But does not that intensification arise out of circumstances offering quite dim prospects for the proletariat? We have seen earlier that we cannot expect ruin of capitalism caused by mismanagement, or its decay, or the appearance of economic limitations that capitalism cannot overcome. Now, however, it is also becoming apparent that the economic power of the capitalist class is growing more and more not only absolutely but also relatively in comparison to that of other classes. The proletariat is therefore becoming economically . . . weaker in relation to capital. Since that is so, where is the proletariat supposed to get the strength it needs to

29. On Kautsky's frequently stated notion that the proletariat represents the interests of the entire society, see "Klasseninteresse—Sonderinteresse—Gemeininteresse," pp. 273–74, and *Die Internationale und Sowjetrussland*, p. 7.

30. See also "Grundsätzlicher Teil" (*Heildelberger Programm*), p. 14 (in *Texte zu den Programmen*, pp. 299–300).

overpower capitalism? We have, to be sure, also seen that . . . the industrial proletariat, too, is becoming ever stronger under the capitalist mode of production. . . . Both classes . . . become ever more powerful, in contrast to the other classes, whose social importance decreases more and more in comparison with [them]. But how is it possible that two antagonistic classes simultaneously become stronger, not merely absolutely but also relatively? . . . The capitalists become ever-stronger in the *economy*, the proletarians in *politics*.

But, according to our conception of history, is not the economy always the decisive factor and politics merely a superstructure dependent on the economy? . . . In reality, the materialist conception of history by no means says that the economically stronger, that is the richer, always proves to be also the socially stronger. It says only that in the final analysis every social change can be explained by an economic change and that no social formation can maintain itself that is not adapted to the given living conditions of men. . . . From the same economic soil there grow forth the most varied tendencies, aiding one another, thwarting one another, combatting or paralyzing one another. They are all economically conditioned, but they are not all of a purely economic nature. In addition to the economic needs and forces, brutal force and intellectual superiority also play a great role in these struggles. Our conception of history does not by any means deny that. It merely accounts for all changes and differences of these kinds of force and superiority, as well as those of the economic needs and forces, by changes of the relations of production.

Let us consider just one example from our own time of how antagonistic different economic tendencies can become that arise out of the same economic basis. *[Kautsky develops this example at some length and summarizes it by saying]* that the historical development of the era of capitalism does not follow only the path of creating ever-larger states and economic areas, but rather proceeds predominantly in the opposite direction, toward division of existing large states and of economic areas delimited by customs duties into numerous smaller ones. Certainly, the first tendency arises out of the economic conditions of capitalist production; but the second, opposed tendency does so no less. The latter is linked with the needs for increased popular education and a higher degree of democracy that result from industrial capitalism. . . . Often enough the two tendencies come into conflict with one another, even though they grow from the same soil. Most of the time, that tendency wins out that, although ultimately grounded in the economy, is directly of a political nature, over the other, which does not merely have an economic foundation, but also arises directly out of economic needs.

In certain circumstances, then, the political factor can become stronger than the purely economic one. To be sure, even the political factor cannot be permanently separated from its economic base. It remains dependent on it.... A state will flourish all the more, ... the more the economically *advantageous* tendencies among the economically *grounded* tendencies appearing within it come to predominate over the others and either suppress the latter or adapt them to themselves. This is the path on which economic necessities assert themselves. It is not as simple as many a critic, and also many a defender, of Marxism believes.

Thus, the economic phenomena of the surface need not always prove to be stronger in politics than the political ones. The fact that the proletariat outgrows capital only in political power, not, however, in economic power, in no way proves the hopelessness of the proletarian struggle for emancipation. It proves only that it is futile to undertake to conduct that struggle with purely economic means, as some social reformers and anarchists, proponents of cooperative associations, founders of colonies, and syndicalists suppose. It is certainly true that many economic organizations of the proletariat prosper, above all, the labor unions, but also the cooperative associations. They become indispensable for keeping the proletariat in fighting trim and for forcing the capitalists to grant various concessions. But they are incapable of overtaking the growth of the economic power of capital and of putting an end to its rule. . . . Only the *political action* of the proletariat constituted as a separate political party is capable of fashioning the class struggle into a struggle for emancipation.

In spite of the growing economic power of capital, the proletariat in several of the large states of Western Europe, especially in Britain and Germany, is close to winning sole possession of governmental power. In many other states, it is advancing rapidly toward this goal. Once in possession of governmental power, the proletariat will be in a position to sever at least one of the two roots of capitalist power: private property in the means of production. . . . But while, with *[its]* abolition, . . . the capitalist mode of production is also abolished, no new mode of production is created. . . . Here politics returns to its dependence on economic conditions, from which it cannot free itself. Here it becomes clear that, while the conquest of governmental power by the proletariat is indispensable, if it is to emancipate itself from the yoke of capitalism, that conquest does not suffice of itself, if certain preconditions are not fulfilled. These are in part directly economic, in part moral and intellectual; we cannot expect them to be present unless they are produced by economically determined conditions of life.

If one of the two roots of capitalist power consists in private property in the means of production, the other consists in the particular form of the production and circulation of commodities. . . . It is adapted to the requirements of the owners of capital, but is indispensable for society as a whole, indeed, even for the wage laborers who are exploited under it. Indispensable, as long as it has not been replaced by a kind of production and circulation of goods that is adapted to the needs of the workers—needs for freedom and equality of rights, for knowledge and enjoyment of life, as well as for adequate food, clothing, and housing—and that satisfies these needs to a higher degree than the present system. *[Kautsky substantially repeats here more briefly what he said in IV:8:10, above.]*

CHAPTER THIRTEEN

The Conditions for the Socialization of Production

If the proletariat is not merely to achieve victory, but also to keep it firmly in its grasp, then the conditions mus ᴊe given that enable it not only to expropriate the capitalist class, but also to replace that class in the process of production and circulation to a sufficient extent, so that the undisturbed continuation of this process is assured. Now, the development of the capitalist mode of production through concentration and centralization of capital is proceeding in a direction that even today is making the individual capitalist increasingly superfluous, namely, by means of joint-stock companies and employers' associations. These restrict more and more the scope open to the much-vaunted initiative of the individual and increasingly replace the competition and the speculation of the individual entrepreneurs with a stable regulation and organization not just of the production but also of the sales of whole branches of industry. This regulation could immediately assume socialist character, once it was carried on not for the purpose of private profit but to meet the demand of society. . . .

But it is precisely the striving after profit that today is sucking as much work as possible out of the workers, in order to make the quantity of surplus value swell to the greatest possible extreme. And that same striving seeks to reduce the costs of production as low as possible. Once the means of production have become the property of a society in which the workers are the ruling class, then . . . the new mode of production should supply just as many products as the old one, indeed, significantly more, if it is to be able to eliminate the immense amount of misery existing today. That will happen only if the workers have certain mental and emotional qualities that impel them to do their best of their own accord, which up to now they have done only under capitalist coercion.

That does not mean that the hours of work should be extended. That would contradict the goal of the emancipation and the intellectual elevation of the workers. . . . Sufficient leisure for all working people is urgently necessary. No less necessary, however, is the highest possible productivity of the labor expended in the shortened hours of work. That can and will be attained, without driving the workers on to work harder, by shutting down all badly organized and equipped factories, by the general use of the most advanced machines and methods, as well as by the productive use of heretofore unproductive or even nonworking elements of the population that are able to work, such as the unemployed, workers in useless, minuscule factories, in superfluous carrying trade, etc.

Finally, it is also urgently necessary that the workers have an adequate understanding of economics, that they be able to grasp economic advantages and necessities as well as economic disadvantages and impossibilities, to distinguish capable from incompetent managers, to get rid of the latter, and to gather gladly about the former and to cooperate with them intelligently. ... But a high degree of moral sensibility is also required, a high degree of solidarity, which sees it as dishonorable, vis-à-vis one's comrades as well as the entire working class and society, not to do one's duty in a factory belonging to a socialist society, that is, a society governed by the working class, whether in the form of property belonging to a cooperative association, to a local community, or to the state.

In the course of the class struggle, the workers learn about economics. Labor unions and labor parties see to that. ... The advances of the workers, the establishment of cooperative associations, guilds, socialized institutions, the formation of factory councils also help impart to larger groups of workers knowledge about the conditions of the process of production and circulation. Before socialists have conquered governmental power, large industrial urban municipalities become very important for accomplishing this end. In such communities, the proletariat comes to power first. There it can first introduce the beginnings of socialist production on a larger scale, if the municipalities enjoy sufficient liberty of action. ... Along with the expansion of the political power of the proletariat as well as the political and economic organizations for militant action, ... there is a growth of the possibilities, the means, and also of the necessities that the proletariat acquire a knowledge of economics and make that knowledge the basis of its activities.[31]

Things are not so simple with respect to the morality the workers need as with regard to the knowledge they require. ... Every particular social activity requires a particular kind of morality and cannot be successfully performed without it. ... The class struggle produces in the worker a high level of morality, ... voluntary discipline within his own organization and solidarity with his comrades-in-arms, ... but also constant distrust, perhaps even hatred of the factory manager, who is either the worker's exploiter or represents him; ... indifference to the interests of the enterprise, the yield of which is harvested only by the worker's exploiter and opponent, the felt

31. On the effects of the class struggle and of democracy on the knowledge and experience and the discipline and solidarity of the proletariat, see also *The Social Revolution*, pp. 81, 184–87; and "Eine ethisch-ästhetische Geschichte der Pariser Kommune," p. 353.

need to give to the latter as little as possible, to get as much as possible
from him, and in this way to diminish the degree of exploitation.

In socialized production, it is a matter of redirecting the ethics produced
in the class struggle . . . to the production process that now becomes a process to increase the well-being of the working class. . . . What the class-
conscious worker has already felt with regard to his union and to his party,
he must now also feel toward the socialized enterprise. . . . The same contempt that he previously felt for the strikebreaker he must now feel for the
worker who attempts to avoid working for the collectivity by deliberately
producing less than he is able to. And he must also have that feeling toward
any individual worker or stratum of workers that make use of especially
favorable circumstances in a socialized enterprise to procure for themselves
extra benefits at the expense of the collectivity of the working class, without
increased productivity on their part.

Changing the proletarian class morality to adapt it to the new relations
of production is not easy. And in contrast to the other material and intellectual preconditions of socialist production, this new morality does not
already arise out of the capitalist mode of production. It can develop only
within the framework of socialist production. That will occur the more
easily, the more the socialized enterprises cease to be an exception within
capitalism, but become sufficiently extensive to influence the thinking and
feeling of the entire working class. . . . The new socialist morality in production will be attainable the more easily, the greater the workers' economic
understanding and the more democracy within the factory. All the more,
the workers will regard the factory as their own. . . . Nothing is more absurd
than attempts to beat into workers by terrorist measures the pleasure in
their work they lack, voluntary discipline and solidarity with the factory.
That can lead only to the result that the workers see the same enemy in the
socialized enterprise as in the capitalist one and oppose it just as stubbornly.
The new morality required by socialism cannot develop in this manner.[32]

. . . The greatest possible wealth of society becomes just as important as
the most far-reaching possible democracy in the factory. The greater the
former, the easier will it be to satisfy far-reaching demands of the workers,
the more readily can the worst misery be eliminated that cries out most
urgently for redress; the greater the benefits that the new regime will be
able to offer immediately to the workers; and the more eagerly will the
workers defend the new regime and be concerned that it prosper. In other
words: *The more the capitalist mode of production flourishes and thrives, the better*

32. Kautsky deals explicitly with the relevant situation under the early Soviet regime hinted
at here in *Terrorism and Communism*, pp. 167–69, 181–82; and in *Bolshevism at a Deadlock*,
pp. 78–84.

the prospects of the socialist regime that takes the place of the capitalist one. That sounds paradoxical from the standpoint of those who suppose that socialism will issue forth from the "collapse," the "failure" of capitalism. It does not, however, contradict the conception that expects the victory of socialism not from the economic decline of capitalism, but from the moral, intellectual, and political advance and increasing strength of the proletariat.[33]

This insight is important for the practice of the proletariat after victory has been won and also already before then for the road it seeks to take to that victory. *[Kautsky quotes from* The Social Revolution, *pp. 97–98, written in 1902, a long paragraph stating that war was not to be desired as a means to bring on the revolution for it would gravely weaken the revolutionary regime and impose difficult tasks on it.][34]* What I had feared in 1902, unfortunately really happened in 1917 and 1918. . . . Communists and social democrats influenced by them rejoiced over the collapse that they thought meant a failure of capitalism and thus its end. Nothing seemed more important to them than to prevent prostrate capitalism from regaining its feet. Every kind of production, with the exception of socialized production, was to be made impossible from then on. That was a terribly dangerous slogan. *[Kautsky quotes from his pamphlet of January 12, 1919,* Richtlinien für ein sozialistisches Aktionsprogramm, *pp. 4–5, declaring that even more urgent than the socialization of production was production itself,[35] and from a report,* Was ist Sozialisierung? *he gave to the second national congress of workers' councils on April 14, 1919, in which he said:]* "Immediate and complete socialization is an empty catchword; if it is impossible, however, then the demand that any and all capitalist production is immediately to be made entirely impossible is no less destructive" *[p. 23].[36]* . . .

At the conclusion of my report of April 1919, I spoke of the "root of the evil" that was responsible for the fact that with regard to socialization nothing had yet happened. As this root I identified: "The division of the proletariat. It was due chiefly to it that a government that arose out of the revolution became dependent on the old bureaucrats, generals, and magnates of capital" *[p. 26].* . . . Without a united proletariat there can be no socialism. A socialist sect, or clique, or conspiracy might under certain circumstances succeed in conquering the state apparatus for itself alone and in holding it fast with all the means of terrorism. In such circumstances, the state ap-

33. See IV:8:10, above.

34. Kautsky expressed the same fear a few months before the outbreak of World War I in *Der politische Massenstreik,* p. 213, and commented on the "moral and intellectual degradation" of the proletariat by war, as he had in 1902, in *Terrorism and Communism,* p. 158.

35. See also *The Labour Revolution,* pp. 132–33.

36. On the inevitability of gradual socialization and the problems this involves for a socialist government, see *Georgia,* pp. 58–69, and, for a different translation, *Selected Political Writings,* pp. 127–36.

paratus will never become a means for the emancipation of the entire proletariat, but only a means for repressing all elements of the working class untouched by sectarianism. It can nationalize the process of production, but it can not democratize it. And only a democratized process of production will be regarded and accepted by the proletariat as one that will emancipate and satisfy it.

And only a united proletariat possesses the strength permanently to maintain its rule under the democratic forms it needs. Whenever the proletariat tears itself to pieces in internal strife, the capitalist class will always be the beneficiary of that strife. Intellectual struggles, struggles over questions of theory, of tactics, of organization, of themselves do no harm; they can be very salutary as a means of compelling clarity of thought. But they become destructive, when they result in an organizational split, and even more so when one proletarian organization moves against another by means of force. The strength of the proletariat in the class struggle, in the struggle for political power, is not least of all a question of organization. And, on the other hand, the socialist reconstruction of production is also a question of organization. Unity of the proletariat is as indispensable in the one case as in the other.

Here, too, can be seen the importance of economic prosperity for the rise of socialism. The unity of the proletariat is threatened by nothing more than by want and unemployment in times of economic depression. . . . Those who have work as well as those who have a clear understanding of the existing relations of power and economic possibilities warn against any test of strength that can be avoided. On the other hand, the others, the unemployed and the ignorant, infuriated by desperation and an unslaked thirst for action, easily allow themselves to be swept away by illusionists and demagogues to outbursts that must of necessity fail and have only one result: the deepening of the rancor and dissension within the ranks of the labor movement.

In the working class, there are always two wings: the prudent and cautious on the one side; on the other, the bold and impatient. These differences do not coincide with different theoretical, tactical, or organizational orientations. Within each of these groupings, both elements can be found. . . . They are both useful, as long as they do not hinder the cohesiveness of the whole body of workers and safeguard it against one-sidedness through their interaction. But their antagonism can become disastrous, if it becomes so intense that it tears the proletariat asunder. That is least likely to happen . . . in periods of economic prosperity.

Capitalist prosperity facilitates socialist measures in yet another way. The greater the capitalists' revenues are as a result of lively circulation, and hence not of increased exploitation of the workers, the more can be taken from them in the form of taxes without disturbing the process of production and without strengthening the tendency to place greater burdens on the workers.

In this way, the state obtains most easily the resources that it needs in order to be able to introduce great innovations in the interest of the masses. In times of prosperity, far-reaching reforms can also be imposed most readily on the capitalists without harming production: reduction of working time, sanitary regulations, etc. For in such times, the entrepreneurs are most likely to have at their disposal the means of bearing the costs resulting from such reforms or of making up for them through technical improvements in their plants. Finally, in times of economic prosperity, innovations in the direction of socialization, for example, newly founded socially owned enterprises, encounter the best preconditions to survive the first difficult years, their apprenticeship, to maintain themselves, and to take root. Therefore we must stress again and again that it is not the economic decline of industrial capital, but its thriving that creates the best conditions for the successful beginnings of a socialist regime.[37] . . .

A proletarian party can achieve control of the government in a country through special circumstances, long before the material, intellectual, and moral conditions are sufficiently developed there to bring about socialist production with extensive self-determination by the workers. Such a regime, too, can bring to the working classes great benefits that a capitalist regime would withhold from them. But it will achieve that only if it forgoes striving for what is economically impossible. On the other hand, whenever it immediately sets about realizing the final goal of socialism, it will always fail; it will either be toppled or it will accomplish the opposite of what it had initially aimed at.[38] Even under favorable circumstances, a proletarian regime will always carefully have to test the ground on which it advances, for its political power and the conditions for socialism will not always exist to the same degree. There, too, many a failure can occur. And the forms of socialism that ultimately, after various trials and errors, prove to be the most suitable may look quite different from those we envision today.

Even occasional setbacks are possible also in the most advanced countries, for example, a temporary transformation of a socialist majority into a minority, perhaps through the desertion of semiproletarian strata or of ignorant proletarian strata to the bourgeois camp, maybe led astray by glittering promises made by the bourgeois parties that surpass the practical accomplishments of what had been the socialist majority. Setbacks due to undemocratic means, to the force of arms, are another matter. We will not discuss them here. . . . Even if such setbacks resulted from a failure, from an in-

---

37. Kautsky had devoted most of his book on *The Labour Revolution* to a section on "The Economic Revolution," including chapters on the forms of sozialization in industry and agriculture.

38. See also *Georgia*, pp. 67–69 (or *Selected Political Writings*, pp. 134–36), and *Bolshevism at a Deadlock*, pp. 73–75, and also IV:9:1d, below.

capacity of the socialist majority, they would prove only that in the country in question the conditions for conquering political power were at the time further developed than those for employing that power for socialist reorganization. That would be far from constituting a failure of the socialist idea as such. After every defeat, the proletariat has so far . . . risen again, more numerous, stronger, and more mature, enriched by what it has learned from its earlier endeavors.

Nevertheless, despite all change of the forms of its activity and its results, its final goal has always remained the same, . . . whether the working class knows it or not. Not an ideal that a theorist has conceived or that a poet has dreamed up and yearned for, but an ideal that is given with its class position and can disappear only with it. Since classes and states have been in existence, every exploited class, if it was capable at all of independent action, has set itself the goal of abolishing its exploitation. Now this goal is being infinitely expanded by the capitalist mode of production, by the forces of production and the proletarian conditions of existence for the exploited which capitalism has created. Now, for the first time in the history of classes and states, the conditions exist that make it possible for the lowest of all classes to free itself and thus to put an end to all class rule. . . . It is still impossible to state definitively when this enormous struggle for emancipation will end and what new social forms it will bring forth. But we can say one thing with certainty: This movement, in the midst of which we are standing and which is carrying us all with it, whether we like it or not, can cease only when an end has been put to any and all exploitation forever. . . . The forces and the conditions for the attainment of this final goal grow ever more from day to day. Thus we may expect it with certainty.

CHAPTER FOURTEEN

The Transformation of the State

The whole immense movement of society that has been called forth by the rise of industrial capitalism and has been carried ever further by the class struggle of the proletariat, cannot proceed without . . . not only bringing about upheavals within the state, but also thoroughly transforming the nature of the state. That has happened already in consequence of the rise . . . of the modern democratic state. As we have seen,[39] this state is already in complete opposition to the essence of the state as it evolved historically, founded from the outset on the legal inequality of the various polities, estates, and classes of which it is made up. . . . But this democratic state

---

39. See IV:7:9, 11 and 12d, above.

does not yet mean the abolition of all classes, but merely the abolition of those differences of social rank that were based on force. It did not from the very beginning eliminate those class differences that had formed within the state and that were of a purely economic nature, that were founded on certain property relations and relations of production compatible with general legal equality.

The democratic state does not prevent the exploiting classes from seizing governmental authority and using it in their class interest, in opposition to the exploited classes. But, . . . the democratic state is by its nature constituted not to be the instrument of a minority, as previous states were, but the instrument of the majority of the population, hence of the laboring classes. Should it become the instrument of an exploitative minority, then that is due not to the nature of the state but to the nature of the working classes, to their lack of unity, their ignorance, dependency, or inability to fight, which are in turn the result of the conditions under which they live. Democracy itself offers the possibility of destroying these roots of the political power of the great exploiters under democracy, something that happens more and more at least for the constantly growing number of wage-laborers. The more that is the case, the more the democratic state ceases to be a mere tool of the exploiting classes. Sometimes the state apparatus begins now to turn against the latter. . . . From a tool of repression it begins to become a tool for the emancipation of the exploited. . . .

Up to now, no majorities have arisen under democracy that were capable of putting through far-reaching innovations. . . . That is certainly a distressing state of affairs. But what is its cause? Quite simply that the socialist parties do not yet have the majority of the population behind them in any state. In present-day society, these parties are the only ones with a program of great innovations. . . . The cause of the distressing state of affairs will not be eliminated by breaking the mirror that shows it to us. . . . Just see to it that there is only one socialist party in every country and that this party has the majority of the population behind it, and both democracy and parliament will immediately become very lively and fertile. And democracy itself offers the best, indeed, the only basis for attaining this condition.

What other political constitution can the critics of democracy oppose to it? Aside from it, in present-day society only one other political situation is at least temporarily possible: that of a lawless *dictatorship* based solely on brutal force. Such a situation can be found even in antiquity, in times of an equilibrium . . . of hostile classes. In the past century, too, we find a situation of balance in the aftermath both of the great French Revolution and of the February Revolution of 1848, and Bonapartism emerging from that situation. . . . Wherever a brisk economic life continued, dictatorship was never able to sustain itself for long. The dictatorships of our time have arisen not in states with a capitalist culture of long standing, but in those with a young industrial capitalism and consequently with an industrial proletariat that is still largely inexperienced. They can maintain their grip on the helm only through methods that increase even more the relative economic backwardness of their states, through growing insecurity, growing constraint of all free movement, . . . through growing isolation of their states and an increase of conflicts with other states. . . .

. . . Dictators can achieve independence from the mass of the population only by relying on an apparatus of power, bureaucracy, police, military, or gigantic gangs of bandits (fasci). This apparatus apparently elevates them to unrestricted autocrats, but in fact degrades them more and more to be its prisoners. Satisfying this apparatus must increasingly be their chief concern, and that is something that is possible only through methods that hinder and constrain any economic advance. This brings every dictatorship necessarily into a growing conflict will all classes of the population. . . . A dictatorship that, thanks to the equilibrium among energetically contesting classes, gains ascendency over them, ultimately has the effect that all class antagonisms recede for the sake of the struggle against it. Today, no dictatorship can maintain itself in power permanently. . . . Its regime will not have advanced the country further than apparently ineffectual democracy. On the contrary, it will leave the country economically, morally, and intellectually weakened. It might hamper for a time the advance of democracy and of the proletariat—often that is its purpose from the start. . . . It is destined . . . to be an episode, painful and filled with sacrifices, but not one that might be able somehow even just to replace democracy, let alone to surpass it in effectiveness.

Democracy is irreplaceable as a means for the emancipation of the proletariat. When it is threatened with force, it can be defended only with force, not with mere persuasion or with the ballot. It must never be surrendered by the militant proletariat. . . . Some people believe that our victory would, at first, not make any change in the nature of the state. It would still remain a means for the repression of certain classes. Only a change of personnel would take place. . . . It would be in complete contradiction to the spirit of a proletariat that has conquered democracy and in numerous mass struggles has made the essence of democracy its own, to use political power for the political repression of its opponents, hence for restricting democracy—as long as its opponents stayed within the bounds of democracy. Measures taken in a civil war against those who have ignited it need not be discussed here. . . .

The state that is governed by a proletarian majority will become . . . the most powerful means for capturing, one after the other, the strongholds of capitalist exploitation and for transforming them into places of free labor. This process must ultimately lead to the end of all exploitation. When that happens, does not the state itself cease to exist? Has it not thereby taken away the ground from beneath its feet, on which it has hitherto stood?

CHAPTER FIFTEEN

The Abolition of the State[40]

[Kautsky quotes a page-long passage from Engels, Anti-Dühring, *pp. 306–307, culminating in the famous phrase:]* "The state is not 'abolished,' *it withers away.*" . . . This statement corresponds perfectly to the Marxist conception of the state as an organ of class rule. . . . No objection can be made against it, if it is taken with the requisite dose of salt. When Engels speaks of the taking possession of the means of production by the state as an "act," one must not conclude . . . that he did not recognize that this transition can only be a more or less slowly advancing process. Immediately thereafter, Engels himself uses the metaphors of a gradual falling asleep[41] and withering away of state power, thus not metaphors of a single act. Also, one may attribute it solely to the condensed, concise *[nature of the]* account, when Engels speaks only of the state as taking possession of the means of production. First, not all means of production can be meant here, but only the large-scale enterprises that require social labor. Second, even these can be taken under management by various representatives of society, by cooperative associations and local communities, as well as by the state. To be sure, however, the state will have to take over the largest and most important sites of production, and those run by local communities and cooperative associations also require suitable legislation from the state in order to come into existence and to thrive. The whole immense social process of production will thus certainly be regulated and directed more and more by the government—to be sure, by a democratic government in the hands of the proletariat.

. . . Engels' remarks . . . require a commentary, for they leave some questions open, about which there should be no misunderstanding. At the conclusion of the statement quoted above, Engels attacks the anarchists, but only because they demand that "the state should be abolished overnight." . . . Anarchists consider the abolition of the state as the precondition for the abolition of exploitation; social democrats, on the other hand, see in the withering away of the state the consequence of the abolition of exploitation.

40. See n. 1 in IV:8, above.

41. The English translation of *Anti-Dühring* says that state intervention becomes superfluous "and then ceases of itself." In the German original, that intervention "schläft von selbst ein," i.e., goes to sleep of itself.

The social situation that finally results, however, is supposed to be the same for the one procedure as for the other. This is not at all what Engels wanted to say. . . .

We must not forget: the state became important for human development not merely as an organization of domination. That is its most conspicuous characteristic and the one that at any given time is most important for those engaged in class struggle, but not its only one. . . . The most important economic and cultural achievements, on which modern socialism rests and which only made it possible, are a direct result of the fact that from the outset the state is greater, and must be greater, than each of the primitive polities, on the conquest of which it is founded; a result of the fact that the state thus creates more extensive trading areas, . . . that it thereby also makes possible the creation of towns and the separation of urban industry from agriculture and finally the creation of art and science. All of that, and thus the foundation of modern socialism itself, disintegrates if the domain of the present-day state is dissolved into its separate elements. That, however, is what anarchism is striving for. The place of the state is to be taken by an immense number of sovereign, small, local communities and cooperative associations, each of which carries on its operations as it sees fit, in isolation or occasionally loosely linked with others. The realization of this, one cannot call it petty-bourgeois, but rather truly prehistoric utopia would lead us directly back into barbarism. It is quite impossible.

The modern democratic state long ago ceased to be an assemblage of mutually resistant elements forcibly held together, which detach themselves from it and make themselves independent as soon as they find an opportunity to do so. On the contrary, in the democratic national state based upon the self-determination of peoples, its individual parts hold together very tenaciously. . . . Forcibly *[separated]* individual parts of a nation . . . cannot find rest until they have achieved unification. This national aspiration is indestructible and irresistible, as is that for democracy and for the emancipation of the proletariat. It springs from the same economic conditions. It means that the era of the liberation of the proletariat will also become an era of the liberation of all oppressed nations, of the joining together of all forcibly separated nations in democratic national states, which will cling closely together without any apparatus of repression and which will live on in socialist society.

The state in this sense will not be made either to fall asleep or to wither away by the abolition of classes. It will victoriously ward off any anarchistic tendency toward dissolution of the state, even if it should still be seriously considered. For at the present time, anarchism is only a part of the history of socialism. . . . Nonetheless, even today the theoretical delimitation [of the Marxist position] from anarchism is still not unimportant for the sake of clarity.

In yet another respect Engels' statement requires an explanation. The expression "the state withers away" could be understood to mean that the state apparatus as such would gradually cease to exist, to function. For some parts that will certainly be true, for example, for the political police, for the military in the case of general disarmament, etc. But other parts of the state apparatus will extend their previous functions all the more, for instance, education, health services, also the promotion of art, insofar as these are carried on by the state. . . . Furthermore, . . . the enormous task of regulating the gigantic mechanism of production of our era will also devolve upon the state—all of this to be done in as democratic, as flexible and unbureaucratic a manner as possible, yet without eliminating all bureaucracy. For no large organization can manage any longer today without bureaucracy, once it has responsibility for tasks requiring specialized knowledge and complete devotion on the part of those entrusted with carrying them out.[42] This transformation will not at all look like a withering away of the state apparatus, but rather like an increase in the number of its functions—as well, certainly, as like a change and even a complete end of some of them.

Engels himself said of the state of the socialist future: "The government of persons is replaced by the administration of things and the direction of the processes of production." The emphasis is here not to be placed on the contrast between *persons* and *things*. The state as it has been up to now also had to administer things, for example, fortresses and arsenals, . . . as well as churches and royal palaces. On the other hand, the direction of processes of production is, after all, nothing other than the direction of producing persons. Rather, the emphasis is to be put on the contrast between *government* (or domination), on the one hand, and *administration* and *direction* on the other. A government means domination when it represents a class that as a minority rules over the great majority through superiority of brutal force, of greater wealth, or of more advanced knowledge. A state directorate appointed by the majority has a different character. If all parts of the population are equally well armed or disarmed, equal in their education and in their property, then the state directorate has at its disposal no means of power vis-à-vis the majority. Nor does it have need of them to execute ordinances vis-à-vis individuals or minorities, since under these conditions the great weight of the majority is irresistible, once it has been unequivocally established by a free election.

The replacement of a government with a mere administration or directorate, such as any organization needs, even given complete equality of its members and complete dependence of the directorate on them—that can certainly be considered as an end of the previous state, at the same time, though, also as a reanimation and strengthening of the traditional state apparatus through a fundamental *change of function*. If the consequences for

42. See also IV:7:13, above.

the state of the abolition of classes are taken into consideration, then one ought to speak not so much of the withering away of the state as of its change of function. . . . If one has a clear grasp of this matter, then the question of how it might be most appropriately designated is less important. . . . The new polity can also be called a state, [or] . . . it can be given a different name, so that its fundamental contrast with the old state is unmistakably expressed. . . .

Let us consider one more point. . . . Engels regards the polity of the classless society as identical with the latter, as the real representative of the entire society. Strictly speaking, however, this can be said only in the sense that the state . . . is now subordinated to society. But the extent of society is by no means the same as that of the state. . . . The capitalist mode of production that is spreading across the world market makes society increasingly synonymous with humanity. . . . Even prior to the World War, in quite diverse areas the need made itself felt to subordinate all or at least some states to certain rules, collectively made and recognized by them, and so to limit their sovereignty. . . . [*Kautsky mentions the Universal Postal Union, the Geneva Convention, the German Customs Union, and the Latin Monetary Union, and then turns to the*] League of Nations, . . . an institution that is necessary and in line with [*historical*] development. . . . It is probable that the League of Nations . . . will ultimately be taken control of by elements that transform it from a tool of the power politics of individual states into an effective tool against the power politics of the large states and for the international union of peoples; into a tool for the peaceful settlement of the problems arising from their living together and for the regulation of economic life, to the extent that it is conditioned by international factors. If the League of Nations maintains itself and grows in strength, then one more task must devolve upon it. There are raw materials that are to be found only in certain locations, but that are becoming vitally necessary for the whole world. . . . The monopoly of their exploitation by particular states can become just as intolerable as private property in the large, crucially important means of production. . . . The taking over by the League of Nations of these natural monopolies of individual states can become no less necessary than the nationalization of those means of production. . . .

It is impossible to predict what shape the history of the League of Nations will take. But one thing is certain: it is indispensable not just for overcoming the dangers of war, but also for the construction of the new society that will take the place of the capitalist one. Already important, it will acquire its full strength only when the elements of the new society have been put into operation and socialist-democratic governments are at the head of the decisively important states of the world. Once we have reached that point, then, along with customs, the customs frontiers will cease to have significance. With wars, the interest in strategic borders will disappear. All the moments will lose their effectiveness that still prevent to such a great degree the drawing of the borders of states solely according to the demands of the self-determination of peoples. Only then will it be possible to establish pure national states everywhere and without exception—other than linguistic enclaves. At the same time, however, the state will also give up a number of important functions to the League of Nations, which will then become the highest organization of society.[43] . . .

At the present time, the state is a very changeable and self-contradictory entity. It is no longer completely the old state, but not yet by a long way the new one. Depending on the nature of their history and the level of their economic development, the various states of our time are very different from one another, and a particular state is not always the same in different situations, not even in the same period of time. . . . We can quarrel about terminology. . . . Perhaps it would be most practical to stick to the term "state" in order to make it clear that it is not a matter of the withering away of the state apparatus that has existed hitherto, but to distinguish the coming state from the preceding *class state* by a special term, like *workers' state* or *social-welfare state*. . . .

Civilization, which made such gigantic advances under class rule, will climb even more rapidly in a classless society, in which the sources of higher learning and skill are made accessible to all. That will be the nature of socialist production, the nature of the workers' state, and thus the nature of socialist society. This situation differs just as fundamentally from the preceding one under the state as the latter differs from the prestate situation. A new epoch of both society and the state is beginning. . . .

Section Nine
Marx's Explanation of the Motive Forces
of Social Development

CHAPTER ONE

Marx's Preface Once Again

a. Class Struggle in History

We have already treated of the classic statement of the materialist conception of history that Marx gives in the preface to his *Contribution to the Critique*

43. On the League of Nations, see also *Sozialisten und Krieg*, pp. 23, 50–53, 61, 630–43, 667–68.

of Political Economy.[1] . . . But we have discussed . . . only the first sentences, which present a general philosophy of historical materialism. . . . The sentences that then follow . . . explain the motive forces and the course of historical development, as Marx saw them when he wrote his book. It would not have been appropriate to set about making a study of these sentences until we had shown the course taken by concrete history up to now. . . . *[Kautsky again quotes the entire Marxian passage except for the first four sentences he had already analyzed at length.]*[2]

This passage differs significantly from the one we considered at the conclusion of Part III. The latter formulates the principles that underlie the *entire* "general process of social, political and intellectual life." On the other hand, the one we are now examining explains . . . in point of fact not the laws of the materialist *conception of history* as such, but only those of *history until now*, which are arrived at by approaching their investigation from the standpoint of this conception of history. Our conception of history can remain the same, and still the laws that have been arrived at for previous history can be modified if facts turn up or become known that were not yet available when the earlier version of these laws was formulated.

. . . Marx says that history up to the present, "the prehistory of human society," was the history of social formations resting on antagonism. . . . "In broad outlines, the Asiatic, ancient, feudal and modern bourgeois modes of production may be designated as epochs marking progress in the economic formation of society." These four kinds of social formations coincide with the four great phases of class society we considered in Part IV. Of social forms that might have preceded these four formations of class society, Marx says nothing. Thus, in 1859, in his explanation of the mechanism of social development, Marx still had only class society in mind.

This conception also dictated . . . *[the assumption]* that the form of movement of society, as it has existed up to the present, is the social revolution. It is said to be caused by the productive forces of society, at a certain stage of their development, coming into conflict with the traditional relations of production or property relations. These relations turn into fetters of the further development of the productive forces. Marx continues: "Then begins an epoch of social revolution." Between this sentence and the preceding one, a connecting link is obviously missing, which Marx omitted, because the connection was made clear by the context. As soon as property relations become fetters on the development of the forces of production, in the interest of further social development there is nothing else to do than break these

1. See III:4:1–6, above.
2. In the following pages, in rendering Kautsky's quotations from Marx's Preface, I have, in the interest of greater accuracy, here and there departed in minor ways from the translation used in "Preface," pp. 425-26, and adhered more closely to that in *MESW*, I, 503–504.

fetters. As soon as that happens, there begins an epoch of social revolution. . . .

The conflict between property relations and forces of production is in reality a conflict between men who own property in the forces of production and those who employ the forces of production and produce. When the owners of the forces of production and those who put them to use, the producers and the consumers of the products created by them, are the same people, no conflict between the forces of production and property relations can arise. Such a conflict presupposes different classes. The social revolution is, then, a result of the defeat of the class of the beneficiaries of the hitherto existing property relations and relations of production by a class that applies the forces of production and, in their application and in the appropriation of the products resulting from their use, feels itself increasingly oppressed by the existing property relations and relations of production.

Thus this analysis is based on the same views that shaped the statement made in the *Communist Manifesto*, that all hitherto existing history has been a history of class struggles.[3] That was a view that could be stated not only in 1847, but also in 1859, without coming into conflict with the recognized science of the time. For only in that same year . . . did Darwin's *Origin of Species* first appear. A short time before, in 1857, the Neanderthal skull had been discovered, the significance of which was for a long while a matter of dispute. The early lake dwellings had been noted in 1854. Only slowly did the elements of an early history of the human race take form from such discoveries and from observations of primitive peoples, a history that long remained unconnected with written history, which was regarded as history proper. . . .

. . . In the *[last]* decade *[of Marx's life,]* however, Marx and Engels eagerly studied early history, as Engels' work on the origin of the family, etc., clearly proves. Some years after Marx's death, the fourth German edition of the *Communist Manifesto* was published. Here, Engels, referring to the sentence under discussion, observes that strictly speaking, it ought to read: . . . "all *written* history" *[p. 67]* was a history of class struggles. This . . . also holds true for Marx's Preface. . . . We must assume that Marx . . . would today make it less general at least on this point.

And probably not just on this point. . . . Research on economic history has shed tremendously much new light on the history of the ancient Orient and of classical antiquity, which allows us to recognize more clearly the social character both of the one and of the other. That compels us to make a further qualification. Even within written history, the law of social revolution is not universally valid. . . . We have seen that in the city-states of

3. See also IV:1:1, above.

classical antiquity, especially in those of Greece, such fierce class struggles often took place that they intensified to the point of bringing about a social overthrow. The proletarians gained control of the government and expropriated the owners, whose property they made their own. But nowhere did there occur a further development leading to new relations of production.[4] The social ideal of the revolutionaries of antiquity lay in the past, . . . : it was the return to the economy of free peasants, to the starting point of the state and the division into classes. . . . That did not, of course, mean social progress. After a few years, at the most decades, the old class distinctions reemerged and the old conditions were reestablished, only with a change of personnel. . . .

With increasing extension of the state, . . . the exploitation of the laboring classes combined ever-greater riches in the hands of the ruling minority. That brought about an often quite fabulous advance of industry, of the arts, of the sciences, thus also of the forces of production. But these increased forces of production were used almost exclusively to satisfy the exploiters' demands for luxuries. Production for the maintenance of the masses changed only slightly. Thus, for the exploited, no new material basis of their work, of their existence, was formed that might have caused them to strive for new forms of production. For the masses, these remained unchanged. The better conditions they longed for lay not ahead of them, but behind them in the good old days when freedom and property had not yet been taken from them.

It is true that a very advanced civilization emerged in the states of the Orient and of classical antiquity, but in each of these states this civilization ended in a cul-de-sac, from which no social revolution could help it escape and which ended with the decay of the state.[5] It was not a revolution from within, but an impulse from without that led out of this cul-de-sac: the conquest of the civilized area by one or more barbarian tribes that breathed new vitality into the old, rotten state, . . . and began a new development of society and the state approximately at the point where that of the supplanted state had also begun. . . . The circuit is not entirely closed, though. . . . The technological and cultural legacy that the victorious barbarians took possession of became somewhat greater from one time to the next, and therefore the society that was set up by the victors on the foundation of this legacy was generally superior to its predecessors, after all. The historical circuit is thus, strictly speaking, a spiral leading slowly upward.

That and not social revolution was the mechanism of social movement up to the beginning of the Middle Ages. Only when Germanic

4. See IV:6:2–3 and 5, above.
5. See IV:5:7c–8, above.

people occupied the Roman Empire did they meet with conditions that, once further developed by them, made a new form of movement of society possible, namely, that effected by social revolution. . . . But we must not generalize the laws of this latter [kind of] development and elevate them to laws governing the entire previous social development. What Marx in 1859 regarded as a general law of social development reveals itself today, strictly speaking, to be only the law of this development since the rise of industrial capitalism. It is only through industrial capital that the unfolding of the forces of production, not so much for the production of luxuries as for mass production, and consequently the revolutionizing of the relations of production as well as of the needs of the working class and their conditions of life and struggle, reach a level that makes these forces of production ever more incompatible with the traditional property relations. Since the end of the Middle Ages, for the first time in the history of the world, the new productive forces come to collide with the traditional system of property. First with the feudal property system; then, since the past century, with the system of property on which commodity production is based.[6]

b. The Impact of Economic Transformations on Ideology

If, then, social forward movement through social revolution is something that is characteristic only of the last few centuries, the sentences in which Marx describes the "ideological" transformations that such a revolution brings in its train do apply to all centuries, not just to those of class society but those of human society in general. They hold good for every change of technological and economic conditions, whether it has been effected by way of social revolution or in another manner. They hold good for every conflict caused by such a change, . . . also for conflicts between dull-minded persons who cannot immediately grasp innovations and those more lively of thought, who easily become enthusiastic about them even before they have been tested. There will always be conflicts of this kind, of course, in every society, even in one entirely without classes. They can also become quite bitter, but can never assume such general and such violent forms as those between classes with antagonistic interests. . . .

6. See IV:7:8 and IV:8:6, above. Kautsky had already a quarter of a century earlier argued that there were no social revolutions before the rise of capitalism. *The Social Revolution*, pp. 21–37.

The sentences dealing with this subject must be read with this modification. Understood in this way, they constitute a general law governing every social development under all social forms, a fundamental law of the materialist conception of history. The sentences in question are the following: "With the change of the economic foundation the entire immense superstructure is more or less rapidly transformed." *[Kautsky also quotes the next two long sentences from Marx's Preface.]* . . . However, . . . prior to the appearance of class society and the state . . . technological progress occurred so slowly, almost imperceptibly, that profound changes of the relations of production and conflicts resulting from them must have been rare. . . . But even when new relations of production came about gradually, without conflict, their changes must have had a revolutionary effect on the consciousness of the men among whom they appeared, must have given to them new outlooks and feelings that could not prevail without conflict with the traditional ones.

c. The Development of the Productive Forces in Society

If we find here one of the most important principles of the materialist conception of history, we must again introduce a qualification as far as the *[next]* sentence is concerned.[7] . . . "No social order ever perishes before all the productive forces for which there is room in it have developed." . . . To this statement, we must object that, while it might well apply to all previous forms of class society, it does not hold true for that of industrial capitalism, hence not for the proletarian revolution. *[It]* was presumably formulated as a result of a study of the bourgeois revolutions. It showed that in the period of its downfall, feudal society was no longer capable of any further development of the productive forces, but rather hindered any further development. Every previous class society also exhibits the same phenomenon, but with the difference that the conditions for the rise of industrial capitalism did not yet exist in them; that they were thus not capable of breaking the fetters on the productive forces through a social revolution in order to free these forces; but that they perished because of these fetters.

Industrial capitalism, however, is a system of exploitation quite different from its predecessors. It does not exploit the masses merely in order to squander the proceeds of the exploitation in luxuries; it seeks constantly to

7. A different and unabridged translation of the rest of this chapter appears in Laidler and Thomas, eds., *The Socialism of Our Times*, pp. 325–34.

increase these proceeds, not only through the methods of absolute surplus value, with which the slave-barons and the feudal lords were also familiar, but also through the methods of relative surplus value, to develop the productive forces, methods of which those barons and lords had no knowledge. Their rule thus resulted in the decay of the forces of production at their disposal, after they had extracted from them what there was to extract. Industrial capitalism, on the other hand, leads to an ever more rapid development of the productive forces. We have seen that economic tendencies counter to this development, which would necessarily bring it to a halt, cannot be expected to arise out of capitalism itself.[8] *[Kautsky summarizes briefly what he had said about crises and the proportionality of production in industry and agriculture in IV:8:7–9, above.]*

... One fact has emerged with increasing clarity in the last few decades: the victory of the proletariat will occur before any of the limits can be reached that some of our theorists have set for the development of the productive forces within capitalism.... The proletariat has come close to becoming the ruling class in some decisively important major states. Thus, it seems out of the question that the capitalist mode of production ... will not perish "before all the productive forces for which there is room in it have developed." In view of the development of the last few decades, this statement is no longer applicable to us. Consequently, we must also modify the comments with which Marx, in the famous chapter on the historical tendency of capitalist accumulation, concludes *Capital*.

... As Marx sees here the tendencies that of necessity lead to the conquest of capitalism, to the "expropriation of the expropriators," he has thereby pointed out the path that economic development is in fact following, the path on which the working class moves with the greatest certainty toward the goal of its emancipation. But we can no longer follow Marx entirely when he goes on to add: "The monopoly of capital becomes a fetter upon the mode of production, which has flourished alongside and under it. The centralisation of the means of production and the socialisation of labour reach a point where they become incompatible with their capitalist integument. This integument is burst asunder. The knell of capitalist private property sounds" [Capital, *I, 929;* MESW, *II, 144*]. It is not from the conflict between the productive forces, for the application of which the capitalist mode of production has become too restrictive, and capitalist property that we expect the end of capitalism; we do not expect this end only when "the monopoly of capital" has become "a fetter upon the mode of production." We believe that we have every reason to be confident that this end will be reached sooner.

8. See IV:8:6, above.

d. Every New Mode of Production Is Tied to Material Conditions

The next sentence of Marx's Preface *[reads]*: "And new, higher relations of production never appear before the material conditions for their existence have matured in the womb of the old society itself." This sentence is certainly in no way less correct than when it was written. . . . It is among the most unassailable principles of the materialist conception of history. Basically, it says the same thing as was stated in the preface to the first edition of *Capital*: A society "can neither leap over the natural phases of its development nor remove them by decree" *[Capital, I, 92]*

. . . In a classless society, no one has an interest or a reason to replace existing relations of production with new ones, unless new productive forces make them appropriate and ultimately necessary. . . . Only in a class society can it happen that a dissatisfied class, when special historical conditions give it the strength to do so, makes the attempt to create new relations of production more favorable to it, even if the conditions for the existence of these new relations have not yet matured in the womb of the old society. When this is not the case, however, the innovations will not be lasting and will rapidly become a plague and will deteriorate, despite all decrees and also despite all terrorism by which the attempt is made to compensate for the lack of the historical preconditions for the new relations of production. This recognition is a sturdy bulwark against all utopian fantasies. It is quite incomprehensible that there are adherents of historical materialism who ignore just this fundamental principle in their practice.[9]

---

9. Kautsky had emphasized in numerous writings that capitalism was a historic necessity and that a successful revolution could only come after a long and slow development and could not be made at will. See his book on the Erfurt Program, *The Class Struggle*, p. 86; his anti-Revisionist works, *The Social Revolution*, pp. 15–20, and *The Road to Power*, p. 6; and his articles in the controversy over the mass strike, "Grundsätze oder Pläne?," pp. 784–88, reprinted in *Der politische Massenstreik*, pp. 141–45; and *Der politische Massenstreik*, pp. 213–22.

He stressed that the conditions for socialism did not yet exist in Russia in his discussion of Russia before the Bolsheviks came to power: "Allerhand Revolutionäres," p. 625, reprinted in *Der politische Massenstreik*, p. 73, and in *The Road to Power*, pp. 18–19; "Die zivilisierte Welt und der Zar," p. 615; "Die Bauern und die Revolution in Russland," pp. 675–76; "Die Differenzen unter den russischen Sozialisten," pp. 73–74; "Triebkräfte und Aussichten der russischen Revolution," pp. 331–33; "Die Aussichten der russischen Revolution," pp. 11–13; "Stockholm," p. 507.

Kautsky then directed the same argument against the Bolsheviks: *The Dictatorship of the Proletariat*, pp. 12–24, 93–100; *Terrorism and Communism*, pp. 161–62; *The Labour Revolution*, pp. 38–39; "Was uns Axelrod gab," pp. 119–21; *Bolshevism at a Deadlock*, pp. 39–45, 78–79; "Georgien und seine Henker," pp. 243–45; "Die Aussichten des Sozialismus in Sowjetruss-

That is certainly not to say that Marxist representatives of the proletariat should reject the opportunity to come to political power, as long as the conditions for the existence of a wholly socialist society do not exist. It does, however, express the obligation for Marxists, wherever they come to power, to determine the extent to which the conditions for the existence of the new society have matured in the womb of the old and to act accordingly in the interest of the working classes. For these, much can be done even before "full socialization" is undertaken.[10]

It may seem striking that in the sentence under consideration here, Marx speaks only of the *material* conditions of existence of the new relations of production. . . . We have pointed out above that the most important of the forces of production is man himself, who first gives rise to the rest of these forces, sets them in motion, and employs them in an appropriate manner. The material forces of production also include certain kinds of labor discipline, organization, knowledge, etc., . . . not just . . . certain inorganic and organic materials and tools, . . . but also . . . certain mental and emotional capabilities in man. These are not, however, brought to maturity in the womb of the old society by some mystical, uncaused, spontaneous movement of the mind, but their appearance is, in the last analysis, due to the newly created technology, hence in this connection in the full sense of the word, to the new material conditions of existence. . . .

Among the preconditions of socialist society that are brought to maturity by capitalist society, *[Marx]* mentions "the revolt of the working class, a class constantly increasing in numbers, and trained, united and organized by the very mechanism of the capitalist process of production itself" *[Capital, I, 929; MESW, II, 144]*. Already in the *Communist Manifesto*, this training and organization of the workers effected by the process of production is described. Thus, the material conditions of existence of the new society must not be conceived of as all too crudely "materialistic." . . .

e. Mankind Sets Itself Only Tasks That It Can Solve

We must examine just one more sentence of the Preface to the *Contribution to the Critique of Political Economy* . . . : "Therefore mankind always sets itself only such tasks as it can solve; since, looking at the matter more closely,

---

land," pp. 440–42 (most of this passage is translated in *Social Democracy versus Communism*, pp. 93–95); *Sozialisten und Krieg*, pp. 296–97, 327–28, 575–77.

10. See also p. 442, above.

it will always be found that the task itself arises only when the material conditions for its solution already exist or are at least in the process of formation." At first glance, this sentence appears to be mystical and obscure. In no case should it be taken to mean that individual men always set themselves only tasks that they can solve. That is not even true for whole classes. In a class society, the different classes set themselves tasks that, corresponding to the antagonism between their interests, are in complete opposition to one another; hence a part of them is necessarily impossible to solve from the start. And have there not been revolutions that failed? Are not most revolutions failures in the sense that the revolutionaries did not achieve in them the goals they were striving for? . . .

Mankind has no brain that could will or think. . . . But precisely because it is a matter of an abstraction, we must not take literally the image used. Mankind cannot set itself tasks at will; however, from time to time, under certain newly appearing conditions, new social relations do emerge that set certain social tasks in the same way for all the men affected by them, hence, one can say, for mankind. It becomes necessary to solve these tasks, if society is to prosper or even just to survive. The new conditions that pose these tasks are the new forces of production resulting from the advance of technology. They not only create the task, but also supply the means for its solution.

The task consists in adapting the social organization to the new means of increased production, a task that can be solved. The solution cannot meet with insurmountable difficulties where there are no class antagonisms and all have the same interest in the most appropriate solution. Where antagonistic classes exist, those classes interested in the preservation of the old order will make the solution more difficult. . . . But, of the classes that confront each other in such cases, that one will most readily gain in strength that is most closely associated with the application of the new forces of production that are superior to the old; that is most likely to discover the social methods and organization best suited to the new forces of production; and that grows in numbers and in importance through these methods and organization. It has the best prospects finally to be victorious and to accomplish the right solution of the social task. . . .

When a new social task appears, individual men undertake to solve it from diverse points of view and with very diverse needs and knowledge. Many of them fail; the same thing happens to entire classes; even whole states can perish. . . . But in the course of all these failures, the amount of experience grows, and the strength of those most interested in the appropriate solution also grows. . . . Thus, when one considers not individual men, classes, or states, but mankind in general, every social task resulting from the emergence of new productive forces has time after time found its solution, which was provided by the same factors that posed the problem.

There is no reason to assume that this will not continue to be the case as society progresses further, especially when it has returned from the class-stage to that of classlessness. . . .

The Further Development of the Materialist Conception of History

That concludes our examination of the sentences in which Marx . . . explains the dynamics of society, so to speak, after he had previously established the constant relationship between economy and ideology, the statics of society, as it were. In fact, the image of the superstructure is possible only *[to describe]* the statics of society; in its dynamics, it ceases to have any substance.

Although it will soon be seven decades old, *[the explanation of]* the dynamics of society presented here by Marx, the summary of the laws of its motion, and the . . . formulation of its statics is still the classical rendition of historical materialism. Time has not passed over it without leaving its mark, however. While some of its sentences have maintained unshaken their unconditional validity, in the case of others we have had to note that new experiences and discoveries have left their validity only conditional, limiting them to particular historical periods. They still explain the historical process and characterize it, but no longer in its full extent, but only certain of its parts.

The practical importance of this formulation for understanding the conflicts of the present time, however, has not been diminished in any way. It was drawn from a profound study of industrial capitalism and of the historical processes leading up to it. It is only for the periods of the past that are more remote from us, for the states of classical antiquity and of the ancient Orient, and especially for the classless age, that not all of Marx's statements hold without qualification. On the other hand, certain economic phenomena that have appeared since Marx's death seem to indicate that one of his assumptions does not necessarily have to hold good for the future without exception: the expectation that a social formation does not perish before it has developed all the productive forces for which there is room in it. But this is still a matter of controversy even among us Marxists. Generally speaking, one can say that the passage of time has affected the account of the materialist conception of history given in 1859 far less than Darwin's theory of the evolution of species that was first published and substantiated in the same year.

Of course, our conception of history, too, must not be protected from ever-repeated reexamination and revisions. On the contrary, it is not a rigid dogma, but a flexible method. In accordance with its own viewpoint, it can only be a child of its times, of certain conditions, and must change with these conditions, must take new experience and knowledge into account and assimilate them. And the mere application of a method helps to develop it ever further. . . . [*We must use it*] in order to gain as much benefit as possible from it for the progress of science and of society. Thus, periodic revisions of Marxism are unavoidable, indeed, they are indispensable. But even if the insights that Marx and Engels gave us are not absolute, eternal verities that must hold good unchanged for all time, nevertheless, they were higher truths beyond those that preceded them and were overcome by them. A revisionism that does not develop Marxism further, but only calls it into question and rejects it in order to return to pre-Marxist ways of thinking, will surely not bring us any scientific progress.

The chief duty of us Marxists at the present time, with regard to the materialist conception of history, is the expansion of its domain. Corresponding to the state of science in their time, Marx and Engels necessarily had to elaborate the materialist conception of history principally as a theory of the history of class societies and class states. Only in their last years did they reach the point where they included the prestate, classless society in the domain of their conception of history, not only occasionally, as they had done earlier, but in a coherent account. The small book by Engels, *The Origin of the Family*, has been left to us as a legacy that shows us the way we must follow in broadening the conception of history passed on to us by our masters.

This is the path I have attempted to tread here. In doing so, I have sought to expand the domain of the materialist conception of history so far that it came into contact with that of biology. I investigated whether the evolution of human societies were not intrinsically related to that of animal and plant species, so that the history of humanity constituted only a special case of the history of life forms, with its own peculiar laws that are, however, connected with the general laws of animate nature. I believe that the common law, to which human as well as animal and plant evolution is subject, consists in the fact that every change both of societies and of species is to be explained by a change of the environment. When the latter remains unchanged, the organisms and organizations that inhabit it also remain unchanged. New forms of organisms and of social organizations arise through adaptation to a changed environment.

While that is generally true, the kinds of adaptation are nonetheless different for the different realms of plants, animals, and men. *Plants* are limited to *passive* adaptation. Changes of the environment, of the climate, of the soil bring about changes in the organisms affected by them through changed nourishment, changed chemical stimuli, and so forth. If these changes are nonadaptive, they cause the organisms gradually to die out; if they are adaptive, they are preserved and finally become hereditary, and new species are thereby established. In the case of other organisms, of *animals*, that have developed the capacities of volition, of cognition, and of locomotion, *active* adaptation is added to this passive one. Changed conditions of life cause animals to use their organs differently. Through this different use, these organs are themselves changed in the course of time. If the changes are adaptive, they are preserved and passed on by inheritance.[11]

In the case of man, however, as we have seen, yet a third form of adaptation to new conditions is added to the first two. Man's intelligence and dexterity reach a degree that enables him to respond to new demands by the conscious *creation of artificial organs*, tools and organizations. An entirely new element is thereby introduced into evolution. Prior to conscious adaptation through the creation of artificial organs, every further development of a species was dependent on a modification of the environment that proceeded independently of it, caused perhaps by geological or cosmic changes on which the organism did not have the slightest influence. That changes for man as soon as he is far enough advanced to make artificial organs for himself. . . . *[These,]* together with the new organizations they have called into being, become a new element of the environment.

When man adapts to his environment, he thereby changes not just himself, as plants and animals do; he also changes his environment. This alteration is his work, but not his conscious work. He consciously creates new organs and organizations in order to solve newly appearing problems. When, however, these organs and organizations become a new environment that poses new problems for man, then that is not to be attributed to man's conscious activity. This new effect of the tools and institutions he has created is very seldom foreseen by him, and even then never in its full extent, and often occurs very much against his will.[12] . . .

Engels once expressed the opinion . . . that man's lack of freedom in history holds good only up to the present time, that it must necessarily disappear in a socialist society. *[Kautsky quotes the passage from* Anti-Dühring, *pp. 309–10, to which he had devoted chapter I:3:10, above.]* The condition in which man confronts "the laws of his own social activity . . . as external, dominating laws of Nature" is abolished for production through the social regulation of the latter. That is doubtless correct. But I cannot completely agree with Engels when he then draws the conclusion that men would thereby achieve control over their living conditions for the first time in history. As far as this control is domination of nature, it has already been accomplished to a high degree by industrial capitalism. On the other hand, to the extent that it is control over the use of the means of production by man (as producer and as consumer), according to plan, without crises, there was such control in early times prior to the emergence of commodity

11. See II:6:2–3, above.
12. See III:3:1 and 11, above.

production. Only the latter brought about anarchy in production and the subjection of men to its laws, which are effective without men being conscious of them. . . .

But Engels goes still further. From the fact that in socialist society men will themselves organize production with full consciousness, he concludes that they will thenceforth also make their *history* completely according to plan, so that "the social causes set in motion by men will have, predominantly and in constantly increasing measure, the effects willed by men."
. . . The further social science progresses, the more accurately will men be able to calculate in advance the effects of their new institutions, insofar as they function as man's organs. But sooner or later, every one of these institutions, detached from the men by whom they were created, must become men's environment, which they encounter as fully formed. The effects they have as such will presumably never be wholly predictable.

. . . In previous history, almost every new technological or economic institution has, in addition to the effects intended by their originators, also brought about unintended effects, if not always immediately, then after the passage of some time, effects that created new social problems. That was precisely what has kept the history of humanity in motion from its beginning onward, and there is no reason why the supplanting of commodity production should change this in any way. Certainly, the means for the solution of social tasks are improving more and more. . . . But along with those means, the tasks, too, are growing more and more. . . . The new institutions *[primitive]* men created for themselves remained predominantly their organs; only to a small degree did they become an environment determining those men. In contrast, how immense is the present-day technological apparatus of society, how extensive are the states, how varied are the areas of their involvement, how closely interwoven, internationally, is all of men's activity, not only their economic and political, but also their cultural one. Not the circumstances of a tribe numbering from two to three hundred people, but those of all of humanity must be taken into consideration today, if one wants to introduce a far-reaching innovation in men's life.

It will be an enormous task, indeed, to regulate according to plan the economic activity of mankind. But we must not by any means expect that it will be possible to foresee all the consequences for men's entire noneconomic life, their scientific and artistic activity, their sexual and social relationships, that will arise out of the efforts to solve that task, or to confront even before their birth the new problems that those consequences bear in their womb. We may assume that the social institutions the victorious proletariat will create will probably have the effect that the proletariat wants to achieve with them, and that it will realize its goal: *the abolition of all exploitation.* But we have no reason whatsoever to assume that with the solution of the present-day problems of society, all social problems will be solved forever. . . . But if the social problems of our time are solved, where then will new problems come from that will cause new movements, if the newly created conditions do not bring them forth, if these conditions do not, in addition to those effects intended when they were introduced, also contain effects that will one day make themselves felt, of which, however, we do not yet have, nor can we have, any inkling?

The final goal of the proletariat is not a final goal for the development of humanity. The law of its motion always remains the same, though: the creation of new institutions for the solution of newly appearing problems. The new institutions solve not only these problems, but also contain in themselves new problems, which in turn make it necessary, in the interest of humanity, to create new institutions. And so on. Thus, like the process of acquiring knowledge, that of social development is also unending—that is to say, a process that lasts as long as humanity, with its abilities and its existing natural environment, persists. An enduringly perfect society is as little possible as an absolute truth. And both the one and the other would mean nothing other than social stagnation and death.

PART FIVE

The Meaning of History

Section One
Uniqueness in History

CHAPTER ONE

The Practical Significance of the Materialist Conception of History

In the course of our investigation, which began almost with the primeval animals, the protozoa, we have arrived at the threshold of the state of the future and have even attempted to cast a glance or two inside that state. But have we not, in doing that, crossed the boundaries set for a conception of history? . . .

. . . All knowledge we obtain . . . is knowledge of the past, . . . for all our insights originate from experiences that lie behind us. In this sense, our entire knowledge, even that of natural science, is of a historical character. Our whole understanding of the past, however, serves to enable us to find our way in the present, . . . to set purposes, goals in the future for our behavior, as well as to show us the means for reaching these goals. . . . The more comprehensive our knowledge of the past is, the farther into the future we can predict the consequences of our behavior in the present, the greater are the goals we set ourselves. The individual researcher might become entirely immersed in the study of the past. That will not prevent the results of his research from influencing the activity of many other men in the present, that is, in their preparation of the future, and thus from influencing the future itself.

Marx and Engels . . . joined theory and practice from the outset, each rendering the other fertile and stronger. *[Kautsky quotes Marx's famous elev-*

enth "Thesis on Feuerbach," p.423; MESW, I, 15, and Engels, "On the History of the Communist League," pp.178–79.] . . . This combination . . . has become exemplary for their disciples and is characteristic of all Marxists, despite all the different shades. . . . Thus Marxism has grown to have its present-day form: that of a theory with the mission to revolutionize science, which it has already profoundly influenced in many ways. At the same time, however, it has also come to be a theory that gives direction to the thought of millions of proletarians of all countries and that also gives direction evermore strongly to the practice of governments where these proletarians are close to victory.

That should not, of course, be taken to mean that every proletarian who belongs to one of the socialist workers' parties is a theoretically thoroughly trained Marxist. That cannot be said even of all their intellectuals. . . . But the principle of the materialist conception of history . . . lives in them and guides their thought and action [that says] that all social and political antagonisms and struggles of our time are in the last analysis antagonisms and struggles among classes. Further, that we must grasp these antagonisms if we want to fight these struggles through and bring them to a satisfactory conclusion. . . .

. . . At the very time of Marx's death, his theory began to be thoroughly thought through by a number of intellectuals in France and Britain, as well as in Germany, and to be applied by them is a systematic manner. And the masses began more and more to free themselves from their Blanquist, Proudhonist, and Lassallean eggshells and increasingly to make the idea of class struggle and of the economic conditioning of its strength and its goals their lodestar. . . . The Second International . . . was from the beginning much more Marxist than the first. . . . Today, the socialist parties have become a power in all industrialized countries, as Marxist parties, as labor parties, as parties of the proletarian class struggle. It is not always Marxist theory, but it is always Marxist practice that gains acceptance in the socialist parties and leads them from one success to the next, if unprecedented catastrophes, such as the World War and its consequences, do not temporarily interrupt the normal course of events, in part abnormally disrupting it, occasionally abnormally furthering it.

We must, of course, precisely from the standpoint of the Marxist conception of history, attribute this enormous success of the Marxist parties in the final analysis not to that conception of history, but to the economic development that makes the proletariat ever stronger and more numerous and intensifies the class antagonisms. . . . Of course, ever-greater and more bitter class struggles would have occurred even without Marxism. The same is true of the formation of workers' parties and their striving after political power. . . . But the fact that this movement became conscious of its ultimate goals and was nevertheless able to cope with its day-to-day tasks, the fact that it was able to combine the sober pursuit of momentary advantages with the enthusiasm inspired by great goals; the fact that is has constantly urged its adherents to strive for an understanding of economics, to seek in that understanding the solid foundation of their activity, and not to let themselves be moved from that firm footing by any emotional exuberance, we owe all of that to the materialist conception of history. It has thereby elevated modern socialism high above both its utopian predecessors and the primitive workers' movements.

And this conception of history has accomplished yet another thing:. . . . Only *[it]* substituted the conscious class struggle of the proletariat for special socialist recipes, made it possible to overcome socialist sectarianism and fragmentation and led the socialists trained in Marxism to look for forms of organization and of struggle for the proletariat and the socialist parties that make it possible increasingly to unite all of the workers and their friends into a compact battlefront and thereby to give the proletariat the maximum of strength that it is capable to developing.

It is certainly true that the materialist conception of history does not determine the direction of social development any more than any other conception of history prior to it was able to do. In the last analysis, this direction is determined by that of economic development. But the tempo of the advance in the given direction of development, the extent of the sacrifices and of the successes in a particular case, . . . depend to a great degree on the level of understanding of the total social process. And for that the materialist conception of history has become extremely significant. Among the factors determining the character of the history of our time, this conception of history, Marxism, is becoming one of the most important. . . .

CHAPTER TWO

The Materialist Conception of History and Historiography

If our conception of history has been almost completely ignored up to now by the leading historians of the present day, that is just because it has acquired such a preeminent position in the history of our time. Its cause has become increasingly identical with that of the proletariat. Thus from the start it was regarded as suspect, dangerous, . . . by all those who feared harmful consequences from the advance and victory of the proletariat. The few intellectuals who have so far joined the class struggle of the proletariat . . . had, like Marx and Engels themselves, not only to add scientific depth to their theories, but also to propagate them. And in their scientific activity, they concerned themselves more with the problems of the present than with those of the past. They engaged in the study of economics more than in that of history. Thus the number of historical works written by Marxists has to date remained quite small. . . .

. . . The starting point for all investigation of the environment is always the individual himself. In accordance with what he experiences, he makes himself a picture of what lies outside himself. . . . In the facts of the past, he sees, above all, what agrees with his experiences in the present. Now it is obvious in the present that the struggles of our times are class struggles. That, one should think, must also make it easier to see the class struggles of the past. And the rise of industrial capitalism, of its mass production and its mass transport, created the conditions for two new sciences, of which there were hardly meager beginnings in antiquity: political economy and . . . statistics. These sciences taught us to discover great laws in society and in particular in economic life, laws that are entirely independent of the individual person, no matter how powerful he might be.

To be sure, the historians need not necessarily know about all of that. Given present-day specialization, work in one discipline is carried on independently of the others. Nonetheless, the economic factor forces itself more and more upon the historians' attention—and economics is itself increasingly becoming a historical science. The expansion of world trade brought about by capitalism makes increasingly available to us knowledge of earlier economic forms in remote regions where primitive peoples have been able to maintain themselves. . . . By means of archaeology, light has been shed on much that was previously obscure in the politics, culture, and economy of earlier ages. . . . The appearance of these new documents from the economy of the past could not but have an effect on historians. *[As examples, Kautsky refers to Karl Lamprecht, Eduard Meyer, and Hans Delbrück and especially to Julius Beloch, whose history of Greece he attacks on a number of points.]* No matter how many economic observations they might record and assimilate, no new conception of history emerges from their work. Their work remains, and must remain, eclectic patchwork, for integrating the individual parts into a unitary total historical context free of contradictions would today mean declaring one's allegiance to the theory of the proletarian class struggle. . . .

CHAPTER THREE

Practical Tasks of Historiography

Like every science, historiography, too, arose out of practical needs produced by life. Recollection of the past was supposed to be of service to the present. The dead were to help the living. *[Kautsky discusses the beginnings of the reciting of history as a form of art serving purposes of entertainment, of education, and of agitation.]* Where deeds that none of the living has ever seen are orally transmitted, . . . the listeners have to rely entirely on the fidelity of the rendering by the later narrator of what the original eyewitness had reported. . . . The inclination to exaggerate in order to enhance the effect is implicit in the artistic, educational, or political intent, . . . until the heroes of the past appear as giant beings endowed with supernatural powers. . . .

A change of this way of transmitting the history of the past is brought about by the emergence of *writing.* . . . Writing made its appearance with the state. . . . In addition to the merchants, it was the rulers of the state who were most likely to seize upon the new means of conferring permanence on words and to employ it for their own purposes. These included above all the greatest possible enhancement of their "charisma," of their prestige. . . . They used writing to proclaim on monuments, visible from afar and made as lasting as possible, the deeds that they had done—or at least would like to have done and promised to do. . . . The more the technology of writing developed, . . . the more uses of writing appeared. Bureaucracy, with its records, arose. . . . The priesthood . . . considered it to be its task to reduce to writing the old traditions. . . . *[All these]* now became sources of history. . . . Finally, the technology of writing had advanced to the point where quite lengthy, coherent accounts were possible, which were recorded on the basis of personal recollections, reports from eyewitnesses, and beyond that on the basis of sources of the kind just mentioned. With that began the real historiography. . . . Writing expands enormously, both spatially and temporally, the area about which information can be gathered in one place and preserved for posterity. . . .

The appearance of writing changes very much the character of reporting about earlier times. It loses its poetic character. But the tendency to exaggerate and to adorn with tendentious additions . . . is strengthened further through the formation of the state and of classes. . . . For reasons of prestige, the monarchs saw to the fabrication of historical reports. The priests of a god . . . sought to increase their power through tales of his miracles. . . . The striving for conquests that is necessarily inherent in the state[1] provided a special reason for the falsification of history. Pretexts from past times were always welcome that provided some historical claim on neighboring areas or established a wrong . . . that was now to be avenged.

Class struggles, too, become objects of historiography. . . . Inasmuch as the art of writing was quite uncommon in the lower classes, the writing of history was predominantly practiced by the exploiters or their creatures and friends. Their position as rulers was presented by the latter as the appropriate reward of their superior morality and intelligence. The practical motives for writing history in this fashion continue to exist as long as states and classes exist. In modern democracy, the lower classes are, to be sure, also

---

1. See IV:6:2–3, above.

able to have their say and by their critique to obstruct excessively crude exaggerations and distortions of the history of our time in newspapers and books. Nonetheless, even today history is still extensively written merely for the sake of sensation or in order to attain didactic and political effects. And yet this state of affairs is characteristic of the most primitive level of historiography.

However, to these original purposes of historiography another one was added at an early time. History was supposed to pass on the *experiences* of the past so that one could learn from them. In particular, it was supposed to show the institutions that had enabled a polity to prosper or had caused it to decline. . . . Whoever wants to offer knowledge, hence wants to draw lessons from the past, must himself seek after knowledge, hence after truth. If he lies about the past, then he misleads his readers or listeners. . . . If history is to instruct us, then it must show us not only the *edifying feats* of our forebears but also their *mistakes.* And it must point out not only the weaknesses of opponents, but also be able to acknowledge their accomplishments. *[Kautsky quotes relevant passages from the prefaces of Livy's* History of Rome, *I, 3–4; Diodorus of Sicily,* Book I/1, 4–5, (I, 7), *and Lissagaray,* History of the Commune of 1871, *unnumbered page of preface.]*

CHAPTER FOUR
History as Teacher

The conception of history as a teacher of nations presupposes the recognition of causal necessities in the lives of nations. Only if the same cause is always followed by the same effect does learning from the experiences of the past make sense. *[Kautsky quotes Thucydides,* The Peloponnesian War, *I, 22 (p.13).]* But . . . history can also become a teacher only with regard to that which repeats itself. . . .

One is most likely to be able to learn from the experiences of the past in specialized fields with simple conditions and limited objectives that change little. That is true of war, for example. . . . Thus modern generals could profitably study the military history of antiquity. . . . That is much more difficult in the field of politics. The state is a far more complex organism than an army; its functions are far more diverse; and the forms and means of politics are far more varied than those of warfare. . . . And the elements that are decisive in politics and enter into conflict cannot simply be commanded by a leader, like an army; each one of them has its own special conditions. . . . The same situations do not recur. . . .

Especially in the most recent period, the view is becoming increasingly untenable that present-day men could derive prescriptions for their own conduct from the tactics and strategy of earlier times. That is less and less true even for warfare, let alone for politics. For industrial capitalism profoundly transforms all conditions so rapidly that every generation, indeed, every decade, is confronted by entirely new conditions and circumstances. *[Kautsky quotes Hegel,* The Philosophy of History, *p. 6].* The appeal to individual outstanding figures and events of the past today serves less scientific than rhetorical and advocatory purposes. . . . *[That]* is very much in opposition to the motive of deriving and providing instruction. Nevertheless, we find that most historians are animated by both motives. . . . An example of this is provided by the history of the French Revolution that Jean Jaurès wrote. I admire and honor this great champion of the emancipation of the proletariat and of humanity as a fighter, as a propagandist, and as a political leader. But I cannot accept his eclecticism as a theoretician. *[Kautsky quotes and comments on passages from the preface of Jaurès,* Histoire socialiste, *I/1.)*

The Singular in History

We have just quoted Hegel, who thought that statesmen and peoples "never have learned anything from history," for every period and its circumstances constitute a special condition that does not repeat itself. One could go still further and say that within a particular historical period every event, every individual is something unique unto itself that does not repeat itself. Must, then, the conclusion be drawn that any search for laws in history is condemned to failure from the outset? This conclusion has in fact very often been drawn. *[Kautsky quotes Meyer,* Geschichte des Altertums, *I/1, pp. 174, 186, as an example.]* If that is correct, then it is certainly impossible to peer into the future on the basis of historical experiences. Then the whole materialist conception of history is also an absurdity. But, of course, if there are no historical laws, if only the uniquely individual, the unpredictable, the fortuitous, appears in history, then it ceases to be a science. . . . Science concerns itself only with the general. Grasping the particular and reproducing it intellectually or shaping it into new forms is the task of art. *[Kautsky quotes Goethe,* Conversations with Eckermann, *p. 14, who defined art in this way, and Beloch,* Griechische Geschichte, *I/2, pp. 7–8, who called historiography, as distinguished from the science of history, an art.]*

. . . The task of the historian is . . . a far more difficult one *[than that of the]* portrait painter. . . . The historian is supposed to describe to us men in the most changeable situations . . . only by means of the study of sources. And he is supposed to make accessible to us and clearly depict for us the entire depth of the mental nature of important historical individuals in all their ramifications. . . . How many people are there who have a clear understanding of their own inner life . . . ? And yet the psyche of a long-dead stranger is supposed to be understood by a historian who is living under-completely different conditions, on the basis of reports by people who were not always close to the one to be described, who were able to pass judgment only on the basis of indirect evidence and could almost never be impartial. . . . Every historian is naturally inclined to see the past from his own standpoint. . . . And yet every age has its own way of thinking and also its own mode of expression. . . .

We humans are social beings and cannot remain indifferent toward other men, . . . if they are of any significance, not even toward those for whom we feel neither personal friendship nor hostility. They appear to us to be either socially valuable . . . or harmful. . . . I have learned that from my own research, even though, with regard to historical personalities, I have always been guided by the principle that we must attempt to study them as products of their circumstances but not try to evaluate them in any way. . . . For the historian, who is supposed to discover only causal relations, value judgments must never be relevant.

But even he who takes this standpoint does not thereby cease to be human. Contrary to his intention, that colors the accounts he gives of men. I could not help becoming fond of Thomas More, for example, and finding Henry VIII extremely unattractive.[2] Personal sympathy and antipathy are further reinforced when political agreement or antagonism enter into the question. . . . It is clear that almost all the authors who serve as our sources see through partisan spectacles from the very start. The difficulty of an objective understanding of historical actors is pushed to the extreme when the historian does not consider the appearance of value judgments as a source of error that must be avoided as much as possible, but rather sees the task of history to be the pronouncement of such judgments. . . .

Difficulties similar to those encountered in the portrayal of particular historical individuals occur in the depiction of particular historical events. . . . Even when the external course of the event is known with certainty, which is very often not the case, it will be as good as impossible to include in the picture of the event all the imponderables that affect the final result, as well as to ascertain the nonobvious influences, confidential agreements, bribes, etc., that preceded that result. . . .

In view of all these difficulties of historiography, it is not surprising that not a few people . . . consider it to be incapable of establishing historical truth. . . . *[This mistrust should be directed only at the kind of historiography]* that is the only one we have been discussing in the present chapter, the one that refuses to search for laws in history and is interested only in the particular, the singular that never repeats itself. . . . This kind of historiography will never provide only the truth, though not pure invention either, but rather

---

2. This is a reference to *Thomas More and his Utopia*, Kautsky's first major attempt to apply the materialist conception of history.

a mixture of truth and fiction, like a work of art. Such works of history will often be products of very skillful and conscientious labor, . . . but we seek in vain in them for a deeper insight into the process of human development if they truly confine themselves to the particular, the singular. Fortunately, that is, as a rule, not the case for historical works spanning a greater period of time. No matter how much their authors strive to limit themselves to the particular, they do not escape from the general.

CHAPTER SIX

The General and the Particular in History

We have just seen that if the particular, the singular, is the sole domain of historiography, then the latter is in reality an art that can provide only a mixture of truth and fiction. That should not be taken as a disparagement of this kind of historiography. There is no rank order among the activities of the mind; science ranks no higher than art. . . . Nor should it be suggested that the historiography of the particular, the singular, is pointless. . . . It is indispensable as the starting point of any science of history. The only question is whether it may not go beyond that starting point. . . .

No doubt, all occurrences and phenomena with which we have to do in history are unique, they do not repeat themselves. . . . We find the same thing in nature. . . . However, . . . on the other hand, we find that there is no individual, no event, that is completely singular, entirely unique. Each one displays features that are found also in other individuals or events, with which it is therefore joined to make a common species. . . . What, then, becomes of the assertion that only the particular is supposed to concern the historian? It cannot mean that he must concern himself only with individuals and phenomena that are unique, but that only what is unique about them may occupy him, not what is general. . . . *[That]* comes down to saying that the historian must not concern himself with collective phenomena, but only with what is unique, and not with the latter in its relationship with other phenomena . . . , through which it would immediately cease to be singular and would be subject to the law of large numbers. . . .

Every phenomenon contains both singular and general elements. . . . It does not depend on the objects, but on the subjective intentions and needs of the observers . . . , whether they are chiefly concerned with the particular or the general in certain phenomena. In addition, it also depends on the conditions under which a phenomenon appears whether we notice the general or the singular in it. . . . As soon as writing has been invented, . . . as soon as technology permits the expansion of the field of observation, it becomes more and more possible to discover general features even in phenomena that are singular for primitive man. . . .

As long as polities remain small, ... *[and]* as long as social conditions change but little so that they are taken for granted, ... no observations are made of numerous similar social phenomena and still less are laws discovered in them. That was changed by the rise of the state and of writing and especially by the lively developments in the politics of the Greek city-states that began in the sixth century. Numerous systems of government of the most diverse kind arose concurrently and successively and invited comparisons and generalizations. ... To be sure, laws in politics were discovered only to a slight extent. In the main, the search was for the idea of the most perfect state. ... Greater advances were made in the area of warfare. ... This domain of history is the first one in which, in addition to the individual and singular, the general is made the object of observation leading to the recognition of laws.

Another domain of social life in which certain observations of general phenomena were made even in antiquity is that of trade. ... In the modern period, ... with the expansion of the sphere of commodity production and with the increase in the number of records about the functioning of economic relations, the material on economics snowballs and the methods of collecting and classifying this material improve more and more. The economic sciences develop, founded upon statistics compiled scientifically and with regularity. ... But is the world that history presents a different one from that of economics, the world of human society? Do other men act in history than in the production process? In point of fact, it was not the nature of the object, but the conditions under which the historians arrived at its observation that resulted in the particular, the singular, being heretofore considered the domain of historiography.

The investigator of the past, in comparison with those who study the present, must struggle with the great disadvantage ... that he must rely on isolated remnants that cannot be reproduced or supplemented and are selected not by the researcher himself but by accident. In the case of today's historical researcher, there is the additional difficulty that the sparse remnants of his sources ... are fragments of material that were themselves already selected by earlier historians, according to their views and interests. The present-day historian might regard other facts as far more important, but he is unable to learn of them. ... The historians of earlier times ... would not have recorded the everyday events and circumstances of their era even if they had been of the opinion, which today is more and more gaining acceptance, that society is determined much more by the quotidian than by the extraordinary. ... These commonplace matters were, after all, quite familiar to the readers. ... All the more must that have been true of the historians who were of the opinion that only the extraordinary was worthy of note. Thus, historians find from the outset only those phenomena recorded in their sources that appear as singular or, rather, they find recorded only those of their aspects that give the impression of singularity. ...

In antiquity, certain thinkers had succeeded in discovering in the "singular" facts of history general relationships, for example, the influence of climate or topography on the character of a people or the conditions and consequences of different systems of government. In the seventeenth century, these reflections are taken up again and carried further. In addition, however, there now emerges the recognition that the most diverse peoples are all developing in the same direction, hence according to certain laws. The first to express this view was the Italian Giambattista Vico (1668–1744). For him, the mainspring of the entire historical process was still . . . a universal spirit, the Divinity. . . . Even Hegel still did not go beyond this world spirit.

On the whole, the eighteenth century was not favorable to the development of historical thought. The conditions of feudal absolutism assumed a form so harmful for society as a whole, . . . the demands of the classes that gathered about the flag of free commodity production and (at first very timidly and insufficiently) of democracy, seemed so . . . reasonable that all the social and political antagonisms of the period appeared to be struggles between reason and irrationality. . . . Seen from this standpoint, all previous history appeared to be merely a collection of instances of stupidity and meanness.

After the French Revolution, . . . the reaction was accompanied by interest in and understanding for the past. At the same time, the historical material was enormously expanded. Lively commerce with the East opened up to Europeans . . . its history, its philosophy, and its languages. A new science arose, . . . that arrived at the discovery of relationships among languages through comparison of different languages and at the recognition of laws of linguistic development through comparison of the different forms of the same language in different periods. . . . Interest in dialects . . . was due in part to the rise of democracy, which gave the educated reason to speak to the people in their own language. On the other hand, it was due also to the reaction against democracy, which was intent on becoming acquainted with the conservative peasants who spoke dialects, in contrast to the . . . revolutionary townspeople, but also . . . on finding in the documents of the past its rationale, which was impossible without an understanding of their language. Thus, one came to discover that language developed in accordance with laws. Owing to its conservative character, however, language also preserved numerous traces of social and technological institutions of the age in which it was formed. Thus linguistic comparison and linguistic history permitted the reconstruction of everyday matters of distant millennia, about which we have no reports. In this way, linguistics also contributed to social history.

. . . In the age of reaction and of romanticism, interest in the legal relationships of earlier times grew. In jurisprudence, there arose the historical school, . . . which again uncovered many instances of society developing in accordance with laws. Legal history prepared the way for economic history, as the law often directly serves economic purposes and cannot be understood without reference to them, quite apart from the fact that its purposes are all, in the last analysis, economically grounded. No less important, finally, was ... archaeology, which began in Italy in the eighteenth century, but moved forward rapidly only in the nineteenth century. It showed what treasures of historical illumination are held by the sites of ancient cultures. . . .

Thus, in the course of the last century the abundance of historical phenomena increased more and more that forced the historian to regard them not as singular, but as general. . . .

General and Particular Laws

. . . We have stressed that there is no phenomenon that is to be understood only as unique. Each one also contains general features. We can, however, also conceive of this in another way. Depending on the context in which we consider a thing or an event, it appears to us as something particular among a number of phenomena of the same kind or as something general that embraces many particular phenomena. The particular and the general are just as much relative concepts as are, for example, the small and the large. . . .

If every particular also represents something general, then it will be possible that, within the framework of a given particular, laws exist for its parts, laws that hold good only within the given particular, particular laws. That is true for particular social formations, modes of production, states, classes, etc., just as for particular ages and stages of culture. Of course, society in general has certain laws that apply to each of its forms. In addition, however, there are also social laws that are peculiar only to particular forms of society. That is one of the insights on which the materialist conception of history rests: one of the most important insights that raise it above the other conceptions of history and of society in general. Insofar as these do not see the hand of God everywhere, which means renouncing all scientific research from the start, they either regard the phenomena of . . . historical life as isolated accidental facts that defy any attempt to discover certain laws in them or they search for natural laws of society and history, that is, laws that hold to the same degree for every form of society, every stage of history, indeed, that are perhaps common to both society and the entire world of organisms. . . .

[Kautsky quotes a long passage from Marx, "Introduction," Grundrisse, pp. 85–88, summarized in its final sentence:] "There are characteristics which all stages of production have in common and which are established as general

ones by the mind; but the so-called *general preconditions* of all production are nothing more than these abstract moments with which no real historical stage of production can be grasped." That holds true for all historical stages of human society. . . . Looking for the general natural laws of society does not in any way make the historical process intelligible to us. Historians are quite right when they refuse to listen to talk of such laws in history. . . .

Neither the seeking after laws that are common to all social conditions nor the collecting of extraordinary particulars from the past is able to provide us with deeper historical understanding. The latter gives us a box of curios; the former, a compilation of commonplaces. The materialist conception of history sees the inadequacy of both these activities. It does not declare them to be useless, but rather insufficient, if they are not supplemented by a search for the particular, the singular in history that is at the same time a generality, a search for the particular historical character of certain social formations and stages of society, which can be explained by certain stages of production. This particular, which is simultaneously a generality, as such also contains its particular social laws.

CHAPTER EIGHT

Historical Laws

. . . In nature, too, certain natural laws cannot always operate, but only when the conditions for their operation are given. This becomes evident even as we consider the aggregate states, the solid, liquid, and gaseous ones. For each of them, there are particular laws that do not apply to the others. . . . And how long did it take until organisms with functions of life and of mind could emerge! . . . Each of these phenomena is governed not only by mechanical and chemical laws, but also by particular "historical" laws that are not always operative, but only when life or mind manifests itself. . . . Thus there are also particular historical laws of human society, particular laws of certain of its forms, for example, of the capitalist form. . . .

Certainly, the much more general laws of mechanics and chemistry also hold for the fields of biology and psychology. But they are insufficient by themselves to explain their phenomena. Similarly, the laws of mechanics, chemistry, biology, and individual psychology also hold good for human society. Yet they do not suffice for the explanation of social phenomena. And thus it can finally be said that, alongside the other natural laws, the general laws that apply to every society are also incapable of explaining a particular social stage or historical period, if we do not, in addition to these laws, also take into consideration the particular laws that specifically apply to this one certain period.

. . . [*The fact*] that here and there Marx declares that his historical laws of society are mere [*tendencies has also been held to*] contradict the concept of a natural law. . . . In reality, every law of nature manifests itself only as a tendency. . . . Every phenomenon is governed by different laws that sometimes support and often thwart, deflect, or hinder each other. Therefore, every natural law can be completely grasped only if in its investigation all interfering factors are artificially eliminated or if they are disregarded by means of abstraction from them. That is true even for such a general law as that of gravity. . . . In this connection, there is a difference between nature and society only inasmuch as social relations are among the most complex ones, so that in their phenomena, more so than in those of nature, individual laws are effective only as tendencies. But whoever draws from that fact the conclusion that the laws of society do not possess the force and validity of natural laws acts like a schoolboy who concludes from his observation of a hot-air balloon that there is no force of gravity. . . .

. . . The materialist conception of history differs from the two great types of conceptions of society that today dominate "bourgeois science." One recognizes only general natural laws governing all societies; the other denies that society is governed by any natural law at all. We call these two kinds of scientific view bourgeois because they have their home among the bourgeois-minded intelligentsia. In contrast to them, we can regard the materialist conception of history as proletarian, because it is recognized almost exclusively in the circles of the proletariat and its intellectual representatives.

As a purely scientific theory, it is, certainly, by no means tied to the proletariat, just as the two other conceptions of society and history are not tied to the propertied classes. But in its practical application, the materialist conception of history today serves the interests of the proletariat, for the assumption that every form of society and of production is historically conditioned, that its laws are valid only for a limited period of time, must make this conception attractive to a class whose interest urgently demands the abolition of that social order and all the more unattractive to those classes having an interest in its continued existence. Of course, these sympathies prove nothing as to the correctness or falseness of the one or the other conception.[3] They do, however, explain why research into the historical character of particular forms of society and of the particular laws governing each of them, which constitutes in our opinion one of the greatest advances of the science of history, has so far gained such a small foothold in bourgeois science.

Classical economics, which reached its culmination in Ricardo, sought after eternal natural laws for all economic activity. In fact, however, it was the particular laws of commodity production that it held to be general economic natural laws. . . . Alongside it, there arose the historical school

3. See also *The Social Revolution*, p. 13, and *Die historische Leistung von Karl Marx*, pp. 10–15.

that sought not after the general, not after economic laws, but after the particular. . . . But this school, too, did not prove to be satisfactory in the long term. The need to grasp the general, that which conforms to law, in the chaos of economic facts, in order to find one's way in them, again came to the fore. But in order not to end up in the Marxist camp, *[economists]* did not advance to research into the particular laws of the different modes of production, but instead returned to a pre-Ricardian position. . . .

The new economic theory, that of marginal utility, dissolves the relation *[of the theory of value]* to production. Both the Ricardian and the Marxist general law of value is applicable only to products that can be increased in number at will through the appropriate expenditure of labor. But other products are also bought and sold that are the only ones of their kind, the pictures of an artist, goods and even attributes of a person that are not products of labor, such as knowledge and conscience, love and loyalty. For all transactions of this kind, the new law of value is supposed to apply to the same degree as for the exchange of commodities that can be multiplied at will, not indirectly, as in the theories of Marx and Ricardo, but directly. But the new school goes back to a point prior not only to production, but also to trade. It is not immediately concerned with value relevant in the exchange of goods, but with the relative importance assigned by an individual to the various goods he possesses. . . . In the place of the natural laws of production and exchange, we are presented with natural laws of the human psyche, needs, desires, calculations that are possible also without any productive activity.

This kind of natural laws of economics was necessarily even less fruitful for grasping the peculiarity of a particular mode of production than that of Ricardo. As for the historical school, it also did not advance us further. But . . . the men of the historical school did not remain unaffected by the achievements of the economists who look for economic laws, and thus some of them succeeded in supplying us with important insights. It does not make much difference whether they are concerned with the recognition of laws or whether they fashion into "ideal types" the general in the particular that they investigate. Bücher, Sombart, and Max Weber went beyond the historical school proper and have done outstanding work, especially the last two. But they would not have been able to do so without Karl Marx. Sombart himself expressly acknowledged that.

Despite all resistance, it is increasingly the spirit of Karl Marx that permeates the economic science of our day and is making it into a historical science—historical, because it looks for the particular, the historical peculiarity of each economic stage. A science, because it seeks for the general; on the one hand, it seeks for what each stage has in common with other stages; on the other hand, within a stage, for the particular laws by which its peculiar phenomena are governed. And while in this way economics is increasingly becoming history, on the other hand, in what we specifically call history, economics is coming to play an ever-greater role; this, too, despite all the resistance of the scholars. . . .

CHAPTER NINE

The Separation of the Particular from the General

In reality, the investigation of the particular cannot be separated from that of the general and vice versa. How can I determine what is particular in a phenomenon, . . . if I do not compare it with other, similar phenomena and remove from it everything that it has in common with them? . . . And vice versa. I cannot come to recognize the general except through comparison of many individual instances and through elimination of everything in them that particularly characterizes each one of them. . . .

[*Kautsky devotes a page to a discussion of Julius Caesar's career to stress how largely it is accounted for by his social background, the political situation in Rome, and the means available to him*]. All of that, however, was not something isolated, singular, that does not repeat itself. . . . What made Caesar a singular phenomenon in these general conditions, . . . was the fact that he was more successful both in political intrigue and in battle than his competitors, all of whom he overcame. Now, somebody had finally to remain as the strongest one. The fact that it was Caesar and no one else is certainly singular and is not explained by reference to general conditions. . . . But is it exactly that which is historically most important about the process of the decline of Roman democracy? We see how little the truly singular means in history and for historiography. It can appear important only to those historians who from the start accept as singular everything in each particular phenomenon about which the sources report, without examining it, and who do not investigate how much of it is of a more or less broad generality.

And yet they constantly encounter cases of agreement of a certain historical phenomenon with other later or earlier phenomena. While conformity with laws is not investigated here, parallels are inferred, analogies are demonstrated, and conclusions are drawn. The general that is established in this manner has the drawback, however, that the historical peculiarity of each of the phenomena that correspond with one another in some points is being disregarded. At one time one sees only the general and then only the particular. Complete understanding of a historical phenomenon, however, is achieved only when both the one and the other in it are taken into account. . . . The materialist conception of history is the first to try systematically in its historical works to separate the particular from the general in each historical phenomenon investigated. This leaves a remnant in which, with the available historical techniques, nothing more can be recognized that is general. For the time being, that remnant must still be considered as accidental, but in relation to the total process it will be insignificant most of the time. . . .

The particular laws of each historical stage become much more important for the course of history and thus also for the understanding of history than not only the accidental singular but also the laws of society common to all historical phases. . . . The history of a particular period is understood the better, the more clearly its particular laws are known. But the peculiarity of a historical period cannot be grasped apart from what it has in common with other periods. . . . Thus, the materialist historian cannot confine himself to the study of particular instances; he must always keep the total historical process, indeed, even prehistory, in mind.

One can arrive at this conclusion from another starting point, too. The factors determining the particular character of an era can be divided into two groups. Some are active, the others are passive factors of the course of history. The ones constitute its motive forces, the others are the inert material that must be moved and formed by them. Their roles correspond to those of adaptation and inheritance in biology. New forms are constituted by new economic conditions and by new needs and abilities that arise out of those conditions and struggle to manifest themselves in new shapes. These forms cannot be created out of nothing, though; they must build on the already existing forms that they encounter and that are adapted to the new requirements by means of the new forces.[4] What is new in a certain era can be explained only by the new economic laws that govern the new economic process peculiar to that era. The old, on the other hand, is a product of the past, indeed, . . . of the entire history of mankind which no age has passed over without leaving its traces. Every age left behind its legacy for the succeeding generations. In order to understand an age, I must be acquainted not merely with its new mode of production, but also with the history of the past out of which it came.[5]

. . . That is also true of practical politics, in which I shall be the more successful, the better I know not just the economic laws of the present, but also the entire history, of which the present is the result. . . . All the better shall I understand the character of the nation in which I am active and the particular forms the new, which becomes necessary, has to assume in this nation. All the more shall I beware of a stereotypical way of looking at things that believes it can impose on the whole world a particular form of the new that originated from the particular conditions of a single country, sometimes under completely abnormal circumstances. . . . The materialist

4. See III:2:12–13, above.
5. See also III:4:2–4, above.

conception of history offers the possibility of learning from *[history]*. And at the same time, it makes the study of history a necessity. For, without knowledge of history, we cannot completely comprehend the present and fully recognize the tasks it sets us.

CHAPTER TEN
The Individual in History

The view that the singular is the domain of history is related to another one that assumes that single outstanding individuals constitute the motive force of history.[6] . . . These two views are not identical. The one concerns the way in which history is to be investigated and presented; the other, with the manner in which history is actually made. But . . . the more I see the determining moment of history in individual persons, the more will history appear to me as a succession of single, accidental happenings. And, on the other hand, the more I confine my concern to such happenings, the more determinative must the influence of single individuals on history appear to me.

The issue is not, of course, whether men make history or not. That is self-evident; no one has denied it. Right at the beginning of his *Eighteenth Brumaire [p.146; MESW, I, 398]*, Marx remarks: "Men make their own history." . . . Strangely enough, there are still people who believe that Marx taught that historical development proceeds by itself, without any help at all from men. Even among socialists, this astonishing conception of Marxism is not rare. . . . Of course, Marx never taught *[this]* nonsense. It is absurd to present the theory of class struggle as a theory of inactivity.

What is at issue here is not the question whether the historical process is effected by men or by some other factors that must be of a completely mystical nature, but . . . whether the historical process is the result of the activity of *all* men in whose presence it occurs or whether the broad masses of men are an inert material that requires an impulse from single outstanding individuals who set them in motion and point them in the direction they have to follow. . . .

The view that preeminent individuals, whose appearance seems like an accident, make history just as they wish is found by historians in their sources. . . . The starting point of history, the heroic epic, makes the fates of

---

6. Kautsky had dealt with the role of the individual in history also in *The Class Struggle*, p. 122; "Was will und kann die materialistische Geschichtsauffassung leisten?," pp. 228–38; *Friedrich Engels*, pp. 5–8; *Vorläufer*, I, xxxi–xxxv; *Sozialisten und Krieg*, pp. 377–79.

peoples dependent on individual heroes. . . . The aesthetic interest in the extraordinary, in the deeds of outstanding men, warriors, princes, giants, expresses itself in the fairy tales that come out of the mass of the people and are of a completely democratic origin. In the case of the heroic epics, there is added to this the singers' interest in praising the families of the great, on whose hospitality they lived. This emphasis on aristocrats and monarchs in the presentation of history was promoted further with the emergence of writing. . . . For a long time, the masses remained ignorant of writing. . . . Historiography remained a privilege of the exploiters and the intellectuals, who, until the rise of modern democracy, were either exploiters themselves, like the churchmen, or servants and parasites of the exploiters. Under those circumstances, all of history became nothing but a depiction of the deeds of aristocrats and monarchs. The masses played only a passive role. . . .

But, certainly, even the strongest democratic feeling does not free the historian from the necessity of writing history as a history of outstanding individuals. Even we Marxists cannot escape from it. . . . How is that reconcilable with our conception of history? If we consider the various social formations that occur within the total sphere of society, then we find that at the head of each one of these an individual is active, in part on the basis of a social institution, of an election or an appointment, or through mere prestige ("charisma"), and that this individual has a decisive influence on their fates. The fate *[of each such formation]* . . . thus depends on a character that appears to be purely a product of accident. . . . That, however, is only one side of the matter. On the other side, we find that there is no particular circle in society that could not be placed in a still larger complex of relations, whether spatial or temporal. The more extended this complex, the more does the individual, the accidental, diminish in importance, and the more is it surpassed by the general, by what conforms to laws. . . . For the standard of living of all the working-class families of a big city, the individual father of a household is wholly irrelevant. It is determined by completely different factors that are not of an accidental nature and in which determinate laws can be ascertained. . . . As enormous as the havoc was that was wrought by the World War ignited by Kaiser Wilhelm's policies, nevertheless the person of Wilhelm II becomes insignificant when we place it, for example, in the total complex of relations of the development of the world by industrial capitalism. . . . Therefore, whether in a historical investigation we take an individual into consideration and follow his activities depends entirely on the extent of the domain encompassed by the investigation. The narrower this domain, the more important do the various individuals appear who act within it.

Least of all can we disregard individual personalities in the practical struggles of the present. Their unique natures and their strength are of the greatest importance for our weal and woe of the moment, . . . as convinced as we might be that none of these individuals is of importance when they are situated in the total historical context extending over centuries.... The most reliable sources for the history of an era are those written by contemporaries or at least by those who were informed by contemporaries of the period in question. Thus, the sources were written not out of historical but immediate interest and cannot help emphasizing within the historical process the activity of individuals who were of special importance for the shaping of the present. But it is the task of the historian to put into a wider total context pictures of a present that have been handed down from the past.... The more he succeeds in doing so, the broader his historical horizon is, the less important for the course of the historical process will the outstanding individuals of history become for him.... Their actions will be judged historically the more effective, the more they correspond to general tendencies of the time, not to the singular tendencies of an eccentric.

Yet, even in considering the present, we must not confine ourselves exclusively to the leading individuals of a social formation, but must take all its members into account.... The fate... of every group of men, up to and including the state, depends not on a single individual, but on the totality of all its members.... The monarch might fancy himself an autocrat!... What he knows of the world, he learns from his servants,... courtiers, generals, high priests, and ministers.... His image of the world is dependent on them and consequently also the decisions he makes. With respect to the composition of this entourage, it is no longer a matter of individual persons but of wider circles like that of all the generals or of the higher ranks of the priesthood, where the law of large numbers becomes operative.... In their totality, something general expresses itself, a certain esprit de corps of the military, of the church, of the nobility, of the bureaucracy. To be sure, these groups are still small.... The individual personality still plays an important role there in influencing the monarch.

But only the monarch's intentions and resolutions are determined by individuals.... These must also be carried out if they are to have an effect. That, however, depends... on innumerable subordinates.... The enormous state apparatus has its own laws of motion and inertia, which even the strongest and most powerful monarch cannot render inoperative at will. ... [Whether] the decrees and laws are effective in the way the monarch intended them to be depends also on the attitude toward them by his "subjects."... Lastly, however, the effectiveness of a law also depends on the conditions in which the subjects live and work.... We have spoken here only of despotism.... In an aristocracy, and all the more in a democracy, the course of state politics is open from the start to the intervention of wider circles.... [That] is true even of the army.... There, too, the final result is one... that is conditioned by the nature of the activity of all the participants in a war.

Individual and Class Struggle

... Despite all their individual differences, men are still fundamentally all organized in the same way; under the same conditions, therefore, they react to the same stimuli and impulses in the same way. . . . And only this similar action of men in society produces historical effects. In comparison, it matters little that every individual will and purpose is subjectively colored, that in addition to what is general each contains something particular that can conflict in some details with other wills and purposes. These details that deviate from the average will as a rule cancel one another; in any case, they remain too weak to be able to play a historical role, in comparison with the common tendencies. . . .

That certainly does not mean that there cannot also be conflicting tendencies in history that acquire great strength and confer on the historical process its character at a given time. . . . Men all react (on the average) to the same stimuli in the same way, *when the conditions are the same* under which the stimulus affects them. In their primitive state, when there is hardly any social differentiation in society, except for the natural one by sex and age-group, men all live under the same conditions, have the same experiences, the same knowledge, the same interests. Then all members of a polity will agree in wanting the same thing and will act to the same end. . . . The expansion of the polity and the division of labor in it cause differences in living conditions, in knowledge, in interests to arise within the polity. This differentiation increases rapidly in the state. From it, there emerge special goals and special actions, which can sometimes foil and oppose each other to a considerable degree. But even then they achieve historical effects only when they are not goals and actions of individuals but of groups. . . . The historical process then appears . . . as the resultant of the special endeavors of a limited number of groups within the society and the polity.

The progress of the division of labor and of the expansion of the state has the tendency to increase the number of these different groups in the polity. But the simultaneous growth of communications within the polity produces, for its part, the opposed tendency, namely, to strengthen the factors that agree with one another as against the ones that differentiate people. . . . As for the occupations, they each lose the more importance relative to the collectivity, the more numerous they become. As that happens, each becomes so very specialized that as a consequence its understanding for the collectivity threatens to become lost. . . . In order to gain this understanding, it now becomes necessary that each person, outside his occupation, especially concern himself with the affairs of the polity. . . .

Thus here, too, the factors of agreement become more effective than the differentiating ones.

Surface appearance, to be sure, shows us a different picture. That is due to the fact that there is a kind of group in society that from the start does not just represent a division, but is founded upon an antagonism to other groups. The essential nature of these groups consists in this very antagonism: *these are the classes.* Where there are classes that are able to struggle, there the class struggles become the most essential content of history. All the local, occupational, individual differences in the state have far less importance than the antagonisms of the classes. Those differences can, to be sure, also be seen within each of the classes; they produce in it diverse tendencies, sometimes conflicting with one another, of a tactical or programmatic nature regarding methods and goals. But that on which the members of the class all agree, what they have in common ultimately always prevails; it is decisive for the formation of the resultant that is characteristic of the general striving of the class. And the ultimate resultant of the direction taken by the politics and the economy in a country is the result of the relations of the forces of the different classes and of the direction followed by each of them. . . .

It is always individuals exercising their will who make history—but it is made by *all* of them, not just by *individual* outstanding personalities. Of course, not all individuals are equally gifted. . . . In human society, there are, in addition to the differences in innate endowment, also those of living conditions, which in one instance promote a given endowment to the highest degree, in another paralyze it completely. In a strongly differentiated society, therefore, the differences in abilities can become very extensive. But the greater or the lesser ability will merely determine the greater or lesser degree of the influence that the individual gains within the class or group in which and for which he acts. His historical influence, though, will depend primarily on the strength of the class or group . . . that he represents. Its entire strength then appears to the historians as the personal strength of its representative. . . . That is true in an especially high degree of individuals who succeed in one way or another in becoming the head of a state apparatus. . . .

There is no question but that a leader must have special qualities if he is to prove himself. Yet these qualities do not by any means need to be ones that are not to be found among his followers. On the contrary, the latter will follow the leader all the more resolutely and unitedly if they, too, possess his qualities. . . . On the other hand, there are no absolute leadership qualities. Every particular situation requires particular attributes. . . .

The ways in which a leader rises differ greatly. When he is chosen by the masses or owes his leading position to his "charisma," . . . those of the existent forces will always become ascendent in the course of the selection process that are best adapted to the needs of the followers and to the requirements of the situation. In this sense, one can say that the right man always appears at the right time, even though at first glance this looks like teleological mysticism. *[Kautsky quotes Engels' letter to W. Borgius (Heinz Starkenburg), p. 503.]* The fact that Cromwell took over the leadership of the English and Napoleon that of the French republic was an accident; but by no means was it an accident that both the one and the other republic ended in a military dictatorship. That was due to the conditions under which they had to maintain themselves. . . . In the one case as in the other, it became a question of life or death for the revolution to prevail in war. . . . The army became the salvation, but also the ruler of the republic, and consequently the most important general in the army, as head of the army, became the head of the state. If it had not been Cromwell, or Napoleon, then it would have been another *[general]*. . . . *[Kautsky quotes Beloch's introduction to his* Griechische Geschichte, *I/1, pp. 2, 4, 5. Beloch]* shows, using different examples, that a particular historical result was inevitable under given conditions, independent of particular individuals, no matter how outstanding they were *[like Columbus and Caesar.]* . . .

When it was stated that the right man always appeared as soon as he was needed, . . . that means only that the class or organization or group that at a given time was the strongest one in the state, governed it, and set its stamp upon it, found each time the leader whom it needed in order to be led in the way it wanted to be. Whether he was the right man for the state or the mass of the people depended on the character of the class or group that raised him and by means of which he was able to prevail. . . .

. . . When offices or possessions are inherited, no selection of the persons who come into the leading positions takes place. . . . They may be wholly incompetent; they may be children or fools. In such cases, it cannot be maintained that finally the right man always finds the right place. However, even under these circumstances a selection can occur, . . . similar to the Darwinist one through the struggle for existence. . . . A firm goes bankrupt, a state collapses, . . . if the accident of hereditary succession puts an incompetent person at the head of a firm or a state in times of grave crises. . . . Entire families are eliminated from the life of the firm or the state in which they had previously played a preeminent role. That does not take place without great harm . . . to the workers employed by the firm that goes bankrupt, to the citizens of the state, the ruling dynasty of which leads it into ruin. This is a very irrational, painful form of selection. But history proceeds in an economical fashion just as little as nature does. . . .

. . . Another difficulty of a historiography that treats exclusively of individuals *[is the following]*. In such an extensive and complex organism as the present-day state, it is never possible to establish in the various historical processes exactly to what extent they are to be accounted for by each of the different persons participating in them; how much each did as a result of current or previous influence from others; how much is due to resistances or to support that he found; how much to the mood of the masses in his own country and its neighbors; how much to the extent of the means of power of his country and of others; how much to the way those means of power were assessed. It is entirely impossible to ascertain precisely what individuals participated in all of that and in so much else besides that is relevant for a leader's historical decision and for its implementation. Much is left to the historian's imagination. And it will always mislead him when it looks only at individual outstanding persons. On the other hand, it will come the closer to the truth, the more it enquires into the collective forces that in the last analysis decide what becomes a historical act and that so very simply—because they constitute only averages—stand behind the individual wills that are so infinitely complex, so fugitive, and often so reticent and thus so difficult to grasp, and that thwart one another.

This way of regarding history is important for the understanding not only of the past, but also of the present. . . . The politics we carry on at any given time will become enormously more effective if we take into account not just the outstanding individuals, but also the collective social forces standing behind them. We will then come to know our own means of power and those of our opponents better, as well as our and their prospects beyond the present. We will then not be seduced . . . into overestimating our own strength and venturing upon tasks to which we are not equal. But we will also not lose heart, . . . if we go beyond the individual and recognize that our cause is so deeply grounded in mass conditions that we are convinced that the future belongs to it. A cause whose success rests entirely on individual personalities is built on sand. . . . It disappears along with them and, historically, has no effect.

CHAPTER TWELVE

The Creative Individual

Does what has been said hold true for all outstanding individuals, . . . *[also for]* outstanding thinkers? . . . We have seen that the thinker does not actually draw from himself the new ideas he produces.[7] . . . The results he arrives at are already indicated to him by the environment. When he deviates from this, he does not function as a leader to enduring new creations but as one who misleads. Those of his new teachings, however, that arise out of a real, profound grasp of what is new in the environment offer nothing that average men would not—indeed, would not have to—achieve sooner or later even without him. When we are accurately informed about the appearance of a new doctrine or an invention, when their beginnings are not

---

7. See III:2:9–13, above.

obscured by myths, we always find that it is not a single person who is striving in the direction of what is new but that many individuals are simultaneously striving in the same direction, though not all do so in the same way. Marx and Engels did not invent socialism, and Voltaire and Rousseau did not invent the Enlightenment. *[Kautsky quotes Beloch*, Griechische Geschichte, *I/1, p. 3, who wrote similarly of the achievements of Pythagoras, Newton, and Stephenson].*

Men will in any case arrive at the discovery of something new, the conditions of which are given. It is only a question of when and how. ... Researchers and thinkers ... are able to spare humanity long and painful detours, to make its development in the direction necessarily given by the external conditions less painful and costly in sacrifices. ... For thinkers, then, the same applies as for statesmen and military commanders. Their individual personalities are not a matter of indifference for social life at a given time. ... For the total historical process, however, any one of them is not decisive. Incidentally, the historical effect of a thinker does not depend on him alone. ... A certain mentality of a society is required if certain ideas are to be adopted by it. New ideas will most readily gain acceptance in it if they satisfy strong, widespread intellectual and emotional needs.

... The extraordinary occurrence in society, which exclusively interests so many historians, remains ... without effect for social development if it remains something extraordinary, something unique. It can occupy us temporarily, but our mental being, our character ... is significantly determined only by influences that act upon us over a long time in the same way. ... And society will be reshaped by the new that appears within it only when the latter succeeds in becoming part of everyday life. Conversely, however, it can also be said that from an isolated, extraordinary event no new knowledge can ensue. Such knowledge is possible only when a process that is new to us is repeatedly observed. ... From the new practice, the new everyday life, there then emerge new insights, new ideas, but also new needs and tasks. ...

Section Two
Will and Science in History

CHAPTER ONE

The Origin of Volition

The assertion that no conclusions about the future can be drawn from history is based on the view that the singular is the domain of history, ... but *[also on the]* view that in social matters our volition at any given time is not determined by our knowledge of the environment, but that, on the contrary, our conception of the environment is a result of our volition. With respect to nature, that would seem nonsensical. In fact, it is supposed to hold good only for the understanding . . . of society, which is considered to be the work of men. Then, from a limited standpoint, society can appear as something we do not have to grasp in order to adapt our behavior to our understanding of it, but as something we (that means every single one of us) have to adapt to our will. . . . This whole view rests upon the theory of free will.[1] At bottom, it excludes from the outset all conformity of human activity to laws and hence also any social science in the sense of a causal science and thus also any prediction of future social phenomena. *[Kautsky devotes more than two pages to quotations from and attacks on de Man,* Zur Psychologie des Sozialismus, *pp. 421, 424, 263, 111, and 105,[2] who argued that social science was a mere product of the will.]*

There can be no doubt that in the last analysis our volition is not determined by our intellectual apprehension of things, but is already there prior to all such knowledge and that it affects the latter in a determining manner. We have seen in Part II that our volition is a result of our innate drives. These are not all always effective and not all always to the same degree. In order for them to begin to function, certain changes must take place in the organism or in its environment, for example, emptiness of the stomach, or the sight of some delicious food, the attainment to sexual maturity, the proximity of a member of the opposite sex, etc. The drives themselves are modified depending on the way of life of the organism, which is a function both of its organs and of its environment. Thus, they are modified to the greatest extent in the case of man as soon as he invents artificial organs that become part of his environment and alter both it and his way of life and thereby also man himself. . . . Volition, then, precedes knowledge. In which areas the latter is gained depends on the former and on the conditions that produce volition, the innate drives of the organism and their modifications by the environment.

CHAPTER TWO

Teleology and Causality

. . . The will . . . which is determined by the drives originating from within the organism . . . is associated with teleological thinking. It concerns itself

---

1. See also III:2:2 and III:4:1, above.

2. The English translation, *The Psychology of Marxian Socialism,* based on the revised 2nd German edition and a further revised French translation, both of 1927, contains only some of the passages quoted by Kautsky—on pp. 492–93, 497, 390–91, and 382. For a highly critical review by Kautsky of de Man's book, originally included in a draft of *Die materialistische Geschichtsauffassung,* see "De Man als Lehrer."

with conditions that ought to obtain. This "ought" can be of very diverse kinds. . . . If the drive is a social one, then the condition that ought to obtain acquires an ethical character, that of an *ethical ideal*.

Human goals that arise solely out of the drives, out of needs, that acquire a certain coloring under certain social conditions, are necessarily undefined, vague. The will takes on a completely different form as soon as it goes beyond mere needs and calls for definite actions to satisfy the needs. Once the will gives rise to actions, it must be necessarily associated with *causal knowledge*. That is not necessary for the setting of goals, but it is necessary for choosing actions to attain a goal. Now the will must no longer be undefined and vague. Acting means nothing other than creating a certain cause in order to achieve a certain effect. . . . Conscious—not instinctual—action is not possible without an understanding of certain necessary causal relations. . . . *[It]* is the function of intellectual apprehension to provide the organism with knowledge of causal relations in the environment. That knowledge enables it to orient its action and hence also its volition that determines this action, corresponding to the goals it set in accordance with its drives and hence in a manner appropriate to achieve its goals. It makes no difference here whether it is a matter of an action in nature or of one in society.[3] . . .

Man may believe that his will is free. . . . He can arrive at this illusion because he does not know the factors that determine his will. But unconsciously, and often reluctantly, he acknowledges through his social activity that men's volition is determined by causal necessities. . . . *[His]* social practice . . . is based on the expectation that men react to certain actions in certain ways. Only on this assumption is action in human society, thus social life, possible.

Of course, our understanding of the environment and also our own ability are always imperfect; thus our behavior will not always be appropriate to gain its end. But it will be more likely to be able to achieve the goal set for it by drive-directed volition, the greater our understanding of reality is. Our volition must therefore be bent on grasping the truth and not on creating illusions. The need to see things as they really are is very strong even among animals. Grasping the truth is necessary to them for their survival.[4] . . .

Now, the "ought" that produces definite actions does not originate solely from knowledge. Instincts, too, can demand certain actions. There are not many instincts in man;[5] but we do find in man, in contrast to the animal, yet a third mainspring for certain behavior: custom, which originates with

3. See also I:4:1–3, above.
4. See II:5:4, above.
5. See II:1:7, II:5:5, above.

other, earlier men and which a later generation encounters ready-made. . . . But regardless of whether it originates with direct knowledge or with knowledge that has been passed down to us and is perhaps already obsolete, our conscious sentiment of obligation is, to the extent that it prescribes our actions, always a result of our understanding of causal relations. . . . However, understanding always makes up only one part of our behavior. It tells us *how* we should act. It does not tell us *that* we should act. The impulse that leads us to act comes from the drives of the individual, which for their part receive their impulses from the external world. An action results just as little from mere knowledge without volition, without a felt need, as a particular action can result from the mere need without a particular perception of the environment. . . .

It is fashionable nowadays to distinguish between two kinds of science: that of nature and that of the mind *[Geist]*. In reality, by the *Geisteswissenschaften* are meant the sciences of society, for the true science of the mind, of the psyche, psychology, belongs to natural science. The difference between the two kinds of science is supposed to consist in the fact that natural science seeks to understand causal relationships, that it is to demonstrate what is, whereas the social sciences and the humanities enquire after ends, investigate what ought to be. Indeed, . . . if man can affect nature only on the basis of knowledge of its *laws*, he can affect other men by means of *commandments*, which he also calls *laws*.

The laws of morality and of the state do not become known to us through observation and investigation of nature, and they do not exist independently of the volition of men. They are proclaimed by men, enforced by men, and are so for human ends—sometimes also for inhuman ends. They are apparently not governed by causality but by teleology. . . . Thus it appears that social research is concerned only with ends and commandments, with laws in an entirely different sense than in the natural sciences. The mode of thinking of men of the law, of jurists, becomes decisively important for this conception of social science, which preponderates all the more, the more widespread legal education is. This conception also requires the assumption of freedom of the will. . . .

The social sciences and humanities include political economy and history. All the others can ultimately be reduced to these two. *[Kautsky quotes Dilthey*, Einleitung in die Geisteswissenschaften, *I, 3 and 5]*. A scientific study of literature and art means nothing other than pursuing literary and art history. And one cannot very well occupy oneself scientifically with politics in any other way than by carrying out historical and economic investigations. . . . And jurisprudence? . . . Its material is the laws . . . but these are made not by jurisprudence, but by politicians and governmental leaders. And the ends that the laws serve originate from life, not from jurisprudence. These laws will be all the better suited to their ends, the more an adequate understanding of the causal relationships of human society exists among the legislators. No matter how much the juridical mode of thinking dominates the social sciences and humanities, they can still ultimately all be reduced to political economy and history. Economic science . . . achieved importance as the theory of the causal relationships in the economic process, and in the study of history, causal relationships are being searched for more and more. . . .

CHAPTER THREE
Pure and Applied Science

A distinction among sciences is certainly to be made, . . . but it is not a distinction between nature and mind or human society, but a distinction between *pure* and *applied* science. Pure science always serves exclusively the discovery of necessary causal relationships; it refrains from any and every setting of ends, in political economy and history, just as in mechanics, chemistry, and biology. On the other hand, applied science always pronounces definite imperatives and makes value judgments about appropriate or inappropriate behavior, no matter whether it is concerning itself with mechanical or chemical matters, with living organisms, or with social phenomena.

These imperatives do not, however, originate from some teleology or other, but from a grasp of causal relationships. To be sure, this understanding is made to serve certain ends. These are ends that do not arise out of any science, neither pure nor applied, but in the last analysis out of the drives that are prior to any science and out of the external conditions under which the needs and desires of men assume their particular forms. *[Kautsky illustrates this with reference to medicine, technology, and political economy]*.

In this regard, the social sciences and humanities are no different from the natural sciences, except for the fact that . . . within class society particular interests appear in the former, while in relation to nature all men have the same interests. And everyone takes an active, practical part in social phenomena, while the study of nature is left as far as possible to experts. As a consequence of the youth of the social sciences and of the disruptive influence of practical interests, pure science is less clearly distinguished from applied science in them than in the natural sciences. . . . A physicist who is only that would not think of trying to construct a locomotive. On the other hand, there is probably not a single political economist who has confined himself to pure theory and has not also concerned himself with questions of practical economics. . . . The difficulty of engaging in the study of economics or history as a pure science . . . is certainly very great. But that is no reason for making a virtue of necessity . . . and for making them out to be entirely teleological sciences, that is, merely applied sciences. That is nonsense, since an applied science presupposes pure science and the laws discovered by the latter. Without knowledge of these laws, all the commandments issued by applied science become nothing but pious wishes. . . .

In light of what has just been said, it is now easy to understand how socialism and science are related to each other. *[There follow nearly seven pages discussing mostly how Marx and Engels differed from pre-Marxian socialists].* Socialism is *applied* science, based upon *pure* science. It would be ridiculous to try to maintain that applied science exists prior to pure science and prescribes for the latter the path it is to follow. Prior to both pure and applied science there exists only the final end arising out of the innate human drives and the particular conditions of life. Science is made to serve this goal, which in this instance is the emancipation of the proletariat. The road leading to this emancipation, however, can be discerned only through scientific labor. . . . If Marxist socialism is not merely the product of an orientation of the will arising out of the drives, but the result of applied science, then the supreme ethical commandment for it is the will to truth. And Marx and Engels always acted in accordance with that commandment. . . .

CHAPTER FOUR
The Power of the Will

. . . For the practical effect of that part of our volition determined by our drives, not only the direction in which it strives is important, but also its intensity. The intensity of our particular drives also depends in part on the individual's inherited physical constitution, in part on the conditions under which he grows up. They determine whether or not the drives for self-preservation preponderate, the social or the sexual drives, those for aesthetic pleasure or those for intellectual knowledge. Man's knowledge cannot, however, directly influence the intensity of his drives, as this knowledge unfortunately does not enable him to select his ancestors or the milieu in which he grows up. . . . Despite all that, the strength of our will can be increased or weakened by the nature of our knowledge. By means of a correct understanding of our environment, of the tasks and of the means that it provides us with, the full strength of our volition is concentrated on the attainment of that which is possible. The impossible is eliminated as a goal, and all waste of will power is thereby avoided. . . .

Regardless how important the intensity of each individual's volition might become for his personal ends, it does not suffice when it is a matter of obtaining large-scale social effects. Then it is above all the unity and uniformity of the volition of many individuals that is important. . . . Assuming that the intensity of the individuals' volition remains constant, the greater the unity of a class, the greater will be the power it is able to muster in the class struggle, the more significant will be the results of its volition.

An indispensable means to this end is a democratic structure of the organizations of the class. Such a structure imposes on the minority the duty
actively to go along with the policies deemed good by the majority, but
on the other hand also gives the minority the right and the possibility of
critically expressing its own standpoint before the entire organization.[6] As
indispensable as this kind of mass organization becomes, it nonetheless finds
its limits when the differences between the majority and the minority become lasting and intolerable. Then the moment draws near when the minority is unable to go along with the policies of the majority. The split of
the organization is imminent.

An attempt to keep the minority in line or to silence it by means of
terrorist coercion can only make the trouble worse. Such coercion can be
carried out only when the party disposes of governmental power. Forbidding a class to study and to test certain views is tantamount to declaring
that it is not of age. A proletariat that is placed in the charge of a guardian
and silently accepts such a disciplinary measure thereby demonstrates its
inability to emancipate itself and thus loses more and more the germs of
the ability to emancipate itself through its own strength that it has already
developed.[7] The proletariat cannot obtain by coercion the lasting, joyous,
and well-considered unity that it must have if it is to prevail against its
many and strong opponents. This unity can be attained not through the
terror of a majority, and even less through the terror of a minority that
rules only by armed force, but only through agreement reached by independent thought.

Such agreement is by no means unattainable. . . . For all the members of
a class, there exists by and large the same environment with the same
problems and the same resources. Within the class itself, the interests, the
living conditions, the means of achieving knowledge are generally the same.
If the main emphasis in the intellectual activity in the class struggle is placed
on the study of the environment; if the ends that are set, the paths that are
followed, are based on the results of this study; if the propaganda among
the masses is aimed chiefly at the dissemination of the knowledge thus
obtained, then the likelihood is greatest that agreement in the way the
proletariat thinks will be attained, at least within its intellectually independent sectors. On the other hand, this agreement will be the more difficult
to achieve, the more mere will, subjective will that appears to be free, is
made the mainspring of historical development and the accidental is sub-

---

6. See also three articles by Kautsky in *Die Neue Zeit* of late 1915, attacking the German
Majority Socialists, collected with responses by two of the latter as *Ueberzeugung und Partei*,
pp. 7–20, 35–42.

7. Kautsky had elaborated this argument against the Bolsheviks in *Terrorism and Communism*, pp. 174–82, and in "Die Gemeinsamkeit des sozialdemokratischen und des kommunistischen Endziels," in Lübbe, ed., *Kautsky gegen Lenin*, pp. 135–36.

stituted for that which conforms to laws. Then the will is not, by superior understanding, directed to activity that is appropriate to an end; then only the needs for quick successes are decisive. When these are not achieved, it can easily happen that they disperse who are guided by mere volition and are not held together by shared knowledge.

In addition to all the great advantages already described that the scientific understanding of our environment brings to the successes of our practical activity, there is, then, also the advantage that a shared scientific theory resulting from investigation of the environment holds a class together. . . . Propaganda must not be a mere appeal to the feelings, to ethical sentiment, but must include the dissemination of new knowledge. It is certainly true that nothing great is accomplished without enthusiasm. But the necessary ethical sentiment must have already been engendered previously, by life, if it is to represent an enduring motive force in a struggle for emancipation. . . . New knowledge . . . spurs men on to strive for further knowledge; it is thought through and discussed, and a new movement starting out from that knowledge is tough and ineradicable, if at the same time the living conditions of the men taking part in it produce and keep alive in them the necessary drive-based forces. The capitalist conditions of the process of production themselves produce the strong urge in the proletariat to emancipate itself. It needs no agitation for that. It does, however, certainly need a clear grasp of the existing conditions in order to know how it should put this urge into action to achieve a lasting success. . . .

CHAPTER FIVE
Marx and Jehovah

[The first three pages of this chapter, like its title, refer to a passage quoted by Kautsky from de Man, The Psychology of Marxian Socialism, *pp. 397–98.]*
A particular scientific view . . . *[or]* knowledge of the environment strengthens our will power when this knowledge shows us that the goal of our volition is attainable. . . . Then it seems quite natural to want to increase the confidence and the strength of people with whom we are cooperating by doing whatever is necessary to paint for them a picture of the environment that is favorable to what they want to accomplish and to withhold from them all information about it that might have a discouraging effect. Such a course of action . . . will always be a shortsighted policy. Illusions cannot be maintained for long, at least not illusions that concern the world of our experience. . . . And one can always expect defeat in a struggle when it is believed that the fighters can be brought to continue the battle only by deceiving them about the situation.

A movement like the Marxist one, which is now eighty years old, cannot be kept going by means of illusions. It has outlived all other socialist orientations and is today the one socialist orientation that is common to all countries with proletarian movements. . . . To be sure, in the proletarian parties of the present day not all members by far are consistent Marxists. Eclecticism and indifference to theory are widespread. But everywhere the politics of the proletariat has become the practical expression of Marxism. . . . Everywhere the labor movement is understood as class struggle, socialism as the goal of the proletarian class struggle, which can end only with the abolition of classes.[8] How could that be possible if the materialist conception of history and the economic theory and practical labor movement that are based on it were not in accord with the conditions of the environment but gave us a false picture of it, of the problems that it poses for use, and of the means it offers to us for solving these problems? . . . Not a decade passes without a "crisis of Marxism;" not a year without numerous "definitive"refutations of Marxism; nor a year without mistakes and inconsistencies on the part of individual Marxists—the greatest danger to our theory. Nevertheless, that theory lives on, from year to year more powerful than ever. It need shrink from the tests of practice as little as from those of science.

Section Three
The Goal of the Historical Process

CHAPTER ONE

Prognoses Derived from Experience

. . . Knowledge of the world has a twofold value for the individual. First, it means the understanding of certain causal relationships. That enables him to set certain causes in order to obtain certain effects. From experiences of the past, however, the individual can also draw certain conclusions about the future. In this manner, he is enabled to prepare himself for coming events, either in order to protect himself against them or in order to exploit them to his advantage. Just as no action is possible without a certain knowledge of causal relations, so too no action is possible without a certain foresight into the future. . . . The foreseeing of what will happen is so important for the self-preservation of the individual and of entire societies and communities, but also so difficult when the coming event is not immediately imminent, that the art of prediction, of prophecy, was regarded as the most desirable and highest kind of wisdom. It was considered to be an emanation of the divinity. . . .

Predictions, prognoses, are not all made in the same way. Three kinds

8. See also V : 1 : 1, above.

can be distinguished among them. One is based on the fact that certain events regularly recur in certain periods of time. . . . The foreseeing of such happenings is quite universal among men and can be found even among the most backward of them. For a long time, of course, such prognoses are of a purely empirical nature, founded upon mere observation of regularities. By different regularities that have been observed independently of one another being placed into an intrinsic relationship, they acquired a greater certainty; they become necessary laws of nature. The prognoses based on such laws thereby acquire the greatest degree of certainty. . . . The second kind of prediction concerns processes . . . that can assume an often quite changeable character, such as . . . rain or wind. *[But]* their frequent recurrence nevertheless ultimately permits the discovery of features through which each of them announces itself. . . . Our life is predominantly determined by prognoses of this, the second kind; they influence our action at every step we take. . . .

The more extensive and diverse human knowledge is, the better it is ordered, the more coherently it is organized in accordance with intrinsic relationships, the greater will be the spatial and temporal area that can be covered by prognoses of this kind, the more does the certainty of the prognoses increase for particular areas, for which predictions had already been made earlier. Absolute certainty, however, will never be attained for prognoses. The world will always be more varied than the picture that we are able to paint of it for ourselves. Nowhere are unexpected disrupting events excluded. . . . But in the case of prognoses of the first kind, such disruptions are as a rule too insignificant to be able to influence our practical behavior. . . . On the other hand, all the various disruptions that menace our prognoses of the second kind can become very important for our practice. . . . We must always regard our expectations of the future as mere probabilities. We have only to strive to make them as well founded as possible, to make the sources of error as small as possible, so that the failures resulting from insufficient foresight do not damage us too badly. He who chooses to refrain from making any prognosis at all, because some prognoses are inaccurate, would either condemn himself to complete inactivity or make his behavior entirely dependent on accident. We cannot manage without prognoses. . . .

Yet a third kind of prognosis is possible, but one that is very rarely made use of. It, too, is based . . . on the fact that a process repeats itself regularly just as in the case of the first kind of prognosis. . . . *[However,]* small deviations constantly occur; they become the greater, the more complex the phenomena are. These deviations can be of two kinds: first, those . . . that cancel each other in their effect, so that in the course of time the recurring process remains fundamentally the same. Thus, the winters of a certain region are sometimes milder, sometimes more severe, but on the whole their character remains the same. . . . In addition to such deviations, though, there are also others that always take place in the same direction, so that they . . . are additive and reinforce each other, . . . *[for example,]* deviations from the previous average temperature . . . that occur in the same direction year in, year out. . . . As a result, there finally appears something entirely new, perhaps an ice age with all its consequences for plants and animals.

The changes occurring with each repetition can be so minimal that for a long time they remain unnoticed, especially if they overlap with deviations of the first kind that cancel each other. . . . But, in the course of the ages, the changes can add up to an enormous total effect and ultimately bring about a condition that is completely different from the earlier one. . . . In this fashion, the constant repetition of the same movement assumes the character of a developmental process. If one succeeds in observing a sufficiently long series of such repetitions, then it becomes possible to discern the direction the development is taking and thus to foresee, to a certain degree, the new condition it will bring into being. . . . The first two kinds of prognosis . . . can only announce the recurrence of phenomena that are already known. The third kind, however, can point to the advent of phenomena that have not heretofore existed. It is much more rarely possible, . . . but on the other hand it opens up to us broader vistas on the future.

Yet the prognoses of the third kind are arrived at, just like those of the first two kinds, only from the observation of numerous repetitions of the same process, thus only from the observation of the past up to the present. . . . Even new phenomena that lie in the future we can come to know only through experience of the old, both that which once was and that which still is. There is no other source of knowledge than that gained from experience. If the new were a product of the creative power of the genius, of that which is nonrecurrent, we would never be able to foresee it, for the singular is unpredictable. Only when it is a matter of phenomena that have repeated themselves, can their recurrence be foreseen and also the further direction of their change, if such a change was already noticeable previously as a regularly occurring phenomenon. That can happen with the greater certainty, the more these processes have been brought into a coherent relationship with the totality of previously observed processes. . . .

CHAPTER TWO

Prognoses in Society

Each of the three kinds of prediction that have been discussed is permissible in all areas of knowledge, in that of nature as well as in that of society considered separately from nature. But for prognoses of the third kind, the prediction of a future development, the conditions are given only rarely.

The employment of prognoses in society is not prevented by the fact that human society is moved by the human will—not, to be sure, by the will of single individuals, but by the volition of all the individuals who are effectively active in it. As in nature, there are also numerous processes in society that repeat themselves incessantly day in, day out, year in, year out, in the same way. These include, above all, the processes of production of material goods. . . . There can, of course, be disruptive occurrences. A slackening of sales can bring a factory to a halt. A fire can destroy the peasant's stores. But, nevertheless, men count on the regular recurrence of the process of production and must do so if a catastrophe is to be avoided.

In economic life, the prognoses of the first of the three kinds distinguished here play the decisive role, to the extent that it is directed to the production of material goods, to the "base" of society in the Marxist sense. Prognoses of the first kind are less easily possible for the superstructure. For higher kinds of intellectual production in science and in art that are of an entirely individual nature they become quite impossible. No law, no prognosis, can be made for the "creative" genius, for what is unique and does not repeat itself. . . . With regard to the geniuses of the past, we can come to understand how they are socially conditioned and can in many instances clearly show that the elements of whatever new thing they brought forth were already present prior to them in new social conditions.[1] But regardless of how far we might succeed in going in this materialist investigation of the life of the mind, it will always permit us to understand only the intellectual and artistic production of the past, not to advance prognoses for that kind of production in the future. . . .

Between the area of material production and that of individual intellectual and artistic production are located those domains of the superstructure in which not single individuals, but masses of people are active. These are primarily the domains of politics, today those of politics in the state, of class struggles, but also of national struggles. . . . Here, as long as the economic foundations remain unchanged, the same processes repeat themselves over and over again, but not in such a regular succession as in the economy and under more complex conditions. In these areas, prognoses are certainly possible and are indispensable for successful work, but not prognoses of the first kind, rather those of the second kind, such as are possible in nature for the weather. They are less certain and . . . each of them applies only to a particular situation and loses its significance and validity as soon as the situation changes. . . .

[How about] prognoses of the third kind, those pertaining to a development in a certain direction? . . . For a long time, the development of human society proceeded so slowly that men were unable to discern it, . . . but assumed that the way they lived was the way things had always been and would always be. . . . A more rapid social development was introduced

---

1. See III:2:12–13, above.

only by the emergence of the state and classes. At first that appears to be only a result of accidental force. The slow economic transformation that only made that forcible change possible was ignored. But, within the state, it now sometimes happened that a faster economic development began that became obvious and even led to prognoses. . . .

If the emergence of the state and classes temporarily resulted in an economic upswing, it was effected for mass production, in contrast to the production of luxury goods, less through an improvement of methods and tools of productions than through increasing the size of the exploited masses of people and through expansion of the arable land worked by them. If its further expansion was impossible, then economic progress began to stagnate. Stagnation became decay where the extent of arable land diminished, perhaps due to neglect of irrigation works or where the sources of cheap workers dried up.[2] This situation could not yield social prognoses of an advance to a higher form of society.

That changed only when the conditions for the emergence of industrial capitalism arose. With it, there came . . . ever more perfect tools also for mass production. It developed the total productive forces of society to the highest degree and did so at rapidly increasing speed that became ever more noticeable and conspicuous.[3] At the same time, the methods of observing mass phenomena in society were improved through the development of statistics. The conditions were thereby formed for social prognoses not of a pessimistic, but of an optimistic sort that . . . prophesied the coming of better times in a new society. But the researchers who operated within the framework of capitalism made no use of the possibility of such prognoses. . . . Industrial capitalism was far superior to dying feudalism; at the time of the latter, it was the most rational mode of production. Thus the thinkers of the bourgeoisie believed that reason had only to discover the natural laws of this mode of production and to make state and society conform to them, and then everything would be in order. . . .

Investigating indications of further economic development that were becoming obvious, in order to derive social prognoses from them, was something that could occur only to someone repelled by the new mode of production because of the horrible misery that it caused, who had nonetheless understood that this mode of production was for the time being a necessity and that its laws could not be overcome by ethical indignation or by subtly elaborated utopias. From this standpoint, it seemed appropriate, especially in an age given to making studies of legal and economic history, to investigate what features of the existing mode of production were universal, common to all modes of production, and what constituted only a

2. See IV:6:5, above.
3. See IV:7:8, above.

historical, transitory category in it; to investigate the existing mode of production as a formation that had gone through a process of development and that bore within its womb further formations; and to examine the extent to which the elements of these new formations were already recognizable at that time and the direction in which they were developing. Thus Marx and Engels arrived at their prognosis of the further development of industrial capitalism. . . .

Unlike bourgeois economists, Marx did not consider the capitalist process of production as one that always repeats itself to exactly the same extent. Rather, he regarded it as a process of reproduction on a progressively increasing scale. Two great causes of progressive expansion are always at work in this process. . . . These two tendencies, that of continuous accumulation and that of technological progress, contradict each other. The former has the effect of increasing, the latter of decreasing the laboring masses. The first tendency proves to be the stronger of the two in this respect. The number of proletarians does not diminish but grows. But the second tendency causes the workers' share in their product to become ever smaller and their exploitation to increase so that the class antagonism between capitalists and workers grows, while the number of proletarians constantly rises. This prognosis is based on the daily recurrence of processes that we can constantly observe. Every day, the accumulation of capital and the growth of the proletariat repeat themselves. Every day, the class antagonism and the class struggle of the two groups are repeated. Every day, experience teaches that the class struggle becomes a political struggle, a struggle for control of the government.

These everyday matters of the present are the basis of the conclusion about the future that the time is inevitably drawing closer when the proletariat will make up the bulk of the nation and will gain control of the government in order to make it serve its struggle for emancipation. Up to this point, the prognosis is scientific and unassailable. So far, no one has been able to oppose to it a different one. Bourgeois science is unable to counterpose to it anything other than the belief that things will always go on the same way they have so far—the very prediction that is wholly absurd from the outset in this era of profound transformations and upheavals in all areas of social life. For the bourgeois masses, this renunciation of any real prediction by bourgeois science means nothing but growing uncertainty with regard to every social movement. . . .

What became most important in the Marxist theory for the proletarian class struggle from a practical point of view was . . . the theory of the expanded process of reproduction and the prediction based on it. . . . The Marxist prognosis created the foundation for joining socialism and the labor movement, for giving to the former the driving force of a united, vigorous mass of men and for pointing the latter toward a lofty goal, not a subjective, arbitrarily invented one, but a goal obtained from observation of the facts that makes possible the uniformity and unity of the advance [*of the working class*] without it going astray.

The present-day workers' parties are the first parties in the world to be formed on the basis of a social prognosis arrived at scientifically and to be guided by it. The Marxist prediction is the first sound prognosis that has acquired practical importance in the history of the world. . . . It was and is still frequently being carped at. But the critics have not succeeded in doing more than that. It has not even occurred to any of them to try to replace it with a different prognosis.

This particular prognosis must not be confused with those I have here designated as belonging to the second kind, the prognoses that no politician can do without. . . . Of course, Marx and Engels also had to make predictions of this kind. They were, after all, not just scientific investigators but also fighters. In this respect, they fared like any other politician. For none of them does each of his predictions come to pass. . . . Their prognoses of nonrecurring extraordinary events, as well as of particular forms and time periods of historical development could not attain the certainty that their forecast of the direction of the general social development had achieved. Yet, even with regard to such predictions, our masters were sometimes surprisingly successful. . . .

We must also not confuse the prediction made by Marx and Engels about the development toward socialism . . . with the entirely differently oriented prognoses of philosophers about the goal of humanity. The kind of prediction to which the Marxist one of coming socialism belongs always remains based on experience. Obtained from experience, it does not reach farther than our experience up to the present allows us to see. Its limits are thereby set. It does not permit one to look into the measureless future, but only to recognize those coming solutions that are to be expected for problems already existing today, as far as the means and the forces for their solution are already developing and observable today.

Now it is certainly impossible to assess exactly, according to the significance that it will later acquire, each of the elements of what is coming that we can already see and to come to know it in all its aspects. It must also be assumed that, in addition to the elements of what is coming that we can observe, others will also become important that we now either overlook or underestimate. Lastly, from every solution of a problem new problems arise that did not previously exist. Thus, in the development of society toward socialism, too, every achievement of the proletariat will certainly strengthen its position, but will also pose new problems for it that have not been perceptible before. That cannot fail to have some influence on the validity of a prediction. . . . It must repeatedly be tested anew, as soon as new facts appear, and must, if necessary, be adapted to these facts and in this way be perfected. Such periodic revisionism is indispensable, but it is worse than useless if it does not go beyond doubts and does not lead to new, more advanced insights. . . .

. . . The further we move away from the economic base, the more uncertain must our prognoses of future development become. It is nonsensical from the start to attempt to make such predictions for the development of literature and art. To try already now to sketch "materialistically" the basic outlines of the future art of socialism is nothing less than it is Marxist. And from a practical viewpoint, it is entirely superfluous that the proletariat . . . as a class battle against certain forms of painting or of literature because they are called "bourgeois." In this regard, even more than in the areas of religion and philosophy, individual taste must remain a private affair. . . . It is already a great achievement if we succeed in discerning in present-day society the developing foundations of the future economic order and of the political order resting on it. Let us not step over the bounds that are set to the materialist conception of history. That can only lead to failures.

CHAPTER THREE

Transcendent Prognoses

The three kinds of prognoses we have observed up to now have all been based on the experience that certain processes repeat themselves under certain conditions. . . . But the human spirit is not content with these predictions. In this area, as in so many others, it tries to go beyond the limits of experience, that is, beyond the limits of knowledge.[4] . . . Whoever feels at home in this realm beyond experience cannot but endeavor to go beyond the bounds of experience in history, too, and to yearn for predictions that reach beyond these bounds, to brood about the goal toward which humanity is striving, about the destiny of humanity, the meaning of history. . . . He seeks an end that mankind serves, to which it draws ever closer. But such an end lies beyond our experience. The search for it is identical with the search for the meaning of life in general.[5] . . .

. . . The notion that the world exists for the sake of man became meaningless long ago. But, thereby the world lost every purpose whatsoever that we can conceive of. The world exists, because it exists. That is all there is to it! But does not the notion then become nonsensical that in the midst of this immense, completely purposeless mechanism, the existence of a few ants or human beings, of all things, should have a purpose? Nevertheless, the majority of men has not yet been able to accept the idea that no other

4. See also I:3:4–9, above.
5. See also I:2:4, above.

ends should have been bestowed on them than those that they set for themselves. *[Kautsky quotes at length from Troeltsch, Der Historismus, pp. 174–75, 177, 83, 85, who asserts that]* despite the fact that it is not discernible, there must be an overall meaning to the world. . . .

CHAPTER FOUR

Astronomical Conceptions of History

[Kautsky quotes a long passage from Troeltsch, Der Historismus, pp. 85–87, who insists that there must be in the universe a multiplicity of "realms of life" or "realms of the spirits"—evidently manlike spirits—each with its own history.]

. . . We can probably assume that in the infinite universe there is an infinite profusion of planets that make organic life possible and harbor it. No less, however, must we assume that the abundance of variations of the conditions of existence that can occur on these planets is also infinite, so that hardly any one of them will ever repeat the life-forms of another and, indeed, will do so the less, the more diverse these forms are. . . . It can be considered as good as impossible that there are also human beings on another heavenly body. . . . If the human race is a singular and extremely minuscule phenomenon in the universe, then so too is its spirit and its history. . . . One must not forget that what we call history is a particular kind of development connected with particular abilities that enable man to create artificial organs for himself. Organisms that have not advanced to the point of possessing these abilities have no history, although they display a development. . . . On the other hand, it is not necessarily true that life-forms that are more intelligent than man must have a history. They might live in such blissful conditions that they do not wish and strive for their change. How should a history then occur? . . .

[Kautsky quotes Delbrück, Weltgeschichte, I, 4, saying:] ". . . the human spirit, which participates in the infinite, the divine spirit, . . . is the center and the essence of the world, the true being, and the whole breadth of the firmament and every secret of nature must and does serve that spirit." . . . Whoever is so firmly convinced of the divine nature of the human spirit and of the history in which that spirit manifests itself . . . has no difficulty in making transcendent historical predictions. Such prognoses, however, are also produced by less religious researchers who can be found even deep within the ranks of socialists. *[Kautsky quotes the concluding sentence of Wells, The Outline of History, p. 1159, referring to future life]* "under the leadership of man, the student-teacher of the universe" . . . stretching out "its realm amidst the stars."[6] . . . Belief in unstoppable, endless progress is, naturally,

---

6. Some editions other than the one cited here do not conclude with this sentence.

most likely to be found among those who are working on that progress, hence in the classes produced by industrial capitalism. They are most likely to share the optimism about the future that the rapid development of the forces of production gives rise to, despite all the suffering and sacrifices that occur in the present.

But . . . why not simply accept the Marxist prediction, which is based on hard facts? It is unfortunately based on such an unpleasant and vulgar fact as that of the class struggle of the proletariat. . . . Our social conditions are certainly too painful and repellent for every thinking and feeling person not to turn against them. But how much more comfortable and agreeable (for nonproletarians) is the prospect of an inevitable advance of humanity resulting necessarily from its nature, hence without strikes and revolutions, without expropriations and similar disgusting things, solely by means of the internal governance by our emotions, by our conscience, which is made ever more sensitive by the progress of time. . . .

Predictions of the continuous progress of humanity are, however, not of an exclusively transcendent nature and are not born merely of emotional needs and moods. In part, they are also conclusions drawn from observed facts. And we must still investigate the degree to which these conclusions are justified. With that, our account of the materialist conception of history shall be concluded.

CHAPTER FIVE

Ascent to Freedom

The great fact adduced by all who believe in the continuous progress of humanity is the steady *growth of civilization [or culture]*, that is, of the sum total of the accomplishments men become capable of through their artificial organs. . . . How trifling is everything man could produce without the aid of the experiences and without the capabilities placed at his disposal through the artificial expansion of his organs. It is infinitesimal in comparison with the enormous intellectual, artistic, and material riches brought to him by his technology. . . . As irresistible as the progress of technology is that . . . of civilization. . . . *[It]* is such a manifest fact that no one doubts it. There is certainly justification for drawing from the facts of this progress until now the conclusion that it will continue indefinitely . . . in all the possibly foreseeable future of humanity.

The only question is what conclusion is to be drawn from that. . . . The pessimists are of the opinion that it is all futile, that men will always remain the same. . . . Since the world process has been recognized as a process of evolution, this view is becoming increasingly confined to the circles of the unthinking and the ignorant. Almost all thinking persons see in the growth of civilization the guarantee for a continuous advance by humanity to higher forms of life. They believe that that is the destiny of mankind. They are, however, not entirely in agreement about what is to be understood by these higher forms of life. This question was treated at length by Müller-Lyer in his book *Der Sinn des Lebens und die Wissenschaft. [Kautsky quotes from pp. 224 ff., 239, 138, 184, 186 (and, in the subsequent chapters 6,7,8, and 10, refers back to some of these as well as to pp. 210, 212, 213), and he quotes Hegel,* The Philosophy of History, *pp. 19, 20, 104, who says (on p.19):]* "The History of the world is none other than the progress of the consciousness of Freedom." Not all who believe in progress define it so exclusively as the obtaining of freedom. But in none of them is the idea of freedom absent. It is with this ideal that we will now concern ourselves. . . .

. . . The concept of freedom as the goal of progress becomes nonsensical if it is understood as the absolute freedom of the individual to act arbitrarily. . . . Living together in society is not possible unless the individual gives up a part of the freedom of movement that he would have if he lived outside of society. This freedom would avail him very little, since, given his nature, man can live only under the protection and with the help of society. And his dependence on society increases with the level of social development and the division of labor. . . . As long as these conditions of social existence obtain, society cannot do without certain rules it imposes on its members. The necessity of these rules is increasing rather than decreasing. Under these circumstances, freedom can never consist in the general absence of rules, least of all in the sphere that is fundamental for society, the economic sphere.

. . . Freedom can, however, also be conceived of as something *subjective*, not as actual complete lack of constraint, but as a *feeling* of a lack of constraint. Such a feeling is compatible with the existence of certain social rules, . . . when the latter are recognized by the individual as necessary and useful and are therefore obeyed just as willingly as are a physician's orders by a sick person. . . . For individuals who are refractory or unmindful of their duty coercion, that is, a constraint of their freedom, might always be necessary. But there will have to be less of this coercion and it will be felt less to be a constraint of freedom, first, the greater the majority of those who establish the rules and the smaller the number of those who resist the rules; and second, the greater the community of interests between the majority and minority. . . . The idea of freedom, then, is a quantitative one. Under conditions that are otherwise the same, freedom in society will be the greater, the greater is the number of those from whom the social commandments originate. . . . The greater the majority of those who support these commandments, the more numerous are those in the state and the society who feel that they are free. . . .

. . . In the last few centuries, freedom has made real advances. . . . But is that to be attributed to the advance of civilization? . . . Freedom marches forward, . . . thanks to the class struggle, first, of all the laboring classes that were awakened to political and social resistance by the progress of industrial capital and later increasingly thanks to the class struggle of the proletariat, which today continues almost alone to hold aloft the banner of freedom. In point of fact, economic progress has the tendency increasingly to deprive the free labor that has taken the place of slavery and serfdom of the little freedom that it bore within itself. The trusts of our day are threatening to establish a new feudalism. It certainly has no prospect of prevailing, though not on account of the progress of civilization, but because of the growth of the political strength of the proletariat. . . .

The struggle of the proletariat for emancipation is leading us now not merely to complete democracy, but also to the abolition of classes and thus of all dependence on individuals, hence to freedom in all respects. It is wrong to say that only after the abolition of classes is complete democracy possible, since it is rather the latter that constitutes the basis for that abolition. That view rests on a confusion of the democratic system of government with freedom. Such a system of government, no matter how far-reaching the democratic rights that it bestows, still does not offer complete freedom. Such freedom becomes possible only through the abolition of classes. . . .

. . . From the formation of the state up to recent times, the course of history moved in the direction of a growing lack of freedom. In the last few centuries, this direction has been successfully reversed. But with this reversal we will not come any farther than where we were already prior to the formation of the state. For before the rise of slavery and the state, the condition of human societies from primeval times onward had been, for hundreds of thousands of years, that of complete freedom, of complete democracy, and of the complete lack of classes and of any kind of individual dependency. . . .

. . . Not civilization, but the proletarian class struggle will bring us complete freedom. We may make this prediction on the basis of phenomena that we can observe even now. But . . . we cannot see beyond the struggle of the proletariat for emancipation, which is taking place before our eyes, and beyond its consequences. To some extent, we can make out the goals of that struggle, but it would be foolish to declare that they are the final goals of humanity, its destiny. The further course of the development of mankind remains completely veiled in darkness for us.

CHAPTER SIX

Ascent to Morality

In addition to freedom, the mere advance of civilization is supposed increasingly to bring humanity other attainments that can be called a rising level of morality. . . . The same idea is expressed by the opinion that the growth of civilization gives us ever more justice in society. . . . Like the yearning for freedom, that for justice is not just subjective, but also purely negative, the rejection of a condition by which one feels oppressed, . . . the preferential treatment of another, to whom a better lot has been granted than to me, even if I am not inferior to him. Underlying the demand for justice, therefore, is fundamentally nothing other than the demand for equality. Inequality is injustice.

The concept of justice is, however, not identical with that of equality. . . . Where inequalities exist, the simple equating of what is unequal can itself again create an inequality and hence be felt to be unjust. Such a thing is possible even within a class. If, for example, the same pay is given for the same work performance, then that means an inequality of income among differentially gifted workers. . . . If, however, every worker receives the same amount, without regard to his productivity, then that again means an inequality, since the industrious must now work for the lazy. . . . The principle of equality is thus . . . not purely formal equality, but an equality that takes the given social conditions into consideration and that is aimed at avoiding new inequalities as much as possible.

The existence of an ideal of justice testifies to the existence of inequalities that are felt to be oppressive. The emergence of this ideal does not at all have to mean moral progress beyond all previous morality. In the beginnings of the human race there existed the greatest equality, not merely legal, . . . social, and economic equality, but to a high degree even natural equality of the individuals of the same sex and of the same age. . . . As civilization advances, however, more and more inequalities appear in society. . . . As soon as the state, classes, and exploitation arise, . . . there is formed among the exploited and oppressed, in addition to the ideal of freedom, also that of justice. The two ideals are not implanted in the human breast by nature: what one possesses does not constitute an ideal. These ideals were produced only by the conditions of a relatively very small part of the time during which mankind has existed. For a long time, the progress of civilization did not advance toward the realization of these ideals. They were realized, rather, before civilization began its advance. . . .

. . . The exploitation of the masses and economic inequality among the individuals of modern society is still continuously advancing. Increasingly, this condition is felt to be unjust; . . . *[that,]* however, is not evidence of moral progress, but merely of a growth of the pressure of inequality. . . . The same factors that are leading to the strengthening of the movement for emancipation will, with increased political freedom, also ultimately gain the strength required to effect economic transformations leading to the abolition of classes. That will certainly mean a movement in the direction of increasing equality and justice. . . . The realization of the demand for morality cannot at all be achieved in any manner other than through the proletarian class struggle and not by any means through the mere growth of civilization. So far, injustice in human society has grown with the growth of civilization. And it is not at all apparent to us that precisely those strata to whom the treasures of modern civilization are most accessible are the ones working most energetically toward putting an end to social injustices. . . .

In addition to being understood as a sense of justice, morality can also be conceived of as solidarity. . . . The advance of civilization could not bring us any closer to this ideal than we already were at the beginning of civilization; it could only for some time move us away from it. . . . The strength of the individual's social drives depends on the social conditions in which he lives. Where he can assure his survival only by associating himself firmly with his comrades, these drives are greatly strengthened. On the other hand, they are weakened when the individual advances best through ruthless egoism at the expense of his fellows. In the course of the development of civilization, the strength of the social drives assumes very different forms and can at one and the same time by very different for different classes and strata. A definite general trend toward the strengthening or weakening of the social drives through the progress of civilization can probably hardly be demonstrated.

Only in one respect can a trend be noted that is growing with the advance of civilization. We can observe an increase of the uncertainty about the way in which the social drives are to be translated into action and about the extent of the circle to which they are to apply. . . . When the horde grows to become the tribe, the extent of the social drives is thereby expanded, but the first uncertainty is also introduced into them as soon as gentes are formed within the tribe. Within the gens, the interest of the family becomes powerful. The social drives apply more to these more narrowly delimited organizations than to the tribe. Then, however, the division of labor and the formation of occupations also take place as well as the combining of tribes into states and the formation of classes. . . . Each of these makes demands on the social drives and affects their strength and their direction. The stronger these drives are, however, the more tormenting are the individual's conflicts of conscience as soon as the different communities or organizations to which he belongs come into conflict with one another. . . . General uncertainty, sometimes also indifference, indeed, cynicism in ethical matters makes its appearance. . . . In primeval times, morality was something self-evident. . . . The further civilization has advanced, the more problematic and uncertain our morality has become.

We may expect that this will change once the antagonisms of classes cease to confuse the polities. Along with exploitation, the antagonisms among nations arising out of exploitative tendencies will disappear. Thus, two of the most important causes of the uncertainty in our present-day morality will be eliminated. But here, too, we cannot base our confidence on the simple progress of civilization but only on the growing strength of the proletariat in its class struggle. . . . Under the new social conditions, the differentiation of human personalities, which up to now has affected only some strata of society, will become a universal phenomenon. Because of this individualism, though, it seems hardly possible that man's feeling of solidarity will ever again attain the intensity it must have had in the beginnings of society.

Ascent to Humanity

. . . We are also told that the quality of *humanity* is among the goals toward which man is striving through his growing civilization. Humanity is no more a clear, unequivocal concept than freedom, justice, and morality. . . . Most frequently, humanity is understood to mean respect for the human individual, gentle customs in opposition to the brutality attributed to prehistoric times. . . . The greatest brutality is the lack of willingness to help members of the polity who are in distress. This kind of brutality is more characteristic of civilization than of the state of savagery.

Most often brutality is regarded as . . . the unscrupulousness and ruthlessness with which the stronger use their physical strength against the weaker in order to . . . have their own way or to give free rein to mere moods. . . . If children are regarded as the weaker ones, then we find that they are nowhere treated as lovingly as among savages. The pedagogy of the cane and the exploitation of children are products of civilization, not of savagery. But among the savages the stronger must also restrain themselves in their behavior toward the weaker adults in the polity, as the whole might of the polity stands behind the weak individual. Only when war and slavery bring about the existence of people who become dependent on masters against whom they have no protection, does it become possible for the ones ruthlessly to do violence to the others. . . . Now lordly manners penetrate family life; the father of the house becomes the tyrant of the house, ruling over wife and child, who regard him with fear and not seldom also with hate, allied against him in the feeling that Freud called the Oedipus complex and that he explained by natural (and quite mystical) sexual relations, instead of accounting for it by certain social conditions.

Brutality from above also produces brutality from below. It assumes the most frightful dimensions when the oppressed attempt to rise up. Civil war becomes the most horrible kind of war. All of that is characteristic of civilization, not of savagery. The age of civilization, of the state and of classes, is the cruelest and most bloodthirsty in the history of mankind.

The kindness toward children and one's fellows that we find at lower levels of civilization is, to be sure, restricted to the members of one's own tribe. With regard to the stranger or the enemy, we find that from early times on any and every cruelty is permitted. . . . Here we do not find a general direction of development. Nonetheless, . . . the mildest forms are more likely to be found in the beginnings of mankind than in later stages. . . . Apes . . . and even predatory animals do not wage war with one another. War is a result of technology, which makes it possible for human societies to increase in number. This produces conflicts among them. And, with weapons, technology provides the means for making the conflicts ever bloodier.[7] The behavior of a people toward its enemies depends to a great extent on its mode of production. The hunter and the cattle-raising nomad who obtain their food by killing animals . . . become accustomed to the spilling of blood and acquire a taste for it. In the case of nomads, an additional factor is robbery as a means of obtaining a livelihood. . . . On the other hand, peasants will be the more inclined to gentleness, the more they engage exclusively in agriculture, the less they obtain their food by slaughtering cattle, . . . the more the animals they keep serve only as draft or productive animals that pull the plow, or give milk, wool, or eggs.[8]

[Kautsky quotes at great length reports of primitive people being peaceable and cooperative, caring and loving, helpful and cheerful, from Nansen, Eskimo Life, pp. 100–103, 116, 162, 56–57 (on the Eskimos of Greenland) and Nordenskjöld, Die Umseglung Asiens and Europas, II, 23, 136, 138, 31 (on the Chukchi of Northeast Siberia); from Waitz, Die Indianer Nordamerikas, pp. 101, 40, and Catlin, North American Indians I, 9, 10; II, 242–45; from von den Steinen, Unter den Naturvölkern Zentralbrasiliens, p. 74 (on the Bakairi of Brazil) and Tschudi, Reisen durch Südamerika, II, 280, 215, 217 (on the Botocudo of Brazil).][9]

. . . In the eighteenth century, it began to appear that, with the growth of civilization, the quality of true humanity also increased, for in comparison with the atrocities of the Wars of Religion of the seventeenth century, and especially of the Thirty Years War in Germany, that century displayed a considerable melioration of customary behavior, at least among the educated. That lasted into the nineteenth century, until compulsory military service, and with it the systematic training of just the most civilized nations to commit the most brutal murder, became established throughout Europe. The result has been evident since the World War, in which the progress of civilization has so far culminated. Nevertheless, we need not despair. We have the best reasons to expect that we are heading toward a condition of general far-reaching humanity. Only we find these reasons not in the mere

7. See II:3:6, above.
8. See IV:3:1–2, above.
9. Kautsky had already drawn on several of these nineteenth-century sources—Nordenskjöld, Waitz, Catlin, and Tschudi—in his early article "Die sozialen Triebe in der Menschenwelt."

progress of technology and of education, but in the growing strength of the proletariat. Owing to its class situation, the proletariat is most filled with respect for the human individual and is led by that situation to strive to attain a condition in which all classes have been abolished and all national antagonisms have been surmounted. Here, again, we put our trust in the proletariat and not in civilization. And here, too, we find that at best we should not expect to achieve more humanity than some primitive peoples have preserved for themselves from prehistoric times down to the present.[10]

CHAPTER EIGHT
Ascent to Health and Strength

... Does men's health improve or deteriorate in the course of the development of civilization? *[Kautsky quotes Waitz, Introduction to Anthropology, pp. 125–126, and Nansen, Eskimo Life, pp. 332–33, and concludes:]* Primitive man remains healthy and strong in the environment to which he is adapted. If it is suddenly changed by force, if new and more unfavorable living conditions are imposed on him, then his otherwise iron-strong health fails.

The growth of civilization certainly brings man increasing understanding of and mastery over nature through artificial organs and institutions. But each of these accomplishments has, in addition to the intended consequences, also unintended, unforeseen ones, and these often result in man paying for his dominion over nature with increasing frailty and sickliness. His artificial organs do not just strengthen his natural organs; they often make their functioning superfluous, causing them and consequently the whole body to atrophy.... Technological progress offers the possibilities of stimulating and deadening oneself with drugs of all kinds.... And to all of that the advance of civilization, with the rise of exploitation and of forced labor, adds continuous overfatigue and undernourishment and horrible squalor of housing....

The very great extent to which filth promotes diseases is generally known today. But just as widespread is the assumption that ... filth disappears as civilization advances. In reality, until recently the opposite was the case. *[Kautsky describes how wild animals keep clean.]* All of that changes mightily for man owing to his civilization, to his turning away from the natural state. *[He covers his bare skin with mud and dirt and, once he can kill animals, with their fat. Clothing leads to further accumulation of dirt and parasites, and fire*

---

10. Kautsky had devoted a chapter to humanizing and brutalizing tendencies, particularly from the eighteenth century through World War I, in *Terrorism and Communism*, pp. 121–57, in which some of the points made here are touched on.

brings ashes and soot.] Filth accumulates when man settles down and do-
mesticates animals that share his dwelling-place with him. . . . Refuse and
excrements . . . now accumulate in one place. . . . All the elements that dirty
the dwelling-place become concentrated when towns are established, and
thus many men, their refuse, excrements, and hearths, are concentrated in
a small space. Filth reaches its peak through the very extensive use of fire
in industry. . . .

That is, to be sure, only one trend of civilization. Soon after the appearance of filth, the struggle against it also begins. . . . The motives for the
endeavor to cleanse the body, clothing, and dwelling-places are of an aesthetic nature. Cleanliness is not yet a hygienic duty. . . . Cleanliness becomes
a hallmark of higher social rank. And the higher social ranks have also
monopolized for themselves all education, and in this sense all civilization,
with the result that poverty and lack of civilization become synonymous;
thus it now appears that cleanliness is a product of civilization. This kind
of cleanliness, however, is only a product of the exploitation of the masses
by a thin upper stratum. It exists only for the latter and then not as a need,
but as a pleasure, as a luxury. . . .

. . . Capitalist industrialism filled the cities with coal soot and crowded
many thousands of the miserably poor together in cramped lodgings with
neither the means nor the need for cleanliness. With that development, the
filth-producing power of civilization had reached its culmination. . . . But
with modern natural science and technology, . . . not only did there arise
the means for dealing with filth in an entirely different manner than previously; filth was also recognized as a danger. . . . And, further, the individual's filth was recognized as a danger not just for himself but also for
his environment. Cleanliness ceased to be a mere pleasure, a luxury; it
became a duty, a social virtue. . . . For the last century, the progress of
civilization has involved progress of cleanliness. . . .

Hand in hand with the pushing back of filth, there goes . . . the rise of
the proletariat, the growing strength of its efforts for a reduced work load,
better nutrition, better housing; as filth is forced back, the proletariat gains
time for sports and the enjoyment of nature, and these cease to be luxuries
of the rich. . . . These factors . . . result in the improvement once again of
the health of civilized humanity. In this regard, too, it is the age of industrial
capitalism that produces the conditions for the advance of society to a higher
level, conditions that were not given in earlier phases of the civilization
associated with the existence of the state.

[Kautsky presents various pre–World War I statistics on mortality from Woy-
*tinsky,*Die Welt in Zahlen, *I, 101, 149, 85, showing that its decline]* begins in
Britain only in the decade between 1871 and 1880 and in Germany even a
decade later *[and that]* the state of health in the countryside, which is backward with regard to culture, surpasses that of the city, which has a higher
level of culture. . . . Only the victory of the proletariat will make it possible

to overcome all the obstacles that even today, due partly to a lack of resources, partly to the impulse to exploitation, still prevent the creation of
healthy living conditions for all men. Only then will the progress of civilization in full measure mean an advance of humanity in health and strength.
But even then we will have to be very satisfied if in the population generally
there will be widely diffused the toughness and endurance as well as the
longevity that used to be found among primitive peoples living in their
ancestral territories unaffected by civilization. . . .

CHAPTER NINE

Ascent to Happiness and Contentment

In addition to physical well-being, civilization should also bring ever more
psychic well-being. *[Kautsky quotes von den Steinen,* Unter den Naturvölkern
Zentralbrasiliens, *p. 57; Catlin,* North American Indians, *I, 61, 84; and
Nansen,* Eskimo Life, *pp. 102–103, describing the primitive people they observed
as happy and cheerful.]* What makes a situation of poverty among civilized
men so frightfully depressing is, besides the physical suffering caused by
it, the fact that the poor man sees the goods piled up all around him that
could easily and abundantly help him and to which his access is cruelly
blocked by his fellow men. Of the latter, no one is concerned about him,
at least no one who is not himself in the same desperate situation. Being
thus abandoned in the midst of a world of riches is the most horrible thing
of all. That is spared to primitive man. . . .

[Kautsky quotes Spencer, The Principles of Sociology, *I, 60, who says of
primitive men:]* "Along with improvidence there goes, both as cause and
consequence, an undeveloped proprietary sentiment." The savage has no
occasion to become acquainted with "the gratifications which possession
brings" *[p. 61].* He produces nothing that would be worth accumulating.
Thus the poor devil of a savage lacks all impulses that could lead him to
surrender his unfortunate happiness in exchange for the delights of worrying
about the increase of his property and of the fear of losing it. *[Kautsky quotes
examples of concern for the preservation of natural resources on the part of the
Cheyenne Indians and the Chagga of East Africa from, respectively Dodge,* The
Plains of the Great West, *pp. 266–67, and Gutmann,* Das Recht der Dschagga,
p. 76.] It is not frivolity and carefreeness that give the savage his happiness,
but rather his lack of proprietary sentiment, his communism. That the latter
can be uplifting and can make people happy is something that the specifically
bourgeois part of science will, of course, never comprehend. . . .

At first glance, it appears odd that the growth of knowledge and of
mastery over nature should result in increasing dissatisfaction of men with
themselves and with the world. . . . It is not culture as such that brings about

that gloomy result. It is a product of the conditions under which more advanced culture, civilization, has until now arisen. The introduction of bondage and of exploitation constitutes the fall of humanity from grace. . . . Prior to the emergence of slavery, of the state and of classes, men were always able to adapt themselves to their environment and their environment to themselves. Their culture did not hinder them in doing this. Rather, the artificial organs they made for themselves became the most important means of adaptation. As long as they were adapted to their environment, and the latter was adapted to them, they were happy. They were not, of course, invulnerable to all misfortunes and distress, but they were nevertheless on the whole content and cheerful.

Slavery and exploitation changed that. The apparatuses of domination and exploitation now become powerful and so far growing ever more powerful means of preventing the masses of the people from adapting men and their environment to one another. They no longer have control over the artificial organs of society, over the means of production. . . . Now the living conditions and the conditions of production of the majority of men among the civilized peoples come increasingly into conflict with their needs. . . . An organism endowed with the capacity for sensation, however, must necessarily feel unhappy when it has to live in an environment to which it is not adapted and to which it is constantly prevented from adapting itself.

The happiness of the ruling and exploiting classes is, however, also disrupted again and again. They do control the means of production and the sources of the necessities of life in general and they do have the power to adapt them to their needs. But this power runs into an obstacle. . . . The laboring masses themselves are the most important means of production for the rulers and exploiters. . . . [*The latter*] must constantly struggle against one kind of resistance or another, and . . . the wildest forms [*of rebellion*] always hang over them like menacing thunderclouds. Furthermore, the differences within the ranks of the exploiters themselves grow with growing exploitation. To the natural differences in ordinary talents are added in their case those in the relations of power resting on the fact that some of them have control over more, others over fewer of the exploited. Individual exploiters and individual families, gentes, and states of exploiters constantly seek to enlarge their areas of exploitation at the expense of other exploiters by force or by cunning. Thus each one constantly feels himself threatened by others and must be armed against them. They live, then, in a constant state of uneasiness and uncertainty, in continuous conflict with large parts of their environment, . . . whether they carry on their struggles with one another on battlefields or in stock exchanges, whether they are threatened by peasant revolts or strikes. . . .

We will be able to return to universal happiness only when we have overcome the consequences of the fall from grace of human society and have achieved a condition without classes and exploitation. Only then will men acquire the power harmoniously to adapt their artificial organs and organizations to their natural needs and to those that have been created by human history and in this way to combine a high level of civilization with a high degree of happiness.

It would, of course, be preposterous to join with Rousseau in raising the cry: Back to Nature. . . . Modern man is a quite different man from the savage; he cannot undo the results of thousands of years of the development of civilization. The natural and social environment of the savage is in no way adapted to the needs of civilized man. He would be extremely unhappy in it. . . . The necessary adaptation of social conditions to the needs of the masses of people in the modern civilized nations can be effected . . . only by the conquest of all critically important means of production and means of culture by the collectivity. The latter will understand well enough how to adapt the forms and employment of those means to its needs, once private property no longer prevents them from doing so. Then we may expect to achieve the Benthamite ideal of the greatest happiness of the greatest number. . . .

Future happiness will certainly have to be of a quite different kind than the primitive happiness of the savages. Of the joys of scientific labor, for example, they could have no notion. On the other hand, they lacked many sensitivities of civilized man. Qualitatively the happiness of the future will certainly differ considerably from that of early times, but we shall be fortunate if in this regard, as with respect to freedom and justice, the quantitative level reached by primitive man is attained.

CHAPTER TEN

Ascent to Perfection

. . . We are supposed to approach ever closer to perfection of man and of the society in which he lives in the course of the development of civilization. . . . The concept of perfection is a relative one. . . . A higher or lower position on the scale of evolution has nothing to do with the degree of perfection.[11] The same is also true of man, of his artificial organs and the social institutions and social relations that he creates in part consciously and that for the rest arise unintentionally as consequences of his conscious creations. The perfection of any one of them will depend on its adaptation to the particular condition constituted by the totality of these factors. Primitive man may be considered to be perfect within a primitive society. . . . He will prove to be extremely imperfect in a higher form of society. On the other hand, primitive society will be in harmony with primitive man, with his needs,

11. See also I: 5 : 3, above.

abilities, and implements; thus it will be perfect for him. In contrast, a society based on exploitation must necessarily always remain imperfect, because it prevent the adaptation of its mode of production and its way of life to the needs and abilities of the great majority of its members.

However, . . . does not our understanding of nature and society grow rapidly? And does not this understanding necessarily enable us to give an ever more perfect form to society? That is an almost universally held view today. [*Kautsky quotes Müller-Lyer, Der Sinn des Lebens, pp. 173, 139, who sees in the development of sociology the key to "a planned development of civilization."*] We need not repeat here what a frightful obstacle to every adaptation of social institutions to the needs of the laboring masses is constituted by the power of the exploiting classes, a power that no "sociology" can break. In the social sciences of our time, the most diverse orientations hold sway, and up to the present day those that preponderate among them are the ones hostile to socialism, for which the "control over civilization" [*expected by Müller-Lyer*] is, after all, only another term. And behind these orientations of social science stand the enormous economic instruments of power of the exploiters, as well as, up to now, political and scientific instruments of power, for example, the universities. . . .

When the obstacles have fallen that have hitherto stood in the way of "control over civilization," will the state of the social sciences attained by then suffice of itself to guarantee that a perfect society will be created? . . . The progress made by the social sciences is enormous compared with the ignorance of earlier times in this area. But this progress appears quite different when it is compared with the extent and the complexity that the social apparatus has achieved relative to that of earlier eras. . . . How simple the social relations were prior to the formation of the state, how easy they were to grasp in their entirety, how easy it was to bring them into harmony with the needs of the members of society! And how little they changed. As a rule, tradition sufficed to master them. Today, relations in modern society are immensely complicated, . . . and every day innovations, often of a thoroughly revolutionary nature, make it increasingly impossible to grasp them in their entirety. In view of this growing wealth of problems, one may well doubt whether the present-day state of economic knowledge will suffice for adapting immediately the entire process of production, with its appendages and offshoots, to the needs of the laboring masses in a manner that completely satisfies them and enables men and social organizations to achieve the maximum that can be attained with the given forces of production. In particular, the statistical description of social relations will have to be tremendously perfected, if we are to be able to solve adequately the problems that arise for us out of present-day society.

But it is not just the degree of our social knowledge that will have to increase significantly, if we are to be able to create something perfect. The diffusion of this knowledge in the masses of the people still has to be enormously extended, if they are to become capable of fulfilling their historical task. For the immense transformation of society that has become inevitable cannot be effectuated from above, by an enlightened absolutism, such as is again becoming fashionable on the Russian and Italian models, by a Messiah. This transformation will be successful only where the masses are willing and able to work on it with the greatest energy and with full understanding.

Before the emergence of the state, the extent of civilization was slight in comparison with the later state civilization, but every member of society participated in it to a high degree. Since that time, civilization has grown gigantically, but this gigantic growth . . . rapidly attained great height, but only little breadth. And this kind of growth is not least of all responsible for the fact that the increase of civilization has up to now not at all yielded those magnificent results that literati and intellectuals have been fond of attributing to it since the eighteenth century. . . . Without a great deal of civilization, it is possible to keep a society satisfactorily going that is, in its fashion, far more perfect than capitalist society, but it can be only a very simple and narrowly delimited one. Present-day society requires an enormous raising of the cultural level of the masses, if it is to become a perfect society. All the elements of civilization that have been created so far must be placed at their disposal. It is the task of the proletariat to conquer for itself this entire civilization. . . .

For the proletarian who wants to hold his own and to serve his class in capitalist society, the possession of modern culture is to a high degree an indispensable aspect of life. He must gain control of this culture, just as he must gain control of the government. Once in possession of both, the proletariat will be able to solve the enormous problem of adapting the capitalist process of production to the needs of the workers in all their various kinds and ranks and thereby to create a perfect society. This society will, however, be more perfect only in comparison with capitalist society, indeed, in comparison with any mode of production founded on exploitation, but not in comparison with every mode of production that has existed heretofore. Great difficulties will have to be overcome before the socialist mode of production will, in its own way, be as perfect as primitive communism was. No one will strive to attain perfection going beyond that, for with it a condition of society can be achieved with which all who live in it are satisfied.

CHAPTER ELEVEN
The Law of Progress

In the world of organisms and societies, there is no general progress from imperfect forms to ever more perfect ones. Only within certain conditions

is there progress from forms that are less well adapted to those that are
better adapted. . . . But do we not all recognize that there is evolution both
in the world of organisms and in that of societies? And does not evolution
mean movement in a certain direction? Do we not all assume that this
direction points upward, from lower to higher forms? Did not Marx and
Engels take over the Hegelian dialectic? To be sure, they turned it off its
head and placed it upon its feet, but they retained the assumption that the
conclusion of a dialectical process, the synthesis, represented an advance to
a higher state.[12] And have I not myself often spoken, and in this book, too,
of higher and lower forms? Hence, development must be an ascent to
something that is above us. Now what else can this be than that which is
more perfect?

What is the motive force that is driving in this direction? . . . *[It can be
explained through a]* modernized Lamarckism that is not, however, mystified
by vitalism and psychism and that sees the cause of the evolution of organisms in the continuous conflict between the organism and its environment, a conflict in which the individual becomes increasingly adapted to
the environment. . . . The whole long process of organic evolution that has
been proceeding on the earth since the beginning of life on it only becomes
explicable through the fact that the environment is constantly undergoing
change and is, moreover, changing in a certain direction. The evolution of
life is conditioned by the evolution of the inorganic world. Only when we
are able to note a continuous advancement to higher forms in this world,
too, do we understand the advancement in the world of organisms.

Now, a development to ever-higher forms as a universal law of the world
is completely incomprehensible for us. Let us assume that the world—not
the solar system, but the universe—had a beginning. . . . As something that
has come into being and was set in motion, it must, however, finally perish
or at least enter into a state of rest, perhaps due to universal entropy, the
complete elimination of all differences in temperature in the universe. An
unending advance to ever-higher forms in the world is incompatible with
this view. But the world can also be conceived of differently. One can avoid
the paradox that it had a beginning, when it arose out of nothing and
received an impulse from nothing, by the assumption that the world is
infinite both in space and time, without beginning and without end. . . .
Then it can never represent either an ascending or a falling direction of
development. Then we must assume that the world has always been in a
state corresponding to that represented by the part of it known to us. In
it, we find at one and the same time all stages of development together—
here glowing clouds of gas, there solar systems that have issued from them
and that are of different ages, including systems whose suns have grown

12. See pp. I:5:3, above.

cold. We may assume that the latter will sooner or later become glowing hot again and will be transformed into clouds of gas. . . . Then there is no development, but only an eternal motion of the world. . . .

Paradoxes cannot be avoided when we make the attempt to grasp the infinite with the finite means of our cognitive faculty. . . . One thing is certain, though: The ascent of the world must either be followed by a decline, or the world knows neither the one nor the other. *[Kautsky quotes Engels, "Introduction to* Dialectics of Nature,*" pp. 56–57.]* What we regard as evolution to higher forms can, then, never be an unending process, but always only proceed in a temporally delimited fashion in spatially delimited parts of the world, in particular solar systems or heavenly bodies, and must in each case ultimately end in a decline culminating in the complete disappearance of all the results of evolution. . . .

The process of development is nothing other than a continuously progressing differentiation of what is homogeneous and combination of what has been differentiated into new, different forms, to make an ever-greater diversity. The mainsprings of this process are gravity and progressive cooling. *[Kautsky describes in some detail how our solar system, originally "a glowing ball of gas," becomes diversified into different elements and different planets. The small ones, among them the earth, form a crust on which water accumulates with chemicals that provide the basis for the appearance of life. Changes in the surface of the earth, including the rise of continents, provide different living conditions.]* This diversity of living conditions necessarily brings forth a diversity of the primeval life-forms that happen to enter into these living conditions and have to adapt themselves to them, if they are not to perish. . . . Owing to the frequent repetition of the process of change of the environment, of immigration and emigration, the number of different species living together in one area soon had to increase greatly. For each of them, all the others became part of its environment, which thereby also became more diverse, and that in turn reacted on the nature of the organisms that lived in this environment and had to adapt themselves to it.

[Eventually, animals develop that live off other organisms. They] need organs of locomotion . . . to be able to pursue their prey, to seize it, and to hold it fast. . . . But . . . the animal must also be capable of recognizing its prey; it must summon up the will to draw its prey to itself; to this end, it must set its organs in motion in a coordinated way and one suited to the end. Thus it happens that organs are formed having mental functions. Mind is born— a new element on the earth that enormously increases the diversity of life on it. . . . The diversity of organic life grows in proportion to the increase of the diversity of conditions on the surface of the earth, and every great change on it that places animals and plants in new conditions calls forth new, more varied life-forms. . . .

With man, . . . there begins a new kind of evolution, independent of the cosmic development that kept the whole evolutionary process of organisms in motion until the emergence of man. His artificial organs and his social institutions . . . change from being his tools into being his environment, which thereby changes itself and again and again creates new living conditions for man to which he has to adapt himself and for which he again thinks up and applies new artificial organs or social institutions.[13] His environment thereby gradually comes to have an enormous diversity, and the problems posed for him by his environment become just as diverse as do the goals that he invents for solving those problems. These goals become ever more comprehensive, every more far-reaching, and increasingly assume the character of lofty ideals. . . .

When we understand progress in this way, then it turns out that is has no definite goal toward which it is directed, for diversity is not to be found in the direction of determinate forms. In this conception of progress, all mysteries of a goal-directedness of organisms or of the spontaneous movement of the mind become superfluous. And that obviates the otherwise inevitable assumption of a world spirit that existed before all organisms and finite minds or spirits and that prescribed to them the goals they had to aim at. The mindless and soulless motive force of the progressive cooling and shrinking of our solar system, and in particular of our earth, suffices to explain all the progress of evolution that we know, until the emergence of man.

With man, there appears a factor of evolution that is by no means without mind and soul—the spirit of invention. But in his case, too, evolution advances to ever-higher forms, that is, to forms that are more diverse and capable of greater accomplishments mindlessly and soullessly insofar as the problems arising out of the new inventions and constituting the impulse to further development were not foreseen and intended, but form a power that operates independently of men's volition and knowledge and, rather, determines their direction.[14] It is on the recognition of this that our materialist conception of history rests. It shows us, to be sure, special laws of the development of society, but it also shows us that these do not contradict the laws of natural evolution, but form, one can say, their natural extension.

CHAPTER TWELVE

The Limits of Progress

We have seen that the meaning of development, of progress, and hence of history consists not in a movement toward a determinate goal of all life, but in a progression toward ever-greater diversity. For organisms and their

13. See III:3:1, above.
14. See III:3:11 and p. 462, above.

creations, however, the latter is bound by the condition that it must prove to be compatible with the primordial purpose of life, the preservation of individuals and of species. But will there not be a contradiction between progress understood in this sense and the transition from capitalism to socialism? . . . Socialism will . . . strengthen the equalizing tendencies of trade among nations as it overcomes their conflicts. . . . No matter how far the protection of rare animals and plants might go under socialism, the progress of agriculture will nevertheless continue to cause the extinction of some of their species and thus decrease diversity in nature. In addition, socialism will also bring about the abolition of classes, of the antagonisms between poverty and wealth with all the many social differences they give rise to. Must life then not become increasingly uniform? Not at all.

The progress of science will continue to press forward again and again to new inventions, to a constantly growing technological diversity. But every technological advance in turn brings new knowledge. . . . *[Man's]* immediate natural environment, as it *is*, might become poorer in life-forms. On the other hand, the nature he *knows* grows daily in its extent and in variety, at a much more rapid rate than the decrease of some wild life-forms. Man's intellectual life, too, thereby becomes ever richer. This increase of intellectual wealth has heretofore been restricted to small circles of people. Socialism will make the rapidly growing diversity of scientific production and of intellectual and artistic production in general accessible to the entire laboring mass of all occupations. It is very possible that the number of occupations will also grow and that thereby, too, the diversity in human society will increase.

Much more important, however, is the following: . . . The advances made by civilization, especially since the emergence of the state, have fragmented the mass of the population into an enormous number of occupations; they have caused great differences in the educational levels of different strata; they have, in war and in peace, thoroughly mixed the very diverse races that were endowed with very different innate abilities and inclinations. And all these advances, together with their consequences, proceed today so rapidly that old and new outlooks become all mixed up with one another for different strata and individuals in very different ways. This continuously progressing differentiation of the ability and the volition of various strata, which manifests itself in each individual in the particular mixture of his personal abilities and inclinations, meets, in industrial capitalism, with a progressive uniformity of the working and living conditions of the mass of the population. Today, only a few have at their disposal the means and the independence to develop fully their abilities and to employ them in accordance with their inclinations.

In this respect, socialism will bring about a fundamental change. . . . The general availability of education will facilitate the full development by everyone of all his potentialities, the promotion of which is in the interest of society. In addition, the increase of the amount of free time at everyone's disposal makes it possible for the individual to make copious use of these fully developed potentialities entirely as he pleases, insofar as they are not socially harmful, at least in his leisure hours, should the opportunity to do so be lacking during the economically necessary working hours. He can employ them either for productive work or merely for appreciative enjoyment in the various fields of science and art, in nature, or in play and sport. In this regard, socialism will offer a hitherto unheard of possibility of the free development of the individual personality. It will do so in a different sense than that for which some modern theorists of education and literati exert themselves so greatly, who encourage each individual to ascribe to himself the greatest importance, to be intent only on his own comfort, and to obey, without inhibition, every one of his drives. . . .

The fullest possible development of the capacities of individual personalities and the greatest possible freedom in the exercise of these capacities in a society without class antagonisms, in the advancement of which all its members have the same interest, must necessarily increase enormously the diversity and productivity of this society. . . . In intellectual and cultural life, in technology, and in the development of the individual, diversity will progress to an extent that will more than make up for all the effects of the elimination of differences among classes and races and the effects of the impoverishment of the wild part of organic nature. . . .

This advance cannot, of course, continue indefinitely. If up to now the progressive cooling of the solar system has resulted in the constant increase of the diversity of the phenomena in it and of the capabilities of the organisms on earth, then the further continuation of this process must, from a certain culminating point onward, cause development in the opposite direction. A long time before all life on earth becomes impossible, it will necessarily begin to atrophy and to become more uniform. Technological progress will not protect man against this, since the energy sources on earth will also necessarily decrease, while the dangers and the obstacles to life increase. . . .

For the time being, *[however,]* no end of human progress can be foreseen. Only the progress of man's artificial environment, however, is to be considered as unending in this sense. The further development of the human organism itself remains confined within narrow boundaries. . . . But ought not the new, more diverse environment react upon *[it]* and make it more varied and more capable than it was in its natural state? From our perspective, especially, this idea must suggest itself very readily. And it would be correct if man's newly and artificially created environment did not have the peculiar twofold character of being simultaneously both man's environment and his organ. His artificial organs and his environment increase simultaneously in diversity, reciprocally conditioning each other, by being at one time the means for the solution of problems and at another time the sources of new problems. With these artificial organs, though, man to all intents and purposes, bars the way to the further development of his natural organs, of his locomotive and sensory organs, which, thanks to artificial organs, he uses not to a greater degree, as in his natural state, but to a lesser one. . . .

Of one organ this not true, however: that . . . which cannot be replaced or perfected by any artificial organ, the organ of the mental functions, the *brain*. The more diverse are the demands made upon this organ, the more varied its functions are, the more diverse must his organ itself ultimately become. Since the days of Neanderthal man, the human brain has certainly developed greatly; it has grown in diversity. . . . But . . . the diversity of accumulated knowledge is growing so rapidly and is assuming such enormous proportions that it has been quite impossible for the human brain to adapt itself in its structure to this alteration of its environment during the relatively short time more advanced human civilization has existed. . . . As a consequence of the inability of the human brain to become more diverse, we find . . . that there is an ever-greater division of the totality of science into special sciences. Onesidedness, the narrow-mindedness of the specialist, is today the greatest danger for our intellectual life. . . .

To be sure, socialism will abolish the monotony of the present-day existence of the broad masses, it will open up to them the whole wealth of diversity contained in nature and culture. It will thereby give the most diverse forms to the functioning of the brains of the masses. Such a state of affairs can, if it operates without interruption through many generations, bring about a general advance in the development of the brain. But this development, too, will not be able to go beyond certain limits, as the hypertrophy of one organ causes other organs to atrophy and is detrimental to the harmony, health, and capabilities of the entire organism. The progress of society, of knowledge, of technology can proceed indefinitely. On the other hand, up to the present, there have been no indications and no reason to expect that the individual members of society will far exceed the measure of natural endowment already attained by the most advanced individuals. . . .

And we have just as little to expect from an elevation of the moral level of individuals, from which so many expect salvation from the troubles of our time. . . . In only one point do the changes in morality exhibit a marked direction. . . . With the progress of technology, the polity expands more and more, and commerce between the different polities grows, so that today, for the civilized peoples, all of humanity stands within the sphere of morality. On the other hand, the uniformity ceases that formerly prevailed within the polity. In it, there are formed families and gentes, occupations, guilds, churches, parties, and, what is more, classes. Each of these organizations and communities provides particular goals and characteristics for man's social drives.

The growing diversity and extent of the domain of the social drives could be regarded as a higher development of morality, if it were associated with an increase in the effectiveness of morality. That is not the case, however. ... The greater the complexity of society becomes, the more difficult does it become to satisfy all the demands of the organizations and communities in it, the interests of which do not always coincide. This is aggravated in the extreme once class antagonisms make their appearance within the polity and, on the other hand, great, universal interests of humanity begin to gain recognition over and above the antagonisms within the polity. ... No era has ever been as rich in internal moral conflicts as our own. When class and national antagonisms have been overcome, many of these conflicts will disappear. But we have no reason to expect that we will thereby achieve a higher morality than the one that has been a part of human nature from its beginnings. ...

Some of my readers will hardly find a conception of history satisfactory that expects unending progress of knowledge and of technology, but not of morality. The needs of the heart, of feelings, they will say, are not met by such a sober outlook. It is too cheerless. ... We assume that the necessary ethical impulses that humanity needs to emancipate itself are not to be acquired only through a process of moral purification, of which there is as yet no evidence. They have always, naturally, existed in men and they are ready to develop fully once the rubble has been removed with which the interregnum of the age of exploitation has covered them over and impeded them, ... once the economic foundations for more advanced forms of social living have been acquired. ...

Of course, our attitude toward a scientific conception must not depend on whether it is consoling or not, but only on whether the facts known to us require that we recognize this conception as correct or not. Science is not religion; its task is not to provide consolation, but truth. And it must proclaim the truth even when it causes us pain. To that extent, then, science is not spared from appearing to be cold, unfeeling, and heartless. The thinker certainly cannot free himself from moral sentiments. He needs a strong moral feeling of duty in order to search indefatigably for the truth and undauntedly to proclaim it even if it does injury to strong interests and inclinations. But this very moral duty to seek the truth must make the scientific researcher insensitive to all other needs and desires that could intrude into science as a disruptive source of error. That duty must, of course, reject all consideration for unethical needs and wants, but must also not let itself be guided by ethical ones, if these are opposed to the truth.

If, however, the research of such a science without heart and without feelings yields results that are not depressing in their effect but edifying, then these must necessarily have a much more encouraging effect on us and arouse much longer lasting enthusiasm than illusions born merely of our emotional needs, the incompatibility of which with our environment soon becomes evident. Thus, the "purely economic" materialist conception of history, which is so heartless and so devoid of all ethical verve, has been able, from its first expressions eighty years ago down to the present day, to call forth in the proletarian masses a more lasting enthusiasm for the struggle for the emancipation of mankind than any other theory before it or any that has existed alongside it. The principal task of scientific knowledge, though, is not that of awakening enthusiasm. The deepest source of all volition and of all enthusiasm is to be found in our innate drives. Scientific knowledge cannot produce enthusiasm, but it can certainly cause the enthusiasm arising out of emotional needs and desires to flame up brightly or it can smother it, depending on whether it shows the goals of that enthusiasm to be attainable or proves the opposite.

The principal task of knowledge is not that of achieving ethical effects, but that of making it possible for men to find their way in the environment that surrounds them and besets them. That is also the principal task of the materialist conception of history. For eighty years, it has enabled those fighting for the emancipation of humanity to employ at any given time the methods and means best suited to that end, without illusions always to set themselves only tasks that can be accomplished. Not everyone, of course, who professes the Marxist conception of history is also capable of properly applying it. But whoever does so as a zealous seeker of the truth, "heartlessly, unfeelingly," without letting himself be blinded by inner or outer needs or wants, such as the desire for power, to him it will bring a rich yield, both in theory and in practice. For the progress of society, of the science of society, and of the organization of society, the materialist conception of history has proved to be our most powerful aid. It teaches us best not merely to *understand* previous history, but also to *make* future history, without any mysticism and equally far removed from passively waiting for future events and from impatient tugging at the chains of necessity in order to skip unavoidable phases of historical development and to do violence to its course.

Bibliography

I. Works by Karl Kautsky

Die Agrarfrage. Hannover: J. H. W. Dietz, 1966. English translation: *The Agrarian Question,* London: Zwan Publications; Madison: University of Wisconsin Press, 1988.

"Die Aktion der Masse." *Die Neue Zeit,* XXX/1 (1911), 43–49, 77–84, 106–17.

"Allerhand Revolutionäres." *Die Neue Zeit,* XXII/1 (1904), 588–98, 620–27, 652–57, 685–95, 732–40.

"Ältere und neuere Kolonialpolitik." *Die Neue Zeit,* XVI/1 (1898), 769–81, 801–16.

"Der amerikanische Arbeiter." *Die Neue Zeit,* XXIV/1 (1906), 676–83, 717–27, 740–52, 773–87.

Are the Jews a Race? New York: International Publishers, 1926. Reprint. Westport, Conn.: Greenwood Press, 1972.

"Die Aussichten der russischen Revolution." *Die Neue Zeit,* XXXV/2 (1917), 9–20.

"Die Aussichten des Sozialismus in Sowjetrussland." *Die Gesellschaft* (Berlin), VIII/2 (1931), 420–44.

"Die Bauern und die Revolution in Russland." *Die Neue Zeit,* XXIII/1 (1905), 670–77.

Die Befreiung der Nationen. 4th ed. Stuttgart: J. H. W. Dietz, 1918.

"Die Bergarbeiter und der Bauernkrieg, vornehmlich in Thüringen." *Die Neue Zeit,* VII (1889), 289–97, 337–50, 410–17, 443–53, 507–15.

Bernstein und das sozialdemokratische Programm. Eine Anti-Kritik. 3rd ed. Bonn: J. H. W. Dietz, 1979.

"Bernstein und die Dialektik." *Die Neue Zeit,* XVII/2 (1899), 36–50.

"Bernstein und die materialistische Geschichtsauffassung." *Die Neue Zeit,* XVII/2 (1899), 4–16.

Bolshevism at a Deadlock. London: Allen & Unwin, 1931.

"Die chinesischen Eisenbahnen und das europäische Proletariat." *Die Neue Zeit,* IV (1886), 515–25, 529–49.

The Class Struggle. New York: W. W. Norton, 1971.

Communism in Central Europe in the Time of the Reformation. New York: A. M. Kelley, 1966.

"Darwin und der Sozialismus." *Die Gleichheit* (Wiener-Neustadt), October 16, 23 and 31 and

November 6, 1875; also in *Der Volksfreund* (Brünn/Brno), October 15 and 29, and November 12, 1981.

Delbrück und Wilhelm II. Berlin: Neues Vaterland, 1920.

"De Man als Lehrer." *Die Gesellschaft* (Berlin), IV/1 (1927), 62–77.

The Dictatorship of the Proletariat. Ann Arbor: University of Michigan Press, 1964. Reprint. Westport, Conn.: Greenwood Press, 1981.

"Die Differenzen unter den russischen Sozialisten." *Die Neue Zeit*, XXIII/2 (1905), 68–79.

"Die Diktatur des Proletariats." *Der Kampf* (Vienna), XXVI (1933), 437–46.

"Drei kleine Schriften über Marx." *Archiv für die Geschichte des Sozialismus und der Arbeiterbewegung* (Leipzig), VIII (1919), 314–29.

"The Driving Force of Social Evolution." *New Leader* (New York), I, no. 31 (June 30, 1928), p. 4, and no. 32 (July 7, 1928), pp. 4–5.

The Economic Doctrines of Karl Marx. New York: Macmillan, 1936. Reprint. Westport, Conn.: Hyperion Press, 1979.

Der Einfluss der Volksvermehrung auf den Fortschritt der Gesellschaft. Vienna: Bloch & Hasbach, 1880.

"Einige Ursachen und Wirkungen des deutschen Nationalsozialismus." *Der Kampf* (Vienna), XXVI (1933), 235–45.

Elsass-Lothringen. 3rd ed. Stuttgart: J. H. W. Dietz, 1919.

"Die Entstehung der biblischen Urgeschichte." *Kosmos* (Stuttgart), VII (1883), 201–14.

"Die Entstehung der Ehe und Familie." *Kosmos* (Stuttgart), VI (1882), 190–207, 256–72, 329–48.

"Die Entstehung des Christenthums." *Die Neue Zeit*, III (1885), 481–99, 529–45.

"Der Entwurf des neuen Parteiprogramms." *Die Neue Zeit*, IX/2 (1891), 723–30, 749–58, 780–91, 814–27.

"Entwurf einer Entwicklungsgeschichte der Menschheit" (1876). In Karl Kautsky, *Die materialistische Geschichtsauffassung*. 2nd ed. Berlin: J. H. W. Dietz, 1929. I, 155–65.

Erinnerungen und Erörterungen. The Hague: Mouton & Co., 1960.

Ethics and the Materialist Conception of History. 4th rev. ed. Chicago: Chas. H. Kerr, 1918. Photocopy: Ann Arbor: University Microfilms International, 1977.

"Eine ethisch-ästhetische Geschichte der Pariser Kommune." *Die Neue Zeit*, XXIV/2 (1906), 351–60.

"Expropriation und Konfiskation." *Der Sozialist* (Berlin), no. 47, November 22, 1918.

"Die Fabel von der Naturnotwendigkeit des Krieges." In *Der internationale Kapitalismus und die Krise*, edited by Siegfried v. Kardorff & al. Stuttgart: Ferdinand Enke, 1932. Pp. 132–50.

"Finanzkapital und Krisen." *Die Neue Zeit*, XXIX/1 (1911), 764–72, 797–804, 838–46, 874–83.

Foundations of Christianity. New York: Monthly Review Press, 1972.

Friedrich Engels. Sein Leben, sein Wirken, seine Schriften. 2nd rev. ed. Berlin: Buchhandlung Vorwärts, 1908.

"Die Gemeinsamkeit des sozialdemokratischen und des kommunistischen Endziels." *Tribüne* (Prague), I (1928), 73–75. Reprinted in *Kautsky gegen Lenin*, edited by Peter Lübbe. Bonn: J. H. W. Dietz, 1981. Pp. 134–38.

Georgia, A Social-Democratic Peasant Republic. London: International Bookshops, 1921.

"Georgien und seine Henker." *Die Gesellschaft* (Berlin), VII/1 (1930), 241–58.

Grenzen der Gewalt. (Anonymously published) Karlsbad: Graphia, 1934.

"Grundsätze oder Pläne?" *Die Neue Zeit*, XXIV/2 (1906), 781–88.

"Grundsätzlicher Teil." In *Das Heidelberger Programm*, edited by Paul Kampffmeyer. Berlin: J. H. W. Dietz, 1925. Pp. 5–26. Reprinted in *Texte zu den Programmen der deutschen Sozialdemokratie, 1891–1925*, pp. 277–328.

The Guilt of William Hohenzollern. London: Skeffington, 1920.

"Gustav Mayers Engels-Biographie." *Archiv für die Geschichte des Sozialismus und der Arbeiterbewegung* (Leipzig), IX (1920), 342–55.

Habsburgs Glück und Ende. Berlin: Cassirer, 1918.

Handelspolitik und Sozialdemokratie. Berlin: Vorwärts, 1901.
Die historische Leistung von Karl Marx. 2nd ed. Berlin: Vorwärts, 1919.
"Hitlerism and Social-Democracy." In *Socialism, Fascism, Communism,* edited by Joseph Shaplen and David Shub. New York: American League for Democratic Socialism, 1934. Pp. 53–102.
"Der Imperialismus." *Die Neue Zeit,* XXXII/2 (1914), 908–22.
"Der imperialistische Krieg." *Die Neue Zeit,* XXXV/1 (1917), 449–54, 475–87.
"Die Intelligenz und die Sozialdemokratie." *Die Neue Zeit,* XIII/2 (1895), 10–16, 43–49, 74–80.
Die Internationale (title on the cover: *Vergangenheit und Zukunft der Internationale*). Vienna: Wiener Volksbuchhandlung, 1920.
Die Internationale und Sowjetrussland. Berlin: J. H. W. Dietz, 1925.
Die Internationalität und der Krieg. Berlin: Vorwärts, 1915.
"Der jüngste Radikalismus." *Die Neue Zeit,* XXXI/1 (1912), 436–46.
"Kannibalische Ethik." *Die Neue Zeit,* XXV/1 (1907), 860–69.
"Karl Kautsky." In *Die Volkswirtschaftslehre der Gegenwart in Selbstdarstellungen,* edited by Felix Meiner. Leizpig: Felix Meiner Verlag, 1924. I, 117–53. Reprinted as "Mein Lebenswerk" in *Ein Leben für den Sozialismus. Erinnerungen an Karl Kautsky* edited by Benedikt Kautsky. Hannover: J. H. W. Dietz, 1954, pp. 11–34.
Kautsky gegen Lenin, edited by Peter Lübbe. Bonn: J. H. W. Dietz, 1981.
"Klassendiktatur und Parteidiktatur." *Der Kampf* (Vienna), XIV (1921), 271–81.
Die Klassengegensätze im Zeitalter der Französischen Revolution. Stuttgart: J. H. W. Dietz, 1919. 1st ed. of 1889 entitled *Die Klassengegensätze von 1789.*
"Klasseninteresse—Sonderinteresse—Gemeininteresse." *Die Neue Zeit,* XXI/2 (1903), 240–45, 261–74.
Kriegsmarxismus (in *Marx-Studien,* IV/2). Vienna: Wiener Volksbuchhandlung, 1918).
"Kriegssitten." *Die Neue Zeit;* XXXIII/1 (1915), 65–76, 97–109.
Krieg und Demokratie. Berlin: J. H. W. Dietz, 1932.
"Krisentheorien." *Die Neue Zeit,* XX/2 (1902), 37–47, 76–81, 110–18, 133–43.
"Kunst und Kultur," *Zeitschrift für Plastik* (Vienna), IV (1884), nos. 9, 10, 12; V (1885), nos. 1, 3, 4, 5, 7, 8.
The Labour Revolution. New York: Dial Press, 1925.
"Lombroso und sein Vertheidiger." *Die Neue Zeit,* XII/2 (1894), 241–50.
"Marxism and Bolshevism—Democracy and Dictatorship."In *Socialism, Fascism, Communism,* edited by Joseph Shaplen and David Shub. New York: American League for Democratic Socialism, 1934. Pp. 174–215.
Die Marxsche Staatsauffassung im Spiegelbild eines Marxisten. Jena: Thüringer Verlagsanstalt, 1923.
"Marx und Marxismus." *Die Gesellschaft* (Berlin), X (1933), 181–200.
Die materialistische Geschichtsauffassung. 2 vols. 2nd ed. Berlin: J. H. W. Dietz, 1929.
"Die materialistische Geschichtsauffassung und der psychologische Antrieb." *Die Neue Zeit,* XIV/2 (1896), 652–59.
"Ein materialistischer Historiker." *Die Neue Zeit,* I (1883), 537–47.
Materialistyczne pojmowanie dziejów. Warsaw: Ksiaźka i Wiedza, 1963.
"Die moderne Nationalität." *Die Neue Zeit,* V (1887), 392–405, 442–51.
Nationalität und Internationalität. (Ergänzungsheft zur *Neuen Zeit*). Stuttgart: Paul Singer, 1908.
Nationalstaat, imperialistischer Staat und Staatenbund. Nürnberg: Fränkische Verlagsanstalt, 1915.
"Eine Naturgeschichte des politischen Verbrechers." *Die Neue Zeit,* XI/2 (1893), 69–77.
"Natur und Gesellschaft." *Die Gesellschaft* (Berlin), VI/2 (1929), 481–505.
"Der neue Liberalismus und der neue Mittelstand." *Vorwärts* (Berlin), no. 47, February 25, 1912.
Neue Programme. Vienna: A. Prager, 1933.
"Eine neue Strategie." *Die Neue Zeit,* XXVIII/2 (1910), 332–41, 364–74, 412–21.
"Die neue Taktik." *Die Neue Zeit,* XXX/2 (1912), 654–64, 688–98, 723–33.

"Nochmals unsere Illusionen." *Die Neue Zeit*, XXXIII/2 (1915), 230–41, 264–75.

Outbreak of the World War. German documents collected by Karl Kautsky and edited by Max Montgelas and Walther Schücking. New York: Oxford University Press, 1924.

Parlamentarismus und Demokratie. 3rd ed. Stuttgart: J. H. W. Dietz, 1920. 1st ed. of 1893 entitled *Der Parlamentarismus, die Volksgesetzgebung und die Sozialdemokratie*.

Der politische Massenstreik. Berlin: Vorwärts, 1914.

"Positive Arbeit und Revolution." *Die Neue Zeit*, XXVII/2 (1909), 324–37.

Die proletarische Revolution und ihr Programm. Stuttgart: J. H. W. Dietz, 1922.

"Reform und Revolution." *Die Neue Zeit*, XXVII/1 (1908), 180–91, 220–32, 253–59.

"Religion." *Die Neue Zeit*, XXXII/1 (1913), 182–88, 352–60.

"Republik und Sozialdemokratie in Frankreich." *Die Neue Zeit*, XXIII/1 (1904–05), 260–70, 300–09, 332–41, 363–71, 397–414, 436–49, 467–81.

Richtlinien für ein sozialistisches Aktionsprogramm. Berlin: J. Sittenfeld, 1919.

The Road to Power. Chicago: Samuel A. Bloch, 1909.

Rosa Luxemburg, Karl Liebknecht, Leo Jogiches. Berlin: Freiheit, 1921.

"Samuel Gompers." *Die Neue Zeit*, XXVII/2 (1909), 677–85.

"Eine Selbstanzeige." *Rote Revue* (Zürich), VII (1928), 161–67.

Selected Political Writings, edited by Patrick Goode. London: Macmillan, 1983.

Serbien und Belgien in der Geschichte. Stuttgart: J. H. W. Dietz, 1917.

"Sklaverei und Kapitalismus." *Die Neue Zeit*, XXIX/2 (1911), 713–25.

Social Democracy versus Communism. New York: Rand School Press, 1946. Reprint. Westport, Conn.: Hyperion Press, 1979.

Socialism and Colonial Policy. Belfast: Athol Books, 1975.

The Social Revolution. Chicago: Chas H. Kerr, 1916. Reprint. Ann Arbor: University Microfilms International, 1978.

Die Sozialdemokratie und die katholische Kirche. 3rd ed. Hamburg: Phönix Verlag, 1947.

Sozialdemokratische Bemerkungen zur Uebergangswirtschaft. Leipzig: Leipziger Buchdruckerei, 1918.

"Ein sozialdemokratischer Katechismus." *Die Neue Zeit*, XII/1 (1893), 361–69, 402–10.

"Die sozialen Triebe in der Menschenwelt." *Die Neue Zeit*, II (1884), 13–19, 49–59, 118–25. Reprinted in Karl Kautsky, *Die materialistische Geschichtsauffassung*. 2nd ed. Berlin: J. H. W. Dietz, 1929. I, 442–75.

"Die sozialen Triebe in der Tierwelt." *Die Neue Zeit*, I (1883), 20–27, 67–73. Reprinted in Karl Kautsky, *Die materialistische Geschichtsauffassung*, 2nd ed. Berlin: J. H. W. Dietz, 1929. I, 424–41.

Die Sozialisierung der Landwirtschaft. Berlin: Paul Cassirer, 1921.

Sozialisten und Krieg. Prague: Orbis, 1937.

"Stockholm," *Die Neue Zeit*, XXXV/2 (1917), 505–12.

Terrorism and Communism. London: National Labour Press, 1920. Reprint. Westport, Conn: Hyperion Press, 1973.

Texte zu den Programmen der deutschen Sozialdemokratie, 1891–1925, edited by Albrecht Langner. Cologne: Jakob Hegner, 1968.

Thomas More and His Utopia. London: Lawrence & Wishart, 1979.

"Triebkräfte und Aussichten der russischen Revolution." *Die Neue Zeit*, XXV/1 (1906), 284–90, 324–33.

Ueberzeugung und Partei. Leipzig: Leipzer Buchdruckerei, 1916.

"Utopistischer und materialistischer Marxismus." *Die Neue Zeit*, XV/1 (1897), 716–27.

Die Vereinigten Staaten Mitteleuropas, Stuttgart: J. H. W. Dietz, 1916.

"Verelendung und Zusammenbruch." *Die Neue Zeit*, XXVI/2 (1908), 540–51, 607–12.

Vermehrung und Entwicklung in Natur und Gesellschaft. 3rd ed. Stuttgart: J. H. W. Dietz, 1921.

Die Vernichtung der Sozialdemokratie durch den Gelehrten des Zentralverbandes deutscher Industrieller. 2nd. rev. ed. Berlin: Vorwärts, 1911.

Von der Demokratie zur Staats-Sklaverei. Berlin: Freiheit, 1921.

Vorläufer des neueren Sozialismus. Bonn: J. H. W. Dietz, vol. I, 8th ed., 1976; vol. II, 9th ed., 1976.

Was ist Sozialisierung? 2nd ed. Berlin: Freiheit, 1920.

"Was nun?" *Die Neue Zeit,* XXVIII/2 (1910), 33–40, 68–80.

"Was uns Axelrod gab." *Die Gesellschaft* (Berlin), II/2 (1925), 117–25.

"Was will und kann die materialistische Geschichsauffassung leisten?" *Die Neue Zeit,* XV/1 (1896), 213–18, 228–38, 260–71.

Wehrfrage und Sozialdemokratie. Berlin: J. H. W. Dietz, 1928.

Die Wurzeln der Politik Wilsons. Berlin: Neues Vaterland, 1919.

"Die zivilisierte Welt und der Zar." *Die Neue Zeit,* XXIII/1 (1905), 614–17.

"Zwei Schriften zum Umlernen." *Die Neue Zeit,* XXXIII/2 (1915), 33–42, 71–81, 107–16, 138–46.

"Zwischen Baden und Luxemburg." *Die Neue Zeit,* XXVIII/2 (1910), 652–67.

II. Works by Karl Marx and Frederick Engels

MESW refers to Karl Marx and Frederick Engels, *Selected Works in Three Volumes.* Moscow: Progress Publishers, 1969.

A. ENGELS

Herr Eugen Dühring's Revolution in Science (Anti-Dühring). New York: International Publishers, 1966.

"Introduction to *Dialectics of Nature.*" In *MESW,* III, 41–57.

"Introduction" (of 1891) to Karl Marx, *The Civil War in France.* In *MESW,* II, 178–89.

Letter to J. Bloch. In *MESW,* III, 487–89.

Letter to W. Borgius (Heinz Starkenburg). In MESW, III, 502–04.

Ludwig Feuerbach and the End of Classical German Philosophy. In *MESW,* III, 335–76.

"On the History of the Communist League." In *MESW,* III, 173–90.

The Origin of the Family, Private Property and the State. In *MESW,* III, 191–334.

"The Part Played by Labour in the Transition from Ape to Man." In *MESW,* III, 66–77.

B. MARX

"The Marx Library" (New York: Vintage Books) consists of the following eight volumes, some of which are referred to by their abbreviated titles below.

Early Writings. 1975.

The Revolutions of 1848. Political Writings Volume I. 1974.

Surveys from Exile. Political Writings Volume II. 1974.

The First International and After. Political Writings Volume III. 1974.

Grundrisse. Foundations of the Critique of Political Economy. 1973.

Capital. A Critique of Political Economy. 3 vols. 1977, 1981.

Capital, "Part VIII: The So-Called Primitive Accumulation." In *MESW,* II, 100–45.

The Civil War in France. In *The First International and After,* pp. 187–236, and in *MESW,* II, 178–244.

A Contribution to the Critique of Political Economy. Moscow: Progress Publishers, 1977.

Critique of the Gotha Program. In *The First International and After,* pp. 339–59, and in *MESW,* III, 13–30.

Economic and Philosophical Manuscripts. In *Early Writings,* pp. 279–400.

The Eighteenth Brumaire of Louis Bonaparte. In *Surveys from Exile,* pp. 143–249, and in *MESW,* I, 394–487.

The Inaugural Address of the International Working Men's Association. In *The First International and After,* pp. 73–81, and in *MESW,* II, 11–18.

Das Kapital. "Volksausgabe." 3 vols. I, Stuttgart: J. H. W. Dietz, 1914. II, Berlin: J.H.W. Dietz, 1926. III, Berlin: J. H. W. Dietz, 1929.

"The Leading Article in No. 179 of the *Kölnische Zeitung,*" *Rheinische Zeitung,* July 14, 1842. In Karl Marx, Frederick Engels, *Collected Works.* New York: International Publishers, 1975. I, 195–202.

Letter to L. Kugelmann. In *MESW,* II, 420–21.

"Preface to *A Contribution to the Critique of Political Economy.*" In *Early Writings,* pp. 424–28, and in *MESW,* I, 502–06.

"Provisional Rules of the First International." In *The First International and After,* pp. 82–84, and, as amended, in *MESW,* II, 19–21.

"Provisorische Statuten der Internationalen Arbeiter-Assoziation." In Karl Marx and Friedrich Engels, *Werke.* East Berlin: Dietz Verlag, 1964. XVI, 14–16.

Theorien über den Mehrwert. 3 vols. 5th ed. Stuttgart: J. H. W. Dietz, 1923.

Theories of Surplus Value. 3 vols. London: Lawrence & Wishart, 1967–72.

"Theses on Feuerbach." In *Early Writings,* pp. 421–23, and in *MESW,* I, 13–15.

C. MARX AND ENGELS

Collected Works. New York: International Publishers, 1975–.

The German Ideology, chapter 1. In *MESW,* I, 16–80.

The Holy Family. In Karl Marx, Frederick Engels, *Collected Works.* New York: International Publishers, 1975. IV, 5–211.

Manifesto of the Communist Party. In *The Revolutions of 1848,* pp. 62–98, and in *MESW,* I, 98–137.

Selected Works in Three Volumes. Moscow: Progress Publishers, 1969.

Werke. 42 vols. East Berlin: Dietz Verlag, 1956–83.

III. *Other Works*

Writings marked with an asterisk are cited only in the Editor's Introduction. All others are cited by Karl Kautsky (or contain writings by him or cited by him), except that more recent editions and English translations have been substituted wherever possible.

Adler, Friedrich. *Ernst Machs Überwindung des mechanischen Materialismus.* Vienna: Brand, 1918.

Adler, Max. Article on Kant's 200th birthday. *Arbeiter-Zeitung* (Vienna), April 22, 1924.

———. *Marxistische Probleme.* 6th ed. Bonn: J. H. W. Dietz, 1974.

———. *Die Staatsauffassung des Marxismus (Marx-Studien, IV/2).* Vienna: Wiener Volksbuchhandlung, 1922. Reprint. Darmstadt: Wissenchaftliche Buchgesellschaft, 1973.

Alverdes, Friedrich. *Social Life in the Animal World.* London: Kegan Paul, Trench, Trubner, 1927.

*Anderson, Perry. *Arguments within English Marxism.* London: New Left Books, 1980.

Aristotle's Constitution of Athens. New York: Hafner, 1950.

Aristotle. *The Politics* (Lord edition). Chicago: University of Chicago Press, 1984.

Avebury, John Lubbock, Lord. *The Origin of Civilization and the Primitive Condition of Man.* Chicago: University of Chicago Press, 1978.

———. *Pre-Historic Times.* 6th rev. ed. New York: D. Appleton, 1900.

Bachofen, Johann Jakob. *Das Mutterrecht.* 3rd ed. Basel: B. Schwabe, 1948.

———. *Myth, Religion and Mother Right. Selected Writings of J. J. Bachofen* Princeton: Princeton University Press, 1967.

Bauer, Otto. *Nationalitätenfrage und Sozialdemokratie.* Vol. 1 of Otto Bauer, *Werkausgabe.* 9 vols. Vienna: Europa Verlag, 1984.

———. "Das Weltbild des Kapitalismus." In Otto Bauer, *Werkausgabe*. 9 vols. Vienna: Europa Verlag, 1976. II, 887–933.

Beetham, David, ed. *Marxists in face of Fascism*. Totowa, N.J.: Barnes & Noble, 1984.

Beloch, Karl Julius. *Griechische Geschichte*. 4 vols. 2nd rev. ed. Strassburg: K. J. Trübner, 1912–27. Reprint. Berlin: de Gruyter, 1967.

Bernstein, Eduard. *Evolutionary Socialism*. New York: Schocken Books, 1963.

Billroth, Theodor. *Wer ist musikalisch?* 4th ed. Berlin: Paetel, 1912.

*Blumenberg, Werner. *Karl Kautskys literarisches Werk. Eine bibliographische Übersicht*. The Hague: Mouton, 1960.

Boas, Franz. *The Mind of Primitive Man*. New York: Macmillan, 1911.

Bogdanoff, A. [A. A. Malinovskii]. *Die Entwicklungsformen der Gesellschaft und die Wissenschaft*. Berlin: Nike Verlag, 1924.

Bottomore, Tom, and Patrick Goode, eds. *Readings in Marxist Sociology*. Oxford: Clarendon Press, 1983.

Braunthal, Alfred. *Karl Marx als Geschichtsphilosoph*. Berlin: P. Cassirer, 1920.

———. "Kautskys materialistische Geschichtstheorie." *Die Gesellschaft* (Berlin), V/1 (1928), 193–212.

Brehm, Alfred. *Tierleben*. 10 vols. 2nd ed. Leipzig: Bibliographisches Institut, 1876–79. Numerous complete and abridged revised editions have been published.

*Brill, Hermann. "Karl Kautsky." *Zeitschrift für Politik* (Berlin), I (Neue Folge) (1954), 211–40.

*Bronner, Stephen Eric. "Karl Kautsky and the Twilight of Orthodoxy." *Political Theory*, X (1982), 580–605.

Bücher, Karl. *Arbeit und Rhythmus*. 6th rev. ed. Leipzig: E. Reinicke, 1924.

———. *Die Aufstände der unfreien Arbeiter, 143–129 v. Chr.* Frankfurt am Main: J. D. Sauerländer, 1874.

———. "Volkswirtschaftliche Entwicklungsstufen." In S. Altmann & al. *Grundriss der Sozialökonomik*. Vol. I: K. Bücher & al. *Wirtschaft und Wirtschaftswissenschaft*. 2nd ed. Tübingen: J. C. B. Mohr. 1924.

Buckle, Henry Thomas. *History of Civilization in England*. 2 vols. From the 2nd London ed. New York: Appleton-Century, 1934.

Bukharin, Nikolai. *Historical Materialism*. Ann Arbor: University of Michigan Press, 1969.

Catlin, George, *North American Indians*. 2 vols. London: Chatto & Windus, 1876.

Chamberlain, Houston Stewart. *Foundations of the Nineteenth Century*. 2 vols. London: John Lane, 1914.

*Cole, G. D. H. *A History of Socialist Thought*. 5 vols. London: St. Martin's Press, 1953–60.

Cunow, Heinrich. *Allgemeine Wirtschaftsgeschichte*. 2 vols. Berlin: J. H. W. Dietz, 1926–27.

———. *Die Marxsche Geschichts-, Gesellschafts- und Staatstheorie*. 2 vols. 4th ed. Berlin: J. H. W. Dietz, 1923.

———. *Die soziale Verfassung des Inkareiches*. Stuttgart: J. H. W. Dietz, 1896.

Daniels, Emil. *Geschichte des Kriegswesens*. 7 vols. Leipzig: G. J. Göschen, 1910–13.

Darwin, Charles. *The Origin of Species and The Descent of Man*. New York: Modern Library, 1936.

Davids, T. W. Rhys. *Buddhism, being a Sketch of the Life and Teachings of Gautama, the Buddha*. London: Society for Promoting Christian Knowledge, 1894.

Delbrück, Hans. *History of the Art of War*. 3 vols. Westport, Conn.: Greenwood Press, 1975.

———. *Weltgeschichte. Vorlesungen gehalten an der Universität Berlin 1896/1920*. 5 vols. Berlin: Stollberg, 1924–28.

de Man, Henry. *The Psychology of Marxian Socialism*. New Brunswick, N.J.: Transaction Press, 1985.

———. *Zur Psychologie des Sozialismus*. Jena: Eugen Diederichs, 1926.

Dilthey, Wilhelm. *Einleitung in die Geisteswissenschaften*. Vol. I (Gesammelte Schriften, I). 8th ed. Göttingen: Vandenhoeck & Ruprecht, 1979.

Diodorus of Sicily. Translated by C.H. Oldfather. 12 vols. London: Wm. Heinemann, 1968.

Dodge, Richard Irving. *The Plains of the Great West and Their Inhabitants.* New York: G. P. Putnam, 1877.

Doflein, Franz. *Das Tier als Glied des Naturganzen.* Leipzig: B. G. Teubner, 1914.

Drumann, W. *Die Arbeiter und Communisten in Griechenland und Rom.* Königsberg: Bornträger, 1860. Reprint. Amsterdam: Liberac, 1968.

Dümichen, Johannes. *Geschichte des alten Aegyptens.* Berlin: G. Grote, 1879.

Espinas, Alfred. *Des Sociétés Animales.* Paris: Baillière, 1878. Reprint. New York: Arno Press, 1977.

Ferguson, Adam. *An Essay on the History of Civil Society.* New Brunswick, N.J.: Transaction Press, 1980.

*Freud, Sigmund. *Civilization and its Discontents.* In *The Standard Edition of the Complete Psychological Works of Sigmund Freud.* 24 vols. London: Hogarth Press, 1953–74. XXI, 64–145.

———. *Group Psychology and the Analysis of the Ego.* In *The Standard Edition of the Complete Psychological Works of Sigmund Freud.* 24 vols. London: Hogarth Press, 1953–74. XVIII, 69–143.

———. *Totem and Taboo. Some Points of Agreement between the Mental Lives of Savages and Neurotics.* In *The Standard Edition of the Complete Psychological Works of Sigmund Freud.* 24 vols. London: Hogarth Press, 1953–74. XIII, 1–161.

Frobenius, Leo. *Vom Schreibtisch zum Aequator.* Frankfurt: Frankfurter Societäts-Druckerei, 1925.

*Geary, Dick. *Karl Kautsky.* Manchester: Manchester University Press, 1987.

*Geary, Richard J. "Difesa e deformazione del marxismo in Kautsky." In Istituto Giangiacomo Feltrinelli, *Annali* (Milan), XV (1973), 81–106.

*———. "Karl Kautsky and German Marxism." In *Rediscoveries,* edited by John A. Hall. Oxford: Clarendon Press, 1986.

Geiger, Lazarus. *Ursprung und Entwicklung der menschlichen Sprache und Vernunft.* 2 vols. Stuttgart: J. G. Cotta, 1868. Reprint. Frankfurt: Minerva, 1977.

Gibbon, Edward. *The Decline and Fall of the Roman Empire.* 3 vols. New York: Modern Library, 1946.

*Gilcher-Holtey, Ingrid. *Das Mandat des Intellektuellen. Karl Kautsky und die Sozialdemokratie.* Berlin: Siedler Verlag, 1986.

Gobineau, Count Joseph Arthur de. *Essay sur l'inégalité des races humaines.* 2 vols. Paris: Firmin-Didot, 1940.

Goethe, J. W. *Conversations with Eckermann (1823–1832).* Translated by John Oxenford. San Francisco: North Point Press, 1984.

Goldstein, Julius. *Rasse und Politik.* 3rd ed. Berlin: Philo Verlag, 1924.

Goode, Patrick, ed. *Karl Kautsky: Selected Political Writings.* London: Macmillan, 1983.

Grosse, Ernst. *Die Formen der Familie und die Formen der Wirtschaft.* Freiburg im Breisgau: J. C. B. Mohr, 1896.

Grunenberg, Antonia, ed. *Die Massenstreikdebatte.* Frankfurt: Europäische Verlagsanstalt, 1970.

Gumplowicz, Ludwig. *Der Rassenkampf (Ausgewählte Werke, III).* Innsbruck: Universitäts-Verlag Wagner, 1929. Reprint. Aalen: Scientia, 1973.

Gutmann, Bruno. *Das Recht der Dschagga.* Munich: Beck, 1926.

Haiser, Franz. *Freimaurer und Gegenmaurer im Kampfe um die Weltherrschaft.* Munich: J. F. Lehmann, 1924.

*Hall, John A., ed. *Rediscoveries.* Oxford: Clarendon Press, 1986.

Hauser, Otto. *Der Mensch vor 100,000 Jahren.* Leipzig: F. A. Brockhaus, 1917.

Heeren, Arnold H. L. *Historical Researches into the Politics, Intercourse, and Trade of the Principal Nations of Antiquity.* 2 vols. London: Henry G. Bohn, 1866.

Hegel, Georg Wilhelm Friedrich. *The Philosophy of History.* New York: Dover Publications, 1956.

Hegel's Philosophy of Right. Oxford: Clarendon Press, 1958.

Helmholtz, Hermann von. *On the Sensations of Tone as a Physiological Basis for the Theory of Music*. New York: Dover Publications, 1954.

Herder, Johann Gottfried von. *Outlines of a Philosophy of the History of Man*. New York: Bergman, 1966.

Herodotus. Translated by J. Enoch Powell. 2 vols. Oxford: Clarendon Press, 1949.

Hildebrand, Richard. *Recht und Sitte auf den verschiedenen wirtschaftlichen Kulturstufen*. Jena: G. Fischer, 1896.

Hilferding, Rudolf. *Finance Capital*. London: Routledge & Kegan Paul, 1981.

Hodgskin, Thomas. *Labour Defended against the Claims of Capital*. New York: A. M. Kelley, 1963.

*Holzheuer, Walter. *Karl Kautskys Werk als Weltanschauung*. Munich: C. H. Beck, 1972.

Hook, Sidney. *Marx and the Marxists*. Malabar, Fla.: Krieger, 1982.

*Hünlich, Reinhold. *Karl Kautsky und der Marxismus der II. Internationale*. Marburg: Verlag Arbeiterbewegung und Gesellschaftswissenschaft, 1981.

*Irrlitz, Gerd. "Bemerkungen über die Einheit politischer und theoretischer Wesenszüge des Zentrismus in der deutschen Sozialdemokratie." *Beiträge zur Geschichte der deutschen Arbeiterbewegung* (East Berlin), VIII (1966), 43–59.

Jaurès, Jean. *Histoire socialiste de la Révolution française*. 7. vols. Paris: Éditions sociales, 1968–73.

Kampffmeyer, Paul, ed. *Das Heidelberger Programm*. Berlin: J. H. W. Dietz, 1925.

Kant, Immanuel. *The Critique of Judgement*. Oxford: Clarendon Press, 1952.

———. *The Critique of Practical Reason*. New York: Garland, 1976.

———. *The Critique of Pure Reason*. New York: St. Martin's Press, 1961.

———. "Idea of a Universal History from a Cosmopolitan Point of View." In *Kant's Principles of Politics*, edited by W. Hastie. Edinburgh: T. & T. Clark, 1891. Ann Arbor: University Microfilms, 1964. Pp. 1–29.

———. *Prolegomena to Any Future Metaphysics*. Indianapolis: Hackett, 1977.

Kardorff, Siegfried von, & al., eds. *Der internationale Kapitalismus und die Krise*. Stuttgart: Ferdinand Enke, 1932.

*Kautsky, Benedikt, ed. *Friedrich Engels' Briefwechsel mit Karl Kautsky*. Vienna: Danubia, 1955.

*———, ed. *Ein Leben für den Sozialismus. Erinnerungen an Karl Kautsky*. Hannover: J. H. W. Dietz, 1954.

*Kautsky, John H. "J. A. Schumpeter and Karl Kautsky: Parallel Theories of Imperialism." *Midwest Journal of Political Science*, V (1961), 101–28.

*———. "Karl Kautsky and Eurocommunism." *Studies in Comparative Communism*, XIV (1981), 3–44.

*———. "Kautsky, Karl." In *International Encyclopedia of the Social Sciences*. New York: Macmillan and Free Press, 1968. VIII, 356–58.

*———. *The Political Consequences of Modernization*. New York: John Wiley & Sons, 1972. Reprint. Huntington, NY: Krieger, 1980.

*———"The Political Thought of Karl Kautsky." Ph.D. diss. Cambridge: Harvard University, 1951.

*———. *The Politics of Aristocratic Empires*. Chapel Hill: University of North Carolina Press, 1982.

*Kolakowski, Leszek. *Main Currents of Marxism*. 3 vols. Oxford: Clarendon Press, 1978.

*Korsch, Karl. "Die materialistische Geschichtsauffassung. Eine Auseinandersetzung mit Karl Kautsky." In K. Korsch, *Die materialistische Geschichtsauffassung*. Frankfurt: Europäische Verlagsanstalt, 1971. Pp. 3–130.

Kropotkin, Peter. *Mutual Aid, A Factor of Evolution*. New York: New York University Press, 1972.

*Kupisch, Karl. "Einleitung." In Karl Kautsky, *Der Ursprung des Christentums*. 16th ed. Bonn: J. H. W. Dietz, 1977. Pp. vii–lii.

Labriola, Antonio. *Essays on the Materialist Conception of History*. Chicago: Chas. H. Kerr, 1908.

Lafargue, Paul. *Le déterminisme économique de Karl Marx*. Paris: M. Giard, 1928.

Laidler, Harry W., and Norman Thomas, eds. *The Socialism of our Time*. New York: Vanguard Press, 1929.

Lamarck, J. B. *Zoological Philosophy*. London: Macmillan, 1914.

Lange, Friedrich Albert. *The History of Materialism*. 3rd ed. New York: Humanities Press, 1950.

Langner, Albrecht, ed. *Karl Kautsky: Texte zu den Programmen der deutschen Sozialdemokratie, 1891–1925*. Cologne: Jakob Hegner, 1968.

*Laschitza, Annelies. "Karl Kautsky und der Zentrismus," *Beiträge zur Geschichte der deutschen Arbeiterbewegung* (East Berlin), X (1968), 798–832.

Lassalle, Ferdinand. "Arbeiter-Programm." In F. Lassalle, *Gesammelte Reden und Schriften*. Berlin: Cassirer, 1919. II, 139–202.

Laveleye, Émile de. *Primitive Property*. London: Macmillan, 1878.

Le Bon, Gustave. *The Crowd*. New York: Viking Press, 1960.

Lenin, V. I. *The State and Revolution*. In V. I. Lenin, *Collected Works*, XXV. Moscow: Progress Publishers, 1974. Pp. 385–497.

Letourneau, Charles. *Sociology Based Upon Ethnography*. New ed. London: Chapman & Hall, 1893.

Lévy-Bruhl, Lucien. *How Natives Think*. New York: Washington Square Press, 1966.

Lewin-Dorsch, Hannah. *Die Technik der Urzeit*, 3 vols, 2d ed. Stuttgart: J. H. W. Dietz, 1919–20.

*Lichtheim, George. *Marxism: An Historical and Critical Study*. 2d rev. ed. New York: Praeger, 1965. Reprint. New York: Columbia University Press, 1982.

Lissagaray, Prosper Olivier. *History of the Commune of 1871*. New York: Monthly Review Press, 1967.

Livius, Titus. *The History of Rome*. Translated by D. Spillan. 4 vols. London: Bell and Daldy, 1870.

*Lübbe, Peter. "Einleitung." In *Kautsky gegen Lenin*, edited by Peter Lübbe. Bonn: J. H. W. Dietz, 1981. Pp. 11–27.

Lübbe, Peter, ed. *Kautsky gegen Lenin*. Bonn: J. H. W. Dietz, 1981.

Lubbock, Sir John. See Avebury, John Lubbock, Lord.

Luschan, Felix von. "Anthropological View of Race." In *Papers on Inter-Racial Problems*. First Universal Races Congress. London, 1911. Pp. 13–24.

———. *Völker, Rassen, Sprachen*. Berlin: Deutsche Buchgemeinschaft, 1927.

Lux, Heinrich. *Etienne Cabet und der ikarische Kommunismus*. Stuttgart: J. H. W. Dietz, 1894.

Luxemburg, Rosa. *The Accumulation of Capital*. London: Routledge & Kegan Paul, 1963.

———. *Einführung in die Nationalökonomie*. In R. Luxemburg, *Gesammelte Werke*, V. East Berlin: Dietz Verlag, 1981. Pp. 524–778.

MacDougall, William. *An Introduction to Social Psychology*. 20th ed. London: Methuen, 1926.

Mach, Ernst. *The Analysis of Sensations*. New York: Dover Publications, 1959.

———. *Knowledge and Error*. Boston: D. Reidel, 1976.

———. *Kultur und Mechanik*. Stuttgart: W. Spemann, 1915.

Matschoss, Conrad. *Die Entwicklung der Dampfmaschine*. 2 vols. Berlin: J. Springer, 1908.

*Matthias, Erich. "Kautsky und der Kautskyanismus. Die Funktion der Ideologie in der deutschen Sozialdemokratie vor dem ersten Weltkriege." In *Marxismusstudien*, II, edited by Irving Fetscher. Tübingen: J. C. B. Mohr, 1957. Pp. 151–97.

Mehring, Franz. *Die Lessing-Legende*. Berlin: Ullstein, 1972. Abridged translation. New York: Critics Group Press, 1938.

*Meiner, Felix, ed. *Die Volkswirtschaftslehre der Gegenwart in Selbstdarstellungen*. Leipzig: Felix Meiner Verlag, 1924.

*Mende, Hans-Jürgen. *Karl Kautsky - vom Marxisten zum Opportunisten*. East Berlin: Dietz Verlag, 1985.

*Messin, F. "Eine neue Revision der materialistischen Geschichtsauffassung." *Unter dem Banner des Marxismus* (Moscow), III (1929), 219–45 and 329–45.
*Meusel, Alfred. Review of Karl Kautsky, *Die materialistische Geschichtsauffassung*. *Weltwirtschaftliches Archiv* (Jena), XXXVII (1933) (Literatur), 185*–94*.
Meyer, Eduard. *Geschichte des Altertums*. 5 vols. Stuttgart: J. G. Cotta, 1953–58.
Mommsen, Theodor. *The History of Rome*. 5 vols. London: Macmillan, 1908. Abridged ed.: New York: Philosophical Library, 1959.
Morgan, Lewis Henry. *Ancient Society*. Cambridge: Harvard University Press, 1964.
Müller, August. *Der Islam im Morgen- und Abendland*. 2 vols. Berlin: G. Grothe, 1885–87.
Müller, Max. *Lectures on the Science of Language*. Delhi: Munshi Ram Manohar Lal, 1965.
Müller-Lyer, Franz Carl. *The Family*. New York: Knopf, 1931.
———. *Der Sinn des Lebens und die Wissenschaft*. Munich: J. F. Lehmann, 1910.
Myers, Charles. "On the Permanence of Racial Mental Differences." In *Papers on Inter-Racial Problems*. First Universal Races Congress. London, 1911. Pp. 73–79.
Nansen, Fridtjof. *Eskimo Life*. London: Longmans, Green, 1893. Reprint. New York: AMS Press, 1975.
Niebuhr, B. G. *Lectures on the History of Rome*. 9th ed. London: Lockwood, 1903.
Noiré, Ludwig. *Das Werkzeug und seine Bedeutung für die Entwicklungsgeschichte der Menschheit*. Reprint of 1880 ed. Wiesbaden: Dr. Martin Sändig, 1968.
Nordenskjöld, A. E. von. *Die Umseglung Asiens und Europas auf der Vega*. 3 vols. Leipzig: F. A. Brockhaus, 1882–85.
Oppenheimer, Franz. *Der Staat*. Vol.II of F.Oppenheimer, *System der Soziologie* 4 vols. 2nd ed. Stuttgart: G. Fischer, 1964.
———. *The State*. New York: Arno Press, 1972.
*Osterroth, Franz. "Karl Kautsky." In F. Osterroth, *Biographisches Lexikon des Sozialismus*. Hannover: J. H. W. Dietz, 1960. I, 156–59.
*Panaccione, Andrea. "L'analisi del capitalismo in Kautsky." In Istituto Giangiacomo Feltrinelli, *Annali* (Milan), XV (1973), 3–25.
*———. *Kautsky e l'ideologia socialista*. Milan: Franco Angeli Libri, 1987.
*Papcke, Sven. "Karl Kautsky und der historische Fatalismus." In *Jahrbuch Arbeiterbewegung*, III: *Die Linke in der Sozialdemokratie*, edited by Claudio Pozzoli. Frankfurt am Main: Fischer, 1975. Pp. 231–46.
*Paschukanis, J. "Die neuesten Offenbarungen Karl Kautskys." *Unter dem Banner des Marxismus* (Moscow), II (1928), 419–37.
Peschel, Oscar. *The Races of Man*. New York: D. Appleton, 1902.
Petrucci, Raphaël. *Les Origines Naturelles de la Propriété. Essay de Sociologie Comparé*. Brussels: Misch & Thron, 1905.
Plato, "Phaedrus." In Plato; *Lysis or Friendship, The Symposium, Phaedrus*, translated by B. Jowett. New York: Heritage Press, 1968.
Plato's The Republic. Translated by B. Jowett. New York: Modern Library, 1941.
Plekhanov, George V. *The Development of the Monist View of History*. Moscow: Progress Publishers, 1972.
Plekhanov, George V. *Fundamental Problems of Marxism*. New York: International Publishers, 1969.
Pliny. *The Natural History of Pliny*. London: Henry Bohn, 1857.
Plutarch's Lives of the Noble Grecians and Romans. New York: AMS Press, 1967.
Pöhlmann, Robert von. *Geschichte der sozialen Frage und des Sozialismus in der antiken Welt*. 2 vols. 3rd ed., Munich: C. H. Beck, 1925. Reprint. Darmstadt: Wissenschaftliche Buchgesellschaft, 1984.
Polo, Marco. *The Travels of Marco Polo*, edited by Thomas Wright. New York: AMS Press, 1968.
Preisigke, Friedrich. *Antikes Leben nach den ägyptischen Papyri*. 2d ed. Leipzig: B. G. Teubner, 1925.

Preuss, Konrad Theodor. *Die geistige Kultur der Naturvölker.* Leipzig: B. G. Teubner, 1914.

★Projekt Klassenanalyse (Horst Arenz & al.). *Kautsky: Marxistische Vergangenheit der SPD?* Berlin: Verlag für das Studium der Arbeiterbewegung, 1976.

★Rappoport, Charles. "Der Autorevisionismus Karl Kautskys," *Internationale Pressekorrespondez* (Berlin), XIII (1928), 1912–13 and 1979–80.

Ratzel, Friedrich. *Anthropogeographie.* 2 vols. 4th ed. Stuttgart: Engelhorns Nachf., 1921–22. Reprint. Darmstadt: Wissenschaftliche Buchgesellschaft, 1975.

——. *The History of Mankind.* 3 vols. London: Macmillan, 1896–1904.

Robertson, John Mackinnon. *The Evolution of States.* New York: Putnam, 1913.

★Rónai, Zoltán. "Kautskys Klassen- und Staatslehre." *Der Kampf* (Vienna), XXII (1929), 464–79.

Rousseau, Jean-Jacques. *Discourse on the Origin and Foundations of Inequality Among Men.* In J.-J. Rousseau, *The First and Second Discourses.* New York: St. Martin's Press, 1964. Pp. 76–248.

★Rubel, Maximilien. "Le magnum opus de Karl Kautsky: 'La conception matérialiste de l'histoire' (1927)." *La Révue Socialiste* (Paris), n.s., no. 83 (January 1955), 4–14, and no. 85 (March 1955), 275–91.

Saint-Simon, Henri Comte de. "New Christianity." In H. Saint-Simon, *Selected Writings,* edited by F. M. H. Markham. New York: Macmillan, 1952. Pp. 81–116.

★Salvadori, Massimo L. "La concezione del processo rivoluzionario in Kautsky." In Istituto Giangiacomo Feltrinelli, *Annali* (Milan), XV (1973), 26–80.

★——. *Karl Kautsky and the Socialist Revolution, 1880–1938.* London: New Left Books, 1979.

★——. *Kautsky e la Rivoluzione Socialista, 1880–1938.* Milan: Feltrinelli, 1976.

Salvioli, Joseph. *Der Kapitalismus im Altertum.* 2nd ed. Stuttgart: J. H. W. Dietz, 1922.

★Schifrin, Alexander (M. Werner). "K. Kautsky und die marxistische Soziologie." *Die Gesellschaft* (Berlin), VI/2 (1929), 149–69.

Schmidt, Conrad. Review of A. Bogdanoff, *Die Entwicklungsformen der Gesellschaft und die Wissenschaft,* in *Vorwärts* (Berlin), October 18, 1925.

Schopenhauer, Arthur. *The Basis of Morality.* 2nd ed. New York: Macmillan, 1915.

Seeck, Otto. *Geschichte des Untergangs der antiken Welt.* 6 vols. 4th ed. Stuttgart: J. B. Metzler, 1920–22. Reprint. Darmstadt: Wissenschaftliche Buchgesellschaft, 1966.

Shaplen, Joseph, and David Shub, eds. *Socialism, Fascism, Communism.* New York: American League for Democratic Socialism, 1934.

Smith, Adam. *The Wealth of Nations.* 2 vols. New York: Dutton, Everyman's Library, 1964.

Sombart, Werner. *Die deutsche Volkswirtschaft im neunzehnten Jahrhundert.* 8th ed. Stuttgart: W. Kohlhammer, 1954.

——. *Händler und Helden; patriotische Besinnungen.* Munich: Duncker & Humblot, 1915.

Somló, Bódog (Felix). *Der Güterverkehr in der Urgesellschaft.* Brussels: Misch & Thron, 1909.

Spencer, Herbert. *The Data of Ethics.* New York: H.M. Caldwell, 1879. Ann Arbor: University Microfilms, 1965.

——. *The Principles of Sociology.* 3 vols. London: Williams & Norgate, 1876–96. Reprint. Westport, Conn.: Greenwood Press, 1975.

Spiegel, Friedrich. *Eranische Alterthumskunde.* 3 vols. Leipzig: Wilhelm Engelmann, 1871–78.

Stammler, Rudolf. "Die materialistische Geschichtsauffassung." In *Handwörterbuch der Staatswissenschaften,* edited by Ludwig Elster & al. 4th rev. ed. Jena: G. Fischer, 1925. VI, 522–34.

——. *Wirtschaft und Recht nach der materialistischen Geschichtsauffassung.* Leipzig: Veit, 1896.

★Steenson, Gary P. *Karl Kautsky, 1854–1938: Marxism in the Classical Years.* Pittsburgh: University of Pittsburgh Press, 1978.

★Steinberg, Hans-Josef. "Karl Kautsky und Eduard Bernstein." In *Deutsche Historiker,* IV, edited by Hans-Ulrich Wehler. Göttingen: Vanderhoek & Ruprecht, 1972. Pp. 53–64.

★————. *Sozialismus und deutsche Sozialdemokratie*. 5th ed. Bonn: J. H. W. Dietz, 1979.

Steinen, Karl von den. *Unter den Naturvölkern Zentralbrasiliens*. Berlin: D. Reimer, 1894. Reprint. New York: Johnson Reprint Corp., 1968.

Stieve, H. "Ueber den Einfluss der Umwelt auf die Lebewesen." *Klinische Wochenschrift* (Berlin), June 24, 1924.

Thucydides. *The Peloponnesian War*. The Crawley Translation. New York: Modern Library, 1982.

Troeltsch, Ernst. *Der Historismus und seine Probleme. Erstes Buch: Das logische Problem der Geschichtsphilosophie*. Aalen: Scientia, 1961.

Tschudi, Johann Jakob von. *Reisen durch Südamerika*. 5 vols. Leipzig: F. A. Brockhaus, 1866–69. Reprint. Stuttgart: Brockhaus, 1971.

Tschulok, Sinai. *Deszendenzlehre*. Jena: Gustav Fischer, 1922.

————. *Entwicklungstheorie*. Stuttgart: J. H. W. Dietz, 1923.

Vorländer, Karl. *Kant und Marx; ein Beitrag zur Philosophie des Sozialimus*. 2nd ed. Tübingen: J. C. B. Mohr, 1926.

Wachsmuth, Wilhelm. *Europäische Sittengeschichte*. 5 vols. Leipzig: F. C. W. Vogel, 1831–39.

Waitz, Theodor. *Die Indianer Nordamerikas*. Leipzig: F. Fleischer, 1865. Reprint. Leipzig: Zentralantiquariat der Deutschen Demokratischen Republik, 1974.

Waitz, Theodor. *Introduction to Anthropology*. New York: AMS Press, 1975.

★Waldenberg, Marek. *Kautsky*. Warsaw: Wiedza Powszechna, 1976.

★————. *Myśl Polityczna Karola Kautsky'ego w okresie sporu z Rewizjonizmem (1898–1909)*. Cracow: Państwowe Wydawn. Naukowe, Oddz. w Krakowie, 1970.

★————. *Il Papa Rosso, Karl Kautsky*. Rome: Editori Riuniti, 1980.

★————. *Wzlot i upadek Karola Kautsky'ego*. 2 vols. Cracow: Wydawn. Literackie, 1972.

Wallace, Alfred Russel. *The Malay Archipelago*. New York: Dover Publications, 1962.

Weber, Henri, ed. *Kautsky, Luxemburg, Pannekoek. Socialisme: La voie occidentale*. Paris: Presses Universitaires de France, 1983.

Weber, Max. *Economy and Society*. 3 vols. New York: Bedminster Press, 1968.

————. *General Economic History*. New Brunswick, N.J.: Transaction Press, 1981.

————. *The Protestant Ethic and the Spirit of Capitalism*. New York: Charles Scribner's Sons, 1958.

————. *Wirtschaftsgeschichte*. 4th ed. Berlin: Duncker & Humblot, 1981.

Wells, H.G. *The Outline of History*. 8th revision. London: Cassell, 1937.

★Wiener, Robert. "Kautskys Darlegung des historischen Materialismus." *Tribüne* (Prague), I (1928), 79–89.

Woltmann, Ludwig. *Der historische Materialismus*. Düsseldorf: H. Michel, 1900.

Woytinsky, Wladimir S. *Die Welt in Zahlen*. 7 vols. Berlin: R. Mosse, 1925–28.

Die Wunder der Natur. 2 vols. Berlin: Deutsches Verlagshaus Bong, 1912.

Index

This index includes the titles of books—but not articles—by Kautsky (not identified by his name), by Marx, and by Engels. Those of other authors can be located by reference to the authors' names.

Abel, 281
Abel, Othenio, 117
Absolutism, 265, 328, 343, 355, 360, 373–74, 379–80, 383–89, 405, 416, 433, 475, 519
Abstraction, xlvii, 32, 40–41, 81, 129, 332, 388, 459, 477–78
Abt, Ernst, 152
Accident, 22–24, 168, 215, 237, 333, 426, 476, 481–83, 487
Accumulation, primitive, 276–77, 358–59, 363, 377, 423
Acquired characteristics, xxxi-*n*, 46, 110, 112–15, 130, 138
Adaptation, xxxvii, xlvi, 45, 54, 108–16, 120–21, 148, 164, 481, 517; active, xxxi, 111–15; among organs, 50–51, 111–14, 184; through artificial organs, xxxi, xxxvii, xliv, 115, 118, 151, 156, 183–85, 213, 216–18, 490, 516, 522; ego and environment, 34–35, 38, 120–21, 169, 217–18; passive, xxxi, 110–11, 115; and perfection, 38; of thoughts, 40–43, 242–44
Adler, Friedrich, 33, 240
Adler, Max, 4, 16, 65, 250, 264
Africa, xxv, 278, 314, 423, 515

Die Agrarfrage, 195*n*
Agrarian policy, 132–33, 195–96
Agriculture, xlvi, 101, 194–96, 289, 294, 442*n*, 447, 456, 512, 523; in city-states, 316, 344, 347–48, 351, 353–54; early, 82–83, 89–90, 155, 158, 177, 193, 203–204, 207, 238, 278–86, 307–10, 318; modern, 133, 260–61, 359, 409, 421–24; in Oriental states, 307–10, 361
Ahriman, 281
Albanians, 290
Alcoholism, 401
Alexander the Great, 339
Alexandria, 17
Alsace-Lorraine, 380
Altruism, 65, 188–89
Alverdes, Friedrich, 87, 99, 152
America, 147, 277, 281, 341, 360. See also United States
Amsterdam, lv-*n*
Anabaptists, 232*n*, 367–69
Anarchism, 106, 250, 427, 436, 446–47
Anatomy, 57
Anderson, Perry, xxiii-*n*
Animal husbandry, 90, 204, 278
Anthropocentrism, 11–12, 37

Anthropogeography, 140, 147–48
Anthropology, xxvii–xxviii, xxx, xxxiv, 56, 146
Anti-Dühring (Engels), xxxii, 7, 26, 35–36, 37*n*, 41, 66, 260, 268–70, 272, 275, 308, 420, 446, 462
Anti-Semitism, 243
Apeman, 60, 121, 123, 156, 217; erect posture, 53, 96, 117, 151, 155; intelligence, 53–54, 151, 153–54; region of origin, 117–18
Apes, 53–54, 57, 60, 64, 87, 92, 117, 151–56, 159, 176, 200, 219, 231, 512
Arabia, 139, 282, 298, 310, 365
Archaeology, 468, 476
Architecture, xlvii, 154, 229, 312
Are the Jews a Race?, xxviii, xxxi-*n*, xxxiii, 48, 52, 123*n*–126*n*, 143, 145
Aristocracy, xlviii–l, 263, 270–71, 292, 298, 315, 396, 483–84; in city-states, 341–55, 389; in early states, 284–86, 297, 308, 321–33, 336–37, 340, 389; mentality, 285–86, 324–26, 342, 363, 366; in Middle Ages, 263, 355, 358, 361–66, 386, 389; in modern times, 367, 369–70, 373–74, 379; in the Orient, 336–37, 340, 343
Aristotle, 113, 325, 346, 348, 354
Arms. *See* Weapons
Army, xliv–li, lix–lx, 237–38, 265–66, 271, 273, 307, 344, 353, 355, 379–83, 394, 405, 430, 470, 484
Art, xxxix, xli, xlvii, 55, 98–102, 105, 129, 134, 141, 229, 232, 238, 240–41, 261, 312–16, 319, 325–27, 332, 351, 357, 447–48, 453, 463, 468–69, 471, 473, 479, 492, 500, 504, 506, 523–24
Artificial organs. *See* Tools
Artisans, 131, 252, 257–58, 313–16, 321, 325–27, 332, 334–35, 344, 348, 354, 359, 362–64, 367–70, 375, 377, 402, 404, 407, 409, 433
Asceticism, 366
Asia, xxv, lvii, 278, 317, 334, 375, 423, 451
Assyria, 231, 257
Athens, 13, 139, 238, 270–71, 273, 317, 345–46, 348–49, 351
Attica, 348, 354
Augustus, 352
Auschwitz, lv-*n*
Australia, 155, 162, 412
Austria, lxix, 141, 203, 360, 380, 405

Avebury, Lord, 87, 93, 162, 179, 203
Aztecs, 277

Baboon, 87, 156
Babylon, 312, 350
Bachofen, J. J., 87
Bakairi, 512
Bakunin, Michael, 175
Banking capital, xlvii, 292, 296–97, 355–56, 358, 433
Baptists, 232*n*, 367–69
Base. *See* Superstructure
Barter, 178–79, 282, 314, 361
Bauer, Otto, 4, 244, 380
Bax, E. Belfort, 4*n*
Beauty, xxxiv, 97–100, 102, 105, 126–27, 154, 220, 312, 325
Beaver, 71, 152, 200
Bedouins, 281
Beetham, David, xxii-*n*, 392*n*, 395*n*
Die Befreiung der Nationen, 288*n*, 375*n*, 380*n*
Belfort-Bax, E., 4*n*
Belgium, 405
Beloch, K. J., 270, 289, 316, 344, 468, 471, 487, 489
Bentham, Jeremy, 517
Berber, 290
Bernstein, Eduard, 4, 165*n*, 420*n*
Bernstein und das soz.-dem. Programm, 398, 420*n*, 421*n*, 426*n*, 432*n*, 433*n*
Billroth, Theodor, 98
Biology, xxviii, xxx, 45–46, 170, 244, 477, 481, 493
Birth control, 424
Bismarck, Otto v., 380, 404
Blanqui, Auguste, 175, 466
Bloch, J., 233
Blumenberg, Werner, xxi-*n*, xxiii-*n*, xxxii-*n*
Boas, Franz, 128*n*
Bogdanoff, A., 240
Bohemia, 360
Bolsheviks, xxx-*n*, 175–76, 413*n*, 457*n*, 495*n*
Bolshevism at a Deadlock, 391*n*, 412*n*, 439*n*, 442*n*, 457*n*
Bonapartism, xlvii-*n*, 405, 444
Borgius, W., 233, 487
Botocudo, 512
Bottomore, Tom, xxii-*n*, 262*n*

Bourgeoisie, xxxviii, l, lviii, 244, 404, 408–409, 416, 419, 442, 451, 501–502
Braunthal, Alfred, xxiii–*n*, 4
Brazil, 201, 512
Brehm, A. E., 60*n*, 71
Bribery, 336, 347, 389, 392, 472
Brigandage. *See* Robbery
Bright, John, 292
Brill, Hermann, xxi–*n*
Britain, lii, 17, 138, 173, 181, 382–83, 404, 415–16, 434, 487, 514; colonialism, lvii, 205–206, 238, 291, 294, 310, 412, 415, 423; industrial capitalism, lvii, 147, 166–67, 190, 292, 368, 370, 389, 402, 423; Puritanism, 173, 360, 367; socialism, lxiii, 189, 392, 406*n*, 436, 466
Bronner, Stephen E., xxii–*n*
Brutus, Marcus Junius, 173, 297
Buckle, Henry T., 147, 297
Buddha, 173
Buddhism, 327
Bücher, Karl, 99, 102, 193, 198*n*, 273, 479
Bukharin, Nikolai, 4, 250–51
Bureaucracy, xlix–liii, lix–lx, lxii, 265–66, 271, 322–23, 331–32, 340, 350, 355, 379–80, 386–87, 389, 391, 396, 405, 411, 440, 445, 448, 469, 484
Bushmen, 155

Cabet, Etienne, 174
Caesar, Julius, xlvii–*n*, 480, 487
Cain, 281
Calles, Elías, 417
Calvinism, 359–60, 367–68, 370, 384
Capital (Marx) xxv, xxxix–*n*, lxiv, 4, 36*n*, 66, 192, 197–98, 214, 234*n*, 250, 276–77, 297, 304, 306, 308, 338, 370, 372, 418–21, 456–58
Capitalism. *See* Banking capital; Commercial capital; Industrial capital
Carlyle, Thomas, 138
Cartels, liii, 253, 293, 410, 417, 420, 432
Carthage, 351
Caste, 262, 284, 416
Catholic Church. *See* Church
Catlin, George, 512, 515
Cato, Marcus Porcius, 173
Cattle-raising. *See* Pastoralism
Causality, 9, 11, 16, 19, 22, 24, 80, 83, 215, 217, 223, 470, 491–93; or function, 33. *See also* Necessity

Celibacy, 330
Celts, 141
Chagga, 515
Chamberlain, H. S., 124, 141
Charisma, 395–97, 469, 483, 486
Chartists, 408
Cheyenne Indians, 515
Chemistry, 9, 52, 477, 493
Chimpanzee, 53, 151–52, 156
China, xlvi, lvi–lvii, 140, 295, 317–18, 331, 341, 401, 412, 414–15, 423
Christianity, xl, lxx, 84, 173–75, 231–32, 284, 310, 355, 360–61, 365–66, 418
Chukchi, 512
Church, 141, 232, 263, 284, 327, 330, 361, 363–66, 368, 373–74, 384, 386, 417, 484, 525
City, 129, 194, 236, 260, 263, 339, 413; of antiquity, xlviii, 326, 342–51, 361–62, 374; early development, xlvii, 311–14, 447; Italian, 362; modern, 335, 379, 385; Oriental, xlviii, 314–15, 332–34, 342, 362, 413–14. *See also* Town
Civil liberties, lxi
Civil war, liv, 337, 376, 392–93, 395, 427, 445, 511; U.S., 214
The Civil War in France (Marx), 266
Class, xlvii, lxvii, 78, 84, 101, 136–37, 163, 165, 290, 511; abolition of, lix–lx, 101, 191, 224, 253–54, 259, 262–63, 307, 351, 411, 443–44, 449, 508–510, 513, 516, 523–24; alliances, 372–73, 405, 415; antagonism, li, 78, 102, 188, 190, 211, 223–24, 239, 245, 250–54, 259, 264, 269, 284, 296, 299, 306–307, 314, 320, 332–33, 335, 337, 345, 371, 388, 411, 415, 426–32, 434, 454, 459, 466, 486, 502, 526; concept of, 250–54, 264; consciousness, l, 367, 398–99, 404, 406, 416, 439; and estate, 263–64; existence of, xlvi, 130, 224, 249–50; and intellect, 131–35; and intellectuals, 397–99; intermediate, 398, 409, 433–34; multiplicity, l, 285, 293, 332, 335, 372; origin of, xlvi, 102, 131, 133, 267–77, 286, 425–26, 453, 501, 509–10, 516, 525; and party, l
Class struggle, l, lix, 6, 101, 192, 224, 249, 259, 369, 371, 407, 411, 432, 438, 441, 447, 454, 466–69, 482, 494, 497, 500, 502, 506–508; in ancient Orient, xlvii, 333, 335, 337; in city-states, xlvii, 345, 452–53; and cooperation, 372–73, 405; and de-

Class struggle (*continued*)
mocracy, l, xlviii, li, 376, 405, 431; in developing countries, 413–18; growth of, lxx, 429; and intellectuals, 252, 327, 397–99, 467; in Middle Ages, 355, 362; motor of history, xlvii–xlviii, 224, 249, 351, 452, 486; against peonage, 297; and proletarian morality, xxix–*n*, lix, 191, 438–39; and violence, xliii–xlix, 376, 392, 428
The Class Struggle, xxv, 375*n*, 398*n*, 405*n*, 420*n*, 427*n*, 432*n*, 457*n*, 482*n*
Clergy. *See* Priesthood
Climate, 53, 76, 108, 147, 176, 182, 279, 475
Cobden, Richard, 292
Cognition. *See* Knowledge
Cole, G. D. H., xxi–*n*
Collective ideas, 81–85, 90–92, 94, 129, 144, 146, 255–56, 301, 326
Colonialism, 190, 195, 238, 243, 276, 291–92, 381, 412, 416, 423
Columbus, Christopher, 487
Commerce, 184–85, 188, 194–95, 300–301, 304–306, 325, 332, 335, 339, 350, 355–56, 371, 385, 422, 474, 479; and cities, 263, 311, 313–15, 326, 361–63; Greek, 298, 342–43, 348; and Jews, 298; and location, 179, 193, 199, 237, 298, 311, 350–51, 361; mercantilism, 238, 292, 373; and morality, 188–91; nations engaging in, 298; and state, xlvii, 294–96; and technology, 180; among tribes, 79, 178, 324; world-, 182, 188, 195, 241, 399, 468
Commercial capital, 292, 296–97, 355–56, 358
Commune, Paris, lxix, 175, 266, 377, 415
Communism: 6, 209, 354, 367–68; in Germany, 440; in Italy, liv, 394; of landownership, 174, 205–208, 294; modern, xxi, li, 175, 320; primitive, 174, 250, 296, 515, 519
Communism in Central Europe, 232*n*
Communist Manifesto (Marx and Engels), 66, 174–75, 205–206, 249, 345, 419–20, 425, 452, 458
Compensation for socialized property, lix, 209, 377–78
Competition, 62–63, 65, 189, 199, 214, 243–44, 333, 358, 371, 437
Comte, Auguste, 65
Congo, 204
Consanguinity. *See* Kinship

Consumers, l, liv, lix, 192, 253, 295, 377, 410–411, 428, 462
Contradiction, 41
A Contribution to the Critique of Political Economy (Marx), xxvii, xxxviii, 225, 227, 234, 239, 246, 249, 304, 450–52, 454–55, 457–59
Cooperatives, xlix, lix, 192, 252, 387, 411, 436, 438, 446–47
Corporation, xlix, liii, 292, 387, 433, 437
Cotton, 168, 190, 214
Craftsmen. *See* Artisans
Crime, 60, 63, 69, 85, 385
Crises, 195*n*, 214, 378, 420–25, 427–29, 456, 462
Critical theory, xxv
Critique of the Gotha Program (Marx), 266, 390–91
Cromwell, Oliver, 487
Crossbreeding, 46–47, 164
Cunow, Heinrich, 4, 93, 209, 277, 281
Customs. *See* Tariff
Cuvier, Georges de, 47
Cyrus, 329
Czechoslovakia, lv–*n*

Daniels, Emil, 310
Darius, 290
Darwin, Charles, xxiv, xxxii–xxxiv, 6, 47–48, 50, 124, 147, 156, 231, 452, 460; on animal morality, 66–67; on animals' sense of beauty, 97–99; descent of man, 53, 65–66; on individual differences, xxxiii, xxxvii, 47–48, 114, 245; and Kautsky's beginnings, 6, 66; and Malthus, 61–62; and Marx and Engels, 6, 52, 66, 452, 460; natural selection, 62–63; on primitive marriage forms, 92; on region of human origins, 117; struggle for existence, 60, 109, 114, 148, 487
Davids, T. W. R., 173
Deism, 10
Delbrück, Hans, 238, 289, 468, 505
Delbrück und Wilhelm II., lxvi–*n*
De Man, Henry, 490, 496
Democracy: in city-states, 345–49, 351–52, 354–55, 374, 396; of conquered peasants, 275, 288, 321–23; in developing countries, lvi–lviii, 375; "formal," li, 374, 387, 393; in medieval towns, lvi, 362; modern, xxviii, xxxv, xlviii–lii, lv, lvii, lxi–lxii,

132, 175, 373–74, 376, 379–90, 392–96, 399, 404–407, 409, 413–15, 419, 427–28, 433–35, 469–70, 475; primitive, 71, 126, 132, 269, 271, 273–74, 321, 323, 328, 396; proletarian struggle for, xlix, lii, 375, 386–87, 393, 404–408, 413, 445, 508; republic, 265–66, 390; value to proletariat, lii–liv, lviii, 174, 375, 392, 410, 421, 445; of victorious nomads, 323

Demography, xxviii, xxx, 49

Desert, 278–79, 281, 308

Dialectic, 34–38, 41, 45, 229, 520; of adaptation, 34–35, 57, 60, 213; critique of Engels, xxvii, 35–38, 54, 218, 225; and evolution, 213, 217–18

Dialectics of Nature (Engels), 521

Dictatorship, xlvii–*n*, lv, lvii, 380, 391–93, 414–17, 444–45, 487; of the proletariat, 390, 392

The Dictatorship of the Proletariat, 375n, 390n, 457n

Digging, 154–56, 158

Dilthey, Wilhelm, 492

Diodorus, 470

Disarmament, 383, 408, 448

Division of labor, lxi, 65, 70, 163–64, 191, 196, 210, 216, 242, 269, 272, 296, 307, 387, 485, 507; among organs, 50, 53, 183–84; occupational, l, 70, 74, 78, 84, 100, 103, 131, 137, 165, 168, 179, 186–87, 211, 223, 254, 257–63, 276, 298, 312, 314, 316, 332, 510, 523, 525; among polities, 78, 179, 187–88, 241, 254, 276; among ruling classes, 284, 301; among sciences, 8, 256–57, 525; between the sexes, 70, 88–89, 131, 135, 158–59, 186–87, 191, 211, 223, 254–55, 276

Dodge, Richard, 515

Doflein, Franz, 67, 75, 87, 99, 110

Dolphin, 111

Drives, xxxv–xxxvi, 42, 59, 107, 490, 492–94, 527; for beauty, xxxiv, 97, 102, 107, 220, 228, 234, 325, 494; conflict among, 105–106; and instincts, 56; for knowledge, xxxiv, 9, 11, 21, 31, 102–106, 220, 228, 234, 302, 491, 494; for self-preservation, xxxiv, 11–12, 21, 29, 31, 38, 40, 56, 59–60, 63–65, 85, 95, 97, 102–107, 220, 226–28, 234, 494, 523; sexual, xxxiv, 11–12, 29, 56, 85–86, 95, 97, 102–107, 220, 227–28, 234, 494; social, xxxii, xxxiv, 56, 65–70, 72, 74, 77–79, 83–85, 95, 97, 102–

107, 208–209, 228, 234, 491, 494, 510, 525–26

Drumann, W., 324

Dümichen, Johannes, 300, 308

Dutch, 205–206, 423

East Indies, 205–206

Eckermann, J. P., 471

Ecology, xxv

Economic and Philosophical Manuscripts (Marx), xxvi–*n*

The Economic Doctrines of Karl Marx, xxv, 165n, 185n

Economics, xxx, xxxvi, lix, 6, 43, 54, 58, 201, 243, 251, 260, 401, 420, 428, 438, 467–68, 474, 478–80, 492–93, 502, 518

Education, xlix, liv, lix, lxii, 90, 229, 301, 303, 379–80, 384–85, 392, 407, 435, 448, 468–69, 514, 523

Egoism, 13, 59–61, 63, 79, 82, 188–89, 191; and historical materialism, xxxv, 3, 104–105

Egypt, 231, 284, 317, 331, 424

The Eighteenth Brumaire (Marx), 175, 265, 482

Der Einfluss der Volksvermehrung, 49n, 203n, 310

Elsass-Lothringen, 380n

Engels, Friedrich, xxi, xxiv–xxvii, xxxiii, lxiv, lxvii, 5, 174, 324, 452, 465–67, 489, 494, 502–503, 521; on classes, xxvii, xlvi, 249, 264, 345–46; conception of history, xlii, lxx, 3–6, 23n, 67, 220, 224–25, 230, 232–33, 404, 461, 487; on contradictions, 41; and Darwin, 6, 52, 66; on dialectic, xxvii, xxxii, 34–38, 54, 217–18, 225, 228, 520; on division of labor, 259–62; economics, 419–20; leap from necessity to freedom, lix, 26–28, 462–63; materialist method, 7–8; on origin of family, 87, 452; on origin of state, xxvii, xlvi, 268–76, 308; on production of life, 234–36; on state, 42, 265–67; on state withering away, 400n, 446–49; "Transition from Ape to Man," 53–54, 75; on village communism, 205–206

England. *See* Britain

Enlightenment, xxxv, 106, 374, 489

Epistemology, 242, 265

Equality, lxii, 269, 346, 374, 437, 444, 448, 509

Equilibrium, 54, 61–63, 75–76, 113, 117–19, 148–49, 157–59, 186, 230, 287

Erfurt Program, xxv, li, 375*n*, 398*n*, 420*n*, 457*n*

Erinnerungen und Erörterungen, xxxii–*n*, xxxiii–*n*, lxix–*n*, 38*n*, 66*n*

Eroticism, 86, 96, 103–104

Eskimos, 203, 512

Espinas, Alfred, 71, 99, 152

Estate, 262–63, 276, 284, 335, 386, 388, 398

Ethics, xxiv, 84, 102–105, 107, 171, 188–89, 191–92, 220, 280, 326, 333, 402, 501; animal morality, 66–67; business-, 189–90; and egoism, 13, 188–89; explanation of, 13, 65–70, 93, 245; and marriage, 94–95; moral law, 24–25, 492; mystical, 14, 43, 68, 97; objection to materialism, 13–14; and progress, 508–11, 525–26; proletarian, 191, 426, 438–39; Puritan, 369–70; and religion, 82–83; and science, 496; and social drives, xxxii, 65–70, 77–78, 83–84, 491, 525

Ethics and the Materialist Conception of History, xxviii, xxxii–*n*, xxxiv, lxvi, 4*n*, 16*n*, 25*n*, 26*n*, 67, 68*n*, 75*n*

Ethnology, xxviii, lxvii, 43, 64

Euphrates, 278

Eurocommunism, xxii

Eurotas Valley, 341–42

Existentialism, xxv–xxvi

Expansion: of hunting grounds, 76–77, 237; of the state, 126, 287–93, 295–96, 300–301, 306, 321–22, 338, 469, 485

Exploitation, 79, 81, 84, 100–101, 124, 258–59, 295, 300, 306, 338, 340, 351, 363, 366, 371, 381, 453, 516; basis of early civilization, 131, 315; capitalist, xlviii–xlix, 251–52, 261, 356–58, 378, 401, 411, 429–32, 441, 445, 456, 502; in city-states, 344, 347–49, 352–54; and democracy, xlviii–xlix, li, 374, 376, 381–82, 387, 444; end of, lix–lx, lxii, 259, 351, 374, 402, 412, 418, 443, 445–46, 463, 510, 516, 526; forms of, xlviii, 282–83, 286, 357, 371, 456; growth of, 312, 429–32, 509, 513, 516; and happiness, 516–17; and monopoly, 258; of peasants, 253, 314, 341–43; prevents adaptation, 516–18; and property, 252, 295, 297; and state, xlvii, 266, 268, 272, 274, 283, 286–95, 319, 322, 332, 337, 386

Expropriation, 251, 377–78, 393, 411

Factory councils, 438

Fascism, xxiii, liii–lv, 394–95, 445

Fatalism, 22

Feminism, xxv

Ferguson, Adam, 65*n*

Feudalism, xlviii, 238, 258, 263, 276, 358, 360, 371–72, 388, 416, 418–20, 451, 455–56, 475, 501, 508

Feuerbach, Ludwig, 26, 35

Filth, lx, 198, 513–14

Finance capital, liii, 292–93, 433

Fire, 153, 161–63, 186–87, 513–14

Five-year plans, xxvi

Flintstone, 160, 177, 180

Florida, 214

Forces of production, xxxviii–xxxix, xli, xlvii–xlviii, 215, 225–28, 234–35, 237–39, 376, 400, 421, 426, 429, 451–56, 458–59, 501, 506

Forest, 53, 75, 151–52, 156, 180, 198, 205, 400

Foundations of Christianity, 173, 231*n*, 232*n*, 274, 350*n*, 353*n*, 355*n*

France, xlvii–*n*, 17, 141, 173, 238, 265–66, 360, 377, 404, 415, 466, 487

Franchise, l, lii, lxi, 404–405, 408

Franklin, Benjamin, 359–60, 368

Franks, 141

Freedom, lxi, 436, 507; of action, 31; of choice, 59; indeterminacy, 24; subjective, lxi, 495, 507–509, 511, 517, 524; of will, 16, 25–26, 29, 31, 59, 150–51, 490–92, 495. *See also* Necessity

Free labor, xlviii, 313, 315–16, 327, 332, 340, 347–48, 356, 358–59, 361, 363–66, 369–70, 374, 376, 387, 445, 508

Free trade, 292, 382, 433

Freud, Sigmund, xxiv–xxv, xxxv–xxxvi, 57–58, 63*n*, 91–93, 106–107, 511

Friedrich Engels, 482*n*

Frobenius, Leo, 204

Fulton, Robert, 167

Functional dependence, 33

Ganges, 278

Geary, Richard, xxii–*n*

Geiger, Lazarus, 128–29

Genesis, 312

Genetics, xxx

Geneva convention, 449

Genius, 64, 163–64, 166, 168, 499–500

Gens, 78, 91, 95, 202, 208, 224, 238, 269–70, 273, 324, 329, 346, 351, 516, 525
Geographical location, 147, 179–80, 193, 196, 199, 237, 298, 311, 368
Geology, 51, 244
Georgia, lxvi, 413*n*
Georgia, 413*n*, 414*n*, 440*n*, 442*n*
Germanic, barbarians, 238, 284, 353, 360, 365, 453–54; languages, 145; tribes, 141, 288
The German Ideology (Marx and Engels), 235, 260
Germany, xxxvii, lxiii, lxvi, 16–17, 105, 124, 138, 141, 169, 205, 406*n*, 409, 415, 436, 466, 512, 514; customs union, 449; empire, li–lii, 380, 404–405, 408, 432; Fascism, lv, 394; mark, 204–206; peasants, 211, 364*n*; revolution, lxv–lxvi, 377, 378*n*, 440
Gibbon, Edward, 310
Gilcher-Holtey, Ingrid, xxii–*n*
Giraffe, 48
Giraud-Teulon, Alexis, 87
Gobineau, J. A. de, 124, 147
God, belief in, 9–10
Goethe, J. W. v., xxviii–*n*, 471
Gold, 105, 305–306
Goldstein, Julius, 137–38
Gompers, Samuel, 406*n*
Goode, Patrick, xxii–*n*, 262*n*
Gorilla, 53, 64, 92, 152–53
Gracchi, 354, 355*n*
Grassland, 53, 151–53, 155–56, 278, 283
Gravity, 478, 521
Greece, xxviii–*n*, xlvii–*n*, 139, 166, 173, 180, 316, 468, 474; class struggles, xlvii, 343–46, 453; democracy, 346–49; location, 180, 298, 341–42, 350; origin of city-state, 341–43; thought, 13, 231, 326–27, 354
Greenland, 201–202, 512
Gregory VII, 330
Grenzen der Gewalt, lv–*n*
Grosse, Ernst, 192
Grundrisse (Marx), xxvi–*n*, 476
Grunenberg, Antonia, 376*n*
Guerrilla warfare, xxvi
Guilds, 78, 259, 334–36, 359, 364, 383–84, 412, 438, 525
The Guilt of William Hohenzollern, lxvi–*n*
Gumplowicz, Ludwig, 123–25, 275
Gutmann, Bruno, 515

Habsburg, 360
Habsburgs Glück und Ende, 380*n*
Häckel, Ernst, 117
Haiser, Franz, 123
Handelspolitik und Sozialdemokratie, 433*n*
Happiness, 327, 515–17
Harem, 330, 339
Harvest mouse, 152
Hauser, Otto, 120, 179
Haxthausen, A. v., 205
Health, 419, 513–15; services, xlix, liv, lix, 385, 419, 448
Hebrews. *See* Jews
Hedley, William, 167
Heeren, A. H. L., 295
Hegel, G. W. F., xxv, xxviii–*n*, xlvii, li–*n*, 6, 26–27, 34–38, 41, 147, 217–18, 264–66, 471, 475, 507, 520
Henry VIII, 105, 472
Hellwald, Friedrich v., 91
Helmholtz, Hermann v., 97
Herder, J. G. v., 275
Herdsmen. *See* Pastoralism
Heredity, xxiv, 45–46, 63, 91
Herodotus, 289, 295, 312, 329
Herr Eugen Dühring's Revolution in Science. See *Anti-Dühring*
Hildebrand, Richard, 206
Hilferding, Rudolf, 292, 421, 433
Hindus, 416
Historiography, xliii, 138, 143, 147, 233, 326, 468–74, 480, 483, 487
Die historische Leistung von Karl Marx, 4*n*, 478*n*
Hitler, Adolf, liv, lv–*n*
Hoangho, 278
Hodgskin, Thomas, 228
Holland, lv–*n*, 205–206, 360, 423
The Holy Family (Marx and Engels), 265
Holzheuer, Walter, xxi–*n*, xxxii–*n*
Homer, 238, 341
Hook, Sidney, xxii–*n*, 230*n*
Housing, liv, 234, 401, 407, 419, 437, 513–14
Hünlich, Reinhold, xxii–*n*
Humanism, xxv, 173
Humanity, 219, 428, 511–13
Hume, David, 22
Hungary, 360
Hunting, 76–77, 82–83, 88–89, 100, 121, 133, 135, 157–60, 177, 186–87, 192, 195–96, 202–204, 207, 209, 237, 260, 278–81, 285, 318, 339, 341, 512

Idealism, xxxvii, xlii, 8, 25, 31, 37, 150, 215, 217, 223, 282
Ideality, of space, 20, 24; of time, 20–21, 24
Ideology, xxxvii, xxxix, xl–xliii, xlv, lviii, lxiv, 228–34, 240, 243–46, 454–55
Imperialism, 195, 291–93, 422–23
Inaugural Address (Marx), 419
Incas, 277, 294
Incest, prohibition of, 91–95
India, xlvi, lvi–lvii, 147, 205–206, 257, 294, 297, 306, 310, 317–18, 412, 414–16, 423
Individualism, xxv, lxi–lxii, 6, 65, 244–45, 367, 511, 524
Indo-European languages, 145
Indus, 278
Industrial capital, xlvii–xlix, liii, lvii–lviii, lx, 105, 147, 208, 238, 251–52, 297, 356, 389, 392–93, 433, 435, 442, 455–56, 460, 462, 506–508, 514, 523; beginnings, 292, 367, 402, 404, 501; "collapse," 420n, 426, 440; destructive effects, 101, 131, 190, 198, 260–61, 377, 400–403, 419; development, lvii–lviii, 174, 379, 385, 409, 422, 429, 432, 443, 454, 468, 483; and dictatorship, lv, 395, 445; expropriation, 251, 377–78, 393, 411, 437, 456, 506; non-European, lvi, 413–18; novelty, lxviii, 322, 327, 355, 357–58, 371–72, 383, 470–71; primitive accumulation, 276–77, 358–59, 363, 377, 423; spirit, xlv–n, 276, 359–60, 363, 368–70, 384; undermining of, 418–25
Industry, xxviii, xxx, 193–96, 238, 260–61, 278, 306, 313, 318, 342–43, 347–48, 350, 355, 369, 371, 373, 409, 421–24, 447, 453, 456. *See also* Industrial capital
Inequality, 443
Inheritance: of acquired characteristics, xxxi–n, 46, 110, 112–15, 130; law of, 105, 202, 269, 324; of office, 268–71, 274, 323, 330, 487
Innovation: and social ideas, 171–74, 176, 182, 216, 222, 488–89; and technical progress, 163–70, 182, 211–12
Instinct, 21, 29, 40, 79–80, 106, 152, 186, 491; and drive, 56, 66, 68, 107; race-, 124–25
Intellectuals, xlvi, 134, 379, 394, 428, 519; not a class, l, 252, 327, 331, 397–99; and clergy, 263, 327, 331, 361, 365, 483; under capitalism, l, 365, 402, 407, 409, 478; in developing countries, lvi, 413–16; medieval, 361, 365; origin of, 254–57, 327; a

privileged class, 134, 483; and science, 327; socialist, 403, 408, 466–67, 478
International: First, 390, 466; Second, xxiv, li, 417–18, 466
Die Internationale, 417n
Die Internationale und Sowjetrussland, 414n, 434n
Die Internationalität und der Krieg, 417n
Invention, xxxviii, 118, 152, 163–71, 213, 215, 226, 255, 357, 371, 488, 522–23
Iron ore, 400, 432
Iroquois, 202, 288
Irrigation works, xlvii, 214, 278–80, 299, 308–11, 317–18, 424, 501
Irrlitz, Gerd, xxii–n
Italy, liv–lv, 273, 285, 361–62, 394, 476, 519

Japan, 423
Jaurès, Jean, 471
Java, 294
Jeremiah, 297
Jerusalem, 350
Jesus, xl, 173
Jews, 139, 141, 173, 180, 231, 281, 298, 349–50, 354
Joint-stock companies, 292, 387, 433, 437
Judicial system, 385
Jurisprudence, 43, 72, 475–76, 492–93. *See also* Law, legislation
Justice, 509–11, 517

Kampffmeyer, Paul, 398n
Kant, Immanuel, xxiv, lxx, 4, 15–17, 19, 22, 24n, 25–26, 31, 65, 67, 97; synthesis with Marx, 4, 16, 25, 67
Kautsky, Benedikt, xxv–n, lv–n, lxviii
Kautsky, Felix, lxviii
Kautsky, John H., xxii–n, xlvii–n, lvi–n
Kautsky, Karl, Jr., lxviii
Kautsky, Luise, lv–n, lxviii
Kautsky, Minna, lxviii
Kinship organization, 74, 78, 91, 144, 187, 208, 210, 223, 236, 323–24, 335
Die Klassengegensätze im Zeitalter der Französischen Revolution, 372, 397–98
Knowledge: and action, 28–30, 80, 255, 465, 491, 497; certainty of, 30–32; derived from experience, 42–44, 149, 219, 255, 465, 499; drive for, xxxiv, 9, 11, 21, 31, 102–106, 220, 228, 234, 302, 491, 494; growth of, xli, 103, 149–50, 164, 179, 215, 219–20, 228–29, 255–56, 301, 326,

379; limits, xxxviii, 17–19, 28, 30, 226, 504, 521; relativity of, 24; specialization, 245, 255–56, 301, 396
Kolakowski, Leszek, xxii–*n*
Korsch, Karl, xxiii–*n*
Kriegsmarxismus, 433*n*
Krieg und Demokratie, lxix–*n*, 75*n*, 188*n*, 277*n*
Kropotkin, Peter, 67
Kugelmann, Ludwig, 265
Kupisch, Karl, xxxii–*n*
Kurds, 290

Labor protective legislation, 214, 403, 419
Labor time. *See* Working time
Labor unions. *See* Trade unions
The Labour Revolution, lxii, lxvi, 195*n*, 375*n*, 378*n*, 390*n*, 398*n*, 411*n*, 440*n*, 442*n*, 457*n*
Labriola, Antonio, 4
Lacedaemon, 342
Lafargue, Paul, 4
Laidler, Harry W., xxii–*n*, 455*n*
Lamarck, J. B., xxiv, xxxii–xxxiii, 48, 520
Lamprecht, Karl, 468
Lange, F. A., 16*n*
Language, 41, 102, 137, 200, 202, 236, 272, 287, 328; closes societies, 73–74, 77, 121, 125, 144, 159, 178, 187; evolution of, 128–32, 153, 168, 185, 206, 299–300, 304, 475; and nation, 145, 379–80; of primitive man, 55–56, 64, 71–75, 80, 99, 157; and race, 145–46
Laschitza, Annelies, xxii–*n*
Lassalle, Ferdinand, li–*n*, 265–66, 466
Latin America, xxv, lvii, 416
Latin Monetary Union, 449
Laveley, Émile de, 205
Law, economic, lxix, 27, 189–90, 194, 198, 243, 258, 392, 399, 413, 418, 468, 479, 481; of history, xlii, 451, 460, 471–72, 474, 476–77, 480, 522; of large numbers, 473, 484; legislation, xl, xlix, 43, 68, 71–72, 95, 106, 144, 201–202, 206, 209, 234, 294, 324, 332, 334, 380, 385, 388, 492. *See also* Jurisprudence; of linguistics, 475; moral, 24–25; of nature, xlii, 24, 27, 52, 170, 215, 244, 319, 338, 477–78, 492, 498, 522; regularity, 72–73. *See also* Necessity; of society, 52, 75–76, 170, 460, 468, 476–78, 522
Leadership, 70–71, 156, 250–52, 264, 269, 272, 328–29, 333, 396, 483, 486, 488
League of Nations, lx, 381–83, 417, 449–50

LeBon, Gustave, 334
Leisure, lxii, 100–101, 131, 134, 136, 326, 339, 407, 437, 524
Lending capital. *See* Banking capital; Usury
Lenin, V. I., xxv, 175, 390*n*
Letourneau, Charles, 202–203
Lévy-Bruhl, Lucien, 10, 81–82, 129
Lewin-Dorsch, Hannah, 152
Liberalism, 404–405
Lichtheim, George, xxii–*n*, xxiii–*n*
Lineage. *See* Kinship organization
Lissagaray, P. O., 470
Liverpool, 168
Livius, Titus, 470
Locomotive, 167, 493
Logic, 240, 242–43
Lombroso, Cesare, 60
London, 367
Louis XIV, 105, 238
Louisiana, 214
Low German, 145
Lubbock, Sir John, 87, 93, 162, 179, 203
Ludwig Feuerbach (Engels), 7, 35, 37, 42*n*
Lübbe, Peter, xxii–*n*, lvi–*n*, 495*n*
Lumpenproletariat, 349*n*, 377, 379, 394, 403
Luschan, Felix v., 117, 125, 128
Luther, Martin, 173, 175
Lux, Heinrich, 174
Luxemburg, Rosa, 192, 304, 376*n*, 421, 425
Luxury, xlvii–xlviii, 101, 105, 132, 178, 188, 295, 312–13, 316–17, 347, 366, 371, 453–55, 501, 514

MacDougall, William, 56
Macedonia, 339, 349, 351
Mach, Ernst, 33, 168, 179
McLennan, John F., 91, 93
Magic, 82
Majority, lxi–lxii, 267, 286, 352, 376–77, 388, 394, 442–45, 448, 495, 507
Malthus, Thomas, 62, 75–76, 424
Manchester, 168
Manchus, lvii, 415
Manifesto of the Communist Party (Marx and Engels). See *Communist Manifesto*
Marginal utility theory, 479
Mark, 204–206, 208, 224, 281, 308–309, 321
Marriage, 86–91, 93–95, 191, 235–36, 285, 324, 339, 380
Marx, Karl, xxi, xxiv–xxvii, xxxiii, lii, lvii–lviii, lxiv, lxvii, 5, 16, 147, 415, 465–67, 494, 502–503; on classes, 249–51, 264, 345–46, 372, 405, 452; conception of his-

Marx, Karl (*continued*)
tory, xxvii, xxxii–xxxiii, xxxv, xxxviii,
xli–xliii, xlvii, xlix, lxx, 3–6, 23*n*, 25, 67,
106–107, 147, 220, 224–25, 227–30, 237,
239, 418, 450–52, 454–61, 477–78, 482;
and Darwin, 6, 52, 66; and democracy,
405; dialectic, 34–37, 217, 225, 228, 520;
on dictatorship, 390–91; on division of labor, 260–61; economics, xxxix, 4, 54,
192–93, 197–98, 205, 355–57, 359, 419–
21, 429, 479; on force, 276–77; materialist
method, 7–8; on oriental despotism, 338;
and socialism, 174, 489; on state, xlix,
265–69, 308
Marxism, xxi–xxvi, xxx, l–li, lvi, lxviii,
400, 436, 461; applied science, xxix–xxx,
494; development, 4–5; a fashion, 5; and
socialism, 174, 466–67, 496–97; success,
lxv, 466, 496–97, 503; in underdeveloped
countries, 4
Die Marxsche Staatsauffassung, 188, 264*n*,
390*n*
Mass, xxxiii, xxxvii, 50–51, 64, 171–72,
222–23, 229, 237, 245, 267, 270, 272,
334–35, 388, 396, 482–83, 486–88, 500,
518–19; strike, 376, 457*n*
Materialism, xlvi, lxx, 8, 217, 223; before
Kant, 17; in Kant, 17, 25; a method,
xxix, lxviii, 6–7, 14, 17, 19, 25, 460–61;
and natural science, xxix, xxxiv, 10–11,
17, 19, 25; rejection of, 9, 12–15
Mathematics, 30, 136–37, 241–42
Matschoss, Conrad, 166–67
Matthew, 173
Matthias, Erich, xxii–*n*, xxxii–*n*
Maurer, G. L. v., 205
Mechanics, 9, 170, 477, 493
Medes, 281
Medicine, xxxvi, xlix, liv, 58, 82, 93, 256,
385, 493
Mehring, Franz, 4
Memory, 59, 299
Mende, Hans-Jürgen, xxii–*n*
Mensheviks, 413*n*
Mental endowment: of classes, 131–35, 212;
of early man, 153, 164; of races, 127–30,
136–38, 142; of sexes, 135–36
Mercantilism, 238, 292, 373
Mercenaries, 271, 322, 329–30, 339–40,
349–51, 353, 355, 373, 395, 416
Merchants. *See* Commerce
Mesopotamia, 214, 310
Messin, F., xxiii–*n*

Metal, 162, 180, 295, 304–306, 344, 416
Meusel, Alfred, xxiii–*n*
Mexico, lvi, 214, 416–17
Meyer, Eduard, 141–42, 255, 282, 300, 468,
471
Middle East, 180
Migrations, 89, 117, 135, 151, 158, 178,
203, 216, 284; cause of racial differences,
118–19, 121; cause of racial mixing, 122–
24, 137; cause of war, 76
Militarism, liii, 194, 402
Mind, adaptation of thoughts, 40–43; conservatism of, xxxvii, 39, 103, 169, 209–
10, 230; and environment, 34, 38–39; impetus to history, 149, 183, 215; opposed
to matter and nature, 9, 150, 154, 215,
217, 522; origin, 14, 521
Mineral wealth, 177–78, 180, 368
Mining, 147, 167, 241, 261, 273, 305–306,
347, 351, 364, 367, 370, 412, 432
Minority, lxi–lxii, 266–67, 272, 286, 294,
320, 349, 352, 376, 442, 444, 448, 495,
507
Mode of production, xlviii, 90, 147, 199,
224, 236–37, 239, 278, 331, 356, 372, 424,
451; concept, xxxix–xl, 197; and mental
character, 219–20, 280–81; and property,
xl, 199; replacement of, 283, 338, 401,
411, 418–21, 424–26, 437, 501–502
Mommsen, Theodor, 141, 264, 273, 295
Monarchy, xlviii, lii, 173, 265–66, 271, 275,
329–32, 334–37, 340–45, 349–50, 362–64,
368, 373, 379, 383–84, 386, 388–89, 405,
415, 469, 483–84. *See also* Absolutism
Money, xlvii, 298, 303–305, 307, 314, 331,
335, 349, 359, 369, 373, 378
Mongols, 295
Monopoly, 177–78, 182, 214, 253, 258, 263,
296, 307, 314, 377, 384, 410, 433, 449,
456
Montenegrins, 290
Montesquieu, C. L. de, 173
Morality. *See* Ethics
Moravia, 368
More, Sir Thomas, 472
Morgan, Lewis H., 120, 147, 163, 202, 210,
249–50, 269, 288
Müller, August, 310–11
Müller, Max, 128–29
Müller-Lyer, Franz, 87, 89, 91, 507, 518
Münzer, Thomas, 232*n*
Munich crisis, xxi
Music, 99–100, 137, 141, 229, 325–26

Muslims, 416
Mussolini, Benito, liv
Mutations, 47–48, 113
Myers, Charles, 128

Nansen, Fridtjof, 201–202, 512–13, 515
Napoleon I, 487
National character, 137–43
Nationalität und Internationalität, 138n, 380n
Nationality, 380
Nationalstaat, 206n, 288n, 380n, 433n
Natural science, xxvii, xxix–xxxii, xxxix,
   xliv, lxvii, 6, 9–11, 14–15, 19, 25, 27, 31,
   45–46, 113, 148, 163, 227, 229, 239–46,
   303, 364–65, 400, 465, 492–93, 499, 514
Natural selection. *See* Struggle for existence
Navigation, 126, 180, 241, 298, 341–42,
   344, 350–51
Nazism, lv
Neanderthal man, 452, 525
Near East, 310, 323
Necessity, 19, 21–27, 31–33, 110, 150
Nechayev, Sergey G., 175
Negroes, 141, 243, 412
Nehemiah, 297
Netherlands, lv–n, 205–206, 360, 423
Neue Programme, 375n, 390n
Die Neue Zeit, xxv, xxxv, lxv, lxix–n, 67
New England, 359
New Testament, 173
Newton, Sir Isaac, 489
Niebuhr, B. G., 139
Nile, 214, 278, 308
Nobility. *See* Aristocracy
Noiré, Ludwig, 99n, 156
Nomads, xlvi, 89, 122, 135, 196, 238, 276,
   278–86, 309, 311, 329, 339, 341, 361, 426,
   512
Nordenskjöld, A. E. v., 512
North America, 206, 412. *See also* United
   States
Novelty. *See* Innovation

Occupation. *See* Division of labor
Oedipus complex, xxxvi, 93, 511
Old Testament, xl, 173
Oppenheimer, Franz, 276, 293
Orangutans, 152–53, 156
Oriental despotism, xlvii, 276, 331, 333–38,
   341, 343, 345–46, 349, 352, 355, 413
The Origin of the Family (Engels), 87, 235,
   249, 268, 270, 324, 452, 461
Ormuzd, 281

Osterroth, Franz, xxii–n
Outbreak of the World War, lxvi–n

Palestine, 180, 298
Palmerston, Lord H. J. T., xxiii–n
Panaccione, Andrea, xxii–n
Pannekoek, Anton, 376n
Papacy, 384
Papcke, Sven, xxii–n
Papin, Denis, 166
Paris Commune, lxix, 175, 266, 377,
   415
Parlamentarismus und Demokratie, li, 275n,
   349n, 375n, 388n, 405n
Parliament, xlix, li–lii, lxi, 387–89, 391–92,
   399, 431, 444
Parties, political, xlix–liii, 372, 387–89, 391–
   92, 399, 406, 408–409, 436, 438–39, 442,
   444, 466–67, 525
Paschukanis, J., xxiii–n
Pastoralism, xlvi, 83, 90, 177, 192, 195–96,
   207, 237, 260, 279–81, 285–86, 289, 293,
   309, 318, 341, 512
Peasants, 101, 131, 133, 206, 238, 258, 281,
   294, 306, 313–15, 324, 386, 512, 516; under capitalism, 260, 358, 372, 377, 404,
   406–409, 424, 433; in city-states, 298,
   344–45, 347, 354; conservatism of, 211,
   475; contrast to nomads, 279–82, 285–86,
   341; a class, 252; in developing countries,
   lvi, 413, 416; early cultivators, 278–79,
   453; and founding of state, xlvi, 276, 282,
   293, 309–11, 321, 425–26; in Middle
   Ages, 253, 361, 364; in Oriental states,
   297, 332–33, 361; and petty bourgeoisie, l
Peloponnesian War, 140, 348
Peonage, 297
Perfection, 12, 37–38, 51, 109, 188, 464,
   517–20
Pericles, 316–17, 351
Persians, 139–40, 231, 270, 281, 289, 295,
   329, 346, 349
Peru, 294
Peschel, Oskar, 117, 128, 152, 179
Petroleum, 400, 416
Petrucci, R., 199–200, 203
Petty bourgeoisie, lxx, 344, 394, 447; under
   capitalism, l, 398, 404, 406–409; and de-
   mocracy, lvi, 413–14; revolutionary,
   xlviii, 367, 369, 371, 375; spirit of, 359–
   60
Phenomenology, xxv
Philosophy, xxxix, lxvii, 9, 150, 169, 215,

Philosophy (*continued*)
232, 240, 243, 245, 255, 265, 302, 326–27, 354, 475, 503–504
Philip of Macedon, 339
Phoenicia, 180, 298
Physics, xxx, 33, 52, 493
Physiology, 57, 94, 146
Pillaging. *See* Robbery
Pinkertons, liv, 394
Piracy, 342, 347, 350
Plaiting, 89, 152–54, 158, 187, 193
Plato, 97, 174, 339, 354
Pleasure, 59, 97–98, 134, 136, 312, 325, 339–40, 366
Plekhanov, George, 4
Pliny, 163
Plutarch, 325
Pöhlmann, Robert v., 354
Der politische Massenstreik, 376n, 398n, 440n, 457n
Polo, Marco, 295
Positivism, xxix
Post, A. Hermann, 87
Pottery, 89, 100, 153, 158, 162
Predictions, lxiii–lxiv, 30, 32, 215, 218–19, 225, 490, 497–504, 506, 508
Preisigke, Friedrich, 331
Press, xlix, li–liii, 387–92
Prestige, 305, 312, 325, 328–29, 333, 469, 483
Preuss, Konrad, 128
Priesthood, 81, 134, 173, 263, 266, 284, 315, 330, 332, 335, 350, 355, 366, 373, 469
Primitive man, 9, 15, 57n, 65, 70–71, 73, 80, 99, 129, 200, 255; adaptable, 54, 119–20; collective ideas, 81–83, 90–92, 94, 129, 255; happiness, 515–17; health, 513, 515; perfection, 517–19; psyche, xxxvi–n, 57–58, 158; sexual relations, 86–88, 92; use of tools, xliv, 152–63, 168
Producers, l, lix, 192, 253, 295, 411, 428, 462
Productive forces. *See* Forces of production
Prognoses. *See* Predictions
Progress, 109, 118–21, 140, 188, 307, 354, 360, 371, 409, 417, 501, 505–508, 519–20, 522, 524; of civilization, 129, 509–10, 513–17, 519, 523; of democracy, xxviii, 382–83, 395; of science and technology, xxviii, 100, 129, 131, 135, 164, 171, 180, 203, 208, 226, 254, 259, 287, 357, 382, 424, 428, 461, 502, 506, 513, 523–26

Projekt Klassenanalyse, xxii–n
Proletariat, lvii, 101; in city-states, 346–49, 353; decline of, 400–402, 407, 410; in East Europe and Orient, lvii, 375, 381, 390, 406, 413–18; growing strength, lxi, 292, 395, 403, 409–12, 419, 425–26, 428–29, 432, 434–35, 438, 440, 443, 445, 466, 503, 508, 510–11, 513–14; industrial, xxix–xxx, xxxv, xlviii, l, lvii, 356, 359, 363, 367, 369, 372, 391, 394, 399, 404, 408, 413, 467; intellectual life, 131–32, 407, 437; unity, 440–41, 495, 502–503
Die proletarische Revolution, 398n, 420n, 427n
Property, 199–202, 268, 294, 297, 376, 378–79, 515; conservatism of, 210–11; development, 205–209; landed, 202–208, 269, 271, 294, 330–31, 342, 347, 354; in means of production, 27–28, 202, 252–54, 257–58, 274, 356, 377, 410–11, 420, 436–37, 449, 452, 516; and mode of production, xl, 199, 208, 213, 227; relations. *See* Relations of production; rights, 201–202, 208–209, 294, 377; and technology, xxxix–xl, 211–13
Proportionality of industry and agriculture, 195–96, 420–24, 456
Prostitution, 213, 339–40, 401
Protective tariff, 194, 253, 383
Proudhon, P. J., 466
Prussia, 238, 265, 404
Psychoanalysis, xxvi, xxxv–xxxvi, 57–58, 93, 107
Psychology, xxx, 3, 477, 492
Punic Wars, 305, 351
Puritanism, 173, 276, 360, 367–70, 384
Pythagoras, 489

Quakers, 232n

Race, xxiv, xlvi; endowments, 123–24, 137–38, 142, 182, 523; and language, 145–46; mixing, 121–24, 137, 143, 145, 523; origin of differences, 117–21; and species, 116; struggle, 125–27, 136, 140, 148; superiority, 124–25, 127–28, 130, 136–37, 303, 324; theorists, 123–25, 127, 143, 146, 148; ties of blood, 143–44
Railways, 140, 165, 170, 182, 195, 228, 241, 383, 416, 422–24
Rappoport, Charles, xxiii–n
Ratzel, Friedrich, 140, 147, 155, 276, 281
Reason, xxxv–xxxvi, 15–16, 68, 106–108, 136, 212, 475, 501

Reformation, xl, 105, 173, 367, 373
Relations of production, xxxviii, xl–xli, xlvii, 225–28, 234, 236–38, 251, 371, 435, 444, 451–55, 457
Religion, xxxix–xlii, xlv–*n*, 42, 78, 81–85, 92–94, 141, 171, 229, 232, 234, 240, 263, 324, 326, 350, 359–60, 368–69, 384, 504–505, 526; wars of, 512
Renaissance, 105
Reproduction, process of, 197–99, 202–203, 214, 502
Republic, lii, 265–66, 343–44, 390, 487
Revisionism, li, 16*n*, 67, 378*n*, 457*n*, 460–61
Revolution, xlvii, lvii, lxv, 211, 283, 396, 413, 459, 506; bourgeois, lvi, 173, 175, 244, 263, 378, 413, 455; English, xlviii, 173, 367–68, 371, 487; French, xlviii, 105, 175, 205, 238, 371, 398, 415, 444, 471, 475, 487; proletarian, lvi, lxvi, 175, 455; Russian, xxv, lvi–lvii, lxv, 377, 393, 457*n*; social, xlvii–xlviii, 337–38, 354, 371–72, 451–54, 456
Ricardo, David, 478–79
Richtlinien, 440
The Road to Power, li, 26*n*, 433*n*, 457*n*
Robbery, 276, 280, 282–83, 285, 289, 293–94, 311, 319, 329, 342, 344, 361–62, 365, 423, 512
Robertson, John M., 140, 318
Romance languages, 145
Romanovs, lvii, 415
Romanticism, 205, 475
Rome, xxviii–*n*, xlvii–*n*, 84, 105, 139, 141, 167, 173, 231–32, 272–73, 295, 297, 317, 345–46, 349–53, 360–62, 366, 401, 418, 453, 480
Rónai, Zoltán, xxiii–*n*
Rosa Luxemburg, Karl Liebknecht, 406*n*
Rousseau, J.-J., 173, 205, 319, 489, 517
Rubel, Maximilien, xxi–*n*, xxii–*n*
Ruskin, John, 138
Russia, 383, 406, 413–15, 519; Revolution, xxv, lvi–lvii, lxv, 377, 393, 457*n*; village communism, 174, 205–206, 294

Sahara, 180
Saint-Simon, C. H. de, 174
Salvadori, Massimo, xxii–*n*, lv–*n*, lvi–*n*
Salvioli, Joseph, 297
Sanielevici, Henri, 117
Savery, Thomas, 166
Schäffle, H. E. F., 70

Schifrin, Alexander, xxiii–*n*, xxxix–*n*
Schmidt, Conrad, 240
Schopenhauer, Arthur, 59
School. *See* Education
Science, xxviii, xxxv, xl, xlvii, 54, 80, 119, 141, 165, 171, 173, 215, 220, 261, 300–301, 307, 314, 328, 351, 357, 371, 384–85, 453, 463, 471, 473, 479, 500, 524; and aristocracy, 134, 326–27; "bourgeois," 478, 502, 515; division of labor, 8, 256–57, 525; and Marxism, xxix–xxx, 461, 466, 494; natural and social, xxx–xxxii, 9, 45, 170, 301, 492; "proletarian," 478; pure and applied, xxix–xxx, 256–57, 493–94; and state, xlvii, 303–304, 325; tasks, 8, 526–27; and value judgments, lxiii, 106, 205, 245, 472, 493, 526. *See also* Natural science; Social science
Scots, 290, 360
Seals, 111, 400
Seeck, Otto, 139, 288
Selected Political Writings, xxii–*n*, 195*n*, 376*n*, 398*n*, 414*n*, 440*n*, 442*n*
Self-preservation. *See* Drives
Semites, 141
Serbien und Belgien, 380*n*
Serfdom, 131, 190, 252–53, 289, 315–16, 332, 347, 352, 356–57, 377, 425, 508
Sex, and intellect, 135–36
Sexual: factor in history, 105, 235–36; mating, 87–95; modesty, 95–96; seduction of aristocracy, 339–40
Shaw, G. B., 138
Siberia, 206, 423, 512
Sicily, 351
Silver, 105, 305–306, 351
Slavery, 122–23, 252, 282, 284–85, 289, 297, 306, 317, 319, 332, 356–57, 456, 508, 511, 516; and business morality, 190; in city-states, 344, 347–48, 352–53, 363–64, 374, 377; disappearance, 352, 361; in early cities, 313–15; first form of exploitation, 272, 282, 286; female, 272–73, 286, 329, 339; and origin of classes, 268–70, 272–75; in U.S., 190, 214
Slavic languages, 145
Smith, Adam, 254
Social contract, 64
Social Democracy versus Communism, 375*n*, 390*n*, 395*n*, 458*n*
Social-democratic movement, lxix–lxx, 175, 406, 408, 410, 414, 417–18, 430, 466–67, 503

Social-Democratic Party, German, xxii, xxiv–xxv, li–lii, lxv, lxviii, 408, 420n, 440n, 495n

Socialism, 356; in antiquity, 354–55; freedom under, 26–28, 426; future, xxviii, xxxv, lii, lvii–lxiv, 101, 133, 174, 191, 195, 214, 219, 250, 260, 263, 307, 320, 398, 418, 425, 427, 442, 450, 497, 503, 523–24; and innovation, 173–75; necessarily gradual, 28, 209, 251, 374, 377–78, 393, 411, 418, 440, 446; presuppositions, 55, 425–27; scientific, xxix–n, lxiv, 467, 494; transition to, lviii–lx, lxii–lxiii, 392, 436, 523; in underdeveloped countries, lvii–lviii, 4, 390, 413; utopian. *See* Utopian socialists

Socialism and Colonial Policy, 414n

Socialization, liv, lix, lxii, 27, 132, 209, 251, 253–54, 377–78, 411–12, 439–42, 449

Social legislation. *See* Welfare policy

Social reform. *See* Welfare policy

The Social Revolution, xxxii, 244, 378n, 398n, 430n, 432n, 433n, 438n, 440, 454n, 457n, 478n

Social science, xxix–xxx, xliv, lviii, lix, lxiv, 9, 17, 25, 31, 43, 45, 106, 218, 245, 326, 463, 490, 492–93, 499, 518, 527

Sociology, 45, 518

Socrates, 324

Solidarity, 280, 298, 438–39, 510–11

Solon, 354

Sombart, Werner, 125, 138, 194, 479

Somló, F., 179

South Africa, 412

Soviet Union, xxx–n, lvii, 391n

Die Sozialdemokratie und die katholische Kirche, 232n

Sozialdemokratische Bemerkungen, 304

Die Sozialisierung der Landwirtschaft, 195n, 196n

Sozialisten und Krieg, lxix–n, 232n, 293n, 376n, 381n, 426n, 433n, 450n, 458n, 482n

Space, 20, 24, 30

Spain, 305, 310, 351, 416

Sparta, 174, 289, 345, 348–49, 351, 354

Speech. *See* Language

Spencer, Herbert, 64, 70, 87, 93, 188–89, 515

Spengler, Oswald, 63n

Spiegel, Friedrich, 141

Spinning machine, 213–14

Stalin, Joseph, lvii

Stammler, Rudolf, 64, 233–34

Starkenburg, Heinz, 233n, 487

State, lxvii, 43, 293, 326, 391, 487, 511; abolition of, lix–lx, 265–66, 446–50; autonomy of, xlvii, 42; and cities, xlvii, 311–14, 447; city-state, xlvii, 276, 317, 341–55, 357, 362, 452, 474; and civilization, 131; concept, 181, 187, 264–67, 388; expansion. *See* Expansion; and irrigation works, xlvii, 308–10; modern democratic, xlviii–xlix, li, liii, 376, 379, 381–89, 410, 431–32, 443–44, 447, 450; and money, xlvii, 305; national-, xlix, 379–81, 447, 450; Oriental, 311, 317, 331, 333–38, 340, 343, 345–47, 349, 355, 357; origin, xlvi, 131, 133, 267–77, 281–83, 286, 308–309, 425–26, 453, 501, 508–10, 516; and property, 208; and science, xlvii, 302–303, 314, 325, 447; and taxes. *See* Taxes; and trade, xlvii, 294–96, 447; and usury, 297–98; and war. *See* War, and state; and writing, xlvii, 299–302, 469, 474

Statistics, 429, 432, 468, 474, 501, 514, 518

Steam engine, 147, 165–67, 170

Steamship, 166–67

Steenson, Gary, xxii–n, xxxii–n

Steinberg, Hans-Josef, xxii–n, xxxii–n, liv

Steinen, Karl v.d., 162, 179, 201, 512, 515

Steinmetz, Rudolf, 63n

Stephenson, George, 167, 489

Stieve, H., 112

Stock market, 389, 516

Stone throwing, by apeman, 156–57

Structuralism, xxv

Struggle for existence, 6, 60, 77, 80, 134, 177, 192, 200; develops drives, 31, 66–67, 79, 97, 104; with environment, xxxiii, 34; Malthusian, 61–62, 148; selection by, 47–48, 50–51, 109–10, 112–13, 487

Sudan, 282, 424

Suffrage, l, lii, lxi, 404–405, 408

Superstructure, xxxviii–xliii, xlv, 170–71, 227–31, 233–34, 240, 435, 455, 460, 500

Surplus value. *See* Exploitation

Survival of the fittest. *See* Struggle for existence

Switzerland, lii, 145, 238, 287, 363, 405

Sympathy, 65, 470

Syndicalism, 436

Tariff, 194, 253, 382–83, 385, 449

Tasmanians, 162

Taxes, xlix, 206, 237, 274, 294, 305–306,

310, 314–15, 317, 322, 329, 331, 341, 348, 353, 361, 373, 385–86, 425, 431, 441

Technology, xlvi, 41, 72, 80, 180, 199; basis of civilization, 136, 216, 224, 318, 506; changes equilibrium of nature, 75, 287; changes human nature, 219–20; determinism, xxxviii–xxxix, xlii–xliii, xlv, 224; development of, xxviii, 11, 27, 56, 83, 98, 100, 102–103, 120, 129, 135, 168, 176, 182, 216, 224, 235, 255, 261, 271, 316, 364–65, 385, 400–401, 407, 459, 514; and economy, xxxix, 192–93, 199, 216, 306; and marriage, 88–89; and migration, 75; and natural science, xxxix–xl, 171, 241–42, 493; and property, xxxix–xl, 211; and relations of production, 226–27; and war, 75, 79, 121, 133, 159, 237, 316, 321, 401, 430, 512

Teleology, 11, 31, 43, 76, 97, 218, 301, 487, 490–93

Terrorism, lxix, 439–40, 457, 495

Terrorism and Communism, 74n, 219, 375n, 428, 439n, 440n, 457n, 495n, 513n

Texte zu den Programmen, 398n, 420n, 427n, 434n

Theories of Surplus Value (Marx), xxv–n, 228

Thessaly, 342

Thirty Years War, 512

Thomas More and his Utopia, 232n, 361n, 365n, 380n, 472n

Thomas, Norman, xxii–n, 455n

Thucydides, 470

Tibet, 327

Tigris, 278

Time, 20–21, 24, 30

Tool, xliii–xliv, 54, 88, 121, 228, 357, 522; and natural organs, 183–85; production of, 54–55, 160; and property, 200–201, 207–208; and trade, 178–79, 295; and weapon, 54, 88, 121, 157, 159–61, 177, 186, 198

Town, xlviii, 263, 361–65, 373–74, 383–84, 386, 514. *See also* City

Trade. *See* Commerce

Trade unions, xlix, liii, 214, 259, 387, 399, 408, 412, 436, 438–39

Trading capital, 292, 296–97, 355–56, 358

Transportation, xlix, 11, 126, 134, 167, 182, 194, 223, 241, 261, 278, 287, 294–95, 306, 311, 361, 373, 379, 383, 401, 419, 422, 430, 432

Trevithik, Richard, 167

Tribute, 274, 282–83, 285–86, 289, 295, 297, 305, 311, 313, 322, 332, 339, 385–86

Troeltsch, Ernst, 142, 169–70, 172–73, 505

Trojan War, 105

Trotsky, L. D., xxv

Tschudi, J. J. v. 512

Tschulok, Sinai, 46, 112

Turks, 310

Ueberzeugung und Partei, 495n

Underdeveloped countries, lv–lviii, 4, 390, 413–17

Unemployment, 395, 401, 420–21, 441

Unions. *See* Trade unions

United States, l, liv, 167–68, 190, 194, 214, 231, 381–83, 394, 405–406, 409, 412–13, 415–16, 423–25, 432

Universal Postal Union, 449

Universities, 384, 518

Usury, 253, 297–98, 300, 324, 332–33, 335–36, 356, 368, 371

Utopian socialists, lxiv, 173–74, 260–61, 402–403, 419, 447, 457, 467, 501

Value judgments, xxix–xxx, lxiv, 205, 472, 493, 526

Venice, 180

Die Vereinigten Staaten Mitteleuropas, 380

Vermehrung und Entwicklung, xxviii, xxxi–xxxii, lxvi, 49n, 51, 61, 75–76, 94n, 99n, 148n, 195n, 203n, 421

Die Vernichtung der Sozialdemokratie, 398n

Versailles, lv–n, 425

Verworn, Max, 33

Vico, Giambattista, 475

Vienna, xxxv, lii, liv, lv–n, lxviii, lxx, 65, 92

Volition. *See* Will

Voltaire, F. M. A. de, 489

Von der Demokratie zur Staats-Sklaverei, 288n, 375n, 390n, 421n, 426n

Vorländer, Karl, 4, 16

Vorläufer des neueren Sozialismus, 232n, 330, 354n, 355n, 361n, 363n, 364n, 367, 368n, 482n

Vries, Hugo de, 47

Wachsmut, Wilhelm, 310

Wagner, Moritz, 117

Waitz, Theodor, 512–13

Waldenberg, Marek, xxii–*n*
Wallace, Alfred Russell, 117, 152
War, lx, 63, 74, 82, 88, 101, 105, 121–22,
    189, 243, 279, 306, 316, 321, 328–29,
    347–49, 352, 362, 380–82, 430–31, 440,
    470, 474, 484, 511–12, 523; and aristoc-
    racy, 133, 258, 285, 297, 322, 329, 339–
    40, 366; and economic conditions, 237–
    39, 282; and industry, 193–94, 196; and
    intellect, 134; and national states, 449–50;
    and nomads, 280, 283; origin, xxxvi, 75–
    79, 159; and race, 125–27; religious, 512;
    and state, 274–77, 282–83, 285, 289–92,
    295–96, 317, 321; and trade, 178; and
    wealth, 272
Was ist Sozialisierung? 378*n*, 411*n*, 440
Watt, James, 165–66
Weapons, 54, 121, 134, 157, 159–60, 177,
    179, 193, 198, 207–208, 237, 269, 279,
    295, 321–22, 329, 333, 344, 382
Weaving, 89, 100, 152–54
Weber, Henri, 376*n*
Weber, Max, xxiv, xlv–*n*, xlviii–*n*, 193,
    273, 276, 296, 305, 334, 342, 344–45, 356,
    359–60, 368–70, 384, 395–97, 479
Wehrfrage und Sozialdemokratie, 394*n*
Weimar Republic, lii
Weitling, Wilhelm, 175
Welfare policy, liii–liv, 354, 383, 403, 408,
    419, 421, 427, 436
Wells, H. G., 505
Westermarck, Edward, 91
Whales, 400
Wiener, Robert, xxiii–*n*

Wilde, Oscar, 138
Wilhelm II, li–lii, 483
Will, 42, 328, 489, 492, 499–500, 521–22,
    527; free, 16, 25–26, 29, 31, 59, 150–51,
    490–92, 495; limits, xxxviii, lxix; and re-
    lations of production, 225–28; power of,
    lxix, 494
Windbreak, 152–54, 193
Woltmann, Ludwig, 4
Wolves, 71
Work: material and social side, 192, 196–97,
    199; for one another, 185–93, 201, 210–
    12, 216–17, 223, 257; with one another,
    185–86, 191–93, 201, 210–12, 216–17,
    223, 257
Working time, liv, 101, 131–32, 197, 261,
    357–58, 401, 407–408, 410, 428, 434, 437,
    442, 514, 524
World purpose, 12–14, 37, 504–505
World War: first, xxiv–xxvi, xxviii, liv, lxii,
    lxv–lxvi, lxix, 138, 194, 292, 380*n*, 394–
    95, 408, 432, 440*n*, 449, 466, 483, 512,
    513*n*; second, xxi, xxiv, lv
Woytinsky, Wladimir, 514
Writing, 41, 73, 102, 136, 241, 299–302,
    304, 307, 325, 335, 384, 469, 473–74,
    483
Die Wurzeln der Politik Wilsons, 406*n*

Yangtze, 278

Zoology, xxx, xxxiv
Zoroastrianism, 281